# Open Computing's Best UNIX Tips Ever

## Ever

Kenneth H. Rosen,
Richard R. Rosinski, and
Douglas A. Host

**Osborne McGraw-Hill**
Berkeley   New York   St. Louis   San Francisco
Auckland   Bogotá   Hamburg   London   Madrid
Mexico City   Milan   Montreal   New Delhi   Panama City
Paris   São Paulo   Singapore   Sydney
Tokyo   Toronto

Osborne **McGraw-Hill**
2600 Tenth Street
Berkeley, California 94710
U.S.A.

For information on translations or book distributors outside of the U.S.A., please write to Osborne **McGraw-Hill** at the above address.

**Open Computing's Best UNIX Tips Ever**

1234567890 DOC 9987654

ISBN 0-07-881924-5

# Table of Contents

## Using FACE as a Standard User Interface

## Some Useful Resources

## UNIX Application Programs

# 2
# Organizing Your System

## Changing Directories

## Listing Files

# 3
# Controlling and Customizing Your Environment

# 6
# Formatting and Printing Text

# 7
# Shell Programming Tips

# 9
# Communications and Networking

# 10
# The Internet

# 14
# Using and Customizing the X Window System

# Acknowledgments

We would like to thank our management at AT&T Bell Laboratories, including Leighton Chen, John Lawson, Randy Pilc, and Karl Martersteck, for their support of this project. We would also like to thank Betty Brokaw for her help with the book review process at AT&T Bell Laboratories.

We thank the following people for their help reviewing material and/or contributing a group of tips: John Navarra, our intrepid technical reviewer, who provided many helpful suggestions, checked our programs, and contributed lots of cool tips, especially concerning tools and the Internet; Avi Gross, who reviewed several chapters in depth and provided lots of helpful suggestions, especially on mail; Bruce McNair, who helped in the area of security; Jonathan Clark, who reviewed material on networking, system administration, and development, and who contributed lots of really useful tips on network administration and porting software to SVR4; Bill Wetzel, who contributed a large collection of tips on program development and on Mosaic; Adam Reed, who contributed a comprehensive set of tips on the X Window System; Mary Bowers, who contributed the questions most commonly asked of UNIX system counselors at AT&T Bell Laboratories; Jim Farber, our coauthor of *UNIX System V Release 4: An Introduction,* who helped us plan this book and who contributed tips on UNIX commands and tools; the editors/maintainers of the FAQ posting on *comp.unix.questions,* Ted Timar and Steve Hayman, for encouraging us to use their FAQ; and Larry Wall, for help with perl.

We would like to thank the following people at Osborne McGraw Hill for their help with this book: Alexa Maddox, Editorial Assistant, who helped manage the project; Vicki Van Ausdall, Associate Editor, who helped coordinate the project; Nancy McLaughlin, Project Editor, who managed the editorial process; Gary Morris, Copy Editor, who ensured consistency and clarity throughout the book; Scott Rogers, Acquisitions Editor, who helped manage the technical review; and last but not least, Jeff Pepper, Editor-in-Chief, who first thought of the project, supported us unwaveringly throughout its development, and helped us see this book to completion.

# Contributors

Ian Benn
Mary Bowers
Dan Busarow
Jonathan Clark
Jim Farber
Randy Goldberg
Avi Gross
Tatjana Heuser
Stephen Marcus
John Navarra
Murray Nesbitt
Elizabeth Poole
Adam Reed
Jim Rogers
Paul Sander
Bill Wetzel
David Wexelblat

# Preface

This book is a gold mine of helpful tips on the UNIX system. Our tips are designed to make your work with UNIX easier, more productive, and more interesting. No matter how experienced with UNIX you are, this book has tips for you. If you're a novice, there are tips to get you started using the many features of UNIX. If you're an intermediate user, you'll find lots of helpful hints for using UNIX more effectively and for broadening your skills. If you're an expert user, you'll find some hidden pearls, and learn about new capabilities that you've been unaware of until now. Everyone buying this book will get many times their investment back, both by saving time and by avoiding frustration getting things done with UNIX. With the tips in this book, you can learn how to use UNIX effectively from scratch, how to become a more experienced user, and how to use lots of different tricks.

The UNIX environment includes much more than the basic operating system. It also includes applications, communications capabilities, programming languages, administrative capabilities, and more. The tips in this book cover many different areas of this rich UNIX environment, including:

- ❑ UNIX system basics and fundamentals
- ❑ Customization of your environment
- ❑ Working with both DOS and UNIX
- ❑ Mail, communications, and networking
- ❑ The Internet and its many resources
- ❑ Text editing and formatting
- ❑ Tools and utilities
- ❑ The X Window System
- ❑ System and network administration
- ❑ Shell and C programming

A tip is meant to be read quickly and easily. You don't have to read lengthy explanations in this book to find useful information. There are different kinds of tips here, each designed to help in a specific way. For example, there are:

- ❏  Quick introductions to UNIX features
- ❏  Comparisons of DOS and UNIX capabilities
- ❏  Sample scripts and programs you can adapt for you own use
- ❏  Answers to frequently asked questions
- ❏  Tricks you can use to perform different tasks
- ❏  Common mistakes to avoid when writing a script or program
- ❏  Summaries of tools available for solving problems
- ❏  Information on how to use Internet resources and where to find them
- ❏  Pointers to where you can find more information

The inspiration for these tips comes from many different places, including our own personal experience, suggestions from UNIX system counselors at AT&T Bell Laboratories, frequently asked questions, articles posted to various USENET newsgroups, contributions from reviewers and friends, and descriptions found in many different books and articles. We've distilled a tremendous amount of information down to tips we think you can really use.

We are interested in receiving feedback from other UNIX users. If you think of any features or problems that should be addressed in future revisions of this book—or, if you have useful UNIX tips of your own—please send them to our Editor-in-Chief at Osborne/McGraw-Hill, 2600 Tenth Street, Berkeley, CA 94710.

# Chapter 1

## Setting Up UNIX Systems

# Getting Started

## TIP 1

## The First Step

If you are a new UNIX user, you may plan to use UNIX on a multiuser system which may have anywhere from two to several thousand different users. Or you may be running UNIX on your own machine. If you are going to run UNIX on a multiuser system, the first thing you need to do is contact the system administrator— the person who manages and maintains your UNIX system. Your system administrator will assign you a logname and an initial password (which you can change later; see Tip 11). He or she will also help you get started, perhaps providing you with an initial *.profile* that sets up your working environment. (See Tip 31.)

If you are going to be running UNIX on your own desktop PC or workstation, first you should read the instructions that came with your system. If you are lucky, your system has already been configured and UNIX system software has been loaded. If your system has been configured, but the software has not yet been loaded, follow the installation procedures provided by your suppliers. If you haven't yet purchased your PC hardware and/or UNIX system software, read Tips 4 and 5. And if you are wondering why anyone would want to run the UNIX system on a PC, read the following tip.

## TIP 2

## Running the UNIX System on a PC

Although most PC users run a version of DOS (Disk Operating System) as their operating system, there are many new versions of the UNIX operating system that are designed for use on a PC. (See Tip 5.) People who have run the UNIX system on large computers or computers with proprietary hardware platforms can now take advantage of the high-volume market of 80386- and 80486-based PCs and their peripherals. This hardware architecture has the advantage that software designed for use on older Intel-based platforms continues to work when new platforms are introduced. An added advantage is that you can set up your PC to run both DOS and UNIX. This lets you run the large amount of DOS software available and enjoy the power of the UNIX system without buying two machines.

# Running Both DOS and UNIX on Your PC

There are several methods for running both DOS and UNIX on a single PC. One common method is to partition your disk with separate DOS and UNIX partitions. You can do this with the **fdisk** command that is part of DOS and is also available on many UNIX systems designed for PC use. Then you should specify which partition your PC should boot from to determine whether you run DOS or UNIX when you start your computer. (For details, see Chapter 13 of this book.)

The other common way to run both DOS and UNIX on a PC is to run DOS under the UNIX system—that is, to make use of a DOS emulator that runs as software on the UNIX system. (See Chapter 13.)

# Setting Up a PC to Run UNIX

If you want to run a standard UNIX on an Intel-based PC, you'll need a configuration with enough capacity to support UNIX system software. There are UNIX-like systems that require little memory and processing power; for example, Coherent will run in 2MB of RAM and 20MB of disk space, and Minix will run on a 286-class processor. We recommend, though, that you start with a bigger machine. A minimal configuration is a 386DX machine with a clock speed of 20MHz, or perhaps 33MHz. This would provide adequate, but not stunning, performance. A 486DX 33MHz or even a 486 66MHz machine would provide much better performance, and with declining PC prices is probably now affordable. You'll need at least 8MB of RAM on your machine, but for better performance you will probably want 12 or 16MB. By the way, you can upgrade to 12 or 16MB of memory by replacing the existing memory or by adding extra SIMMS. You'll need 120MB of hard disk space as an absolute minimum, but you'll probably want 300MB to store a reasonable number of programs and your data.

When choosing a PC to run UNIX, you should look for machines with an EISA bus and a SCSI (Small Computer Systems Interface), which will help you avoid peripheral and driver problems. We also recommend that you buy a tape drive to be used for system backups and to help with software installation.

# TIP 5

# Choosing UNIX System Software

There are many versions of PC UNIX system software, each designed with a different goal in mind. Some are feature-rich, some provide standard platforms, and others are cheap, or even free (but with the necessary trade-offs in features and support).

One of the most important versions of UNIX system software is SVR4.2 (also called Destiny) developed by UNIX Systems Laboratories. SVR4.2 was built with SVR4 as a base and ease of use on PCs as the overriding goal. SVR4.2 provides a graphical desktop manager with icons representing common tasks. You can use a mouse to select a task and then run it. This includes many important system administration tasks.

Solaris 2.1 from SunSoft is another attractive version of the UNIX system for Intel-based machines that is built on SVR4. Solaris contains many of the features of the SunOS that extend the capabilities of SVR4. Solaris includes a sophisticated graphical user interface, system administration via a graphical interface, graphics libraries, and enhanced development tools. Although some reviewers consider Solaris 2.1 the most attractive and complete UNIX system for PCs, it does require a fully configured system. One reviewer recommended running Solaris on a 486 50MHz system with at least 16MB RAM (or 32MB RAM for many graphics-intensive applications) and a hard drive with at least 340 and preferably 500 MB! Solaris and much of Sun's software are available on CD-ROMs.

An excellent source of information on UNIX system software for Intel-based PCs can be found in the article "PC-clone UNIX Software Buyer's Guide," posted periodically to the newsgroups *comp.unix.pc-clone.32bit, comp.unix.sys5.r4,* and *news.answers.* This article provides reviews and useful details about many different versions of UNIX for use on PCs. (See Chapter 10 of this book for information on reading netnews to learn how to access such articles.)

# TIP 6

# Configuring Your UNIX PC

Most DOS software will run on any PC clone with peripherals, but the UNIX system is trickier. Before setting up your system, you'll have to make sure there are device drivers to support the peripherals you'll need—display, tape drive, SCSI controller, networking cards, and so on. You should either buy a system already configured and equipped with all the necessary device drivers, or at least make sure that these device drivers are available for the UNIX system software you plan to use. You can get information of this kind in the netnews group *comp.sys.intel.* (See Chapter 10 for tips on reading netnews.)

# Dialing In to a UNIX System

**TIP 7**

To access your UNIX system from a terminal or a PC over the telephone network, you will need a modem. This modem can be a separate box or a PC board. Modern modems run at speeds varying from 1200 to 9600 bits per second (bps), with some newer modems as fast as 14400 bps. With the slower speeds, you may find it frustrating to carry out some common tasks. For instance, while editing a document using a 1200 bps connection, you may get ahead of your keystrokes. With a 2400 bps connection, you may find that your system is slow in redrawing the screens used by a graphical application. The moral of all this is that you should use one of the higher speed modems if you possibly can. The new 9600 bps modems will probably meet your needs and their cost is rapidly declining.

Most commercial and public-domain terminal emulation packages can be used to access UNIX host computers. In fact, terminal emulators often come packaged with popular DOS or Macintosh software. To dial in to your UNIX system with a terminal emulation package, you must have the correct communication settings. First, you have to set the right speed. This depends on your modem and the modem used by your host computer. You have to set the type of terminal that you want to emulate on your PC: vt100 is a common choice, but other possibilities provide better functionality. (Once logged in, you will use the TERM variable to tell your UNIX system what kind of terminal you are emulating; see Tip 39). You must also specify the number of data bits, stop bits, and parity; whether flow control is on or off; whether parity check is on; and possibly other things. To find out the correct settings, you should contact your system administrator or look at the specifications describing what the UNIX host computer expects.

Once you have set up your terminal to a modem, or your PC with a terminal emulation package with the correct options, you can dial in and establish a connection to your UNIX host computer. Once this connection has been made, you can log in just as you would if you were directly connected. You'll receive the following prompt:

```
login:
```

This will be followed by another prompt:

```
password:
```

When you have entered the correct password for your login, you will be able to run UNIX system commands. Note that once you are logged in to a UNIX host, you can remotely log in to other UNIX machines that have network connections to this host. (See the tips in Chapter 9 to learn how this is done.)

## TIP 8

# Logging In to Your UNIX System

People who use most DOS, DOS/Windows, or Macintosh systems don't have to supply a password when they log in. However, since the UNIX system started as a multiuser system, it has always required that a user provide a password.

For UNIX system novices, when you access a UNIX system it first asks for your login. This is the logname assigned to you by your system administrator. (If you have a single-user system, you will need to set up your system and assign yourself a password; see Chapter 11 of this book.) Then you will have to enter your password. Your initial password is usually assigned by your system administrator. You will be able to change this later. (See Tip 11 for details.) The UNIX system checks whether you have entered the correct password for the login you provide. If you have entered both the correct login ID and password, you will be able to start entering UNIX system commands. Here is a sample of how this works when user Juanita, who has the password ioxbt13, attempts to log in (note that for security reasons, the password is not displayed in a real login):

```
login: juaanita
password: ioxbt13
Login incorrect
login: juanita
password:  pxbt13
Login incorrect
login: juanita
password: ioxbt13
UNIX System V........
```

In the first case, the login ID was incorrect (an extra "a"); in the second case, the login ID was correct, but the password was incorrect. In the third case, both were entered correctly, and log in was completed, so the system responded with the system welcome information.

It's worth noting that UNIX is case-sensitive—that is, it distinguishes between upper- and lowercase characters. The password ioxbtl13 is not the same as IOXBTL13. In some operating systems, such as DOS, upper- and lowercase characters are treated as equivalent. Remember UNIX is CaSe SeNsItIvE.

# The Basics of Logging Off

When you are finished with your session and wish to leave the UNIX system, type

```
$ exit
```

This will log you off. To see that you have logged off successfully, wait for the system to give the login prompt:

```
$ exit
login:
```

You should always log off when you have completed your work. Leaving your terminal unattended and still logged on lets other people use your system; this could result in serious damage to your resources. Also, you shouldn't just turn your machine off or hang up your telephone connection, since someone might be connected to your still active logon session. So always log off with **exit**.

Sometimes you may want to do some special things when you log off. See Tips 24 and 173 for some help in this area.

# How to Turn Off Your UNIX System Computer

Users who have experience with personal computers, including those who use DOS, are in the habit of shutting down their computer system by turning off the machine. Since DOS is mainly a command interpreter, file manager, and program loader, this does not normally cause a problem. Unless a program is being executed, turning off the machine does no harm. With more complex operating systems such as UNIX, the system itself runs many different processes and holds many files open. Turning off such systems will almost always result in damage to the file system or the system administration processes.

Don't shut down your system by turning off the power! Before turning off your machine, you must do the following: Become superuser (if you don't know what this means, then you shouldn't be shutting the machine down), and then run the **shutdown** command. On SVR4 systems the command is

```
#  /usr/etc/shutdown
```

On previous versions of UNIX, the command is

```
#  /etc/shutdown
```

All files will be closed and all processes halted. You will then see this message:

```
Reboot the computer now
```

At this point, you can turn off the machine.

In UNIX System V Release 4.2, the UNIX desktop, the special user interface incorporated into SVR4.2, makes it easier to shut the system down. First, save all open files, quit all of your applications, and then double-click on the shutdown icon on the UNIX desktop. You'll see two confirmation questions, and then this text message:

```
Reboot the computer now
```

At this point, turn off the computer.

# Now That You Are Connected

## TIP 11

# Changing Your Password

If you are a user on a machine with a system administrator, that person will assign you a password you can use when you first log in. This password may be something you will have trouble remembering or it may be intended for temporary use. This means that you will want to change your password after you have successfully logged in for the first time. It's also a good idea to change your password periodically to keep your system more secure. If you keep the same password for a long time, it's more likely that someone will guess it or determine it by trial and error, or that it will fall into the hands of some malicious person. And, if you're on a multiuser system, the system administrator may have your account set up so you are forced to change your password after a certain period has elapsed, commonly six months or a year. In any case, it's easy to change your password. Just use the **passwd** command. When you run this command, you are prompted for your old password. Only when you have entered this correctly are you able to tell the system your new password. This prevents someone from changing your password when you are logged in and leave your office for a coffee or health break.

Once your old password has been entered correctly, you are prompted for your new password. (For information on selecting your new password, see Tip 12.) After entering your choice for a new password, you must reenter it. Only when you type your new password the same way twice does the system recognize it. Here is an illustration of how the **passwd** command works, showing how you can change your password from boz3puc to acy8xum. (Notice again that passwords are not displayed to the user).

```
$ passwd
passwd: changing password for roxanne
Old password: boz3puc
New password: acy8xum
Re-enter new password: acy8xum
```

*On some systems, once you have changed your password you won't be able to change it again until a specific number of days (often 7, 14, or 30) have elapsed. This number is specified by the system administrator in the /etc/passwd file. So make sure you can live with your new password for at least a little while!*

You should also note that most systems use password aging. This means your password will expire after a particular number of days specified by your system administrator. You will be warned that your password will expire each day for a particular number of days before it does. If you don't change your password yourself by the time it expires, you will be forced by the system to change it using the same procedure illustrated with the **passwd** command.

# Guidelines for Selecting Your Password

The best kind of password is one that is difficult for someone else to figure out, but at the same time reasonably easy to remember. Unfortunately, most people pick passwords that are easy to remember, but also easy for other people to guess. For example, people might use the names of family members, family pets, street names, and so on—all strings that someone who knows them might guess. You also want to pick passwords that are resistant to attack by computer programs that generate likely passwords.

You may find the following hints useful in choosing passwords intelligently.

❑   Do not use any parts of your name or the name of a family member, friend, or pet, or any nicknames for these individuals.

❏   Do not use any part of your birthdate, address, automobile licence plate number, telephone number, or similar personal information.

❏   Do not use a word that might be found in a dictionary of any kind, such as an English language dictionary, a Spanish language dictionary, a technical glossary, and so on.

❏   Make sure your password contains characters that are not all the same type. That is, use characters of at least two of the following types: lowercase letters, uppercase letters, digits, and punctuation marks.

❏   Consider a combination of letters and digits that will render your password pronounce-able—for example, wud28zab, 1fup0yut, kux1tro, and so on. This will make it easier for you to remember it.

Make sure you can easily remember the password you choose and never leave it written down anywhere near your terminal.

# What If You Forget Your Password?

**TIP 13**

If you forget your password, no one will be able to tell you what it is. This is because the UNIX system stores passwords in an encrypted form. So the system administrator can only access the encrypted version of your password and cannot recover your password from this encrypted version. The only way for the system administrator to let you log in again is to give you a new password!

# Using UNIX System Commands

**TIP 14**

The UNIX system provides a large number of different commands for your use. Each of these commands is a program that carries one or more tasks. Generally, your command line will start with the name of the command, following by the option or options you want to use, if any, followed by the argument or arguments, if any. Options are usually specified with a – (minus sign). For example,

```
$  ls -l  memo
```

is a command line containing the **ls** command with the –1 option, and with *memo* as its sole argument. This causes information about the file memo in your current directory, if it exists, to be listed in long form. Command lines don't necessarily require arguments. For example,

```
$ ls -l
```

is a command line containing the **ls** command with the −l option. This causes the files in your current directory to be listed in long form. And command lines don't require options. For example,

```
$ ls memo
```

is a command line containing the command **ls**, no options, and the argument *memo*. This command will print the name of the file *memo* if it exists in the current directory. If this file does not exist in the current directory, you'll see a message like this:

```
memo: no such file or directory
```

Many commands, such as **ls**, have many different options. Using these options you can often do a wide variety of tasks. You can learn what a command and each of its options do by reading the manual page on this command, which you should be able to find online and in the appropriate UNIX System Reference Manual.

# Six Simple Commands to Get You Started

If you are new to UNIX, you'll need a few commands to play with to get used to it. Here are six simple commands that you might want to learn first. Look them up in the manual, read about them in a book on UNIX, and play with them.

| Command | Function |
|---|---|
| **banner** | Displays up to 10 characters in large letters |
| **cat** | Prints the contents of a file on the screen |
| **date** | Tells you the date and time with a 24-hour clock |
| **echo** | Prints its argument on the screen |
| **pg** | Prints contents of a file on the screen in chunks |
| **wc** | Tells you the number of lines, words, and characters in a file |

For example, to print "New Jersey" on your screen, use

```
$ echo "New Jersey"
```

To print this string in large letters, use

```
$ banner "New Jersey"
```

If *memo 12* is a file, you can display its contents all at once on your screen, using

```
$ cat memo12
```

To see the contents of this file in chunks, type

```
$ pg memo12
```

You will see the number of lines, words, and characters in the file *memo 12* if you run

```
$ wc memo12
```

Finally, if you run

```
$ date
```

you'll get the current date and time (according to your system's clock).

# TIP 16  Demystifying Command Names

To new users of UNIX, the set of common commands seems mysterious and confusing. Novices sometimes complain that it is difficult to get started learning UNIX commands, and as a result the system is not considered very user-friendly. This is partly because of its history. UNIX was originally invented by and for sophisticated computer scientists. It was simpler and more efficient for both these users and their computers to use short, even cryptic, commands than fuller, more verbose ones.

You can remove some of the mystery that surrounds UNIX, and make it easier to learn and use commands, if you remember that most if not all UNIX commands are acronyms, abbreviations, or mnemonics that relate to longer descriptions of what the commands do. For example, **ls** *li*sts the names of your files, **wc** does *w*ord *c*ounts of files, **rm** *r*e*m*oves files, **mv** *m*o*v*es files, **mkdir** *m*a*k*es *dir*ectories, **rmdir** *r*e*m*oves *dir*ectories, **ed** is an *ed*itor, **vi** is a *vi*sual editor, and so on. Although there aren't consistently followed rules in making up command names, you'll find it useful to try to learn the command names by associating them with the mnemonic acronym for their functions.

# Stopping the Execution of a Command

When you run a command on the UNIX system, and don't put it in what is known as the background (see Tip 23), you won't get a prompt to run another command until the execution of this command is completed. To stop such a command, you need only press the BREAK or DELETE key. The UNIX system will halt the execution of the command and return a prompt awaiting your next command. On some systems, you may have to type CTRL-D to interrupt the command.

# Running a Series of Commands with One Line

You can run a series of UNIX commands by putting them on the same line separated by semicolons. For example, if you want to list the files in your current directory, see the current date and time, pause for 30 seconds, and then list the current users of your system, you would type

```
$ ls; date; sleep30; who
```

If you want to run a series of commands in the background, you'll need to group these commands using parentheses and put an ampersand after the grouping, as in this example:

```
$ (ls; date; sleep30; who) &
```

Here, you will get a prompt back and the three commands will run in succession in the background, giving you their output only when all three have completed. If you were to type

```
$ ls; date; sleep30; who &
```

you would first get the output of **ls**, then the output of **date**, and there would be a 30-second pause. Then you would get a prompt while the **who** command ran, and finally the **who** command would report its output.

# Where Does Input to a Command Come From, and Where Does Output Go?

On the UNIX system, the input to a command is called the standard input and the output of a command is called standard output. Unless you tell the UNIX system otherwise, standard input comes from the keyboard and output goes to the terminal display. For example, if you want to alphabetize a list of words, you could run the **sort** command, list a series of words one on a line, type CTRL-D to indicate the end of input, at which point the **sort** command would send the alphabetized set of words to the display. Here is an example:

```
$ sort
dog
cat
rabbit
iguana
CTRL-D
cat
dog
iguana
rabbit
```

Instead of taking the standard input from keyboard input, you can tell a command to take its standard input from a file. To do this, you would use the < (input redirection) symbol. For example, if the file *words* contained the four words "dog", "cat", "rabbit", and "iguana", one per line, you would get the same result by typing

```
$ sort < words
```

You may also want to send the standard output of this command to a file instead of displaying it on your terminal. To send the standard output of a command, use the > (output redirection) symbol. For example to put the output of the **sort** command in the file *swords,* taking the input from the keyboard, you would use

```
$ sort > swords
```

Finally, to take the input from the file *words* and put the output in the file *swords*, you would type

```
$ sort < words > swords
```

# Using cat to Create a File

Before you learn a text editor, such as **vi** or **ed**, you may want to create files. You can use the **cat** command to do this. For example, to create a file named *test,* type

```
$ cat > test
```

Then type the lines you want to put in the file *test,* hitting RETURN after each line. You may use BACKSPACE to erase what you've typed on a line and change that line, but once you type RETURN you can't change the line. When you are finished, type the end-of-file character CTRL-D on a line by itself. This terminates **cat** and closes the file *test.* If you want to put more lines in the file *test,* type

```
$cat >> test
```

By using the >> symbol, you will append the file *test* rather than writing over it.

# Putting Error Messages in a File

When you run a program you may get an error message instead of the output you expect. Such a message is usually sent to you through a logical channel, called standard error, that is separate from standard output. For example, when you run

```
$ rm memo6
memo6:  No such file or directory
```

the message you receive is sent to you via standard error.

*Standard error is also used in a variety of other ways, such as sending comments, help messages, or prompts. Usually, and by default, standard error is sent to your terminal screen. This is desirable since in most cases you will want to see error messages. However, you can redirect your standard error so that it is sent to a file rather than displayed on your screen. This is done differently depending upon which kind of shell you are using.*

To redirect standard error in the Bourne shell (**sh**) or Korn shell (**ksh**), you include the digit "2" followed by the > symbol and the name of the file where you want standard error sent. Here 2 is the file descriptor for standard error and > is the usual symbol for redirection. For example, the command

```
$ cat memo6 2> errors
```

doesn't produce any output on your screen when the file *memo6* doesn't exist. However, it does put a message in the file *errors*. If you list the contents of *errors* using **cat**, the results would look like this:

```
$ cat errors
cat:  cannot open memo6
```

With the C shell (or related shells such as **tcsh**), the procedure is a little different since you use the symbol &> to redirect the standard error. Therefore, the previous example becomes:

```
$ cat memo6 &> errors
```

# TIP 22 — Pipes

The UNIX system gives you an easy way to use the output of one command as the input to a second command. You can do this with a pipe (I) operator. For instance, to count the number of login sessions on your system, you can pipe the output of the **who** command to the command **wc –l**, which counts the number of lines of output. For example,

```
$  who | wc -1
48
```

tells you that there are 48 login sessions active on your system.

# TIP 23 — Running a Command in the Background

Usually when the shell runs a command, it waits until this command has been completed before it resumes its dialog with you. So, when the shell is running a command you cannot interact with it—for example, you cannot issue another command. To get around this problem, you can run commands in the background. To do this, put an ampersand (&) after your command. When you run a command in the background, the shell will continue its dialogue with you while it carries out the command. For example, to sort the extremely large file *employees* in the background, you would type

```
$ sort employees &
```

You probably will want to direct the output of this command to a file instead of having it show up on your screen while you are interacting with the shell. You may also want to run error messages in a second file instead of seeing them on your screen. So, with **sh** or **ksh**, you should use

```
$ sort employees > list  2> error.out &
```

To redirect the output of the command to a file, the error messages to a different file, and to put the whole thing in the background when running **csh** or **tcsh**, use:

```
$ (sort employees > list  &> error.out) &
```

To determine which shell you are running (if you don't know), see Tip 32.

# How to Keep a Job Alive After Logging Off

## TIP 24

Ordinarily, when you log off, any jobs you are running will terminate, even if you have set these up as background jobs. You can use the **nohup** (*no hang up*) command to run a job so that it will keep running after you log off. So, if you type

```
$ nohup sort employees > list 2> error.out &
```

and then log off, this command will run. Make sure that you include the & to make the job run in the background. The next time you log in, you'll find the output of the **sort** command in *list* and the standard error in *error.out*.

# Fixing Your Typing Mistakes

When you want to erase a single character on a command line, use your erase character. In UNIX SVR4 the backspace, or CTRL-H, is the erase character. Note that in earlier and other versions of the UNIX system, the # character is the erase character. If this is true on your system, you may want to change it to the backspace character. (See Tip 164 to learn how this is done.)

When you want to erase an entire line, use the kill-line character, which on most UNIX systems is the @ character. When you type the kill-line character, everything you have typed on the current line is deleted and your cursor is positioned at the beginning of the next line. You can also change the kill-line character to something other than @, but some people continue to use @ for this purpose. Since the @ character is used in addressing electronic mail, many people will use CTRL-U or CTRL-X as the kill character. Tip 164 explains on how to change the kill character to something else.

# What If You Really Want an At Symbol (@) in a File?

Unless you have changed your kill-line character, whenever you type @, the at sign, it deletes your current line of input. But what if you really want to put the at sign in your command line or in a file? To do this, you will need to type a backslash (\) before you type @. This tells the UNIX system that it should ignore the special meaning of the at sign as the kill-line character and treat it as a literal character. For example, if you type

```
38 computers @ $54,323 each
```

the system will ignore everything preceding the at symbol, give you a new line, and consider your input to be this:

```
$54,323 each
```

But if you type

```
38 computers \@ $54,323 each
```

the system will not consider the at sign a kill-line character, and will accept your input as you wish.

# Reading the News on Your System

**TIP 27**

The system administrator of most UNIX systems alerts users to useful or necessary information about the system via UNIX system news. Sometimes when you log in to your system you will get a message that tells you that there is news for you to read. Here is an example:

```
TYPE "news" to READ news:  DWB3.2
```

To read this news, run the **news** command. This will give you this news article as well as any other you haven't read, in order from newest to oldest.

Sometimes you may have already read a news item, but need to read it again because you didn't pay enough attention the first time you saw it. Maybe you just didn't care about the subject when you first read it, but now it is crucial to your life. To see all the news items on your system, including the ones you've already read, just type

```
$  news -a
```

The –a option tells **news** to show you every news item available on your system.

# Lock Your Terminal to Prevent Pranks

**TIP 28**

You should never leave your terminal unattended and logged in to UNIX. If you are away, any passerby can execute any command you are allowed to execute. Your private or proprietary files can be read, sent to a printer, or mailed to another location or company. Your files can be altered or deleted. If a malicious prankster issues the command **rm -r \*** from your terminal, all of your files will be gone.

Only your imagination limits the kind of pranks that can be played. For example, the following command will make the system pause for 100 seconds every time you try to list your files.

```
function ls {
sleep 100;/bin/ls $*
}
```

One way to prevent this sort of thing from happening is to use a terminal-locking program. For example, on many systems a program called **lock** is available that will lock your keyboard, unlocking it only when you reenter your password. You should have this or a similar program (perhaps with a different name such as **tlock**) on your system; ask your system administrator for the details. If you don't have such a program, you should be able to find a terminal-locking program in the public domain, or in a book on UNIX system security.

You should be sure to use **lock** or a similar program if you leave your desk for even a few minutes. The following example shows how **lock** works.

```
$lock
Password:
Sorry
Password:
```

The terminal is locked, and no commands or input are attended to.

To unlock your terminal, enter the same password you use to log in. If a wrong password is entered, the word "sorry" appears, along with another "Password:" prompt. If there are a number of wrong attempts (usually three), the system logs you off automatically. Some versions of **lock** do not require that you use your login password. You can enter any string as a locking password.

# Setting Up Your Environment—The Basics

## TIP 29

## Setting Up Your .profile

Use your *.profile* file to customize your environment. To do this, you include commands, define shell variables, and set values of shell variables. Typical things that you'll want to do include setting up the path used to find commands (see Tip 43), setting your terminal type, changing your prompt, defining some variables used by programs that you run, and running some commands. For example, you might want to run the **date** command to see the current date and time, the **news** command to see any news on the system that you haven't yet seen, and the **who** command to see who's logged in to the system.

It's simple to set the value of a shell variable in the System V Shell. This tip emphasizes **ksh** and **sh**; see Tip 36 for an equivalent with **csh** or **tcsh**. You need only type a shell variable name followed by an equal sign (=) and its value. For example, to set your UNIX System Shell prompt to a plus sign (+), you would include the following line in your *.profile:*

```
PS1=+
```

You can also define your own shell variables. For example, to move files from various directories in your file system to the directory */home/fred/book/new,* you can define the shell variable NEWBOOK using the line

```
NEWBOOK="/home/fred/book/new"
```

Once you do this, you can move a file from any point in your file system to this directory with the command

```
$ mv filename $NEWBOOK
```

It is necessary to export all shell variables that you set in your *.profile* unless these variables are automatically included in your environment. For example, to export the variable NEWBOOK, you would include the following line in your *.profile:*

```
export NEWBOOK
```

# Exporting Variables

**TIP 30**

Your environment is the collection of all the settings of all the variables the UNIX shell uses. Remember to export any variable you set in your *.profile*. Export puts the value of that variable in your environment, which in turn makes it available to other shell programs.

If you want to see the current settings of shell variables, type the **env** command. The shell will list all the current variables and their settings.

# TIP 31

# A Basic Template for Your .profile

When you log into UNIX, the commands in a file called *.profile* are executed. This sets up various options, sets variables used by the shell, and executes specific programs (like **news**) for the user. Every user needs a *.profile*. We are going to suggest two that you may wish to use—one in this chapter and one in Tip 184. The first is a generic *.profile* that will work for most users, and can be customized or extended as you wish:

```
##  A Generic .profile suitable for all new users and most general
#  users of UNIX systems.
#
#
#  Set default file permissions to read & write for user only
    umask 066
# Refuse messages sent from other terminals
    mesg n
# Set default terminal characteristics
    stty sane tabs nl0 cr0 echoe erase '^h'
    stty kill
# Set and export PATH variable
    PATH=${PATH}:${HOME}/bin
    export PATH
# Set and export path for directory changes
    CDPATH=:${HOME}
    export CDPATH
# Set general mail variables
    MAIL=/usr/mail/${LOGNAME}
    MAILCHECK=60
    MAILPATH=${MAIL}:${HOME}/rje%"New file has just arrived in rje."
    MAILPATH=${MAILPATH}:/usr/spool/uucppublic/${LOGNAME}%\
    "New file has just arrived in ~uucppublic/${LOGNAME} directory"
    export MAIL MAILCHECK MAILPATH
# Define program used for paging
    PAGER=/usr/bin/pg
    export PAGER
# Set WWB variables
    PATH=${PATH}:/opt/wwb/bin
# Set KSH variables
```

```
    ENV=${HOME}/.kshrc
    HISTFILE=${HOME}/.sh_history
    HISTSIZE=999
    SHELL=/usr/bin/ksh
    export ENV HISTFILE HISTSIZE SHELL
# Customize prompts
    PS1="+"
    PS2="--> "
    export PS1 PS2
# Customize vi screen editor
# To set 'numbers' in VI uncomment (delete the #'s) from the next 2
    lines:
#       EXINIT='set nu showmatch warn wrapmargin=5 smd'
#       export EXINIT
# To disable the EXINIT variable altogether, uncomment (delete the #)
# from the next line (if you want to use your .exrc, for example):
#       unset EXINIT
# Offer to display current system news items
echo "\nDo you want to read the current news items [y]?\c"
read ans
case $ans in
 [Nn][Oo]) ;;
 [Yy][Ee][Ss]) news | /usr/bin/pg -s -e;;
 *)        news | /usr/bin/pg -s -e;;
esac
unset ans


#  Exec into the korn shell
exec /usr/bin/ksh
```

# What's Your Login Shell?

**T**IP
**32**

The shell is the part of the UNIX system that you use to control the resources of your operating system. Not only is the shell your command interpreter, but it also provides job control functions and is even a programming language! As the UNIX system developed, several different shells were introduced. UNIX System V incorporates several of the most important of these: **sh**, the standard UNIX System V shell (sometimes called the Bourne shell, the job shell **jsh**, the C shell **csh**, and the Korn shell **ksh**. The C shell was originally developed by Bill Joy as part of Berkeley UNIX and has its adherents among people used to working with a BSD version of the UNIX system. The Korn shell, developed at Bell Labs by David Korn, provides a compatible superset of the features of the System V shell with most of the features of the C shell, and has many other enhancements. The job shell **jsh** adds job control features to the System V shell.

Your login shell is the shell program that is automatically started for you when you log in. Your login shell is determined by the last field in your entry in the */etc/passwd* file. To see what this is, type the following line, where *logname* is your logname.

```
$ grep logname /etc/passwd
```

The output of this command will be the line in the */etc/passwd* file corresponding to your login. The fields in this line are separated by colons. Here we only care about the field after the last colon. If your login shell is the System V shell (Bourne shell), you will see either */bin/sh* or no entry (since this is the default login shell); if your login shell is the Korn shell, you will see */bin/ksh;* if your login shell is the C shell, you will see */bin/csh;* and so on.

If you'd like to change your login shell, ask your system administrator to change the last field in the line in */etc/passwd* corresponding to your logname. Or, if you have superuser privileges, make this change yourself. On some systems, normal users can make this change by executing the change shell command:

```
$ chsh
```

We recommend you set your login shell as the Korn shell since it is compatible with the System V shell, incorporates most of the features of the C shell, and has many other useful enhancements. However, if there are a lot of C shell experts at your location, you may prefer to make the C shell your login shell.

# T**I**P 33

# Useful Shell Variables

If your login shell is the System V shell or the Korn shell, the file *.profile* is executed when you first log in. By convention, you set several shell variables that will be valid for your entire login session here. For example, the variable TERM contains the name of the terminal you're using, PATH contains the sequence of directories that should be searched in command execution, and so on. Often there are dozens of such variables in a *.profile*. You will find it useful to set many of these variables in your *.profile*. The following table lists many of these variables.

| Variable | Purpose |
|---|---|
| CDPATH | Lists in order the subdirectories that the shell searches through when you change directories. (See Tip 47.) |
| DISPLAY | Used by the X Window System to identify the display server used for X applications. (See Chapter 14.) |
| EDITOR | Specifies your preferred editor. (See Tip 42.) |
| ENV | Identifies the pathname of the initialization file executed whenever a new Korn shell is started. (Applies only to **ksh;** see Tip 186.) |
| HISTFILE | Identifies the pathname of file holding the Korn shell history list. (See Tip 177.) |
| HISTSIZE | Indicates the number of commands stored in the Korn shell history list. (See Tip 176.) |
| HOME | Identifies the pathname of your login directory. (See Tip 61.) |
| LOGNAME | Indicates your login name. |
| MAIL | Identifies the pathname of the directory containing your mail. (See Tip 184.) |
| MANPATH | Lists directories containing manual pages. (See Tip 171.) |
| PAGER | Specifies your preferred screen display program (such as **more**). |
| PATH | Lists directories that the shell searches for commands. (See Tip 45.) |
| PS1 | Defines the primary shell prompt. (See Tip 142.) |
| PS2 | Defines the secondary shell prompt. (See Tip 384.) |
| SHELL | Identifies the pathname of the shell. |
| TERM | Defines your terminal type. (See Tip 39.) |
| TZ | Stores time zone information. (See Tip 198.) |
| VISUAL | Specifies your preferred visual editor (such as **vi** or **emacs;** see Tip 181). |

The convention is that these variables have names that use all uppercase letters.

# Finding the Value of a Shell Variable

**TIP 34**

To find the current value of a shell variable, use the **echo** command with the name of the variable preceded by a dollar sign ($) as the argument. For example, to find the current value of the variable $TERM, you would use the command

```
$ echo $TERM
vt100
```

Here, the output vt100 indicates the current value of the variable $TERM is vt100. When you use the System V shell, you can see the values of all your shell variables using the **set** command.

# Setting Up Your .login File (for C Shell Users) and Your .cshrc File

When the C Shell starts up, it looks in two files, *.login* and *.cshrc,* for a set of initial commands and variable definitions. Your *.login* file should have those commands and variable definitions that only need to be executed at the beginning of your session.

Your *.cshrc* file should include commands and definitions that you want executed every time you run a shell, not just when you log in. It should include alias definitions and definitions of variables used by the shell, but that are not environmental variables. To set the value of an environmental variable, use the **setenv** command. For example, to set the value of TERM to vt100 you would use the command

```
% setenv term vt100
```

To set the value of an ordinary variable in the C Shell, you define it by using the **set** command followed by an equal sign and the value you are setting. For example, to specify that the last eight commands you executed are saved, you would set the value of the *history* environmental variable to 8, using the command

```
% set history = 8
```

# Useful C Shell Variables

The C Shell uses some of the same environmental variables as the System V Shell, but it also uses a number of other useful environmental variables. Some of these are variables that you either set to on or to off. Such variables are called *flags*. For example, the *notify* variable lets the C shell know whether to tell you onscreen if a background job terminates. The line

```
set notify
```

will make the shell tell you as you soon as a background job terminates. Here is a list of some of the C shell variables you might want to set in your *.login* or *.cshrc* files. (See Tip 35.)

| Variable | Purpose |
| --- | --- |
| cdpath | Lists order subdirectories shell searches through when you change directories. |
| echo | When set, the shell shows command line after all substitutions are made. |
| cwd | Indicates the pathname of the current directory. |
| history | Specifies the number of command lines saved. (See Tip 179.) |
| savehist | Specifies the number of command lines saved on log out. |
| ignoreeof | Prevents CTRL-D from ending the shell. (See Tip 199.) |
| noclobber | Prevents the redirection character (>) from overwriting files. (See Tip 196.) |
| noglob | Prevents wildcard expansion from taking place. (See Tip 154.) |
| notify | Causes the shell to inform you immediately when a background job terminates. |
| path | Specifies a list of directories for shell searches. |
| user | Indicates your logname. |
| prompt | Specifies the command line prompt. (See Tip 144.) |
| status | Indicates the exit status of the last command. |

# A Template for Your .login File

TIP 37

Here is a sample *.login* file that you can use as a basis for your own:

```
# change interrupt character to Ctrl-C and allow clean backspacing.
if (-t 0) then
    stty intr '^C' echoe
endif
# Set the X server to the host where we logged in on.
if ($?DISPLAY == 0) then
    if ($?REMOTEHOST) then
```

```
            setenv DISPLAY ${REMOTEHOST}:0
        else
            setenv DISPLAY :0
        endif
endif

# Set the Terminal type
    echo -n "Terminal type: "
    set term = $<
else
        echo -n "Terminal type: <xterm>"
        set term = $<
endif
if ($term == "") then
            set term = 'xterm'
endif
setenv TERM 'tset - -Q $term'
#ignore the end of a file
set ignoreeof

# Logout if left idle too long
set autologout = 200

# Display the date
date

# List of aliases

            alias print lpr
            alias printer lpq
            alias m more
            alias mroe more
            alias h history
            alias bye logout
            alias d /bin/date
            alias e emacs
            alias k /bin/kill -g
# make all removes interactive.
            alias rm /bin/rm -i
            alias ls ls -F
            alias ^L 'clear'
            alias dir ls
```

```
        alias ll  ls -la
        alias pd dirs
        alias cd 'cd  \!* ; pwd ;echo " " '
        alias read  'more \!*'
        alias cl clear
        alias lo logout
        alias f finger
        alias del  'rm  -i'
        alias mv "mv -i"
        alias cp "cp -i"
# Prevent dump cores
limit coredumpsize 0
```

# A Template for Your .cshrc File

Here is a sample *.cshrc* file that you can edit to meet your own needs:

```
# aliases
# list directories in columns with delimiters
alias ls 'ls -CF'

# Remember last 100 commands
set history = 100

# For interactive shells, set the prompt to show the host name and
# event number.
if ( $?prompt ) then
        if ( -o /bin/su ) then
                set prompt=`hostname -s` \!# "
        else
                set prompt="`hostname -s`\!% "
        endif
endif

# ad to path
setenv PATH $PATH':/usr/local/bin:~randy/bin'

# figure out how deep this shell is (How many logouts needed to exit).
```

```
if ($?level == 0) set level = 0
@ level = $level + 1
setenv level $level

# put hostname and level on the prompt
setenv HOSTNAME 'hostname | sed ' s/\..*//''
if ($level == 1) then
    set prompt = "$HOSTNAME% "
else
    set prompt = "${HOSTNAME} $level% "
endif

# Supress Core dumps

limit coredumpsize 0

alias LOGOUT logout
#turn on history to last 20 commands
set history=20

# all files will be created with permission mask 077
umask 077
```

# TIP 39

# Setting Your Terminal Type

Screen-oriented programs, such as the **vi** editor, need to know what kind of terminal you're using. The way that you tell UNIX your terminal type is by setting the value of the TERM environmental variable. For example, in the standard UNIX System V shell, you would type

```
$ TERM=vt220; export TERM
```

to set your TERM variable to vt220. If you use the C shell, you would type

```
% setenv TERM vt220;
```

If you use the same type of terminal all the time, you should put the appropriate line setting your terminal type in your *.profile* or your *.login* if you use the C shell. If you use different terminals—for example at home, in the office, or on the road—then you can query for the terminal type each time you log in by putting the following script in your *.profile:*

```
# Set terminal type....
echo -n "What Terminal are you using?>\c"
read TERM
```

The "\c" characters keep the cursor on the same line as the query, and the characters you type are taken as the value of TERM. If you want to see the value of your TERM variable, you need only type

```
$ echo $TERM
```

# Does Your System Know about Your Type of Terminal?

Your system will probably have the information programs need to know about your terminal, unless you have a relatively uncommon, extremely new, or exotic type of terminal. You can check to see whether a terminal description exists for your terminal by looking for the name, number, or manufacturer of your terminal in the */etc/termcap* file which contains the *termcap* terminal database and/or in the *terminfo* database in the */usr/share/lib/terminfo* directory.

For instance, if you have an AT&T 5425 and want to know whether your system has information about this terminal in */etc/termcap*, run the command

```
$ grep 5425 /etc/termcap
ATT4425|ATT5425|att5425|4425|5425|tty5425|att4425|AT&T 4425/5425:\
(more lines of input with terminal data)
```

This tells you that 5425 is a value of TERM that your system understands and that it is interchangable, as far as */etc/termcap* is concerned, with several other values of TERM such as att4425, att5425, and tty5425.

You can also look in the terminfo database on your system to see whether it knows about your terminal type. The directory */usr/share/lib/terminfo* contains separate files for each terminal type understood by your system, with all terminals with names beginning with a particular character stored with the directory */usr/share/lib/terminfo/character*. For example, terminals beginning with "b" or "5" would be stored, respectively, in directories */usr/share/lib/terminfo/b* and */usr/share/lib/terminfo/5*. For example, if you have a new brand of terminal named "zippy", you would run

```
$ ls /usr/share/lib/terminfo/z
```

and see whether "zippy" was in your output. Similarly,

```
$ ls /usr/share/lib/terminfo/6
```

would tell you whether there is a *terminfo* file for your 699 terminal. (By the way, on older versions of System V and other versions of UNIX, you should look in */usr/lib/terminfo* rather than */usr/share/lib/terminfo*.)

# Working with a Color Display

**TIP 41**

If you have a terminal with a color display, you need to make sure you provide a value of the TERM environmental variable that includes support for color. For example, when you run UNIX on a 386-class PC, you might want to set the value of TERM to be 386AT. If you are using the X Window System, you can use some standard commands to manage the color of screen output. (See Chapter 14.)

However, if you are not, you may be able to control some aspects of your color display. On some versions of the UNIX system, including some built with UNIX System V Release 4 as their base, you can use the **setcolor** command to set the default colors for the background and foreground of your display. Unfortunately, **setcolor** does not work the same on different UNIX versions, with some versions of **setcolor** using coded names of colors, allowing different color intensities, and so on. But as an example, to produce red characters on a white field on most systems, you would type

```
$ setcolor white red
```

You will need to experiment to find a combination of background and foreground colors that you find pleasing. Once you do so, you might want to add a **setcolor** command to your *.profile* or *.login* file.

If you want to get deeper into using colors, you might want to change the colors of specific messages or how screen-based applications use color. To do so, you'll need to use escape sequences for colors which depend on the version of UNIX you are running and the terminal you are using. See your manual for details.

# Setting Your Editor

Your *.profile* is also the place to set the variables for editing. If you use the **vi** editor, you can also set up the editor options you wish to use as your defaults. Here is an example:

```
#  Initialize Ex/Vi Editor variables.
EDIT=ex
EDITOR=vi
ED=vi
VISUAL=vi
EXINIT="set report=1 noterse ws wm=21 nu eb aw ic"
export EDIT EDITOR ED VISUAL EXINIT
```

This sample sets **vi** and **ex** as default editors, and sets their options so that all changes are reported, long messages are given, searches wrap around the end of the file, lines auto-wrap and break at a space 21 characters from the edge of the screen, all lines are numbered, errors are noted by a bell, and upper and lower case of characters is irrelevant in searches.

*Four different environmental variables are defined for editors here. The reason different variables for editors are needed is that different programs use different variables for editors.*

# Organizing Your PATH

The shell variable PATH defines the sequence of directories that should be searched to find a command. If you issue a command, like **ls**, your UNIX system goes to the first directory in your PATH to look for it, then to the second, if it's not in the first, and so on. Since the list of directories is searched sequentially, you can speed up the apparent performance of your system by organizing the PATH variable. Put the directories for frequently used system commands (like */usr/bin*) at the beginning of the PATH so they can be found quickly.

# Use a Short PATH

Keep the list of directories in your PATH as short as possible. You want to include a path for commands you use frequently without including all possible directories. For example, if you use a command rarely, it's quicker to alias it to a full pathname (see Chapter 3 for information on aliases), than to include its directory in PATH. The reason for this is that looking in that seldom-used directory for other commands that you issue will slow your performance down.

This is most noticeable when you make typing errors in entering a command. If you type **vu** filename when you meant **vi** filename, the shell will search every directory in the PATH before it gives you the error message:

```
/usr/lbin/ksh:  vu: not found
```

Keep the PATH short and you'll spend less time waiting for error messages from the shell.

# Specifying Your PATH

Here is the format for setting a PATH variable:

PATH=*directory list*

where *directory list* consists of a list of directories separated by colons.

For example, here is a common PATH for a SunOS v6 UNIX system:

```
PATH=/bin:/usr/bin:/usr/5bin:/usr/ucb:/opt/bin:/opt/dwb:/home/you/bin
```

Instead of entering your PATH as one long line, use the following approach:

```
PATH=/bin
PATH=$PATH:/usr/bin
PATH=$PATH:/usr/5bin
PATH=$PATH:/usr/ucb
PATH=$PATH:/opt/bin
```

```
PATH=$PATH:/opt/dwb
PATH=$PATH:$HOME/bin
```

This extends the PATH by repeatedly setting it to its previous value plus one new directory. This makes it easy to review the directories you include in your PATH and to eliminate or rearrange them if needed.

# Don't Put the Current Directory in PATH!

Notice that this PATH does not include the current directory—that is, the shell does not look in the current directory for a command. The reason is that including the current directory (specified as ".") in the PATH introduces security risks. Assume for a moment that you are in some directory. You want to see what's there, so you issue the **ls** command. Assume further that a prankster has put a command file named ls in that directory, but it executes this command line:

```
rm -r $HOME/*.
```

If the shell executes the prankster's **ls** command before the system command, you will have just deleted all your files.

For this reason, it's strongly suggested that you not put the current directory in PATH. Instead, execute commands in the current directory by using this format:

```
$ ./command
```

If you feel you must put the current directory in your PATH, put it at the end. That way any standard system command will be encountered before a command of the same name in the current directory.

# Changing Directories the Easy Way with CDPATH

You can use the CDPATH variable to make it easy to move from directory to directory. In this variable, you list in order the directories that the shell searches to find a subdirectory to change to when you use the **cd** command. For example, if you set

```
CDPATH=$HOME: $HOME/projects: /books/math
```

then when you issue the command

```
$ cd tips
```

**cd** first looks for a directory named *tips* in */home/bart*, then in */home/bart/projects*, then in */books/math* (if */home/projects* is the home directory).

# Using FACE as a Standard User Interface

# Let FACE Do Most of the Work for You

**TIP 48**

Suppose you don't want to have to remember where commands and files are located in the UNIX file system. UNIX System V, Release 4 has a built-in option that allows novice and casual users to operate under a menu-driven environment called *FACE* (Framed Access Command Environment). This menu interface was available under Release 3.2, but has been enhanced to allow for additional functions such as system administration and extended mail handling. For information on using FACE for system administration, see Chapter 11 of this book.

The FACE environment is set up so you can continually select submenus within menus until you reach the activity you want to perform.

The following page shows an example of a FACE screen.

Remember that all the work you do until you get to this point is just setting up the correct environment. If you are unsure about what you are doing when you reach this point, you can always back out of the menus one at a time, even up to the initial menu.

There are a number of FACE tutorials in textbooks about UNIX SVR4. One of the better ones is Chapter 5 of the *UNIX System V Release 4 User's Guide,* by the UNIX Software Operation (Englewood Cliffs, NJ: Prentice-Hall, 1990).

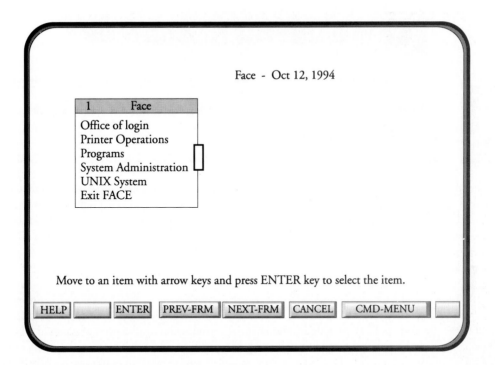

```
                          Face  -  Oct 12, 1994

          ┌─────────────────────────┐
          │  1          Face        │
          ├─────────────────────────┤
          │ Office of login         │
          │ Printer Operations      │
          │ Programs                │
          │ System Administration  ⎕│
          │ UNIX System             │
          │ Exit FACE               │
          └─────────────────────────┘




        Move to an item with arrow keys and press ENTER key to select the item.

   ┌──────┐  ┌─────┐ ┌──────┐ ┌───────┐ ┌────────┐ ┌────────┐ ┌────────┐ ┌──┐
   │ HELP │  │     │ │ENTER │ │PREV-FRM│ │NEXT-FRM│ │CANCEL │ │CMD-MENU│ │  │
   └──────┘  └─────┘ └──────┘ └───────┘ └────────┘ └────────┘ └────────┘ └──┘
```

# Using the FACE Function Keys

**TIP 49**

There are two type of function key labels available under FACE. There are the labels for moving from menu to menu, and those within a specific form. Regardless of which type you are looking at on your screen, they are both self-explanatory. These function keys are mapped to specific control key sequences, depending on whether you are in a form or at the menu level. Hitting the appropriate control key sequence will do the same thing, but may cause unexpected results if you hit the wrong sequence at the wrong time. Until you become proficient at using control key sequences, you are better off using the function keys to move around.

FACE depends on having the appropriate function key mappings in order for them to work properly. If you are having trouble using them, look at the TERM= statement in your *.profile,* or try to remember what you entered during login. You may have to change your terminal type to match the one expected by FACE.

# Some Useful Resources

## How Do You Manage to Learn All the Details about UNIX?

The real answer to this question is that you don't learn all about UNIX. There are so many commands, options, languages, and so on that are part of UNIX, it's unlikely that anyone knows all the details. It's not uncommon for someone to be an expert about one part of the system, but to know little about other parts. Perhaps one of the reasons for the propagation of UNIX is that everyone can be a UNIX expert on some topic. There are several things you can do to learn the basics and to develop your own special areas of expertise.

Find a good introductory book on UNIX. Of course our preference is *UNIX SYSTEM V, Release 4: An Introduction*, by Ken Rosen, Richard Rosinski, and James Farber (Berkeley, CA, Osborne-McGraw-Hill, 1990). In that book, we provide a comprehensive introduction to all aspects of standard UNIX. New users, or anyone new to some feature or program, will find it useful. There are also many other useful introductory books on the UNIX system, as well as a wide range of books on specialized and more advanced topics. You will find a large selection of such books at many bookstores that cater to a technical audience, such as those associated with universities, near companies employing lots of computer professionals, and some of the newer 100,000-title bookstores sprouting up in the more prosperous parts of the U.S.

If your area doesn't have a good source of UNIX system books, you can find out about these books by reading reviews in the magazines that cover the UNIX system. (See Tip 54.) You will find a comprehensive listing of UNIX system books on netnews, which is periodically posted to the newsgroup *news.questions.answers*. You can also peruse the booklet *A Selected Bibliography of UNIX and X Books*, by Tim O'Reilly (Sebastopol, A: O'Reilly and Associates, 1993), which provides a useful annotated bibliography of UNIX system books organized into various categories. You can find this booklet at trade shows, such as UNIX Expo. You will also find it useful to look through various publishers' catalogs.

## The UNIX System V Release 4 Document Set

If you had all the volumes in the *UNIX System V Release 4 Document Set*, you could fill a shelf in your bookcase! However, you'll probably only need a few of these volumes for your particular purposes.

This Document Set contains three series of books, *General Use and System Administration*, *General Programmer's Series*, and *System Programmer's Series*. This series of books is published by UNIX Press, and is available from the Prentice-Hall Publishing Company.

The *General Use* and *System Administration* series includes *The Product Overview and Master Index*. This book contains an introduction and summary of features of Release 4. It also describes the Document Set and has an overall index and permuted index that combines all the separate permuted indices. There are two volumes in this series that you may want if you are a general user. These are the *User's Guide* and the *User's Reference Manual.* The *User's Guide* presents an overview of UNIX and has several useful tutorials on some common tasks. The *User's Reference Manual* describes the UNIX system commands intended to be run by users, as opposed to by programs. System administrators will want to have the *System Administrator's Guide*, which describes how to perform administrative tasks and the *System Administrator's Reference Guide*, which contains manual pages on administration commands. General users who need to use networking facilities such as TCP/IP and file-sharing systems will want the *Network User's and Administrator's Guide*, as will system administrators who need to manage these networking facilities.

If you are a developer of application programs you will want the appropriate volumes from the *General Programmer's Series*. These include *Programmer's Guides for ANSI C* and *Programming Support Tools*, *Character User Interface* (FMLI and ETI), *Networking Interfaces*, *POSIX Conformance*, and System *Services and Application Packaging Tools*. You will also want the *Programming Reference Manual*, which describes the commands needed by programmers.

If you are a UNIX system programmer and need to migrate a computer program from an earlier version of the UNIX system to SVR4, or if you want to run programs for different versions of UNIX on the same machine, you will want the appropriate volumes of the System Programmer's Series. These include the *ANSI C Transition Guide*, the *BSD/XENIX Compatibility Guide*, the *Device Driver Interface/Drive-Kernel Interface (DDI/DKI) Reference Manual*, the *Migration Guide*, and the *Programmer's Guide: STREAMS*.

# Using the Manual Pages

**T** **IP**

**52**

To learn more about how UNIX system commands work, you should read the manual.
UNIX manuals, either printed or online, provide good, brief descriptions of UNIX system commands, how they work, and their options. Poring over the manuals is often the easiest way to answer a question.

The UNIX system has traditionally included online documentation via the manual page. The manual pages on UNIX System V are organized into different categories, as shown in the following table:

| Section | Category |
|---------|----------|
| 1 | User commands |
| 1M | Maintenance commands |
| 2 | System calls |
| 3 | Library routines |
| 4 | Administrative files |
| 5 | Miscellaneous |
| 6 | Games |
| 7 | Special files and I/O |
| 8 | Adminstrative commands |

Besides the official online documentation supplied with your system, you may find manual pages written by the developers of programs available on your system. You can write your own manual pages for programs you develop. (See Tip 170.)

To see the manual pages on a particular command, use the **man** command. For example, to see the manual pages on the **ls** command, type

```
$ man ls
```

Sometimes, an entry occurs in more than one section of the manual. In this case, if you type only **man** and the command name, you'll be shown the entry in Section One of the manual. To see other section entries, include the section number of the manual pages as the first argument to the **man** command. For example,

```
$ man chmod
```

will show you the listing for the **chmod** command in Section One, and

```
$ man -s2 chmod
```

will show the Section Two entry for **chmod**.

# Using the Permuted Index

**TIP 53**

Sometimes, you're not sure what the correct command name is to perform a particular task. While some UNIX system commands are logical (for example, **find** finds a file for you), others are not (for example, **grep** finds an expression within a file for you). Because of this, UNIX system command reference guides use a feature called the permuted index. This type of index is useful when you have enough information to start looking up the command by using descriptions of it, or keywords. There is a master index of all commands in the *UNIX System V Release 4 Product Overview and Master Index* that is part of the *UNIX System V Release 4 Document Set*. There are also indices for each one of the individual reference manuals—the *User's Reference Manual*, for example.

The structure of the permuted index is an alphabetical listing of these keywords associated with the commands covered in the manual. Looking at a page of a permuted index, you see that the center section of the three-part entry for each command is what is in alphabetical order. The right part of the entry is the command that performs the function and the section of the manual where it can be found. The left part of the entry consists of additional keywords that may be used to look up the same command to reaffirm that you have the correct command.

Let's take the **awk** command as an example. You are looking for the command to do pattern scanning and processing. You may look for the words "pattern", "scanning", "language", or "processing" in the center section of the alphabetical entries. Under each one, you see the **awk** command listed to the right. To the left of the keyword, say "pattern", you will see the command as well as the other keywords, in this case "scanning" and "processing". Looking under each of the other two entries will result in the cross-referencing of the remaining two keywords, hence the term permuted index. For the awk listing, you'll see each of these entries alphabetized in the *User's Reference Manual:*

|  |  |  |
|---|---|---|
| language awk | awk pattern scanning and processing | awk(1) |
| scanning and processing | language: awk pattern | awk(1) |
| processing language: awk | pattern scanning and | awk(1) |
| awk pattern scanning and | processing language | awk(1) |
| language: awk pattern | scanning and processing language | awk(1) |

where the entry is alphabetized in the listing under the word in the center section.

# Some Useful Periodicals

**TIP 54**

There are quite a few useful magazines and journals devoted to the UNIX system. Perhaps the most useful is *UNIXWorld,* which includes product reviews, tutorials, industry news, and feature articles on technology trends. (Note that *UNIXWorld* changed its name to *Open Systems World* as of January, 1994.)

You might also want to read *UNIX Review,* which is aimed at system integrators, resellers of *UNIX systems,* and engineering and scientific users. This magazine contains information on UNIX system products and tutorials, and feature articles on important technical issues. The *UniForum Monthly Magazine* is another useful magazine on the UNIX system. It includes product information, standing columns, case histories, interviews, and feature articles on UNIX system issues.

For a description of more than 30 different periodicals with articles on the UNIX system, see the *Open Systems Product Directory* published by UniForum.

# Attend UNIX Meetings

**TIP 55**

You will also find it useful to attend conferences, seminars, and trade shows which are devoted to the UNIX system or to computers. You can find a comprehensive list of such events in the *Open Systems Product Directory.* Some of the larger events held annually are UNIX Expo, which is primarily a trade show where you can see the newest UNIX system platforms, the Usenix Association Winter and Summer Technical Conferences, which include workshops and technical talks, and the UniForum Conference and Trade Show which combines a trade show with tutorials and technical sessions. You can consult magazines on the UNIX system for an up-to-date listing of such events. (See Tip 54.) By the way, you'll often find a good selection of UNIX system books at such shows.

# Read the UNIX Groups on Netnews

**TIP 56**

The Internet is a global communications network that acts as an information superhighway for computer users. Netnews, a service on the Internet, is a bulletin board service that covers literally thousands of topics. If you have access to netnews, you have an excellent way to learn more about UNIX by reading the newsgroups devoted to the UNIX system. Some of these newsgroups are general in scope, while others deal with particular areas, such as shell programming or system administration. Listed here are some of the interest groups that are related to UNIX:

| | |
|---|---|
| comp.sources.unix | comp.unix.amiga |
| comp.std.unix | comp.unix.wizards |
| comp.unix.aux | comp.unix.bsd |
| comp.unix.cray | comp.unix.dos-under-unix |
| comp.unix.questions | comp.unix.osf.misc |
| comp.unix.ultrix | comp.unix.osf.osf1 |
| comp.unix.aix | comp.unix.pc-clone.bit |
| comp.unix.admin | comp.unix.pc-clone.bit |
| comp.unix.large | comp.unix.sys |
| comp.unix.misc | comp.unix.sys.misc |
| comp.unix.programmer | comp.unix.sys.5.r3 |
| comp.unix.shell | comp.unix.sys.5.r4 |
| comp.unix.xenix.sco | comp.unix.solaris |
| comp.unix.xenix.misc | comp.unix.user-friendly |
| comp.unix.internals | comp.security.unix |

To learn how to access these newsgroups and how to post articles to them, see the appropriate tips in Chapter 10 of this book. You can become a spectator and participant in wide-ranging UNIX discussions.

# Finding a Local Expert

**T I P 57**

Finally, perhaps the most useful thing you can do is find a local expert. Since everyone can be an expert in some aspect of UNIX, most places have at least a few UNIX experts who can help you. Some large universities and corporations may have counselors whose job it is to help with UNIX questions. Don't be bashful in asking for help. Reciprocate; help others when they ask for your advice.

# Organizations to Join

**TIP 58**

You may also find it helpful to join one of the various organizations devoted to the UNIX system, such as a local, regional, or national user group. One of the largest of these organizations is the UniForum Association. This organization publishes the annual *Open Systems Product Directory*, which contains a wealth of information about UNIX system products, services, and information sources. It also publishes a magazine, a newsletter, and technical guides; and sponsors conferences, trade shows and seminars, and user groups throughout the United States and the rest of the world. You can reach UniForum at:

> UniForum
> 2901 Tasman Drive, #201
> Santa Clara, CA 95054
> telephone: (800) 255-5620 or (408) 986-8840
> fax: (408) 986-1645

The user groups affiliated with UniForum include groups in Argentina, Australia, Brazil, Canada, Chile, China, Denmark, Hong Kong, India, Israel, Italy, Japan, Kuwait, Mexico, New Zealand, Puerto Rico, Singapore, South Africa, Taiwan, and the United Kingdom. You can find the addresses and telephone numbers of each of these groups in the *Open Systems Product Directory*. In the United States, there are affiliated user groups in the following areas: Alabama, Southwest U.S., Chicago, Michigan, upstate New York, Ohio, Oklahoma, Dallas/Fort Worth area, Houston, Seattle, and the Washington, D.C. area. Again, the contact information for these groups is listed in the Open Systems Product Directory.

The USENIX Association is an organization devoted to furthering the interests of UNIX system developers. It holds conferences and workshops and publishes a technical journal and a newletter. The contact information for USENIX is

> USENIX Association
> P.O. Box 2299
> Berkeley, CA 94710
> telephone: (510) 528-8649
> e-mail: uunet!usenix!office

# UNIX Application Programs

## How to Find UNIX Application Programs

**T**IP
**59**

There are several different ways to obtain UNIX application programs. When looking
for programs of interest, first look at the programs and utilities that are already available on your system.
If you are on a multiuser system, it will help to ask other users and your system administrator what is
available on your system. You should also browse around in the directories that contain add-on
programs. The next thing you might want to do is look for public-domain or publicly available software
available over the Internet. There is an amazing variety of free UNIX system software available on the
Internet—see Chapter 10 for details on how to obtain such software. Another obvious thing is to
check with your UNIX system vendor to see if they have application programs of interest to you.
Finally, you can buy commercial applications programs. The following tip tells you where to look for
such programs.

## Finding Commercial UNIX Software

**T**IP
**60**

There are several good places to look for commercial UNIX system software programs.
One of the best is the *Open Systems Products Directory*, published annually by UniForum. This directory
lists commercial software available for the UNIX system, along with other products for UNIX systems.
Applications software is divided into several categories, including accounting, system, communications, horizontal and vertical, application development tools, and database management. Horizontal
software includes a wide range of applications, including computer-aided design, data visualization,
decision support, electronic data interchange, geographical information systems, image processing,
mathematical optimization, office productivity tools, optical character recognition, order entry, report
generation, spreadsheets, word processing, workflow automation, and many other types of programs.
Vertical software includes applications packages for many different industries, including advertising,
agriculture, banking, education, engineering, government, health care, hotel management, insurance,
law enforcement, lawn and tree care, legal, library systems, medical and dental, real estate, retail/point-
of-sale, and trucking.

System software includes such areas as archiving, backup, CD-ROM file management, compilers,
debuggers, device drivers, performance monitoring, programming languages, and security. Commu-

nications software includes such areas as device interfaces, LANs, PC-to-UNIX programs, and terminal emulators. Applications development tools include a wide range of products, including application generators, artificial intelligence/expert systems, language translators, simulators, utility programs, and X Windows tools.

Another good source is the *UNIX System V Product Catalog*, published by UNIX International. This catalog lists more than 1400 system software programs, 4000 horizontal applications, and 4000 vertical applications for more than 60 industries. The catalog also contains information on companies that provide training, consulting, porting, and other services for UNIX System V. You can order this catalog (at a moderate price) from UNIX International, 20 Waterview Blvd., Parsippany, New Jersey 07054.

Magazines such as *Open Systems World* and *UNIX Review* are also good places to look for information on commercial software products for the UNIX system. Often, these magazines publish articles that compare and contrast different software programs providing similar functions.

# Chapter 2

## Organizing
## Your System

# Creating and Removing Files and Directories

## TIP 61

## Tips on Organizing Your Files

UNIX has a hierarchical file system. That is, your file system can contain *directories*—which can in turn contain other directories called *subdirectories*—and *files*.

The most basic aspect of organizing your system is organizing the directories and files you'll be using. First, don't just dump all your files and programs in your home directory (*/home/you* where *you* is your logname). This will work for a while, but you'll soon find it's inefficient to have everything in one big heap. You should get in the habit of regularly reorganizing your directories and files so that they match natural categories in the material you are working on. You might want to follow the same conventions used in UNIX SVR4 when you name your own directories under the home directory, since these conventions make it easy to organize your system. Here are some of the conventions you might want to follow.

❑ Create a mail directory in your home directory (*/home/you/mail*) . This directory should contain a copy of all the saved mail you've sent and received, mail saved in files named after the sender and after the project referred to, the file *mbox,* and your outbox.

❑ Create a *bin* directory to hold useful utility programs. Originally *bin* was a contraction for *bin*ary, but now *bin* directories are used to hold any useful utilities, including shell scripts.

❑ Create a *lib* (for *lib*rary) directory to hold material that you or your programs need to refer to frequently. For example, templates for memos, sets of macros for text formatting, and so on should be kept in the *lib* directory.

❑ Create a *src* (for *sour*ce) directory to contain the source code of programs.

❑ Create a *man* (for *man*ual pages) directory to contain manual pages for your own commands.

❑ If you do any system administration, you should create an *sbin* (for *s*ystem *bin*aries) directory to hold system administration programs.

# How to Name Files

**T**IP
**62**

Files on the UNIX system are identified by their names. A filename is a sequence of any characters, except slashes and null characters. (There are some additional characters you should avoid in naming files; see Tip 64.) In the UNIX system, uppercase and lowercase letters have different meanings, so the files *TEMP, Temp,* and *temp* are all different. (Note that DOS considers uppercase and lowercase letters the same.) You should pick descriptive names for your files. In UNIX SVR4, filenames can be up to 14 characters. Other versions of UNIX allow filenames up to 256 characters. The extra overhead of typing a few extra characters is worth the convenience of being able to find your stuff later. For example, it's unclear what a file named *letter17* might contain, whereas *hcohen_4.23* indicates this file contains a letter to Harvey Cohen written on April 23.

You might also want to use file extensions when you name UNIX system files. For example, you might name a file containing a memo on videophones using the mm macros *videophones.mm.* (See Tip 63 for more on filename extensions in the UNIX system.)

# Filename Extensions

**T**IP
**63**

There are some standard conventions that everyone uses in naming files on UNIX systems, and there are some good suggestions that are helpful, but not universal. One thing to keep in mind when naming a file is to use a filename extension. Unlike DOS, the UNIX system has no special rules about filename extensions. In DOS, a file such as *memo1.txt* is considered a file named *memo1* with the extension *.txt,* where the extension tells DOS the file type. DOS treats the filename separately from how it treats the extension or a filename with an extension. Although the UNIX system does not follow such conventions, some programs either produce or expect a file with a filename extension. For example, in program development, files that contain C language source code must have the extension *.c; filename.c* would indicate a C language program. Likewise, object files are always given a *.o* extension, and assembler files a *.a* extension. These conventions are required by the UNIX C language compiler.

People sometimes expand these conventions to use extensions in other ways. Although not universal, it is common to use a *.mm* extension (*filename.mm*) with text files that are to be formatted with the mm macros package, and *.ms* (*filename.ms*) if the file is prepared with the ms macros package. Similarly, files formatted with Latex (an enhanced version of the TeX text formatting system) are indicated with a *.xx* extension. This is useful only if you or your coworkers use several different formatting or macro packages. Occasionally, people will use a *.sh* extension (*filename.sh*) to indicate that a file contains a shell script.

The following table lists the filename extensions expected or produced by various programs, together with some filename extensions in conventional use.

| Extension | File Type |
|-----------|-----------|
| .a | Archived or assembler code |
| .au | Audio file |
| .c | Source of a C program |
| .csh | C shell script (convention) |
| .enc | Encrypted (convention) |
| .f | Source of a Fortran program |
| .F | Source of a Fortran program before preprocessing |
| .gif | gif file (picture) |
| .gl | gl file (animated picture) |
| .gz | Compressed with the **gzip** command |
| .h | Header file |
| .jpg | jpeg file (picture) |
| .mm | Text with mm macros (convention) |
| .ms | Text with ms macros (convention) |
| .o | Compiled and assembled code (object file) |
| .ps | PostScript source code (convention) |
| .s | Assembly language code |
| .sh | UNIX System V Shell program (convention) |
| .tar | Archived using the **tar** command (convention) |
| .tex | Text formatted with TeX commands |
| .txt | ASCII text (convention) |
| .uu | Uuencoded file |
| .xx | Text formatted with Latex commands |
| .z | Compressed using the **pack** command |
| .Z | Compressed using the **compress** command |

If you choose, you can use filename extensions other than the common ones. For example, you could use *.shell* instead of *.sh* for files containing a UNIX System Shell script. But you should not (or cannot) change the filename extensions expected or produced by programs.

# Characters to Avoid in Filenames

You can use any ASCII character in a filename except two: the / (slash, also called the virgule), which has a special meaning under UNIX; and the null character. The slash acts as a separator for directory and filenames on the system. Even though any other ASCII character can be used in a filename, it's a good idea to avoid the use of many of them. For example, the shell interprets certain characters as having special meaning. If you use these characters in a filename, this special meaning has to be turned off when you want to refer to the file. The characters to avoid are listed here:

| | |
|---|---|
| ! (exclamation point) | @ (at sign) |
| # (pound sign) | $ (dollar sign) |
| & (ampersand) | ^ (carat) |
| ( ) (parenthesis) | { } (braces) |
| ` " (single or double quotes) | * (asterisk) |
| ; (semicolon) | ? (question mark) |
| \| (pipe) | (space) |
| < > (arrows) | (backspace) |
| \ (backslash) | (tab) |

Note that you cannot create a file named . (dot) or .. (two dots), since these names are reserved for the current or parent directory.

# Tips for Naming Directories

Most people like to use a particular convention for naming directories so that they can distinguish whether a name refers to a directory or an ordinary file. For example, some people give directories names that are all uppercase letters, that only begin with an uppercase letter, or that have the extension *.d* or perhaps *.dir* instead. For example, if you choose names beginning with uppercase letters for directories, and names beginning with lowercase letters for regular files, you'll know that *Memos, Programs,* and *Misc* are directories, while *memo9, program3, letter, notes.13,* and *a.out* are all regular files. You should create your own convention for naming directories and stick with it.

You may want to organize your home directory with some of the conventions found in UNIX SVR4, using the same names for subdirectories of your home directory as are used in the root directory; see Tip 61 for details. Note that you can find out which of the files in your current directory is itself a directory by using the **ls -l** command. (See Tip 86.)

# TIP 66 — Using Wildcards When Specifying Files

Wildcards are a useful shorthand for specifying one or more files. The shell provides three wildcards for files: the \* (asterisk), which matches a string with any number of characters, including zero characters; the ? (question mark), which matches any single character; and [...] (brackets), which enclose a character list or range for matching. To illustrate how the \* is used, note that you can match all files with names that end with ".c" by using \*.c, all files containing the string "letter" with *\*letter\**, and all files beginning with "memo" with *memo\**.

To illustrate how the ? is used, note that you can match all files that start with the string "version" followed by a single character using *version?*. Similarly, you can match all files that start with the string "program." followed by a single character with *program.?*. This includes all the files with C-like extensions, including *program.c, program.o, program.h,* and *program.a.*

To see how brackets are used, note that *[mMemo]* matches both the files *memo* and *Memo; program[1-4]* matches the files *program1, program2, program3,* and *program4;* and *temp[a-z]* matches all files with the name temp followed by a single lowercase letter (such as *tempd*). You can also use combinations of wildcards—for example, *\*memo?* will match any string that ends with memo followed by a single character, such as *bookmemo1, memo2, Xmemo9,* and so on.

There are a couple of exceptions to the way wildcards work. One important fact to note is that hidden files, those with names that start with a . (dot), are not matched unless the dot is supplied. So *\*profile* does not match *.profile,* but *.\*file, .prof\*,* and *.profil?* do. Another exception is that wildcards won't match / (slash), since this character is used between the names of directories in a path and is also the name of the root directory.

DOS users should note that wildcards work differently in DOS than they do in UNIX. For example, to match all files in a DOS directory, you have to use \*.\*, since the \* does not match a string with a

. (period) in it. In UNIX, the * will match any string except those that begin with a . or have a / (slash) in them.

# A Wildcard Pattern That Matches All Hidden Files

Suppose we want to match all hidden files, that is files that begin with a . (dot).

If we use .??*, we will match all files that begin with . (dot) followed by two or more characters. This misses not only . and .., but also files with two-character names beginning with ., such as *.a* and *.1*. We can match these files using *.[!.]*, which matches all files with names that have two characters where the first character is a dot and the second is any character other than a dot. This works in the Korn shell and in some other newer shells. You can also match these files using *.[^A--/-^?]*. Here the range of characters inside the brackets starts at the ASCII CTRL-A character (represented by ^A), goes up to - (dash), continues at / (slash), and goes through the ASCII DEL character, ^?, which is produced by pressing the DELETE key. Consequently, you can use either

```
.??* .[!.]
```

or

```
.??* .[^A--/-^?]
```

# A Wildcard Pattern That Matches All Files Except . (the Current Directory) and .. (the Parent Directory)

It's surprisingly tricky to find an expression with wildcards that matches all files except . (dot) and .. (dot dot). Note that *matches all files that don't begin with . (dot) and .* matches all files that do begin with . (dot). But this includes . (dot) and .. (dot dot), which we don't want to match.

To match files that start with . (dot) and are followed by anything other than a dot, use *.[!.]\**. This is understood by the Korn shell; some other shells use a ^ (carat) instead of a !. Unfortunately, this misses files that start with .. (dot dot), such as *..a*.

The expression *.??\** lets us match files that begin with . (dot) and are followed by at least two characters. This avoids the files . and ..; it also misses filenames that start with . (dot) but are only two characters long, such as *.a1*.

Putting all these things together, we can match all files except . and .. using the following three patterns:

```
.[!.]* .??* *
```

# What's in the UNIX System V File System?

Your own file system is part of the larger UNIX file system, which is already present when you are added as a user. You should know about this file structure since you can access files outside your own file system tree. UNIX's file system varies according to which variant of UNIX you are using. We will describe key elements of the UNIX System V Release 4 file system here. If you use a different version of UNIX, you should consult the appropriate manuals to learn about the file system on your machine.

Important directories in the UNIX SVR4 file system include

❑ */* (the *root* directory)   The main directory of the entire file system

❑ */stand*   The directory containing the standard programs and data files used in booting the system

❑ */sbin*   The directory containing programs used in booting the system and in system recovery

❑ */dev*   The directory containing device files, including terminals, printers, and storage devices

❑ */etc*   The directory containing system administration and configuration databases

❑ */opt*   The directory that is the root of the file system of add-on applications

❑ */home*   The directory containing the home directories of all users—for example, */home/fred* is the home directory of user fred

❑ */spool*   The directory containing the directories for spooling files, or saving them for later processing, including

> */spool/lp*   Contains spooling files for line printers
>
> */spool/uucp*   Contains files queued for the UUCP System
>
> */spool/uucppublic*   Contains files deposited by the UUCP System

❑ */tmp*   The directory containing all temporary files used by UNIX

❑ */var*   The directory containing files with variable uses in the system, including

> */var/adm*   Contains system logging and accounting files
>
> */var/mail*   Contains user mail files
>
> */var/news*   Contains messages of common interest
>
> */var/opt*   The root of a subtree of files for add-on application packages
>
> */var/tmp*   Contains temporary files
>
> */var/uucp*   Contains files for the UUCP System

❑ */usr*   The directory that contains a variety of user-accessible directories, including

> */usr/bin*   Contains executable programs and utilities
>
> */usr/sbin*   Contains executable programs for system administration
>
> */usr/games*   Contains game programs
>
> */usr/lib*   Contains libraries for programs and programming languages
>
> */usr/share/man*   Contains online manual pages
>
> */usr/ucb*   Contains the BSD compatibility package binaries

# What Are the Hidden .*rc Files?

You may have encountered hidden files with names that end with rc, such as *.cshrc, .kshrc, .mailrc, .exrc,* and so on. Why do these filenames end with *rc?*

The answer is that rc stands for *run command,* which comes from the **runcom** command in one of the early operating systems (called CTSS) from which UNIX evolved. The **runcom** command was used to run commands from batch files. Analogously, *.*rc* files are used to initialize or customize the environment for a particular program. For example, *.cshrc* customizes your C shell environment, and *.kshrc* your Korn shell environment.

## Changing Directories

# Finding Your Current Directory and Changing Directories

If you need to know what your current directory is, just run the **pwd** command. For example, the following shows you that the current directory is */home/xavier/memos*:

```
$ pwd
/home/xavier/memos
```

The UNIX system contains several methods and some useful shortcuts for changing directories.

First, note that when you use the **cd** command with no argument, you are returned to your home directory. Let's say your home directory is */home/fred*. When you are in the directory */home/fred/memos*, you will find the following sequence:

```
$ pwd
/home/fred/memos
$ cd
$ pwd
/home/fred
```

Note that the **pwd** command prints the name of the current directory. DOS users should remember that the **cd** command works differently in DOS than in UNIX. The **cd** command in DOS tells you what the current directory is, instead of changing to your home directory as it does in UNIX.

To change to a subdirectory of the current directory, simply use the **cd** (change directory) command with the name of the subdirectory as the argument. For instance, to change from the directory */home/fred* to its subdirectory */home/fred/memos*, just type the following line:

```
$ cd memos
```

To change to a directory from anywhere in your file system, you can always supply **cd** with the full pathname to this directory. For example, to change to */home/fred/memos/april* from */home/fred/vouchers,* you need only use the following command:

```
$ cd /home/fred/memos/april
```

Since .. (dot dot) refers to the parent directory of your current directory, to move to that parent directory, type

```
$ cd ..
```

So we would have

```
$ pwd
/home/fred/memos/april
$ cd ..
/home/fred/memos
$ cd ../..
/home
```

For an additional shortcut for changing directories, see Tip 72, which gives an easy way to change to the previous directory; Tip 73, which shows how to use an abbreviation for users' login directories; and Tip 47, which shows how to use your CDPATH environmental variable to facilitate the move from directory to directory.

# Changing to Your Previous Directory

**TIP 72**

Sometimes you may want to change back to your previous directory, that is, the one you were working in before you changed to your current directory. If you use the Korn shell, you don't have to give **cd** the name of the previous directory to do this. You need only type

```
$ cd -
```

For example, suppose you changed from */home/nancy/memos* to */home/nancy/programs/old*. If you use cd -, you will change back to */home/nancy/memos*. If you then run a few commands without changing your current directory, using cd - again will put you back in */home/nancy/memos*.

Unfortunately, this capability is not part of the C shell.

# Using an Abbreviation for a Login Directory

Suppose you want to change to the subdirectory */memos/new* in the home directory of user djf, */home/djf*. Instead of using this command,

```
$ cd /home/djf/memos/new
```

you can use the abbreviation ~djf for the login directory of the user djf, and then use the following command:

```
$ cd ~djf/memos/new
```

Using the *~logname* abbreviation makes it unnecessary to know the full pathname of the home directory of this user. Also note that a tilde (~) without a logname is the abbreviation for your home directory. So, you can change to your directory *memos/new* using

```
$ cd ~/memos/new
```

# Running a Command in Another Directory

You may need to run commands in a different directory than your current one, taking files from that directory as input and producing output in that directory. You don't have to change to that directory to run commands in it. Instead, you can use a subshell. You can change directories in the subshell and when your subshell is terminated, you are still in your original current directory. For example, suppose you are in your directory */home/ralph* and want to run a command in the subdirectory results. You might do something like this:

```
$ (cd results; sort -n * > report)
```

This command line sets up a subshell. The current directory of the subshell is first changed to *results,* and then the **sort** command is run in this subshell, producing a file *report* in the subdirectory results. When this command line has run, you are still in */home/ralph.*

# Creating and Removing Directories

**T**IP
**75**

A file doesn't have to already exist when you ask UNIX to put something into it, since UNIX will automatically create the file. However, a directory must already exist before you can put files into it and doesn't cease to exist until it is removed. If you create a directory, then remove all its files, it will still exist.

The DOS commands **mkdir** (or **md**) and **rmdir** (or **rd**) are very similar to the UNIX equivalents **mkdir** and **rmdir**. However, the UNIX commands offer more options and are more powerful. To create a directory (in either operating system), type

```
$ mkdir dirname
```

The new directory will be created as a subdirectory of the current directory. In UNIX, you can create several new directories at once by using the -**p** option. For example, to create a directory called *projects* containing a subdirectory called *local,* type

```
$ mkdir -p projects/local
```

To remove a directory in DOS, you must first delete all subdirectories and erase all files. The UNIX commands are more flexible. The basic command for removing a directory is **rmdir**. (The command **rm** is for removing files, although it can also remove directories.) The directory will be removed if you type

```
$ rmdir dirname
```

# Removing Files

To remove a file in DOS, you would use the **del** or **erase** command. How does this work in UNIX?

The DOS **del** command erases a file—either a single file specified by a filename or a group of files specified by a wildcard. For example, to erase all the files in the current directory, you would type

```
erase *.*
```

In this case, DOS will ask whether you are sure that you want to do this.

The UNIX command for removing files is **rm**. It includes a number of options that make it more powerful than the DOS **del** command. For example, you can use the **-f** option to remove all of the files in a directory (without a warning prompt). You can also remove all of the files and subdirectories in a directory with

```
$ rm -r *
```

If there are any write-protected files in any of the directories, you will be prompted before they are removed.

# Restoring a Lost File

You need help! By mistake, you issued the following command in the directory where you stored your thesis:

```
$ rm *
```

How can you recover the last six years' work?

Standard UNIX systems do not have an **undo** command to rescue you. But there is hope if you are on a multiuser system with a system administrator. Call your system administrator and ask to have all the material in that directory restored from the last backup. That way, you have lost only the work done since the last time the system was backed up. If you are your own system administrator, turn quickly to Chapter 11 to see how to restore the directory yourself. If you haven't been making backups, you are out of luck.

# Preventing Disaster with rm *

The command **rm** * is so powerful that an innocent typo can have terrible consequences. If you want to get rid of all the files with a *.doc* suffix (*able.doc, baker.doc, dog.doc,* and so on), you can use the following command:

```
$ rm *.doc
```

But if you mistype and hit the space bar before the .doc, as in:

```
$ rm *  .doc
```

all your files will be removed and then you'll see the error message:

```
rm: .doc non-existent
```

In this example, you can be more cautious by typing

```
$ rm -i *.doc
```

This invokes the **-i** (*i*nteractive) option of the **rm** command, which prompts you for confirmation before it removes each of the files.

# Removing Files with Funny Characters in Their Names

Suppose you have a file with a funny character in its name. How can you delete this file?

One way is to use

```
$ rm -i pattern
```

where the pattern matches only the names of files you want to remove. For example, to remove all files with names that begin with the string "123" followed by the ASCII bell character CTRL-G (^G), you should use

```
$ rm -i 123?
```

This command asks if you want to remove each file matching the indicated pattern, such as *1234*, *123a*, *123+*, and *123^G*. You answer **n** when asked if you want to remove one of these files, until you come to *123^G,* which you do want to delete.

You can also use

```
$ rm -ri .
```

This command asks you file by file whether to remove each file in the directory. Answer **y** to the problem file and **n** to everything else. This may be inefficient since you will have to answer whether you want to delete each of the files in every subdirectory of your current directory (.). To avoid this, you might want to make these directories unsearchable using **chmod a-x**, remembering to make them searchable again when you're through.

If the funny character in your filename is a / (slash), you've got a messy problem. This is extremely unlikely, but if you end up with a file like this, see your local guru.

# Removing Files with Names That Begin with –

If you create a file whose name begins with a – (dash), you will have trouble dealing with it. In particular, the command **rm**, as shown below, will not work.

```
rm -file
```

The reason is that the initial – is treated as an option flag, and the command will act as if you are trying to invoke a nonexistent option. This problem is not restricted to **rm**. Most commands will get confused by a filename that begins with –.

Your easiest solution is to find some way to refer to the file that doesn't begin with a dash. For example, you could use

```
$ rm ./-file
```

For many commands, you can use the end-of-options argument --, to stop the command from processing anything that follows it as an argument. Suppose you wish to print the string "-xyz" to your screen (or to standard input). The following expression will give an error message:

```
$ echo -xyz
```

The correct expression to print the string would be

```
$ echo -- -xyz
```

# Using find to Remove Files

Another way to remove a file with a troublesome filename is to use the **find** command to execute another command on any file that matches its argument, as shown here.

```
$ find . -type f ... -ok rm '{}' \;
```

In this example, ... uniquely identifies the file. The trick is to come up with an option to **find** that will do this.

One way to uniquely identify the file you want to remove is to use **ls -i** . to get the inode number of files in the current directory, and then use that number with the **-inum** (*i*node *num*ber) option of the **find** command. An example of this follows.

```
find . -inum 1358 -ok rm '{}' \;
```

Use the **-ok** option for protection; it prompts you for confirmation of the command before executing it. If you think the filename has a funny character in it, you might want to use **-exec** instead of **-ok**, since this avoids the prompting. However, this also eliminates your safety check.

Of course, you can use the same approach if you want to perform some other command, such as moving the file:

```
$ find . -inum 1358 -ok mv '{}' newname \;
```

## Listing Files

# TIP 82

# How to List the Files in a Directory

In DOS you can use the **dir** command to list the contents of the current directory, not including any hidden system files. The output of the DOS **dir** command includes the name and size of a file and the date of its last modification.

To list the files in a UNIX system directory, use the **ls** command. Without an option, this command will print the names of all the files and subdirectories in your current directory, except hidden files. (See Tip 83 to learn how to include such files in the list.) For example,

```
$ ls
NOTES   letter9.3   memo7.7   memo8.13
```

shows that the current directory contains *NOTES*, which in this case is a subdirectory, and *letter9.3, memo7.7,* and *memo8.13*, which in this case are all files.

If you want to know if a particular file or subdirectory exists in your current directory, give **ls** the name of this file as an argument, as shown here.

```
$ ls letter9.2
letter9.2 not found
$ ls letter9.3
letter9.3
```

This tells you there is no file with the name *letter9.2* in your current directory, but there is a file with the name *letter9.3.*

The **ls** command has an amazing number of options you can use to list files in different ways. If you use a version of UNIX other than SVR4, you will find that these options may work differently than described here, so you should consult the **ls** manual page to see how they work on your system.

For example, you may want to have your files listed with their names sorted alphabetically across rather than down the screen. To do this, use the **-x** option to **ls**. To have files listed one per line, use the **-1** (one) option. To list all files, including hidden files, use the **-a** option. (See Tip 83.) To list files so that nonprintable characters show up in octal form, use the **-b** option. (See Tip 84.) To get only the names of files and their sizes, use the **-s** (*size*) option. To get more detailed information about the file, use the **-l** (*long*) option. (See Tip 86.)

You can also combine options. For instance, **ls -al** will provide a detailed list of information about all files, including hidden files; **ls -abl** will provide the same, as well as nonprintable characters in filenames will be shown in octal form.

# Listing Hidden Files

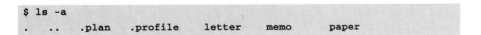

The **ls** command doesn't list your hidden files. This is because when you list the files in a directory, you normally don't want to list hidden files. (This is, after all, one of the reasons they are hidden.)

However, if you want to list all of the files in a directory, including hidden files such as your *.profile,* use the **ls** command with the **-a** option. An example of **ls -a** output is:

```
$ ls -a
.    ..    .plan    .profile    letter    memo    paper
```

The output shows the current directory, represented by . (dot), the parent directory represented by .. (dot dot), the hidden files *.profile* and *.plan,* and the three files *letter, memo,* and *paper.*

# Listing Files So That Nonprintable Characters Appear

Sometimes a file will have a nonprintable character in its name. When you use **ls** to list your files, these nonprintable characters won't show up. When you try to delete such a file, using what you think is its filename, you will get a message that no such file exists. How do you avoid this problem?

The answer is to use the **-b** option of the **ls** command. When you use this option, nonprintable characters are printed with the octal \ddd *notation*. For example, suppose you have a file that you've accidentally named *memo1^G* (the last character here being the ASCII bell character CTRL-G). When you list your files, you see one with the name *memo1*. If you already had a file named *memo1*, you'd see *memo1* twice when you ran the ls command! But if you run ls with the **-b** option, your output will include the string "memo1\007" for this file, since \007 is the octal notation for the ASCII bell character CTRL-G.

# Listing Files in the Current Directory, Its Subdirectories, and So On

If you are a DOS user, you may use the **tree** command to display your file system. Although there is no precise equivalent in UNIX, you can use the **-R** (*recursive*) option to the **ls** command to list all the files in your current directory, along with all the files in each of its subdirectories, and all the files in the subdirectories of these subdirectories, and so on. An example of this follows.

```
$ ls -R
Memos     lettera   letterb    note1    note2    note3
./Memos
memo1    memo2     memo3
```

There are a couple of other ways to list all the files in your current directory or under it in your directory tree. The **find** command is specifically designed to descend through your file system starting at a specified point. If you tell it to print the names of files it finds, you'll get a full listing of files in subdirectories. The command you use is as follows.

```
$ find . -print
```

The **du** (*d*isk *u*sage) command also provides information about all files under a directory.

```
$ du -a
```

gives you both the name and size of all files under the current directory.

Whether you use **find** or **du** depends on what you think is most natural and convenient, and on what information you want to see besides the filenames.

# Getting Detailed Information on Your Files

TIP 86

Suppose you want to find a file that you changed last month, or you want to find your largest or smallest files. How can you do this? You can get the type of detailed information you need to answer such questions by using the **ls** command and the -l (*l*ong) option, which produces detailed information about the files in your current directory. Here is an example of this.

```
$ ls -l
total 28
drwxr-xr-x  3  moby  group3  340  Oct 30  01:44  Misc
-rwxr-x---  1  moby  group3  586  Feb 13  18:18  memo1
-rw-rw-r--  1  moby  group3  102  May  1  12:00  notes
-rwxrwx---  1  moby  group3   82  Jun 13  08:01  letter
```

The output you'll get shows one line per file, with the name of the file appearing in the last field. The permissions for the file are shown in the first field. (See Tip 129.) The second field shows the number of linked copies of that file. The third field shows the owner of the file and the fourth the group the file belongs to. The fifth field shows the size of the file in bytes. The sixth shows the last time the file was changed.

# TIP 87

# Finding Your Oldest Files

Suppose you want to find your oldest files, perhaps in order to clean out your system by deleting some files. When you use the **ls** command with the -t option, you will have the files in your current directory listed in order of their modification time, with files you've changed most recently listed first. The files at the end of your list become possible candidates for deletion.

# TIP 88

# Counting the Files in a Directory

You can get a count of the number of files in a directory by piping the results of running the **ls** command with the -l option to the **wc** command with the -l option. Note that this will not count the hidden files in that directory. For example, to count the number of nonhidden files in your directory programs, run

```
$ cd programs
$ ls -l | wc -l
43
```

This shows that there are 42 nonhidden files in the directory programs, since there is one line for each file, plus one line, for a total of 43.

If you want to include the hidden files in the count, run

```
$ ls -al | wc -l
46
```

This output shows that there are 3 hidden files, since there are 42 nonhidden files and 45 total files in the current directory.

# Finding Out When a File Was Created

Unfortunately, there is no way to know the creation time of a file since that information isn't stored anywhere. However, files have a last-modified time, which is displayed in the output of **ls -l**; a last-accessed time, which is displayed in the output of **ls -lu**; and an inode change time, which is displayed in the output of **ls -lc**. Although this inode change time is often referred to (even in the manual pages for some commands) as the file's creation time, this is not correct since the inode change time is set by a number of commands, including **mv**, **ln**, **chmod**, **chown**, and **chgrp**.

# Listing the Size of a File

Murray Nesbitt of the University of Toronto has suggested using the following shell script to list the files in bytes.

```
ls -l ${1+"$@"} | awk '{tmp += $5}  END  {print tmp}'
```

This command prints the contents of the fifth field in the output of **ls -l**; you can modify this script to print other information provided by **ls -l**. To set this up, put this command as the single line in a file—say, *fsize*. Then make this file executable and make sure your PATH contains the directory the file is in. Then, for example, to find the size in bytes of the file *memo1*, use

```
$ fsize memo1
```

(See Chapter 7 for information on shell programming and Chapter 8 for information on the **awk** command used in this command.)

John Navarra of Northwestern University suggests the following script, named *files*.

```
/bin/ls -l $* | awk '{
    print $4,"\t",$8
    sum +=4
}
END {print "Total: ",sum, "bytes {" NR " files) "}' -
```

You can use *files* to get the size and filename of each file in a directory matching a wildcard pattern, together with a running total at the bottom. For example,

```
$ files /bin/n*
```

will give a list of the size in bytes and filename of each file in */bin* that starts with the letter "n" and will give the total bytes in these files and the number of such files.

# How Much Space Is Left on Your Disk?

How does UNIX determine the amount of free space available for a file system?

When you use the DOS **dir** command, you get the amount of free space on a disk, along with a listing of all the files in a directory and their sizes. DOS also provides the **size** command, which shows the size of individual files. UNIX offers two powerful commands for viewing disk usage: **df** (disk free) and **du** (disk usage).

The **df** command shows the total number of free blocks (a block is 512 bytes) on the disk. If you run the **df** command with no arguments, you will get information on all the file systems, including both local and remote. You can determine the number of kilobytes the file system has available, the number used, the capacity, and where the file system is mounted. If you want information on a particular file system, give this file system as the argument. For example, for information on the free blocks in the directory */usr/tmp*, type

```
$ df /usr/tmp
```

The **du** command gives more detailed information about the disk space taken up by the directories and subdirectories. It tells you how many kilobytes a directory and each of its subdirectories occupy. To get only the storage occupied by the directory, without splitting out the amount each subdirectory occupies, add the -s (*s*uppress) option to **du**. To find out how much space each file occupies, add the -a (*a*ll) option to **du**.

# Working with Files

## Compressing Files

**T IP**

**92**

Let's say you are running out of file space and your telephone bills for transferring large files are using up your lunch money. What can you do to make your files smaller without losing information?

One thing you can do to save space for storing large files and to save transmission time is to compress them. When you compress a file, you produce a new file with the same information as the original file, represented using fewer bits. The UNIX system includes several utilities for compressing files, including **compress** and **pack**.

Of these two, **compress** usually produces a smaller file. The following example shows how **compress** is used. To compress the file *dictionary* using **compress**, use the command

```
$ compress -v dictionary
dictionary:  Compression: 51.43% - replaced with dictionary.Z
```

This command replaces the file *dictionary* with the file *dictionary.Z*. Note the use of the -v option to determine the compressed file is 51.43% smaller than the original file. To recover the original file from the compressed version, you need only use the following command line:

```
$ uncompress dictionary.Z
```

## Concealing Filenames

**T IP**

**93**

Is there a way to make the name of a file invisible? That is, to hide it so it won't show up when someone runs the **ls** command?

The answer is yes and no; you can hide a filename from the **ls** command, but you can't make it invisible to a knowledgeable user. The standard way to hide a filename is to precede it with a . (dot). If a filename begins with a dot, that name is not displayed when you use an ordinary **ls**.

This feature is often used to hide files you need, but don't want cluttering up the screen. For example, you probably have several of these already:

| | |
|---|---|
| *.profile* | Startup file when you log in |
| *.kshrc* | Startup file for the Korn shell |
| *.mailrc* | Preferences and aliases for mailx |
| *.exrc* | Preferences, macros, and abbreviations for ex/vi |
| *.news* | Date of the last time you read news |
| *.login* | Startup file for the csh |
| *.lastlogin* | Date of your last login session |

If you use the **-a** option to **ls**, these files are displayed. For example, **ls -a** shows just the filenames, and **ls -al** shows names, permissions, dates, owner, and other information.

Although these files are hidden, they are not invisible to the experienced user. You can make them more invisible by giving a file an unprintable name. For example, using control codes as a filename will hide it. Naming a file ^A^B (CTRL-A CTRL-B) will cause **ls** or **ls -a** to leave a blank in place of the filename. The filename won't be printed, but it's obvious that something is there. You can combine these two by using a name like . ^A (dot CTRL-A), so that **ls -a** will show two lines containing a single dot.

You can be more clever and manipulate the terminal. You can look up the escape sequence for your terminal that erases a line and moves up a line, and use that for your filename. But that's easily defeated as well. In fact, since the command sequence

```
$ ls -a > tmp
$ vi tmp
```

puts all the filenames in *tmp,* the **vi** editor will show all the special characters that might be there.

# Splitting Big Files into Pieces

Suppose you have a file so big you can't run it on your editor. Is there a way to split it into smaller files?

You can use the **split** command if you have a really large file that you want to split into pieces. For example,

```
$ split addresses
```

will split the file addresses into pieces, each with 1000 lines. The first piece will have the name *addresses.aa,* the second piece the name *addresses.ab,* the third *addresses.ac,* the 27th *addresses.ba,* and so on. If you want each piece to have 500 lines, you would instead use

```
$ split -500 addresses
```

# How to Use tmp and .tmp Files

Many programs use a tmp file to capture some output for later examination. It's a good idea to treat any file named *tmp, .tmp,* or *.tmp1234* as temporary and ephemeral. Often, tmp files are used in shell programming to hold intermediate or temporary data, and are quickly deleted. Don't put anything that has value beyond your current login session in a tmp file, and delete any tmp files you see in your own directories.

On most systems there is also a directory, */tmp,* that is used generally as temporary space for a variety of programs. Sometimes users will put large files in */tmp* rather than in their own directories. (If a system charges for disk storage used, */tmp* is generally not included in the charge, so putting something there means it can be stored free.) When */tmp* is filled, programs that use it can't be run. As a result, system administrators regularly clean out */tmp,* usually getting rid of all files a day or more old. Again, don't put anything of value in a */tmp* directory. Note that on most systems, */tmp* is automatically cleared when the machine is rebooted.

# TIP 96

# What to Do with Confidential Files

If you are like most people, you will have some files on your system that you'd like to keep private. For example, you may have an up-to-date resumé and letters applying for new jobs, salary information, files with April Fools' jokes that would get you in trouble if anyone knew you were the culprit, and so on. One thing you can do is set up a directory called *personal* and put all your private files in that directory. Then if you set the permissions on that directory so that no one else can read, write, or execute any of these files, only you or a superuser will have access to them. You can do this with the command

```
$ chmod  700 personal
```

To keep these files secret even from superusers, such as system administrators, you will need to encrypt each file. (See Tip 97 to see how this is done.)

*Encrypting files will not make the files completely secure, but will only make them resistant to compromise. A serious codebreaker, using sufficient effort, will be able to read your encrypted files.*

# TIP 97

# Encrypting Files

You can encrypt files by using the **crypt** command. When you use **crypt** to encrypt a file, no other user, not even the superuser, will be able to read this file without the encryption key.

To use **crypt** to encrypt a file, you must supply an encryption key. Although there are several ways to do this, the best way is to have **crypt** prompt you for this key. For example, suppose you want to encrypt the file *letter* and put the encrypted version of this file in *letter.enc*. Here is how you do it.

```
$ crypt < letter > letter.enc
Enter key:  2xz8b
```

Here, **crypt** prompted you for an encryption key. You supplied 2xz8b as this key. Once you have encrypted your file, you will want to remove the unencrypted version. In this case, you would use

```
$ rm letter
```

```
$ rm letter
```

To decrypt the encrypted file, you simply run **crypt** again. This time you recover the original file *letter* from the encrypted file *letter.enc* by using

```
$ crypt < letter.enc > letter
Enter key:  2xz8b
```

The reason decryption works this way is that in the method used by the **crypt** command, decryption is carried out by the same method used by encryption, using the same key.

If you forget the key you used to encrypt a file, then you are out of luck. No one, not even your system administrator, can help you recover your encrypted file, without some serious cryptanalysis.

The other ways to supply the encryption key to **crypt** have some serious security weaknesses. You can supply the key as part of the command line, for example, using

```
$ crypt 2xz8b < letter > letter.enc
```

But someone running **ps -a** at the time you issue this command will see your encryption key. What if you use the CRYPTKEY environmental variable, by including the line

```
CRYPTKEY=2xz8b
```

in your *.profile* and encrypt using **crypt -k** to use the value of CRYPTKEY as the encryption key? Someone could find the value of this key by gaining access to your *.profile*.

Note that because of U.S. government regulations, the algorithms used by **crypt** vary, depending on whether you have a version of UNIX produced for use in the United States and Canada or elsewhere. This means that a key used to decrypt encrypted files in one part of the world may not work elsewhere.

You should also note that files encrypted using **crypt** are vulnerable to serious attack. There is even a package called the *Crypt Breaker's Workbench,* available on the Internet, that performs this cryptanalysis. So, the files you encrypt using **crypt** are really only resistant to attack and are not totally secure.

# Moving and Copying Files and Directories

## TIP 98

## How to Move a File

The UNIX system provides a command **mv** that you can use to rename a file or to move it to a different place in your directory tree. For example, to rename the file *memo1* to *memo.93* in your current directory, you would use the command

```
$ mv memo1 memo9.3
```

To move a file to another place in your directory tree, you give **mv** the full pathnames of the old and new files. Similarly, to move the file */home/abigail/file1* to */home/abigail/misc/notes,* you would use the command

```
$ mv /home/abigail/file1 /home/abigail/misc/notes
```

If you are a DOS user, note that in DOS there is no single command that performs the same functions as the **mv** command in UNIX. In DOS, you can give a file a new name in the directory using the rename command. But to move a file to another place in your directory tree in DOS, you must first use the **copy** command to copy the file where you want to put it in your directory tree and then you use the **del** command to delete the original copy.

## TIP 99

## Some Tips for Moving Files

It's possible to make a bad mistake when renaming files using **mv**. For example, you can accidentally overwrite an existing file if you try to rename a file with a filename that already exists. To avoid this problem, use the -i (*i*nteractive) option to **mv**. When you use this option, **mv** tells you when it would have to overwrite an existing file to perform the requested task. Then it gives you the option of overwriting the existing file. For example,

```
$ mv -i memo1 memo93
mv:  overwrite memo93?
```

If you type **y** after the question mark (?), *memo93* will be overwritten with the contents of *memo1*. If you type **n** (or almost anything else the system shouldn't interpret as "yes"), the file will not be overwritten.

You can also use **mv** to move an entire directory with one command. For example, to move the directory *Book93*, including all its subdirectories and files, to the directory *Oldbook,* you can use the command

```
$ mv Book93 Oldbook
```

# Copying Files

**TIP**
**100**

Let's say you want a second copy of a file, perhaps as a backup copy you can refer to if you accidentally change the original file in a way you didn't intend. To copy a file on the UNIX system, use the **cp** command. If you are a DOS user, you should note that the UNIX **cp** command is analogous to the DOS **copy** command.

For example, to make a backup copy of the file results called *results.bck,* use the command

```
$ cp results results.bck
```

If the file *results.bck* doesn't already exist, it will be created and the contents of *results* copied to it. If *results.bck* already exists, its contents will be overwritten with those of *results*.

You can put a copy of a file in a subdirectory of the current directory by providing the name of that subdirectory as the target, as shown here.

```
$ cp results Data
```

In this example, *Data* is a subdirectory of the current directory, and will put a copy of the file results in the subdirectory *Data.* You can also make copies of several files in a subdirectory by listing their names, followed by the name of the subdirectory, as arguments. For example,

```
$ cp memo1 memo2 memo3 memo4  Documents
```

will make copies of the files *memo1, memo2, memo3,* and *memo4* and put them in the subdirectory *Documents.* Note that copying a file is different than moving a file since copying a file does not delete the source file. You need to give the **cp** the name of your source file followed by the name of your destination file.

# How to Copy Files and Directories Without Messing Up

To make a copy of a file on UNIX systems, use the **cp** command. For example, you may want to make a copy of a file to use as a backup file, as shown in this example.

```
$ cp memo memo.bk
```

This puts a copy of the file *memo* in the file *memo.bk.* You should be careful when you copy files, since the destination file will be overwritten if it already exists. To avoid this problem, UNIX SVR4 provides the **-i** (*i*nteractive) option, which warns you before it overwrites an existing file. An example of this follows.

```
$ cp -i memo memo.bk
```

This command won't make a copy of memo with the filename *memo.bk* if it already exists unless you say you want to do this when it asks.

DOS uses the **xcopy** command to copy all the files in a directory. In UNIX you can copy an entire directory with one command by using the **-r** (*r*ecursive) option of **cp**. For example, to make a copy of the directory structure under *projects* in the directory *newprojects,* use the command

```
$ cp -r projects newprojects
```

# Making a File Easily Accessible by Others

Let's say you want to let your friend Donna access one of your files as easily as she would one in her own home directory. To do this, you can give a file a second filename without making a second copy of the file as you would when you copy it. Use the **ln** (*link*) command, which makes a symbolic link between directory entries, as shown here:

```
$ ln addresses  /home/donna/addresslist
```

This command will make the file addresses in your current directory accessible as *addresslist* in the directory */home/donna/addresslist*. However, there will only be one actual copy of this file. Note that any changes to the contents of the file affect it under either name. You can only link files if they are on the same file system.

# How to Concatenate Two Files, and Append a File

DOS uses the **copy** command to copy files, producing the same results as the UNIX **cp** command. However, the DOS **copy** command does more than just copy files. You can use it to concatenate two files—that is, produce a file containing the contents of the first file followed by the contents of the second file. You can also use the DOS **copy** command to append the contents of a file to an existing file.

On the UNIX system, the **cp** command will not append a file or concatenate two files. But there are easy ways to do these tasks using the **cat** command. To append a file, use the **cat** command and the **>>** (append) redirection symbol. For example, to append the contents of the file *notes9.23* to the file *labnotes*, type

```
$ cat notes9.23 >> labnotes
```

To concatenate two files, use the **cat** command with the two files as arguments (in the appropriate order), followed by redirection to a third file. For example, to concatenate the files *notes1* and *notes2*, putting the result in *notes*, use the command

```
$ cat notes1 notes2 > notes
```

# Moving All Filenames That Match a Pattern under a Directory

Instead of moving all files under a specific directory, you may want to move all files that match a particular pattern. For example, you may want to move all files in the current directory and its subdirectories that have the extension *.txt* in their names to a single new directory.

To accomplish this task, use the find command. In the following example, the command moves all files ending in *.txt* to the directory *newdir*.

```
$ mv `find . -name '*.txt' -print` newdir
```

It uses the "command substitution" feature of the shell. The command in inverted quotes,

```
$ find . -name '*.txt' -print
```

is executed and its output (in this case the names of all files under the current directory with extension *.txt*) is substituted in the **mv** command.

# Comparing Files and Directories

# How to See the Differences between Two Directories

Suppose you've put the files for a project in one of your directories and made copies of these files in another directory. After doing this, you changed some files in one of the directories but forgot to change the corresponding files in the other directory. Can you figure out what you did?

You may have two directories with similar contents. For instance, one of your directories may contain all the files for a certain project and a second directory may contain backups of these files. If you need to figure out which files are different in these two directories, you can use the **dircmp** (*dir*ectory *com*pare) command. When you use this command with the two directories as arguments, **dircmp** will list the filenames unique to each of the two directories and then tell you whether or not files with the same filenames in the different directories are the same.

Here is an example of how **dircmp** works. (The output has been edited down from two pages.)

```
$ dircmp NewDirectory and OldDirectory
Oct  4 11:25 1993  NewDirectory only and OldDirectory only
./file4                         ./file3
Oct  4 11:25 1993  Comparison of NewDirectory and OldDirectory
directory       .
same            ./file1
different       ./file2
```

This shows that there is a file called *file4* in *NewDirectory*, but no file with that name in *OldDirectory*, and that there is a file called *file3* in *OldDirectory*, but no file with that name in *NewDirectory*. It also shows that the files named *file1* in *NewDirectory* and *OldDirectory* are the same, but that the files named *file2* in the two directories are different.

# How to See the Differences Between Two Files

Let's say you forgot whether the file *memo1* or the file *memo-1* contains the latest version of a document. There are easy ways of figuring this out.

Sometimes you may have two files that are very similar. You may not even be sure the files are actually different. For instance, one of your files may be the latest version of a memo you are writing and another may be a backup copy.

If you just want to know whether the two files are identical, use the **cmp** command. This command will tell you the first position in the file where the files differ. In the following example:

```
$ cmp memo memo.1
memo memo.bck differ:  char 11, line 38
```

```
$ cmp memo.1 memo.2
```

the files *memo* and *memo1* differ first in the 11th character of their 38th line and the files *memo.1* and *memo.2* are identical, since **cmp** produces no output when run with these two files as arguments.

To actually see all the differences between two files, use the **diff** command. This command compares the files line by line and prints the differences, telling you how the text of the first file would have to be changed to match that of the second.

# Comparing the Number of Lines and/or Words in Two Files

Suppose you have two versions of a file and you have forgotten which one contains additional material—either material you added to it and not to the other, or material you deleted from it and not from the other. Instead of running the **diff** command to actually see the lines that are different in the two files, you may only want to know which one contains more lines, or maybe which one contains more words. Suppose the two files are *memo9.12* and *memo9.13*. To find out which contains more lines, run the command

```
$ expr `wc -l memo9.12` - `wc -l memo9.13`
8
```

Since the output tells you how many more lines *memo9.12* has than *memo9.13*, you have learned that *memo9.12* has eight more lines. If the result was negative, then *memo9.13* would have more lines than *memo9.12*. Similarly, to find out which file contains more words, run the command

```
$ expr `wc -w memo9.12` - `wc -w memo9.13`
35
```

This shows that *memo9.12* contain 35 more words than *memo9.13*.

## Viewing and Printing Files

## How to Display a UNIX File

On the DOS system, you use the **type** command to view the contents of a file. On the UNIX system, you use the **cat** command. When you use the **cat** command, the printable ASCII characters in the file are displayed. Nothing else besides these characters is displayed, such as a header giving the filename and other information. If you want to see nonprintable ASCII characters, such as the ASCII bell character CTRL-G, use **cat** with the -v option. You can get rid of repeated blank lines when you view a file by using **cat** with the -s (*squeeze*) option. If you want to include a header when the contents of a file are displayed, use the **pr** command. (See Tip 116.)

## Displaying the Contents of Non-Text Files

The DOS Shell utility provided with DOS versions 5 and 6 provides a way to view files in ASCII and hex side by side. How can you view a non-text file in UNIX?

UNIX has two powerful commands for extracting information from non-text files: **strings** and **od**. The **strings** command can be used to identify ASCII strings in a binary file—for example, to identify the file or pick out error messages that give you a clue about how to use the file. To use it to find the ASCII strings in the file *temp,* type:

```
$ strings temp
```

It may be useful to pipe the output to **more** or an output file if it fills more than one screen.

The other command that translates files into readable form is **od**. It prints an octal dump of the contents of a file, including nongraphic characters such as NEWLINE and TAB. This can be useful in identifying these characters—for example, if you need to strip them out of a file. The following string shows how to get an octal dump of the file *temp.*

```
$ od temp
```

The **od** command takes a number of options that modify the format of the display. For example, to display bytes as single-byte characters, use the following command.

```
$ od -c temp
```

If *temp* contains the lines:

```
one
two
```

the output of the last **od** command would be

```
0000000000  \r \n o n e \r \n t w o \r \n
0000000014
```

# Fixing Ragged and Uneven Lines in a File

Let's say you have a file with some really short and some really long lines. Is there some way to neaten it up so the lines are about the same length?

If your file has a lot of ragged lines, you may not even be able to display or print it, since the ends of long lines may not show up on a normal-sized page. The **fmt** command will even out the lengths of lines in a file. When you run the command

```
$ fmt notes > notes.fmt
```

the file *notes.fmt* will contain the contents of the file *notes* with each line having up to and as close to 72 characters as possible. Note that **fmt** does not change blank lines or lines starting with dots. You can have **fmt** produce lines with a number of characters different than 72 (or as close as possible). For example, to produce lines not exceeding and as close to 50 characters as possible, use

```
$ fmt -w 50 notes > notes.fmt
```

## Looking at the Start or End of a File

Suppose you forgot which of your files contains some meeting notes. If you can look
at the first few lines of each of your files, you could solve your problem. Is there a way to do this? Also,
you have a copy-to list at the end of one of your memos. Is there a way to look at the last few lines of
your files to find this list?

You can use the **head** command to view the first few lines of a file and the **tail** command to look at
the last few lines of a file. In the following example, the first ten lines of the file *memo* will be displayed
on your terminal.

```
$ head memo
```

To see only the first four lines, you would type

```
$ head -4 memo
```

Similarly, to view the last ten lines of the file *memo,* run

```
$ tail memo
```

To view the last five lines, run

```
$ tail -5 memo
```

## Viewing Long Files

When you run the **cat** command to view one of your long files, the contents scroll by
before you can read them. What can you do?

Sometimes you want to see what's in one of your files, but you don't want the entire contents displayed
on your screen all at once. This is especially true when the file you are interested in is extremely long.
With high-speed connections, you would have to be as quick as Commander Data on the Starship
Enterprise to read everything displayed when you use the **cat** command to display a long file. One
solution is to press CTRL-S to make output pause while you read the contents of your screen and CTRL-Q

to resume scrolling. However, this can be awkward to use and you may not be able to stop scrolling where you really want to stop.

A better solution is to use a pager, which lets you scroll through a file screen by screen. If you're a DOS user, you may use the **more** command, which lets you page through files. On the UNIX system, there are several different pagers. The UNIX system **more** command displays a file one page at a time. For example, to page through the file *food,* type

```
$ more food
```

This will show you the first screenful of text in *food* and then a prompt. If you press the ENTER or RETURN key at this prompt, it scrolls up to display the next line. If you press the SPACEBAR, it will display the next page.

The UNIX system **pg** command is a more versatile pager than **more**. Just as with **more**, you can use the **pg** pager to see the contents of a file one screen at a time. You can also use **pg** to move back and forth between different screens of output and to search for patterns in the file. For example, to see the contents of the file *output* one screen at a time, type

```
$ pg output
```

You will be shown the first screenful of this file. To see the next screen, press the ENTER or RETURN key. If you want to move forward eight screens, type **+8**; to move back four screens, type **-4**. You can also see a screen 12 lines ahead with **+12l** and a screen 15 lines back with **-15l**.

You can search for a particular pattern by using **pg**. For example, to see a screen with the next occurrence of the word "results" while using **pg**, type

```
/results/
```

# Checking the Progress of a Program That Writes Its Output to a File

Let's say you want to check on the progress of a program that writes its output to a file. For example, suppose you have a program that transfers files from several different computers on a network into the file report. By issuing the command

```
$ tail report
```

you will see the last ten lines of the file report. This should tell you how much progress your program has made. If you want to see new input as it comes in, you can issue the command

```
$ tail -f report
```

This will show you the last ten lines of report, pause for a while, and then show you the new lines in the file *report*.

# Printing Files

**T I P 114**

The UNIX system provides the lp system for printing files. Although the lp system contains many programs, as a user you only need to know about three of these: **lp**, the basic command used for printing files; **lpstat**, which checks the status of **lp** print jobs; and **cancel**, which cancels **lp** print jobs. Here we'll show you how to print files by using **lp**; in Tip 115, we'll explain how to use **lpstat** and **cancel**.

To print a file on a particular printer, use the **lp** command with the **-d** option. For example,

```
$ lp -d laser addresses
request id is 1-1011 (1 file)
```

This prints out the contents of the file *addresses* on the printer laser. If you don't provide a printer, **lp** will use the default printer for your system; ask your system administrator which printer this is. You can also specify your own default printer if you use the LPDEST variable. For example, if you want to use your printer laser9 as the default, put the following line in your *.profile:*

```
LPDEST=laser9; export LPDEST
```

# Checking the Status of Print Jobs, and Canceling Them

You sent some jobs to the printer and want to find out their status. You also want to cancel one of these jobs. How can you do these things?

You can use the **lpstat** command to check the status of your print jobs. You'll get back the request IDs of the print jobs and status of these jobs. (The request ID of a print job is displayed on the screen when this request is issued.) If you want to see the status of printers, give **lpstat** the **-p** option.

To cancel a print job, use the **cancel** command. You just need to give **cancel** the request ID of the print job you wish to cancel. For example,

```
$ cancel laser1-147
```

cancels the print job with request ID laser1-147. You can cancel all your print requests to a particular printer using the **-u** option. For example, the following code will cancel all print jobs sent by alice to the printer laser1.

```
$ cancel -u alice laser1
```

All print jobs requested by alice, regardless of printer, are canceled by

```
$ cancel -u alice all
```

# Doing Some Simple File Formatting with pr

If you want to put a header on every page of a file, you can use the **pr** command, as in the example shown here.

```
$ pr addresses
```

In this example, the contents of *addresses* will be displayed on your screen, with each page beginning with a header containing the date, time, name of the file, and page number.

You can have **pr** print its output in multiple columns. For example, to print the contents of addresses on your screen in three columns, use

```
$ pr -3 addresses
```

You can also customize the heading at the top of each page with the -t option. For example,

```
$ pr -t "Address List" addresses
```

will put the heading "Address List" at the top of each page of the output; the normal page header will not be printed. You can double-space the output using the **-d** option and print line numbers using the **-n** option. You can also specify the page layout using the **-w** option to specify the width, the -l option to specify the page length, and the **-o** option to specify the left margin offset. For example,

```
$ pr -d -n -w50 -o5 -l65 addresses
```

will print the file *addresses* to the screen, double-spaced, with line numbers, with a line width of 50 characters, a left margin offset of 5 characters, and a page length of 65 lines.

To print the output of **pr** on your printer, just pipe the output of your **pr** command to the **lp** command. For example,

```
$ pr -d -n -w50 -o5 -l65 addresses | lp
```

# Numbering the Lines in a File

You can easily number the lines of your text files.

Suppose you want to number the lines in your file *note* and put the copy of this file with numbered lines in *note.num*. The simplest way to do this is to use the **nl** (*n*umber *li*nes) command as follows:

```
$ nl note > note.num
```

# TIP 118

## Copying What You Do

There is a handy way to copy everything you do to a file. You need only use the **script** command. To use this command, you type the command name and the name of the file in which you want the transcript of your session stored. If you do not supply a name, a file typescript will be created for this purpose for you. For example,

```
$ script session1
```

will put everything in your session, including escape sequences sent to your terminal by programs, in the file *session1*. You can stop the recording of your session in this file by pressing CTRL-D.

You can play back your session using the **cat** command. When you do this, you will see what happened during your session. This can be quite hard to follow if you used an interactive program, such as a screen editor, in your session.

# Finding Files and Finding Out What's in Them

# TIP 119

## Finding Out What's in a File

You have an old file in one of your directories and don't remember what it is. What should you do to figure out what this file is?

How can you tell what's in a file? If you regularly clean up and reorganize your files, you need to be able to see what's inside a file before deciding to move or delete it. Don't simply try to use **cat** to display the file on your screen, or **vi** to show it to you using an editor. If the file is a binary object file, using **cat** will do strange things to your terminal, as random bits may be interpreted as control or escape sequences. Even if it's a text file, using an editor to glance at a file simply takes too long.

The following commands are helpful in keeping your files organized. Suppose you want to figure out what is in your file *octerb,* which has a cryptic filename. First, use the command:

```
$ file octerb
```

The **file** command looks in the file for a code number (called a "magic number") that identifies the type of file. Examples of types of file are a text file, an nroff file, a binary program for a specific machine type, ASCII text, a directory, English text, and so on. You can look at the file */etc/magic* for a list of all the file types that are identified on your system. For example, you may get the following:

```
$ file octerb
octerb      sparc pure dynamically linked executable
```

If the file is a compiled program for the machine you are using, the **file** command will indicate this. If the file is not a program for your machine, **file** will indicate the machine type in some cases, or will simply respond:

```
filename       data
```

If the file is not a binary file, you can use the **head** command to view the first several lines. For example,

```
$ head filename
```

will show the first 10 lines of the file, and

```
$ head -20 filename
```

will show the first 20 lines. You can use the **tail** command to show you the lines at the end of the file. Using **head** and **tail** should give you enough information to figure out what the file contains. If you don't have the **head** command on your system, the following command line will do the same thing (and would make a good alias or function).

```
$ sed 10q filename
```

If the file is a binary file, consult the following tip.

# Finding Out What's in a Binary File

TIP
120

Suppose you have a file that you know is a binary file. You might want to delete it, but want to make sure it isn't something you need. What should you do?

Sometimes you may find a binary file in your directories, and not know what it is. It may be an old program you've forgotten about, or junk left over from when you moved to a new machine. Before you delete it, you may want to try to find out what it is. The first thing you should do is use the **file** command. For example,

```
$ file aberdf
aberdf    sparc pure dynamically linked executable
```

If the file is a compiled program for the machine you are using, **file** will indicate this. If the file is not a program for your machine, **file** will indicate the machine type in some cases, or will simply respond:

```
acerdf     data
```

Next, you can try the character mode of the **od** (*o*ctal *d*ump) command. For example,

```
$ od -c acerdf
```

will show, on each line, 16 bytes of data interpreted as if it were ASCII text. If you look through this output, you should be able to see familiar text such as error messages, or a usage message. If the file contains neither a program for your system, nor any recognizable text, then probably you can delete it.

# How to Find Patterns in Files

You want to find all the lines in one of your files that contains the word "verification." How can you do that?

The UNIX system provides several tools for finding a pattern in a file, including the **grep** (for *g*lobally search for *r*egular *e*xpression and *p*rint), **egrep** (*e*xtended *grep*), and **fgrep** (*f*ixed *grep*) commands. For example, if you want to search a file, or a group of files, for lines that contain a particular pattern, you can use **grep**. You just need to give **grep** the pattern you want to search for as the first argument to **grep** and the names of the files to search as the second argument. For example,

```
$ grep verification rfp
The target platform must support speech verification.
```

located the pattern "verification" in the file *rfp*. You can tell **grep** to ignore the case of letters by giving it the **-i** option. For example,

```
$ grep -i unix chapter1
only be found in UNIX System V Release 4.2, which is available
is part of the UNIX system and is not part of DOS or the Mac OS.
The name of the package is gnunix and the current release is 8.1.
```

# Using a File's Contents to Find It in Your Current Directory

Suppose you want to find one of your memos on speech technology that contains the word "Spanish." All your memos are in files with names that start with the string "memo." How can you find the right file?

You can use **grep** to locate a particular file in your current directory based on its contents. For example, if you know that one of your memos on speech technology contains the pattern "Spanish," you can locate this file by using

```
$ grep Spanish memo*
memo8:  The system must support speech synthesis in Spanish.
memo9.13:  Spanish food will be served at the International Food
```

This tells you that the memo on speech technology that mentions "Spanish" is *memo8*.

# Searching for Regular Expressions

You don't have to give **grep** the exact pattern of characters that you want to search for. Instead, you can give it a regular expression. For example, suppose you want to find all lines that contain the reference to ProjectX, ProjectY, or ProjectZ, and the names of these projects could be followed by one or more digits. In this case, you would use

```
$ grep 'Project[X-Z][0-9]*' memo
```

# Searching for More Than One Target at Once

Let's say you want to find lines in one of your files that contain the words "French," "Spanish," or "Portuguese." You can't use a single **grep** command to do this. Is there another command you can use?

You can use either **fgrep** or **egrep** to search for more than one target pattern in a file or group of files. For example, to search your memos for strings matched by the regular expression *memo\**, in your current directory for lines containing either "French," "Spanish," or "Portuguese," use

```
$ fgrep "French
Spanish
Portuguese" memo*
```

You need to put each target string on a separate line when you use **fgrep**. You can't give **fgrep** a regular expression to match; you must give it a specific target pattern. However, **fgrep** works very rapidly.

If you want to search for more than one pattern—where one or more of the patterns is a regular expression—in a file or group or files, you should use **egrep** instead of **fgrep**. For example, you can find all lines in the file *animals* that contain either "cat" or "dog" by using

```
$ egrep "cat|dog" animals
```

Here, "|" is the alternation operator. Similarly, you can find all lines in the file *memo* that contain a string of one or more digits or the string "XZ" by using

```
$ egrep "([0-9]+*)|*XZ*)" memo
```

Here the + character is used by **egrep** to denote one or more repetitions of the preceding characters, so that "[0-9]+" is used to represent a string of one or more digits.

# Finding a File with a Particular Name

You know you have a file named *memo1* somewhere in your files, but don't remember where it is. How can you find it?

You may have misplaced a file with a particular name in your file system. If you need to locate it, use the **find** command. When you use **find,** you search through the contents of a directory and all of its subdirectories. For example, to search for the file named *memo1* in your current directory (.), use

```
$ find . -name memo1 -print
```

Here, you have used **-name** to have **find** match files with the filename *memo1* and **-print** to have **find** print the pathname of files named *memo1*. If you want to find all the files in your current directory or in the file */temp/memos* with filenames matched by the regular expression *memo\**, use the command

```
$ find . /temp/memos -name "memo*" -print
```

# Finding Files in Your Directories

When you have set up directories corresponding to discrete projects or work activities, you'll find that you still need to have some way to locate files that may not be where you think they are. UNIX has a function that uses the **find** and **print** commands to locate files for you. If you type **ffind filename**, it begins looking in the current directory, and descends into all subdirectories; it will print the relative pathname of every file that has the letters "filename" as part of its name.

```
function ffind
          {
          find . -name \*$@\* -print 2}/dev/null
          }
```

If you don't know where you've placed your letter to Roy, but are sure that the word "roy" is somewhere in the filename, use the command:

```
ffind roy
```

You'll see all possible alternatives:

```
./royals
./royalties
./bin/royco
./junk/roy.let
```

# Finding a File That Contains Certain Stuff

Maybe you didn't put Roy's name in the name of the file holding his letter, and maybe you don't remember what you called the file. Now you need to find the files that refer to "roy" inside the file, not just in the filename. The function **files_with** uses **find** and **grep** to search through your files to find the right one:

```
function files_with {
find . -type f -print | xargs grep -l -i -s $@ 2>/dev/null
}
```

You use this command in a similar way to the **ffind** command (presented in Tip 126):

```
$ files_with roy
```

The output looks like this:

```
./mail/mbox
./mail/outbox
./dept/rbb.1fq
./dept/faq.rbb
```

and provides a listing of all the files that contain the word "roy."

# Finding Where in the Files the Stuff is Hiding

Let's complicate the situation. Suppose you find that you have many big files that contain the word "roy." You don't want to look through every one of them to find what you're looking for; you certainly don't want to have to check through them with an editor. What can you do? The function **locate** shows you the line in each file where the term appears:

```
function locate {
find . -type f -print | xargs grep -n -i -s $@ 2>/dev/null
}
```

If you run the command **locate pete**, **find**, **print**, and **grep** are invoked with the right set of options. The output looks like:

```
./mail/mbox:20:people's heads. Fortunately, Pete was there all day
./mail/mbox:21:trying to do the same thing! Because of Pete
./mail/outbox:173:There are many competent vendors
./mail/outbox:1558:6. Title: Peter Norton's Guide to UNIX
./mail/outbox:1559:    Authors: Peter Norton and Harley Hahn
./dept/pss.1dq:89:Competencies and Technology Transfer, before
./dept/funding:11:Pete (and Jim also). I need some help from
./dept/funding:19:Pete needs these items before noon tomorrow.
```

Each line of output specifies the relative pathname of the file and the line number in the file where the string occurs, then prints the line for you to inspect.

## Permissions

# All About Permissions

If you are on a multiuser machine, you will want to restrict who can read or change your files and who can run your programs. You can do this on the UNIX system by the use of *permissions*. The three basic permissions in the UNIX system are *r* (for *r*ead), *w* (for *w*rite), and *x* (for *ex*ecute). These permissions are used for both files and directories, but with different (but somewhat analogous) meanings. (Note that there are some special types of permissions besides *r*, *w*, and *x*; these are discussed in other tips). When a user wants to read a file, for example, to display its contents with the **cat** command, the *r* permission must be given to that user.

When a user wants to write new data to a file or change the file, the *w* permission must be granted to that user. When a user wants to run a file as a program or shell script, the *x* permission must be granted to that user; for shell scripts, the *r* permission must also be granted to that user. A user can see which files are in a directory only if that user has *r* permission on the directory. A user can add, copy, remove, or rename files only if he or she has *w* permission on the directory. And the user must have *x* permission to be able to access the directory when accessing files in the directory.

Permissions on the UNIX system are set on three levels: first, for the owner of a file or directory; second, for members of the group of the owner of a file or directory; third, for everyone other than the first two. You can see the permission setting of the files and subdirectories of the owner of the current directory by running the command

```
$ ls -l
```

You can read these permissions by examining the first ten characters in each line of output of this command. The first character tells you the type of file, with a "-" (dash) indicating a file and a "d" indicating a directory. The next three characters (characters 2-4) specify the permissions granted to a user. Characters 5-7 specify the permissions granted to the group. The last three characters (characters 8-10) specify the permissions granted to all others. For example, the first ten characters of the line

```
-rwxr-x--x   1 linda       1988 Nov 11 12:12 script
```

tell you the permissions set for the regular file *script,* owned by linda. Since the owner's permissions are *rwx*, linda has read, write, and execute permissions. Since the group permissions are *r-x*, members of linda's group are granted read and execute permissions, but not write permission, for *script*. And since the others' permissions are *--x*, everyone else is granted execute permission, but not read or write permissions, for *script*.

Permissions can be represented by a three-digit octal number. This octal number has one digit representing the owner's permissions, one representing the group's permissions, and one representing the rest of the world's permissions. To find these octal numbers, use the three bits that correspond to whether permissions are granted, with a 1 representing a permission that is granted and a 0 representing one that isn't granted. In our example, the second, third, and fourth characters are *rwx*; this corresponds to 111, which represents the octal digit 7 (since 7 = 4 + 2 + 1). The fifth, sixth, and seventh characters are *r-x*; this corresponds to 101, which represents the octal digit 5 (since 5 = 4 + 0 + 1). The eighth, ninth, and tenth characters are *--x*; this corresponds to 001, which represents the octal digit 1 (since 1 = 0 + 0 + 1). So, the permissions on the file script can be represented by the octal number 751.

# Changing Permissions

**TIP 130**

If you are the owner of a file, or root, you can change the permissions of a file by using the **chmod** (*ch*ange *mod*e) command. You can tell **chmod** which permissions to change in several different ways. For example, to grant execute permission to members of the group of the owner of the file *script,* use the command

```
$ chmod g+w script
```

The g+w tells **chmod** to add (+) write permission (w) to members of the group (g) of the owner of the file. You could do the same thing with the command

```
$ chmod 771 script
```

since this changes the octal number representing the permissions to 771, which corresponds to *rwxrwx--x.*

For another example, suppose you want to remove the write permission for group members. You could use

```
$ chmod g-w script
```

or

```
$ chmod 711 script
```

since this would make the permissions on script correspond to *rwx--x--x.*

DOS users should note that the UNIX **chmod** command changes permissions, while the DOS **chmod** command changes a different type of file attribute, namely whether a file is hidden, read-only, or archived.

# What Permissions Should You Set on a Directory?

You will want to set the permission on directories in different ways depending on what they contain. Some of the most common situations are the following:

1. If you have a directory containing public information that can be modified by anyone, assign it *rwxrwxrwx*, or 777, permissions.

2. If the directory contains confidential personal files and no one else should be able to do anything with them (including list them), give the directory *rwx------*, or 700, permissions.

3. If the directory contains files confidential to a team of people, where the team members make up the group of the owner of the directory, give the directory *rwxrwx---*, or 770, permissions.

4. If the directory contains public files that are managed by a team of people, where the team members make up the group of the owner of the directory, give the directory *rwxrwxr-x*, or 775, permissions, since the only permission you do not want to grant is for others to alter the files.

5. If the directory contains files that are public, but you don't want anyone else altering them, give the directory *rwxr-xr-x*, or 755, permissions.

6. If the directory contains programs that you want others to be able to use, but you don't want anyone knowing what else is in this directory, give the directory *rwx--x--x*, or 711, permissions. This grants members of the group of the file's owner and others the ability to search for and use files in the directory, but not to list or modify the files in the directory.

# You Can Set File Permissions Automatically

Setting the permissions of a file in the correct way is one of the most important things you must do to keep your system secure. But it would be a pain to have to set these permissions correctly each time you create a file. Fortunately, there is an easy way to automatically set the permissions of a file when it is created. You can do this by putting the umask command in your *.profile* (or your *.cshrc* if you are a C-shell user). The argument you provide to the **umask** command specifies in octal notation the permissions you want turned off, rather than the permissions you want turned on. For example, to turn off the write permissions for members of the group of the file's owner and the read and write permissions for others, you would turn off permissions corresponding to *----w-rw-*, or 026. So, to automatically shut off these permissions whenever you create a file, type

```
umask 026
```

in your *.profile*. Then, whenever a file is created it is given 666-026=640 permissions, corresponding to *rw-r-----*. Your choice of umask depends on your security needs. Here are some guidelines.

1. On a system where you don't want anyone else to read or modify your files, use a **umask** of 066, which turns off the read and write permissions for members of the group of the file's owner and all others.

2. If you want members of the group to be able to read your files, but not change them, and don't want others to read or change them, use a **umask** of 026.

3. If you want members of the group to be able to read or change your files, but don't want others to read or change them, use a **umask** of 006.

4. If you want members of the group to be able to read or change your files and want others to be able to read them but not change them, use a **umask** of 022.

5. If the only people you don't want to give the ability to change your files are people outside the group, use a **umask** of 002.

# Who Owns a File?

**TIP 133**

Each file has an owner associated with it. To find out who this owner is, run the **ls -l** command. (See Tip 86.) Moreover, there are some basic rules you should know to figure out who owns a particular file. First, any file you create is owned by you. Furthermore, any copy of a file you make, no matter who the original owner is, is also owned by you. (Of course, you need read permission to copy it.) When you rename a file with **mv** (in the same file system), its owner does not change. When you append to an existing file, using the >> operator, its owner doesn't change. When you edit a file with **vi**, its owner doesn't change, although when you use **emacs** to edit a file, in some circumstances (such as when you replace a file with its backup), you may become the owner of the file. You can always see who the owner of a file is by using the **ls -l** command, as stated earlier.

Sometimes you may want to change the owner of a file—for example, when you need to take over the editing of a paper that someone else was previously editing. If the previous owner moves the file to your home directory, you don't become the owner. However, you can become the owner of a file if you make a copy of it. The problem with this is that you must have read permission on the file. There is a better way to change the owner of a file, based on the **chown** (*ch*ange *own*er) command.

In general, only the owner or the superuser can change the ownership of a file. To use **chown**, you give it the logname of the new owner and the name of the file. For example, to make lori the owner of the file *paper*, you would type

```
$ chown lori paper
```

By the way, you can change the ownership of all the files in a directory by using **chown** with the **-R** option. To give lori the ownership of all files in the directory **Programs**, you'd use

```
$ chown -R lori Programs
```

# Which Group Are You In?

You can determine which groups you are in by using the **groups** command. For example,

```
$ groups
department41
projectX
```

tells you that you are in the groups *department41* and *projectX*. If your system doesn't have the **groups** command, you could look for your logname in the */etc/group* file. You will find lines for each group that you are in. For example,

```
$ grep zeke /etc/group
department41::422:zeke,oscar,nana,lingo,wool
projectX::118:astrid,betty,robin,yolanda, zeke
```

tells you that you are in these two groups. Note that the group *department41* has group ID 422 and the group *projectX* has group ID 118.

When you log in, you are assigned to your primary group. This is the group whose group ID is the fourth field of your entry in */etc/passwd*. For example, if this fourth field is 422, which is the group ID of *department41*, you are in the group *department41* whenever you log in. If you need to change your group, and are a member of that group, use the **newgrp** (*new group*) command. For instance, to change to the *projectX* group, you would type

```
$ newgrp projectX
```

Of course, you have to be a member of this group to be able to change your current group to it.

# Protecting Files from Deletion by Other Users

When someone has write permission on a directory, he or she can move and remove files. This can be a problem, since someone who doesn't own a file may remove a file owned by someone else. To prevent this, System V Release 4 uses the sticky bit permission on directories. When this permission is turned on for a directory, users other than the owner of the file, the owner of the directory, and the superuser, cannot move or remove files in this directory even if other permission settings would normally allow this.

The command you issue to set the sticky bit on the directory *tmp* is:

```
$ chmod +t tmp
```

# Changing the Permissions on All Files in a Directory

There is an easy way to change the permissions of all files in a directory. You can do this by using the **-R** option to the **chmod** command. For instance, the following command makes all the files (and directories) in the directory *Programs* readable and executable by everyone, but writable only by the owner of the directory:

```
$ chmod -R 755 Programs
```

If you use a version of the UNIX system that doesn't support the **-R** option of **chmod**, you can change the permissions of all files in *Programs* by using this command:

```
$ find Programs -exec chmod 755 {} \;
```

# Tips on Changing Groups of Filenames

## Changing the Extension of a Group of Filenames

How do you move all files with the filename extension *.foo* to files with the same name except with extension *.bar*?

This tip, and the rest of the tips in this chapter, come from the FAQs prepared by Ted M. A. Timar in the newsgroup *comp.unix.questions*.

To construct an answer, first note that the command **mv *.foo *.bar** won't solve this problem, since the shell expands wildcards before it runs commands. Hence, "*.foo" and "*.bar" are expanded before the **mv** command is carried out. For example, if the files in your current directory ending in *.foo* are *a.foo, b.foo,* and *c.foo,* the Standard System V Shell executes this command to

```
mv a.foo b.foo c.foo *.bar
```

which isn't going to do what you want, even if you have a directory actually named *\*.bar*. In the C Shell, when you run this command, the shell prints "No match." because it can't match "*.bar".

Depending on your shell, you can move all files ending with *.foo* to files with the same base name, but ending with *.bar,* with a loop to move each file individually, by using **mv**. If your system has the **basename** command that strips pathname components, leaving only the name of the file, you can change the filenames by using the following shell script in the Standard System V (or Bourne) Shell:

```
for f in *.foo; do
```

```
     base=`basename $f .foo`
     mv $f $base.bar
done,
```

If you use the C shell, use the following shell program:

```
foreach f ( *.foo )
    set base=`basename $f .foo`
    mv $f $base.bar
end
```

Some shells have their own variable substitution features, so instead of using the **basename** command, you can use simpler loops, such as the following C Shell program:

```
foreach f ( *.foo )
    mv $f $f:r.bar
end
```

If you use the Korn shell, the following shell script will work:

```
for f in *.foo; do
    mv $f ${f%foo}bar
done
```

# Changing Base Names for a Group of Files

If the **basename** command isn't available on your system or you want to do something like rename files matching the wildcard expression *foo.** to change their base name to *bar* instead of *foo*, you can use the **sed** command to strip apart the original filename in other ways. The general looping idea is the same. You can also convert filenames into **mv** commands with **sed**, and pipe the results to **sh** for execution. You can try

```
$ ls -d *.foo | sed -e 's/.*/mv & &/' -e 's/foo$/bar/' | sh
```

Vladimir Lanin has written a program called **mmv** that does this job. It was posted to *comp.sources.unix* in April 1990 and can be found in the archive of this newsgroup. It lets you use

```
$ mmv '*.foo' '=1.bar'
```

You can use an archie server (see Chapter 10) to find an archive site with this program and then use anonymous ftp to copy it.

# Changing the Case of a Set of Filenames

Suppose you want to translate the letters in a set of filenames from all uppercase to all lowercase. How can you do this?

Shell loops like the ones in the previous tip can also be used to translate filenames from upper to lowercase or vice versa. Here are some shell scripts for the C, Bourne, and Korn shells, respectively, that translate uppercase letters to corresponding lowercase letters.

C Shell:

```
foreach f ( * )
    mv $f `echo $f | tr '[A-Z]' '[a-z]'`
end
```

Bourne Shell:

```
for f in *; do
    mv $f `echo $f | tr '[A-Z]' '[a-z]'`
done
```

Korn Shell:

```
typeset -l l
for f in *; do
    l="$f"
    mv $f $l
done
```

# Translating Funny Filenames

Some of your files have funny filenames—for example, including embedded blanks. What should you do to translate uppercase letters to lowercase letter?

Here is a shell script to use:

```
for f in *; do
  g=`expr "xxx$f" : 'xxx\(.*\)' | tr '[A-Z]' '[a-z]'`
  mv "$f" "$g"
done
```

The **expr** command will always print the filename, even if it equals **-n** or contains a System V escape sequence like **c**.

(By the way, some versions of the **tr** command require the square brackets ([ and ]), while others don't. It's harmless to include them in this example, since versions of **tr** that don't want the square brackets will just translate "[" to "[" and "]" to "]".)

# Using the perl Language to Change Filenames

If you have the **perl** language available on your system (see Chapter 8 for information on **perl**), you will find quite useful the **rename** script, written by Larry Wall, the author of the **perl** programming language. It can be used to accomplish a wide variety of filename changes, and it employs the same notation used in many UNIX text editors.

```
#!/usr/bin/perl
# rename script examples from lwall:
#       rename 's/\.orig$//' *.orig
#       rename 'y/A-Z/a-z/ unless /^Make/' *
#       rename '$_ .= ".bad"' *.f
#       rename 'print "$_: "; s/foo/bar/ if <stdin> =~ /^y/i' *
```

```
$op = shift;
    for (@ARGV) {
    $was = $_;
    eval $op;
    die $@ if $@;
    rename($was,$_) unless $was eq $_;
    }
```

For example, to translate all names that are lowercase to uppercase, use

```
$ rename 'tr/a-z/A-Z' *
```

To rename all files that match the wildcard expression *.doc* (that is, files with names that end with the filename extension .doc), you can

```
$ rename 's/\.doc$//' *.doc
```

See the book *Programming perl* by Larry Wall and Randal L. Schwartz (Sebastopol, CA: O'Reilly and Associates, 1990) to learn how you can use **rename** to change filenames in other ways.

# Chapter 3

# Controlling and Customizing Your Environment

# Customizing Your Prompt

## Setting Your Prompt

You seem to use the **pwd** command a lot. Does UNIX offer a way to set your prompt so that it shows the current directory? DOS lets you do this with the **PROMPT** command, so how is it done on a UNIX system?

You can set your prompt by setting the primary prompt variable PS1 in your *.profile*. If you are using **ksh**, here's the command:

```
PS1="\$PWD  $ "
```

The \ (backslash) is essential. Your prompt will now look like this, if you are in the directory */home/you/mail:*

```
/home/you/mail $
```

## Setting Your C Shell Prompt

The prompt displayed by the C shell is the value of the environmental variable *prompt*. Use the **set** command to set your prompt, as shown here:

```
set prompt="ralph%"
```

This sets the prompt to

```
ralph%
```

You can also do more sophisticated things. For example, the following example changes the prompt to the current working directory, followed by a % symbol:

```
set prompt="`pwd`%"
```

So, if the current directory is */home/fred/books,* the prompt would be

```
/home/fred/books%
```

You can also have only the last directory in your current pathname as your prompt, using the following C shell command:

```
set prompt="${cwd:t}%"
```

With the same current directory as before, this would lead to the following prompt:

```
books%
```

The same effect can be accomplished in **ksh** with this command line:

```
PS1="\${PWD##*/}% "
```

# Setting Your Prompt under csh

How can you set the prompt to include your system name and the current directory if you're using **csh**?

The following command sequence will put both the name of the machine you're using and the current directory in your prompt with **csh**. Put these lines in your *.cshrc:*

```
set prompt="<\! `hostname`: $cwd >"
alias cd 'cd \!*: set prompt = "<\! `hostname`: $cwd >"'
```

This resets the prompt to the current host machine and directory every time you do a **cd**.

The screen will look like this on machine mach1:

```
mach1: /home/you/mail >
```

# Setting Your Prompt If You Use an Xterminal

If you're using **csh** and sometimes use an Xterminal, try the following in your *.cshrc:*

```
if ($TERM == xterm)  then
      alias cd 'cd \!*; echo -n ]0;"${HOSTNAME}" : $cwd"; set\
      prompt=${HOSTNAME}": $cwd> "'
else
      alias cd 'cd \!*; set prompt=${HOSTNAME}": $cwd> "'
endif
```

This gives you an appropriate prompt when you're on your Xterminal.

# Setting Your Prompt under .csh—the Deluxe Version

This next variation on the **pwd**-prompt tip runs the risk of providing too much information. This one requires that you run **csh**, and uses two lines of screen real estate for every prompt! Try it in **csh** on SVR4, but don't put it in your *.cshrc* unless you're sure you like it.

```
set cwd=`pwd`
set machname=`uname -n`
set subprompt='$ '
set prompt="${subprompt} ${machname} ($$) ${user} \! ${cwd}\
${subprompt} "
```

Your two-line prompt will look like this:

```
$ mach1 (824) yourlogin 12 /home/yourlogin
$
```

Here, *mach1* is the system name, *824* is the process number of your shell, *yourlogin* is your login name, *12* is the current event number, and */home/yourlogin* is the current directory.

## Aliases

## Aliases

An alias is an alternate name for a script, program or command. Both the Korn shell, **ksh**, and the C shell, **csh**, support aliases. Aliases are used for three reasons. One is to reduce the amount of typing you do. If you always use a command with certain options, such as the combination shown here,

```
ls -alt
```

you can create a single-character alias for the whole command and its options:

```
alias l='ls -alt'
```

Now, whenever you issue the command **l**, you'll get the longer **ls -alt** version.

A second use for aliases is to rename a command that you find difficult to recall. Some of the UNIX system commands have obscure, historical names—**grep**, for example—and an alias allows you to change them:

```
alias search='grep'
alias del='rm'
```

This example makes the command **search** equivalent to the command **grep**, and **del** an alias for **rm**.

A third purpose of aliases is to avoid path searches. When you issue a command—for example, **col**—the shell searches through all the directories in your PATH to find the command. If you alias the command name to its full pathname, the search will be avoided and the command will start faster. For example, to substitute the entire pathname for the command name, type this line:

```
col='/usr/opt/dwb/bin/col '
```

# Some Useful Aliases

Here are some sample aliases that have proven useful. Alter the pathnames to correspond to those on your system. Use these as a model for the aliases that you create.

```
# ksh aliases
#    Multiple aliases can be included in one logical line.
#    (Note that newline is escaped.)  The -x option to alias
#    is used to export the aliases to scripts run under the
#    login ksh. Note also that there can be no space between
#    the '=' and the strings.
alias -x at='at 2>>.atjobs' \
        col='/usr/opt/dwb/bin/col ' \
        int='typeset -i' \
        ls='/bin/ls -logt' \
        md='/bin/mkdir' \
        mmx='/usr/opt/dwb/bin/mmx -1' \
        more='/usr/opt/exptools/bin/more -s' \
        nroff='/usr/opt/dwb/bin/nroff ' \
        ps='/bin/ps 2>$LOGTTY'\
        tbl='/usr/add-on/dwb/bin/tbl ' \
        trace='set -x' \
        untrace='set +x' \
        xit='exit;exit'
# define aliases to avoid path searches
alias -x calendar=/usr/bin/calendar \
        stty=/bin/stty \
        tee=/bin/tee \
        wc=/bin/wc
```

# Some Tips on Using Aliases

Aliases are convenient, but have their faults. Too frequent use of aliases can make your system idiosyncratic. Your commands won't work in the standard way the manual describes them, because they are no longer normal commands. The advantage of having one command with multiple options decreases if you alias command-option groupings. If you have aliased a standard command, and now want to use its traditional version, use the command **unalias**, as shown here:

```
$ unalias ls
```

If you want a list of all active aliases, including those defined by the shell itself, type

```
$ alias
```

A popular parody of UNIX systems from a few years ago claimed that UNIX system users spent their time discussing "what the **print** command is called this week." Aliases make it even easier to make silly changes in the system.

Aliases can also affect other parts of the system, if used without caution. The **grep** command looks into files and finds patterns there. Perhaps a better name for **grep** on your system would be **find**. You could rename the command by typing this:

```
alias find='grep'
```

Sometime soon, however, you'd notice that the UNIX system **find** command didn't work correctly. If you use aliases, make sure you look through the permuted index in the manual to be certain you're not using the name of an existing command in your alias.

Finally, aliases are simply renamings of commands. They are not as powerful as shell scripts or functions. The shell will not pass arguments or positional parameters to an alias as it does to scripts and functions. The arguments to an alias are simply appended ("glued") to it.

# Ignoring Your Command Spelling Mistakes

TIP
150

You can use aliases to make your system ignore your mistakes in spelling commands. For instance, suppose that when you want to run the **more** command, you often type "mroe", and sometimes "moer". If you put the following aliases in your *.profile,* or your *.cshrc* if you are a C shell user, you will be able to run the **more** command by typing "more", "mroe", or "moer":

```
alias mroe='more'
alias moer='more'
```

# Temporarily Ignoring Aliases

Suppose you have written an alias to redefine **ls**, so that when you type **ls**, your system runs **ls -al**. But during one of your sessions you want to run **ls**. You can run the default **ls** command by typing a backslash before the string **ls**:

```
$ \ls
```

This works in both the Korn and C shells. If you need to run the default **ls** command throughout your current session, you will probably want to use this command line:

```
$ unalias ls
```

# Aliases in the C Shell

To write an alias in the C shell, you use a syntax that does not employ the equal sign to make assignments:

```
% alias name definition
```

For example, to define **ls** as **ls -al**, you would use

```
% alias ls ls -al
```

When the definition involves more than running a command with options, you should enclose the definition in single quotes. For example, if you have set up the following alias:

```
% alias address 'cat ~/addresses | grep -i'
```

then

```
% address xerxes
```

runs the following command:

```
% cat ~/addresses | grep -i xerxes
```

# Aliasing rm -i

You can be cautious when deleting files by aliasing the **rm** command so that it always uses the interactive (-i) option. To do this, add the following line to your *.profile* or your *.alias* file:

```
alias rm='rm -i $@'
```

This will make all uses of **rm** interactive.

# A Specific Alias for rm *

Dave Korn, creator of the Korn shell, provided the following alias for **rm**. It is interactive only when you use the * character, but not if the filename ends with *.o* or *.BAK*. In **ksh**, this alias sets the **no global** option, defines a function called **_rm**, and aliases **rm**.

```
alias rm='set -o noglob;_rm'

function _rm
{
    trap 'set +o noglob' 0       # restore filename expansion on exit
    set +o noglob                # re-enable filename expansion
    option=
    case $1 in
    -[fri]|-[fri][fri]|-[fri][fri][fri])
        option=$1
        shift
        ;;
```

```
*)
        for i in "$@"
        do   case $i in
                *\*.o)
                    ;;
            *\*.BAK)
                    ;;
            *\*.CKP)
                    ;;
            *\**)
                    if    test -t
                    then option=-i
                    fi
                    ;;
            *)
                    esac
        done
esac
/bin/rm $option $*
}
```

# A Better Alias for rm

**TIP 155**

There is some disadvantage to using **rm -i** aliases. If you change the basic way that commands work, you or others could come to view this new use as standard. When you are on a new or different system, **rm \*** may result in a disaster. This is especially problematic with a new user who has been trained on your system. To avoid this, define a new command, **del**, that is interactive, and leave **rm** alone:

```
alias del='rm -i $@'
```

# Undoing a Deletion

**TIP 156**

These aliases and functions make it harder to make a mistake with **rm** *, but files that are removed are still gone forever if they haven't been backed up. Is there any way to undo the deletion if you change your mind later?

It's possible to define a new command that will do just that. For example, create a new directory in your home directory to save old files in; call it *.saved*. Since the filename begins with a dot (.), the name won't normally be displayed when you list your files with **ls**. Next, create a function that moves files to this directory instead of removing them, as shown here:

```
function del {
        mv $* $HOME/.saved/$*
        }
```

If you ever change your mind, look in the *.saved* directory, find the file, and move it back. The following alias will move it to the current directory:

```
function undel {
        mv $HOME/.saved/$* ./
        }
```

# Improved del and undel

**TIP 157**

The last tip gives the general idea of how to delete files to a special directory and then undelete them by moving them back. To be really useful, however, you'd want this to work much better. The following example defines two scripts, **del** and **undel**, which work as described earlier. But they also do several other things: perform error checking to see if the file exists; show the contents of *.saved* if the file doesn't exist; provide some user feedback about what the file is doing; change the file modification date to indicate when it was moved; and handle directories. Much more useful!

```
#!/bin/ksh
#################################################
#
```

```
#   del - This is a replacement/adjunct to rm.
#
#   When you del <file> the file is touched, and
#   moved to $HOME/.saved  The filename is expanded
#   to include the process number so that a (mostly)
#   unique name is attached to each file. If <file>
#   is really a directory, del complains; if <file>
#   doesn't exist, del tells you. This really needs
#   to be extended to cover rm -r as well, but
#   it doesn't do that now.
#
#   This is especially useful with a demon (using at, or
#   login checking) that deletes a file in $HOME/.saved
#   when it is a week old.
#
################################################

here=`pwd`

case $0 in
del)
#   If there is no argument used with del, then just list the
#   contents of $HOME/.saved
    if [ -z "$1" ]
    then
    ls -lus $HOME/.saved
#   If del is called with arguments, test each one.
#   If it's a file, then tell the user it's being deleted
#   and change its modification date, but just move it
#   to $HOME/.saved. Append the current
#   process number to the filename.
    else
    for i in $*
    do
        if [ -f $i ]
        then
            echo  deleting $i
            touch $i; mv $i $HOME/.saved/$i$$
#   If the argument is a directory, then save the
#   name of the current directory, change into the new directory,
#   make a list of the files there, change back to the prior
#   directory, and move each of the files to $HOME/.saved.
```

```
            elif [ -d $i ]
            then
            oldpwd=`pwd`
            cd $1
            files=`echo *`
            cd $oldpwd
            for i in $files
            do
                    if [ -f $1/$i ]
                    then
                            mkdir $HOME/.saved/$1;
                            mv $1/$i $HOME/.saved/$1/$i$$
#   If one of the items in the new directory isn't a file,
#   then reinvoke del on the new directory.
                    else
                            del $1/$i
                    fi
            done

#   If there is nothing in a directory (i.e., all its files have
#   been moved to .saved), then remove the directory
empty=`ls $1`
if [ -z "$empty" ]
then
    rmdir $1
fi
            else
                    echo del: file $i does not exist
            fi
    done
    fi
    ;;


undel)
#   If there is no argument used with undel, then just list the
#   contents of $HOME/.saved
    if [ -z "$1" ]
    then
    ls -lus $HOME/.saved
#   otherwise, change directory to $HOME/.saved and move the named
#   files to the current directory
    else
```

```
        cd $HOME/.saved;
        for i in $*
        do
        i=`basename $i`
             if [ -f $i ]
             then
                   echo  restoring $i
                   touch $i; mv $HOME/.saved/$i $here/$i
             elif [ -d $i ]
             then
             cd $i
             files=`echo *`
             for j in $files
             do
                   j=`basename $j`
                   if [ -f $j ]
                   then
                            echo restoring $here/$j
                            mv $HOME/.saved/$i/$j $here/$j
                            touch $here/$j;
                   else
                        undel $j
                   fi
             done
             empty=`ls $i`
             if [ -z "$empty" ]
             then
                   rmdir $HOME/.saved/$i
             fi
             else
                   echo undel: file $i does not exist
             fi
        done
        fi
        ;;
esac
```

To use this script, put it in a file called *del*, and link it to *undel*, i.e., **ln** *del undel*.

# Shell Functions

## Using Shell Functions

**T**IP **158**

In **ksh** and **csh**, shell functions provide another way to customize your UNIX system environment. For the most part, shell functions are just like shell scripts, so a shell programming book, or the tips in Chapter 7 of this book, apply to functions as well. The most important difference between functions and scripts is that all functions are automatically loaded by the shell when you log in. That means the shell can execute them directly; it is not necessary for the shell to fork off another process to execute a script. Since a new process need not be started, and the commands need not be read in, functions execute much faster than scripts do.

This is also true for regular shell scripts that call functions. When a shell script encounters a function, the function is executed directly without forking another shell. Several examples of functions will be described in subsequent tips. Use functions for commands that you'll use frequently, and in which saving process overhead is helpful. For this reason, you want to keep your functions small with a single purpose. If you define all of your functions in a single file (called *.functions*) and put a line like the following in your *.profile* or *.kshrc*, then all those functions will be loaded when **ksh** starts.

```
. $HOME/.functions
```

## Customizing File Lists

**T**IP **159**

The UNIX system command **ls** allows more command line options than any other command. It's also among the most frequently used. It's easy to define a function to provide **ls** output in exactly the format you would like. The function shown next lists the current directory and contents, if none are specified. The output is printed in columns, sorted by modification time, with the size in blocks indicated. Directory names have a / (slash, or virgule) added at the end, and executable files are indicated by an * (asterisk) at the end.

```
function l
{
```

```
    if [ $# != 0 ]
    then ls -sCFt $*
    else ls -sCFt ./
    fi
}
```

# A Useful Function for Listing Files

The most common command pairing by users is the **cd** command immediately followed by the **ls** command. If you find yourself frequently changing directories, then seeing what's there, use the following function and alias:

```
function _cd {
    cd $1; ls -sCFt;
    }
alias cd=_cd
```

This example illustrates an important point about functions and aliases in **ksh.** Since **cd** is a built-in shell function, you can't write a function of your own with the same name. You can, as in this example, write a function with the capabilities you want, and then alias it to some other name.

# Using the UNIX System as a Wristwatch

If you don't wear a wristwatch, but you do have a UNIX machine on your desk, there is an easy way to check the time.

Here is simple little function called **t**, that displays the current time for you. Since it is a function, it executes quickly. It can't be called **time**, because that's the name of an existing UNIX command. Here it is:

```
function t {
date +%r
}
```

If you had created a file named *t,* which contained the command line **date +%r**, you would get the same output. However, the shell would create a process to run **t**, and a second process would be created to execute the **date** command. The shell itself directly executes the function **t**, saving two extra processes.

# Viewing Functions and Aliases

Suppose you have many, many functions and aliases—too many, actually, to remember. How can you tell whether one of your commands is an alias, a function, or a shell?

There is a built-in command in **ksh**, called **whence**, that helps you do this. If you issue the following command, you'll see the complete command, if it's an alias or shell, and the function name if it's a **ksh** function.

```
whence filename
```

The **-v** (*verbose*) option gives more information, as shown here:

```
$ whence t
t
$ whence demon
/home/you/bin/demon
$ whence nroff
/usr/add-on/dwb/bin/nroff
$ whence -v t
t is a function
$ whence -v demon
demon is /home/you/bin/demon
$ whence -v nroff
nroff is an exported alias for /usr/add-on/dwb/bin/nroff
```

On some systems, the command **whence -v** is aliased to **type**.

# Viewing Functions and Aliases—Deluxe Version

The following function, called **show**, is an enhancement of the built-in command **whence**. But **show** provides much more information, especially about **ksh** functions.

```
function show
{
    typeset XxX
    if test x$1 = x
    then print 'usage: show variable-name'
        return 1
    fi
    # test for functions
    typeset -f $1
    test $? -eq 0 && return
    # test for aliases
    XxX=`whence -v $1`
    if test $? -eq 0
    then print $XxX
        return
    fi
    # get export status
    XxX=`typeset | grep " $1\$"`
    if test $? -ne 0
    then XxX="local $1"
    fi
    # get value and print result
    eval print "\"$XxX = \${$1:-### NOT SET ###}\""
}
```

If you run the command on a function, shell script, or alias, you get these responses:

```
$ show t
function t
{
date $ %r
}
```

```
$ show demon
demon is /home/you/bin/demon
$ show nroff
nroff is an exported alias for /usr/add-on/dwb/bin/nroff
```

# Controlling and Customizing Your Terminal

## Setting Your Terminal Options

**TIP 164**

You can use the **stty** (for *set tty*) command to set your terminal options. You probably will want to put some **stty** commands in your *.profile* to set up your terminal in the way you want. There are about 70 different options you can set, but only a few are things you may want to set. For example, this command line will set up your screen terminal so that characters are eliminated from your screen when you erase them using the BACKSPACE key:

```
$ stty echoe
```

And the following command expands the tab setting to eight spaces and preserves tabs when you are printing:

```
$ stty -tabs
```

The command

```
$ stty ixon
```

will turn on flow control, whereas

```
$ stty -ixon
```

will turn it off.

You can set the terminal bit rate to 9600 bps by using

```
$ stty 9600
```

You can set the window size to 30 rows and 75 columns (in terms of characters) by using

```
$ stty rows 30 columns 75
```

You can also use **stty** to specify the keys you want to use for certain control functions. For example, you can designate CTRL-H (BACKSPACE) as your erase character by typing this:

```
$ stty erase \^H
```

You can use CTRL-X as your kill character (instead of @) by typing this:

```
$stty kill \^X
```

And you can use CTRL-C as your end-of-file character by typing this:

```
$ stty eof \^C
```

You can reset your erase and kill characters back to # and @, respectively, by using

```
$ stty ek
```

Finally, you can check all your terminal settings by using

```
$ stty -a
```

# TIP 165

# Clearing Your Screen

Sometimes bizarre things will happen to your terminal display. For example, your display could switch to inverse video, it could repeatedly flash, display nonsense characters, show characters from a graphical character set, and so on. Logging off and logging on again will cure most problems, although problems with the terminal itself won't be corrected this way. If your screen is messed up, but you have a shell prompt, and your system supports *termcap*, the first thing you can try is to clear your screen. If your system supports *termcap*, you can do this, and fix some other display problems, by typing this command line:

```
$ clear
```

If your system supports *terminfo*, you can clear your screen and fix other problems with this command line:

```
$ tput clear
```

# Fixing a Deranged or Frozen Terminal

**TIP 166**

There are quite a few things that can make your terminal become deranged, including nonprintable characters in the output of a command directed to your terminal, line noise, program bugs, and so on. You might see graphics characters, flashing characters, inverse video, or your screen might become locked. How can you get your terminal back to normal?

One thing you can do is log off and log in to your system again. When you log in, your system will reset your terminal options to values that work for your terminal. However, there are some things you can do without logging off.

The simplest thing you can try, if you are able to get a shell prompt, is to clear your screen. See Tip 165 to learn how to do this.

You can also try using this command line:

```
$ stty sane
```

This will reset your terminal using a set of **stty** options that work on most terminals most of the time. This won't reset your terminal to exactly the way you want it, but may give you the opportunity to continue working and to reset your terminal options as you wish. By the way, you may have to type ^J (CTRL-J), the newline character, to get a prompt and to execute this command if your terminal does not interpret the ENTER or RETURN key as the newline key.

Another thing you can do if you can get a shell prompt and your system uses *terminfo* is to use this command, which will send the appropriate reset command to your terminal.

```
$ tput reset
```

If that doesn't work, try the following:

```
$ tput init
```

This will completely reinitialize your terminal settings according to the type of terminal in the variable TERM.

# What If Your Terminal Is Hung or Locked?

If your terminal seems to be locked, you might have accidentally pressed your SCROLL LOCK (or HOLD SCREEN) key. If so, press it again, and your terminal will return to normal. If this doesn't work, press SCROLL LOCK again to undo the first time you pressed it. You also may have accidentally pressed CTRL-S, which stops output. If so, press CTRL-Q to restart output.

If neither of these work and you are logged in remotely, you may have some loose wires. Check the connections to your modem or computer and make sure nothing is loose. If you have a modem, you can tell whether your terminal is sending and receiving data by looking at the SD (*Send Data*) and the RD (*Receive Data*) lights, respectively.

# Changing Your Terminal's Tune

If you would like a memory-resident program that changes the frequency of the beep in a PC that runs UNIX, there is a device driver available from *ftp.win.tue.nl* with the path *pub/sysvX86/speaker.shar.Z* that allows you to play tunes on your speaker.

# Controlling Screen Emphasis

**T**IP
**169**

You can use the **tput** command to control your terminal's characteristics. The **tput** command uses the *terminfo* database to determine which special commands and escape sequences perform which actions on your terminal, and then translates into those sequences. For example, different terminals use different commands to set BOLD or UNDERLINE or FLASHING, and so on.

If you set shell variables to the following **tput** values, you can control screen attributes in simple ways:

```
BOLD='tput smso'
OFFBOLD='tput rmso'

echo "${BOLD}You have mail:${OFFBOLD}
```

Look in the manual under TERMINFO (5V) for a list of terminal characteristics and their codes.

To put your prompt in bold, use this:

```
PS1=${BOLD}${PWD} ${UNBOLD}
export PS1
```

# Writing Your Own Manual Pages

**T**IP
**170**

For many of the program and shell scripts you've written, you'd like to provide manual pages so that other users don't have to call you. You can prepare instructions, and format them so that they actually look like UNIX documentation.

UNIX system manual pages are formatted with **nroff** and **troff**, and written with the **man** macros. Check the book *UNIX System V Release 4: An Introduction,* by Ken Rosen, Richard Rosinski, and James Farber (Berkeley, CA: Osborne/McGraw-Hill, 1990) for an example of how to use these macros. You can create your manual with a command line like this one:

```
$ nroff -man filename > man-name
```

This command will produce a formatted file.

You can also use the following command to view a description of the strings, macros, and registers defined by the **man** macro package:

```
man man
```

# TIP 171

# Finding Your Own Manual Pages

Let's say you've written manual pages, formatted them all, and even put them in your own manual directory. But the **man** command doesn't seem to know about them. How do you tell **man** where they are?

The search of the **man** command is specified by the MANPATH environmental variable. Set it in your *.profile,* and don't forget to export it. The following sequence will add your directory *$HOME/man* to the existing MANPATH variable:

```
MANPATH=$HOME/man:${MANPATH}
export $MANPATH
```

This order will cause your manual directory to be searched first, before the system man files. This is useful if you have different versions of standard commands on your system.

# Tips on Logging Off

# TIP 172

# Logging Off—Basic Version

If you are remotely logged into your UNIX system, there are a number of ways to log off: typing ^D (CTRL-D), turning off the terminal, hanging up the phone, and so on. Depending on your local configuration, some of these ways might inadvertently let another user into your account. For example, if you were connected via a phone line and a modem, and you hung up, the next caller into the system could be connected to that port before the UNIX system disconnects it. To avoid this, get into the habit of using the following command to log off when you are on a dial-up connection:

```
stty 0
```

On workstations such as Sun or HP, this doesn't work the same way as on a dialed-up connection. If you are using **ksh**, an alternative is **exit**, a shell built-in command that will log you off.

The commands **exit** and **stty 0** are *not* equivalent. Since **exit** terminates the shell that called it, if you put **exit** into a shell script, it terminates that script. On the other hand, **stty 0** drops the connection to your terminal, regardless of the fact that it was called by a child shell.

# Setting Up a .logout File

**TIP 173**

If you use **csh**, the file *.logout* is automatically executed when you log off. If you use another shell, you'll have to arrange to have that happen. An easy way to do this is to create an executable file called *.logout* in your home directory, where you can put scripts like those above. To get this file to execute when you log off, use the **trap** command in your *.profile*.

Including the following line as the first line in your *.profile*

```
trap 'echo That's all Folks' 0
```

will cause your screen display "That's all Folks" when you log off, and the line shown here

```
trap '/home/you/.logout' 0
```

will execute *.logout* in your home directory when you log off.

# Logging Off with a Logout Script

**TIP 174**

You can build the **stty 0** command into a logout script that does other things for you. For example, the following script captures the date and time you logged off, as well as the directory you were in when you logged off:

```
date > $HOME/.last_login;
```

```
pwd > $HOME/.last_dir
echo "********************************************************"
echo '*****'   $LOGNAME logged out at `date`  '*****'
echo "********************************************************"
stty 0
```

## Logging In Again After Logging Off

Using a *.logout* script can let you go directly to the last directory you were working in when you next log in. Simply put the following line in your *.profile* file:

```
cd `cat $HOME/.last_dir`
```

Including this line in your *.profile* is especially useful if you use long pathnames, as we suggest. For example, if you are working in */home/you/thesis/draft/second/section2/chapter7* before logging off, you'll be placed back there on your next login.

## Customizing Your Command History

## Changing the Size and Location of Your History List

One of the nice features of **ksh** is its command history and command editing features. By default, the Korn shell stores your 128 most recent commands in the history list. You can change the number of commands stored in this list by changing the value of the HISTSIZE variable. For example, to make this 200 commands, type the following:

```
$ HISTSIZE=200; export HISTSIZE
```

The default location for the history list is *$HOME/.sh_history*. You can change this file using the variable HISTFILE. For example, to change this location to *$HOME/.ksh_history*, type

```
$ HISTFILE=$HOME/.ksh-history;  export HISTFILE
```

# Using the History List

**T**IP
**177**

If you're using the Korn shell, **ksh**, you can set **ksh** variables, as shown in the following example. The variable HISTFILE holds the record of the last commands you entered; HISTSIZE is the number of commands kept in the history.

```
HISTFILE=$HOME/.sh_history
HISTSIZE=512
SHELL=/bin/ksh
export ENV HISTFILE HISTSIZE SHELL
```

If you are using a nonwindowing terminal, entries like those above will be fine. On a windowing terminal, some people find using just one history file confusing. All the commands you typed in all of the windows are merged. Each shell and window will have its own command history list if you put the following line in your *.kshrc:*

```
HISTFILE=$HOME/.history$$
```

Since each window you use has its own history file, you may find you have dozens of *.history* files in your *$HOME* directory. Remember to delete the ones from previous logins. You may want to do this at logout by adding a line like this one:

```
rm $HOME/.history*
```

to your logout script.

# What If You Need an Exclamation Point (!) in a C Shell Command Line?

Sometimes you may need to use exclamation points (!) in commands. How can you get the C shell not to interpret this exclamation point as the current history character? One way is to precede each ! that you want treated literally with a \ (backslash). For example, suppose you want to send a mail message to att!jersey!lola. You would type

```
% mailx att\!jersey\!lola
```

If you need to use exclamation points frequently, you may want to change the C shell history character to something besides the exclamation point. You can do this by setting the *histchars* variable. This variable consists of two characters. The first is the history character, which by default is !, and the second is the modification character, which by default is ^. The following example shows how *histchars* is used:

```
% set histchars='#,'
```

This command line changes the history character to # (pound sign) and the modification character to , (comma).

# Controlling How Many History List Commands are Saved and Listed (C Shell Version)

The C shell variable history is used to set the number of commands saved by the shell. For example, if you want to save the last 100 commands, include the following line in your *.cshrc* file:

```
set history=100
```

To list all the commands stored by the shell, use this:

```
% history
```

If you want to see the last 20 commands, type

```
% history 20
```

and if you want the 100 commands in the history in reverse order, type

```
% history -r
```

# Using Your History List in ksh

The most frequent use of a **ksh** command history is to rerun previous commands without having to retype them. To run your last command again, type

```
$ r
```

You can run the last command in the background by typing this:

```
$ r &
```

And you can run the command before the last command with this:

```
$ r -2
```

The space between the r and the -2 is essential.

To run a command several places back in the command list, you need only remember how the command started. For example, to run the last command that started with **grep**, type

```
$ r grep
```

# TIP 181

# Editing the Command Line in ksh

The **ksh** also allows you to edit previous commands and then rerun them. This is useful when you make typing errors or need to rerun a long command line with some small changes—changing the filename, for example, in a text processing command. The way to think about this capability is that you are editing your history list, and executing the command that you edited.

First pick a screen editor, either **vi** or **emacs**. (See Chapter 5.) Set the shell variable VISUAL to pick one of these editor command sets. Use

```
VISUAL=vi
```

to select the vi commands, and use

```
VISUAL=emacs
```

to select **emacs**. Note here that you are not actually selecting the **vi** or **emacs** editors. You are telling the Korn shell which set of built-in editing commands to use. You don't need to specify the pathname of the editor, merely which editor commands you'll use. Set VISUAL in your *.profile,* and command line editing will be enabled for the length of your session. Note that **ksh** gives you the equivalent of a one-line screen editor that uses either the **vi** or **emacs** command sets.

For either editor, you should proceed as if the history list rather than the command were on your screen. In **vi**, press the ESC key to get out of input mode, use the **h, j, k,** and **l** keys to move around the list, and use **vi** deletion and substitution commands to change items on the command line. Multiline shell scripts entered at the command line are treated as a single long command by the command line editor. The script shown here

```
for i in *
do
      print $i
done
```

becomes the following single command line:

```
for i in *^Jdo^Jprint $i^Jdone
```

^J is the CTRL-J character.

# Using Your History List in csh

**TIP 182**

You can use your C shell command history list to rerun old commands and to form new commands from ones you ran previously. There are lots of ways you can use the command history to run commands; here we illustrate some that you may find useful.

To run your last command again, type

```
% !!
```

You can now rerun your last command in the background (if it wasn't run there previously) by using

```
% !! &
```

You can run the command you ran before your last command (that is, your second most recent command) with

```
% !-2
```

You can run a particular command from your command history with the exclamation point followed by the number of this command in the history list. For example, you can run command number 17 of your history list by typing

```
% !17
```

You can select the command name and throw away everything else, including options and arguments, with !:0. For example, if your last command line was

```
% ls -l Memos
```

Then you can use

```
% !:0
```

to run the **ls** command.

You can run the last command line containing a particular command by putting this command name after the exclamation point. For instance,

```
% !cat
```

will run the most recent command with **cat** in the command name, which is probably the last **cat** command you ran.

You can also repeat the last command with an editing change.

# Controlling Your Jobs

## Job Control Basics

You can use the job control commands of the job shell **jsh** to list all your current background jobs, suspend or resume a job, and move a job from background to foreground, or vice versa.

To list all your current jobs, type this:

```
$ jobs
[1]   +   Running                 troff -mm chapter1 &
[2]   -   Suspended               sort employees > list &
```

Here you have two jobs running. Each one has a job number that's listed first on the line showing this job. To terminate a job, all you need to do is use the **kill** command, supplying the job number after a percentage sign (%). For example, to **kill** (terminate) the job with job number 2, type

```
$ kill %2
```

You can also **kill** the most recent background job running a particular command. For example, to terminate your most recent background job running **troff,** use

```
$ kill %troff
```

You can suspend the job you are running in the foreground by pressing CTRL-Z. To stop a job, use the **stop** command; to resume a stopped job, running it in the background, use the **bg** command; and to resume a job in the foreground, use the **fg** command. If you have more than one job in the background, use **fg %1** or **fg %2**, and so on.

# Customizing Your Korn Shell Environment

## A More Elaborate .profile for ksh Fans

**TIP 184**

Here is a template for a more extensive *.profile:*

```
##################################################
#
#   A more extensive, all-purpose .profile that does lots
#   of neat stuff.
#
##################################################

# define basic environmental variables
HOME=${HOME:-`/bin/pwd`}              # set HOME on login only
HOME=/home/you
MAIL=/usr/mail/$LOGNAME

MYBIN=$HOME/bin
#  Set PATH variable
PATH=$HOME/bin
PATH=$PATH:$HOME/lib
PATH=$PATH:/bin
PATH=$PATH:/usr/bin
PATH=$PATH:/usr/lbin
PATH=$PATH:/usr/add-on/local/bin
PATH=$PATH:/usr/add-on/dwb/bin
```

```
PATH=$PATH:/usr/add-on/wwb/bin


PAGER=pg
MAILCHECK=1

#  Specify search path for directory changes.
CDPATH=:$HOME:
#
export HOME MAIL HORRR MYBIN PATH CDPATH
export PAGER MAILCHECK

# define korn shell variables
ENV=$HOME/.kshrc
HISTFILE=$HOME/.kshhistory
HISTSIZE=512
SHELL=/usr/bin/ksh
export ENV HISTFILE HISTSIZE SHELL

# CUSTOMIZE PROMPTS

    UNDERLINE=`/usr/bin/tput smul`
    NORMAL=`/usr/bin/tput rmul`

    PS1="`uname -n`:${UNDERLINE} \${PWD} ${NORMAL} "

    PS2="> "
    export PS1 PS2


# printer variables - undelete and alter where appropriate
#BIN=56
#DEST=HO
#FORMS=8by11
#export BIN DEST FORMS

#  Refuse messages sent from other terminals.
mesg n 2>/dev/null
#
```

```
#  Initialize Ex/Vi Editor variables.
EDIT=ex
EDITOR=vi
ED=vi
VISUAL=vi
EXINIT='set notimeout w300=4 w1200=23 report=1 noterse ws smd \
nomesg wm=21 nu eb aw magic ic sh=/usr/bin/ksh \
|map #3 Gi/\<^[A\>^["add@a|map #2 1G!Gvispell^[ \
|map! ZZ ^[ZZ|map #7 i\fB^[ea\fR^[|map #8 i\fI^[ea\fR^['
#
export EDIT EDITOR ED VISUAL TERMCAP EXINIT
#  Get and Set TERM variable.
   echo 'Terminal?   \c'
     read TERM

export TERM


#  Default tty characteristics:
stty ixon kill ^X erase ^H icanon echo echoe echok -hupcl -tabs ixon
  ixoff ixany cr0 nl0
stty eof ^Z
#
#
#  Default file protection is rw-------.
umask 066


#  Change directory into last directory
#  used in last login session.
#    THIS IS USED WITH LOGOUT COMMAND, EG.:
#    logout:
#    pwd > $home/.last_dir
#    stty 0.

cd=`cat $HOME/.last_dir 2> /dev/null`
#
#  Exec into the korn shell
exec /usr/bin/ksh
```

# TIP 185

# A Sample .kshrc File

When the *.profile* above is executed, it invokes the Korn shell **ksh**. When **ksh** starts, it executes the commands in *.kshrc*, which set up its options and environment. Here is a sample *.kshrc* that is suitable for most uses of **ksh** as your primary shell:

```
##########################################################
#
# .kshrc: executed when ksh is explicitly invoked
#
##########################################################


# set ksh options
set -o monitor          # use builtin job monitor features
set -o vi          # set builtin cmd line editor
set -o markdirs          # indicate directories with '/'

# set ksh variables
CDPATH=:$HOME:/usr
MAILCHECK=1
MAILPATH=$MAIL?"^Gyou have mail":$HOME/rje?"check rje ^G"
MAILPATH=$MAILPATH:/usr/spool/uucppublic/$LOGNAME?"check uucp ^G"
TMOUT=0
export CDPATH MAILCHECK MAILPATH TMOUT


EDITOR=/usr/bin/vi
ED=$EDITOR
FCEDIT=ED
HISTSIZE=512
HISTFILE=$HOME/.kshhistory
export EDITOR ED FCEDIT HISTSIZE HISTFILE


# read alias and functions files
. $HOME/.alias          # read alias file
. $HOME/.functions # read function file
ENV=.kshrc1
export ENV
```

# An Alternate ksh Environment

Notice that in the preceding tip, the environment ENV is set to a new *kshrc* file, *.kshrc1,* and that environment is exported (made available to other programs). When you use the Korn shell **ksh** as your primary shell, you will normally want to use monitoring, command line editing, mail checking, and all the other helpful features. Typically, you will also want to have access to all of your aliases and function definitions. However, this may not always be true. Let's consider two kinds of users. The first kind uses a windowing terminal and creates several shells, each associated with a different window. This user wants to have all of the **ksh** definitions and variables available in every window. This user should have the same **ksh** environment for every shell, and should set the ENV to *.kshrc* at the end of the *.kshrc.*

A second user does not use a windowing terminal. This user uses a primary shell as the command interpreter, and spawns other shells only to execute scripts or to place commands in the background. For this user, it is unnecessary to have all of the shell variables defined. Even the PATH variable can be left undefined so that shell scripts do not result in PATH searches. In fact, on a heavily used system, defining all of these will slow down the creation of new shells.

However, it makes sense to have aliases and functions used in such shell scripts. Since the variables and so on are not used in these subshells, one can define an environment that doesn't use them. The following *.kshrc1* is an example of such a **ksh** environment definition:

```
###################################################################
##   .kshrc1 - Alternate Environment for ksh
###################################################################


# set ksh variables
PATH =""
CDPATH=:$HOME:/usr
export PATH CDPATH


# read alias and functions files
. $HOME/.alias          # read alias file
. $HOME/.functions # read function file
ENV=.kshrc1
export ENV
```

# Finding Out Which Processes Are Running

Sometimes you will need to find out which processes are running on your system. For example, you may have a runaway process that you want to terminate or you may need to determine your terminal number so you can send yourself a message later in the day. You can use the **ps** (process status) command to find out all the active processes running on your machine.

If you run the **ps** command with no options, you will get a list of all the active processes associated with your ID. For example, the following list tells you that you have three processes active, all attached to terminal ID *term/94*.

```
$ ps

   PID TTY      TIME COMMAND
  8852 term/94  0:17 vi
  9215 term/94  0:01 ps
  6870 term/94  0:04 ksh
```

You can also see all the active processes running on your SVR4 system by typing this:

```
$ ps -ef
```

The active processes on BSD systems can be listed with

```
$ ps -aux
```

# Killing Processes

After viewing the list of processes running on your system associated with your login, you may want to terminate, or kill, some of them. For instance, you may want to stop a large job, such as formatting a document, before it is finished, or stop a process that may be running out of control. You can terminate any process that you own using the **kill** command. To kill a process, you need to know its pid (*process ID*), which you can get from the **ps** command output.

Most of the time, running the kill command with a pid will kill the process with this pid. So the following will generally kill the process that has 1888 as its pid:

```
$ kill 1888
```

You need to know that running the **kill** command in this way won't always do want you want. For instance, you may want to kill all the child processes of the process as well as stop a runaway program. You can do this by listing the pid of the process followed by the pids of all its children. (You can find all processes that are children of a particular process using the **ps** command also.)

You should also know that running the **kill** command with no option does not always kill the process specified. The reason for this is that using the **kill** command always sends one of the 31 SVR4 signals to the process. When you don't use an option, the **kill** command sends the process the default signal 15 (the TERM signal), which is a software termination signal. Some processes do not accept this signal, and hence do not terminate when you run the **kill** command with their pid. For example, if you are logged on twice, you *can't* terminate one of your sessions by simply using the **kill** command and the pid of the shell process of the second session.

To unconditionally terminate a process, use the **kill** command with the **-9** option. This sends the process signal 9, the KILL signal, which immediately and unconditionally kills the process. So, to kill process 4433 immediately and unconditionally, type this:

```
$ kill -9 4433
```

# Keeping a Process Running After You Log Off

Usually when you log off, all the background processes you created during your session are killed. To prevent this from happening, you can use the **nohup** command, which gets its name from "*no hangup*." You will want to use the **nohup** command when you have a process you expect to run for a very long time, perhaps hours or even days. To run a command so it won't be terminated when you log off, first type **nohup** followed by your usual command line (ending with an **&** to indicate a background job).

If you have one or more pipes in your command line, you will need to put **nohup** after each pipe as well, so that none of the processes following a pipe is killed when you log out. Or you can build a shell script that runs the sequence of commands and then run this shell script using **nohup**. For example, you might type the following:

```
$ nohup sort longfile &
889
Sending output to nohup.out
```

Here, your output is sent to the file *nohup.out* in the current directory. This is done since the output of the **sort** command cannot be sent to your terminal once you've logged off.

Another example using nohup is shown here:

```
$ nohup cat articles | nohup sort | nohup lp &
```

In this command line, **nohup** appears after each pipe to ensure that none of the processes produced by the command line are killed when you log off.

# TIP 190 — Scheduling Your Processes

You can schedule when commands are executed using the **at** command. All you need to do is specify the time in one of many acceptable ways, and then list the commands you want to run at that time, one on a line, terminating your list by including CTRL-D on a separate line.

Here are some examples of acceptable times:

```
0911 April 3     (9:11 AM on April 3)
3:33 pm Feb 29   (3:33 PM on February 29)
noon today       (12:00 PM of the same day)
5 am tomorrow    (5:00 AM of the next day)
```

So, to run the **sort** command on the filenames at 3 AM on September 15, you might type the following:

```
$ at 0300 September 15
sort names
CTRL-D
```

# Sending Yourself a Reminder Message

**TIP 191**

You can use the **at** command to send yourself a reminder message, assuming that you will still be logged on to your terminal and in the same session. To do this, use the **ps** command to find out the terminal number associated with your session. Then use the **at** command with the time specified in one of the formats understood by the **at** command. Here is an example:

```
$ at 3:28 pm today
echo "^GMeeting with the Director at 3:30 PM^G" > /dev/term/32
CTRL-d
```

Enter this code, and if the terminal of your session is */dev/term/32,* and your session is still active at 3:28 PM (of the same day), the bell on your terminal will ring (caused by echoing ^G, the bell ring), the message "Meeting with the Director at 3:30 PM" will be echoed to your terminal, and then the bell will ring again.

# A del and undel Demon

**TIP 192**

Help! All of the files you've ever "deleted" (see Tip 157) but actually just moved to another directory are now jammed into your *$HOME/.saved* directory. Do you have to go through the whole directory and manually remove each file?

The **del** command alters the modification date of the file when it is moved to *.saved*. Thus you know when it was moved. Use the following script to automatically get rid of deleted files. This script removes them when they are seven days old, but you can give yourself more time. Put this script in an executable file located in *$HOME/bin/demon.*

```
#  demon for del command

cd $HOME/.saved;
find . -atime +7 -exec /bin/rm -r {} 2> /dev/null \;

at 6 am tomorrow 2>/dev/null <<%
$HOME/bin/demon
%
```

You have to run the job manually the first time, but then it sets up an **at** job to run itself at 6 AM each day.

# A Potpourri of Tips on Customization

## Blocking Online Messages

Receiving a message from someone using the **write** command can be extremely annoying. You may be working on some important memorandum or developing some new program when all of a sudden you hear a beep and text appears on your screen in the middle of your work. You can use the **mesg** command to control whether you are willing to accept write messages and requests to establish talk sessions. To refuse these messages, type

```
$ mesg n
```

Since the message status returns to **y** when you log off, you probably will want to put the following line in your *.profile* to make sure that online messages are refused during all your sessions:

```
mesg n
```

## Avoiding Typing Long Filenames with Filename Completion

The C shell has a popular and useful feature called filename completion. To enable this feature, set the toggle variable *filec,* using the following command:

```
$ set filec
```

When this variable is set, you need only type the first part of a filename in a command line. Type the command you want to run, followed by the first part of the filename, followed by ESC ESC (press the escape key twice). For example, if your current directory contains the files *newhampshire, newjersey, newmexico,* and *newyork,* you can print out the contents of *newjersey* by typing this:

```
$ cat newj [ESC][ESC]
```

newj will be expanded to newjersey *by filename completion. Keep in mind, however, that when more than one filename starts with the specified pattern, filename completion doesn't select any of the filenames.*

If you use CTRL-D instead of ESC ESC, as shown here,

```
$ cat new CTRL-D
```

the command will print out all the filenames that have "new" at the beginning, including *newhampshire, newjersey, newmexico,* and *newyork.*

# How to Avoid Creating Large Files

Sometimes a command will create an extremely large file that will clog your system.
This can happen when the output of a command is much larger than you expect or a program gets out of control from a bug. When you use the Korn shell, you can use the **ulimit** command with the -**f** option, supplying the upper limit in terms of 1000s of bytes. For example, you can avoid creating files larger than 10 megabytes by using this command:

```
$ ulimit -f 10000
```

If you use the C shell, you can use the command string **limit filesize,** giving the maximum filesize in terms of megabytes by using the abbreviation m. For example, this command line prevents the creation of files larger than 10m:

```
$ limit filesize 10m
```

# Preventing Files from Being Overwritten (Korn Shell)

When you use the Korn shell, you can prevent an existing file from being overwritten by the redirection of the output of a command. You do this by setting the *noclobber* toggle variable to on (a toggle variable has two possible values, on and off).

To turn on *noclobber* in the Korn shell, type

```
$ set -o noclobber
```

To see how this works, suppose you have a file named *temp* in your current directory. If you try to overwrite *temp* by redirecting output, you'll get a message that it already exists. Here is an example:

```
$ who > temp
temp:  file exists
```

# Preventing Files from Being Overwritten (C Shell)

When you use the C shell you can prevent an existing file from being overwritten by the redirection of the output of a command. You do this by setting the noclobber toggle variable to on (a toggle variable has two possible values, on and off).

To turn on the *noclobber* variable, type

```
$ set noclobber
```

Then if you have a file named *temp* in your current directory and you try to overwrite it with the output of a command, you'll get a message telling you that the file already exists. For example,

```
$ who > temp
temp:  file exists
```

If you really do want to overwrite the file *temp,* you can do this using >! (the redirection symbol >, followed by an exclamation point, !). For example, the following command line will put the output of the **who** command in the file *temp,* overwriting whatever the file held before:

```
$ who >! temp
```

# Setting Your System's Time Zone

TIP
198

You can set the time zone of your system using the TZ environmental variable. The internal format used by your UNIX system is universal or Greenwich Mean Time. Your system determines the local time using the value of TZ. For example, the following command line specifies that the time zone is EST (Eastern Standard Time), which is 5 hours earlier than Universal Time, with a switch to EDT (Eastern Daylight Time) for part of the year:

```
TZ=EST5EDT
```

On some systems, time zone data is kept in the directory */usr/lib/zoneinfo.* By browsing through the files in this directory, or its subdirectories, you'll find values for TZ for different places in the world. If you can find this information, you can set the time of your system to any location for which there is such information. If you often need to know what time it currently is somewhere else in the world, you can write an alias to do this.

# Avoiding Accidental Logoffs

TIP
199

You can accidentally log off by pressing CTRL-D when you only meant to terminate another command. You can avoid these accidental logoffs when you use either the Korn shell or the C shell by turning the *ignoreeof* toggle variable on. To do this in the Korn shell, use this command:

```
$ set -o ignoreeof
```

Include this line in your *.profile* file to have this toggle variable set each time you log on.

To do this in the C shell, use this command:

```
%  set ignoreeof
```

To avoid typing this line each time you log on, you should include it in your *.cshrc* file.

When you have set *ignoreeof,* you can terminate your shell by typing **exit** instead of CTRL-D.

# How to Know Which Version of a Command Will Run

Sometimes you may have different versions of a particular command on your system, with the same name, but in different directories. For example, you may have written a shell program **ls** in your *bin* directory, */home/fred/bin,* that lists the files in your current directory in a particular way that you like. Which **ls** command will run when you enter **ls** on the command line? The one in */home/fred/bin,* the standard UNIX SVR4 command in */bin,* or some other version?

The answer is found in your PATH variable. Your system searches for your command in the directories in your PATH in the order in which they are listed. So, if the directory */bin* containing the **ls** command is listed before */home/fred/bin* in your PATH (and it should be for security reasons!), when you type **ls** you will run the standard **ls** command on your system. To avoid this problem, you should have given your version of **ls** a different name!

On some UNIX systems, there is a useful utility called **which**. If your system has this command, you can determine which version of a command will run. For example, to determine which version of **ls** will run, you would type

```
$ which ls
/bin/ls
```

The **which** command is particularly useful on systems such as UNIX SVR4 with BSD compatibility packages and versions of SunOS with System V compatibility packages, where there may be two different versions of a command, one with System V origin and the other with BSD origin. If the **which** command isn't available on your system, you can obtain one from the software included in *UNIX Power Tools* by Jerry Peek, Tim O'Reilly, and Mike Loukides (Sebastopol, CA: O'Reilly and Associates, 1993).

# A Fortune a Day?

**TIP**
**201**

Many UNIX systems contain a directory called *usr/games* with a variety of different amusements. If you work at a large and/or serious corporation where game playing and humor are discouraged, you may find that this directory is not present on your UNIX system or that all the files in it have been made nonexecutable. But if this directory is present and its programs are executable, you can get an electronic fortune by running the fortune command, as shown here:

```
$ /usr/games/fortune
You will win the lottery today.
```

To get a fortune when you log in each day, make sure you put *usr/games* in the PATH in your *.profile* and put a line containing the **fortune** command in your *.profile*.

# Chapter 4
## Mail Tips
## and
## Tricks

# Types of Mail Readers

## TIP 202

## UNIX System Mail Packages

There are many different ways to read mail on UNIX. You can use the **mail** command, the **mailx** command, enhanced mailers such as **Elm**, **mush**, or **mh**. You can even read mail with a text editor such as **emacs**. (See Tip 209.)

The reason so many UNIX mail packages exist is that the **mail** program, the original UNIX system mailer, was very primitive. It provided a combined User Agent (UA) (to interact with the user) and Transfer Agent (TA) (to interact with the mail network). It had few features, and required that mail senders know the path from their machine to the recipient's machine.

In response, several different enhanced mail packages were developed with the aim of providing a better UA to e-mail. BSD provided **mail** with profiles, aliases, folders, and other neat features. AT&T's version of **mail**, called **mailx**, was made available in addition to the original **mail** program in UNIX System V. The **mailx** program is used extensively by UNIX System V users, with only old-time UNIX users sticking with the **mail** program.

In addition, a large number of enhanced mail packages have been developed for the UNIX system, each providing its own special features and capabilities. Some of the more popular of these are **mush** and its commercial progeny, **Z=mail**, **Elm**, and **mh**. (See Tips 203, 204, and 205 for more information about these mailers.) One of the newest capabilities in UNIX system mailers is support for multimedia mail, including audio and images. This support is provided by MIME (see Tip 206), with MIME capabilities integrated into many of the popular UNIX mailers.

## TIP 203

## What Is Elm and Where Do I Get It?

**Elm**, another commonly used enhanced e-mail package, provides a user agent intended to work with any UNIX System Mail Transport Agent, such as **rmail** or **sendmail**. **Elm** provides a screen-oriented user interface, with lots of useful features, including listing a table of contents of your mail, printing sequentially numbered pages of mail output, and an auto-reply feature for people on vacation. **Elm** has a reputation of being easy for novices to use, and it requires considerably less configuration than **mush**. Information on **Elm** can be obtained from *archive-server@DSI.COM*. You can also find a large amount of useful information on **Elm** in the newsgroup *comp.mail.elm* and the FAQs (frequently asked questions) that are posted periodically to this newsgroup and to *news.answers*. The book *UNIX Communications, Second Edition* by Bart Anderson, Bryan Costales, and Harry Henderson (Carmel IN: Howard W. Sams, 1991) also contains a useful chapter devoted to **Elm**.

You can obtain **Elm** via anonymous ftp from many different sites. Currently, these sites include *wuarchive.wustl.edu* in */mirrors/elm* (North America), *ftp.cs.ruu.nl* in */pub/ELM-2.4* (Europe), *ftp.demon.co.uk* in */pub/unix/mail/elm* (UK), *ftp.adelaide.edu.au* (Australia), and *NCTUCCA.edu.tw* in */packages/mail/elm* (Taiwan). You should consult *comp.mail.elm* and use **archie** to find the latest information on these archive sites. When you get the Elm distribution you will find some useful documents, including the *Reference Guide*, the *User's Guide*, and the *Filter Guide*.

# What Is mush and Where Do I Get It?

TIP 204

**mush**, the Mail User's Shell, provides a complete environment for e-mail. It has a full screen user (**vi**-like) interface and a command line mode. In line mode, you can recall previous commands using a history file, and you can use pipes to connect different mush commands. Furthermore, in line mode you can use the **pick** command to search for messages by sender, subject, date, content, and in other ways. (See Tip 211.) **mush** contains a scripting language so you can build your own library of mail handling commands.

An enhanced version of **mush** is commercially available as **Z-mail**. You can learn about **Z-mail** and **mush** by consulting the book *The Z-Mail Handbook* by Hanna Nelson (Sebastopol, CA: O'Reilly and Associates, 1991). **Z-mail** won the *UNIX World Magazine* "Product of the Year Award" for 1991. The commercial version has two character modes as well as Motif and OpenLook Graphical user interfaces. You can learn more about **mush** by reading the newsgroup *comp.mail.mush*. Further details are available from *argv@zcode.com*.

You can obtain a public domain version of **mush** from a variety of anonymous ftp sites, including *ftp.uu.net* in */usenet/comp.sources.misc*, *usc.edu* in */archive/usenet/sources/comp.sources.misc*, *keos.helsinki.fi* in */pub/archives/comp.sources/misc*, and *ftp.waseda.ac.jp* in */pub/archives/comp.sources/misc*.

# What Is mh and Where Do I Get It?

*Mail Handler*, known as **mh**, is a mailer user interface available in the public domain. Key features of **mh** include its ability to be used from a shell prompt, and the fact that each of its commands can utilize the capabilities of the shell—for example, pipes, redirection, aliases, history files, and many others. You can use **mh** commands in shell scripts and call them from C programs. Furthermore, to use **mh** you don't have to start a special mail agent. **mh** puts each mail message in its own file, the name of which is the message number of the message. This means that you can rearrange messages by changing their filenames, and that standard UNIX system file operations can be used on messages.

For more information on **mh** you can consult the book *mh & xmh: E-mail for Users & Programmers, Second Edition*, by Jerry Peek (O'Reilly and Associates, 1992). (**xmh** is an X-Windows version of **mh**; see Chapter 14.) You can also consult the newsgroup *comp.mail.mh* and the FAQs posted periodically to this newsgroup and to *news.answers*.

You can obtain **mh** via anonymous ftp from several different sites including *ftp.ics.uci.edu* in *mh/mh-6.8.tar.Z* and *Louis.udel.edu* in *portal/mh-6.8.tar.Z*. (See Tip 600 to find out how to copy files via anonymous ftp and how to make them available for use.) Consult *comp.mail.mh* or use **archie** for updated information on these archive sites.

# What Is MIME and Where Do I Get MIME Software?

The *Multi-purpose Internet Mail Extensions (MIME)* is a specification for the interchange of messages that contain text in languages with different character sets and multimedia content, such as audio and images.

You can obtain **metamail**, a public domain implementation of MIME, from *thumper.bellcore.com* in *pub/nsb/mm.2.6.tar.Z*. This program was designed to be easily integrated into the mail systems used on UNIX systems. Most users don't use **metamail** directly, but rather a version of their favorite mailer with **metamail** integrated into it. For example, the latest versions of **Elm** and **mh** both include support for MIME.

For more information, consult the newsgroup *comp.mail.mime* and the FAQs on MIME posted periodically to this newsgroup and to *news.answers*.

# Reading Mail

## Reading Your Mail

**TIP 207**

When someone sends you mail, the UNIX system stores it in a mailbox identified by your login name. When you issue the command **mailx**, this mailbox is read, and its contents are organized by messages. When reading mail, it allows you to save, delete, or respond to messages. Its flexibility allows you to customize its operation for easier use.

When **mailx** is first run, it checks a file—*/usr/lib/mailx/mailxrc* on some systems, */lib/Mailrc* on others—which contains systemwide defaults, then checks your own startup file (*$HOME/.mailrc*) to personalize your use of **mailx**. It's best to have few or no parameters set in the system *mailxrc* file, and in fact, its presence is optional. If there are no systemwide settings, then each user can set default parameters as desired.

The first parameter to set is a pager. If you have long mail messages, they'll tend to scroll off the screen before you finish reading them. To set up your favorite pager, put a line in your *.mailrc* file like this:

```
set PAGER="pg -e"
```

This paginates the messages into screen-sized chunks. (See Tip 225 for more information on your *.mailrc* file.)

## Organizing Mail That You Have Received

**TIP 208**

Let's say you often read mail during the course of the day. How can you organize the mail you receive?

Using the **s** (*save*) command just appends everything to the file *mbox*. That means you have one big heap of mail that's not sorted. To find anything, you must remember when it arrived and search through a huge *mbox*.

If you use **mailx**, you can save mail messages to specific files, simply by using the following command sequence at the question mark prompt to specify the file in which you want a message saved:

```
? s filename
```

One difficulty with this command is that **mailx** assumes you want to store the message in a file in the current directory. Therefore, you'll find that you've stored messages from the same person or on the same topic in several different directories. To avoid such chaos, make sure you always save messages in the same directory. There are a number of ways to do this. You can set an environment variable for **mailx** in your *.mailrc* file. If you set

```
folder=$HOME/mail
```

then **mailx** knows you want to save messages in that directory. When you want to specify that a message be saved in a file in that directory, you add a + (plus sign) at the beginning of the filename. Thus,

```
? s october
```

will save the message in the file *october* in the current directory, but

```
? s +october
```

will save it in *october* in *$HOME/mail.*

A less cumbersome way to save messages in *$HOME/mail* is to create an exported alias for your **mail** command in the following way:

```
$ alias -x   ckmail='cd   $HOME/mail;/usr/bin/mailx;cd   -'
```

or in some shells:

```
$ alias ckmail='OLPWD=$PWD; cd $HOME/mail; /usr/bin/mailx; cd $OLDPWD'
```

Now whenever you read mail with the **ckmail** command, you'll automatically be placed in the *$HOME/mail* directory. Every time you save a message to a file, that file will be in the *mail* directory. To make things easier to find, save each message in a file named after the sender, as well as in a file named after the project to which the message refers. In that way, you can easily find a message.

You can also accomplish the same thing, but faster, with the following **ksh** function:

```
function ckmail
```

```
{
if mail -e
        then
                (cd $HOME/mail;/usr/bin/mailx)
        else
                echo "No mail at this time"
fi
}
```

This function has the added advantage of not putting you into the **mail** program unless you actually have mail.

# Using Unipress emacs to Receive Mail

**TIP 209**

The **emacs** program is much more than just an editor; it provides a full environment for most activities people do on UNIX, including sending and receiving mail. While in **emacs**, you don't need to exit, or to start another shell in order to send and receive mail. Unipress **emacs** features an emulation of Berkeley **Mail** from the Berkeley version of UNIX.

To check for mail in Unipress **emacs**, simply press CTRL-X R to start the mail reader. If there is mail, you get a list of your messages in one window, and the first message is displayed in another window. While you are in this mail environment, the following commands are active:

| Command | Meaning |
| --- | --- |
| p | Previous message |
| n | Next message |
| f | Scroll other window down |
| b | Scroll other window up |
| m | Start new message |
| r | Reply |
| s | Save |
| x | Exit |

# Using Elm to Eliminate Annoying Mail

Electronic mail used to consist of short, mostly valuable messages from people you knew and worked with. As e-mail has spread in popularity and use, it's taken on some of the qualities of junk mail. Because it's so easy, people now send outrageous mail: listings of all courses taught by a particular company, lists of all memos and letters written and received by a particular organization, notes saying "how about lunch?" sent to hundreds of people, useless communications from upper management, and so on. How can you avoid receiving such mail, rather than having to read and delete it after it arrives?

Unfortunately, the standard UNIX mailers **mail** and **mailx** do not have the ability to prescreen mail messages. This feature is one that's badly needed in big organizations that depend on UNIX mail. The **Elm** mailer (see Tip 203) contains a "filter" utility that can take actions based on the sender, subject, addressee, and so on before the mail is placed in your mailbox. If you have the **Elm** mailer on your machine, use the command **man filter** to see its operation.

Basically, you create a *.forward* file that contains the command:

```
|/usr/bin/filter
```

or

```
"| /usr/bin/filter -o /dev/null"
```

You also create the file *.filter_rules* in your home or *.elm* directory. This file contains a set of if-then rules that specify what to do with each piece of mail.

# Searching Messages with the pick Command

The **mush** and **mh** mailers provide **pick**, a command you can use to search different components of messages. For instance, in mush line mode, you can search for messages from Maria using the following command:

```
pick -f Maria
```

Here the **-f** option tells **pick** to look for messages where the "From:" field contains the string "Maria".

You can search for messages about a particular subject using the **-s** option. For instance, the following command will search for any message that has the string "Tips" in its subject line:

```
pick -s -i Tips
```

Here the **-i** option tells pick to ignore case, so that messages with "tips", "Tips", and so on will be found.

## Sending Mail

# Composing and Editing a Response to Mail

Let's say whenever you try to send someone a response to a mail message, you make several typing errors and the message looks like it was sent by an illiterate. Is there a way to edit you response before it goes out to the world?

You can edit the outgoing message, or even compose the whole message within an editor, by typing either of the following commands on a line by itself:

```
~e
```

or

```
~v
```

The **~e** command evokes your preferred line-oriented text editor on the message, while **~v** calls up your preferred screen editor. You set your editor preferences within the *.mailrc* file, as shown here:

```
set EDITOR=/bin/ed VISUAL=/usr/bin/vi
```

Now when you respond to a message, the "To:", "Subject:" and "Cc:" fields will be moved to a file called *tmp,* which is used by your editor:

```
To: hal@mach.xyz.com

Subject: Response to your meeting note.

Cc: bill



~

~

~

~

~

~

~

~

~

~

~

~

~
"/tmp/Re19253" 3 lines, 71 characters
```

Now you can type your message into **vi**, exit **vi** (using ZZ or :wq) when you're done, and send the message with ^D (CTRL-D). You can set the values of the EDITOR and VISUAL variables in your environment, rather than in the *.mailrc*. The sample *.profile* in Tip 3.1 does just that.

# Including the Body of the Message That You are Responding To

Suppose you want to be able to refer to the material in a message without having to retype it. Is there a way to include the original message in your response?

There is a **mailx** command that does exactly that. When you respond to a message, follow the steps laid out in the preceding tip. Before you go into the editor however, issue the ~**m** command. This will read the message into the buffer, then use ~**v** to edit the whole file. For example, the following code reads in the 25 lines from the message:

```
To: hal@mach.xyz.com
Subject: Response to your meeting note.
Cc:bill
```

```
~m
Interpolating 25
(continue)
```

A ~v command evokes **vi** on the whole *tmp* file:

```
To: hal@mach.xyz.com
Subject: Response to your meeting note.
Cc:bill


        From hal Sun May   2  12:08 EDT 1995
        From: hal@mach.xyz.com
        To: you


        Bill asked me to check if you plan to attend the lab
        meeting this Monday. Let me know if you are going to
        be there or not.


        hal
~
~
~
~
~
~
~
~
"/tmp/Re19253"  23 lines,  977 characters
```

Compose your response in **vi**, and the original message will be sent along with your answer.

# Sending a Mail Response

You can set two parameters in your *.mailrc* to assure that **mailx** asks for the subject line and copy to list whenever you send mail. Simply use the following line:

```
set asksub askcc
```

Once you have set these variables, when you respond to a message, you'll see lines similar to this on your screen:

```
? R
To: hal@mach.xyz.com
Subject:
```

Always fill in the "Subject:" line. It's easier to handle mail if you know who the sender was and what the message concerns. Don't put the whole message in the subject line. Although you can have a "Subject:" line up to 1024 characters long, it's difficult for the recipient to read, respond to, and file such messages. When you fill in the "Subject:" line, you'll be prompted for the "Cc:" (Copy To) list, as shown here:

```
To: hal@mach.xyz.com
Subject: Response to your meeting note.
Cc:
```

After providing a "Copy To" list (press RETURN if you don't want copies sent to anyone else), you're given a blank line on which to start typing your message.

```
To: hal@mach.xyz.com
Subject: Response to your meeting note.
Cc:bill
```

To send a simple message, just type away. When you get to the end, press CTRL-D and the message will be sent.

# **T** **IP** **215** **Sending Blind Carbon Copies**

With **mailx** you can send blind carbon copies to recipients whose names you do not want included in the "Cc:" list. When you send someone a blind carbon copy, the mail will be sent to them, but their names will not appear anywhere on the output message seen by the other recipients. This is particularly useful when you want to clue someone into something that other people don't want them to know. You can set this option by using the following statement in your *.mailrc* file:

```
set askbcc
```

This will cause the following line to appear on your screen after the "Subject:" and "Cc:" lines:

```
Bcc:
```

After the colon, you list the e-mail addresses of people who should receive blind carbon copies.

# Some Other Useful mailx Options

**TIP 216**

There are a number of other options that can be automatically set in your *.mailrc* file, or can be explicitly set at the shell level via the **set** command. Some of these are listed here:

| Name | Function |
| --- | --- |
| debug | Enables debug mode. |
| dot | Treats a single period on a line as an EOF code. |
| metoo | Sends a message to your login, just as to other recipients. |
| quiet | Suppresses mail welcome and version messages. |

Any of these internal mail variables can easily be unset with the **unset** command. For example, suppose you are having problems in **mailx** and want to do some debugging. Your sequence might look something like this:

```
$ mailx
set debug
(....some debugging work effort)
$ unset debug
```

This last command resets the *debug* variable to its default state, which is *nodebug*.

# Responding to Mail to the Author or to the Author and All Recipients

**TIP 217**

When you read an e-mail message, you can respond to the sender or to all of the recipients of that message. Here are a few useful things to know about responding to mail.

After you've read the mail, the command mode prompt (? by default) appears on the screen. Using **mailx**, if you type **r**, you can usually respond to *all* of the people who received that message; if you type **R**, your response goes *only* to the sender. Notice the difference, and note that the easy command, **r**, is probably not the one you want. This however, depends on the way that your administrator has set up the variable *flipr* in your environment. The reason for this variable in the first place is that **mail** works exactly the opposite way! Many people used **mail** for a while, then moved to **mailx**. The difference in mail response formats can cause amusing and, in some cases, annoying results.

Don't send replies to all recipients unless there is a good reason. If someone invites you to a meeting, or tells you about an event, use the appropriate response to reply to the sender; don't use the wrong one that will tell everyone your intentions. This can be particularly irritating when you inadvertently reply to a broadcast message intended for an entire complex, choose the wrong form of the reply, and send it back to all of the original recipients!

You can check out the setting of *flipr* for either **mail** or **mailx** easily by picking a message with just a few recipients. Enter **r** and see what is displayed back to you. If more than just the author's name appears, then *flipr* is set so that **r** responds to all recipients. If only the author's name appears, then *flipr* is reversed, meaning **R** replies to all recipients. In either case, if you don't want to send the response to the listed recipient(s), you can answer the send confirmation prompt by saying no. This will send the message to your *dead.letter* file, and no harm will be done.

If you are the only user on the machine, you can change the meaning of **r** and **R** to your personal taste by setting *flipr*. If, however, you are on a multiuser machine, you should learn what the others are using, and use that convention to be consistent.

# Sending a Quick Mail Message

Let's say you often want to send one person a short e-mail message. Is there an easy way to do this without getting into the **mailx** program?

The following shell script uses **mailx** (and therefore gives you all of its options and aliases for sending mail), but with a simple command line interface. The **tm** command interprets the first argument as the message recipient and the rest of the line as the message.

```
############################################################
#
#  tm - telephone message # #  tm sends a message to the recipient
#  with some convenience not provided by Mail
```

```
#
#  Usage: tm [name [message]]
#  tm sends a one line message to the named
#  person, where the name is either a login ID or
#  Mail alias.
#  OR
#  Usage: tm name
#  name is a one word login ID or Mail alias.
#  tm then prompts you for a message terminated by
#  a double <F132
.
#  OR
#  Usage: tm
#  If you invoke it as tm
#  without any arguments, it prompts you for
#  the addressee, as well as the message.
################################################################

##   Initialize it
##

trap 'if [ -f $HOME/.tmp$$ ] ;/bin/rm -f $HOME/.tmp$$;exit 1' 1 2 3 15


##
##   Get Name
##

if [ -z "$1" ]
then echo "TO:\c"
     read PERSON
     if [ -z $PERSON ]
     then echo "Usage: tm [name [message]]"
exit
     fi
else PERSON=$1
   shift
fi


##
##   Get Message
##
```

```
if [ -z "$1" ]
then
    echo "Enter Message terminated by a double "<CR>."
    echo "MESSAGE:\c"
    while [ true ]
    do
        read MSG
        if [ -z "$MSG" ]
        then break ;
        else
        echo $MSG>>$HOME/.tmp$$
        continue;
        fi
    done
else
    echo "$*">>$HOME/.tmp$$
fi


##
##  Send Message
##

echo Mail being sent to $PERSON.
if mailx $PERSON < $HOME/.tmp$$
then
    /bin/rm -f $HOME/.tmp$$;
else
    /bin/mv $HOME/.tmp$$ $HOME/dead.letter
    mail $LOGNAME <<-!ERROR!
    Cannot send to $PERSON
    Message moved to $HOME/dead.letter
    !ERROR!
fi
```

# Saving Your Outgoing Messages

Is there some way to automatically send yourself carbon copies of all mail messages you send?

If you place the following line in your *.mailrc* file, all of your outgoing messages will be appended to the *outbox* file.

```
set record=/home/you/mail/outbox
```

Note that your name will not appear in the "Cc:" line in the mail header.

# Sending a File to Another User

It's easy to send a file to another user with **mailx**. For example, to send the file *report* to user jan on your machine, use this command:

```
$ mailx jan < report
```

Similarly, to send this file to *wendy@cs.ucsc.edu,* use

```
$ mailx wendy@cs.ucsc.edu < report
```

# Sending a Set of Files to Another User

There are often occasions when you wish to bundle up a set of files and directories and send them off somewhere. For example, if you are moving to a new machine, it's convenient to send files from your old machine named "mach" to your new one named "mach1". If you are working collaboratively with others, you may have need to send them batches of stuff. This is the procedure for sending all the files, subdirectories, and so on in the directory *notes* to login ID user on UNIX system mach1:

```
$ cd notes
$ find . -print | cpio -ocvdm >file.cpio
$ uuto -mp file.cpio mach1!user
$ rm file.cpio
```

The -**m** option on **uuto** sends you mail when the transfer has been accomplished; the -**p** option copies the source to the spool directory before transmission. This is crucial to assure that the **rm file.cpio** doesn't remove the *cpio* file before the system gets around to sending it.

On the receiving system, here is what the recipient should do to retrieve the material, assuming that the received files are to be put in a new directory called *newnotes*.

```
$ mkdir newnotes
$ cd newnotes
$ uupick
from system mach:  file file.cpio ? m
39 blocks
$ cpio -icvdm <file.cpio
$ rm file.cpio
```

## Using Unipress emacs to Send Mail

To send mail from within Unipress **emacs**, simply press CTRL-X and then type M. **emacs** opens up a mail buffer and presents you with a screen that contains a "To:" line for the address. Next comes a subject line, and after that the area in which you type the message. CTRL-C sends the message.

## Customizing Your Mail Environment

## Using Mail Aliases to Cut Down on Typing

As the name suggests, *aliases* are alternative names for people you wish to send e-mail to. Using aliases makes sending mail easier and faster. The simplest and most common purpose of aliases is to save typing time. If you have someone you correspond with via e-mail, a brief alias will make it easier to send mail to that person. For example, by using aliases, you can send e-mail by name rather than by the full electronic address. Suppose you send a lot of mail to your friend sandy, who has the login sla. Instead of remembering the login sla you can put the line

```
alias sandy sla
```

in your *.mailrc* file. To send mail to your friend sandy via **mailx**, you can use the command

```
$ mailx sandy
```

Obviously, aliases are also helpful when someone's mail address is long. For instance, the line

```
alias yvette  att!arch!montana!yvx
```

lets you send e-mail to your friend Yvette at *att!arch!montana!yvx*, using the command

```
$ mailx yvette
```

Replacing a difficult to remember string with a nickname is a frequent use of aliases. For example:

```
alias dilbert scottadams@aol.com
alias rush 70277.2502@compuserve.com
alias bill PRESIDENT@WHITEHOUSE.GOV
alias al VICE.PRESIDENT@WHITEHOUSE.GOV
```

Using the aliases dilbert, rush, bill, and al, shown here, you can send mail to the creator of the Dilbert and Dogbert cartoons (Scott Adams), the flamboyant and controversial political rabble-rouser (Rush Limbaugh), the President of the United States (Bill Clinton), and the Vice President of the United States (Al Gore), respectively.

# Using Aliases for Groups of People

**TIP 224**

Aliases are also used to define groups of people to receive messages. Rather than send out individual messages to each person in the lab group, you can define a group in an alias and let **mailx** send your message to each. Notice that you can nest aliases. In this example, a lab group is made up of five people, while the department is made up of the lab group and four others.

```
alias dept lab.grp khr jmf rrr pat.s
alias lab.grp bill hal lin kwame mary
```

To use an alias, you put the definition in your *$HOME/.mailrc* file. If many of the people on your machine work together, defining a set of common aliases in the system startup file will make them usable by all. This makes it easier for a group of people to maintain an alias list because only one copy exists. If you declare an alias in your personal *.mailrc* that has the same name as one in the system *mailrc*, yours will be used, since **mailx** reads your *.mailrc* after the system *mailrc*.

Note that with **Elm**, to use a group alias, each user in the group must have a previously defined alias or a valid address on the current machine.

# T**IP** 225    A Sample .mailrc File

When you start **mailx**, it tries to execute commands first from the systemwide options file */usr/lib/mailx/mailrc*, then from your own customization file *$HOME/.mailrc*. The common use of these files is to set up personal options and define alias lists. If an error occurs in the startup file, the remaining lines are ignored. Here is a sample *.mailrc* entry that sets the variables described in this chapter.

```
set PAGER=pg
set from askcc asksub metoo prompt="?>:"
set crt=20
set quiet hold
set header append dot keep save showto
set folder=/$HOME/mail
set MBOX=$HOME/mail/mbox
set record=/$HOME/mail/outbox
set toplines=10
set EDITOR=/bin/ed VISUAL=/usr/bin/vi

alias dept lab.grp khr jmf rrr pat.s
alias lab.grp bill hal lin kwame mary
```

The space between setting variables and defining aliases is there only to make it easier to read the *.mailrc* file. If you group variables and aliases into clusters, you'll find it is easier to read and maintain the file.

# A Sample elmrc File

When you use the **Elm** mail reader, you can set preferred options for reading mail in your *elmrc* file that **Elm** puts in your *.elm* directory. You can put comments in this file by typing a pound sign (#) at the beginning of the line. You can use the following sample *elmrc* as a guide for creating your own *elmrc*.

```
# display messages on your screen
print = cat
# set editor
editor = vi
# specify where to save mail
maildir = ~/Mail
# prefix sequence for indenting included messages
prefix = >
# how to sort folder
sortby = Reverse-Received
# automatically include replied-to message into buffer
autocopy = on
# save messages, by login name of sender/recipient
savename = on
# set defaults for processing messages
# make yes the default for the delete message prompt
alwaysdelete = ON
# make yes the default for the keep unread mail in incoming mailbox prompt
alwayskeep = ON
# use an arrow to indicate the current message
arrow = ON
# set directory name for received mail
receivedmail = Rmail
# set your user level to 1 for intermediate user
userlevel = 1
# set pathnames for signatures for local and remote mail
localsignature = Mail/.localsig
remotesignature = Mail/.remotesig
```

# A Sample .mushrc File

When you use **mush** mailer, you can use your *.mushrc* file to set the values for mush variables, to define mail aliases, macros, and command-line aliases. You can insert comments in your *.mushrc* by putting them after a # (pound sign) , which can appear anywhere on a line. Here's a sample abbreviated *.mushrc* that you can use as a basis for your own.

```
# put you in your editor when sending and replying to mail
set autoedit
# prompt for the subject of outgoing messages
set ask
# attach a signature file to all messages you send
set autosign = "~\.signature"
# set some useful command aliases for line mode
cmd P print
cmd D delete
cmd PK pick -i -d +1/1
# have mush keep last 20 commands in mush history file
set history = 20
# set some mail aliases
alias jeff  Jeff Pepper <pepper@osbmgh.com>
alias wayne  Wayne Yuhasz <wayne@crc.com>
```

## Forwarding Mail

# Forwarding Mail to Other UNIX Systems

People often have logins on several UNIX systems. Although most of your colleagues send e-mail to the primary login, you may still get messages sent to the other logins. Here is a way to forward and consolidate mail so that it all comes to the same place, as long as all the systems are UNIX machines capable of sending mail to one another. Use the message forwarding facility of **mailx**. Place the following as the first line in your mailbox:

```
Forward to mach3!you
```

Once this line is present in your mailbox, all of your mail will be forwarded to user *you* on *mach3*.

This method works if you have an existing mail file. A more general method of accomplishing the same thing is to use this command to turn forwarding on:

```
$ mail -F mach3!you
```

Similarly, you must use the following command to turn forwarding off:

```
$ mail -F ""
```

The pair of double quotes ("") are mandatory to provide a null argument. This does the same thing as in the preceding examples, but it is more general. On some systems, mail is configured so that the mail files are deleted when empty. Using **mail -F** to manage forwarding will work even if you don't have a mail file.

When you use **mail -F**, the **autoforward** function can act on any new mail received. The **autoforward** function forwards the mail to the recipients you designate in your **mail -F** command.

# Forwarding Mail to a Group of People

**TIP 229**

You can also use the forwarding option to forward mail to a group of people. Let's say that your group has a general e-mail address that can receive messages on a variety of topics. These messages need to be directed to several people for proper handling or response. For example, Bill might want to see all messages to review the variety of mail received. Sally needs to handle the ones asking for more information, and Chris follows up on all the noninformational messages. To forward mail to several people at once, use a command like this one:

```
$ mail -F "bill,sally@mach2,mach1!mach7!chris"
```

You can use either commas or spaces to separate the recipients. Pick one and use it consistently. Since commas are easier to see, we've used them in this example. The list of recipients cannot exceed 1024 characters. When forwarding to a list, it is necessary to enclose the whole list in double quotes ("") to assure that **mail** takes the list as a single argument.

# Handling Mail When You Are on Vacation

Suppose you are about to embark on a month-long hiking and rafting expedition in the Australian Outback. You can't handle e-mail while on this trip, but don't want people to think badly of you if you don't reply to their mail. Short of telling everyone you know you'll be away, is there a way to deal with this problem?

Yes, you're in luck. The **vacation** command automatically replies to your incoming mail. If you type the command with no arguments (as shown here), the program will run interactively, and prompt you for information it needs.

```
$ vacation
```

To run **vacation**, create a file named *$HOME/.forward* that contains the following line:

```
"|/usr/ucb/vacation you"
```

In this example, the word "you" refers to your login name. A message contained in the file *$HOME/.vacation.msg* is created, and will be sent to anyone who sends e-mail to you. The message file takes this form:

```
Subject: Away from my desk
From: you (via the vacation program)
I will be enjoying an extraordinary month
of hiking and rafting, and will NOT be
available. Your mail regarding "$SUBJECT"
will be read when I return
```

When you want to turn on the **vacation** message, run the following command:

```
$ vacation -I
```

This starts **vacation** and creates two files, *.vacation.pag* and *.vacation.dir,* which will contain the list of people who sent you mail. **vacation** does not reply to every message, but rather responds to a sender then waits some designated amount of time before sending the message to the same person again. The default interval is one week, but this can be changed from the command line when **vacation** is initialized. The flag **-tN**, as in

```
$ vacation -I -t5d
$ vacation -I -t8w
$ vacation -I -t12h
```

will change the duration to 5 days, 8 weeks, or 12 hours, respectively.

# E-Mail Addressing

## Understanding E-Mail Addresses

**TIP 231**

Unfortunately, there are many different forms of e-mail addresses. Different addresses use different symbols, including @, !, and %. The Internet format for e-mail addresses uses the at sign, "@". For instance, the address *khr@detroit.att.com* is the e-mail address of the user khr on the system *detroit.att.com.*

Another common e-mail format is that used by the UUCP System. This format uses the exclamation mark "!", also called a bang, and specifies the routing of e-mail. For instance, the e-mail address *michigan!afs* is the e-mail address of the user afs on the system michigan. This address can be used to send mail to the user afs on michigan from a user on the system colorado as long as there is a UUCP connection between colorado and michigan. If there is no such connection, but there are UUCP connections between colorado and arizona and between arizona and michigan, e-mail to afs on michigan from a user on colorado can be addressed as *arizona!michigan!afs*.

The symbol % is used to provide routing information for e-mail on the Internet. It is used to specify a particular mail gateway to be used when a mail message is routed to the recipient's system. For example, sending a message to *anita%arizona@nevada* sends a message to the user anita on the system arizona, routing this message to the gateway system nevada.

# TIP 232

# Why Mail Fails

There are many different reasons why an e-mail message may not reach its intended recipient. When you send an e-mail message but it does not get through, you may get a message back telling you that the mail failed. For example, when you try to send a message to *rex@abacus,* you may receive a message with a line like this one:

```
550   rex@abacus... User unknown
```

This indicates that your message did reach the remote system abacus, but no user with login rex is known. Maybe you have misspelled the login, or that login is no longer in use.

Similarly, you may receive a message with a line like the following:

```
550   abacus (TCP)... 550   Host unknown
```

This means that the message never reached the host abacus.

Another message you may receive when your mail fails is this one:

```
554 <rex@abacus>... Service unavailable
```

This message means that the mailer service between the machines is unavailable, at least temporarily. Try again a little later, and if the mail still does not complete, you may have to ask your postmaster about the status of the machine you are attempting to reach. (See Tip 234.)

# TIP 233

# Finding a Path to a Remote System

You can use the **uuname** command to list the systems your system is directly connected to. For example, if there is a line with the character string "bosky" in the output of the **uuname** command on your system, you can send mail to the user *homer* on machine *bosky* with the address *homer@bosky.* Note that to find this line you would use the following command:

```
$ uuname | grep bosky
```

If "bosky" is not in the output of **uuname**, you will need to use an intermediate system as a backbone. If your system has the **uuhosts** command implemented, you can try to find a path to *bosky*, using the following command:

```
$ uuhosts bosky
```

The output of this command may provide you with a path to *bosky*. If your system does not have the **uuhosts** command, or if you do not receive a path to *bosky* when you use this command, you can use the map of backbones available from the USENET to find backbones to which your system is connected.

# Consulting the Postmaster

Almost every system that receives e-mail has a mailbox, called postmaster, read by its system administrator. You can send a message to this mailbox to request help reaching a particular user on the system. For example, suppose you are trying to send mail to jsmith on the system *phoenix*, but that your mail messages to *jsmith@phoenix* are all bounced back to you as undeliverable. You could send an e-mail message to *postmaster@phoenix* describing your problem. You may learn that jsmith is not the login of anyone on *phoenix*, but that *jesmith* is a login of a user on phoenix. Or you could learn that *jsmith* has a closed account.

It may be useful to send a mail message to the postmaster whenever you are having a problem with e-mail involving that system. For example, you may have trouble using gateways to reach a system or using that system as an intermediate gateway, or with an abusive system user who sends out junk or offensive messages.

# Sending UNIX Mail to CompuServe

Let's say you have a friend on compuserve. You know her ID number, but never succeed in sending her mail. If you type the following,

```
$ mail 12344,232@compuserve.com
```

then the rest of the message just bounces. What are you doing wrong?

The trick is to change the comma to a period. For example, the following command will send the mail correctly to your friend:

```
$ mail 12344.232@compuserve.com
```

## TIP 236 — Sending Mail to Users on the Bitnet

Let's say you want to send mail to a friend in Italy. He's told you that he is on Bitnet at *csuc_xx@alamo01.cineca.it*. You try sending mail to him but it doesn't work. How should you change this address so your mail will reach him?

Bitnet addresses do not usually follow the Internet dot addressing style. On some systems, you can simply send mail to this address:

```
csuc_xx@alamo01.cineca.it.bitnet
```

If your sendmail understands the mail-exchangers, the mail will be gated to Bitnet. Many sites have a Bitnet delivery mechanism configured in their *sendmail.cf* file. If yours does not, you need to translate the address, and send the mail through a gateway. For example, we would translate your address to the one shown here:

```
csuc_xx%alamo01.cineca.it.bitnet@cunyvm.cuny.edu
```

The *cunyvm.cuny.edu* gateway would then handle delivery. Otherwise, you could send it to this address:

```
csuc_xx%alamo01.dnet@dectcp.cineca.it
```

dectcp would then gateway your mail to Bitnet.

In short, you should be able to enter either of the above address forms to send mail to your friend in Italy.

# Finding Someone's E-Mail Address

## Finding E-Mail Addresses

Trying to find someone's e-mail address can be quite frustrating. What should you do when you want to send an electronic message to someone on the Internet when you don't know the address? Fortunately, there are several different methods for finding an e-mail address. Among these methods are **whois**, a directory of e-mail addresses together with an application for accessing it (see Tip 242); the Usenet-address Server at MIT (see Tip 241); **fred**, an interface to X.500 directory services (see Tip244); the *Knowbot Information Service* (see Tip 243); the **finger** command (see Tip 240); the **netfind** program, which searches through a variety of databases (accessed with telnet at *bruno.cs.colorado.edu*, by means of login netfind); and the White Pages Pilot Project (which offers its user's handbook via anonymous ftp at *uu.psi.com*). You can also use the new Internet Network Information Center (InterNIC) Directory and Database Services, which provides white page directory services based on X.500. (See Tip 669 for more information on the InterNIC.) When you use the InterNIC directory service you supply the name, department, organization, and country of the person whose e-mail address you need using a menu-driven interface.

For a survey of these and other methods, as well as for updates to the status of these methods, you can consult the news article, "How to Find People's E-mail Addresses" posted periodically to several newsgroups, including *news.answers, soc.net-people,* and *comp.mail.misc.* (For more specific information concerning finding e-mail addresses for students and employees at colleges and universities, see Tip 239.)

## What If You Know the Remote Host but Not the User Name?

If you know the name of the remote host where someone has a login, but you are not sure of his or her user name, you can use **telnet** to talk directly with the sendmail port. (See Tips 589-593 for more information on **telnet**.) For example, if you were on the system bhutan, you might use the following code:

```
$ telnet nepal 25
Trying 129.111.99.32
Connected to nepal

Escape character is '^]'
220 nepal sendmail ready
250 nepal Hello bhutan, pleased to meet you
vrfy igor
550 igor... User unknown
vrfy igors
250 Igor Smith <igors@nepal>
```

In this example, you first use **telnet** to connect to the sendmail port 25 on the remote host *nepal,* and then try to verify the user name, *igor,* your best guess for the user name of the person to whom you wish to send e-mail. After receiving the message that igor is an unknown user, you try igors and receive the reply that Igor Smith has the e-mail address *igors @nepal.* This may be the user you want.

# How to Find E-Mail Addresses of Users at Universities

You can see how to find e-mail addresses of students and employees of universities and colleges in the periodically posted article "College E-mail Addresses," a FAQ which can be found in *news.answers, soc.answers, soc.college,* and *soc.net-people.* This article gives a general introduction for locating e-mail addresses on the Internet. More importantly, it provides detailed information on finding e-mail addresses for users at a large number of universities and colleges, including some in Europe.

Many universities have an accessible campus phone book. You may be able to access this phone book by using Gopher (see Tip 676), by logging into a Telnet port, or by using a command on the campus machine. You will need to run the command used for accessing addresses; this is commonly called **ph.** You can look up e-mail addresses by name, by department, and so on, with this command.

# Using finger to Find an E-Mail Address

Sometimes you can use the **finger** command to find someone's e-mail address. Although the typical use of **finger** requires a user's e-mail address, some organizations have set up their systems to forward a request for information on a user with a particular userid from the generic address of a domain. Some systems are set up to forward this request to individual machines. For example, to find out about the user with userid heg on a machine in the domain *math.unj.edu,* you might try this command:

```
$ finger heg@math.unj.edu
```

The system might forward this to the system *gauss.math.unj.edu* where *heg* is a valid userid.

Some systems also let you use a surname or a full name to find a user. For example, to find out about user Hector E. Govno, who you know is in the Mathematics Department at the University of New Jersey, you might try this:

```
$ finger Govno@math.unj.edu
```

or this:

```
$ finger H.Govno@math.unj.edu
```

You may need to use the middle initial for some sites, or replace the periods between parts of a name with underscores.

# Finding Someone with the USENET User List

Another way to find someone's e-mail address is to consult the USENET user list kept by MIT. This list includes the names and e-mail addresses of all posters to newsgroups that enter MIT news servers. The server at MIT tries to read the name and e-mail address of the poster of each news article it receives.

For example, to find the e-mail address of Homer Simpson you can send the following e-mail message to the MIT USENET user list server:

```
mail-server@pit-manager.mit.edu:
send usenet-addresses/simpson
```

In this message, you ask the USENET user list server to list the contents of the "From:" field of news articles that contain the string "simpson". The server will reply with a mail message that lists the "From:" fields that contain the string "simpson". You might get lucky and find Homer Simpson's e-mail address in the reply. Here is an abridged response received from the USENET user list server when such a request was made:

```
Nannette.Simpson@eng.sun.COM (Nannette Simpson)    (Nov 11 92)
simpson@aplcen (David G. Simpson)  (Nov 11 92)
simpson@moonchild.rtp.dg.com (Guy Simpson)  (Oct 11 93)
Scott.Simpson@f904.n250.z1.fidonet.org (Scott Simpson)    (Sep 14 92)
jim.simpson@canrem.UUCP (Jim Simpson)  (Feb 23 93)
simpson@teecs.UUCP (Libby Simpson)      (Oct 11 92)
simpson@altair.math.uiuc.edu (Stephen Simpson)    (Aug 21 93)
simpson@bnr.ca (Scott Simpson)      (Oct 11 92)
simpson@math.psu.edu (Stephen G Simpson)     (Nov 24 92)
simpson@teda.Teradyne.COM (Garret Simpson)  (Oct 2 92)
simpson@bcrka333.bnr.ca (Scott Simpson)      (Aug 2 93)
Simpson@p0.f1.n310.z199.nacjack.gen.nz (Simpson)  (Mar 1 93)
simpson@wabwrld.UUCP (Homer Simpson)    (Nov 11 93)
simpson@ee.rochester.edu (Kevin Simpson)     (Mar 11 93)
jim.simpson@dosgate.UUCP (Jim Simpson)  (Feb 23 93)
simpson@tesla.uwaterloo.ca (Simpson KF Lam)  (Sep 1 93)
simpson@minotaur.sdd.trw.com (Scott Simpson)     (May 1 93)
simpson@matt.ksu.ksu.edu (Phillip C Simpson)     (Apr 21 93)
simpson@parc.xerox.com (Bob Simpson)   (Aug 1 93)
simpson@aplcen (Simpson David G.)  (Oct 16 93)
ssammy@simpson-01.cs.strath.ac.uk (Paul Sammy 3rd Year iE)   (Feb 12 93)
zawada@dcs.qmw.ac.uk (Simpson)      (Jul 1 93)
zawada@softage.demon.co.uk.demon.co.uk (Mark D Simpson)     (Oct 11 92)
fsimpson@gandalf.rutgers.edu (Floyd Simpson)     (Jul 1 93)
nik@infonode.ingr.com (Nik Simpson)    (Feb 12 93)
tsimpson@athena.mit.edu (Troy W Simpson)     (Sep 21 93)
```

Notice that we succeeded in finding the e-mail address of Homer Simpson, although he may not be the one who works in a nuclear power plant. Note that not only were people named Simpson picked up by this request; so were users on systems with the string "simpson" in their names!

# The whois Program

**TIP 242**

If your system has the **whois** command, you can find directory information about a
person by issuing this command with the last name of that person. An example is shown here:

```
$ whois rosen
Rosen, Kenneth (KR111)              rosen@bermuda.att.com
   AT&T Bell Laboratories
   101 Crawfords Corner Road
   Holmdel, New Jersey 07733-3030
   (908) 555-1234
   Record last updated on 2-May-94.
```

You can also use search strings to look for people. When you do this, put a period (.) at the end of the
string. For example, the command line **whois ros.** will find Kenneth Rosen, as well as everyone else
in the directory whose last name begins with the string "ros".

If you do not have the **whois** command on your system, you can access the NIC directory by using
the **telnet** command to log in to *nic.ddn.mil.*

# Knowbot Information Service

**TIP 243**

The *Knowbot Information Service* (*KIS*) is a server that knows about a large number of
white pages servers. The nice thing about KIS is that it can look for a person's address in many different
databases using a single set of commands. You can use KIS by logging on to port 185 of either of the
systems *nri.reston.va.us* or *sol.bucknell.edu.* (See Tip 589 to learn how to do this.)

Once you are logged on, you can search for a person by typing his or her name at the prompt. KIS
will look for this person's address by contacting a series of different white page servers, including the
whois database at the Network Information Center, European databases, databases for commercial
e-mail systems, and so on.

Although the KIS is powerful and easy to use, it is a prototype system. It may undergo changes, the
systems providing it may change, and it may become harder to access. Even so, KIS is a useful way to
try to find someone.

# fred—An X.500 Directory Service

**fred** was developed as a friendly interface to X.500 directory services. You can access **fred** by logging in to the system *wp.psi.com* via **telnet**. You need to log in using the name *fred*; no password is required. Once you log in to **fred**, you can run a whois request at the fred> prompt, supplying the name of a person and the organization the person belongs to. For example, shown here is a request to find the e-mail address of Doug Host, who works for AT&T.

```
fred> whois host -org att
```

You can use wildcards with **fred**, as shown in this example:

```
fred> whois host -org a*
```

This is a request for the e-mail addresses of people named "Host" at organizations that begin with the letter "a".

You can have **fred** search for e-mail addresses using phonetic matching of names. To do this, use the following command:

```
fred> set soundex on
```

In this way, you can search for the e-mail address of someone whose name you don't know how to spell by taking your best guess.

You can also access **fred** using electronic mail. To do so, send an e-mail message to *whitepages@wp.psi.com* and put your request in the subject line of your message. After a relatively short time, you will receive an answer to your request.

# How to Use an Organization's Mail Server to Find Someone

If an organization employs a mail server you can often reach someone working at that organization without knowing that person's full e-mail address. The mail server will either correctly route the mail to the intended recipient by translating the name to the full e-mail address or respond with a message that the mail failed. For example, you might be able to reach someone named Alexander Bell at AT&T using the address *a.bell@att.com*.

The system *att.com* might translate this address into the full e-mail address and send on the message. If the name supplied in the e-mail address is ambiguous, the mail server might send back a message that the mail failed and supply a (possibly incomplete) list of potential recipients, which may help you find the full e-mail address of the intended recipient.

For instance, if there were two different Alexander Bells, say Alexander G. Bell and Alexander H. Bell, you would get back a message from *att!postmaster* that might tell you what Alexander G. Bell's e-mail address is. How much help you get from a mail server depends on the software used by that organization to route mail.

## Filtering Mail

# How to Turn On an Arbitrary Mail Surrogate

**TIP 246**

How can you have your incoming mail filtered through a script that does more than the **vacation** or **autoforward** functions?

You can do many interesting things by writing a simple shell script and setting up things so that the script is called whenever new mail arrives. This tip explains how such surrogates are written/invoked, while Tips 247 and 248 give specific examples of such scripts.

The first step is to write a program, using a shell script or a C program, that expects to get the mail message as the standard input. You can optionally have it expect to get additional information on the command line such as the e-mail address of the sender of the message, the type of the message (e.g., text or binary), and what it says on the subject line. Assuming you have a shell script, it can start with something like this:

```
$ cat $HOME/bin/my_surr.ksh
# My surrogate should be called as:
#        my_surr.ksh %R %S
# The script saves the information using variables.
```

```
FILE=$HOME/.mail$$
FROM=$1; shift
SUBJECT="$*"

# Capture the contents of the mail message.
cat > $FILE

# Do things with the mail message, using the sender/subject or by
# using tools like grep, cut, etc to dig information from the file.
...

# Clean up.
rm $FILE
```

The section shown as "..." can be replaced by your own code, according to what you need done. To turn on the surrogate, you can enter something like this:

```
$ mail -F "|$HOME/bin/my_surr.ksh %R %S"
```

or you can combine this with autoforwarding to recipients by entering the following line:

```
$ mail -F "user, attmail!user2, |$HOME/bin/my_surr.ksh %R %S"
```

You can turn off the surrogate by typing:

```
$ mail -F ""
```

# Autoforward Combined with Autoanswer Surrogate

What do you do if you are going away on vacation and have some mail that must be handled while you are gone and both your secretary and boss want to see it?

The **vacation** program handles only the former case. One solution is to type something like this:

```
$ mail -F "mysecretary, attmail!myboss, |C=0;S=2;F=*;\
/usr/lib/mail/vacation2 -o %R -M msg_file"
```

Enter all that on one line, and then place text in a file with a name like *msg_file*, so that it looks like this:

```
$ cat msg_file
I am not able to answer your message until I return from vacation.
In the meantime, copies of your messages have been forwarded to
mysecretary and attmail!myboss.
```

A more casual version follows. First, create a file like *$HOME/bin/surrogate* and make it look something like this:

```
$ cat surrogate
# Used as a mail surrogate with arguments: return-address, subject
# Save original message in a mailsave directory for reading
# when you return in a unique filename that looks like:
#          $HOME/mailsave/021093122241
MSG=$HOME/mailsave/`date +%d%m%y%H%M%S`
cat >$MSG

# Determine sender and subject from command line.
SENDER=$1; shift; SUBJECT="$*"

# Forward message to list of people maintained in $HOME/.af
cat $HOME/.af | while read RECIPIENT
                do
                     ( echo "Subject: forwarded - $SUBJECT\n"
                       cat $MSG
                     ) | mail $RECIPIENT
                done

# Generate auto-answer message and return for every message.
( echo "Subject: AUTOANSWERED - $SUBJECT\n"
  cat $HOME/msg_file
) | mail $SENDER

# Pause a second to guarantee unique filenames for the saved
# message and return a successful exit code.
sleep 1; exit 0
```

There are many good enhancements to such a script, but it does a reasonable job in forwarding to an arbitrary number of recipients (one per line in *.af*) and also in answering the sender. One use of this is to create a mailing list. Note that the original messages are stored in files you can read when you return.

# TIP 248 — Maintaining an Information Source

What if you have data in files that you want to make available to people who are not on your machine? One method is to create a simple account with a mail surrogate, as we will describe in this tip. Although this can be enhanced to meet your needs, the model is to create files for each topic and allow remote users to add new files, request current files, and delete them by using an appropriate "Subject:" line in their message. When adding files, the information will be in the mail message (header and all).

```
$ cat surrogate
# Surrogate called with sender and a subject that looks like:
#         add name
#         request name ...
#         delete name

SENDER=$1; shift
VERB=$1; shift
FILES="$*"
MSG=/tmp/msg$$
cat >$MSG

cd $HOME/database

case $VERB in
add )
cat $MSG >> $FILES
    ;;
  request )
    for file in $FILES
      do
        if [ -f $file ]
          then
            echo "--------$file as requested----------------"
            cat $file
          else
```

```
        echo "+++++++$file not found++++++++++++++++++"
   fi
 done | mail $SENDER
;;
delete )
 rm -f $FILES
 ;;
* )


 ;;
esac
```

# Using the procmail Mail Processing Program

You can filter your mail and do a variety of other mail processing tasks using the **procmail** program. With **procmail** you can create mail servers and mailing lists; sort your incoming mail into separate folders; preprocess your mail; start a program when mail arrives, such as playing different chimes on your workstation when different types of mail arrive; selectively forward incoming mail; and so on.

You can obtain **procmail** using anonymous ftp from *ftp.informatik.rwth.aachen.de* as the compressed tar file *pub/unix/procmail.tar.Z*. (See Tips 600 and 606.) It is also available in *comp.sources.misc* archives from a wide variety of anonymous ftp sites.

# Chapter 5

# An Overview
## of Editors

## Editor Basics

# What Editors Are Good For and Why There Are More Than One

Editors exist because people spend more time creating and modifying text than performing any other task on a computer. Creating program documentation, writing letters, and even writing programs and creating their input text files for testing all require editing. To edit files, you can either use a line editor, such as **ed**, or a screen editor, such as **vi** or **emacs**. There are tips in this chapter for both forms of editors.

Most people do their editing using either **vi** or **emacs**. However, a surprising number prefer line editors. In any case, it's important to understand how line editors work, since screen editors also let you use line editor commands.

There is also a stream editor called **sed**, which uses much the same syntax as **ed**, but allows you to handle bigger files. In addition, it lets you build a script to perform repetitive tasks on the contents of a file one line at a time. Tips on **sed** are given in Chapter 8.

# Basic Differences between Line Editors and Screen Editors

A line editor is one that works on the current line, and treats all other text relative to this line. This type of editor was prevalent when there were few screen-oriented devices on which to display the file you were editing. The original UNIX line *ed*itor, **ed,** was built as a little language that used simple (although sometimes cryptic) command strings to manipulate text.

Screen editors became popular with the introduction of CRTs. These made it possible to see not only the current line, but an entire screenful (typically 23 lines) of surrounding text, thus putting the current line in context. An early effort at this was the **ex** editor, written by Bill Joy at Berkeley. Written as an extension of **ed, ex** enabled the viewing of a screen of text under the *vi*sual option. From this came the ability to enter the editor in *vi*sual mode directly, under the editor called **vi.** All of these editors had separate input and command modes, meaning that all things in input mode were treated as new text (except the command needed to get out to command mode), and all things in command mode were treated as commands to change, delete, and display text, or go into input mode.

Another editor, called **emacs**, was developed as a screen editor with a single mode, where everything was treated as input unless preceded by a special character, which told the editor that this was a command. A very powerful editor, **emacs** also allows extensive interaction with other UNIX capabilities. See Tips 300-320 to learn about **emacs**.)

# Why You Should Know about ed Even If You Use a Screen Editor

**TIP 252**

Even though you may think that you will never use **ed**, there are many good reasons why you should become familiar with **ed** and its command structures. First, some of the **ed** commands can be used within each of the other editors, so if you forget how to perform some task under a screen editor, you can use the equivalent **ed** sequence. Second, *string searches* (looking for a particular word or string) and *substitutions* (replacing or deleting a word or group of words) use the same constructs in all of the editors. In fact, issuing *global* commands, which may be difficult in other editors, is actually easy in **ed**. Many **vi** users still use the **ed** global commands within **vi**. Third, the syntax used within **ed** is used by other UNIX processes that do some form of editing within them such as **grep** (for searching in files), **diff** (for comparing files), and **bfs** (for processing large files). Finally, you can use line editing commands, such as those used in **sed**, to put together scripts that carry out batch editing on files, such as with **sed**. (See Chapter 8 for tips on **sed**.)

As an example, in **vi**, where **ed** subcommands begin with the : (colon), the command sequence

```
:/Waldo
```

would search the text to find "Waldo," the same way that

```
/Waldo
```

would under **ed**. Also, you can use **ed** commands instead of some **vi** commands in the event that you forget them. For example, if you forget that the command structure to write and quit under **vi** is

```
ZZ
```

you can do the same thing with this **ed** sequence:

```
:wq
```

# Editing with ed

## Creating and Writing Files under ed

**TIP 253**

To create a file under **ed**, type the **ed** command followed by the name of the file you wish to create. The editor will respond with a question mark (?) and the filename to indicate that this file does not exist, and then you can append text. The command **a** enters input mode, and everything up to a line with a single dot (.) is put into the file. The contents can then be written with the **w** (*w*rite) command and the file exited (*q*uit) with the **q** command. So the sequence

```
$ed newfile
?newfile
a
this is some input text
followed by more input text
and even more input text
.
w
77
q
$
```

will put three lines of text (which the editor replies contains 77 characters) into the file *newfile* and save it.

## Modifying Text in Files Using ed

**TIP 254**

Once you have created a text file, you will probably need to be able to modify it. You may want to reorder text, change wording, correct spelling mistakes, or simply delete unneeded text.

In the previous example, the text can be modified to make the word "more" into the string "some more", remove occurrences of the word "text", and delete the last line by a combination of string searching, substitution, and deletion:

```
$ed newfile
77
/more
followed by more input text
s/more/some more
followed by some more input text
1,$s/text//p
and even more input
d
1,$p
this is some input
followed by some more input
w
49
q
$
```

Note that the file is now recognized by **ed**, that results of searches and changes are displayed back, and that the editor updates the character count after writing.

# Using ed to Make Global Changes to Text

**TIP 255**

There are times when you need to change a word or phrase every time it appears in a document. Perhaps you need to change "my" to "our" everywhere. The sequence

```
1,$s/my/our
```

will apply the change only to the first occurrence in each line in the file. While changing only the first occurrence may be acceptable in certain situations, if you want to catch every occurrence, you should use the **g** (*g*lobal) option:

```
1,$s/my/our/g
```

This will change all occurrences of the word "my" to "our".


# Using vi

## TIP 256

## Inserting Text into a File with vi

If you are just learning to use **vi**, it is helpful if you have already used **ed**. The environments are very similar; both have an input mode for entering text and a command mode for editing text. Both have a uniform method for moving between the two modes. The method for entering input mode depends on where you wish to place the input. The following table lists the commands and where they place your cursor for input:

| | |
|---|---|
| a | Appends text immediately after current cursor position |
| i | Inserts text immediately before current cursor position |
| A | Appends text to end of current line |
| I | Inserts text at beginning of current line |
| O | Opens line above current one for input |
| o | Opens line below current one for input |

Having a choice of single character commands allows you to begin inputting above, below, in front of, or behind the current cursor without having to move it.

Once you have entered input mode, the way to return to command mode is by hitting the Escape key (labeled ESC). If you are not sure what mode you are in, hit the ESC key, since there is no damage done if you are already in command mode. In normal operation, **vi** will beep if you hit ESC when in command mode.

# Making Simple Changes and Deletions in vi

The editor **vi** has a simple command structure for modifying text in your files. The two basic commands are **r** (*r*eplace) and **c** (*c*hange). The replace commands allow you to replace either a single or multiple characters:

| | |
|---|---|
| r*n* | Replaces the current character with character *n* |
| *x*r*n* | Replaces the next *x* characters with *n* |
| r*string*(ESC) | Replaces characters with *string* until ESC is hit |

The change commands act similarly:

| | |
|---|---|
| cw*string*(ESC) | Changes current word to *string* until ESC is hit |
| c$*string*(ESC) | Changes from cursor to end of line with *string* |
| *n*cw*string*(ESC) | Changes *n* words to *string* |
| *n*c$*string*(ESC) | Changes *n* lines to *string* |

If you have inadvertently entered things that you did not want to enter, a simple way to delete them is to place the cursor on the first unwanted character, and hit **x** (lowercase "x") once for each character you want to delete. You will see a character disappear each time you hit the key. There is another way to do this, by hitting **d** (lowercase "d") and then **l** (lowercase "l") for each character, but the **x** method is simpler since it involves only one keystroke.

If you want to delete an entire line or set of lines, you only need to place the cursor on the line to be deleted and hit **dd** (two lowercase "d's"). Since the cursor is automatically moved to the line immediately following the one you just deleted, you can repeat this to delete subsequent lines. When the cursor is at the bottom of the file, **dd** will put the cursor on the line immediately preceding, since there are no more below.

# Writing Out a File in vi

Writing a file under **vi** is also easy. There are two ways to do it. The first is by hitting **ZZ** (two capital "Z's"). This method not only writes the file, but quits the **vi** session as well. The second method is to use the **ed** equivalent to write the file, as shown here:

```
:w
```

Normally under **ed**, the **w** (write) and **q** (quit) commands are issued separately; under **vi**, they can be combined into one command. So the command

```
:wq
```

writes and quits the file the same way that **ZZ** does.

# Recovering a File You Were Editing When Your System Crashed

One of the most frustrating things is to lose work when your system crashes or when your remote connection goes up in smoke. Fortunately, when you are editing files with **vi** and your editor session is killed, for whatever reason, your editor buffer is preserved in a special directory (often */usr/preserve*). In addition, in many cases you will get a mail message from your system that will tell you that a copy of the editor buffer of the file you were editing has been saved. The message will also tell you how to use the **-r** option of **vi** to *r*ecover this session.

For example, suppose you were editing the file *todo* using a terminal session with a remote phone connection and the line is dropped. The system will save your session. To recover it, you would type

```
$ vi -r todo
```

If you don't remember the name of files you were editing when your session was abruptly ended, type

```
$ vi -r
```

You'll get back a list of the files saved and the time they were saved. If you forget to retrieve one of these saved files for more than a few days, it may be gone, since your system administrator will remove these saved files at regular intervals.

# Editing Encrypted Files

You can encrypt a file using the UNIX **crypt** command available with the Security Administration Utilities which is distributed only in the United States. This command provides you with some additional security, suitable for private or personal materials, but not for situations that require a truly high level of security. The reason for this is that messages encrypted using this command are vulnerable to sophisticated cryptographic attack.

You can edit a file encrypted with **crypt** using the **vi** editor with the **-x** option. When you use **vi** with this option, you will be asked for the encryption key. Once you supply this, you will be able to edit the file. If you supply the incorrect key, you will get a garbled file. Here is an example of how this works:

```
$ vi -x resume
key: lin91xev
```

Note that this same option is available for the **emacs** editor.

## Cutting and Pasting with vi

# Collecting Material into a Named Buffer

You can cut and paste a series of words, sentences, paragraphs, and so on, and literally assemble a new sequence of text by using the named buffers. For example, to delete twelve lines into a buffer *g*, use the following command:

```
"g12dd
```

Typed this way, the command overwrites whatever was in the buffer to begin with. In the following command, the twelve lines will be deleted and appended to the existing contents of buffer *G*. Notice the uppercase buffer name:

```
"G12dd
```

This provides an easy way to do a major restructuring of a document. For example, you can move blocks of text to an appendix by appending them all to a named buffer, moving to the end of the file, and putting the contents of the buffer at the end.

# TIP 262  More Cutting and Pasting into Buffers

You can cut a range of text to one of the named buffers, where the range does not cover an integer number of lines. For example, in the following text, you can cut text from one place to another in the named buffer *a*. Using a file containing

```
aaabbbbbb
bbbbbbbbb
bbbbccccc
```

let's cut the "b's" out and save them into buffer *a*, using four steps.

First, position the cursor at the beginning of the range to be cut (**1Gfb** will work in this example). Second, mark the location with marker **a.** Third, move to the end of the range. Finally, cut the range and put it into buffer *a*. The sequence would look like this:

```
1Gfb
ma
Gfc
"ad`a
```

# Undeleting Text and Undoing Changes in vi

**TIP 263**

When you use the delete commands in **vi**—for example, **dw** (*delete word*), **dd** (*delete line*), and so on, the text that you delete is automatically saved. The commands **u** and **U** *undo* these changes. The **u** command restores the work that you are editing by undoing the last command that changed the text. For example,

| | |
|---|---|
| 8dd | Deletes 8 lines |
| u | Restores the 8 lines |
| u | Deletes them again |
| u | Restores them again |

# Restoring a Changed Line in vi

**TIP 264**

While the **u** command restores the last change, the U command undoes all of the commands that influenced a line. This works only on one line, and only while the cursor remains on that line; if you move to another line, **U** now will apply only to that line. For example,

| | |
|---|---|
| dw | Deletes a word |
| 2x | Deletes 2 characters |
| U | Restores the word and the 2 characters |

# Undoing All the Changes Made in a Session

**TIP 265**

There may be a time when you find that you've made several changes in a document, but that you liked it better before the changes. How can you get rid of all the changes that you made? At least two ways are available. The command

```
:q!
```

exits **vi** and throws all the changes away. The command

```
:e!
```

is similar, except that with this command you remain in **vi**, with the file in the same state as when you began the editing session. This is one command that you can't undo.

# Undoing Some Deletions but Not Others

What if you realize that you need the material (maybe a whole paragraph) you deleted three commands back? Is there a way to undo deletions made several commands ago? Luckily there is. The undo commands work because **vi** saves the text into a numbered buffer every time you use a delete command. The most recently deleted material is in buffer 1, that deleted by the previous command is in buffer 2, and so on. You can retrieve this saved text by using the **p** or **P** commands as follows:

```
"1p
```

This example puts the contents of buffer 1 into the document below the current line, while

```
"4P
```

puts the contents of buffer 4 above the current line. Your last 9 deletions are saved this way. Those beyond 9 are not available.

# Reviewing Deleted Material in the Numbered Buffers

If you're actively working on editing a file, it's unlikely that you'll remember whether a change was in the 5th or 8th edit. Is there a way to review the contents of all the numbered buffers? You can do this with a special use of the . (dot) command. Normally the . command simply repeats the last command that you typed. An important exception exists with numbered buffers, as shown here:

```
"1p
```

In this example, the contents of buffer 1 are put into the file. A . command now will put in the contents of buffer 2, another . will insert buffer 3, and so on. So if you type

```
"1p.......
```

you'll put into the file the contents of all 9 buffers in order. You can search for deleted text by combining the . and **u** commands:

```
"1pu.u.u.u.u.u.u.u.
```

This will insert the contents of buffer 1, undo that, put in buffer 2, undo that, put in buffer 3, and so on. Stop when you see the material you want to restore, and move on.

# Eliminating Columns of Characters

**TIP 268**

Let's say you have large data files in which data are stored in columns, and want to get rid of, say, the first 40 characters on a line and keep the rest. This can be done in the following (not very elegant) way:

```
:%s/^.........................................//g
```

The problem is that one has to type 40 dots to get rid of 40 characters. There is a more straightforward way to do this operation, but don't try it with **vi** commands. Pipe the file to **cut**, as shown here:

```
!!cut -c41-
```

The **awk** command offers another way to do this:

```
awk '{print substr($0,41,length($0))}' < file > outputfile
```

This prints only columns 41 to end of the line to the output file.

# Setting Options in vi

There are dozens of different options that can be set in **vi**, and three different methods to set them. Here's what you need to know to be able to use options effectively. You can set options while in **vi**, as shown here:

```
:set ic
```

This will set the **ignore case** option for that session. Searches in **vi** will find words or patterns regardless of whether they are in upper- or lowercase letters.

You can collect all of your options, set, and export them as a shell variable. In the Bourne or Korn shells, the following example will set options for numbering all the lines, ignoring the case of letters in searches, and ignoring the special meaning of regular expression characters such as ^, $, *, and so on.

```
EXINIT="set number ignorecase nomagic"
export EXINIT
```

This is how you would accomplish the same thing with the C shell:

```
setenv EXINIT="set number ignorecase nomagic"
```

If you put the above lines into your *.profile,* these options will apply to all of your login sessions.

# A Sample EXINIT Entry

Here is a sample entry for an EXINIT variable that provides a good start on useful **vi** option settings, and includes the macros discussed in the tips in this chapter.

```
EXINIT='set notimeout report=1 noterse ws smd nomesg wm=21\
nu eb aw\ magic ic sh=/usr/1bin/ksh|map #3\
Gi/\<^[A\>^["add@a|map #2 1G!Gvispell^[|map! ZZ ^[ZZ|map #7\
i\fB^[ea\fR^[|map #8 i\fI^[ea\fR^['
```

# Using a .exrc File to Set vi Options

**TIP 271**

A third way to set options is to collect them in a separate file called *.exrc*. It is recommended that you put all your **vi** options in *.exrc* files, although there are advantages and disadvantages to doing this. The disadvantage (over using an EXINIT shell variable) is that it takes slightly longer to start with an *.exrc* for options. Instead of simply reading a shell variable, **vi** has to open a file and read it. The advantages, however, are that it's easier to maintain and change settings in an *.exrc* file than in a long shell variable, that it removes unnecessary stuff from your *.profile,* and most important, that it allows you to have different custom settings of **vi**. If you need to use different options under different conditions, an *.exrc* allows you to do this. For example, in writing business memos, you may use certain abbreviations; for personal letters, you may disable the sections option; and for C programs, you can set the autoindent option. If you place a different *.exrc* file in various subdirectories, then **vi** uses those options when you're editing a file in that subdirectory.

# Using Comments in .exrc Files

**TIP 272**

As you can see from the sample EXINIT entry in Tip 270 above, the syntax of abbreviations and macros is not easy to read, and is difficult to remember. You may write a brilliant macro and then forget what it does. To make your *.exrc* files easier to read and understand, you can put comments in the file describing what the macros do. The comment character is " (the double quote) as the first character on a line. Even simple macros benefit from some description:

```
" go to end of file and insert a new line

map K Go
```

# Making Sure vi Reads the .exrc File

**TIP 273**

For some users, it may appear that, for some inexplicable reason, **vi** is not reading your *.exrc* file at start time. If there is an *.exrc* file in your home directory, it should be read. Make sure you don't also have a EXINIT variable set. If you do, this will be used in preference to the *.exrc* file. Simply unset the variable, or better, delete it from your *.profile*. Everything should work again.

# Displaying the Current Option Settings

If you have different options set at different times, you may want to check them. To see a value of a specific option, type

```
:set ai?
:set nu?
```

This will display the current setting of the **ai** and **nu** options. To display all the values of all the options you have changed, type

```
:set
```

And to see the values of all the options, type

```
:set all
```

# Getting vi Input from a Pipe

Is there any way to get **vi** to accept its input from a pipe? Let's say you want it to take the output of some command (like **grep**) and send it to **vi** for editing.

You can run **ex** from a pipe (or redirect *stdin* from a file). **ex** and **vi** are generally the same binary, but **ex** is a line/command-oriented editor as opposed to a visual editor. The following example will work, but won't give you what you want:

```
for file in file1 file2 file3
do
```

```
    ex $file <<STUFF
    %s/./\u&/g
    w
    q
    STUFF
done
```

The editors **vi** and **ex** look to *stdin* for commands but expect to process those commands on text that they'll find in a file. By the same token, when you run **ex** with a *here* document as the input source, the *here* document contains the commands, not the text to operate on. The same goes for a pipe and for any other way of delivering *stdin*. You can't easily use **vi**, **ex**, or **ed** to edit the contents of *stdin*. Use **sed**, **tr**, **awk**, or **perl** instead.

# Using ex Scripts to Edit Standard Input

**TIP 276**

The last tip says that you can't easily use **vi**, **ex**, or **ed** to edit *stdin*. What if you don't know **sed**, **tr**, **awk**, or **perl**? Is there another easy way to do it? You can write **ex** scripts, but you have to pass along *stdin* in a tricky way. Here is an example that takes three files containing all lowercase characters, and uses an **ex** script to convert them to all uppercase. The three files contain these strings:

```
$ cat file1 file2 file3
lower case characters in file 1
lower case characters in file 2
lower case characters in file 3
```

Next we create an **ex** script called **upcase** that contains the **ex** commands:

```
$ cat upcase
%s/./\u&/g
w
q
```

and a shell called **upit** which applies the **ex** script to the files:

```
$ cat upit
for file in file1 file2 file3
do
```

```
    ex - $file < upcase
done
```

Now if we run the shell script **upit**, and check our test files, voila:

```
$ ./upit
$ cat file1 file2 file3
LOWER CASE CHARACTERS IN FILE 1
LOWER CASE CHARACTERS IN FILE 2
LOWER CASE CHARACTERS IN FILE 3
```

The **ex** scripts have been used on the files provided in *stdin*.

# Using the abbr Command to Reduce Typing in vi

You can save some typing of frequently used long phrases by using the **abbr** command. In **vi**, the **abbr** command translates short strings (*abbr*eviations) into long strings. The **map** command replaces a sequence of commands with a short macro name. Place both abbreviations and map macros in either the EXINIT variable set in your *.profile,* or in a separate file *$HOME/.exrc*. If you have both an EXINIT and an *.exrc* file, **vi** will consult only the EXINIT variable, and ignore anything in the *.exrc.* If you find yourself frequently typing Neuromusculature Research Institute of Massachusetts Institute of Technology, you can abbreviate it to "nrm" with this command:

```
:abbr nrm Neuromusculature Research Institute of Massachusetts\
Institute of Technology
```

Whenever you type "nrm", **vi** will substitute the longer expression. Don't overuse this strategy; **vi** begins to seem a little out of control if it expands many **abbr** expressions. Most important, select a short letter combination that is very unlikely to be entered in natural typing. Selecting "an" as an abbreviation would mean that all attempts to type the article "an" would be converted to a new long word.

# Displaying Unprintable Characters in vi

To display unprintable characters in a **vi** session, place the cursor at the beginning of a line, and type the command:

```
:1
```

The current line will be displayed at the screen bottom. Unprintable characters will be shown as two character codes—for example, tabs will be shown as ^I (CTRL-I), control characters as ^X (CTRL-X), and Escape as ^[ (CTRL-[). Each line ends with a $, which represents the carriage return-newline. The command takes a numeric argument, so that

```
:5,101
```

shows lines 5 through 10. To display all of the lines (of a small file, for instance), you can type

```
:1,$1
```

# Right Justification in vi

It is possible to justify text in **vi** so the right-hand edge of the text isn't so ragged by using the *wrapmargin* feature of **vi**. This feature automatically breaks each line before the edge of the screen. You can set the amount in your *.exrc* file.

```
set wm=20
```

This command will cause the line to break at the space following a point 20 characters from the right edge of the screen.

# TIP 280 — Replacing Tabs with Spaces in a File

Let's say you like to use tabs in just about every session of **vi** you work with. Is there a macro that could replace the tabs with the appropriate number of spaces in a file?

One way to do this is to go into **ex** mode and issue a regular expression editor command:

```
:g/^I/s//    /g
```

This finds every tab (^I) in the file and substitutes four spaces. Alternatively, you can map a free key, such as g, to a macro. This macro will replace all the tabs with four spaces. You can include such a mapped macro in your EXINIT variable or in the *.exrc* file:

```
:map g :%s/^I/    /g^M
```

The CTRL-I (^I) and CTRL-M (^M) sequences are generated by preceding each with a control V—that is, ^V^M puts a ^M in the line.

Yet another alternative is to use **expand** from within **vi**. For example, to expand tabs to four spaces throughout the file, do the following:

```
1G
```

This will move the pointer to the beginning of the file. Then, to send the whole file to "expand -4," which does the expansion, use the following coding:

```
!Gexpand -4
```

# TIP 281 — Making Text in vi Look Neater

If you collaborate with other writers who use different settings in **vi** (for example, different wrap margin settings), or if you import files from other systems (for example, from DOS WORD), your text will look shaggy. Worse, it is hard to move, or wrap across the screen, when the lines are of different lengths. This is a common problem faced by all **vi** users, because newlines are a fixed part of the text. You can write your text and let it get as messy as you like, and then run it through a text formatter like **fmt**. You can do this by piping individual paragraphs through the text formatter, as shown here:

```
!}fmt
```

Or you can pipe the whole document through it, as shown here:

```
1G
!Gfmt
```

# Evening Up Text in vi

You can neaten the appearance of a file typed with **vi** by doing a partial formatting of the file. This is especially useful for sending e-mail. You can type in a long message and then format it with the **nroff** command. When **nroff** is invoked without any **nroff** command macros, it simply formats the material as a single block of text.

If you want to convert 25 lines of a file into a neat text block, go to the beginning of the text section and issue the command:

```
!25!nroff
```

This will send the next 25 lines to **nroff**, and the output of **nroff** will replace those lines.

# Line Numbering in Text Files

If you are looking for a program that lets you take a text file and generate another file with the line numbers embedded in it, the following command should do the job:

```
$ pr -t -n filename
```

Of course, you should redirect the output into another file if you want to make use of it:

```
$ pr -t -n filename > file
```

# TIP 284

# Using Line Numbers When Editing

The entry of text with **vi** is straightforward; a good typist can enter *insert* mode and keyboard away. Similarly, the mechanics of editing and the changing and moving of text can be done conveniently within **vi**. Some of the tips in this chapter show how to define macros to do large-scale edits. But many people find it harder to creatively edit, revise, and write on a screen than on a paper copy. This is not the executive aversion to keyboards; it is harder to work because the structure of the document is lost on a terminal. This script, called *num*, prints a copy of the file with each of the lines numbered, and a formatted (troffed) version of the file:

```
# num filename - prints out numbered version of text.
for i in $*
do
cat $i | pr -nh $i | prt
troff -Tpost $i | prt -l troff -d 4s
done
```

If you set the line numbering option in **vi** (using the command **:set nu**), then the printed numbered file and the **vi** version will correspond. Mark up the paper copy as you normally would. To transfer the editorial changes to the electronic version, start from the end of the file and make all the changes. You have to start from the end, because changes and deletions alter the line numbers in **vi** from the change to the end of the file. If you work from the end forward, this won't matter.

# TIP 285

# Editing More Than One File at a Time

You may have useful notes or other material distributed among several files. Using the multiple file editing capability, and the named buffers in **vi**, you can move material among these files, cutting and pasting, inserting and deleting, to put together a final version. You can edit multiple files by using the following command:

```
vi file1 file2 file3 file4 file5
```

The command

```
:n
```

edits the next file in the command line list. The command

```
:n file4
```

would move directly to *file4*. When you get to the end of the list, the command

```
:rew
```

(for rewind) starts at the beginning of the list with *file1*. If you forget the filenames that are in the command line list (not unusual if you have normal, complex names), then the command

```
:args
```

will print on the bottom line of your screen the whole list that you are editing. The current filename is enclosed in brackets, like this:

```
file1      file2      [file3]      file4      file5
```

# Writing Files When Editing Multiple Files in vi

TIP 286

When you are editing multiple files, **vi** will not let you move from one file to the next unless you have written out any changes made to the first file. Before you switch files, you could issue a w (*w*rite) command, as shown here:

```
:w
```

or you could use

```
:n!
```

or

```
:n! file2
```

to insist that **vi** switch files without checking for changes. An easier alternative is to set the **autowrite** option for the whole session, or better, for all editing sessions. Put the following line in your *.exrc:*

```
:set aw
```

# Writing Out a Text Block in vi

**TIP 287**

The easiest way to write out a block of lines to another file, without having to count the lines or find the first and last line numbers, is with the following sequence of commands:

```
mx
???G
"ay'a
:e filename
dG
"ap
1Gdd
:w
:e #
```

The context of this sequence is as follows: go to the beginning of the block; mark it (**mx**); go to line *???* (**???G**); yank from the current position to the mark and put in named buffer a (**"ay'a**); edit the file (**:e filename**); put in the contents of buffer a (**"ap**); delete the first blank line (**1Gdd**); write the file (**:w**); and go back to editing the first file (**:e #**). Of course, the **dG** command is only required if the file exists.

Alternatively, if you want to write to the file *foo* from the current line to mark x, just use

```
'x w foo
```

# Using vi to Move Text Between Files

**TIP 288**

Some DOS-based editors have a "clipboard" feature that lets you move text between files.

For example, you can edit two files, put something in one file on the clipboard, and move it to the other file. Here is how to do the same kind of thing in **vi**. The numbered buffers in **vi** are used to automatically save deleted material. There are also 26 named buffers (named *a, b, c, d, ..., z*) that are under your control. Further, the contents of these buffers are preserved when you switch between files. The following sequence of commands allows you to cut and paste between files:

```
vi filename1 filename2
```

starts **vi** with two files to edit. The command

```
"a15y
```

yanks 15 lines into the buffer named *a*. The command that switches to the next file is

```
:e #
```

And the command

```
"ap
```

puts the contents of buffer *a* into the second file below the cursor position.

# Using the map Command to Write Macros in vi

**TIP 289**

A macro is a sequence of commands—a little program—within **vi** that you can execute. For example, you may find yourself deleting large sections of text, and moving them to the end of the file for use in an appendix. Rather than type the same command sequence repeatedly, you can define a macro with a simple name that stands for the entire sequence, as shown here:

```
:map v (d)Gp
```

This example creates a macro called **v** which goes to the beginning of the current sentence, deletes from that point to the end of the sentence, then goes to the end of the file and puts the deleted material there. Every time you type the letter **v**, while in command mode, this sequence will be executed.

# TIP 290 — Inserting Formatting Macros in vi

One use of macros in **vi** is to insert formatting commands that are needed by the **nroff** and **troff** formatters. For example, to make a word bold, place the string "\fB"(start bold font) at the beginning of the word and the string "\fP" (return to previous font) at the end. Rather than issue these commands for each change in editing, you can define a macro which does it automatically when you press F7 (function key seven), as shown here:

```
:map #7 i\fB^[ea\fP^[
```

# TIP 291 — Creating a "Write File and Quit" Macro

When you write a macro, you may want it to be a replacement or enhancement of an existing command. For example, the **ZZ** command writes and quits the file, but only when you are in command mode. You may want the **ZZ** command to write the file and quit in both command and input modes. You could do this with

```
:map! ZZ ^[:wq
```

This macro exits input mode, writes the file, and quits the editor if two uppercase "Z's" are typed. This makes the command work consistently in both editing modes.

# Selecting a Macro Name

**TIP 292**

When you are enhancing an existing command, it is appropriate to use the existing command name. It's a mistake to do that if you are trying to define a new command. However, since most keys are **vi** commands, it's difficult to avoid collisions with existing commands. Safe choices are the letters "g" and "v", which aren't used as commands, and any of the function keys. You can specify a function key in **vi** by referring to it by number—for example, #1 is function key number 1, #2 is 2, and so on, regardless of the terminal you are using. So the macro

```
:map #1 d)
```

means that when you press function key #1, the rest of the current sentence will be deleted. You can also use multiletter commands in macros. In this case, the whole command name must be typed within one second. You can eliminate this time limit by setting the **notimeout** option, but this is not recommended. With **notimeout** set, **vi** appears to slow down in input mode. In reality, it just waits to display any letter combinations until it is clear that they are not part of a macro. But this means that letters do not appear on the screen immediately when typed.

# A Macro That Executes a Program

**TIP 293**

This tip combines several of the things we've shown in earlier tips. The following macro executes a shell script and appends the output of the script to the end of the file. This one is especially useful because it checks for misspelled words. First, you need to create a file in a directory that is in your PATH that contains the following script, called *vispell:*

```
tee ./vis$$
echo SpellingList
trap '/bin/rm -f ./vis$$;exit' 0 1 2 3 15
/usr/bin/spell vis$$| comm -23 - $HOME/lib/myspelldict|tee \
-a $HOME/lib/spell.errors
```

This script runs the **spell** program, eliminates any words you have included in your own dictionary (located here in *$HOME/lib/myspelldict*), and adds all the errors to another file, *spell.errors,* that you can check manually later.

The following macro associates the second function key (#2) with a command sequence:

```
:map #2 1G!Gvispell^[
```

The sequence adds the output of *vispell* to the end of the file, and then exits input mode. When you run this macro by hitting the F2 function key, you end up with a list of misspelled words, one per line, at the end of the file.

# Using the Contents of a Buffer as a Macro

You can also execute the contents of a named buffer as though it were a macro by using the **@a** command (this will execute the contents of buffer *a*). This is useful if you don't know precisely what the macro should say. This macro searches for whatever is on the last line of the file, as shown here:

```
map #2 Gi/\<^[A\>"add@a
```

This example says to go to the end of the file, add the characters \< to the beginning of the line, and append the character > to the end of the line. Then delete the line into named buffer *a* and execute the contents of the buffer as a macro—that is, search for the word. Used with the macro in Tip 293, it finds the first occurrence of the misspelled word in the file; the **vi** command **n** finds the next occurrence of the same word, and so on.

# Cancelling a Macro

If you have set a macro in your *.exrc* or EXINIT, but decide you don't want it operating during a specific **vi** session, you can cancel the macro by using the **unmap** command. The command that cancels macros in command mode is

```
:unmap macroname
```

To cancel input mode macros, use

```
:unmap! macroname
```

# Programming with vi

There is a useful feature for code completion in **vi**. If you want to make an **if** construct, type your predefined abbreviation "qii". When you type the space after qii, **vi** replaces it with

```
if ( @ )
{
} /* end if ( @ ) */
```

Suffering from coding style guidelines? Let the editor do it for you!

To make a multiline abbreviation substitution, put this in your *.exrc* file for that **if** replacement.

```
:abbr qii if ( @ )^M{^M} /* end if ( @ ) */^[kkF@cw
```

In this example, ^M is CTRL-M and ^[ is ESC. The macro is broken down as follows:

| | |
|---|---|
| :abbr qii | Abbreviate 'qii' |
| if ( @ )^M | Place this into the editor buffer, and hit CR. |
| {^M | And this... |
| } /* end if ( @ ) */ | And this... |
| ^[ | Press ESC to go into command mode. |
| kk | Move up two lines. |
| F@ | Backward 'F'ind the @ char. |
| cw | Change word. |

Check out some of the already created macros for C. Here is a list drawn from the INDEX file in the *macros/* directory at the VI/EX archives around the world:

| Macro | Purpose and Source |
|---|---|
| c.template.Z | Vi C-mode. Mitchell Wyle. |
| cmacros | Small and quick C-macros. CED. |

| Macro | Purpose and Source |
|---|---|
| commentC.tar.Z | Very good way to do C-comments. Rob Hutten. |
| cvi.Z | C syntax-sensitive editing. Bo Thide. |
| generals | General, text, mail, C, Modula-2. Compiled by M. Lamoureux |
| goodies.tar.Z | Find the previous word, emacs-mode, C-mode, and others. M. Neitzel. |

For more information about the files in the archives fetch the INDEX file. If you need more information, you are welcome to send e-mail to *Ruben@uib.no*.

# vi Macros for Inserting and Removing Comments in C Code

Here are two more *.exrc* macros that insert comments around a line, or remove the comments around a line in a C program:

```
" Insert C comments around a line
map ^C :s/.*/\/*&*\///^M

" Remove C comments around a line
map ^R :s/[/*][*/]//g^M
```

# Getting vi Macros

The EX/VI archives contain a lot of useful tools for editing and formatting with EX/VI. Ove Ruben R. Olsen (e-mail: *ruben@uib.no*) maintains the EX/VI-archive and the *Comp.Editors* FAQ posting on the Internet. The VI/EX archives can be found at:

**Europe:**

| | |
|---|---|
| Main site: | *alf.uib.no (129.177.30.3)* |
| Filearea: | *pub/vi* |
| Peak hours: | 07.00 am GMT to 03.00 pm GMT |

**Japan:**

| | |
|---|---|
| Mirror site: | *utsun.s.u-tokyo.ac.jp (133.11.11.11)* |
| Filearea: | *misc/vi-archive* |
| Peak hours: | 01.00 am GMT to 09.00 am GMT |

**USA, Canada and Mexico:**

| | |
|---|---|
| Mirror site: | *cs.uwp.edu (131.210.1.4)* |
| Filearea: | */pub/vi* |
| Peak hours: | None |
| Mirror site: | *ftp.uu.net (192.48.96.9)* |
| Filearea: | */pub/text-processing/vi* |
| Peak hours: | None |

**Australia, New Zealand,
and the Rest Down Under:**

| | |
|---|---|
| Main site: | *monu6.cc.monash.edu.au (130.194.1.106)* |
| Filearea: | */pub/Vi* |
| Peak hours: | Not relevant |

For more information about the files in the archives read the INDEX file. For those without **ftp**, send an e-mail message to *Ruben@uib.no* with the subject header GET HELP.

# A Function for Automatic Backup of Edited Files

New users of an editor, as well as cautious writers, will often make a backup copy of an important file before they begin editing it. If they later regret the changes and deletions made, the backup copy preserves the file in its original form. The following little function does this automatically. Invoke it as **v** *filename,* and it makes a copy of the edited file with the characters with .BAK appended to the filename:

```
function v {
for i in $*
do
     if [ -f $i ]
     then
             tmp=`basename $i`
             echo Backing Up $tmp
             /bin/cp $i ./$tmp.BAK
     fi
done
/usr/bin/vi $*
stty echo;
}
```

Notice that this allows only one backup copy with the same name as the file with the .BAK extension. If you edit the file a second time, the backup file will be overwritten.

There are several good places to look for more information about **vi**. These include *The vi User's Handbook* by M. I. Bolsky (Murray Hill, NJ: AT&T Bell Laboratories, 1984) and *Learning the vi Editor* by Linda Lamb (Sebastopol, CA: O'Reilly and Associates, 1990). You can also read the articles in the newsgroup *comp.editors.*

## An Overview of emacs

## What Is emacs, and How Is It Different from vi?

The text editor **vi** has many useful features. It has different modes of operation depending on whether you are entering material or correcting it. For example, **vi** allows you to edit several files at a time, but only one is open at a time. It supports multiple buffers for use in editing, allows you to abbreviate frequently typed words, and provides an easy-to-use macro facility that lets you write sequences of commands and bind them to a simple name.

The screen editor **emacs** was also developed according to a particular philosophy of computing. Originated by Richard Stallman as editor *mac*ros in 1975, **emacs** has grown as a result of Stallman's philosophy, now represented by the Free Software Foundation (FSF), and the GNU project. (*GNU is Not U*NIX): Stallman has insisted that **emacs** be given away, requiring only that enhancements be given back so that **emacs** may continually improve.

One result of this openness is that although there are only a few versions of **vi** (and they have the same user interface), there are many versions of **emacs**. Furthermore, **emacs** has evolved into an entire user environment. Many people stay in **emacs** for their entire login session; everything they want to do on UNIX can be done in **emacs**. You can open all of the files in your directory and simultaneously edit them. You can manage your files and directories: creating, deleting, and moving files is simply editing the file system. You can read and send mail from **emacs**. You can enhance **emacs** using its built-in programming language. You can write and execute shell or C programs. You can edit binary (program) files. You can even customize **emacs** so that it has some of the same commands as **vi**.

As we have mentioned, one of the problems with **emacs** is its many different versions, each with its own set of commands. These versions often vary considerably from each other. Of the multiple versions, some of the most popular are GNU Emacs, UniPress (Gosling's) Emacs, Freemacs, Micro-Emacs, and Epsilon. In this book, we will include tips on GNU Emacs and UniPress Emacs. For a discussion of these different varieties and their features, see the *UNIX Desktop Guide to Emacs* by Ralph Roberts and Mark Boyd (Indianapolis, IN: Hayden Books, 1992).

# How Can You Find emacs to Use on Your System?

The first thing to do is check to see if you already have it. On large UNIX systems (by "large," we mean one in which someone else is the system administrator), **emacs** may already be available. If so, it's probably in one of the standard directories in your PATH. To find out, simply type

```
$ emacs
```

and see what happens. It may not be in your PATH, or perhaps the system administrator has renamed it. Try to find it using the **ffind** function described in Tip 126; if you go to the root directory (**cd /**) and execute

```
$ ffind *emacs*
```

the correct pathname should appear on your screen (if **emacs** exists on your system).

# How Can You Get emacs If It Is Not Already Installed on Your System?

Since there are dozens of versions of **emacs**, you have many alternatives. One is to check netnews (see Chapter 10) to learn about current **emacs**. There is one *comp.emacs* group, and a dozen *gnu.emacs* groups. If you have access to the Internet, read the net to find out about current status.

You can get GNU **emacs** from the Free Software Foundation, 675 Massachusetts Ave., Cambridge MA, 02139, U.S.A. The FSF does not charge for software, but it does charge for distribution costs. A cheaper way to get GNU **emacs** is by anonymous ftp from MIT. See Chapter 10 on how to use anonymous ftp; the command sequence you need is shown here:

```
$    ftp prep.ai.mit.edu
$    login: anonymous
$    Password: your user name
$    cd gnu
$    cd emacs
$    binary
$    get filename
```

Incidentally, you can browse here to get other GNU project software.

An MS-DOS version of **emacs** called **Freemacs** is a subset of GNU **emacs**, and supports a full programming language for **emacs** modification. You can get **Freemacs** by anonymous ftp from *grape.ecs.clarkson.edu.*

# Is There a Commercial Source for emacs?

There are many people who will not want to use ftp for the **emacs** sources. Downloading, unpacking, compiling, and installing complex software is not something all UNIX users want to spend their time on. Some corporations forbid their employees to use Freeware, Shareware, or anonymous ftp because of the security risks. Commercial versions of **emacs** are available. An early port of **emacs** to UNIX was done by James Gosling; it is similar to GNU **emacs** except that it has a simpler programming language (M-Lisp) and a different set of default commands (different user interface). The current descendant of Goslings **emacs** is sold by UniPress Software, a firm in Edison, NJ. Other versions of emacs are available commercially. Check the newsgroup *comp.emacs*, the books mentioned in Tip 304, and the *Open Systems Product Directory* (see Tip 58) to learn about these.

# Where to Learn More About emacs

A good source for learning about the different versions of **emacs** from a beginner's to advanced level is the *UNIX Desktop Guide to Emacs*, by Ralph Roberts and Mark Boyd (Hayden Books, 1992). You can find more information about GNU **emacs** by consulting the book *Learning GNU Emacs* by Debra Cameron (O'Reilly and Associates, 1992). You should also read the newsgroups *comp.emacs, gnu.emacs,* and *comp.editors* for articles on **emacs**. The FAQs on GNU Emacs are another valuable resource. These are posted periodically to *comp.emacs*.

# Manipulating Text in Files with GNU or UniPress emacs

Since **emacs** is a single-mode editor, all characters are treated as input unless preceded by a control character sequence. The sequence

```
$ emacs dougfile
```

opens up the file *dougfile* for input. When you are done entering text, the control sequence

```
^x^s
```

(CTRL-X CTRL-S) will save the current buffer in the file *dougfile*.

There are several commands you can use to delete text in GNU **emacs.** These include the following:

| | |
|---|---|
| CTRL-D | Delete the next character. |
| CTRL-K | Delete the current line. |
| DEL | Delete the previous character. |
| ESC-D | Delete to the next end of word. |
| ESC-K | Delete to the end of the sentence. |

There are several commands you can use to delete text in UniPress **emacs.** These include the following:

| | |
|---|---|
| CTRL-D | Delete the next character. |
| CTRL-H | Delete the previous character. |
| CTRL-K | Delete to the end of the line. |
| ESC-D | Delete the next word. |
| ESC-H | Delete the word to the left. |

To move the cursor in GNU and UniPress **emacs,** you can use certain commands which are common to these two versions of **emacs.** Here are some of them:

| | |
|---|---|
| CTRL-P | Move to the previous line. |
| CTRL-N | Move to the next line. |
| CTRL-F | Move forward (right) one character. |
| CTRL-B | Move backward (left) one character. |
| CTRL-A | Move to the beginning of the current line. |
| CTRL-E | Move to the end of the current line. |
| ESC-A | Move to the beginning of the previous sentence. |
| ESC-E | Move to the beginning of the next sentence. |
| ESC-F | Move forward (right) one word. |
| ESC-B | Move backward (left) one word. |
| ESC-] | Move to the end of the current paragraph. |
| ESC-[ | Move to the beginning of the current paragraph. |
| ESC-< | Move to the beginning of the buffer. |
| ESC-> | Move to the end of the buffer. |

# Getting Help in GNU emacs

One of the first things you should do when learning how to use GNU **emacs** is to use the interactive help file that explains a set of basic commands. To access this help file, press CTRL-H T.

GNU **emacs** includes several help facilities. When you press CTRL-H C, **emacs** prompts you for a key sequence. When you enter this sequence, **emacs** displays the name of the command bound to that key sequence. When you type CTRL-H A, **emacs** will prompt you for a string. When you enter this string, **emacs** will display all the functions that contain this string. To get a description of the functions, you can use the **describe-function** command by pressing CTRL-H F.

# Getting Help in UniPress (Gosling) emacs

There are several way to get help when using UniPress **emacs**. The simplest way is to press ESC-?. **emacs** will prompt you for a keyword, and then then display a list of commands with names containing the keyword. To get further help, you can use the **describe-command** feature. If you give **describe-command** the command that you want more information on, it will display the manual entry for that command. For example, to get the manual entry on the **spell** command, press ESC-X, and then type **describe-command spell**.

# Correcting Typing Mistakes with GNU or UniPress emacs

There are several useful **emacs** commands that you can use to fix typing mistakes. One common typing error is transposing letters—for instance, typing "hte" instead of "the". You can correct such typing mistakes using the **transpose-character** command. This command exchanges the two characters on either side of the point. To run this command, press CTRL-T.

You can also transpose two words using the **transpose-word** command. This exchanges the word in front of the point with the previous word or the word under the point. To run this command, press ESC-T.

# Searching for Text in GNU or UniPress emacs

You can search a file for a particular string using CTRL-S to search forward and CTRL-R to search backward. When you enter either of these commands, **emacs** prompts you with

```
Search for:
```

at the bottom line of the window and waits for you to type in the search string. You must press ESC after this string. You can repeat your previous string by using either CTRL-R or CTRL-S with an empty search string.

# Replacing Text in GNU emacs

You can do a global search and replacement using the **replace-string** command. When you press ESC-X, type **replace-string**, and then press ENTER, **emacs** prompts you for the old string to replace and the new string you want to replace it with. After you enter these strings, **emacs** replaces all occurrences of the old string that come after the point in the current buffer with the second string. If you want to replace the string everywhere in the buffer, you have to move the point to the beginning of the buffer before proceeding with the replacement process.

If you want to search for and interactively replace a string, you should use the **query-replace** keypress (ESC-%). When you issue this command, **emacs** prompts you for the old string to replace and the new string to be used as the replacement. At each occurrence of the old string, **emacs** puts the cursor after the string and gives you nine different options that tell **emacs** whether to make the replacement, to continue, to go back to the last replacement location, and so on.

# Replacing Text in UniPress emacs

You can do a global search and replacement by pressing ESC-R. **emacs** will then prompt you for the old string that you want to replace, and the new string you want to replace it with. After making this replacement globally, **emacs** reports back to you telling you how many times this replacement was made.

If you want to search for and interactively replace a string, you should use the **query-replace-string** command (ESC-Q). When you issue this command, **emacs** prompts you at the bottom of the window for the old string to replace and the new string to be used as the replacement. At each occurrence of the old string, **emacs** puts the cursor after the string and gives you four options: change this and go to the next occurrence, change this and all other occurrence, change this one and stop, and don't change this one and stop.

# Using emacs to Insert Control Characters into Your File

Suppose you want to put a control character which is the same as an **emacs** command in one of your files. How do you do this?

The answer is simple. You use the **quoted-insert** command, CTRL-Q. This command tells **emacs** that the next character you type is text and not part of an **emacs** command. So, to put CTRL-A into your file, press CTRL-Q CTRL-A.

# How to Mark a Region and Delete It, Move It, or Write It Out in GNU emacs

In **emacs**, a region is defined as the space between the current point and a mark. The mark is set with the command **set-mark** associated with the keystrokes CTRL-@ (^@). If you want to delete the entire region, use the **kill-region** command (CTRL-W). If you move the current point and use the **yank** command (CTRL-Y), the deleted material will be restored at the new point. To write out a marked region, set the mark, move the current point, and use the **write-region** command. This command does not have a default keyboard binding, so to execute the command, press ESC-X and then type **write-region**.

# Exiting a File in emacs

The **exit-emacs** command sequence will let you leave the **emacs** editor. To exit, type the control sequence

```
^X^C
```

When you do this all your changes will be lost, since the contents of the buffer are not written to a file. To save your changes, use

```
^X^F
```

This will write the file you were editing and exit **emacs**.

# How Can You Use emacs for File Management?

In **emacs**, you can determine your current directory by pressing ESC-X, then typing **pwd**. The full pathname will appear in the last line on the screen.

If you want to change the directory for any buffer, press ESC-X and type **cd**. Your path will appear in the last line at the bottom of the screen. Edit the path and hit RETURN. You'll be in the new directory.

To invoke the directory editor on the current directory, press ESC-X and type **dired**.

You'll see a listing of files similar to that provided by **ls -l** on the screen. While in **dired** you can operate on the files; for example, you can mark a file for deletion, undelete it, find a file and load it into the buffer for editing, create a new file, copy or rename a file, and so on.

# Your Terminal Is Using Control-S/Control-Q for Flow Control. How Can You Disable It Within emacs?

**emacs** often uses CTRL-S in its internal commands. There could be a problem with this, because the same commands are used for flow control, suspending data flow to the computer host. This should already be taken care of by your system administrator, but if it hasn't been, use this **lisp** command:

```
(set-input-mode nil t)
```

# Editing with Multiple Windows in UniPress emacs

One of the nice features of **emacs** is that you can use several editing windows at the same time. For example, if you are editing a file, you can use the **split-current-window** command, CTRL-X 2. This puts two windows on your screen, each associated with the same buffer. You can arrange to see two different parts of the file in these windows. Although you will be working in only one of the two windows, you can see both. When you need to switch between the two windows, use CTRL-X N to go to the next window and CTRL-X P to return to the previous window. You may want to yank some text from one of the windows, move to the other window, and insert that text at some point in the buffer in this second window.

When you are finished working in two windows, use the command CTRL-X 1 to delete all windows except your current ones.

To edit two different files in two windows, use the **visit-file** command: CTRL-X CTRL-V. When you enter this command, you will be prompted for the name of the second file and a buffer containing that file will be placed in the second window.

# TIP 318

# Keyboard Macros in GNU emacs

It is quite easy to create and use keyboard macros in emacs. These are macros that are made up of a sequence of keystrokes. When you give such a macro a name, you can have emacs execute this sequence of keystrokes whenever you use the macro. To define a keyboard macro, first use the **start-kbd-macro** command, CTRL-X (. All the keystrokes you enter until you type the **end-kbd-macro** command, CTRL-X ), are stored as the macro. You can name your macro using the **name-last-kbd-macro** command. Since keyboard macros are lost when you end your **emacs** session, you should include any you want to use permanently in your *.emacs* file. (See the following tip.)

# TIP 319

# What to Put in Your .emacs File.

Like other editors, **emacs** allows you to initialize variables in a file. The *.emacs* file lets you define keys and functions as well as change default variables. Lines used for comments are preceded by a semicolon, and these should be used liberally throughout the *.emacs* file for clarity. Here is an example of a GNU **emacs** *.emacs* file.

```
; set the fill-column variable
(setq fill-column 60)
; turn off the auto-save-default variable
(setq auto-save-default-nil)
; disable keystroke echoing
(setq echo-keystrokes zero)
; set the default-major-mode to text
(setq default-major-mode 'text-mode)
```

Here is another example of an initialization script to put in your *.emacs* file to set the *load-path* variable:

```
(setq load-path
      (append
       (list (concat (getenv "HOME") "/lib/gnuemacs/lisp")
             (concat (getenv "HOME") "/lib/gnuemacs/lisp/non-local"))
       load-path))

(load "emacsinit")
```

# Using Functions in emacs

**T**<sup>IP</sup>

**320**

emacs briefly moves the cursor to the matching left parenthesis when a closing right parenthesis is typed. This is often convenient for checking that parentheses have been matched correctly. However, this feature only works if the matching parenthesis is on the current screen, and only at the moment that the right parenthesis is first typed.

The following **elisp** function moves the cursor from wherever it may be in the document to the matching (left or right) parenthesis. Invoking it twice will return the cursor to its original position. If the cursor is not over a parenthesis, or no matching parenthesis exists, an error message will result. Note that characters considered as possible matching parentheses are defined in the syntax table for each mode, and will therefore be different in c-mode from text-mode. This function is bound to the Meta-' key.

```
(defun goto-matching-paren ()
    "Move cursor to matching paren."
        (interactive)
        (let* ((oldpos (point)) (blinkpos))
          (condition-case ()
             (setq blinkpos (scan-sexps oldpos 1))
             (error nil))
```

```
      (if blinkpos
        (setq blinkpos (1- blinkpos))
        (condition-case ()
          (setq blinkpos (scan-sexps (1+ oldpos) -1))
          (error nil)))

      (setq mismatch
          (/= (char-after oldpos)
          (logand (lsh (aref (syntax-table)
                                  (char-after blinkpos))
                      -8) 255)))
    (if mismatch
        (progn
          (setq blinkpos nil)
          (message "Mismatched parentheses"))
        (if blinkpos
        (goto-char blinkpos)))))

(global-set-key "\e`" 'goto-matching-paren)
```

Versions of **emacs** other than GNU also have their own *.emacs* initialization files with similar constructs, the major differences being the names used for functions and the default variables. It's best to get an **emacs** reference manual, such as the one by Roberts and Boyd (See Tip 304), to understand the requirements and variations within your own version.

# Chapter 6

## Formatting and Printing Text

# Options for Formatting Text with UNIX

## Document Preparation on the UNIX System

You have lots of choices when you need to prepare documents in the UNIX system. You can use a What You See Is What You Get (WYSIWYG) word processor, a desktop publishing system, such as Interleaf or Framemaker, or the traditional UNIX approach to document preparation, a text formatter.

You can use a commercial WYSIWYG word processor like *WordPerfect* or *Word* on your UNIX system, much as you would on a DOS system. WYSIWYG word processors combine editing and text formatting into a single special purpose program. As you edit a document with a WYSIWYG word processor, the program shows you the way your document will look when printed. This style of word processing is appealing since it is often easy to use, reduces the number of steps in producing a document, and gives you the opportunity to see your document in final form as you write it.

But WYSIWYG word processing has some disadvantages. In particular, it links together two different operations into a single program, thus making it impossible to select an editor independent of the formatter. It often creates a document file format that can only be read by the original program, or must be translated into a compatible format. It limits the author/producer to a few styles and formats supported by the program. If you want a style or format not thought of by the original programmer, it is difficult or impossible to realize it.

Desktop publishing systems generally include everything a word processor program has, including a WYSIWYG editor and other related tools. They also include a range of tools supporting the production of large documents, including books. These products usually have tools for creating and including graphics, color, and other types of input. They also include tools for managing large document projects. Because of their wide utility and power, desktop publishing systems are more expensive than word processors. You can get information about UNIX system desktop publishing systems from the *Open Systems Products Directory*, published by UniForum. (See Tip 58.)

Text formatting systems, including **troff** and TeX, are extremely flexible and powerful, but they work much more like programming languages than like word processors. When you use a formatting system, you insert your text along with various commands. In most cases, you don't see what your output looks like until you print it or display it on your screen. However, a good formatter can be used to customize your documents in just about any way you choose. The penalty you pay for this degree of customization is the necessity of writing code and having to print or display documents to see them in draft form.

# How Do You Use the troff System?

**TIP 322**

To do word processing with the traditional UNIX text processing tools, you first use your favorite editor to create a file that contains your input along with the commands needed to format your document. These commands come from the troff system, which includes a series of tools, languages, macro packages, postprocessors, and formatting programs.

To do your editing, you can use **emacs**, **vi**, **ed**, or any other editor with any of the formatters. You insert your text together with different kinds of commands. These commands can be troff commands, commands from one or more different macro packages, or commands from a preprocessor.

You can do just about anything with troff commands. However, formatting a complicated document using just these commands would be extremely time consuming and may cause you nightmares since you would have to use large numbers of such commands in complicated ways. In fact, formatting a complicated document using troff commands is similar to writing a complicated computer program. To avoid this problem, you can use macro packages with macros that do many common formatting tasks, and preprocessors with tools for formatting special input, such as tables, equations, and line drawings. See Tip 329 to get started using troff commands, Tip 338 to learn about different macro packages, and Tip 341 for particulars about the memorandum (mm) macros, and Tip 354 to learn about preprocessors.

Once you've written your file, you should run the appropriate command line to either display your finished document on your screen or to print it. (See Tips 347 and 348.)

# Why Use the troff System to Format Documents in This Day and Age?

**TIP 323**

Text processing with the troff system is not WYSIWYG, but rather You Asked For It You Got It (YAFIYGI). Because the editors and formatters use standard ASCII UNIX file formats, any UNIX tools can be used on a document file. You can search it with **grep**, use the file as standard input to other programs, append to it material from standard output and so on. Unlike word processing programs that use their own file formats, document files are available for all UNIX tools to operate on.

A further benefit of YAFIYGI over WYSIWYG is that it separates markup from format. Markup consists of the codes and symbols used to designate a part of a document. For example, a symbol for a paragraph or a title is part of the markup for a document. The format is the particular way that these markup symbols are interpreted by the typesetter. For example, you (or your publisher's style) may want a title to be centered and in 14 point Times Roman bold type, or flush left in 10 point Helvetica. Similarly, different styles may require that a paragraph be indented 10 spaces on the first line or that it be flush with a skipped line, or that it be set in some other style. In a WYSIWYG editor, the markup is invisible and linked to the format. Consequently if you want to change some aspect of the format, the change must be made manually throughout the document. Since the troff system separates markup and format, you can change the format of the whole document by changing a single macro definition.

The flexibility and power of the troff system result make it popular for serious document production— for example, scientific journals, newsletters and brochures, viewgraphs, slides, as well as the usual manuscripts, notes, memos, and letters. For most people, the value of this flexibility outweighs the effort needed to learn the troff system. If someone asks if you can get a document to look like a particular sample, the correct answer is, "It's troff, I can make it do anything!"

# TIP 324 · Learning More About the troff System

As you might expect, since the troff system provides such a rich environment for formatting text, there are a lot of details to look up. You can learn more about the troff system by consulting the manual pages of the commands in the troff system. You can also consult one of the many books devoted to text processing using the troff system. Some of these that you may find useful are:

*AT&T UNIX System Documenter's Workbench Software Release 3.1.* Murray Hills, NJ: AT&T Bell Laboratories, 1990.

K. Christian, *The UNIX Text Processing System.* New York: Wiley, 1987.

D. Dougherty and T. O'Reilly, *UNIX Text Processingh.* Indianapolis, IN: Hayden Book Company, 1988.

S. L. Emerson and K. Paulsell, *troff Typesetting for UNIX Systems.* Englewood Cliffs, NJ: Prentice-Hall, 1987.

Narain Gehani, *Document Formatting and Typesetting on the UNIX System.* Summit NJ: Silicon Press, 1987.

Narain Gehani and Steven Lally, *Document Formatting and Typesetting on the UNIX System— Vol II.* Summit, NJ: Silicon Press, 1988.

Brian Kernighan, "The UNIX System Document Preparation Tools: A Retrospective." *AT&T Technical Journal,* Volume 68, Number 4, 1989.

M. Krieger, *Word Processing on the UNIX System.* New York: McGraw-Hill, 1985.

Michael Lesk, "Typing Documents on the UNIX System," *UNIX System Research Papers, Tenth Edition, Volume II.* Saunders College Publishing, 1990.

K.P. Roddy, *UNIX nroff/troff, A User's Guide.* Englewood Cliffs, NJ: Prentice-Hall, 1987.

# Where Can You Get troff?

**TIP 325**

In the past, the troff system was always bundled with UNIX system software. But newer versions of the UNIX system often don't include **troff**. To remedy this, you can use an old version of the troff system, a public domain version of the troff system, or a commercial product that includes the troff system along with a variety of enhancements.

Although UNIX SVR4 doesn't include **troff** as part of its standard package, if the SVR4 BSD Compatibility Package is installed on your system, you can use the BSD version of **troff**. You will find this included in the directory */usr/ucb*. Although this older version of **troff** is not the most complete, it may meet your needs.

You can obtain a useful variant of the troff system, called **groff**, from the Free Software Foundation. This software is available from several archive sites and is provided on the disk included with the book *UNIX Power Tools,* edited by Jerry Peek, Tim O'Reilly, and Mike Loukides (Sebastopol, CA: O'Reilly and Associates, 1993). But if you want the latest and greatest troff system tools and software support, you should buy a commercial version of the troff system. You may want to purchase the *Documenter's Workbench,* which was developed by AT&T Bell Laboratories where **troff** was invented. The *Documenter's Workbench* is commercially available from a variety of UNIX system providers and Novell Corporation's UNIX System Laboratory; the latest version is Release 3.2. It includes a wide variety of useful tools, including many troff preprocessors and postprocessors, and specialized macro packages. Besides the *Documenter's Workbench* there is a variety of other commercial troff systems, listed in the *Open Systems Products Directory.*

# What Is nroff, and When Do You Use It?

The programs that translate your document with commands and text into output for printing or display are called **troff** and **nroff**. You use the **troff** program when your output device is a typesetter, a laser printer, or a bitmapped display. You use **nroff** when your output device is a line printer or line-oriented display. The **nroff** program provides a subset of the capabilities of **troff** that work with line-oriented devices.

# What Is TeX, and Where Can You Get It?

TeX is a set of software programs used for typesetting text, designed especially for typesetting material containing mathematical equations. TeX typesetting can be done on a wide range of computers, including UNIX systems, DOS PCs, and Macintoshes. You can get TeX software free of charge from a number of sources or you can purchase commercial versions of TeX that provide a wider range of features, better interfaces, and support.

You can get TeX software for the UNIX system either via anonymous ftp over the Internet or by ordering it through the University of Washington (and paying a small fee). To obtain TeX software via anonymous ftp, you probably want to read the instructions for doing so. These instructions can be found in the file *FTP.nwc*, which you can access via anonymous ftp in *./pub/tex* on *ftp.cs.umb.edu*. Anonymous ftp sites that support TeX include the Comprehensive TeX Archive Network (CTAN). Each of these sites supports archives of a comprehensive set of TeX system software, including many useful tools and macro packages. You can use anonymous ftp to obtain the TeX software you need from any of the CTAN sites. The current CTAN sites, and the directories containing TeX software are *pip.shsu.edu* with TeX root directory *./tex-archive*, *ftp.tex.ac.uk* with TeX root directory *./pub/archive*, and *ftp.uni-stuttgart.de* with TeX root directory *./soft/tex*. You can also get TeX software for UNIX from other archive sites including *ymir.claremont*, *ftp.cs.ruu.nl*, and *wuarchive.wustl.edu* (in the directory *./decus/tex*).

# Can You Translate a troff Document to TeX or Vice Versa?

Sometimes you may have a document that was prepared in **troff**, but you work in a TeX environment. Or you may have a TeX document and want to convert it to **troff**. Is it possible to do this? The answer is that while it is not possible to convert such documents entirely from **troff** to **TeX** or vice versa, there are some useful conversion programs that do some of the job. The problem is that many commands, inline escape sequences, and preprocessor code cannot be easily translated using an automated program. In any case, if you need to translate a troff document to **TeX**, you should begin by running the **tr2tex** program. If you need to translate a TeX document to **troff**, you should begin with the **texi2roff** program. Both programs are available in the public domain. To find sources for these, consult the newsgroup *comp.text* or use the archive server to find archive sites for them. You can get information on translation programs between **troff** and **TeX**, and **TeX** variants, in the newsgroups *comp.text.tex* and in the FAQs (frequently asked questions) from this newsgroup.

# Using troff Commands

# Some Useful troff Commands for Customization

The troff system lets you customize your document in lots of different ways. We'll describe some of the most common ways in this tip. For details on the full set of troff commands, see the "troff User's Manual" included in the *Documenter's Workbench Manual*.

You can set the length of your printed page using the **.pl** command. For example, to make your page 10.5 inches long, use

```
.pl 10.5
```

You can adjust the length of lines using the **.ll** command. For example, to make your lines 7 inches wide, use

```
.ll 7
```

You can center a group of lines using the **.ce** command. For example, to center the next five lines, use

```
.ce 5
```

You can cause a break, which stops the filling of the current line, by using

```
.br
```

You can begin a new page with

```
.bp
```

You can stop lines from being right adjusted, so that lines will be ragged right, by using

```
.na
```

See Tips 330 and 331 to see how to change the font and the point size, respectively, using troff commands.

# TIP 330 — Changing the Font

There are two ways to change the font in a troff document. You either use a troff command or an inline escape sequence. Each font is specified by one or two characters—for example, R represents Roman, H represents Helvetica, B represents Roman Bold, CW represents Constant Width, and HB represents Helvetica Bold. For example, to change to Helvetica, you use either the command

```
.ft H
```

or the inline escape sequence \fH. To change to Helvetica Bold, use either the command

```
.ft HB
```

or the inline escape sequence \f(HB.

There is a useful representation of the previous font, P. So to change to the previous font (that is, the font you were using before you changed fonts the last time), you can use either the command

```
.ft P
```

or the inline escape sequence **\fP**.

The fonts available to you depend on your output device. So you will need to find out which fonts are supported by your printer or display.

# Changing Point Sizes

You will probably want to change the point sizes of characters in your documents.
The point sizes available in troff documents depend on your output device, with almost all printers and many displays supporting point sizes of 6, 7, 8, 9, 10, 11, 12, 14, 16, 18, 20, 22, 24, 28, and 36. Many newer devices support many more point sizes, especially if they support scalable fonts. You can use the **.ps** (point size) command to change point size. For example, the following command will change the point size to 14:

```
.ps 14
```

You can also change point sizes using the inline embedded command **\sN**, where N is the point size. Here **\s14** will change the point size to 14. Note that if your printer supports point sizes up to 64, you will need to use the inline command **\s(64** to change to point size 64, since otherwise the point size will change to 6, and the 4 will be considered input.

# Printing Text Lines Starting with a Period

One of the tricky things in **troff** is printing out lines that begin with a period. Normally, troff considers lines beginning with a period as commands. To tell **troff** to treat such lines as text, you can start such lines with a backslash followed by an ampersand (\&). This combination of characters produces a character with zero width, or, put differently, a null character taking no space. So, if you want to include the line

```
.ps
```

in your troff output, you would have the line

```
\&.ps
```

in your input file.

# Putting Comments in troff Files

Sometimes you may want to put comments in your troff code. There are several ways to tell **troff** to ignore these comments, so it doesn't consider them text or commands. One way is to use the troff **.ig** command. You put **.ig** on a separate line and following this with one or more lines of comments. You then put .. (dot dot) on a separate line following your comments. An example of a comment inserted in a document with **.ig** is shown here:

```
.ig
This is the 10/13 version of the RFP  for woodpecker houses
..
```

You can also put your comments in a line by starting this line with a .\" (dot backslash double quote). So you could insert the same comment as before with

```
.\" This is 10/13 version of the RFP for woodpecker houses
```

Finally, you can include comments at the end of a line of troff input. Anything following a \" (backslash double quote), as shown here, is ignored in a line of troff text.

```
.ps 15   \"This command changes the point size to 15
```

# Putting Accent Marks in Documents Formatted with troff

You may need to put letters with marks in your documents. One way to do this in the troff system is to use the escape sequences supported by the mm macros. You put the escape sequence for an accent immediately after the letter it is used with. There are seven escape sequences for this purpose, shown in the following table:

| Accent Mark | Escape Sequence | Example |
|---|---|---|
| grave accent | \\*' | è |
| acute accent | \\*' | ó |
| circumflex | \\*^ | ô |
| tilde | \\*~ | ñ |
| cedilla | \\*, | ç |
| lower-case umlaut | \\*: | ö |
| upper-case umlaut | \\*; | Ö |

For example, to produce an e with an acute accent, your input is e\\*', and to produce an n with a tilde over it, your input is **n\\*~**.

# How Do You Print Non-ASCII Characters?

Sometimes you may want to use a special character not included in the ASCII character set. For example, you may want to use the registered symbol, the copyright mark, Greek letters, bullets, or other special symbols. You can insert such characters in your troff document if they are represented with a four-character escape sequence of the form \\(*xy*, **where** *x* and *y* are two characters, or \\N'*access code*', where *access code* is a number. Some of the characters you might want that are represented with escape sequences or access codes are:

| Character | Input |
|---|---|
| ® (registered symbol) | \\(rg |
| © (copyright symbol) | \\(co |
| ™ (trademark symbol) | \\(tm |
| ¶ (paragraph mark) | \\(pg |
| £ (pounds sterling) | \\(ps |
| ¥ (yen) | \\(yn |
| – (minus sign) | \\(mi |

| Character | Input |
|---|---|
| ± (plus-minus sign) | \\(+- |
| ∪ (union sign) | \\(cu |
| ∞ (infinity symbol) | \\(if |
| ☜(left-hand index) | \\(lh |
| ☞(right-hand index) | \\(rh |
| ■ (box) | \\(bx |
| ♣ (club) | \\N'167' |
| ♦ (diamond) | \\N'168' |
| ♥ (heart) | \\N'169' |
| ♠ (spade) | \\N'170' |
| ¿ (inverted question mark) | \\N'191' |
| ¡ (inverted exclamation mark) | \\N'161' |

You can also produce the Zapf Dingbats by using access code formats or alias names. See Tip 336 for details.

The *Documenter's Workbench Software Manual* contains a comprehensive list of non-ASCII special characters and the escape sequences or access codes needed to produce them.

# Using the Zapf Dingbats

**TIP 336**

Typesetting on UNIX systems with **troff** allows you to use a wide variety of different fonts and typographical effects. For example, you can easily use the Zapf Dingbats symbol set to insert special character symbols into a document. To be able to print the Zapf Dingbats, you should have a printer—for example, a Postscript printer—that supports this character set. Similarly, to display them on your screen, your display must support this character set, most likely using bitmappings.

The Zapf Dingbat font is represented by ZD. So, to tell **troff** to change to this font, use either the **.ft** command or the inline escape sequence **\f(ZD**.

An example of using a Zapf Dingbat character is the following string definition for producing a right-hand pointing finger, ☞ .

To define the string \(*rh as the right-hand symbol, put the following line at the beginning of your file:

```
.ds rh \f(ZD*\fP
```

Then, when you need the pointer anywhere in your file, use the string \f*rh.

Here we have defined a string, **rh,** and set it to the Zapf Dingbat character that corresponds to an ASCII "*".

The *Documenter's Workbench Software Manual* contains a complete list of the Zapf Dingbats. Each Zapf Dingbat can be produced either by an assigned alias character, such as * for the right-hand symbol, and by a character access code, which in the case of the right-hand symbol is 42. So, to produce a right-hand symbol, use either of the two strings \f(ZD* or \f(ZD\N'42'.

To see all the Zapf Dingbat fonts, try putting the following lines in a file and using the appropriate troff command line:

```
This is a test.
.nf
.ft ZD
1234567890-=qwertyuiop[]asdfghjkl;'zxcvbnm,./

!@#$%^&*()_+QWERTYUIOP{}ASDFGHJKL:"ZXCVBNM<>?
 '~\\|

.fi
```

# Inserting Trademark and Service Mark Symbols in a Document

If you use trademarks and service marks in your writing, legal convention is to include the mark the first time the word is used in a book or article.

To get the ® (registered trademark) symbol to print after the word UNIX, add the following to your file immediately after the first use of the word UNIX in your document.

```
UNIX\v'-.5m'\s-2\(rg\s0\v'+.5m'
.FS *
UNIX is a trademark of Novell.
.FE
```

The string starting with the backslash in the following example produces the <sup>SM</sup> (service mark) after the word "WORD".

```
WORD\v'-.5m'\s-4SM\s0\v'+.5m'
```

If you plan to use the service mark often in a document, you may save typing by placing the following three lines in the beginning of your document:

```
.de Sm
\v'-.5m'\s-4SM\s0\v'+.5m'
..
```

Once you've done this, you can call the macro at the appropriate point in your text. For example:

```
Using the word here
.Sm
followed by more text.
```

## troff Macros

# Using troff System Macro Packages

**TIP 338**

Macros are small programs that have been previously defined to handle some standard document formatting functions. The troff system will handle both troff commands and macros when it processes a file. Generally, a macro begins with a dot (.) and consists of one or two uppercase letters. Since a dot never appears at the beginning of a line in normal text, it is a good choice for macro labels.

There are a number of different macro packages available for your use. The most common of these are the *mm macros* designed for producing standard documents such as letters, reports, memoranda, papers, manuals, and books. The *ms macros,* which predate the mm macros, are used for a similar purpose and are still used in some places. The *me macros* also do similar things and are common in many BSD environments. The *man macro* package is used to format UNIX system manual pages. The *mv* and *mview* macro packages are used to format viewgraphs and slides (also called foils, overheads, or transparencies). All of these macro packages are available with the Documenter's Workbench, except the me package, which you will find in the BSD Compatibility Package of SVR4.

# Where Can You Find troff System Macros on Your System?

You may want to determine which troff macro packages are available on your system. In order to use a macro package, **troff** must be able to access these macros in the file *tmac.name* in the directory */usr/lib/tmac*, with *mname* the name of the macro package. For example, **troff** looks for the definition of the mpictures macros in the file */usr/lib/tmac/tmac.pictures*. If you actually need to look at macro definitions, say as inspiration in writing your own macros, you should note that the files in */usr/lib/tmac* often contain **.so** commands that switch the input stream to the file where these macros are defined. Looking at these commands, you will be able to find where the macro definitions are located on your system.

# Writing Your Own Macros

You can define your own macros using the troff **.de** command and syntax. The first line of the definition is **.de**, followed by the label for the macro. Make sure the name you use doesn't interfere or collide with existing macro definitions. To assure this, you can avoid all names with the form **.X** (single uppercase letter), **.XX** (two uppercase letters), and **.Xx** (one upper- and one lowercase letter). Your macro names can be of the form **.xX** (one lower- and one uppercase letter). For example, since **.PH** is the mm Page Header macro, if you define your own paragraph header macro, you should not use **.PH** as its name. Instead, use **.pH**. To define this macro, begin with the line **.de pH**, and follow it with the troff commands that you want to include each time you start a new paragraph, ending with a line containing dot dot (..). For example:

```
.de pH          \" Define Paragraph Heading     Usage:     .pH "Title"
.sp             \" Skip a space
```

```
.I                   \" Italicize
.Iti +10             \" Indent this line 10 spaces
\&\\$1               \" Insert Heading
.R                   \" Return to Roman font
..                   \" End macro definition
```

After making this definition, when you include the macro in your file, as shown here,

```
.pH "Next Point    "
This is the next point that I intend to make in this manuscript.
```

you'll get this in your formatted document:

Next Point
This is the next point that I intend to make in this manuscript.

A good tip for writing your own macros is to look at the definitions of those in the macro packages included with your troff system. (See Tip 339 to learn how to find these.)

## TIP 341 — Useful Macros in the mm Package

There are close to 100 different macros defined in the Memorandum Macros. Here is a summary of the most commonly used macros, with a brief description of the arguments they take, and what they do:

| Macro | Purpose |
|---|---|
| .2C | Two-column processing. |
| .AS [*arg*][*indent*] | Abstract start. If *arg* is 0, then the abstract is printed on page 1, and no cover page is printed; if *arg* is 2, the abstract appears only on cover page. |
| .AE | Abstract end. |
| .AF [*company-name*] | Alternate first-page format. |
| .AU "*name*" [*initials*][*loc*] [*dept*][*ext*][*room*][*arg*][*arg*] [*arg*] | Author information is printed on the cover sheet or in the "from" field. |
| .AT "*Title*" | Author's title. |

| Macro | Purpose |
|---|---|
| .B [*arg*][*previous font*] | Bold font. If no arguments are included, the font is switched to bold until another font command is given. If the first argument is given, it alone is printed in bold, and the previous font is reinstated. |
| .BL [*indent*][1] | Bullet list, indented by the amount specified. If the second argument [1] is specified, no blank lines separate list items. |
| .DS [*fmt*][*fill*][*rt-indent*] | Begin a static display. The first argument controls the left margin format; 0 or L means no indent, 1 or I means indent, 2 or C means center each line, and 3 or CB means center display as block. The second argument controls the fill mode; 0 or N means no fill, 1 or F means fill. The third argument specifies the indent from the right margin. |
| .DE | Display end. |
| .EQ [*label*] | Equation start. |
| .EN | Equation end. |
| .FC [*closing*] | Formal closing. |
| .FS [*label*] | Footnote start. |
| .FE | Footnote end. |
| .H *level* [*heading text*] | Text headings; levels 1-7 supported. Heading 1 is set off from text; heading 2 is placed above the following text. Settings of 3-7 produce underlined or italicized headings. |
| .IA [*name* [*title*]] | Inside address start. |
| .IE | Inside address end. |
| .LE | List end. |
| .LO *type* [*notation*] | Letter options. |
| .LT [*type*] | Letter types. |
| .MT [*type*] | Memorandum type. |
| .OP | Force odd page. Causes the text that follows to begin on an odd-numbered page. |
| .P [*type*] | Paragraph marking. |

| Macro | Purpose |
|---|---|
| .PH [*arg*] | Page header. *arg* has three parts, specifying the left, center, and right content of the header. |
| .PF [*arg*] | Page footer. *arg* specifies the footer content. |
| .S [*size*][*spacing*] | Sets point size and vertical spacing. |
| .SG [*initials*] | Signature line. |
| .SK [*pages*] | Skip one or more pages. The exact number is specified in *pages*. |
| .SP [*lines*] | Skip vertical lines. *lines* is the number of lines to be skipped; the default is 1. |
| .TE | Table end. |
| .TL | Title of memo. |
| .TP | Top of page. |
| .TS [H] | Table start. If a table header is needed on each page of a multipage table, use the H argument. |
| .WA name [*title*] | Writer's address start. |
| .WE | Writer's address end. |

Some of these macros combine to do common tasks. For instance, the macros **.WA**, **.WE**, **.IA**, **.IE**, **.LO**, **.LT**, **.FC**, and **.SG** are used to write letters (see Tip 350), and the macros **.TL**, **.AF**, **.AU**, **.AT**, **.AS**, **.AE**, **.MT**, **.SG**, **.NS**, and **.NE** are used to produce memoranda (see Tip 351). You can find a complete set of the memorandum macros in the *Documenter's Workbench Software Manual*.

# Using the mm Macros to Insert Proprietary Markings in troff Documents

You can put proprietary and other markings in documents using the mm macros. You use the **.PM** macro followed by a type. Possible types are P or 1 for PROPRIETARY, RS or 2 for PROPRIETARY (RESTRICTED), RG or 3 for PROPRIETARY (REGISTERED), CP or 4 for "SEE COVER PAGE" message, CR or 5 for a copyright notice, and UW or 6 for an unpublished work marking. For example, you could use

```
.PM P
```

or

```
.PM 1
```

# Formatting Lists with the mm Macros

The mm macros support lists in a wide variety of formats. To format a list, you first must choose a list initialization macro. Here are the choices:

| Macro | Type of List |
|---|---|
| .AL [type] | Numbered list; types are 1 (default) for positive integers, A for uppercase letters, a for lowercase letters, i for lowercase Roman numerals, I for uppercase Roman numerals |
| .BL | Bullet list |
| .DL | Dash list |
| .ML [mark] | Marked list; user selects arbitrary string of one or more characters as list item mark |
| .RL | Reference list; items are consecutively numbered with numbers in square brackets |
| .VL | Variably marked list; mark defined for each item after **.LI** |

Each item in a list is preceded by a **.LI** command and the entire list is terminated using a .LE command. An example of the formatting of a short list is shown here:

```
.BL
.LI
Africa
.LI
Antarctica
.LI
Asia
.LI
Australia
```

```
.LI
Europe
.LI
North America
.LI
South America
.LE
```

## Using the mm Macros to Create a Title Page

The following lines, inserted at the beginning of your troff code, will produce a centered title on page one. The text will start on the second page, but it will be numbered "1".

```
.PH ""
.PF ""
.DS
.sp 4.5i
.DE
.ce 1
.ps 16
TITLE
.nr % 0
.PH "''- % -''"
.SK
.ps 12
.sp
```

## Using the mm Macros to Emphasize Text: Bold, Italic, and Underline

There are three normal ways that text is emphasized in a document: bold, italic and underline. Often all three are called for by a particular style sheet. When you use the mm macros, you can produce bold text using **.B** and italic text using **.I**. For example, the following code will bold or italicize the material inside the double quotes:

```
.B "Bold Stuff"
.I "Italic Stuff"
```

You can use commands within running text to do the same—for example, \fBBold Stuff\fP changes the font to bold for "Bold Stuff" and then resets it to the Previous font style. Using \fIItalic Stuff\fP does the same for italic font.

Underlining is not a font type, and does not have a predefined macro. Here is a macro that does the trick—place the following three lines near the top of your document:

```
.de us
\\$1\l'|0\(ul'
..
```

Once you have included these lines, whenever you need words underlined you can call the **.us** macro and surround the words with double quotes. For example, the following code will cause the word "simple" to be underlined:

```
underlining can be
.us "simple"
```

# Checking a Document That You've Formatted with mm Macros

There is a useful command, **checkdoc**, for checking whether you've used the mm macros properly. You can use this command to find mismatched macro pairs, macros out of sequence, missing arguments for mm macros, and a wide variety of other formatting errors. For example, if *memo1* is a file containing troff code using the mm macros,

```
$ checkdoc memo1
```

will produce as output a list of errors in your use of the **mm** macros with line numbers and descriptions of problems.

# Displaying Your Formatted Document on Your Screen

If you have an ordinary terminal and not a bitmapped screen, you won't like what you see when you display a document formatted with the mm macros. This is because the output will contain a lot of control characters. These control characters show up because your terminal can't backspace, can't produce bold characters, can't do reverse line overlays, and so on. To get something readable, put your output through a filter that eliminates these distracting control characters, carrying out reasonable alternative actions. The UNIX system has such a filter, the **col** command. So to display a document you have formatted using the mm macros on your terminal screen, type

```
$ mm memo | col -b
```

Here, the **-b** option to col is used to take care of the backspace characters (CTRL-H) since your terminal can't backspace.

If you do have a bitmapped display, you can view the output of **troff**, with or without the mm macros. You need only run the appropriate troff command line and pipe the output to the appropriate display program for your terminal. This display program could be a PostScript previewer. If so, make sure you use the appropriate command line to produce PostScript output.

# Printing Documents Containing mm Macros

There are a variety of commands you should know to print documents formatted with the mm macros. For example, to print your file *memo* formatted with the mm macros using **troff** (assuming here that you have a laser printer), use

```
$ mmt memo | lp
```

If you have a line printer and run **nroff** instead, use

```
$ mm memo | lp
```

If you want to invoke one or more **troff** (or **nroff**) command line options, you should use **troff** (or **nroff**) directly. For instance, the following command line will print out pages 7-11 of your document formatted with troff commands and the mm macros:

```
$ troff -mm -o7-11 memo | lp
```

# Including PostScript Images in troff Documents

You can include images created with PostScript in your troff documents using the mpictures macros. Use the **.BP** (*b*egin *p*icture) macro to do this. Give this macro the name of the file containing the PostScript code, the height and width the PostScript page should occupy, a position option, an offset amount, some additional options, and a label for the display. Text will fill any space around the PostScript picture. For example,

```
.BP globe.ps 3 4 r 1 o "The World"
```

is used to include the page described by the Postscript file *globe.ps* in a 3 x 4-inch space, 1 inch from the right margin, with a box around it (from the o flag), with the caption "The World".

There are two other related macros, **.EP** (*e*nd *p*icture) and **.PI** (picture include), used for controlling the placement of PostScript pages and text, which you may want to use if **.BP** can't do all the things you need.

If you use the **.BP**, **.PI**, and **.EP** macros in your troff document, you should use the following command line to print out your document:

```
$ troff -mm -mpictures -Tpost file | dpost | lp
```

# Using the mm Macros to Write a Letter

You can format business letters using a set of mm macros designed for this purpose. The template for the formatted letter looks like this:

```
.WA "writer's name"
writer's address
.WE
.IA
recipient's name and address
.IE
.LO type [notation]
.LT [type]


Body of letter


.FC [formal closing]
.SG
```

This will produce a standard business letter. The option you give to the **.LT** command tells mm the style of letter you want. The possible types are BL (for *blocked format*), SB (for *semi-blocked* format), FB (for *full blocked* format), and SP for *(simplified format)*. You may want to experiment to see which style you prefer. The **.LO** command can be used with the following types: SA (*salutation*), AT (*attention* line), SJ (*subject* line), RN (*reference* line), and CN (*confidential* notation).

When using these macros you must include the **.WA**, **.WE**, **.IA**, **.IE**, and **.LT** macros in the order shown and all **.LO** macros must come before the **.LT** macro.

# TIP 351

# mm Macros for Formatting Memos

You can format business, academic, and professional memoranda using the mm macros. In general, memoranda include a block of information about the author, a title, a memorandum type, an abstract, the body of the document, a formal closing, a signature line, an approval line, and a copy to list. The following is a template for producing a memorandum:

```
.TL
title of document
.AF [company name]
.AU name [initials] [location] [org] [phone] [room] [arg] [arg] [arg]
.AT [author title]
.AS


body of abstract (optional)
```

```
.AE
.MT [memorandum type]

body of memorandum

.FC "formal closing"
.SG
.AV "name of approver"
.NS

list of recipients

.NE
```

Some of the possible memorandum types are 0 for a memorandum with no heading, 1 (default) for a memorandum with the heading TECHNICAL MEMORANDUM, 2 for a memorandum with the heading INTERNAL MEMORANDUM, 3 for a memorandum with the heading ADMINISTRATIVE MEMORANDUM, 4 for a released paper, and "string" for a memorandum with the specified string as the heading.

For the memo to be generated properly, the macros at the beginning must be in the right order. The only required macros are .TL (*title*), .AU (*author*), and .MT (*memo type*).

# Putting References in Documents

**TIP 352**

You can put automatically numbered references in your document using the mm macros. To put in a reference, type the string \*(**Rf** after the text to be referenced. Then put in the .RS (*reference start*) macro, followed by an optional string if you wish to use this as a subsequent reference. Finally, insert the text of the reference, followed by the .RF (*reference finish*) macro. The following example shows how to input references:

```
the mating habits of aardvarks.\*(Rf
.RS aA
A. Avocado and A. Asparagus, The Mating Habits of Animals with
Names that Start with the Letter A, McGraw Hill, N.Y. 1995
.RF
```

You could refer to this same reference later in the document with

```
the mating habits of agoutis.\*(aA
```

The same reference number that was used originally will be printed after the specified text.

# Putting Headings in Memos

**353**

You can use the mm macros to put headings in memos. The instruction you use for a heading is

```
.H heading level [heading text]
```

The first argument you give the .H command is the level number of the headings. The major sections of the document are first level headings, the subsection of these major sections are second level headings, and so on. The second argument of the .H command is the optional heading text. The first and second level headings are printed in italic text, each followed by a blank line. The third through seventh level headings are printed in italic text, each followed by two horizontal blank spaces. For example,

```
.H 1 "Overview of the Smell-a-Phone Project"
.H 2 "Background"
.H 3 "History"
.H 3 "Technology"
.H 3 "Market"
.H 1 "Conclusion"
```

produces

```
1.  Overview of the Smell-a-Phone Project

1.1  Background

1.1.1  History
1.1.2  Technology
1.1.3  Market
```

```
2.  Conclusion
```

You can also produce unnumbered headings by using the .HU macro. Headings will be printed in italics. For example,

```
.HU "Smell Peripherals for Multimedia PCs"
```

produces

*Smell Peripherals for Multimedia PCs*

# Preprocessors to troff

## What Are troff Preprocessors?

**TIP 354**

The troff system includes a variety of special-purpose formatting programs that operate on a source file producing output that is then sent off to **troff**. For example, the **tbl** preprocessor is used to format tables, the **eqn** preprocessor to format mathematical formulas, the **pic** preprocessor to format line drawings, and the **grap** preprocessor to format various types of graphs. There are a number of other preprocessors available, including one used to format phonetic symbols and another used to format chemical structures. You might want to ask your local experts if they know about a particular type of troff preprocessor that you may need.

## A Template for Tables

**TIP 355**

A *table* is a rectangular arrangement of entries. The **tbl** preprocessor to **troff** can be used to produce complicated tables. When you format tables using **tbl**, you include **tbl** instructions and table entries together with troff commands, macros, and text.

The structure of **tbl** code for a table follows a general model that looks like this:

```
.TS
global option line;
row format line 1
row format line 2
...
last row format line
data for row 1
data for row 2
...
data for last row
.TE
```

The beginning of the table is marked by the **.TS** (*t*able *s*tart) macro and the end by the **.TE** (*t*able *e*nd) macro. The global option line is used to describe the overall table layout. It consists of a list of global options separated by commas, ending with a semicolon. Options that you can use include *center*, which centers the table; *expand*, which makes the table as wide as the current line length; *box*, which encloses the table in a box; *allbox*, which encloses each item in the table with a box; *doublebox*, which encloses the table in two boxes; and *tab(x)*, which changes the data separator character. (See Tip 356.)

The first row format line specifies the format of the first line of the table. The second row format line specifies the format of the second line of the table, and so on. The last row format line specifies the format of all remaining rows of the table. Each line in the format section contains a key letter, which may be accompanied by modifiers, to describe each column of the table. Key letters include *l* (*l*eft justify), *r* (*r*ight justify), *c* (*c*enter), *s* (*s*pan), *n* (*n*umeric data), *a* (*a*lphabetic data), and ^ (expand entry from previous row). If key letters in a formatting line are separated by vertical bars, the entries in the formatted table are separated by vertical lines.

To learn how to put text blocks in tables, see Tip 358. To learn how to change the format of a table in the middle of the table, see Tip 357.

To learn the full set of options for formatting tables, you should consult a good book on the troff system. (See Tip 324.)

# Changing the Table Data Separator Character

The default character used to separate data in tables is the TAB character. Many people dislike using this character for this purpose because it is not visible and causes a number of blank spaces to appear on input lines between data elements. There is an easy way to change this separator. You only need to change the character used as a separator in the line of global options following the **.TS** (*t*able *s*tart) macro. For example, to change the table data separator from TAB to : (colon), include this in your global option line:

```
tab(:)
```

# Table Format Changing

If you want to change the format of a table in the middle of the table, you can use the **.T&** (table change) macro. When you do this, each table input line is close to its corresponding format line. What you need to do is include **.T&** on a separate line, preceding the lines of data whose format you wish to change. You then follow this line with the desired number of row format lines. Note that you can't change the number of columns, the space between columns, or the global options using the **.T&** macro. Also, because of a peculiarity in troff system software, you can't use **.T&** to change formats of lines after the first 200 lines of a table!

# Putting Text Blocks in Tables

Sometimes, you will want to put a whole block of text as an entry into a table. It's inconvenient to type this block as a simple string between tabs (or whatever character you are using as a data separator). To include a block of text as a table entry, you only need to precede it by the two characters "T{" (T left brace) and end it with the two characters "T}" (T right brace). As an example, assuming that the : (colon) is the data separator, the following sequence is used to include the block of text on the lines between the text block instructions:

```
:T{
one or more lines
of text in the same block
T}:
```

# TIP 359 Including Footnotes Within Tables

The troff system formatters take care of footnote formatting and numbering and are easily evoked with a simple macro call. It's somewhat more of a challenge to include footnotes inside a table. The following example shows you a way to do it. Note that you need to use \\*F instead of \*F inside the table.

```
.nf
TEXT-TEXT-TEXT
TEXT-TEXT-TEXT\*F
.FS
Footnote before table
.FE
TEXT-TEXT-TEXT
.TS
box, tab(;);
l l.
Item1;Item2
Item3\\*F;Item4
Item5\\*F;Item6\\*F
.TE
.\" you have to subtract the (number of footnotes
.\" within the Table - 1) from :p. Here, number of
.\" footnotes = 3, so we subtract 3-1= 2 from :p
.\" as follows:
.nr :p -2
.FS
footnote #1
.FE
```

```
.\" remember to include a ".nr :p +1" before each
.\" .FS that describes a footnote inside the table
.\" (after you're done with the very first one of
.\" them - like footnote #1 in this example)
.nr :p +1
.FS
footnote #2
.FE
.nr :p +1
.FS
footnote #3
.FE
More TEXT-TEXT-TEXT\*F
.\" You won't need any ".nr :P +1"'s for regular
.\" text footnotes...
.FS
Footnote after table
.FE
TEXT-TEXT-TEXT
.fi
```

# Checking Your tbl Code

**TIP 360**

If you have a troff file containing tbl code, you should check whether there are errors
in this code before printing your documents. The first thing you can do is to run the **checkdoc**
command to find some of these possible errors, such as whether each .TS is followed later by a .TE.
To find other errors in tbl code, run the **tbl** command and throw away its output by sending this
output to */dev/null*. Error messages produced by the **tbl** command will be displayed on your screen.
For example, to find tbl errors in the file *paper*, run

```
$ tbl paper > /dev/null
```

Once you have eliminated errors in tbl code, you should display your formatted document on your
screen, if you can, before printing it, since your tbl code may not work as you expected it to.

# TIP 361

# Putting Equations in troff Documents

The *eqn preprocessor* is a powerful tool for putting mathematical expressions, such as equations, in your troff documents. You can use **eqn** to insert equations in two ways—on separate lines or in lines of text. To format equations that go on separate lines, start with **.EQ** on a separate line, put in your eqn code, and conclude with **.EN**.

The following is an example of eqn code for an equation on a separate line:

```
.EQ
x sub 1 + y over z  ~=~ alpha sup 2
.EN
```

Here, "x sub 1" is eqn code for x with the subscript 1, "y over z" is eqn code for the fraction of y over z, the tildes around the equal sign tell **eqn** to put a blank spaces on either side of the = symbol, and alpha sup 2 is eqn code for the Greek lowercase letter alpha raised to the second power.

To produce an inline equation with **eqn**, you need to use equation delimiters that tell **eqn** where equations start and where they end. For example, to use dollar signs as these two delimiters, use

```
.EQ
delim $$
.EN
```

Then you would put the following in your troff code to produce the same example:

```
$x sub 1 + y over z ~=~ alpha sup 2$.
```

One of the most common eqn errors is not having your equation delimiters in the appropriate places, so be sure to start and end every inline equation with a delimiter. For more details on how to use **eqn**, see the *Documenter's Workbench Software Manual,* or a book on the troff system such as those recommended in Tip 324.

# Check Your eqn Code Before Printing Your Document

Since eqn code can be rather complicated, you should check to see whether you have any errors in this code before you print your document. First, use the **checkdoc** command. This will find a good number of errors in eqn code. Then you should run the **eqn** command and discard the output by sending it to */dev/null.* Error messages produced by **eqn** will be displayed on your screen. For example, to find eqn errors in the file *primepaper,* use the command line

```
$ eqn primepaper > /dev/null
```

Since eqn code can contain lots of errors, you might want to put your error messages in a file and then read them later. You do this using the command

```
$ eqn primepaper > /dev/null  2> eqnerrors
```

You can look in the file *eqnerrors* to see the errors in your eqn code.

# Printing troff Documents Containing tbl and/or eqn Code

If you want to print a file containing equations formatted with mm macros and with eqn code, use the command line

```
$ eqn file | troff -mm | lp
```

If your file also contains tables formatted with **tbl**, use

```
$ tbl file | eqn | troff -mm | lp
```

# Templates for Some Common Formatting Tasks

## A Deluxe Internal Memorandum Template

Most users find that they prepare the same kinds of documents over and over. We all write letters, memos, notes, and so on, which should have the same basic form from instance to instance. You can customize the look of your own memos and letters by using the mm macros with a set of extra troff commands inserted. The following is a deluxe template that does many things, including:

- ❏ Keeping right margin ragged (unjustified).

- ❏ Specifying large bold headings for first and second level.

- ❏ Specifying Helvetica for text and headings.

- ❏ Setting the point size to 11 and vertical spacing to 12 points.

- ❏ Setting printable page dimensions.

- ❏ Setting an end-of-file macro to print the last page number.

- ❏ Setting a blank page header.

- ❏ Setting the page footer to include page number and date.

- ❏ Placing graphic (multiweight) line and title on top of second and succeeding pages.

```
.ND ""
.SA 0
.ds HF 3 3      \"designates bold print for 1st & 2nd level headings
.ds HP 13 13    \" 13-point type for 1st & 2nd level headings
.ds BU \s+2\(bu\s0
.nr Hs 2        \"causes a space after 1st and 2nd level headings
.tr ~           \"translates tilde to unpadded space
.fp 5 B         \"specify use of Helvetica fonts
.fp 4 HB
.fp 3 HB
```

```
.fp 2 HI
.fp 1 H
.S 11 12        \"font size 11 for text, 12 points for vertical spacing
.ll 6.5i            \"line length set to 6.5 inches
.pl 10.5i          \"page length set to 10.5 inches
.em ee          \"Set end of file macro to ee
.de ee          \"End of file macro
.af % 1          \" ensure Roman font
.tm LAST \\n%   \"Print number of last page on >&2
..
.PH ""
.PF "''\\\\nP'\\\\*(DT'"
.TL ""
A Proposed Possible Preliminary Outline of Suggested Alternative
 Considerations for a Conceivable Tentative Recommendation; Draft 0.1
.AU "Ima Programmer" IMP "MIT 1J-322" Architecture 617-555-1212 \
 "email=imp@foo.mit.edu"
.AS 2 5
**ZZ To Be Completed In a Later Draft ZZ**
.AE
.FD 10
.MT ""
.de TP                          \"MultiWeight Line on top of Page
.sp 3.3P
.po -.75i
\l'45P'
.po
.po -.25i
.ps 80
.vs 0
\l'20.75P'
.br
.ps 9
\v'-4p'Best UNIX Tips\v'4p'
.sp 3P
.po 1.0i
..
.P
 TEXT GOES HERE

.SG "" 1
.ig
```

```
Copy to
..
.NS

.NE
.ig
Copy (with att.) to
..
.NS 1

.NE
```

# A Template for Generating a Note

**TIP 365**

You may often send people short notes on notepaper. The following template allows you to do this using UNIX to type and format the note. This template uses troff commands to define a set of macros that create a piece of notepaper stationery. A logo and an affiliation block is placed as it would be on standard stationery. This example generates AT&T stationery; replace the material in the first two lines with the codes for your own organization's logo.

```
.if !\nl=1 .ie t .ds l% \s36\(LH\s0
.el .ds l% AT&T
.PH "'''' "
.tr ~
.po +1.0i
.ll 3.8i
\v'+2.0i'
.\"
.\" define eb macro to draw the box, use 'mk a' to define top left
.\"
.de eb
.sp -1
.nf
\h'-1.0n'\L'|'\\nau-1'\l'\\n(.lu+2n\(ul'\L'-|'\\nau+1'\l'|0u-1.0n\(ul'
.fi
..
.de mS
.mk a
```

```
.sp 2
\h'+2.5i'\*(1%
.br
\h'+0.3i'\l'+9.0c'
.br
\h'+0.3i'\fB\\$1\fR\h'|\n(.lu-8m'\n(mo/\n(dy/\n(yr
.sp
.ev 1
.in +0.3i
.ll 3.5i
..
.de mE
.br
.ev
.sp |6.5i
.ps 7
.vs 8
.nf
.in +0.3i
.ft R
AT&T Bell Laboratories
Crawfords Corner Road
Room 1T-932
Holmdel, N.J. 07733
Phone: (908) 555-1212
FAX:   (908) 555-1313
E-Mail imp@att.com
.in
.sp
.ps
.eb
..
..
.mS "Ima G. Programmer"
.\" ——————— EDIT BELOW THIS LINE ONLY ———
.ft H
.ps 11
.sp 2
.nf
Rich,
.fi
.P
```

```
Here is the notepaper macro.
.P
Enjoy.



Ima



.\"  —————— EDIT ABOVE THIS LINE ONLY——————
.mE
```

## TIP 366 — Using the UNIX System to Print Labels

To print labels using the UNIX system, create an address file with three addresses across the page. A label, plus the space that separates it from the next label, takes up six spaces. Therefore, if an address has four lines, change the **.sp 3** line to **.sp 2**. Be sure tabs separate the columns; blanks won't work. Eleven sets of three labels will fill one page. Insert an

```
.SK
```

command to start the next page. Send the file to the printer with the following command:

```
$ nroff filename | opr -txr -f/XRLABL/
```

Here is the template:

```
.PH ""          \"removes page numbers
.po 0           \"move left margin to edge
.nf             \"turn off fill mode
.ta 35 69       \"set tab positions
name <tab>              name <tab>              name
street <tab>            street <tab>            street
city, state zip <tab>   city, state zip <tab>   city,state zip
.sp 3           \"leave three blank lines
```

# Entering Labels Interactively

**TIP**
**367**

The following script will let you enter a single address at the keyboard, specify the number of copies of the label you want, and run off that number.

```
#################################################
##
##  labeler
##  generates labels with name and address
##  creates file temp$$ and removes on next run.
##
#################################################
echo "Enter first line of label (e.g. name), then CR:\n"
read n
echo "Enter second line (e.g. street addr), then CR:\n"
read a
echo "Enter third line then CR:\n"
read cs
echo "Enter fourth line then CR:\n"
read s
echo "Enter last line, or CR if none:\n"
read x
echo "how many labels? \c"
read nl
cat /a17/rrr/bin/xs > temp$$
count=1
while
    test "${count}" -le "${nl}"
do
    echo $n'\n'$a'\n'$cs'\n'$s'\n'$x'\n\n' >> temp$$
    count=`expr ${count} + 1`
done
opr -f label1 temp$$
/bin/rm temp$$
echo "${nl} labels printed; labeler done"
```

# Including Full Page Art in a Manuscript

**TIP 368**

Suppose you need to include a full-page photo in a document. Let's say you want your text to go up to page 48, the photo to appear on page 49, and the text to resume on page 50. When you use the .SK macro (to skip a page), it doesn't work. How can you skip a full page in your document?

When you use **.SK**, text processing is stopped at that point, the rest of the page (1-59 lines) is left blank, and the page is ejected. So, using **.SK** gives you a partially blank page; **.SK 2** gives you a partially blank page followed by a full blank page, and so on. (Clearly, you don't want this.) To fill the entire page and then leave a blank page, use a floating display, as follows:

```
.DF
.sp 60
.DE
```

This will create a floating display of 60 blank lines, which will be output on the page following the point where the command is issued.

# Error Messages in the troff System

**TIP 369**

In **troff**, the normal error-handling macro is called )**D**. It prints on the standard error a warning that includes the line number in the file in which the error occurred, then the troff processor terminates. This forces you to fix errors sequentially through the file. You don't even see error messages from mistakes until you've corrected any errors that happen earlier in the file.

There will be cases in which you'll gladly pass over some early nonserious errors to see if **troff** will process the whole file. To do this, define a new error handling macro, )**d**, and call it in your own macros:

```
\"   This internal macro is like )D except it only
\"      issues a warning:
.de )d
.tm *****************************
.tm WARNING: input line \\n(.c: \\$1
.tm *****************************
..
```

When you invoke the )d macro the line number and filename will be displayed on your screen, but **troff** will continue processing the file.

# How Long Will Your Document Be?

Sometimes you'd like to know how long a memo or manuscript is without having to print the whole thing. Unlike a WYSIWYG word processor, you can't tell how long your document will be from your input file. How can you tell how many pages are in a long memo? You can use the **.em** macro to run troff commands at the end of the file. The following macro should be placed at the beginning of your file. If you use a command line such as this one,

```
$ troff -mm filename > /dev/null
```

nothing will be printed. When **troff** has finished, a message like "LAST PAGE IS NUMBER 321" will appear on your screen.

```
.em ee              \"Have end-of-file macro call ee
..
.de ee              \"Define ee macro
.af % 1             \" ensure Roman font
.tm LAST PAGE IS NUMBER \\n%   \"Print number of last
   \"page on standard error
..
```

Whenever you actually print the file, the "LAST PAGE IS NUMBER 321" will also be printed on the standard error.

# Using Source Files with troff Code for Large Projects

You don't have to have all your troff code and input in one file. For example, you may have an extremely large document or a special macro package. Putting all the troff code in one file will make this file too long or will make it awkward to modify. To make your troff input more flexible, put different parts of your troff codes in separate files. Then build a small file that includes for each file of troff input a separate line containing the **.so** (*source*) command followed by the name of that file. For example, to structure the troff code for a book, put troff code for the different portions of a book in separate files. If you also want to use a customized package of macros called bookmacros, your file *book* would look like this:

```
.so bookmacros
.so Preface
.so Contents
.so Chapter1
.so Chapter2
.so Chapter3
.so Index
```

To process this file, run the **xpand** command before running any preprocessors. For example,

```
$  xpand book | eqn | tbl | troff -mm | lp
```

puts the source files in, then runs the resulting output through **eqn**, then through **tbl**, then through **troff** using the mm macros, and then prints out the contents. (Note that on some systems, you will need to use either the **soelim** or **soxpand** command instead of **xpand**.)

# Entering the Current Date and Time in a troff Document

Often, in the last stages of writing a manuscript you need to make frequent changes and print out copies. At these times its useful to be able to include the current date and time in the printed document when it is run off. There may be significant changes between the 8 A.M. and 6 P.M. versions of the text.

It's easy to put the date into your document. The mm macros define a string, \(*DT, that holds the current date. The only trick to its use is to figure out the proper number of \ marks in calling the macro. In running text will insert the date at that point. In a table, two backslashes (\\) may be needed. To insert the date in the page footer requires four backslashes. This footer prints the word "DRAFT" and the current date on the bottom of every page:

```
.PF "'DRAFT''\\\\*(DT'"
```

To put in the current time is a little trickier, because **troff** doesn't know the current time. Here is a solution. Add this line to the front of your document:

```
.sy date '+TIME: %H:%M' >/tmp/mytime
```

This causes **troff** to have UNIX run the **date** command and place the output in a file. Next, include the following line where you want the time printed:

```
.so /tmp/mytime
```

The file *mytime* will be read into your document at that point.

# Using Number Registers

**TIP 373**

You can use number registers to keep running counts during troff processing. The following example shows how this is done.

Style sheets for manuscripts for academic journals often require the author to indicate the approximate placement of figures and tables in the manuscript by including a banner containing the sequence number of the table or figure. Here are two macros that insert the banners, and keep track of the figure and table numbers by using number registers, incrementing them each time the macro is called.

```
.nr x 0          \"Insert table about here
.de hT
.nr x +1
.ne 6
.DS 2


_____


Insert Table \\nx about here

_____

.DE
..


.nr y 0          \"Insert figure about here
```

```
.de hF
.nr y +1
.ne 6
.DS 2
_____

Insert Figure \\ny about here
_____
.DE
..
```

The two macros are called **hT** and **hF** (for *here's Table* and *here's Figure*). The name is made up of a lowercase followed by an uppercase letter to avoid collisions with mm or ms macros, which by convention avoid lowercase-uppercase macro names.

Each macro first sets a number register to zero. Within the body of the macro, the number register is incremented, we check to see that there are at least 6 lines left on the page, and then we put a centered display into the manuscript that includes the number.

# Generating an Index for a Formatted File

To generate an index of terms for a file, two UNIX commands are used: **subj** and **ndx**. First issue the following command:

```
$ subj file > subjectfile
```

This results in *subjectfile* containing a list of the subjects (nouns) found in the file. Next you need to edit *subjectfile* to remove the words you don't want in the index.

The command

```
$ ndx subjectfile "troff -Tpost -mm file" > index
```

will generate an index corresponding to the page numbering that will result when the file is run off with the command **troff -Tpost -mm file**. The following command will produce a subject-page index of *chap1 chap2*:

```
$ ndx subjectfile "nroff -mm -rW60 -rN2 -rO0 chap1 chap2" > indexfile
```

in the resulting index, the page numbers correspond to those in the document produced by this command:

```
$ nroff -mm -rW60 -rN2 -rO0 chap1 chap2 > indexfile
```

Finally, you can edit the index for more readable output. Add these two lines to the beginning of the file:

```
.ta 6.0iR
.tc .
```

Then, globally change ... to tabs. In **vi** or **ed** you can use this command line:

```
:g/\.\.\./s//< tab char>/g
```

# Increasing Readability of Columnar Information

**TIP 375**

You can arrange text input in columns by setting tabs in your document. If the columns are long, you can increase their readability by filling the area between the columns with dots. The following example uses the **.tc** command to place dots in the area between the two columns of a table:

```
Agenda
.sp
.ta 5.0i
.tc \.
.nf
Introduction          Smith
Software Overview Jones
Hardware Overview Delta
Functional Requirements          Baker
Maintenance Software             Charlies
Remote Command Architecture      Smith
.fi
```

## Spelling and Grammar

# Checking the Spelling of Words in a File

The UNIX system includes a command that checks the spelling of the words in an ASCII file. When your run **spell** on a file, the output is a list of words that the **spell** command has determined are spelled wrong. For example,

```
$ spell memo
```

would produce the following list:

```
hte
sytem
Chung
DMAD
Ramanathan
SYstem
XSpell
```

Note that **spell** handles uppercase and lowercase letters in the way you probably want it to. For instance, **spell** considers hare, Hare, and HARE to be spelled correctly, but hArE, HarE, and HaRe to be spelled incorrectly.

# Customizing Your Spell Dictionary

Since you may often use words, proper names, and acronyms that **spell** considers to be spelled incorrectly, you may want to create a personal spelling list. To tell **spell** which words you want it to ignore, you can create a file *okspell* containing these words in the proper format. To do this, put the following words, one on a line, in the file *temp*, and then run the **sort** command:

```
$ sort temp > okspell
$ cat okspell
Chung
Ramanathan
XSpell
```

To run the **spell** command so that it ignores the words in *okspell*, type the following:

```
$ sort +okspell memo
hte
sytem
```

# But What About British Spelling?

**T IP 378**

The spelling of English language words varies in different parts of the world. For example, inthe British Commonwealth, the spelling "centre" is used rather than "center" in the U.S. If you want spell to use the spellings of words in the British Commonwealth all you have to do is to run **spell** with the -**b** option. So if your memo contains the words "centre," "center," "theater," and "theater" (and no other words spelled incorrectly or differently in U.S. or British English), here is what you will find when you run **spell** and **spell -b**, respectively:

```
$ spell memo
centre
theatre
$ spell -b memo
center
theater
```

# Checking for Grammatical Errors

**T IP 379**

The *Writer's Workbench* is a software package you can use to check and analyze your writing. Originally written at AT&T Bell Laboratories, you can now purchase it from NCR and other vendors.

If you have the *Writer's Workbench* installed on your system, **wwb** will analyze the contents of your file memo. Type

```
$ wwb memo
```

This runs a collection of programs that check for spelling errors, incorrect punctuation, double words, poor word choice and possibly misused phrases, and split infinitives. It runs a program that gives you a readability score that indicates the number of years of schooling someone needs in order to read your document. Finally, it determines whether you have an appropriate distribution of sentence types, passives verbs, and nouns formed from verbs.

You can run the parts of **wwb** separately. To check for spelling errors run **spellwwb**; to check your punctuation, run **punct**; to find double words, run **double**; to find split infinitives, run **splitinf**; to check word usage, run **diction**; to check for sexist language, run **sexist**; and to produce statistics on writing style, run **style**.

# Chapter 7

# Shell Programming Tips

# Why Program in Shell?

## UNIX Programming in Shell or in C?

**TIP 380**

UNIX systems provide several alternatives for use in programming, including shell scripts and C programming. How do you decide whether to use shell scripts or C programs for a particular task?

If you are writing an application in which speed of execution and performance are important, you should code your program in C because it executes so much faster. There are times when programming with **ksh** is not suitable for everything, but a main **ksh** program with a couple of special C utilities will solve most programming problems. With something as powerful as **ksh,** all you need is the shell, and your programs will run virtually anywhere.

It's easy to write a quick shell script, particularly for relatively small utility programs of the kind most people need. Shell scripts are frequently easy to write (especially if you use other tools like **sed** and **awk**). They help in quickly getting a small program running. They are tremendously powerful in automating mundane tasks.

A further advantage of shell programming is that with a shell script, the source code and the executable program are in the same place. One result is that it's also easier to maintain a shell script. When the script gets too large, however, it's easier to debug C than a script using **sh/sed/awk**. There are better debugging tools for C (a weakness of shell programming which still needs to be fixed—but see Tip 428.).

## Selecting Which Shell to Use

**TIP 381**

Your system has several different shells available, including **sh** (the Bourne *sh*ell), **csh** (the *C sh*ell), and **ksh** (the *K*orn *sh*ell). Which one should you use? Does it matter which one you're proficient in?

At one time, compatibility with other users at your location was an important reason for selecting a particular shell. Since SVR4, however, these three shells are available on virtually all systems. It does make a difference which shell you use, however.

If you will be doing any system administration, you must learn **sh**, the Bourne shell, since several UNIX control files require that language. If you intend to do any serious shell programming, you probably should avoid **csh**, the C shell. Although it has many supporters from BSD systems, there are too many common actions which are difficult or impossible in **csh**. For example, you can't manipulate file descriptors beyond redirecting them to *stdout* ; you can't trap any signals except SIGINT; quoting is especially awkward; and so on. Programming in **csh** is just harder. A long description of these problems is regularly posted as a UNIX FAQ (Frequently Asked Question) in *comp.unix.questions,* available via anonymous ftp from *convex.com* in */pub/csh.whynot.*

Many people use **ksh**, the Korn shell, as their default. It is a superset of the Bourne shell, so learning it doesn't interfere with doing system administration with **sh**. It has many powerful extensions over **sh**, which make it especially easy to program in.

There are several other shells, such as **tcsh**, **bash**, and **zsh**, available on different systems. For the most part, these are very similar (in some ways equivalent) to the shells we discuss in this chapter. For example, **tcsh** is a superset of **csh**, and most of the tips that we provide about **csh** are relevant to **tcsh** users as well. Similarly, **bash** and **zsh** are functionally equivalent in many ways to **ksh**. If you use **bash**, many of the **ksh** tips will work with **bash**, most likely with the same script.

# Determining Which Shell You Are Using

**TIP 382**

How can you determine which shell you are using, and how can you change it if it's not the right one? There are two different ways to figure out which is your default shell. The easiest and most straightforward is to look in the */etc/passwd* file. You can search that file for the entry that corresponds to your login. The final field in the line indicates the shell that is used as your default. For example, the following code shows the listing for one of the authors, indicating that **ksh** is the default shell.

```
$ grep rrr /etc/passwd
rrr:x:4392:6837:41221F-R.ROSINSKI(HOS971)386:/home/rrr:/usr/bin/ksh
```

If the entry for the shell is blank, your shell is whatever is the default for your system, most likely either **sh**, **ksh**, or **csh**.

If you can't check your */etc/passwd* entry (because users don't have access to it on your system), you can still determine which shell is your default by exercising features that differ among the different shells. For example, **ksh** has a variable called RANDOM which is not available in either **sh** or **csh**. Also, **sh** and **csh** handle a call to RANDOM in different ways. If you are using **ksh** and try to print the value of RANDOM, you will see its value, as shown here:

```
$ echo $RANDOM
10450
$
```

Doing the same thing while running the Bourne shell gives just a blank line:

```
$ echo $RANDOM

$
```

With **csh** as your default, you'll get an error message:

```
$ echo $RANDOM
RANDOM: Undefined variable.
$
```

# TIP 383

# How Do You Get a Random Number?

You saw one use of RANDOM in Tip 382. More frequently, it's used to get a random number generated by the Korn shell. The RANDOM variable contains a random integer between 0 and 32,767 (inclusive). Each time this variable is accessed, its value is changed, following a uniform distribution:

```
$ echo $RANDOM
16748
```

To produce a uniform random variable from a different range, you can normalize the value produced by RANDOM.

# Writing and Running Shell Scripts

**TIP 384**

In its most basic form, a shell script is simply one or more commands that the shell executes for you. There are a number of ways provided to handle I/O, to do some conditional testing ("if *xxx* then *yyy*"), and to manipulate numeric and string variables. The easiest way to enter a shell script is simply to type it in at your terminal. For example, here is a simple way to invite five people to lunch using e-mail.

```
for i in bill mary joe fred ted
>do
>print "Time for Lunch,  I'll Buy!!" | mail $i
>done
```

If you enter this script at your terminal, you'll notice that the second through fourth lines are preceded by the ">" character. This indicates that a command line has been continued onto a second line. Its value is contained in PS2, the *secondary prompt,* and can be set to anything you like. When you finish the command (with the word "done"), the whole thing is executed by the shell. If you do this a lot, you may want to create this script in a more general way and use it repeatedly. To do so, put the following information in a file:

```
#  lunch - Invite people to have lunch
#  USAGE: lunch lognames

for i in $*
do
     print "Time for Lunch,  I'll Buy!!" | mail $i
done
```

You can use this script to invite anyone, by simply issuing the command:

```
$ lunch bill fred joe
```

In this command, *lunch* is the name of the file containing the script.

# Executing Shell Scripts

You just did exactly what you were told to do in the last tip, but you can't run the script. What's the catch?

There are a couple of reasons why your script wouldn't execute. First, you may have gotten an error message that said

```
ksh:  lunch:  not found
```

This is likely to have happened if you followed an earlier tip not to put the current directory in your search path. Since the shell won't look in the current directory, it can't find your script. Execute the script by giving a pathname that specifies the current directory (./) as the place to look for *lunch,* as here.

```
$ ./lunch
```

You may have gotten another error message:

```
ksh:  lunch:  cannot execute
```

To get the script to execute under these conditions, you need to make the file readable and executable by using the **chmod** command:

```
$ chmod +rx lunch
```

Alternatively, you can directly spawn a subshell to execute the script.

```
$ ksh lunch
```

In this case, the file needs only to be readable for **ksh** to read it and execute the commands found there.

# Passing Arguments to a Shell Program

When you run a shell program, several positional parameters are set. The parameters represent things that are on the command line:

| Parameter Name | Meaning |
|:---:|:---|
| $0 | Name of the program or function |
| $1 | Name of the first argument |
| $2 | Name of the second argument |
| $3 | Name of the third argument |
| $N | Name of the Nth argument |
| $# | Number of the positional parameters |
| $* | All the command line arguments |
| $@ | Each of the command line arguments |
| $$ | Process ID of the shell |

If you always provide the same number of arguments in the same order to your shell program, you could use the positional parameters to pass information to parts of your program.

# The Difference Between $* and $@

TIP
387

The two shell parameters $* and $@ are often used interchangeably because they often work the same way. However, they are not the same, and using one when you mean the other can cause a problem. $* means all of the command line arguments are to be read by the shell as one long string; $@ means that each of the arguments is to be read as a separate string. Here is an example:

```
## para1 - prints out values of command line arguments

for i in "$*"
do
   print $i
done
```

Then,

```
$  para1 one two buckle my shoe
one two buckle my shoe
```

On the other hand, the following behaves differently:

```
## para2

for i in "$@"
do
  print $i
done


$ para2 one two buckle my shoe
one
two
buckle
my
shoe
```

If the Internal Field Separator (IFS) is equal to a space, and if $* or $@ are not quoted as they are here, they behave exactly the same. If you are doing string manipulation, however, treating all the arguments as one string is very different from treating each of the arguments as a separate string.

# Creating Temporary Filenames

**TIP 388**

You can use variables set by the shell to create fairly unique names for temporary files. The **schedule** program in Tip 436 assembles a copy of your schedule in a temporary file, mails it to you if it's correct, and allows you to edit it if it's not. The temporary file in this script is called *tmp$$*, which stands for the letters "tmp", followed by the process number of the shell executing this script. Since it's unlikely that two simultaneous processes could have the same process ID number, the filename will be unlikely to conflict with another. If you run the script a second time, *tmp$$* will be a different name since it'll have a different process number.

# Checking Positional Parameters

**TIP 389**

It's common to write short, one-line shell scripts for your own use, but if you start to share them with others, you'll find yourself adding options and new bells and whistles, including checking for errors that you'd never make. Here is a template for growing such one-line scripts. **packall** shows a common way for shell script to check for the number of positional parameters, set some variables based on them, and then hand everything off to a UNIX command line. If a directory pathname is given, the command line starts in that directory.

```
################################################################
##
##   Packall
##   This program packs an entire directory structure
##   or substructure. If no arguments are given, the
##   current directory is assumed to be the starting
##   point. If a directory pathname is given,
##   packall starts in that directory. Arguments are
##   passed to pack; the args -, and -f are the only valid ones.
##
################################################################

PATH="."
FLAGS=""

## Check to see if there is a second argument to the command,
## If there is not, then check to see if the first is a readable file
## if its not, treat the first arg as flags to the command.
if [[ $2x = x ]]
then
     if [[ $1x != x ]]
     then
          if [[ -r $1 ]]
          then
               PATH=$1
          else
               FLAGS=$1
          fi
     fi
else
     PATH=$2
     FLAGS=$1
fi
/bin/find $PATH -exec echo " " \; -a -print -a -exec \
/usr/bin/pack $FLAGS {} \;
```

# Aliases, Functions, and Scripts

# When to Use Aliases, Functions, or Shell Scripts

An *alias* is a shorthand synonym for a command string. For example, if you always use certain options when you call a UNIX command, you can save some typing by constructing an alias. The following example shows two advantages in using aliases.

```
alias l='ls -lt'
alias m='/usr/add-on/exptools/bin/more -s'
```

First, use of an alias saves some typing; second, use of appropriate aliases can make commands execute faster by avoiding a search through your PATH for the command. It makes little sense to put the directory */usr/add-on/exptools/bin* in your PATH if **more** is the only program you use in that directory. Providing the full pathname as an alias speeds up execution of **more** and reduces the number of directories searched for other commands.

A *function* in shell programming is a small, well-defined script analogous to a function or subroutine in other programming languages. In **ksh**, functions have two major advantages. First, they execute in the current environment, which means they have access to all the variables of the script that invokes them. Second, they execute faster than a script because they are loaded only once when they are defined, and not each time they are run. To take advantage of functions, you should put the definitions in your *.profile,* or in a file (*.functions*) called by your *.profile.* By doing this, the functions will be defined whenever **ksh** is invoked. Some useful functions that show the syntax used to define them are given throughout this book.

Suppose you need to convert from hexadecimal to decimal, and vice versa, and you find that calling the **dc** (*d*esk *c*alculator) program is just too slow. This function provides a fast alternative:

```
## Decimal to hex conversion. function hex {
    typeset -i HeX
    (( HeX = 16#0 ))
    while [ $# != 0 ]
    do
        (( HeX = $1 ))
```

```
        print -n "0x${HeX#16#}   "
        shift
    done
    print -
}


## Hex to decimal conversion
function dec {
    typeset -i DeC
    (( DeC = 0 ))
    while [ $# != 0 ]
    do
        (( DeC = 16#${1#0x} ))
        print -n "${DeC}   "
        shift
    done
    print -
}
```

# Identifying Command Pathnames, Aliases, and Functions

You have aliases, shell scripts, functions, built-in commands, and UNIX system programs that you use. You've used the **alias** command to change some of the systems programs to work in your own unique ways. How can you tell what any particular command really is?

The **whence** command is used to find out what a command name corresponds to. If you use the command **whence name**, the full pathname for that command is displayed. For example,

```
$ whence cat
/usr/bin/cat
```

displays the full pathname for the **cat** command. You can also use the -v option to find out exactly what type of item each name is. The Korn shell, **ksh**, will indicate whether the name is an alias, a built-in, exported alias, a function, a program, a reserved word, a tracked alias, an undefined function, or not found. An example is shown here:

```
$ whence print
print
$ whence -v print
print is a shell builtin
$ whence pager

$ whence -v pager
pager not found
$whence -v l
l is a function
```

See also Tip 162, and the **show** function defined in Tip 163. It shows the entire definition, not just the type.

# Aliases in sh

**TIP 392**

The capability to use aliases exists in both **ksh** and **csh**. However, there is no aliasing facility in the Bourne shell, **sh**. You can get most of the advantages of aliases, however, by cleverly using shell variables. You can define a shell variable to be equivalent to a command string:

```
l="ls -sxFt"
export l
```

Now, invoking that variable is equivalent to issuing the longer command:

```
$ $l
total 280          3 tom           2 wdfreq*       6 mmxit*
   6 rough*        6 ix*           6 proofer*      6 draft*
  12 spell.errors  2 index/        2 wwb/          2 exx*
   4 linus.man     4 frame.mm*     2 fnote.mm      2 note.mm
  38 tdc*          2 mydraft*      2 frame.rrr     2 troffit*
  12 termcap*     12 termcap.skel* 2 tabmrk*       2 trs100
  16 vmca*         4 xs*           2 roughit*      2 termcap0*
```

You need to invoke the value of the variable to run it, so "$l" is necessary—"l" alone won't work. If you define a set of these variables in your *.profile,* you need to export them to make them available to subshells. This "aliasing" for **sh** works only with simple commands and options. It won't work for compound commands using pipes, for example.

# Shell Programming Concepts

## Writing Loops in sh and ksh Scripts

**TIP**
**393**

The easiest way to write programs in any language is to model your program after a previous one. That is, it's easier to rewrite and connect scraps of earlier code than to reinvent a program segment from scratch. There are three ways to write loops in shell. This tip provides simple templates that describe the syntax of each in **ksh** and make them easier to use.

The **while** loop continues until some condition is met.

```
integer x=1  #declare x an integer, initialize in to 1

while ((x <=4))
do
    print "The value of x is $x"
    ((x = x + 1))  #increment the loop counter
done
```

This example loops four times and prints the value of the *x* variable in each loop.

The **until** construct is the opposite of **while**. It continues to loop until some condition has been met.

```
integer x=1  #declare x an integer, initialize in to 1

until ((x > 4))
do
    print "The value of x is $x"
    ((x = x + 1))  #increment the loop counter
done
```

This loop continues until *x* is greater than 4.

The third looping mechanism is the **for** loop, which specifies a set of values for the loop variable.

```
for x in 1 2 3 4
do
```

```
print "$x"
done
```

# Using for Loops in String Lists

Since the **for** loop handles its own indexing, it is one of the easiest to use. In addition, since it can be used with string variables as well, it becomes an important way to manipulate lists of strings. For example, here is our familiar way to mail a message to multiple people:

```
for x in joe dan bill bob fred
do
      print "Hello, this is a test message" | mail $x
done
```

# Using for Loops with Internal Field Separators

**for** loops of the kind used in the preceding tip work because the elements in the string "joe dan bill bob fred" are separated by spaces, and the default Internal Field Separator (IFS) assumed by the shell is a space. You can set the value of IFS to anything you wish and use it to segment long strings whose elements are not separated by spaces. For example, the PATH variable consists of a set of directory names, each set off from the others by a colon (:). You can isolate each of these elements by using the following script:

```
IFS=":"
for i in $PATH
do
print $i
done
```

# Making Conditional Tests

To make conditional tests in **sh** and **ksh**, you use if-then-else concepts. The syntax for such tests is

    if *command*
    then
        *commands*
    [elif *condition*
    then
        *commands*]
    [else
        *commands*]
    fi

The parts marked in brackets are optional. The **if**, **then**, and **fi** are required.

It's useful to understand how conditional testing works on UNIX systems. Every command returns an exit status when it completes. By convention, a command returns a zero (0) when it completes successfully, and a non-zero value, usually one (1) when it fails. Sometimes these values are also called "true" for 0 and "false" for non-zero. With conditional tests, *command* is evaluated; if 0 (true) is returned, then the body of the **if** is executed. If non-zero (false) is returned, then the **elif** or **else** sections are executed.

# Using the exit Command in Shell Scripts

When you write complex shell scripts, you should include explicit exit statements. The command **exit** alone returns the exit value of the command that preceded it. If you place an **exit** at the end of a script, the appropriate value will be returned when the script ends. This is actually a redundant use of **exit**, because **ksh** will do the same thing as the shell executes. You'll see this use in several of the scripts in this book; however, we've been redundant at times in order to be consistent in using **exit**.

The **exit** command will return specific values at your direction. For example, **exit 3** will return a value of three (3) when **exit** executes. Use this capability in error handling. For example, identify an exit on error by having the command return a specific value. To terminate a section of a script that handles user error, you should normally use

```
exit 1
```

## Using case to Test Several Conditions

**TIP 398**

If you need to distinguish among many alternatives with multiple **if**, **elif**, **elif**, and so on, commands, it's easier to make the same comparisons with the **case** command. The format for a **case** command is

```
case WORD in
    pattern1)   command list;;

    pattern2)   command list;;

    pattern3)   command list;;

esac
```

The value of *WORD* is successively compared against *pattern1,* then *pattern2,* then *pattern3,* and so on. When a match is found, the command list is executed up to the double semicolon. Upon reaching the double semicolon, the **case** statement ends, and the value of the command list that **ksh** executed is returned.

## Using case to Test Script Options

**TIP 399**

In the old days, real programmers took care of option handling by themselves, most often using **case** statements. You'll still find examples and templates which use **case** to set option flags, as in the following example.

```
case $1 in

    -x)    xflag=1;;
    -y)    yflag=1;;
    -b)    echo "buckle my shoe"
esac
```

Don't do this! Use **getopts** instead. You shouldn't waste your time trying to capture UNIX command syntax with a set of **case** commands; **getopts** was developed to do this one thing well. See Tips 418-422 on using **getopts**.

# Rules of Thumb for Using case

TIP
400

Use **case** statements instead of long **if, elif, elif, elif,** and so on, sequences. **case** statements are much easier to read and to follow than strung-out **else ifs**.

Use **case** commands to put together long lists of possible values of a variable, but put the most likely values at the top of the list of patterns. Since pattern matching stops once one match occurs, having a long list doesn't usually affect performance very much.

You can combine alternative patterns using the vertical bar (|) to separate them, as shown here.

```
case WORD in
    tomayto | tomahtoe)    command list;;

    potayto | potahtoe)    command list;;

esac
```

The | acts as an "or" symbol reminiscent of the C language. However, if you use the |, don't assume it acts like the | in C. In particular, the order in which these are evaluated is not defined in **ksh**, whereas in C, the order is left to right.

Where reasonable, include a default or two. You can handle a null value of a variable, if one is possible, with something like the following:

```
    "")    print -u2 "$WORD must have a value"
```

You can check for user errors with a general purpose default. For example,

```
*)   print -u2 "Inappropriate Response
     print -u2 $ERROR_MSG
```

If you are using a **case** statement to execute a list of commands depending on the name of the script ($0), as in Tip 413, you don't need a default. The script will be executed only if it's called by one of the names in the **case**.

# Evaluating with test and [ ]

**TIP 401**

The shell provides a built-in command, **test**, to evaluate expressions. **test** is most often used in **if ... then** statements to determine whether a certain condition is true, and then to take some action, depending on the answer. **test** is the original Bourne shell command, supplanted by the use of [ ] or [[ ]]. They are equivalent forms, with the [[ ]] being easiest to read and follow in a program. Spacing is critical in making tests with [ ] or [[ ]]. There must be a space on either side of the bracket operator. You can make compound tests by using the *and* (-a), *or* (-o) and not (!) operators. See Tip 402 for examples.

# Making Numeric Comparisons

**TIP 402**

The Korn shell provides several different ways to make comparisons between pairs of numbers or pairs of strings. For numeric comparisons, these are:

$a == b$ ($a$ equals $b$)
$a != b$ ($a$ does not equal $b$)
$a < b$ ($a$ is less than $b$)
$a > b$ ($a$ is greater than $b$)
$a <= b$ ($a$ is less than or equal to $b$)
$a >= b$ ($a$ is greater than or equal to $b$)

One difficulty in shell programming is that there are several similar, but confusingly different, ways to make these comparisons. The following **if** statements are all equivalent:

```
if ((a == b))
if test $a -eq $b
if let "$a == $b"
if [ $a -eq $b ]
if [[ $xz -eq $b ]]
```

Standardize your own programming on the first form. You'll see the other forms, especially those using **test**, **-eq**, or **let** in older shell scripts, but you'll avoid errors in your own scripts if you always use the $((a == b))$ form.

# Making Numeric Comparisons II

Here is a summary of numeric comparisons:

| Test | Returns True If: |
| --- | --- |
| ((*number1* == *number2*)) | *number1* equals *number2* |
| ((*number1* != *number2*)) | *number1* does not equal *number2* |
| ((*number1* < *number2*)) | *number1* is less than *number2* |
| ((*number1* > *number2*)) | *number1* is greater than *number2* |
| ((*number1* <= *number2*)) | *number1* is less than or equal to *number2* |
| ((*number1* >= *number2*)) | *number1* is greater than or equal to *number2* |

# Making String Comparisons

There are several ways to make string comparisons, and the inconsistency with numeric comparisons is often a source of error. The string comparison operators are:

*s1* = *s2* (*string1* equals *string2*)
*s1* != *s2* (*string1* does not equal *string2*)

*s1* < *s2* (*string1* precedes *string2* in ASCII sorting order)
*s1* > *s2* (*string1* follows *string2*)

-z *s1* (*string1* is of zero length—that is, *string1* is null)

-n *s1* (*string1* is of non-zero length—that is, *string1* exists.

A common mistake to avoid is confusing the numeric and string equals. For comparisons between strings, use the = operator—for example, [[ *s1* = *s2* ]]. With numbers, a single equal sign means assignment (that is, ( *a* = *b* ) means set *a* to be the same as *b*). To make comparisons of numbers, you must use ==.

A second source of confusion comes from the role of white space in making comparisons. In making comparisons of numbers in double parentheses, white space is irrelevant. The following are all equivalent:

```
((a==b))
(( a==b ))
(( a == b ))
```

In making string comparisons however, white space is critical. Each operator must be separated from its neighbor by a space. The comparison

```
[[ $s1 = $s2 ]]
```

will work correctly, whereas the closely similar ones shown here will not:

```
[[$s1 = $s2]]
[[ $s1=$s2 ]]
```

Although shell syntax doesn't require it, you should adopt a consistent approach to both forms. Always separate operators by spaces in both numeric and string comparisons.

Notice a third inconsistency. In making comparisons between numbers, you don't need to use a $ (dollar sign) in front of a variable name to indicate its value, whereas with string comparisons you do.

# Making String Comparisons II

Here is a summary of string comparisons:

| Test | Returns True If: |
|------|------------------|
| [[ *string1* = *string2* ]] | *string1* is equal to *string2* |
| [[ *string1* != *string2* ]] | *string1* is not equal to *string2* |
| [[ *string1* = *pattern* ]] | *string1* matches *pattern* |
| [[ *string1* != *pattern* ]] | *string1* doesn't match *pattern* |
| [[ *string1* < *string2* ]] | *string1* comes before *string2* |
| [[ *string1* > *string2* ]] | *string1* comes after *string2* |
| [[ -z *string1* ]] | *string1* is null (has zero length) |
| [[ -n *string1* ]] | *string1* is non-null (has non-zero length) |

# Making File Comparisons

TIP
406

The Korn shell, **ksh**, provides a means for determining the nature of particular files using the normal **test** comparisons. For example,

```
[[ -f filename ]]  # Returns true if filename is a regular file.
[[ -x yourfile ]]  # Returns true if yourfile is executable.
[[ -r private ]]   # Returns true if private is readable.
```

Use the following to evaluate status of files and directories in shell programs.

| Test | Returns True If: |
|------|------------------|
| **-r** *file* | *file* exists and is readable. |
| **-w** *file* | *file* exists and is writable. |
| **-x** *file* | *file* exists and is executable. |
| **-f** *file* | *file* exists and is a regular file. |
| **-d** *file* | *file* exists and is a directory. |
| **-c** *file* | *file* exists and is a character special file. |
| **-b** *file* | *file* exists and is a block special file. |
| **-p** *file* | *file* exists and is a named pipe (fifo). |
| **-u** *file* | *file* exists and its set UID is set. |

| Test | Returns True If: |
|------|------------------|
| **-g** *file* | *file* exists and its set group ID is set. |
| **-k** *file* | *file* exists and its sticky bit is set. |
| **-s** *file* | *file* exists and has size greater than zero. |
| **-L** *file* | *file* exists and is a symbolic link. |
| **-O** *file* | *file* exists and its owner is the effective UID. |
| **-G** *file* | *file* exists and its group is the effective group ID. |
| **-S** *file* | *file* exists and is a special file of type socket. |

For example:

```
if [[ -r $filename ]]
then print "$filename is readable"
     exec 9< $filename
     read -u9 line
     print $line
fi


if [[ -x $filename -a ! -d $filename ]]
then print "$filename is executable"
     ksh $filename
fi


if [[ -s $filename -a -x $dirname -a -d $dirname ]]
  rm $filename
fi
```

## Handling Basic Shell I/O

# Reading Input into a Script from the Keyboard

You can use **read** to capture user input from the keyboard into a shell variable. The easiest way to do this is simply to prompt the user for input and catch it with **read**:

```
print -n "Enter Terminal Type:"
read TERM
print "Your terminal is a $TERM"
```

You can do the same thing in a single command. If you give the name of a variable followed by a question mark and a prompt, **ksh** will write the prompt to standard output and capture the input. Don't leave any spaces between the variable name, the question mark, and the prompt.

```
read TERM?"Enter TerminalType:"
print "Your terminal is a $TERM"
```

If you use **read**, but don't specify a variable, then the input is captured in the shell variable REPLY.

```
print -n "Enter Terminal Type:"
read
print "Your terminal is a $REPLY"
```

# Confirming Actions with User Input in Shell Scripts

You can write shell scripts that enhance the operation of standard UNIX commands by doing some simple checking of the command line parameters and asking for user confirmation. For example, the **cp** command will overwrite a file whether you intended to or not. Here is a script that defines a new command, **copy**, which checks to make sure that it has two arguments, checks to see if the second filename already exists, and if it does, uses the **read** command to get confirmation before it overwrites the file.

```
# Copy a file
if [ "$#" != 2 ]
then
        print "Usage: copy from to"
        exit 1
fi

from="$1"
to="$2"
```

```
# See if the destination file already exists

if [ -f "$to" ]
then
        print "$to already exists; overwrite (y/n)?\c"
        read answer

        if [ "$answer" != y ]
        then
            print "$from not copied"
            exit 0
        fi
fi

# If destination doesn't exist or "y" was typed

cp $from $to            # proceed with copy
```

# TIP 409
# Reading Standard Input from a File

This example, **utoword.sh**, combines the use of the **read** command with a little bit of conditional testing to do simple string processing. Users who need both DOS and UNIX systems are sometimes disturbed by the incompatibility in text file formats supported by popular editors. UNIX ends each line with a new line and carriage return, while DOS editors such as WORD use only carriage returns to delimit paragraphs. In this script, **read** accepts a line from the standard input and puts it on the standard output without the carriage return. A return is output to delineate a paragraph if a blank line is encountered in the input.

```
# This is a UNIX sh/ksh shell script to convert a "text" file with many
# lines per paragraph to a one-line-per-paragraph format suitable
# for importing to Word for Windows. The algorithm is in sh/ksh
# and should have the input file fed in on standard input.
#
# utoword.sh <input_file >output_file
# Created by Avi Gross

IN_PARA=no          # flag used to mark whether the state of
                    # the program is currently in a paragraph
```

```
while read line
  do
    if [ "$line" ]         # line has contents - non-blank
      then
    if [ "$IN_PARA" = "no" ]
      then                 # this is first line of paragraph
        IN_PARA=yes        # set flag as being IN_PARA paragraph
        echo "$line\c"     # write first line, no CR
      else                 # this is 2nd or more line
        echo " $line\c" #
    fi
      else                 # this is a blank line
    if [ "$IN_PARA" = "yes" ]
      then                 # this is first blank line
        IN_PARA=no         # turn off paragraph flag
        echo "\n"          # write TWO carriage returns
      else                 # this is 2nd or more blank line
        echo ""            # write a blank line
    fi
    fi
  done

# now handle the case where the file ends with a non-blank line
# by writing a return in that case.
[ "$IN_PARA" = "yes" ] && echo
```

# Reading a File for Input

**T**I**P**
**410**

By default, the Korn shell and the **read** command take their input from the standard input. You can easily get input from a file into a script, however. To do this, use the **exec** command to create a new file descriptor and associate it with a file. Then **read** can be used with the **-u** option to read from that file descriptor. For example, this script, *head,* takes a number of lines as its first argument and a filename as its second. It opens the file and reads and prints that number of lines.

```
USAGE: head no.of_lines filename
#  Associate a file descriptor with filename
exec 9< $2
#  file descriptor number 9 is connected to filename
```

```
integer i=0
while ((i < $1))
do
read -u9 line
print "$line"
((i = i + 1))
done
```

# TIP 411

# Redirecting Output

Occasionally you'll get some unwanted text displayed on your screen when you run a shell script. Usually this is the result of the standard error being sent to your screen. Normally, you'd want to see error messages, but when running a shell program in the background, for example, the error messages just distract you. Sometimes, you may want to collect all the error messages in one file. The way to do this is to redirect the standard error to a place other than your screen.

In UNIX, file descriptor 0 is the standard input, file descriptor 1 is the standard output, and file descriptor 2 is the standard error. To direct the standard output, you use the > operator, as shown here:

```
$ ls -l comptech > filename
```

This example will run the **ls** command with the -l option and place its output into a file. If you look into that file, you'll see something like this:

```
-rw-r--r--   1 rrr        41131      2331 Mar 27  1993 comptech
```

If the file didn't exist, we'd see the error message displayed on the standard error which is attached to our screen. We could redirect the standard error to a different file, so that all error messages would go into the error file. To do this, use the 2> operator, which says to redirect file descriptor 2. To send errors from the **ls** command to an *errorfile,* you could say

```
$ ls -l compblech 2> errorfile
$ cat errorfile
compblech: No such file or directory
```

# Handling Shell Script Output

You can redirect standard in, out, error, and the other file descriptors as shown in
Tip 411. You can also control a terminal's characteristics within a shell. Tip 164 in Chapter 3 used the
**stty** command to set the terminal characteristics for the login shell. You can use **stty** within a shell
script to control terminal characteristics during execution of that subshell. For example, **stty ignbrk**
will result in the shell ignoring any BREAK characters, so a user could not break out of the shell; **stty
-echo** will turn off input echoing on the screen. Here is a prank that uses **stty -echo** to turn off output
echoing at a critical time to pretend it's the login routine. Someone walking up to an unattended
terminal running this prank would inadvertently give his login and password away.

```
##  Prank login
##

clear
while true
do
stty ignbrk
print "login:\c"
read logname
stty -echo
print "Password:\c"
read passwd
print "\n"
print "Fatal Error: No root file system"
print "#$%%^&*(&*()(++^~~~$%%%*((~(~"

print $login $passwd | mail you
stty 0

done
```

# A Way to Make Maintenance of Similar Programs Easy

You will often have similar programs that are related to one another, and that should be maintained
in the same way. Suppose you had four programs used for text formatting: **final**, which generated three

copies of a final version of the manuscript; **proof**, which generated one version; **draft**, which generated a double-spaced version of the file; and **rough**, which printed out the raw file with line numbers, page numbers, and headers. You should maintain all these together, making similar changes in all. UNIX provides an easy way to do this. Make one copy of the file—let's call it *final*—and link that copy to several program names, as shown here.

```
ln final proof
ln final draft
ln final rough
```

Now you have one file that has four names associated with it. Since the positional parameter $0 stands for the name of the program used on the command line, you can have different processing done depending on what program name was used, by switching on $0 in a **case** statement. Now there is only one file to maintain, but a different part of the script runs, depending on the command name.

```
####################################################
##
##  This shell processes an entire manuscript in
##  several different ways depending on the name
##  that is given to it.
##
####################################################


for i in $*
do

case $0 in

final)    # final
            (tbl -TX $i | nroff -cm\
            -rA3 -rE1 -rN2 -rU1 -rL66 -rW67 -rO0 -TX \
            | lp -c -m -n3) 2>>/tmp/$LOGNAME.$$;

;;


proof)    #proof
            (tbl $i | nroff -cm -rA2 -rN2 \
            -rE1 -rC3 -rL66 -rW67 -rO0 -|\
            col | lp -n1 )  2>>/tmp/$LOGNAME.$$

;;
```

```
draft)   #draft
         (tbl $i | nroff -cm -rA2 -rN2 \
         -rC4 -rE1 -rL66 -rW67 -r00 -| col \
         | lp -n1 )  2>>/tmp/$LOGNAME.$$



;;



rough)   #roughit form
         (nl -bt -p $i | pr -d -h $i | lp -n1 \
         -t$i ) 2>>/tmp/$LOGNAME.$$



;;
esac
done
```

# Handling the Unexpected

## Removing Temporary Files from a Shell Program

When you use temporary files in a shell program, it's important to remove them at the end of the program. A common way to do this is simply to include a line like this at the end of the shell script.

```
/bin/rm tmp$$
```

This doesn't quite do what we want because there are several ways for a program to finish, and placing the line **/bin/rm tmp$$** at the end of the program will only be successful if the program gets to that command. The tmp files will be left around if the program is terminated before it reaches the **rm** command, if you interrupt the program, hang up your modem, or log out while the program is running.

The solution is to use the **trap** command. As its name suggests, **trap** traps system interrupts until some command can be executed. A few of the various system interrupts are provided in the following table:

| Signal | Abbreviation | Meaning |
|--------|--------------|---------|
| 1 | HUP | Hangup |
| 2 | INT | Interrupt |
| 3 | QUIT | Quit |
| 9 | KILL | Kill |
| 15 | TERM | Terminated |

The command

```
trap '/bin/rm tmp$$;exit 1' 1 2 3 9 15
```

will trap the signals summarized in the table, and will execute the **/bin/rm tmp$$** command before exiting. This means that all tmp files are deleted even if the program terminates abnormally.

# TIP 415

# Conditional Execution in a Trap

The **trap** command will execute any command that we wish before the program terminates. Perhaps we don't want to simply remove our tmp files when the script is interrupted. We ought to be able to do other things like writing a file to the disk. This is easy using the template above, as shown here:

```
trap 'cat tmp$$ > $HOME/.schedule;/bin/rm tmp$$;exit 1'1 2 3 9 15
```

This example writes the tmp file to the file *.schedule* in the user's *HOME* directory, then deletes the file and exits. But what if there already was a file called *.schedule*? We wouldn't want to overwrite it incautiously. We can put conditional tests in the **trap** command to prevent this. We'll use this code scrap later in a script that prompts for a schedule and mails it to others.

```
trap 'if test -f tmp$$
    then
        if test -f $HOME/.schedule
          then
            echo "$HOME/.schedule already exists!  Do you"
            echo "wish to overwrite (save this schedule) ? (y/n) >\c"
            read overpermit
            if test \( $overpermit = 'y' -o $overpermit = 'yes' \)
          then
                cat tmp$$ > $HOME/.schedule
```

```
                    echo "schedule saved in $HOME/.schedule"
                    /bin/rm tmp$$
                    exit 1
            else
                    echo "schedule not saved"
                    /bin/rm tmp$$
                    exit 1
              fi
            else
                    cat tmp$$ > $HOME/.schedule
                    echo "schedule saved in $HOME/.schedule"
                    /bin/rm tmp$$
                    exit 1
          fi
      fi
      exit 1' 1 2 3 15
```

This sample of code checks to see whether there is a tmp file and whether the *.schedule* file already exists. If there is a tmp file but no *.schedule* file, then *tmp$$* is removed. If *.schedule* already exists, the user is prompted to see whether the existing file should be overwritten before exiting.

# Handling User Errors in Shell Scripts

TIP
416

When other people start to use your shell programs, you'll need to provide some user support. If the program is not used properly, it should inform the user of his or her error. This tip provides several different ways to do this.

The first suggestion is to provide a usage message if the user simply types the command name. This provides an easy way to remind the user of the correct syntax. If you simply type a standard UNIX command that normally takes arguments, you get a usage message. For example, the UNIX system command **uuto** takes as arguments a filename and a destination address. The order is arbitrary and easily forgotten.

```
$ uuto
Usage: uuto [-m] [-p] [-E] files remote!user
```

This demonstrates the UNIX convention for usage messages. The command and its necessary arguments are specified, and any optional arguments are enclosed in brackets ([]). You can include the same kind of help in your programs by using the following template. It replaces $0 with the name of the program, and prints the usage message on the standard error if there are no arguments.

```
$USAGE="$0 [options] arg1 arg2 arg3"
if [[ $# < 1 ]]
then
     print -u2 $USAGE
     exit
fi
```

When a shell program takes arguments, you should provide a simple help message if the user forgets them. Change the words "arg1, arg2, arg3" to something that is meaningful in your application.

# TIP 417 — Providing a Menu of Alternatives

Within **ksh**, you can provide a user with a menu of choices, and allow him or her to select one of them. There are three components to menu selection in **ksh**. The tertiary prompt string (PS3) contains the value of the string used to prompt the user to make a selection. The **select** command displays a series of options, each preceded by a number, and the whole list followed by the value of PS3. The REPLY variable contains the value of the selection made by the user. If REPLY is empty, then **select** displays the menu alternatives again; **select** will then execute a compound command.

The following script is called **author**. If it is invoked with a file or set of files, it edits them using **vi**. When it is invoked with no arguments, it offers the user a preselected list of files to edit. Notice that the file being edited doesn't have the same name as that in the menu. You can provide simple choices to the user and translate them into something else in the **select** command.

```
# author - edits a file
# If no file is specified, author prompts with a menu
# of preselected files
# USAGE: author [filename]

if [[ $# < 1 ]]
then
PS3="Which Chapter would you like to edit?"
select menu in chap1 chap2 chap3 chap4
do
     case $menu in
          chap1)
          vi uno
          break
```

```
        ;;
        chap2)
        vi dos
        ;;
        chap3)
        vi tres
        ;;
        chap4)
        vi quat
        ;;
        *)
        print -u2 "wrong choice - get help"
        break;;
    esac
done
print "GOODBYE"
else
vi $*
fi
```

The **csh** does not have a select operator, so if you want to provide menus to a user, you need to construct them from other shell programming concepts. The following example provides a template for a **csh** menu.

```
#   csh version of author - edits a file
#   If no file is specified, author prompts with a menu
#   of preselected files
#   USAGE: author [filename]

if [[ $# < 1 ]]
then
  while (1)
    echo "1)chap1"
    echo "2)chap2"
    echo "3)chap3"
    echo "4)chap4"
    echo -n  "Which Chapter would you like to edit?  "
    set a = $<
    switch ($a)
    case 1*:
        vi uno
        breaksw
```

```
    case 2*:
        vi duo
        breaksw

    case 3*:
        vi tres
        breaksw

    case 4*:
        vi quat
        breaksw



        default:
        echo  "wrong choice - get help"
        exit 1
    endsw

print "GOODBYE"
   end
else
vi $*
endif
```

# Setting Shell Program Options

## Setting Options with getopts

Use the built-in command **getopts** to read options into a shell program. **getopts** checks the argument list for options; if options aren't provided, the positional parameters are used instead. The advantage to using **getopts** is that the command provides a simple way to use standard UNIX command options syntax in your shell programs. An option begins with a + (plus) or a – (minus); two minuses, —, indicate the end of the options. Each time **getopts** is invoked, it places the next option letter in a variable with that name.

The variable OPTIND contains the number of the next argument to be processed.

```
#getopt1 example

while getopts xyz args
do
  case $args in
      x)   xflag=1;;
      y)   yflag=1;;
      z)   zflag=1;;
  esac
done


print "xflag = $xflag; yflag = $yflag; zflag = $zflag"
```

If we run this program example, it prints the values of the variables that were set based on the command line. It uses UNIX syntax for the options, so they can be grouped or left separate, just as in standard commands.

```
$ getopt1 -xyz
xflag = 1; yflag = 1; zflag = 1

$ getopt1 -x -y -z
xflag = 1; yflag = 1; zflag = 1
```

If an option isn't used on the command line, it is left unset:

```
$ getopt1 -x
xflag = 1; yflag =; zflag =
```

# Turning Options On and Off

**TIP**
**419**

By convention, using – (a minus sign) before an option means turn it on; using + (a plus sign) means turn it off. (It's exactly the opposite of the way common sense would dictate, but originally options were off by default and only turned on, and the sign picked to do this was –. To keep consistent with the old usage, + and – are now counterintuitive.) **getopts** prepends + to the option name if a + is in the command line.

```
#getopt2 example

while getopts xyz args
do
  case $args in
      x)   xflag=ON;;
      +x)  xflag=OFF;;
      y)   yflag=ON;;
      +y)  yflag=OFF;;
      z)   zflag=OFF;;
      +z)  zflag=OFF;;
  esac
done


print "xflag = $xflag; yflag = $yflag; zflag = $zflag"
```

Running this example gives us this sample output:

```
$ getopt2 +x -y +z
xflag = OFF; yflag = ON; zflag = OFF
```

# Handling Errors with getopts

**TIP 420**

The examples provided in earlier tips will read valid option values and set variables based on those options. However, neither of these examples handles errors. How can you deal with the case of a user entering the wrong option?

In **getopts**, if you place a :(colon) before the option list, then **getopts** sets the value of arg to ? if the user specifies something other than x, y, or z; and it sets the value of OPTARG to the name of the undefined option. For example:

```
#getopt3 example

while getopts :xyz args
do
  case $args in
      x)   xflag=1;;
      y)   yflag=1;;
```

```
        z)  zflag=1;;
        \?) print "$OPTARG is not a valid option";;
  esac
done


print "xflag = $xflag; yflag = $yflag; zflag = $zflag"
```

Notice that the ? in the **case** statement has to be preceded by a \ (backslash) in order to prevent the shell from interpreting it as a wildcard. If you now run the example with an invalid option, you get

```
$ getopt3 -ax
a is not a valid option
xflag = 1
```

# Setting Command Line Arguments

TIP
421

The examples of **getopts** in Tips 418-420 have shown how to set variables on or off by setting command line options. Often, you'd like to specify the value of some variable on the command line. To tell **getopts** that the option requires an argument, place a : (colon) after the option name. This capability also allows you to provide error messages to the user if he or she misuses the options. For example,

```
#getopt4 example

while getopts :x:yz args
do
  case $args in
      x)  xflag=$OPTARG;;
      y)  yflag=1;;
      z)  zflag=1;;
      :)  print "You forget to specify $OPTARG"
          exit 1;;
      \?) print "$OPTARG is not a valid option";;
  esac
done


print "xflag = $xflag; yflag = $yflag; zflag = $zflag"
```

This example will set xflag to the value of the argument to the *x* option, if it is provided, but remind the user if it is not. It will also provide an error message if an invalid option flag is used.

```
$ getopt4 -x 400 -yz
xflag = 400; yflag = 1; zflag = 1

$getopt4 -xyz
You forget to specify x
```

# Avoid Confusing the Two Uses of : (Colon) when Using getopts

Although it is a powerful shell built-in, **getopts** is used less often than it should be. People avoid it in part because of two sources of confusion that make it hard to use. The first, the reversal of the intuitive meaning of + and - to mean turn off and turn on, has been discussed in Tip 419. The second source of confusion comes from the multiple meanings of the :(colon) used in **getopts**. You can place colons anywhere in the list of options, and, unfortunately, the meaning of the colon changes depending on where in the list it occurs.

If the colon precedes the list of options, it means set the value of arg to ? if there is an unexpected option on the command line.

```
getopts :xyz arg
```

If the colon follows an option, it means that **getopts** should expect an argument right after the option.

```
getopts xyz:
```

These uses can be combined in cases where both meanings are appropriate. In the following example, each of the options requires an argument and sets arg to ? if an invalid option is used.

```
getopts :x:y:z:
```

# Testing Shell Variables

Is there a way to test a shell variable to tell if it's an integer or a string?

All shell variables are strings. What we can test is whether the string qualifies as an integer or not.

In **sh** and **ksh**:

```
case $variable in
[!0-9+-]*|?*[!0-9]*) echo not an integer ;;
# If the first character is neither a sign nor a digit, or if
# any character after the first isn't a digit, it is not an integer.
"") echo null string ;;
*) echo integer ;;
esac
```

In **ksh**:

```
typeset -i holder
if (holder=$variable)
then echo integer
else echo not an integer
fi
```

# Checking Shell Variables

Is there a way to define an environment variable only if one doesn't exist? Suppose you want to do something like the following:

```
if ($VARIABLE doesn't exist) then set VARIABLE = initialvalue
```

Just checking to see if VARIABLE has a value doesn't work, since if VARIABLE doesn't exist, the shell script will terminate with an error. What you need to do is take advantage of the shell's ability to do parameter expansion. The following expression

```
${parameter:-string2}
```

uses the value of the parameter as it is set; otherwise it is set to string2. The expression

```
${parameter:+string2}
```

is a way of using an alternate value for a parameter. In this case, if the value of the parameter is unset, or null, it is set to null. If the parameter is set, that parameter is reset to string2.

The expression

```
${parameter:?string2}
```

provides a way to check for and display unset shell parameters. In this example, if the parameter is unset, then string2 is displayed in the standard error.

# A dir Tree Program

Suppose you are looking for a program that will traverse the directory tree of a system and put this information into some sort of neat form.

This appeared in *UnixWorld* a couple of years ago:

```
#!/bin/sh
# @(#) dtree - prints a directory tree

dir=${1:-.}
(cd $dir ; pwd)
find $dir -type d -print | sort -f |
sed -e "s,^$1,," -e "/^$/d" -e \
"s,[^/]*/\([^/]*\)$,\`—-\1," -e "s,[^/]*/, |      ,g"
```

Output from the **dir** script looks something like this:

```
/mach5/rrr

`
`-----.Data
`-----.saved
  |        `-----rje
  |        `-----examples
`-----1001
  |        `-----12-93doc
`-----BCS
  |        `-----harvard
```

```
    |       `-----travel
`-----bin
`-----dept
`-----funding
    |       `-----1992
    |       `-----1993
    |       `-----1994
`-----group
`-----image
    |       `-----data
`-----letters
`-----lib
    |       `-----phonevouch
    |       `-----wwb
`-----mail
`-----speech
    |       `-----data
`-----supr
    |       `-----92.grp
    |       `-----93.grp
    |       `-----94.grp
    |       `-----address
    |       `-----rrr
`-----tech
```

Another alternative is **utree**, a utility from Peter Klingebiel available by anonymous ftp from *ftp.uni-paderborn.de* in */unix/tools* as *utree3.04-um.tar.Z.*

## Debugging Shell Scripts

## Debugging a Shell Script

How do you debug shell scripts? Is there a UNIX script debugger to solve the problem without editing the script? Or even an automated editor that inserts **print** statements?

Unfortunately, debugging shell scripts isn't easy, and there are few tools that help do it. The first thing to do is run the script with the **v** and **n** options to the shell. The **v** (*verbose*) option displays each line of the script as it's read by the shell, and the **n** (*noexec*) option has the shell read the line and check for syntax errors without executing the command. An advantage to doing this over just running the script is that the shell will check the syntax of legs of an interactive program that might not be exercised ordinarily.

```
$ sh -vn <script> or  % csh -vn <script>
```

This should reassure you that you've made no silly syntax errors. If you do get an indication of an error, keep in mind that the notification can refer to something several lines away from the actual error. If the error is unmatched parentheses, quotes, or **if-fi**, you'll have to search for where the missing token goes.

If the script is syntactically correct, but still doesn't run correctly, you can run it in the *trace* mode as

```
$ sh -x <script> or % csh -x <script>
```

This displays the statements as they are executed and the values of the intermediate expressions and variables before each is executed. If this produces too much information, try the following in **sh** or **ksh**:

```
set -x          #turn on command echoing

lines of code under question

set +x          # to turn off command echoing.
```

The equivalent under **csh** is this:

```
set echo        #turn on command echoing

lines of code under question

unset echo      # to turn off command echoing.
```

# TIP 427

# Using print Statements in Debugging

A final resort if you can't find an error in a shell script is to insert a plethora of **print** statements. These can vary from statements that print the values of variables at various points in the program (for example, print "$x $y $z $2 $3 $#"), to messages that tell you what parts of the script have been executed (for example, "Go to the second **if** statement with $x $y $z $2 $3 $#"). This is the usual, awkward way to try to figure out what's wrong with it, and it eventually works.

In addition to printing the values of variables that you use in your script, remember that you can also print values of variables set by the shell. For example, the variable _ (underscore) contains the last argument of the previous command. You can use **print $_** to see how far your script has gotten.

The shell variable ERRNO contains the value of the error number of the most recently failed system call. If you use

```
print $ERRNO
```

at the point where your script breaks, you'll see the error number from the failed system call. These error numbers are system-dependent, so you need to look them up in your manual to see what problem this error number corresponds to.

In similar fashion, you can print the values OPTARG and OPTIND to see whether **getopts** is working the way that you expect.

# Finding a Shell Debugger

**TIP 428**

Although there is no debugger for shell programs available as a part of UNIX, relevant tools are available. For example, the "Answers to UNIX " column by Ray Swartz in the January 1993 issue of *UNIX World* provides a shell debug program **shdbg**, which lets you interactively execute shell programs line by line.

If you are using the perl language, there is a debugger available for it as well.

# ksh Debugging

**TIP 429**

The Korn shell provides an additional feature that makes finding errors in **ksh** a little easier. The fourth prompt string variable, called PS4, is used when debugging these scripts. When you debug a script (by using **set -x** or **ksh -x**), the shell puts the value of PS4 before each command being executed.

The default value for PS4 is + (the plus sign), so normally you'd see each line of your script preceded by a + as it executes.

You can change the value of PS4 to any variable that might be useful in debugging. For example, adding the lines

```
set -x
PS4='[$LINENO]+ '
```

will print the line number of each command as it is executed. If you have a long script, this helps identify where a problem is located.

# Making Shell Programs Run Efficiently

## TIP 430

## Avoid PATH Searches

Most users' PATH variables include six or eight directories, each containing dozens of files. The sample *.profile* that we included in Chapter 2 contains several. When you issue a command in a script, these directories are searched to find the command and load it. Eliminating this search will make scripts run faster. Specify common commands by giving the whole pathname, rather than just the basename. You can enforce some discipline on yourself by setting the PATH variable in a script to eliminate searches.

```
PATH=""
```

will force you to define full paths for all your commands. Since this only affects the environment of the shell script, your basic command environment is unaffected.

You could also define the full pathname of a program as a shell variable at the beginning of the script, and then substitute the variable for the name of the command that you are executing.

```
troff=/usr/bin/troff
tbl=/usr/bin/tbl
eqn=/usr/bin/eqn
```

```
$eqn $* | $tbl | $troff -mm | lp
```

# Use Shell Built-Ins

**TIP 431**

You can speed up the execution of your shell programs if you use shell built-ins wherever possible in place of UNIX system commands. For example, the following short script uses the output of the **ls** command to set up a list of files, then executes a command on each.

```
for i in `ls`
do
command list $i
done
```

Using the built-in shell expansion of * eliminates the need to spawn a new shell to run **ls**, and makes the script more efficient, as shown here:

```
for i in *
do
command list $i
done
```

# Have Commands Open Their Own Files

**TIP 432**

A common inefficiency in users' shell scripts is the use of the **/usr/bin/cat** command to provide input to other commands. For example, one of the scripts in Tip 413 was originally written with the following command sequence:

```
cat $* | tbl | nroff -cm#\   # etc.
```

This will work, of course, but it's very inefficient. The shell has to search for the location of **cat** (specifying **/usr/bin/cat** would have been better), even though the command is unneeded. The following does the same thing faster:

```
tbl $* | nroff -cm#\   # etc
```

# TIP 433
# How to Organize Command Sequences

When you arrange a series of UNIX commands in a pipe line, pay attention to the order in which they occur. Put first in the pipe line commands that decrease the amount of input the most. If you have a large phone book and wish to create an alphabetical list of the people who are at one location, the following command will work:

```
$ sort phonebook | grep Ithaca > Ith_file
```

However, this is very inefficient. Why sort the whole phone book when the search will throw most of it away? The following minor change improves it significantly:

```
$ grep Ithaca phonebook | sort > Ith_file
```

# TIP 434
# Use the Right Search Tool

UNIX provides three system commands to do searching. Although these commands have similar functions and are sometimes thought of as equivalent by users, they have some important differences. Picking the right one for your application will make your search commands and scripts more efficient. **egrep** searches for full regular expressions of the type defined by **ed(1)**. **grep** searches for limited regular expressions, and therefore is faster than **egrep**. **fgrep** can't handle regular expressions at all, but only searches for strings.

It's often thought that **fgrep** stands for *f*ast **grep**, and that it's faster than either **grep** or **egrep** because it only searches for strings, not regular expressions. But this is not the case! **fgrep** is actually the slowest of the three. Use **fgrep** when there is a specific advantage to doing a string search. For example, it's easier to use **fgrep** to search a file for characters (like *, ?, ^, $, .,) that have special meaning in regular expressions.

# Subshell Startup

With **ksh**, when you execute a script with an explicit call, as in:

```
$ ksh -x script
```

the file referred to by the ENV variable (that is, *.kshrc*) is processed. If **ksh** executes a script without a separate ksh call, the ENV is not read, but exported aliases, arrays, and functions, and the history list are inherited by the subshell running the script. This increases the speed with which shell scripts run compared with **csh**. When **csh** starts a subshell, the ENV variable (*.cshrc*) is always executed. If you use **csh**, you can force it to start a subshell without executing either the *.cshrc* or the *.login* (if it is a login shell) files by specifying the **-f** (*fast* start) option.

```
$ csh -f script
```

Of course, this won't work if your script uses any aliases defined in the *.cshrc* file.

# A Schedule Notifier That Puts It All Together

Here is a long, useful shell script that uses many of the concepts that have been discussed in previous tips. The **schedule** command prompts the user to list his or her entire whereabouts for the week, and mails off that information to $SUP. The error checking is rather extensive here and covers many possible problems. This script was originally written by Hal Zenner.

```
############################################
## schedule- Prompts the user for the week's
## activities and sends the information to
## an interested party, designated "sup".
############################################

DATE=`date '+%m/%d/%y, %r'`
ED=${ED:=/usr/bin/vi}
SUP=sup
SUPLOG=machname!sup
```

```
BAILOUT="Schedule *NOT* sent to $SUP"

trap 'if [ -f tmp$$ ]
        then
          if [ -f $HOME/.sched ]
            then
              echo "$HOME/.sched already exists!  Do you"
              echo "wish to overwrite (save this schedule) ? (y/n) >\c"
              read overpermit
                if [ \( $overpermit = 'y' -o $overpermit = 'yes' \) ]
                  then
                  cat tmp$$|sed -e "/^          $/d" > $HOME/.sched
                  echo "schedule saved in $HOME/.sched"
                  /bin/rm tmp$$
                  exit
                else
                  echo "schedule not saved"
                  /bin/rm tmp$$
                  exit
                fi
          else
              cat tmp$$|sed -e "/^          $/d" > $HOME/.schedRRR
              echo "schedule saved in $HOME/.schedRRR"
              /bin/rm tmp$$
              exit
          fi
      fi
      echo $BAILOUT
      exit 1' 1 2 3 15
echo "
                        SCHEDULE PROGRAM:

Enter CR if you will be in the office;

Enter LOCATION (e.g., VAC, Home, etc.) if you will not be in.\n
If you enter a location, you will be prompted for a telephone number.
    If you don't know a number, enter a CR.\n\n"
while true
  do
    while [ -z "$startweek" ]
      do
        cal
```

```
        echo "For week starting (enter date or q to quit) >\c";read
              startweek
      if [ "$startweek" = 'q' ]
        then
          echo $BAILOUT
          exit 1
      fi
    done
  cat > tmp$$ <<!
Schedule for $LOGNAME
Schedule completed $DATE
For week starting $startweek

!
  for day in Mon Tues Wed Thur Fri
    do
      for time in A.M. P.M.
        do
          echo "$day\t$time\t> \c";read x
          if [ -n "$x" ]
            then
              echo "\ttelephone no > \c";read tele
            else
              x="In Office"
              tele=""
          fi
          echo "$day\t$time\t$x\n\t\t$tele\n--------">>tmp$$
        done
    done
    echo "\nPlease check your schedule --"
    cat tmp$$|sed -e "/^                    $/d"
    while true
      do
        echo "\nIs it correct? (y/n) >\c";read correct
        if [ $correct = y ]
        then
          echo "Do you wish to send the schedule to $SUP? (y/n)
                >\c";read send
            if [ $send = 'y' ]
              then
                cat tmp$$|sed -e "/^                    $/d"|mail $SUPLOG
                echo bye
```

```
                            /bin/rm tmp$$
                            exit
                        else
                          if [ -f $HOME/.sched ]
                            then
                              echo "$HOME/.sched already exists!  Do you"
                              echo "wish to overwrite (save this schedule)
                                    ? (y/n) >\c"
                              read overpermit
                      if [ \( $overpermit = 'y' -o $overpermit = 'yes' \) ]
                      then
                          cat tmp$$|sed -e "/^        $/d" > $HOME/.sched
                                  echo "schedule saved in $HOME/.sched"
                                  /bin/rm tmp$$
                                  exit
                      else
                        echo "schedule not saved"
                        /bin/rm tmp$$
                        exit
                      fi
                        else
                          cat tmp$$|sed -e "/^        $/d" > $HOME/.sched
                          echo "schedule saved in $HOME/.sched"
                          /bin/rm tmp$$
                          exit
                        fi
                  fi
                else
                  $ED tmp$$
          fi
      done
done
```

# Chapter 8

# UNIX Tools

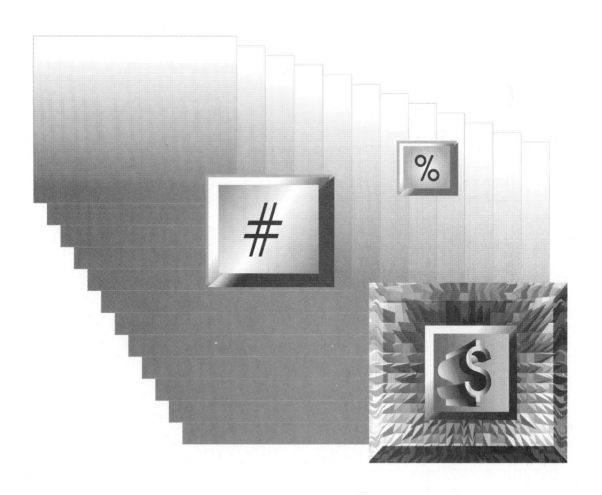

# Cutting and Pasting Files

## Cutting Fields from a File

**TIP 437**

There are times when you only need to use some of the information in a file. An example would be a file where each record consists of a name, a room address, a telephone number with area code, and a title, and you only want the name field, or the area code of the phone number. The **cut** command allows you to do this. With the **cut** command, you can select either entire fields or columns of data.

A *field* is a grouping of data separated by some delimiter. While the default delimiter is a blank space, you can also specify the delimiter based on some other character, such as a tab, a comma, or a semicolon. To cut fields, specify the **-f** option with the number(s) of the field(s) you want. Let's say you have the following file of fellow workers called *coworkers* where each field is separated by a blank space:

```
adams,john 1A222 908-555-1876 manager
davis,mary 1B315 908-555-1395 manager
jones,alfred 2N643 201-555-9831 programmer
nelson,bob 5K185 908-555-3194 technician
smith,ann 3D485 201-555-8406 analyst
young,neil 4J164 908-555-6548 operator
```

and you want only the names to be extracted. Since the field containing the names is the first field, the following command will produce the desired result:

```
$ cut -f1 coworkers
adams,john
davis,mary
jones,alfred
nelson,bob
smith,ann
young,neil
```

If you want to extract the names and put them into the file *workernames,* you can do this with

```
$ cut -f1 coworkers > workernames
```

# Cutting Multiple Fields from a File

You can cut multiple fields from a file by specifying the fields or a range of fields. The following example extracts the name (field 1) and the title (field 4) from the *coworkers* file:

```
$ cut -f1,4 coworkers
adams,john manager
davis,mary manager
jones,alfred programmer
nelson,bob technician
smith,ann analyst
young,neil operator
```

# Cutting Columns of Data from a File

Suppose you had the same *coworkers* file, but each field was a fixed length, meaning the fields all started in the same column for each record. The file might look like this:

```
adams,john      1A222    908-555-1876    manager
davis,mary      1B315    908-555-1395    manager
jones,alfred    2N643    201-555-9831    programmer
nelson,bob      5K185    908-555-3194    technician
smith,ann       3D485    201-555-8406    analyst
young,neil      4J164    908-555-6548    operator
```

If you want to extract the name and phone number, you can use **cut** with the -c option. The -c option tells **cut** the starting position of each column you want and the length in characters. Since the name starts in column 1 and is 14 characters, and the phone number starts in column 25 and is 12 characters, the command and its results would be

```
$ cut -c1-14,25-36
adams,john     908-555-1876
davis,mary     908-555-1395
jones,alfred   201-555-9831
nelson,bob     908-555-3194
```

```
smith,ann        201-555-8406
young,neil       908-555-6548
```

# TIP 440 — Using cut As Part of a Pipe Sequence

The **cut** command is also useful when you want to use only part of the output of another command. Suppose you have a structured file called *recipes* in which you keep a list of all your favorite dishes. You have over 40 beef recipes, all starting with the word "beef", followed by a 14-character field denoting the type of beef dish. You could build a new file called *dishtypes* using a combination of **grep** and **cut** with this sequence:

```
$ grep beef recipes | cut -c9-22 > dishtypes
```

This would contain

```
$ cat dishtypes
au legumes
bouillon
burgundy
cajun style
charcuterie
endicott
...
```

# TIP 441 — Pasting Information Together in a File

You may need to combine information from separate files into a single file. You can do this with the **paste** command. For example, suppose you have a file called *military* that contains the names used in military language to represent letters of the alphabet, and a second file called *radio* with similar representations in amateur radio language. To merge them into a file called *lingos* and see how they compare, do the following:

```
$ paste military radio > lingos
$ cat lingos
```

```
alpha      able
bravo      baker
charlie    charlie
delta      dog
....       ....
```

Using **paste**, you were able to take the one-column *radio* file and the one-column *military* file and make a two-column *lingos* file.

You can specify field delimiters in **paste**. This is especially useful if you are creating a file in which you want to eliminate "white space." The next tip shows you how this can be done.

# Using paste with Standard Input

**TIP 442**

You can build files dynamically using a combination of **paste** and the standard input, denoted as – (minus sign) on a command line. Using our previous file *coworkers* to build a list of holiday gift suggestions called *giftlist*, the command

```
$ paste coworkers  -  > giftlist
```

will read a line from the file *coworkers* and wait for you to key in a response. You would type in your suggestion and hit the carriage return, which will display the next name and wait for your next response. You do this until you reach the end of the file. A sample *giftlist* output file might be

```
$ cat giftlist
adams,john   desk set
davis,mary   calendar
jones,alfred  footrest
nelson,bob   ashtray
smith,ann   paperweight
young,neil   stapler
```

# Using paste to Get Multicolumn Output

**TIP 443**

You can use the **paste** command to take the output of a command and arrange it in multicolumn format. For example, you can get four-column output from the **ls** command, using

```
$ ls | paste - - - -
```

# Using cut and paste to Reorganize File Information

You can use the **cut** and **paste** commands together to extract information from one or more files, and then merge this data with existing data in another file. Suppose you have a file called *states* that contains the names of the fifty states, their capitals, and the zip codes of the capitals that looks like this (note that the fields are delimited by semicolons):

```
$ cat states
Alabama;Montgomery;36193
Alaska;Juneau;99803
Arizona;Phoenix;85009
Arkansas;Little Rock;72207
(other 46 entries)
```

You also have a file called *abbrevs* containing the two-letter abbreviations for the states:

```
$ cat abbrevs
AL
AK
AZ
AR
(other 46 entries)
```

You could compose a file called *maillist* containing the capital as the first field, the state abbreviation as the second field, and the zip code as the third field of each record by performing the following sequence:

```
$ cut -d; -f2 states > temp
$ cut -d; -f3 states > temp2
$ paste temp abbrevs temp2 > maillist
```

The contents of the file *maillist* would then be

```
$ cat maillist
Montgomery AL 36193
Juneau AK 99803
```

```
Phoenix AZ 85009
Little Rock AR 72007
(other 46 entries)
```

This could be a useful file for a shell program that built automatic mailing labels.

# Doing Character Translations

## Using the tr Command to Translate Characters

**TIP 445**

The **tr** (*t*ranslate) command is used to translate characters in standard input to other specified characters in standard output. For example, you can translate every occurrence of the letter "J" to "H" in the file *junk,* putting the result in *newjunk,* using

```
$ tr J H < junk > newjunk
```

You can change all the lowercase letters in the file *note* to uppercase letters, putting the result in *NOTE,* using the command

```
$ tr "[a-z]" "[A-Z]" < note > NOTE
```

Here you need to use square brackets to specify ranges of characters; you need quotation marks to prevent the shell from interpreting the brackets. The **tr** command maps each letter of the first range of characters to the corresponding letter in the second range of letters.

Another common use of **tr** is to change the field separator in a file of data. For example, suppose lines of the file *phonelist* contain the name of a person, followed by a colon, then his or her office number, then a colon, then his or her telephone number. The command

```
$ tr : 'CTRL-I' < phonelist
```

will send to standard output the file with the colon field separator replaced by the tab character.

# Removing Multiple Consecutive Occurrences of a Character

You can use the **tr** command with the **-s** (for *s* queeze) option to remove multiple occurrences of a character in a file. For example, to change each occurrence of "QQ" and all longer multiple occurrences of "Q" in the file *names* to "Q", putting the result in *names.1*, you can use

```
$ tr -s Q < names > names.1
```

Similarly, you can change all occurrences of multiple blank spaces to a single space, using

```
$ tr -s " " < names > names.1
```

# Changing End-of-Line Characters for Macintosh Text Files

The lines of text files in the Macintosh operating system end with a carriage return. Transferring such files to a UNIX system can be done in many different ways. However, once the file is on a UNIX system, working with it is really unpleasant unless the carriage returns used to mark end of lines are changed to the newline character expected by UNIX. You can use the **tr** command to make this end-of-line character translation. Since the octal codes for carriage return and newline are \015 and \012, respectively, use the following command to make the necessary translation:

```
$ tr '\015' '\012' < macfile > unixfile
```

# Encrypting Characters with a Substitution Cipher

You can use the **tr** command to implement a substitution cipher where each letter is replaced by a different letter of the alphabet. For example, you could encipher the file *message* containing all uppercase letters, using the command

```
$ tr '[A-Z]' KTADBJRVCZXQWUFENSYIOLPHGM < message
```

The mapping of plaintext letters to ciphertext letters in this example is given by the order of the 26 letters of the alphabet. For example, each "A" is translated to a "K", each "F" is translated to a "J", and each "X" is translated to an "H".

A commonly used substitution cipher is the famous rot13 cipher used to encipher netnews articles by shifting letters 13 positions. For example, to encipher the file *message* with rot13, you can use

```
$ tr "[a-m][n-z][A-M][N-Z]" "[n-z][a-m][N-Z][A-M]" < message
```

# Deleting Characters with tr

You can use the **-d** option of **tr** to delete specified characters. This option is normally used to delete nonprinting characters from a file. For example, to delete all digits from the file *salaries*, you could use

```
$ tr -d "[0-9]" < salaries
```

You can combine the **-c** (*c*omplement) option and the **-d** (*d*elete) options to delete all characters other than those listed. For example,

```
$ tr -cd "[0-9]" < data
```

will delete all characters in the file *data* except digits. This means that all letters, punctuation marks, spaces, carriage returns, other nonprinting characters, and so on, are deleted from the file.

# Translating All Characters in a Range to the Same Character

You can translate all the characters in a range to the same character by using an * (asterisk) after the character you want to use to replace all characters. For example, to replace all uppercase letters with a question mark, you can use

```
$ tr '[A-Z]' '[*?]' < file
```

## Translating All Numbers in a File to a Single Number Sign

Suppose you want to remove every number in a file, replacing each with a single number sign (#). Let's say you have a list of people in the file *customers* with their PINs and you want to create a list of the people with #'s replacing the PINs. You could use the command

```
$ tr -s '[0-9]' '[#*]'  < customers
```

## Getting a List of All the Words in a File

You can get a list of all the words in a file, with a count of how many times they appear, by first using the **tr** command with the -s option to translate every space (of one or more blanks) to a newline, then sorting the output into alphabetical order, and finally removing rendundant lines. For example, to get a list of all the words in the file *chapter1* listing how many times each word appears, you can use

```
$ tr -s '<SPACE>' '\012' < chapter1 | sort | uniq -c
```

## Renaming Files from Uppercase to Lowercase Letters

You just moved a large number of files from a different machine into your UNIX system. All the filenames are in uppercase. How can you rename them all into lowercase without having to manually enter every filename?

The following script uses a **for** loop and the **tr** command to do this:

```
for i in $*
do
    lcfile=`echo $1 | tr "[A-Z]" "[a-z]"`
    cat {$i} | tr -d '\015' > ${lcfile}
    rm {$i}
done
```

Here's an alternate way to do the same thing, using **ksh**:

```
    typeset -l lcfile
    for i
    do lcfile=$i
        tr -d '\015' < $i > $lcfile
    done
```

This is actually more efficient than the first method because it saves spawning a process to run the **cat** command.

# Sorting Files

## Sorting a List of Names

**TIP 454**

If you have a file called *contacts* containing a list of unalphabetized names, one name per line with the last name given first, you can use the **sort** command to order the names alphabetically, as shown here.

```
$ sort contacts
```

This will send the list of alphabetized names to standard output.

If you have multiple files of this type—say, *contacts.dec*, *contacts.nov*, and *contacts.oct*—you can create a file *contacts* containing a merged list of names in alphabetical order by using

```
$ sort contacts.oct contacts.nov  contacts.dec > contacts
```

# Specifying the Output File

You do not have to use the right arrow (>) to specify where you want to put the output of the **sort** command. Instead, you can use the **-o** option to specify an output file for a **sort** command, as shown here.

```
$ sort -o people names
```

This example sorts the lines of the file *names*, where each line contains one name per line, putting the output in the file *people*.

You can replace the input file with the sorted output file using **-o**, followed by the name of the file you are sorting. For example, to replace the file *names* with the sorted version of the file, use the following command:

```
$ sort -o names names
```

# Sorting by Numbers

You can sort a file where each line starts with a number by using the **-n** (numeric) option of **sort**. For example, suppose you have a file *words*, where each line starts with a number, giving the number of times the word following it appears in this book. To put the lines in the file in order so that the least common words are listed first, use

```
$ sort -n words
```

To get the list in descending order of frequencies, use the **-r** (*reverse*) option together with the **-n** option:

```
$ sort -rn words
```

# Sorting on a Particular Field

Suppose you have a file *report* where each line contains two fields, a customer name
and the number of widgets they bought from you, where the two fields on each line are separated by
a tab. You want to produce a file listing these customers in descending order of how many widgets
they have bought from you. You can produce such a file by telling **sort** to skip to the second field to
do its sorting (and of course to sort in reverse numeric order). To do this, use

```
$ sort -rn +1 report
```

Similarly, if you have a file *addresses* where each line contains four fields—name, phone number, city,
and state—separated by tabs, and you want to sort by state in alphabetic order, use

```
$ sort +3 addresses
```

If the fields of your file are separated by some other character than tabs or spaces, you can tell **sort** to
use this other character as the field separator with the **-t** (*t*ab) option. For example, if the lines in the
file *addresses* had fields separated by the % (percentage mark), you would use

```
$ sort -t% +3 addresses
```

# Sorting on More Than One Field

Suppose you have a file *people* that contains a list of addresses, where each line contains
the first name of a person, a blank space, his or her last name, a tab, his or her telephone number, a
tab, and his or her e-mail address. For example, a line of this file looks like this:

```
Lola Montez   304-555-6666        lam@arts.uwv.edu
```

Let's say you want to sort this file using the last name first, then the first name, and then the e-mail
address. You would use

```
$ sort +1 -2 +0 -3 people
```

The options tell **sort** to first sort on the second field (last names), not to sort on the phone numbers, then to sort on first names, and then not to sort on e-mail addresses.

## TIP 459 — Eliminating Redundant Lines

Suppose you want to merge three different files, each listing people's contact information in the form described in the last tip. Some people may be listed more than once and you only want one entry per person. That is, you want to eliminate redundant lines to get only a single line for each person. You could do this in two different ways.

First, you could sort the file as was done in the previous tip and pipe the output to the **uniq** command, which eliminates redundant lines. The command line you use is

```
$ sort +1 -2 +0 -3  people1 people2 people3 | uniq > people
```

Suppose you end up with more than one entry for a particular person; for example, there may be entries in the file for a single person with different e-mail addresses. You want to eliminate all but one of these entries. You can use the -**u** (*u*nique) option of **sort** to do this.

```
sort +1 -2 +0 -3 -u people1 people2 people3 > people
```

## TIP 460 — Counting Occurrences of Lines

Suppose you want to count the number of people who live in each state in a file *members*, where these people are listed with the state given in the fifth field of each line. To do this, you could first use the **cut** command to select only the fifth field, then use the **sort** command, and finally the **uniq** command with the -**c** (*c*ount) option. The command line to use is

```
$ cut -f5 members | sort | uniq -c > statecount
```

# Doing Batch Editing with sed

## What Is sed?

The stream editor **sed** is a powerful tool you can use to filter text files, making global editing changes. **sed** applies each editing command to a line before it moves on to the next line of input. In this way, **sed** can easily make changes to very large files because the entire file doesn't have to be read into memory and processed. Thus, **sed** is a very quick and efficient tool for making a series of changes to one big file or many little files.

When you use **sed** to edit a file, you do not change the file. Instead, you transform the lines of the file, line by line, and send the transformed version of the file to standard output.

Also, unlike other editors such as **ed**, an editing command in **sed** is used on every line of the text. That is, you do not have to make a command a global command. For example, if you use the **sed** command

```
$ sed 's/computer/fish/' memo
```

you will change the first occurrence of the string "computer" to "fish" on every line of the file *memo*. To change *every* occurrence of "computer" to "fish", including subsequent occurrences on each line, you would use

```
$ sed 's/computer/fish/g' memo
```

Note that the editing commands in **sed** command lines are placed in single quotes. This is done because the editing command list is an argument to the **sed** command and it may contain special characters, spaces, newlines, and so on. (See Tip 462.)

## Put Quotes Around Arguments in the Command Line

If you are going to be using **sed** from the command line, it is customary, and most of the time necessary, to enclose the expressions in single quotes to avoid characters that have special meaning to the shell. For example,

```
$ sed 's/^/^I/g' report
```

will put a tab (^I or CTRL-I) at the beginning of each line in the file *report*. Without the quotes, the shell would try to interpret the "^" character.

# Selecting Lines in sed

**463**

A **sed** command may include an address that specifies which lines an operation should act on. You can specify addresses either by giving line numbers or by using patterns described using regular expressions. For example, you can delete the first 100 lines of the file *notes* by using

```
$ sed '1,100 d' notes
```

An example of using a regular expression to specify a pattern is shown here.

```
$ sed '/Project X/ d' notes
```

This deletes all lines containing the string "Project X".

# Adding Text Using sed

**464**

To add text in **sed**, you can use the sed **a** (*a*ppend) or the sed **i** (*i*nsert) command. For example, the sed **a** command

```
/AT&T Bell Laboratories/a\
101 Crawfords Corner Road\
Holmdel, New Jersey 07733
```

will add the two lines shown after each line containing the string "AT&T Bell Laboratories". Here the sed **a** command is followed by a backslash to escape the first end of line; a backslash follows the first line of text to be appended, indicating a newline. If you used the sed **i** command instead, the new lines of text would be inserted before the current line.

To run this sed **a** command on the lines of the file *memo*, you can put it in the command line, using

```
$ sed 'instruction' memo
```

where 'instruction' is the sed **a** command given earlier. You may prefer to put this command in a script file, say *sedscript*, and use the command line

```
$ sed -f sedscript memo
```

# Changing Lines Using sed

You can use the sed **c** (*c*hange) command to change lines in a file. For example, the **sed** instruction

```
1,50c\
\
SECRET INFORMATION DELETED\
\
```

will replace the top 50 lines of a file with a blank line, followed by "SECRET INFORMATION DELETED", followed by another blank line.

To use sed **c** to change the lines in the file *report*, you can use a command line of this form:

```
$ sed 'instruction' report
```

where the instruction is the sed **c** command. You may prefer to put this command in a script file, say *sedscript,* and use the command line

```
$ sed -f sedscript report
```

# Some Common sed Mistakes

Because **sed** processes information line by line, any time you ask **sed** to make substitutions, you must be careful of the order in which you proceed. For example, if you have a **sed** script which does the following substitutions,

```
s/first/second/
s/second/third/
```

what you might expect to happen—all the strings "first" would change to "second" and all the strings "second" to "third"—would not happen because the first thing that's done is all strings "first" are changed to "second" and then all strings "second" are changed to "third". Thus, what you wind up doing is changing both the strings "first" and "second" to "third". The proper **sed** commands here would be

```
s/second/third/
s/first/second/
```

Another example of a potential problem with **sed** is the following. Suppose you want to delete everything in the file *notes* from the first line to the first blank line. You might use the command

```
$ sed '1,/^$/d' filename
```

(Here you have used ^$ to represent a blank line since it is the start of line ^, followed immediately with the end of line $). However, if there were no blank lines in the file, there would be no output, because **sed** would have deleted all lines. Contrast this with a screen editor such as **vi**, where a similar command would have given an error because no blank line was found.

# Qualified Pattern Matching and Substitution in sed

**sed** allows you to qualify which lines you want to make changes on by specifying a pattern. In this way, you can make global changes to a file only on those lines which match some descriptive pattern. For example, to change all occurrences of the string "Massachusetts" to "MA" in the file *addresses* only on lines which also contain the string "Boston", you can use the following command:

```
$ sed '/Boston/s/MA/Massachusetts/g' addresses
```

**sed** also allows you to not substitute on lines which contain a pattern but to make the substitution on other lines. For example, to change all occurrences of "&" to "and" on lines which do not contain "&&", you could use the following **sed** command:

```
$ sed '/&&/!s/&/and/g' filename
```

In this way, you avoid changing the string "&&" to "andand".

# Making a Substitution on the nth Occurrence of a Pattern

**sed** also allows you to make a substitution on the *n*th occurrence of a pattern in a line. For example, given a file *customers*, where each line contains three fields separated by tabs, you can substitute a space for a tab at the second occurrence of TAB in a line by using the command

```
$ sed 's/CTRL-I/ /2' filename
```

# Extracting Wanted Lines Using the -n Option

Unless you specify otherwise, **sed** operates on every line in the file and returns modified (or unmodified) text to standard output. However, if you just want to return those lines that are changed by the **sed** program itself, you can use the **-n** option.

This is a desirable feature if you just want to work on portions of a file or extract portions of a file. For example,

```
$ sed -n '/pattern1/,/pattern2/p' filename
```

will print those lines which fall between pattern1 and pattern2 in *filename*.

```
$ sed -n '/pattern1/,/pattern2/!p' filename
```

will print those lines which do not fall between pattern1 and pattern2 in *filename*.

# Using Script Files with sed

Putting long editing scripts on the **sed** command line is very awkward. Instead, you can create an editing script that contains a list of **sed** commands in the order you want them executed and use the **-f** option to **sed**. For example, suppose you have put your **sed** commands in the file *script*:

```
$ cat script
s/Drive/Dr./g
s/Street/St./g
s/Avenue/Ave./g
s/Boulevard/Blvd./g
s/Route/Rte./g
```

To make the editing changes in these lines to the file *addresses* in the order listed, putting the result in *newaddresses,* use the command

```
$ sed -f script addresses > newaddresses
```

# Changing the Internal Delimiter Used by sed

The / (slash) character is normally used as the internal delimiter in **sed**. This is not a necessity. In potentially confusing circumstances, changing this delimiter to something else makes commands much more readable. For example, consider the lines

```
$ sed 's/\/home\/u3/\/User\/u2/'
$ sed 's:/home/u3:/User/u2:'
```

Here the first command line is hard to follow because of the slashes and backslashes, while the second line, which uses the colon as the delimiter, is much easier to understand.

# Using the "&" Character for the Last Pattern Matched

**TIP 472**

When doing substitutions, the current pattern in the pattern space can be retrieved using the "&" character. For example, suppose the file *phonelist* has the following lines:

```
312-931-1523
708-332-4343
708-451-8812
312-478-1234
```

You can put parentheses around the area code of each phone number using the command

```
$ sed 's/^[0-9][0-9][0-9]/(&)/' phonelist
```

# Using sed with Speed and Efficiency

**TIP 473**

Because **sed** does things to a file one line at a time, you need a way to tell **sed** to stop processing altogether once a specified action has taken place. For example, if you want to print just the first ten lines of the file *employees,* you could use the command

```
$ sed -n '1,10p' employees
```

But if *employees* is a very big file, this command would not be very efficient, because even though **sed** would only print the first 10 lines, it still reads until the EOF. Instead, you want to do something like this:

```
$ sed 10q filename
```

Here is an example comparing the time used by **sed** to operate on a big file in these two ways:

```
$ wc -l bigfile
37224 bigfile
$ time sed -n '1,10p' bigfile > /dev/null
3.3 real       1.0 user       2.2 sys
```

```
$ time sed '10q' bigfile > /dev/null
0.2 real          0.0 user          0.2 sys
```

If you didn't redirect output to */dev/null*, after it prints the first 10 lines, you can observe **sed** noticeably hanging while it reads the other 37,214 lines!

For example, if you just wanted to print the 1000th line of the file *phonelist,* you could use

```
$ sed -n 1000p phonelist
```

But, again, **sed** still reads in contents of the file until the EOF is reached. Comparing this again:

```
$ time sed -n 1000p bigfile > /dev/null
1.8 real          1.2 user          0.5 sys
$ time sed "1000!d
> q" bigfile > /dev/null
0.1 real          0.0 user          0.0 sys
```

We see the latter option is much more efficient.

# Applying a Series of Edits to the Same Line

Sometimes it is difficult (or impossible) to describe a series of edits you would like to do on one line or a group of lines. For this reason, you can write **sed** scripts that do the series of edits, one after another, on those lines.

For example, if you want to strip out all the backspaces (^H), blank lines, and page separators from a man page, you could use the following **sed** script called *sed.man:*

```
s/^H//g
/^$/d
/Sun Release/d    # this is the page separator for Sun man pages
```

You could use this script in a pipeline in the following way:

```
$ man date | sed -f sed.man > date.man
```

The -f option tells **sed** to take its options from the filename specified next.

For example, if you just wanted your script to apply to a certain range of lines in the input file, you could enclose those commands in braces and specify which lines you wanted to operate on, as shown here.

```
/pattern1,/pattern2/ {
sed commands
    ...
    }
```

This will tell **sed** to apply the commands only on the lines between pattern1 and pattern2.

# Learning More About sed

**T IP 475**

**sed** is a surprisingly useful tool. To learn more about **sed**, you may want to consult the book *sed & awk: A Nutshell Handbook* by Dale Dougherty (Sebastopol, CA: O'Reilly and Associates, 1990). There is also a lot of useful material on **sed** in the book *UNIX Power Tools*, edited by Jerry Peek, Tim O'Reilly, and Mike Loukides (O'Reilly and Associates, 1993).

# Using awk

# What Is awk?

**T IP 476**

The **awk** program was first developed by *Aho, Weinberger,* and *Kernighan* in 1977 as a pattern-scanning language. Since then it has been expanded extensively. It has grown into a useful toolkit for modifying files, searching and transforming databases, generating reports, and for a tremendous variety of other tasks. **awk** is designed to work with structured files and text patterns. It is particularly useful for working with files containing information structured into fields, since it contains features for breaking input lines into fields and for comparing these fields to patterns that you specify.

Although you can do many things with a one-line **awk** command line, you will want to learn the **awk** programming language in order to develop longer and more complex awk programs. This programming language includes such features as control instructions, functions, built-in variables, and so on.

# TIP 477 — What Are nawk and gawk?

One of the problems has been that awk programs built using one version of **awk** don't work the same, or won't work at all, using later versions. To take care of this problem, UNIX System V Release 4 includes two versions of **awk: nawk** (for *new awk*), the version first introduced with UNIX System V Release 3.1; and **awk**, the older version, which is also called **oawk** (for *old awk*) on some systems. The intention in future releases of UNIX System V is to change things so that **awk** refers to the newer version, now called **nawk**.

The **nawk** program includes many enhancements over earlier versions of **awk**. These enhancements include many additional built-in variables, including FILENAME, RS (for *record separator*), ORS (for *output record separator*), and NR (for *number*). Also, there are many new built-in functions in **nawk**, including functions for indexing operations on input records and for discarding the current record and reading the next input record; letting you create your own user-defined functions; and writing to files instead of to the standard output.

The **gawk** program is a public domain version of **awk** that is part of the GNU system. It has some features not found in **awk** or **nawk**. (See Tip 489 on AWKPATH, for example.) Programs written for **nawk** will also run in **gawk**. You can get a copy of **gawk** via anonymous **ftp** from *prep.ai.mit.edu* in the directory */pub/gnu*. Be sure to obtain a copy of the large gawk tutorial when you get **gawk**. A copy of **gawk** is also included on the disk that you get when you buy the book *UNIX Power Tools*.

# TIP 478 — Getting Started with awk

Like any computer language, **awk** can be intimidating at first. However, its structure follows a simple design of pattern-action statements, and if you already know the C language, learning **awk** is a breeze. A pattern-action statement tells **awk** to test every line of input for a particular pattern and to perform the corresponding action whenever the pattern matches the input line.

The simplest awk program is one that does not look for any pattern in the input file at all, but instead takes a single action before looking at the input file. For example,

```
$ nawk 'BEGIN {print "hello world"}' anyfile
```

or similarly,

```
$ nawk 'END {print "this is the end"}' anyfile
```

The next simplest program looks at the input file and evaluates some of **awk**'s built-in variables, such as FILENAME or NR (the number of records). To test this, create a text file with several lines of text, separated by newlines, and call it *awktest*. Then type

```
$ nawk 'END {print FILENAME; print NR}' awktest
```

You should get as output the name of the file followed by the number of lines you typed in. If you want to see the pattern-matching features of **awk**, create a file that consists of a list of words or phrases, separated by newlines, and call it *awktest2*. Include in the list a particular string such as "12345". Then type

```
$ nawk '/12345/ {print $0}' awktest2
```

This will print each record that contains the string you specified. In **awk**, $0 stands for the entire record.

If you omit the name of an input file, **awk** will take its input from standard input. You can type a line at a time at the keyboard and your awk program will operate on it. This is especially useful for testing one-line programs while you are learning the syntax or trying to understand regular expressions.

# Making Sure awk Has a Source of Input

**TIP 479**

**awk** needs standard input in order to run! Before the main awk script is run, it needs a source of input to process. Thus, nothing will be output until a line of input is read in. The exception is the commands in the BEGIN section. These commands are processed before input is read in, but unless an EOF is received by **awk**, the program will just hang. For example, the awk program

```
$ awk '{print "Hello, World" }'
```

doesn't do anything because there is no source of input. The BEGIN directive does do processing before a line of input is read:

```
$ awk 'BEGIN {print "Hello, World" }'
```

But since no EOF is received by **awk**, it will hang there. So, you have to use something like

```
$ echo "" | awk '{print "Hello, World" }'
Hello, World
```

or the equally ugly:

```
$ awk 'BEGIN {print "Hello, World" }' < /dev/null
Hello, World
```

# Specifying and Matching Patterns in awk

# Using Regular Expressions to Specify Patterns in awk

You can specify patterns in **awk** in many different ways. The simplest kind of pattern matching in **awk** is searching for a particular string. To look for lines containing the string "slug", enclose this string in slashes as follows:

```
/slug/
```

Next, you can match patterns using regular expressions. Use the same regular expressions that are used by **egrep**. For example, to match all lines beginning with the string "Example", use

```
/^Example/
```

To match all lines ending with the word "newts", use

```
/newts$/
```

To match all lines containing one of more uppercase "Z"'s, use

```
/Z+/
```

To match any lines containing the string "memo" followed by a digit, use

```
/memo[0-9]/
```

# Using Comparison Patterns for Strings in awk

You can use string comparison patterns in **awk**. These are patterns where you compare two elements. These can be comparisons of numbers or strings.

You can test whether two strings match using the == operator. For example, you can test whether the third and fourth fields of a record match by using

```
$3==$4
```

You can use the ~ (tilde) to test whether one string contains another. For example, you can test whether the first field begins with "Qu" with

```
$1 ~ /^Qu/
```

Using the != operator, you can test whether strings are not the same. For example, you can match any line where the second field in not the string "Manager", by using

```
$2 != "Manager"
```

You can use the <, <=, >, and >= operators to compare two strings using the standard alphabetical order for ASCII characters. For example, suppose you have a file you use to keep your address book, with last names in the first field. You can match records with last names following "Thompson" in alphabetical order with

```
$1 > "Thompson"
```

# Using Range Patterns in awk

You can use range patterns in **awk** to match any line after a match of the first pattern and a match of the second pattern, including the starting and ending lines. For example, to match all the lines in a file for names between Yaakon and Yumax, where the lines begin with names of people in alphabetic order, use

```
/^Yaakon/,/^Yumax/
```

# Using Type Comparisons in awk

**awk** does automatic type comparisons. Since variables are not declared with a certain type (as they are in C), **awk** tries to figure out what type of comparison you want to do, based on the syntax of the expression. Thus, $1 > "character" is an expression that determines whether the character value of $1 is greater than "character". An expression like $1 > 5 will do an integer comparison.

For example, since **awk** supports string comparisons, you can do something like this:

```
$ awk '$1 > "D" {print $0}' filename
```

This will print out all lines whose first record begins with a letter "larger" (in ASCII sorting sequence) than "D".

# Matching a Pattern Over Two Lines

Matching a pattern over a range of lines is not easily done in **awk**. Therefore you need a processing control statement that will process the next line without doing anything else (like returning to the top of a loop or script when done). Use **getline** for this. You can read in the next line of input and do pattern matching (or any other operation) on that line.

For example, using the awk **getline** statement, you can construct a program based on the following template:

> */pattern1/* {
>     *do something*
>     ...
>     getline
>     if ( */pattern2/* )
>     *do something*
>     *else*
>     *do something else*
> }

Here, **getline** gets the next line from input. It does not transfer control back to the top of the script but resets $0 to the next line read in. Therefore, a new pattern2 can be tested for on the next line.

# A Warning with Pattern Matching: Lines Can Match More Than One Pattern

With **awk**, you can do a sequential pattern match on lines and apply actions to them. Thus, the next line is not read in until *all* the tests are done in the script. Unless you are careful, however, you might wind up doing more than what you intended.

Suppose you have the following code in the following template:

```
/pattern1/ { do something }
/pattern2/ { do something else }
```

If the current line matches both pattern1 and pattern2, then both "somethings" will be done—which might not be what you want. For example, consider the following awk script called *shellreport*, which determines the number of users who use **csh** and **tcsh** as their login shells on your machine:

```
$ cat shellreport
#!/bin/sh
awk '
```

```
BEGIN { FS=":"; print
        "===============================================" }

$NF ~ /tcsh/  {
     ++tcsh_count
}
$NF ~ /csh/  {
     ++csh_count
}
END { totalcount=tcsh_count+csh_count
     printf("%d entries scanned. %d total found (%.2f %).\n", NR,
totalcount,                   (totalcount / NR)*100)

}' /etc/passwd
```

However, there is a problem with this script. When you run it, you get the following:

```
$ shellreport
===============================================
94 entries scanned. 94 total found (100.00 %).
```

Now, you know for sure that 100% of the people don't use **csh** or **tcsh** for their login shell because you don't! So what's going on? The problem is that the string "csh" is contained in the string "tcsh". Thus, the **tcsh** users are getting counted twice! And it turns out (oddly enough) that this combination of **csh/tcsh** users is exactly 94 or 100% of the entries! You need to modify your script so that you do more exact pattern matching.

For example, if you use the full pathname, you are guaranteed a unique match. You can check this with the following commands:

```
$ grep '/bin/csh' /etc/passwd | wc -l
     70
$ grep '/bin/tcsh' /etc/passwd | wc -l
     12
```

Here you see that if the **tcsh** users were counted twice (12*2), you would get 70+24=94 users who used **tcsh/csh** as their login shell! In reality, 12 other people use something else besides **tcsh/csh**. Therefore, changing the pattern matching string to the full pathnames in the script above will work as expected.

# Matching One of Two Patterns in awk

**TIP 486**

You can use the alternation operator "|" to match lines containing either of two different patterns in **awk**. It allows either pattern1 or pattern2 to be sufficient for an action to occur. For example,

```
$ awk '$1 ~ /(pattern1|pattern2)/ {print $0}' filename
```

prints out all lines whose first field matches pattern1 or pattern2. This is like the **egrep** alternation (|) operator.

# You Want to Search for a Pattern in a Text File. Should You Use vi, awk, grep, or sed?

**TIP 487**

These commands have overlapping uses. The one that you use in a particular search depends on how you want to specify the pattern. Of these four commands, **awk** gives you the most general control over the pattern you specify. For example, it can be a string, a group of strings such as all those starting with a particular letter, or a number that fits into a range. Here are some typical **awk** patterns:

| Pattern | What it matches |
|---------|-----------------|
| /Chicago/ | Any occurrence of Chicago in the record. |
| /^Peoria/ | Peoria when it occurs at the beginning of a line. |
| /Chicago\|Peoria/ | Any occurrence of Chicago or Peoria. |
| $2 ~ /Hawaii/ | The second field in the record matches Hawaii. |
| $2 !~ /USA/ | The second field does not match USA. |
| $4 > "k" | The fourth field follows k in alphabetical order. |

Because **awk** accepts regular expressions, you have full control over the patterns that you specify.

# Tips on Running awk Programs

## How Do You Run an awk Program?

Many useful awk programs are just a few lines long. You can run these short programs directly by putting the program in the command line. For example, if you have a simple database of names, addresses, and phone numbers, you can print out a list of the first field in each record with the command

```
$ nawk '{print $1}' phones
```

This will display on the screen the first field in each record. If you wish to direct the output to another file, you can type

```
$ nawk "{print $1}" phones > namelist
```

If your awk program is longer than one line, it will be easier to save it as a text file and put the name of the file in the **awk** command line, preceded by -f. In the previous example, if you save the program as *printfirst*, then you can run it as

```
$ nawk -f printfirst phones > namelist
```

Note that the **-f** option used before the program name is not the same as the -F option used to specify a field separator. It is like the -f option in **sed**.

If you have a multiline program that you don't expect to use repeatedly, you can type it in directly. You get the prompt from the shell and the secondary prompt on each succeeding line. You type each pattern-action statement on its own line. Don't forget the closing apostrophe at the end of the program, followed by the input file and any output file if needed.

## Using the AWKPATH Environmental Variable in gawk

You can specify a directory search path for **gawk** to use when the file specified with the **-f** option is not in the current directory. The default value of AWKPATH is

```
.:/usr/lib/awk:/usr/local/lib/awk
```

With this value of AWKPATH, when a file is specified using the -f option, **gawk** searches the current directory, then the directory */usr/lib/awk,* and finally the directory */usr/local/lib/awk* to find this file. The obvious advantage of using AWKPATH is to avoid including the possibly lengthy absolute pathname of the file specified with -f in the command line.

# How Do You Initialize and Use Variables in awk?

You don't have to initialize variables. String variables are set to null by default and numbers are set to zero. Variable names can be any sequence of letters and digits, beginning with a letter. They can include the underline character. They must not duplicate any of the built-in variable names, such as NR, RLENGTH, or RSTART. Here is a short program that uses variables. Suppose you have an input file that contains numbers to be averaged—for example, a file of people and their hours worked for each day.

```
Mary   8.0   6.7   8.7   7.8   8.9   8.2
John   7.8   7.7   9.0   5.6   7.8
Jack   7.8   8.6   7.4   9.1
```

If you want to compute the average number of hours for each person, you have a small problem of different numbers in each list. Here is an awk program to take the average.

```
sum=0                          # for clarity
i=2                            # start at the second field
while (i<=NF) {                # loop in each record
sum += $i                      # add number to the sum
i ++                           # go the next field
          }                    # stop when i=NF
average=sum/(NF-1)             # compute the average
print "The average hours for " $1 " is " average}  # print the average
```

This program uses the user-defined variables *sum, i,* and *average,* as well as the built-in variable NF (number of fields in the record). There is no pattern statement because we want **awk** to take this action for every line of the input.

# Passing in Parameters on the Command Line in awk

To write awk scripts that take command line parameters or shell variables, some special arrangements have to be made to get **awk** to correctly interpret how the variable is to be evaluated. In some cases, **awk** will not behave properly.

The following shows a relatively simple method:

```
$ awk -f shellreport shell=bash /etc/passwd
```

This invokes the awk script *shellreport* for the shell which is set to **bash**. The script *shellreport* counts how many people use **bash** in */etc/passwd*; it is a modification of the script in Tip 485 on matching more than one pattern. However, there are drawbacks to this method.

First, pattern matching can't be done on *shell*. For example, suppose our script looked like this:

```
BEGIN { FS=":" }
$NF ~ /bash/ { print $0
++count }
END { print count " Entries found for " shell }
```

Then *shell* will be substituted in the END statement, but putting */shell/* in the pattern match won't work. So the line

```
$ awk -f shellreport shell=bash /etc/passwd
```

would not be correct.

Second, the BEGIN statement is unaffected by these variables as well. If we add a BEGIN statement,

```
BEGIN { FS=":"; print "Report for shell" shell }
$NF ~ /bash/ { print $0
++count }
END { print count " Entries found for " shell }
```

then the variable *shell* would not be interpreted in the output. The reason is that variables are not available to the script until after the first line of input is read.

Consider the following, more complex method, which uses imported shell variables:

```
#!/bin/sh
shell=$1       #set $1 as the shell variable to be used in awk
awk -F: '      #set field separator to a ':'
$NF ~ /'"$shell"'/ { ++count }
END { print count " entries found for shell '"$shell"' " #print results
}'
```

This program incorporates a shell script wrapper around the awk program and passes the shell variable to the awk script. The variable must be enclosed in '"$shell"' quotes. In this way, **awk** never sees the string '$shell' as a variable and the shell will expand its value for you. In this way, you can pass the shell as a command line argument.

In **nawk** and **gawk**, you can use

```
nawk 'BEGIN { FS=":" }
$NF ~ shell { ++count }
END { print count " Entries found for "shell }' shell=$1 $2
```

Note that **nawk** and **gawk** allow you to pass in these parameters directly from the shell.

Putting everything together we can now provide the following awk script called *shellreport*. You can use this script to determine how many users use each login shell, generating a report for each partition on your system. With simple modifications, you can make this script work for your machine's setup.

```
#!/bin/sh
# shellreport    Report what percentage of users use shell for each
#                partition and in general.  The /etc/passwd file is
#                used by default to get the information
#
# Usage: shellreport shell [filename]

shell=$1       #set $1 as the shell variable to be used in awk
datafile=$2    #set $2 to datafile to be used as input.


awk '
BEGIN { FS=":"; print "<<<Report for '"$shell"'>>>"
            print
        "==============================================" }

# Use '\/' to make sure pattern /shell is searched for. Csh and sh would
```

```
# otherwise be the same.
$NF ~ /\/'"$shell"'/  {
     if ( $6 ~ /u1/ ) ++u1count
     else if ( $6 ~ /u2/ ) ++u2count
     else if ( $6 ~ /u3/ ) ++u3count
     else ++othercount
}
END { totalcount=u1count+u2count+u3count+othercount
    u1percent=(u1count / NR)*100
    u2percent=(u2count / NR)*100
    u3percent=(u3count / NR)*100
    otherpercent=(othercount / NR)*100
    print("Directory   No. Entries   Percent on Partition")
    printf(" u1 \t\t %d \t\t %.2f\n", u1count, u1percent)
    printf(" u2 \t\t %d \t\t %.2f\n", u2count, u2percent)
    printf(" u3 \t\t %d \t\t %.2f\n", u3count, u3percent)
    printf(" other \t\t %d \t\t %.2f\n", othercount,otherpercent)
    print("===============================================")
    printf("%d entries scanned. %d total found (%.2f %).\n", NR,
          totalcount,
(totalcount / NR)*100)


}' ${datafile:-/etc/passwd}      #use /etc/passwd if $2 is not defined


$ shellreport tcsh
<<<Report for tcsh>>>
===============================================
Directory   No. Entries   Percent on Partition
 u1            15              0.23
 u2            262             3.99
 u3            213             3.24
 other         4               0.06
===============================================
6569 entries scanned. 494 total found (7.52 %).


$ shellreport csh
<<<Report for csh>>>
===============================================
Directory   No. Entries   Percent on Partition
 u1            18              0.27
 u2            2695            41.03
 u3            2608            39.70
```

```
other            9              0.14
=================================================
6569 entries scanned. 5330 total found (81.14 %).
```

Notice that in general you will have to edit this script to make it work with the *usr* partitions on your machine. If your machine doesn't have separate *usr* partitions, you can just delete the part of the script that does this calculation.

# More on Passing Shell Parameters into awk Scripts

Testing the value of shell-imported variables in an **if**() statement in **awk** is a little tricky. You will need another set of quotes around your variable: ""*$variable*"". However, some versions of **awk** allow for a *variable=value* statement on the command line, but it too has limitations. Still, although it is a bit painful, you need some method of passing in shell variables in all circumstances to an awk script.

Unfortunately, passing shell variables in an **if**() statement is not possible with the syntax described. Namely,

```
if ( '"$variable"' )
```

is not correctly interpreted in **awk**, because the shell will strip off all the quotes around $*variable* and substitute its value. Therefore, we have two alternatives. First, the YASQ (yet another set of quotes) approach

```
if ( "'"$variable"'" )
```

will do the trick.

Second, some versions of **awk** accept a *var=value* syntax on the command line and you can pass "fake filenames" as variable settings. For example, the line above in your script would become

```
if ( variable )
```

and the last line of the script would become

```
}' variable=value -
```

This feature is undocumented but is mentioned in the UNIX FAQ which is posted periodically to *comp.unix.questions.*

*Some versions of* **awk** *will cause variable settings encountered before any real filenames to take effect before the BEGIN block is executed, but some won't, so neither way should be relied upon.*

*When you specify a variable setting,* **awk** *won't automatically read from* stdin *if no real files are specified, so you need to add a "-" argument to the end of your command.*

# TIP 493

# Using the next Statement to Pass Control Back to the Top

The **next** statement returns control of the script back to the top. Thus, the **next** statement in **awk** is very useful for scripts where you want to continue doing something until something else is true. It is sort of like a **do-until** loop except that you jump all the way back to the top of the script.

For example, given a file that is grouped in blocks, you can print a certain block of information in the following simple way:

```
awk '
/blockpattern/ { wanted = wanted - 1; next }
wanted == 0 { print }'
```

Assuming you want the third block (counting from 0), when a line matching *blockpattern* is read in, the *wanted* variable gets decremented and the **next** statement passes control back to the TOP of the script (contrast with **getline**). Thus, *wanted* gets decremented, and processing continues until the next line matching *blockpattern* gets read in. This continues until *wanted* == 0 and the lines are printed.

# Piping awk Output Through Standard UNIX Commands

awk output can be piped directly through standard UNIX commands. This is very useful because sometimes a certain operation is either impossible or just extremely tedious or inefficient to code in **awk**. Therefore, you can let other UNIX tools do that work for you.

For example, you can pipe the output to a UNIX command as follows:

```
END { for (w in count) print w | "sort -r" }
```

prints each word in the *count* array in reverse sorted order.

# Doing Some Common Tasks with awk

# How Do You Maintain a Simple Database Using awk?

You can use **awk** to manage a database where you can search for a target or combination of targets, sort entries, and add and delete entries. First set up your database, using **vi** or another editor. Create the file as a text file with each record as a separate line. If you wish to have spaces within a field—for example, in a field with a first and last name—you will need to use something other than a space, such as a comma or semicolon, to divide the fields.

Suppose your database is contained in the file *projects* and each line contains four fields: the name of the project, the type of project, the date due, and the name of the project manager. For example, the first entry might be

```
videophones, programming, mid-December, Anne Jackson
```

If you want to see all the projects where the due date contains the string "December", you can type

```
$ nawk '/December/ {print}' projects
```

If you wish to see all the entries in which the name contains "video" and the project manager is "Jackson", you can type

```
$ nawk -F, '$1 ~ /video/ && $4 ~ /Jackson/ {print}' projects
```

# Does awk Work with a Text File that Does Not Have Newlines?

**awk** sets a newline as the default record separator. If you give it an input file without newlines, it will read the file as one long record. There may be situations when this is acceptable—for example, when searching a file for a particular word or phrase. In this case, each word will be a separate field (since the default field separator is a space). If you wish to see if a text file contains a particular word, such as "assignment", you could use

```
/assignment/ {print "found the word"}
```

This awk program will not tell you at which field position the word occurred, because **awk** does not store the current field number as a built-in variable. (Interesting point here—you cannot add a counter in the action statement to count the position of the field within the record, because **awk** has a built-in mechanism to read the fields. You can only specify actions that occur within each record, or before or after the entire input file is read.) You might think that a statement like

```
print $NF
```

would tell you the current field number, but instead it gives you the last field in the record.

# How Do You Use awk to Add a New Field to a File?

You can use the **getline** function to add a new field. **getline** tells **awk** to read input one line at a time, either from the keyboard or from an input file. It automatically splits the line into fields, which can then be selectively added to your file. Suppose you have a file called *oldfile* that contains three fields of information, and a file called *newfile* that you wish to add as the fourth field of each record. You can type

```
getline new < "newfile"        # get a line from the newfile
$4 = new                       # assign it to the new fourth
                               # fieldprint $0}
# send the entire new line to output
```

When you run this awk program with *oldfile* as the input file, it will create a new file and send it to standard output, such as an output file that you specify.

# How Do You Tell awk How Many Fields Your Database Contains?

You don't have to—**awk** is a self-contained programming language that is specialized for reading input one line at a time and separating it into fields, either with a default field separator of a tab or space or with a field separator that you specify when you call **awk**. Any awk program automatically reads the input lines, separates them into fields, labels the fields $1, $2, $3, and so on, and takes actions that you specify on the fields. If you don't specify a pattern, **awk** will take an action on every line in your input. If you don't specify an action, the default action is to print each line to the screen (unless you specified an output file when you called the awk program).

# Directly Accessing the Last Field of a Variable Length Record in awk

You want to access the last field in a record, but you don't know how long this record may be. Is there a way to do this in **awk**?

You can use the $NF variable to access the last field in a variable length-sized record. Thus, if you don't know how many fields are in your record, or if the record size changes, $NF will get you the last record. Let's say you have the following list of names in the file *authors*:

```
Victor Hugo
Ernest Hemingway
James Joyce
F. Scott Fitzgerald
Sir Walter Scott
```

Suppose you wanted to print the last name first, followed by a comma, followed by the rest of the name. Since the records are of variable length, you can't simply reverse $1 and $2. So, the answer is the statement:

```
$ awk '{ print $NF",", $1,$2}' authors
```

This will produce the listing as follows:

```
Hugo, Victor
Hemingway, Ernest
Joyce, James
Fitzgerald, F. Scott
Scott, Sir Walter
```

# Changing the awk Field Separator

You have a file that you want to read with an awk program, but the fields are delimited by semicolons. How do you change the field separator?

There are two ways to change the field separator in **awk**. The first way is to use the -F option to specify a different field separator in the command line. For example, if you wish to call an awk program that reads the first field of each record of the file *customers,* with a field separator being a semicolon, the command line would be

```
$ nawk -F; '{print $1}' customers
```

If you are using the -F option along with the **-f** option, which specifies that the awk program is stored in a file instead of being typed in directly, the -F and **-f** options can be in either order on the command line.

The other way to change the field separator is inside the awk program, in a BEGIN statement. This way is more useful if you need to change the output file separator also—for example, if you are reading a file, making some change to it, and sending the result to an output file. If the input file separator is not the default, then you must specify both the input and output file separator, or else the output file will not have the proper separator. The syntax for this is to place a BEGIN statement at the beginning of your awk program, containing specifications for both FS and OFS. For example,

```
BEGIN {FS=";";OFS=";"}
```

This would be the first line in your awk program, followed by the remainder of the program. It tells **awk** to reset the field separators as its first action, before it begins the basic cycle of reading each line of each input file.

Note that in the command line, the option is -**F**, whereas in the BEGIN statement, it is FS. The BEGIN statement, like all built-in variable names in **awk**, must be in uppercase.

# Using awk as a Sorting Tool

**T**IP **501**

You have a list of names with the first name followed by the last name. How can you change the order to last name, first name, so that you can sort them into alphabetical order?

**awk** provides a simple way to do this. It will automatically read each line, separate it into two fields divided by the space between the two names, and then take the action you specify of switching the order of the two fields. Here is a sample program.

```
temp=$1; $1=$2; $2=temp; print}
```

You can either run this in the command line or put it into a text file and call it with the -**f** option as discussed in Tip 488.

## Is awk a Good Tool for Converting a Text File from One Format to Another?

**awk** is an excellent tool for this purpose. It is specialized for reading lines of text and taking action on each line. When you are changing a file from one format to another, you may need to change the field delimiter, strip one or more fields from each record, change the order of two fields, or add a new field from another file. **awk** provides commands to do all of these. Field delimiters are discussed in Tip 500. If you wish to strip the first field from each record, you can type

```
{$1=""; print $0}
```

This will take each record, set the first field equal to the null string, and send the new record to standard output.

## Converting Between Uppercase and Lowercase Letters in gawk

Converting text between uppercase and lowercase is a common thing to do. Unfortunately, this operation is difficult in **awk**, but easily done in **gawk**, with the **toupper**() and **tolower**() functions.

For example, to convert strings from uppercase to lowercase, and vice versa, use the **toupper**() and **tolower**() functions as follows:

```
$ gawk '{print toupper($0) }' -
foo
FOO
blah blah blah
BLAH BLAH BLAH
```

To change the case of letters in strings in **awk** without these functions requires a messy script of **substr**() manipulations.

## Arrays in awk

## awk Is Said to Have Powerful Array Structures. How Do These Work?

Unlike C, **awk** provides associative arrays which allow sets of data to be associated with each other by field. When a file is read in, **awk** parses it into its component fields and records and allows us to associate one field to another. This is very useful for defining relationships between fields. The associative arrays in **awk** are very powerful, because they can take strings as subscripts, unlike many programming languages that allow only numbers as subscripts. **awk** provides a simple notation for associative arrays and a straightforward command for stepping through an entire array.

For example, the first and fifth fields of */etc/passwd* (the usernames and fullnames) can be associated with the assignment

```
fullname[$1]=$5
```

In addition, looping over an associative array is a bit different than the normal procedure:

```
for (i=1; i<=NR; ++i) print array[i]
```

And an associative array looks like:

```
for ( item in array ) print array[item]
```

Suppose you have a database of addresses and you wish to count how many people live in each state. The states are listed according to their two-letter abbreviations. You need to look at each record, identify the state, and increment a count for that state. When all the records have been counted, you want to display the totals. Here is part of an awk program to accomplish this, using three states for the example. The array is called *count*; it takes each state name as a subscript.

```
/PA/    {count["PA"]++           # increment the array indexed PA
/CA/    {count["CA"]++           # increment a different index
/RI/    {count["RI"]++           # put in as many as you want
END {for (s in count) print s, count[s]}   # this steps through
                                 # the array and prints each one
```

The END pattern matches after all the records have been read, and takes the action of printing each state name, followed by the count of its records. The user-defined variables are the array *count* and the variable *s*. Notice that you don't have to define the array; you simply assign values to its elements. If instead of printing all the elements of the array, you only wanted one, you could print it with the command

```
print count["PA"]
```

# Using Sorted Output of Associative Arrays in awk

When making up an associative array, the items in the array are not necessarily stored in the order they are assigned. Thus, if you print them, don't expect the output to be in the same order as the input. **nawk** and **gawk** seem to handle this problem better, but even with them, if the original data is not sorted, the output will not be either. The last point may seem picky, but the primary point is that the **awk** output in this case is counterintuitive.

For example, assume you have a file with the numbers 1-15 in it, with one number per line in order. Here is a script which will read the file into an associative array and print it.

```
array[NR] = $1
}
END {
    for ( item in array)
        printf("%s\n", array[item] )
}
```

Here is the output of 'showarray' using **awk**:

```
$ awk -f showarray 15nums
13
```

```
2
14
3
15
4
5
6
7
8
9
10
11
12
1
```

As you can see, the numbers are not printed in the same order they were read in. This is because a hashing table is used to store the values of the array. The output is returned in a fairly random order and not sorted the way we might expect. **gawk** will do the sorting for you or you could pipe the **awk** output through the **sort** command. However, if the numbers in the file were *not* in order to begin with, neither **gawk** nor **nawk** will print the numbers in the same order as the order of the file.

# Creating and Manipulating Arrays

**TIP 506**

You can create and manipulate arrays using the awk **split** function. **split**() can be used to parse any string into elements of an array. In this way, you can build up an array manually (like the following example) or extract subfields from various entries by passing an array to it: **split**(*string, array, separator*). Here is an example:

```
numbers="zero, one, two, three, four, five, six, seven, eight, nine,
        ten"
split(numbers,integers,",")
```

This will create an array of 'strings' (zero through ten) which takes a number as an argument and returns the proper 'string' notation.

# A Potpourri of Tips for Programming with awk

## One-Line if-then Statements in awk

In **awk**, you can use one-line **if-then** statements of the following form:

```
expression1 ? expression2 : expression 3
```

When a statement of this form is used, if expression1 is true, the expression has the value of expression2; otherwise, it has the value of expression3. This is the standard C convention for **if-then-else**. For example,

```
$2 > 100000 ? ++sixfigures : ++fivefigures
```

can be used to compute the number of salaries in a company above $100,000 and the number below $100,000, where the salary is found in the second file of an employee salary record.

## nawk Supports the do-while Loop (Which Guarantees at Least One Pass)

A **do-while** loop has one important advantage over any other type of loop—it guarantees one pass through the loop. Any time you are going to be reading in data for at least one pass, the **do-while** loop is a better alternative than another loop because testing is done AFTER the first line is read in.

*Of course, if you are going to assure at least one pass, you might want to do some error checking first!*

# The Number and Array of Command Line Arguments

You can get the number and array of command line arguments using the ARGC and ARGV variables, respectively. These two variables are analogous to the standard C **argc** and **argv** variables. They are used to get information from the command line. Without these two variables, command line processing is much harder. Frequently, you want to test for the number of arguments and for various options in your script. ARGV and ARGC make this process easier.

Unless the parameters specified on the command line are of the form *var=value*, **nawk** will treat each element of ARGV as the name of the next input file. If the entire program is written in the BEGIN section, this is not really a problem since it is executed before input is read.

# Special Codes and Escape Sequences in awk

There are special escape sequences used by **awk** for nonprinting characters such as tab and newline. The following table shows some of the special escape sequences used by **awk**:

| Escape Sequence | Description |
| --- | --- |
| \a | Alert character (usually the ASCII BEL) |
| \b | Backspace |
| \n | Newline |
| \r | Carriage return |
| \t | Horizontal tab |
| \ddd | Character represented in octal form (1 to 3 digits) |
| \character | Any literal character |

# Getting C-like Formats in awk

You'd like to get C-like type formats (%d, %g, %f, and so on) and length designations (%.2f, %-1.14g, and so on) in **awk**. Can you do this?

The answer is yes. **awk** has a **printf** function just like that in C, with type formats, length designations, and justifications. For an example, see the *shellreport* script in Tip 491.

# Closing Open Files and Pipes in nawk and gawk

The **close** (*expr*) function is used to close an open file or pipe. The argument **expr** can be any filename or command expression. However, to **close**() the expression correctly, the value of **expr** must be exactly equal to the string that was used to open the file or run the command.

For example, to get the last word from */usr/dict/words* and store it in the variable *lastword*, we would use

```
nawk BEGIN {
    "tail -1 /usr/dict/words" | getline lastword
    close("tail -1 /usr/dict/words");
    print "The last word in /usr/dict/words is: " lastword
}' /usr/dict/words
$ lastword
The last word in /usr/dict/words is: zygote
```

Thus, we've closed the pipeline with the exact string that was used to open it. Once something is successfully closed, the next call to **getline** would reopen the file or command. Thus, **close**() is necessary, for instance, if you want to write a file and then read it later in the same program. In addition, in some versions of **awk**, there is a limit to the number of files and pipelines that can be opened at any one time during execution of the program. In these situations, **close**() is necessary to keep the number of open processes to a minimum.

# Using the delete Statement in awk

**nawk** supports a **delete** statement to delete array entries before they get passed as filenames to the rest of the script. The reason you want such a statement is to prevent **nawk** from trying to open command line arguments as filenames after the BEGIN section (because input processing is done after the BEGIN section, as mentioned above). For example,

```
BEGIN {
    for ( i=1; i < ARGC; ++i ) {
        do something

    delete ARGV[i]
    }
}
    rest of script
    ...
```

# Getting the Current Date in an awk Program

How can you get the current date in a awk program?

There are several ways to do this, depending on your version of **awk**. For example, you could use

```
time=`date`
awk '
BEGIN {print "'"$time"'"}
...
```

or

```
awk '
BEGIN {print TM}
' TM="$time" filename
```

These versions will work in **nawk** or **gawk**. In **awk** you will have to wrap the awk script in a shell script and assign the date to an **awk** variable:

```
#!/bin/sh
awk -e 'BEGIN {
date="'`date`'"
}
{
print date
}'
```

In **nawk**, you could also use

```
nawk 'BEGIN { "date" | getline; date=$0}
    {
            print date,$0
    }'
```

# TIP 515 — Generating Random Numbers in nawk

Random numbers are frequently used in games, simulations, random executions, and so on. Direct access to random numbers is provided in **nawk** or **gawk** using the **rand()** function. This function generates a pseudorandom floating-point number between 0 and 1. Before using **rand()** in an awk program, you should use the **srand()** function, which initializes the seed used by **rand()** to generate pseudorandom numbers. If you use **srand()** with no arguments, it will use the current time of day as the seed. Here is an example that shows how to use **rand()** to get a pseudorandom integer between 1 and 100, inclusive.

```
# select.awk - selects random integer between 1 and 100, inclusive
BEGIN {
srand()
select = 1 + int(rand()*100)
print select
}
```

Here we have constructed a random integer between 1 and 100, inclusive, by first setting the seed used by **rand()** with the **srand()** function, multiplying by 100 the random number between 0 and 1 (exclusive) computed by **rand**(), taking the integer part of this number to give us a pseudorandom number between 0 and 99, and then adding 1 to give us a pseudorandom number between 1 and 100.

# Testing for Patterns Using match() Function Variables

The **match (s,r)** function is used to find the leftmost longest substring of the string s matched by the regular expression r. It returns the index where the matching substring begins, or 0 if there is no matching substring. **match (s,r)** also sets the variables RSTART and RLENGTH. RSTART is the indexing position, and RLENGTH is the length of the matched substring. For example, to look for the string "book" in "matchbook", we would use **match(matchbook, book)**. The value of RSTART would be 6 since "b" is the sixth letter of the word, and the value of RLENGTH would be 4 since the word "book" is four characters long. **match(s,r)** is very useful for testing and extracting patterns from a file since we can use any of **nawk**'s regular expressions.

For example, a **grep**-like function, **nawkgrep**, can be written:

```
nawk '
match($0, pattern) {
    print NR, substr($0, RSTART, RLENGTH)": "$0
}' pattern="$1" $2
```

This function searches through input (given from $2) and try to match the given line to the pattern given by "$1". It then prints out the line number, the matching substring, and the line for which the pattern was matched, as shown in this example:

```
$ nawkgrep '([Bb]ook|store)' testfile
2 store: I need to go to the store.
5 book: There are many good UNIX books available at the bookstore.
10 Book: Are you in the Book of the Month club?
11 book: This book has some really great tips!
```

Here we are looking for the string "Book or book" or the string "store" in a line. Notice that the 5th line of the file contains two matching strings but the line was printed out only once. The string "book" was found first in the line, so that the string is the one reported for the line.

# TIP 517

## Global Substitutions in nawk

The **gsub(r,s,t)** command acts as a global **sub()** command by globally substituting "s" for "r" in string "t". Thus, when a problem calls for many global substitutions on a line, **gsub()** is much more efficient than **sub()** because it does all substitutions at once. So you are better off using **gsub()** rather than **sub()** whenever possible.

Here is a script that uses **gsub()** to turn all uppercase letters in a file to lowercase.

```
nawk '
# set up lower and upper case variables
BEGIN { lower="abcdefghijklmnopqrstuvwxyz"
        upper="ABCDEFGHIJKLMNOPQRSTUVWXYZ" }
{
  # see if there is a match for one or more capital letters.
  while ( match($0, /[A-Z]+/) )
        # loop over all capital letters in line
        for (i=RSTART; i <= RLENGTH+RSTART; ++i)  {
            # find ITHCAPITAL letter in line
            ITHCAPITAL=substr($0, i, 1)
            # find position of ITHCAPITAL in upper
            if (CHAR = index(upper, ITHCAPITAL))
                #globally substitute ITHCAPITAL for its corresponding
                #lowercase buddy. Global substitution saves time.
                gsub(ITHCAPITAL, substr(lower, CHAR,1))
            print loopcounter
            ++loopcounter
        }
  # print line out
  print $0
}' $1
```

We will use this script on *testfile:*

```
$ cat testfile
ThIS IS a TeST
```

Notice that we have a loopcounter variable to determine how many passes it took to get the job done on *testfile*. With **gsub**, the answer is

```
$ lower testfile
1
2
3
this is a test
```

However, if you were to replace **gsub**() with **sub**(), you would need eight passes.

# Using the Improved getline Statement of nawk

You can pipe the output of a standard UNIX command directly into the **getline** command and assign a value to a variable. The following program, which looks up the full name of a user in */etc/passwd*, illustrates the use of **getline**. Notice that $0 is not set in this example; no splitting is done on the line. Also, there is no associative array between fields in */etc/passwd*. Thus, this program is much faster than an **awk** equivalent.

```
nawk '
BEGIN {
    "whoami" | getline name
    FS=":"
    }
    {
        if (name == $1 ) {
            printf("%-10s %s\n", $1, $5)
            exit
        }
}' /etc/passwd
```

Here is a useful table of values **getline** sets in different circumstances.

| Form | Sets |
| --- | --- |
| getline | $0, NF, NR, FNR |
| getline var | var, NR, FNR |
| getline < file | $0, NF |

| | |
|---|---|
| getline var < file | var |
| cmd \| getline | $0, NF |
| cmd \| getline var | var |

# TIP 519 — Creating User-Defined Functions

The advantage of defining your own functions is obvious. Any time you have a series of steps you want to perform repeatedly throughout your program, a function is an ideal way to handle this. The only other alternative is to repeat your code many times.

Some versions of **awk** (and **nawk** and **gawk**) support user-defined functions of the form

```
function name(list) {
    statements
return(expression)    [optional]
}
print integers[0]='zero'
```

For example, we can write a simple **max()** function that returns the greater of two characters:

```
$ cat max
echo $1 $2 | nawk '
{
print max($1, $2)
}

function max(m,n) {
        return m > n ? m: n
}'

$ max 1 5
5
$ max -1 -2
-1
$ max a A
a
$ max 1 a
```

```
a
$ max 1.22 24.2
24.2
```

Notice that **max** can be used with much more than just integers or floating point numbers. It can also return the ASCII max.

# Some Useful awk One-liners

Here are some really useful **awk** one-liners that you'll be able to use in many situations. They give a glimpse of what **awk** can do with a very simple bit of coding.

You can print out the total number of records in a file using

```
awk '{nf+=NF} END { print nf }' filename
```

This is the same as **wc -w** *filename*.

You can print out the total number of characters in a file using

```
awk '{nc+=length($0) } END { print nc + NR }' filename
```

NR, which is a newline by default, is added to the total to get all the newlines.

This is the same as **wc -c** *filename*.

You can print the number of lines containing the string *string* using

```
$ awk '/string/ { lines++} END { print lines}' filename
```

You can print the text between *pattern1* and *pattern 2* using

```
$ awk '/pattern1/,/pattern2/ { print $0 }' filename
```

# Your awk Program Is Not Running Correctly. What Did You Do Wrong?

**awk** can be difficult to troubleshoot because its error messages are not very specific. Here are some things to check if you have a problem.

❑ There must be a space between the final single quote in the command line and anything else that follows it.

❑ A filename on the command line is not enclosed in quotes. If you use a filename inside a program, it must be enclosed in quotes.

❑ When you specify an input file on the command line, it does not need a left arrow (<), but the output file on the command line must have a right arrow (>).

❑ The awk program in the command line is surrounded by single quotes.

❑ Inside an awk program, the action statement is surrounded by braces ( {} ).

❑ If an action statement takes more than one line, the opening brace must be on the same line as the pattern statement. The closing brace can be on a line of its own.

❑ Regular expressions are enclosed in slashes.

❑ If you modify a field or create a new field, you must include a print statement to send the new record to standard output.

❑ To compare the value of two variables, use ==. To assign a value to a variable, use =.

❑ Check the number of open files or pipes; **awk** supports only a limited number of open files at a time. You can use **close()** to close files after you are done with them. (See Tip 512.)

# How Do You Remember the Syntax of awk—When to Use Braces or Slashes or Apostrophes?

The program on the command line goes in apostrophes and the action statements go in braces. Multiple-line statements can be typed in, and lines after the first will have the secondary prompt.

Regular expressions go within slashes, but not all patterns are regular expressions. Comments begin with the # sign and end with the newline, as always. In a program, comments are important. Don't use a single quote in a comment; the shell will interpret it as the end of the awk program.

# Finding Out More About awk

**TIP 523**

To find out much more about **awk**, you should consult *The AWK Programming Language* by Alfred V. Aho (Reading, MA: Addison-Wesley, 1988). This book provides a comprehensive description of the awk language and gives many illustrative examples. You should also consult the book *sed & awk: A Nutshell Handbook* by Dale Dougherty (O'Reilly and Associates, 1990). Another excellent source of information is the gawk tutorial; you can obtain it via anonymous ftp from *prep.ai.mit.edu* in */pub/gnu/gawk-doc-2.15.2.tar.gz.*

# Using perl

# What Is perl?

**TIP 524**

**perl** (for *P*ractical *E*xtraction and *R*eport *L*anguage) is a programming language designed to make it easy to manipulate text, files, and processes. It provides a concise way to carry out a variety of jobs that are difficult to do with a C program or a shell program. **perl** was originally developed as a data reduction language that could be used to scan large files of text, invoking commands to retrieve data and creating easily understood reports from the information extracted. As **perl** developed, capabilities were added that can be used to manipulate files themselves, not just their contents. Further capabilities were added to manipulate processes, control the flow of data between processes, and so on.

**perl** was designed to do many things with the C programming language and using a shell. Consequently, it provides a useful tool for building programs that cannot be done easily using just C or just the shell.

# TIP 525

# The Top Twelve Reasons to Use perl

The **perl** programming language has become extremely popular and is widely used. Here are some of the reasons for this:

❏ It's free.

❏ It's available on a number of platforms, including anything that looks, acts, and smells like UNIX and in addition, Amiga, Macintosh, VMS, OS/2, and MS/DOS.

❏ It is much less buggy and more portable than shell scripts or awk or sed programs.

❏ It generally takes less time to code a perl script than a corresponding C program.

❏ Pattern matching and textual manipulation often outperform a C program and blow away shell scripts.

❏ It can do everything **awk**, **sed**, or a shell can do and much, much more.

❏ There is more than one way to do something with **perl**. There are usually many ways to accomplish a task.

❏ You don't need any special compiling instructions to run a perl script.

❏ There are no built-in limitations on how long array sizes can be, on variable lengths, subroutine recursion limits, on the use of binary data, or on file sizes.

❏ You have the ability to write secure programs that detect which data is taken from unsecured sources.

❏ It comes with a built-in symbolic debugger.

❏ There is plenty of online documentation, and there are people on the Internet willing to help you.

In short, **perl** is a nice comfortable place between C programs and shell scripts.

# TIP 526

# Where Can You Get perl?

**perl** is in the public domain and is available from several different sites, including *uunet.uu.net* in the archive file *gnu/perl-4.0.10.tar.Z, tut.cis.ohio-state.edu* in the directory *perl/4.0,* *jpl-devvax.jpl.nasa.gov* in the directory *pub/perl.4.0*. It is also available from the *comp.sources.unix* archive. You can also obtain **perl** using anonymous uucp from *osu-cis* and *uunet*; see *Programming perl* by Larry Wall and Randal L. Schwartz (O'Reilly and Associates, 1991) for details.

# Using the perl Interpreter

To write **perl** scripts, you need some way for **perl** to interpret them. The standard way to do this is to use the "# !" syntax for specifying the name of the interpreter at the top of the file. However, some systems do not support this, so you will have to do something like this:

```
$    #!/bin/sh
eval `exec /usr/bin/perl -S $0 ${1+"$@"}`
        if $0;
        (your script goes here).
```

# Getting Information from the Terminal in perl

**perl** provides a very easy way to grab a line of input from the terminal using the <STDIN> operator. In this way, interactive programs can easily be written. For example:

```
$ #! /usr/bin/perl
print "What is your name? ";
$name = <STDIN>;
print "Your name is $name";
```

# Getting Rid of the Last Character of a Variable in perl

Use the **chop**() operator to get rid of the last character from a variable. In many cases where input is being assigned to a variable name, the trailing newline is retained. **chop**() provides an easy way to get rid of it. As an example,

```
$ #! /usr/bin/perl
print "What is your name? ";
$name = <STDIN>;
chop($name);
print "Your name is $name";
```

results in the output

```
$ What is your name? john
Your name is john$
```

Notice that we got our shell prompt back on the same line.

# Using String Versus Numeric Tests in perl

When performing tests between two strings, use the following string operators:

| | |
|---|---|
| eq/ne | string equality/inequality |
| lt/gt | string less than/greater than |
| le/ge | string less than or equal to/greater than or equal to |
| cmp | compare two strings. Returns -1, 0, or 1. |

When performing tests between two numbers, use the following numeric operators:

| | |
|---|---|
| ==/!= | numeric equality/inequality |
| </> | numeric less than/greater than |
| <=/>= | numeric less than or equal to/greater than or equal to |
| <=> | compare two numbers. Returns -1, 0, or 1. |

For example:

```
print "What is your name? ";
$name = <STDIN>;
chop($name);
```

```
if ( $name eq "John" ) {
    print "I know you, you are $name.\n";
} else {
    print "I don't know you $name.\n";
}

print "What is your age? ";
$age = <SYDIN>;   ;
chop($age);
if ( $age < 30 ) {
    print "$age isn't so old! \n";
} else {
        print "Hmm, getting up there in years huh?\n";
}
$ name
What is your name? John
I know you, you are John.
What is your age? 35
Hmm, getting up there in years huh?
```

*If we didn't use the* chop() *operator here, the string equality would fail because of the newline.*

# Matching Patterns in perl

**TIP 531**

Use the =~ operator to match a pattern and the !~ operator to nonmatch a pattern.
These operators are very useful when looking for patterns in a variable, a record, a field, and so on.
They test patterns not only for the "normal" regular expression syntax but also for extended regular
expressions in the perl library.

Here is an example:

```
print "What is your name? ";
$name = <STDIN>;
chop($name);
if ( $name =~ /[Jj]ohn/ ) {
    print "I know you, you are $name.\n";
} else {
```

```
        print "I don't know you $name.\n";
    }
```

In this way, both "John" and "john" will be recognized as valid names.

As another example, you can make the test a little fancier using the perl word boundary operator and the ignore case operator:

```
print "What is your name? ";
$name = <STDIN>;  ;
chop($name);
if ( $name =~ /John\b/i ) {
    print "I know you, you are $name.\n";
} else {
    print "I don't know you $name.\n";
}
```

This will allow any upper- and lowercase combination of the word "John" and ensure that the character following the last character in "John" is not another letter. So this expression will be successful on anyone named John:

```
What is your name? JoHn NaVaRRa
I know you, you are JoHn NaVaRRa.
```

# TIP 532 — Assigning Elements to an Array in perl

In **perl**, array variables begin with an @ symbol so they are distinguished from regular variables which begin with a $. We can assign elements directly into the array as follows:

```
@known_names = ("Joe", "John", "Jeff", "Jen" );
```

This creates an array *known_names* with four elements. However, single elements in the array are referred to with the "$" notation. Thus, $known_names[0] is "Joe". Note that the array subscripts begin with 0 just as in C. Using arrays is a very powerful method of storing many variables in one chunk, but **perl** does this a little differently than other languages. As an example, here is a program that recognizes the individuals in the array but no one else.

```
@known_names = ("Joe", "John", "Jeff", "Jen" );
```

```
print "What is your name? ";
$name = <STDIN>;
chop($name);

for ( $i=0; $i<=3; $i++ ) {
    if ( $name eq $known_names[$i] ) {
        print "I know you, you are $name.\n";
        exit(0);
    }

}
    print "I don't know you $name.\n";
```

# Centering Text in perl

Centering text is a breeze in **perl**. Assume you have a standard 80-column terminal and you would like to center each line in the following file:

```
$ cat titlepage
The Dark and Stormy Night
by Lyle Leavitbe
10/13/93
```

You can center the lines of this file using **perl** as follows:

```
$ perl -pe 'print " " x ((80-length()-1)/2)' titlepage
            The Dark and Stormy Night
                 by Lyle Leavitbe
                    10/13/93
```

This script figures out, based on the length of the input line, how many blanks are to precede it. Notice the **-p** command line option. It is the concise way in **perl** to wrap an input loop around your script and print lines.

This little script also makes a nice macro in **vi**. You can add this line to your *.exrc* file:

```
map v :.!perl -pe 'print " " x ((80 - length() - 1)/2)'^M
```

Whenever you want to center a line, you can position yourself anywhere on the line and just hit "v".

# Editing Files in Place with perl

**TIP 534**

**perl** provides an **-i** option that's useful in conjunction with the **-p** option in letting the user edit a file in place and save a backup copy with an extension at the same time. In the preceding tip, we could have edited the file *titlepage* in place (saving the original to a file *titlepage.orig*) with the command

```
$ perl -pi.orig -e 'print " " x ((80-length()-1)/2)' titlepage
```

To see how this worked, we can display the files *titlepage* and *titlepage.orig*.

```
$ cat titlepage
                The Dark and Stormy Night
                    by Lyle Leavitbe
                       10/13/93
$ cat titlepage.orig
The Dark and Stormy Night
by Lyle Leavitbe
10/13/93
```

# Using Subroutines in perl

**TIP 535**

Functions in **perl** are known as subroutines. A subroutine can be put anywhere in the program and can be used repeatedly. Subroutines can take parameters and return values just like C functions. Subroutines offer huge capabilities!

In **perl**, all calls to a subroutine start with "&" and they are defined using the "sub" keyword. For example:

```
#!/usr/bin/perl
```

```
        print "What is your name? ";
        $name = <STDIN>;
        chop($name);
        &test_name($name);

        print "What is your age? ";
        $age = <STDIN>;
        chop($age);
        &test_age($age);

sub test_name {
        if ( $name eq "John" ) {
                print "I know you, you are $name.\n";
        } else {
                print "I don't know you $name.\n";
        }
}

sub test_age {
        if ( $age < 30 ) {
                print "$age isn't so old! \n";
        } else {
                print "Hmm, getting up there in years huh?\n";
        }
}
```

# Building and Processing Lists with Built-in Functions

**perl** comes with many built-in functions that enable you to manipulate multiple items (known as lists) with single commands. For example, suppose you wanted to print, in reverse order, all the text files in your directory. The first thing you need to do is pass in a list of arguments from the command line and build an array (or list) of the text files. Then you can sort and print them in reverse order.

Here is our first script called *lst* (for *l*ist *t*ext files):

```
$ cat lst
#!/usr/bin/perl
while (@ARGV) {
        $file = shift @ARGV;
        push(@textfiles, $file) if -T $file;
}
print join(' ', reverse sort @textfiles), "\n";
```

We construct a loop that runs over all the arguments in the @ARGV array (which we provide from the command line) and subsequently set the value of $file to the next argument on the stack. If $file is a text file, as determined by the -T option in the **if** statement, it is "pushed" onto the @textfiles array.

*For those of you who are familiar with **pushd** and **popd** in the shell, the action of the **push**() function is just the same for arrays.*

Once all the text files are determined, we use the **reverse**() and **sort**() functions to reverse sort the @textfiles array. Then we use the **join**() function to insert a space between each element in the @textfiles array, which we then print. Here is a run:

```
$ /bin/ls -F  # Notice there are 6 text files and one directory
a       able    b       blah/   c       d       e
$ lst *
e d c b able a
```

However, in typical **perl** fashion, this script can be written in more than one way. Here is another version of the script using the built-in **grep**() function:

```
$ cat lst
#!/usr/bin/perl
print join(' ', reverse sort grep(-T, @ARGV)), "\n";
```

perl's **grep** function is much more powerful than the normal family **grep** functions (**egrep**, **fgrep**, **grep**). Besides its ability to use perl's extended regular expression syntax, it can also use the test operators (-T in this case).

Notice also that we did not use parentheses in the **reverse**() and **sort**() functions. It is permitted to insert them to improve readability (and make Lisp programmers happy), but this is unnecessary.

Be warned, however, that this feature in **perl** does have some disadvantages. (See Tip 541.)

# Creating New Filehandles

To create a new filehandle in **perl**, use the **open**() function. By default, the STDIN, STDOUT, and STDERR filehandles are automatically set up when your perl script is executed. However, to read in data from a file, you will need to create a new filehandle. Reading in data from a file is very useful—especially if you have more than one program that needs the data. Using your script above, which recognizes "known names", instead of putting the names in an array, put them in a file called *known_names* and run the script:

```
#!/usr/bin/perl

        print "What is your name? ";
        $name = <STDIN>;
        chop($name);
        &test_name($name);

        # print message if known name is not found.
        print "I don't know you $name.\n";

sub test_name {
        open(KNOWN_NAMES, "known_names") || die "Can't open name
file.  $!\n";
        while ($known_name = <KNOWN_NAMES>) {
                chop($known_name);
                if ( $name eq $known_name ) {
                        print "I know you, you are $name.\n";
                        exit(0);
                }
        }
}
```

The **test_name**() subroutine now tries to open the file *known_names* under the filehandle *KNOWN_NAMES*. If successful, each line of the file is sequentially read into the $known_names variable and is tested against the $name variable received from STDIN. If the test succeeds, the recognition message is printed. If the test fails, the next line is read in and tested. If all tests fail, the unrecognized message is printed.

```
$ cat known_names
John
Jeff
Jen
```

```
Joe
$ name
What is your name? John
I know you, you are John.
$ name
What is your name? Goofy
I don't know you Goofy.
```

# TIP 538

# Splitting a File into Fields

The powerful perl function **split**() allows you to split up a file into fields based upon a field separator you pass to **split**(). The field separator can be any complicated pattern you want—including some regular expression. Thus, a file can be easily tokenized, given a series of **split**() routines. Here is an example that splits up the *etc/passwd* field into its component parts and print a summary for a given username:

```perl
#!/usr/bin/perl
print "Which username do you want to lookup? ";
$username=<STDIN>;
chop($username);
open(PASSWD, "/etc/passwd") || die "Can't open passwd file: $!\n";
while (<PASSWD>) {
      ($login, $passwd, $uid, $gid, $fullname, $home,
       $shell)=split(/:/);
      if ( $username eq "$login" ) {
           print "\n.....Info for $username.....\n\n";
           print "uid:     $uid\n";
           print "gid:     $gid\n";
           print "name:    $fullname\n";
           print "home:    $home\n";
           print "shell:   $shell\n";
           exit(0);
      }
}

print STDERR "Couldn't find $username in /etc/passwd.\n";
exit(1);


$ lookup
Which username do you want to lookup? navarra
```

```
.....Info for navarra.....

uid:    2124
gid:    20
name:   John Navarra
home:   /home/cartan/navarra
shell:  /bin/bash
```

# Using the if-elsif Construct in perl

Unlike C, **perl** has an **if-elsif** construct because there are no case statements in **perl**.
The **if-elsif** construct is needed in order to achieve this. A common mistake in **perl** is to write something like this, which is illegal:

```
if ( expression1 ) {
    do something;
} else if ( expression2 ) {
    do something else;
}
```

Instead, you need to write:

```
if ( expression1) {
    do something;
} elsif ( expression2) {
    do something else;
}
```

# Simple Debugging Checks

The **-c** and **-w** command line options to **perl** are two simple but useful methods to
check the validity and "correctness" of your perl script. These options are by no means extensive—you
will have to run the perl debugger for that. For example,

```
$ perl -c scriptname
```

checks for correct syntax, while

```
$ perl -w scriptname
```

prints warning messages for certain inconsistencies.

# Your perl Program Is Not Running. What Did You Do Wrong?

Here are some things you might check if your perl program is not running.

❏ Make sure your program is both executable and readable. **perl**, like other scripting languages (including **sh**, **awk**, and **sed**) uses an interpreter. Therefore, you need both read and execute permissions to run a perl program.

❏ Make sure that you are invoking your perl script. Unless you want to dereference a previous UNIX command, make sure that your perl script is not the name of a standard UNIX command, such as **test**. Also, make sure the perl script is actually in your PATH or you might get funny results or an error message from the shell telling you it cannot find your script.

❏ Make sure all variables begin with a "$". It is a common mistake to make an assignment such as

```
response='yes';
```
instead of

```
$response='yes';
```

❏ Make sure calls to subroutines begin with "&". For example

```
var=&max($one,$two);
```
is the correct call to a subroutine which finds the greater of two numbers.

❏ Remember, == and != are numeric tests, whereas eq and ne are string tests.

❏ Don't forget those trailing semicolons! You C programmers won't fall for this, right? ;-)

❏ Don't forget to use **chop**() when assigning variables the output of a command. For example,

```
$tty=`tty`
```
preserves the trailing newline, whereas

```
chop($tty=`tty`)
```
chops it off, making $tty suitable for other manipulations. (See Tip 529 for more info on **chop**().)

❏ Don't forget the "$" in the looping variable in a **foreach** statement. For example,

```
foreach $arg(@ARGV) {
      &process($arg);
}
```
is the correct way to loop over an argument list and process it.

❏ Use the **if-elsif** construct correctly. **perl** does not have case statements and there is no elif or fi as there is in shell programming. (See Tip 539 for more information on **if-elsif** constructs in **perl**.)

❏ The price to pay for being able to disregard unneeded parentheses in **perl** is that it forces things that look like functions to be functions—that is, only those arguments in ()'s are evaluated. Thus we have:

```
$ perl -e 'print (1+2)*3'
3
```
and

```
$ perl -e 'print ((1+2)*3)'
9
```
The latter result is probably what you intended but in the first case, **perl** saw the ()'s and only looked at what was in the domain of the **print**() function.

❏ Check the syntax and debug your code. Use the **-c** and **-w** options to print syntax errors and other warnings about your script. If all else fails, try the perl debugger (**-d** option).

# Learning More About perl

**TIP 542**

One of the best ways to learn more about **perl** is to consult the book *Programming perl* by Larry Wall (the creator of **perl**) and Randal L. Schwartz (O'Reilly and Associates, 1991). This book provides a comprehensive overview of **perl** and gives many useful tips for programming with **perl**, including a description of how to program common tasks.

You should also consult the newsgroup *comp.lang.perl*, which contains a discussion of the **perl** language and questions and answers about **perl**. You may find the FAQs posted in this newsgroup and in *news.answers* helpful.

Since **perl** is a tool that continues to evolve as its author adds new features, you probably should consult the latest version of the manual page on **perl**. If you end up doing a lot of programming with **perl**, we suggest you pick up a copy of the *Quick Reference Guide to perl* by Johan Vroman, which is included when you buy *Programming perl* and can obtained on the Internet as a PostScript file.

# Tips for Mathematical Calculations

# Doing Arbitrary Precision Arithmetic

**TIP 543**

The UNIX system provides a useful tool, **bc**, for doing arbitrary precision arithmetic—that is, for performing calculations to as many decimal places as desired. For example, you can find the 50th power of 2 as follows:

```
$ bc
2^50
1267650600228229401496703205376
```

You can use control statements with **bc**, including **for**, **if**, and **while** statements. For example, to compute the first twenty powers of 3, you could use

```
$ bc
for(i=1;i<=20;i=i+1)3^i
```

```
3
9
27
81
...
```

# Doing Base Conversions in bc

You may need to convert numbers from decimal to hexadecimal or from binary to decimal, and so on. **bc** is a useful tool for doing this sort of base conversion. To make these conversions, use the bc **ibase** (for *input base*) command to set the base for input and the **obase** (for *output base*) command to set the base for output. You need to use the **obase** command first; otherwise you will need to write the base you want output in terms of the input base. The defaults for both the input and output bases are 10.

For example, to convert numbers to hexadecimal (from decimal), do something like this:

```
$ bc
obase=16
46
2E
```

Here the uppercase letters A, B, C, D, E, and F are used to represent the hexadecimal equivalents of the decimal numbers 10, 11, 12, 13, 14, and 15, respectively. To convert hexadecimal to binary, you would do

```
$ bc
obase=2
ibase=16
A2B8
1010001010110100
```

# Writing Programs Using bc

You can write a program in **bc** and put the program in a file. To run this program, give bc the name of the file. For example, the program **modexp** can be used to compute the remainder of a large power of a number when it is divided by a particular integer; this computation, called modular exponentiation, is used in public key cryptography.

```
# modexp:   x(b,n,m) computes (b^n) mod m
define x(b,n,m){
auto i,j,y,z,d[]
for (i=0; n>0; i++){
    j=n%2
    n=(n-j)/2
    d[i]=j
}
z=1
y=b%m
if (d[0]==1)z=*y
for (j=1; j<=i; j++){
    y=(y*y)%m
    if (d[j}=1) z=(z*y)%m
return(z)
```

Once you put this program in the file *modexp,* set this command line to use it:

```
$ bc modexp
```

You can then use the function **x(b,n,m)** within your **bc** session. For example, once you have done this, to find the remainder of the 1000000th power of 2 when it is divided by 65337, enter

```
x(2,1000000,65337)
```

This causes the bc program **modexp** to run, giving you the following result:

```
12088
```

# TIP 546

# Factoring Integers

If you get the impulse to factor an integer and if this integer has 14 or fewer digits, you can use the **factor** command. For example:

```
$ factor 11111111111111
11111111111111
    11
    239
    4649
    909091
```

If you ask **factor** to factor an integer with more than 14 digits, it will reply with "Ouch!". If you must factor larger integers, you might want to use a mathematical computation program such as Maple or Mathematica or obtain a public-domain factorization program.

## Yes!

# Getting Agreement with yes

**TIP 547**

The UNIX philosophy began the emphasis on modular tools that did one thing very well, and could be connected to other tools. One of the best examples of such tools is yes. yes is a program that does one thing well: it provides an infinite series of yeses (actually y). This is useful for interactive programs that require some confirmation before proceeding. For example, if your system is set up so that the **rm** * command is always interactive, you can avoid having to respond with y to each request to delete a file by using the following command line:

```
$ yes | rm -i *
```

In this case, **yes** terminates when the **rm** command finishes, so no infinite loop occurs.

**yes** sends a letter "y" as its default, but will optionally send any string. The command **yes no** will generate an infinite sequence of the string "no". For example, if you know you really don't want to delete any of your files, then

```
$ yes no | rm -i *
```

will keep them all around.  :-)

# Chapter 9

# Communications and Networking

# Sending Messages, Talking, and Chatting with Other Users

## TIP 548

## Writing Messages to Other Users

You can send a message directly to the terminal of another user on your system with the **write** command. Everything you type at your terminal will be copied to the screen of this user. For example, to send a message to user lola, you would use the command

```
$ write lola
```

If lola is logged in, the bell of her terminal will ring twice and the following message will be displayed on her screen:

```
Message from ratso
```

If she wishes to communicate, she can enter

```
$ write ratso
```

and you can continue a conversation until one of you presses CTRL-D or DEL to end the conversation. When you have completed one of your messages, type **o** (for *o*ver) to let the other person know that it's time to reply. When ending such a conversation you might want to type **o-o** (for *o*ver and *o*ut). The **write** command translates nonprintable characters before sending them to the other person's screen. This prevents you from sending control sequences that do nasty things to the other person's terminal.

You won't be able to use **write** to send messages to all users, since many users don't normally accept messages. One reason is that unwanted messages are disruptive and can mess up the screen someone is working on. To turn off messages, put the line

```
mesg n
```

in your *.profile* or *.login*.

# Sending a Message to Everyone on Your System

**TIP 549**

You can send everyone on your system a message using the **wall** command. One way to use **wall** is to create a file, say *invitation*, containing your message, then run the command

```
$ wall < invitation
```

However, people who are refusing messages by setting **mesg** to **n** (*no*) will not get the message.

# Using talk for Online Communication

**TIP 550**

You can use the **talk** program to communicate with another user on your local machine or a remote system. The **talk** program uses a split-screen interface. For instance, if abby, logged in to the system vermont, wanted to establish a talk session with user fred on the system nevada, she would use the command

```
$ talk fred@nevada
```

If fred is logged on to the system nevada and he is accepting messages, he will receive a message like:

```
Message from Talk_Daemon@vermont at 03:13
talk:  connected requested by abby@vermont
talk:  respond with:  talk abby@vermont
```

If fred responds with the command

```
$ talk abby@vermont
```

a **talk** session is set up between them.

Each person in this talk connection is given a window that is either the top or bottom half of the screen, with a dashed line separating the two halves. One nice feature of **talk** is that both people can type messages simultaneously. Once you reach the bottom of your window in a talk session, the cursor moves back to the top of the window and overwrites whatever was there before.

# Problems with talk

**551**

Sometimes you will not be able to set up a **talk** session with a remote user. Here are some possible reasons.

One possibility is that the other user is refusing to accept messages by setting the **mesg** command to **n** (*no*). If you attempt to talk to such a user, you will get the message

```
[Your party is refusing messages]
```

*You can use **finger** to see whether someone is accepting or refusing messages. (See Tip 582.)*

You may also try to set up a **talk** session with someone who is not currently logged in. When this happens, you'll get the message

```
[Your party is not logged in]
```

You also may not have a connection to the remote machine where the user you want to talk to is. For example, if there is no Internet connection from your machine to the machine *silakka.fi,* you may get a message like

```
silakka.fi is an unknown host
```

Sometimes different versions of the **talk** command are incompatible for technical reasons. If this is the case, you may get a message like

```
[Checking for invitation on caller's machine]
```

The solution to this is to make sure the versions of **talk** on your machine and on the remote machine can communicate. You might look on your machine for the program **ntalk** (*new talk*), which was designed to take care of such problems. If you do not have the ntalk program on your machine, you can obtain it via anonymous ftp from *ashley.cs.widener.edu* in */pub/src/network/ntalk.tar.Z* and */pub/src/network/ntalkd.tar.Z,* for the program and the daemon, respectively. Or, you might use **ytalk**, an enhanced version of **talk** that also takes care of incompatibilities between systems. (See the next tip.) Ask your system administrator for help with this.

# Using ytalk

**TIP 552**

The **ytalk** (for *Yenne talk*) was developed by Britte Yenne as an enhanced version of **talk**. It is compatible with the original and newer versions of **talk**. It also lets you hold group conversations among three or more people. To use **ytalk** to set up a conversation with another person, say *pilar@taco.mex,* you would use

```
$ ytalk pilar@taco.mex
```

The screen will be divided into two halves and the user ID of the user you are talking to will be shown at the top of the half of the screen devoted to her conversation.

To talk to more than one person, give all their addresses on the talk command line. For example,

```
$ ytalk pilar@taco.mex xerxes@persia.ir cervantes ra@ag.rutgers.ed
```

sets up a five-way conversation between you and the four other users listed. The screen will be split into five parts with the user ID of each participant shown at the top of the part of the screen devoted to his or her part of the conversation.

You can add or delete users at any time by using ESC to bring up a menu. On this menu you can type **a** to add a new user, **d** to delete a user, and **o** (for *o*utput) to put everything from a user into a file.

You can get a copy of **ytalk** via anonymous ftp from *bongo.cc.utexas.edu* in */pub/ytalk.*

# The UNIX Chat Line

You can have an online conversation with several people using the Internet Relay Chat (IRC) facility. Generally, people convene on electronic chat lines to talk about particular topics. To use the chat facility, you must have the client **irc** program on your system. If you don't already have it, you can obtain it via anonymous ftp from either *fanhope.andrew.cmu.edu* or *cs.bu.edu* in the directory */irc/clients*. You will find client irc software in this directory for UNIX, DOS, Macintosh, and other systems.

Once you have chat client software on your system, you can connect to one of several different chat servers. Some of these servers are *csd.bu.edu, ucsu.colorado.edu, ug.cs.dal.ca* (in Canada), *nic.funet.fi* (in Finland), *vesuv.unisg.ch* (in Switzerland), and *munagin.ee.mu.oz.au* (in Australia).

You can also try out **irc** by using **telnet** to remotely log in to *bradenville.andrew.cmu.edu*. Since this system has limited resources and is often unavailable, you should only access **irc** this way to try it out.

# Starting Out with the Internet Relay Chat

Once you have connected to an IRC server, you can use a variety of commands. To issue commands, first type a / (slash). For example, to see a list of available channels, type

```
/list
```

The list of channels will include their names, topics, and number of users. To join a particular channel, use the **join** command. For example, to join the channel #hottub, type

```
/join #hottub
```

Once you do this, all lines you type that do not start with a slash are sent to the channel you joined.

You can leave a channel using the **leave** command. For example, to leave #hottub, type

```
/leave #hottub
```

To be on multiple channels at the same time, you will need to run the command

```
/set novice off
```

and then issue **join** commands for each channel you want to participate in. (Taking part in more than one chat at the same time can be bewildering.)

You can get help with IRC commands by typing

```
/help
```

You can get a brief introduction to the Internet Relay Chat by typing

```
/help intro
```

You can see who is taking part in a particular chat using the **who** command. For example,

```
/who #hottub
```

shows who is currently taking part in the #hottub channel and

```
/who *
```

shows you who is joined to your current channel. To end your chat session, type

```
/quit
```

# Learning More About the Internet Relay Chat

TIP
555

You can learn more about **irc** by reading tutorials obtainable via anonymous ftp from *cs.bu.edu* in the directory */irc/support*. Look for files with names matching *tutorial.\**.

Also, you can usually find the sources for chat client software on the newsgroup *alt.irc*. In addition, you can learn about some active chat lines on the Internet when you read this newsgroup. You should read the FAQs about the Internet Relay Chat that are posted periodically to the newsgroups *alt.irc* and *news.answers*.

# Using the UUCP System

## Sending Files via uuto

**TIP 556**

One of the best commands for transferring files between UNIX systems is **uuto**. Give the **uuto** command the name of the file, followed by the bang-style address of the recipient. For example, to send your file *mushrooms* to ellen on jersey—jersey being a system your machine knows how to set up a **uucp** connection with—you would use

```
$ uuto mushrooms jersey!ellen
```

If you include the **-m** option to **uuto**, mail will be sent to you telling you that your file was successfully copied on the remote system.

A useful tip when sending files via **uuto** is to use the **-p** option to copy these files to the spool directory awaiting copy to the remote system. If you don't do this and you either delete or change the files before they are actually sent by the UUCP system, you won't send the file that you intended. For example,

```
$ uuto -m -p mushrooms jersey!ellen
```

will copy your file *mushrooms* to ellen on jersey as the file exists when you issue this command, sending you mail when the file is successfully copied to the spooler. Getting this mail message back is important if file permissions are restricted so that you cannot copy files to the remote system.

It's also useful to know that you can send directories via **uuto**. For example,

```
$ uuto -m -p fungus jersey!ellen
```

will send the entire contents of your directory *fungus* to *jersey!ellen*.

# Retrieving Files Sent to You via uuto

**TIP
557**

When someone sends you files using the **uuto** command, you will receive a mail message telling you that you have received files in the public directory for files sent to you. You can use the **uupick** command to retrieve and move these files. When you run the **uupick** command, you will receive a prompt from **uupick** asking you what you want to do with each file. Here is an example:

```
$ uupick
from system jersey: file molds ?
```

If you respond to this prompt with an **m** (*move*), the file *molds* will be moved to your current directory and you will be told how many blocks were used for this file. For example:

```
m
16 blocks
```

If you want to move this file to the subdirectory *fungus* of your current directory, you would instead respond with

```
m /fungus
16 blocks
```

A useful tip for retrieving files via **uupick** is that you can retrieve all the files that were sent to you via **uuto** from the same system by responding to the **uupick** prompt with **a**. For example,

```
$ uupick
from system jersey: file molds ? a
180 blocks
```

retrieves all files sent to you from jersey, including *molds,* moving them to your current directory from the public directory where they were sent.

# How to Transfer Files to a Remote System via uucp

You can transfer a local file to a remote machine using the **uucp** command, as long as your local system knows about the remote system and this transfer is allowed. (See Chapter 12.) For example, you can send the file *numbers* in your current directory to the remote system acme, giving it the pathname */var/home/zox/numbers*, by using

```
$ uucp numbers acme!/var/home/zox/numbers
```

# How to Transfer Files Between Remote Systems Using uucp

You can transfer a file between two remote system using **uucp** as long as both remote systems are known to your local system, if you have permission to execute the **uucp** command on the remote site from which you are transferring the file. For example, you can send the file */var/home/kramer/report* on the system uranus to the system neptune, giving it the pathname */var/home/jerome/report*, by using

```
$ uucp uranus!/var/home/kramer/report  neptune!/var/home/jerome/report
```

# How to Transfer Files to Machines Not Known to Your Machine

You can still use **uucp** to send a file to a machine not directly connected to yours via **uucp** as long as you know a route to that machine. For example, if your machine doesn't know about the remote host xaxa, but you know that you can reach xaxa by connecting to wawa, then to yoyo, then to bozo, and finally to xaxa, you can send your file *report* to xaxa, giving it the name */var/home/ned/report*, by using

```
$ uucp report wawa!yoyo!bozo!xaxa!/var/home/ned/report
```

*You will need permission on all intermediate systems; see the tips in Chapter 12 for details.*

# You Can Abbreviate Home Directories When Transferring Files

You can use the abbreviation *~logname* to specify the home directory of users on remote machines when transferring files with **uucp**. For example, the command

```
$ uucp report omega!~ina/report
```

puts your file *report* in the file *report* in the home directory of the user ina on omega. Here, the home directory of ina must be writable by others.

# Giving a uucp Job a High (or Low) Grade of Service

On some systems there are different grades of service from the UUCP system. These grades specify the priority of uucp jobs. For example, your system may have three grades of service: high, medium, and low. You can transfer your file report with high priority using

```
$ uucp -ghigh report cuba!/var/fred/cronder
```

If you wanted to give this low priority, you would use **-glow** instead. The priority you give a uucp job determines how the system queues it among the uucp jobs awaiting completion; here jobs with high priority receive the highest priority and are completed before other uucp jobs.

To see the grades of service available to users, run

```
$ uuglist -u
```

# Which Machines Can Be Directly Connected to Yours via uucp?

You can find out which other systems your system can directly connect with using **uucp** by running the **uuname** command. When you run

```
$ uuname
```

you'll get a list of all these systems; this list can be extremely long since your machine may be able to directly connect to hundreds or thousands of other systems and each system is printed on a separate line. To see whether your system can connect with a particular system via **uucp**, you can pipe the output of **uuname** to a **grep** command. For example, to see whether your local system can directly connect to the remote system malta, run

```
$ uuname | grep malta
```

If the output of this shows the name "malta", then your system can directly connect to malta via **uucp**. If the output is null, then it cannot.

# How to Check Your uucp Jobs

You can use the **uustat** command to check on the status of your **uucp** jobs. The output of **uustat** will tell you the status of all your recent **uucp** commands. For example,

```
$ uustat
jerseyZ01f7 10/14-14:23 S jersey ken 1384 /home/ken/UNIX/TIPS/part9
```

tells you that the uucp job with job ID jerseyZ01f7 was requested at 14:23 on 10/14 to jersey by the user ken, it was sent (S), 1384 is the size of the file, and */home/ken/UNIX/TIPS/part9* is the file being sent. If the file was requested, but has not been sent, the S in this output line would be replaced with an R.

# Spooling a uucp Job

When you issue a uucp command to transfer a file to a remote system, this file may not be sent immediately. If you want to send the version of your file as it exists when you request the transfer, give **uucp** the -C option. This causes **uucp** to copy your file to the spool directory */var/spool/uucp*. This copy is what is sent to the remote system. For example, to send the current version of the file *part9* to the remote system burma, giving it the pathname */var/home/larry/burma*, use

```
$ uucp -C part9 burma!/var/home/larry/burma
```

*Be aware that you can do the same thing using the* **-p** *option to the* **uuto** *command.*

# Cancelling a uucp Job

You can kill a **uucp** job if it hasn't yet been sent. Use the **-k** option of **uustat**; and you will need the uucp job ID of the request. For example, if you want to kill the uucp job with job ID jerseyZ01f7, you would use

```
$ uustat -kjerseyZ01f7
Job: jerseyZ01f7 - successfully killed
```

# Running Commands on Remote Machines with uux

You can use the **uux** (for *UNIX-to-UNIX* execution) command to run a command on a remote machine (as long as this is allowed; see Chapter 12). For example, you can collect files from different computers on your UUCP network, send these files to a remote host, execute a command on this remote host, and send the output to a specified system.

To see how **uux** works, suppose you want to get the file *spiders* in */home/linda* on the remote system nono and the file *arachnids* in */home/susie* on the remote system nini and concatenate them to a file named *8legs* in */home/kermit* on the remote system pipi. You would run

```
$ uux "!cat nono!/home/linda/spiders nin!/home/susie/arachnids > \
  pipi!/home/kermit/8legs
```

## Calling Remote Systems

# Using cu to Connect to a Remote System

You can use the **cu** (*c*all *UNIX*) command to call a remote system and to connect to this system. You can connect via **cu** to any system known to yours by name. In particular, the remote system has to have an entry in the */etc/uucp/Systems* file on your machine. For example, if you want to connect to the system yak and yak is known to your system, you would type

```
$ cu yak
```

If the connection is made, you'll see

```
Connected
login:
```

You can now log in on yak with your login and password (which you must have). If for some reason the connection fails, you will get a message to that effect. For example, if you attempt to connect to a remote system using **cu** and this system is not included in the *Systems* file, you'll get the message

```
Connection failed:   SYSTEM NOT IN Systems FILE.
```

# Calling Remote Systems Using
# Telephone Numbers

You can call a remote system using **cu** by giving it a telephone number to dial. Your system will dial using an automatic calling unit. To give **cu** a telephone number, use the = character to wait for a secondary dial tone before dialing the rest of the number, the - character to pause for four seconds before dialing further, and the digits 0-9 and the symbols * and # from the telephone keypad. If you use a * or - in your telephone number string, remember to use quotes around the phone number so that the shell will not interpret these as shell metacharacters. For example, suppose you have to dial a *9 to get an outside line. To reach a remote computer by dialing in to it at (201) 555-1234, you would use

```
$ cu "*9=12015551234"
```

You will either succeed in connecting to the remote system and get a login prompt or you will get a message that the connection failed.

You can select the line speed of the connection using the -s (*speed*) option. For example,

```
$ cu -s9600 9=18095550123
```

is used to set up a connection at 9600 bps to the computer with telephone number (809) 555-0123, where a 9 is required to get an outside line.

# TIP 570

## Transferring Files During a cu Session

You can transfer ASCII files during a cu session. To do so, use cu ~ commands. To transfer a file from the remote host to which you are connected, use the cu ~%take command. During your cu session, once you type ~%, **cu** will put the name of your local system between ~ and %. You then type the rest of the command. For example, suppose you have logged in to the remote system reno using **cu** from your local host juneau. You can transfer the file article on reno to your system, giving the file on your machine the name *oldarticle*, by using

```
~[juneau]%take article oldarticle
```

You can also transfer a file from your local system to the remote system during your cu session with that system. For example, to transfer the file named *memo7* to reno, naming it *memo.old*, use

```
~[juneau]%put memo7 memo.old
```

*This works only when the remote system is a UNIX machine. It is also not a very reliable method.*

# TIP 571

## How to Run a Command on Your Local System During a cu Session

You can run commands on your local system during a cu session using the tilde sequence *~!command*. After you type ~!, **cu** will put the name of your local system between the ~ and !. After running your command on the local machine, terminate this shell on the local machine using the **exit** command. This will return you to your cu session with the remote machine. When you do this, **cu** echoes a ! character. You can also run a command on your local machine and send its output to the remote system using the tilde sequence *~$command*.

# How to Change Your Current Directory on Your Local System During a cu Session

You can change the current directory on your local system during a cu session with a remote host by using the cu ~%cd command. For example, to change the current directory on your local system tuna to */home/lisa/devices* from */home/lisa*, use

```
~[tuna]%cd devices
```

This change will persist during your cu session unless you use the cu ~%cd command again. (Using the command ~!cd does not work since this command will be executed in a subshell; the change of directories with this command will not persist once the subshell ends.)

# Using cu to Set Up a Direct Connection to a Modem

You'd like to connect to your modem on *ttyb* to check the settings, such as the number of rings it waits before auto-answering. There is also a table of commands you can use on the back of the modem. How do you send commands to the modem and get the answers back?

You can use **cu** to do this. You need to set up the modem in direct mode. You can do this by modifying the uucp file *Devices* in */etc/uucp*. (See Tip 773; you'll need to have root permissions to do this.) For example, you might put the following line in this file:

```
Direct ttyb,M - 2400 direct
```

You now execute the following command:

```
$ cu -l ttyb -s 2400
```

You will now have a direct connection with your modem. Note that on some systems you can use **sysadm** or **sysadmsh** to do this.

## TIP 574 — Calling Remote Terminals Using ct

You can call a remote terminal attached to an auto-answer modem using the **ct** (*c*all *t*erminal) command. Use the same options and syntax as **cu**. Here is an example:

```
$ ct -s2400 7015559876
```

uses a 2400 bps line to dial (701) 555-9876.

You may want to use the **ct** command to automatically call out from your system at work to your terminal at home at night, saving you the cost of a phone call. To do this, you can use an **at** job. For example, the script

```
at 9:00pm
ct -s4800 9=5558888
```

will call your home terminal at 555-8888 (getting an outside line with 9 and waiting for dial tone) at 9 P.M.

## TIP 575 — Using tip to Call Remote Systems

The **tip** (for *T*elephone *I*nterface *P*rogram) command is available on some, but not all, UNIX systems. The **tip** program contains all the functionality of **cu**, as well as many other features. One of the major advantages of **tip** over **cu** is that you can use **tip** to transfer files to and from machines running operating systems other than UNIX, such as DOS. The **tip** program uses three special files: the */etc/remote* file on your system that defines the systems, modems, and lines known and used by **tip**; the */etc/phones* file on your system that lists phone numbers for different remote sites; and the *.tiprc* file in your home directory in which you set up your personal preferences for using **tip**.

If there is an entry for a remote machine in */etc/remote,* you can give **tip** the name of this machine to set up a connection. For example, if there is an entry for the system mongolia in */etc/remote,* you can call mongolia by using

```
$ tip mongolia
```

You can also use **tip** to call a remote system by giving the telephone number of this remote system. The **tip** program will use the information in the */etc/remote* file for the default system named tip0.

Once you are connected to the remote host mongolia, you can log in on this system using the appropriate login sequence. Once your session has been established, you can either enter commands on the remote host or use tip ~ commands such as ~., which disconnects the connection, ending the tip session; ~^Z, which suspends the remote connection, allowing you to run commands on your local system; ~c, which you can use to change the current directory on your local directory; ~p, which you can use to send a file to a remote UNIX machine; and ~t, which you can use to retrieve a file from a remote UNIX machine.

# Transferring Files to and from a Remote UNIX Machine Using tip

**TIP 576**

When you have set up a tip connection with a remote UNIX host, you can transfer a file from this machine using the tip ~t (*t*ake) command. For example, to transfer the file *memo1* from the remote host mackerel to which you are connected via **tip**, use

```
$  ~[take] memo1
```

Here, when you type ~t at the mackerel prompt, **tip** expands this to ~[take]. Once you give the name of the file you want to transfer and press ENTER or RETURN, **tip** will transfer this file and tell you how many lines were transferred and how long it took.

To transfer a file to the remote UNIX machine, use the tip ~p (*p*ut) command. For example, to transfer the file *memo2* to mackerel, use

```
$  ~[put] memo2
```

Here, when you type ~p at the mackerel prompt, **tip** expands this to ~[**put**]. Once you give the name of the file and type ENTER or RETURN, **tip** transfers the file, telling you how many lines were transferred and how long it took.

# Setting Up Your .tiprc File

Use your *.tiprc* file to set the variable you want to use in tip sessions. Here is a sample

*.tiprc* file:

```
# Sample .tiprc file
disconnect=logout
record=session.tip
script
nobeautify
```

This *.tiprc* is used to set variables used by **tip** to do the following. **tip** will send the string "logout" when it disconnects its connection to a remote host. It specifies that everything captured during a connection will be appended to the file *session.tip*. It also specifies that unprintable characters not be discarded in the captured file.

# Transferring Files to and from a DOS PC with tip

If you want to connect to a remote DOS system using **tip**, there should be a line in */etc/remote* telling **tip** how to make the connection. Suppose this has been done for the DOS PC pc31. To connect to pc31 using **tip**, type

```
$ tip pc31
```

If this connection is successful, you will get the C: prompt on pc31. To transfer a file, say *C:chap1.doc,* to the local UNIX machine, first use the tip ~s command to set the *eofread* variable to the C: prompt. Do this with

```
~[set] eofread=C:
```

Here, **tip** expanded ~s to ~[**set**]. Next, use the tip ~< command used to transfer a file from a machine not running UNIX. Do this with

```
~< Filename: chap1.doc
```

Here, **tip** expanded ~< into ~< **Filename:**. After you type ENTER or RETURN, you will get a prompt asking you to list a command for the remote host. You should use the DOS type command, as follows:

```
List command for remote host: type chap1.doc
```

When you press ENTER or RETURN, **tip** will transfer the file to your local UNIX host. Once the file has been transferred, it will see the DOS C: prompt and it will know the transfer is complete. It will then tell you how many lines were transferred and how long it took.

To transfer a file to the DOS PC, first set the *eofwrite* variable to the character that DOS uses to mark the end of a file, CTRL-Z, using the tip ~s command as follows:

```
~[set] eofwrite=^Z
```

Next, use the DOS **type** command to set up the DOS machine to put the transferred file in the file *C:memo.txt* as follows:

```
C: type > memo.txt
```

Send the file */home/anna/memo* to the remote DOS machine using the tip ~> command as follows:

```
~> Filename: /home/anna/memo
```

When you press ENTER (or RETURN), **tip** transfers the file. Once it completes the transfer, it sends the DOS machine the CTRL-Z character, which puts the end-of-file character for DOS at the end of the file. The **tip** command will tell you how many lines were transferred and how long the transfer took.

# Setting Up an /etc/remote File

**579**

The */etc/remote* file is used to define the systems, lines, and modems used by the **tip** command. This file contains an entry for each remote machine to be contacted using **tip**, along with one special entry for the virtual system tip0, used when you give **tip** a telephone number instead of the name of a remote host. For example, an */etc/remote* file might contain the following lines:

```
tip0:dv=/dev/cua1:at=hayes:br#9600:
michigan:pn=3135558888:tc=tip0:
dingo:pn=@:tc=tip0:
pc31:pn=5557654:dv=/dev/cua2:at=hayes:br#1200
```

Here, the first line starts with the name tip0, which is the special machine name used by **tip** when you do not give a machine name. Next, the device (dv) used by the modem for **tip** is specified; here it is */dev/cua1*. Then the type of modem (at) is specified; here it is the Hayes-compatible modem type. Finally, the bit rate (br) is specified; here it is 9600 bits per second.

The second entry tells **tip** that to call the remote system michigan, the phone number 313-555-8888 should be used and that all other settings should be the same as with tip0; this is specified with tc=tip0.

The third entry tells **tip** to look in the file */etc/phones* to find the telephone number to reach dingo (see Tip 580) and to use the settings in tip0.

The fourth entry again gives all the information required by **tip** to reach the remote DOS PC named pc31.

For example, when you have your */etc/remote* set up this way, and you type

```
$ tip 9085552365
```

the **tip** program finds the line for tip0 in */etc/remote* and uses the information specified there to dial 9085552365. Specifically, it dials this number using the Hayes-compatible modem at */dev/cua1*, setting the modem to run at 9600 bits per second.

# Setting Up an /etc/phones File

When an entry in */etc/remote* has pn=@ in it, **tip** knows to look in the */etc/phones* file on your system. For example, the */etc/phones* on your system may look like this:

```
dingo     809-555-3333
dingo     809-555-2222
coli      813-555-1111
coli      813-555-0101
coli      813-555-0102
```

When you run

```
$ tip dingo
```

**tip** finds the line for dingo in */etc/remote*. It sees the pn=@ setting and then looks in */etc/phones* to find the number to dial. Since 809-555-3333 is the first number specified for dingo in */etc/phones*, this is the first number it dials, using the modem connected to */dev/cual* at 9600 bps. If this is unsuccessful, it then tries the second number specified for dingo, 809-555-2222.

# Connecting to a Modem via tip

If you have access to a UNIX system via a direct link and this machine has a 19200 bps modem on it, you can use the **tip** command to use this modem from the shell. For example, if your modem is connected to */dev/ttya*, to be able to use **tip** to connect to it, modify the "hardwire" line in */etc/remote* to set the device as */dev/ttya* and set the baud rate to 19200 bps. Then to connect to the modem, type

```
$ tip hardwire
```

You will be connected to the port and modem. Any command you type will be received by it.

# Fingering

## TIP 582

## Fingering a User

You can use the finger service to obtain information on a user on a remote host on the Internet. The information you can obtain varies from host to host. The information about a remote user that you can get using the **finger** command includes this person's user ID, full name, phone number, and office location, as well as whether the user is currently logged in, whether the user has read mail, the last time the user has logged in, and other customized information. For example, to get information on the user iat on *ogre.uri.edu*, you would run

```
$ finger iat@ogre.uri.edu
```

Here is what the output may look like:

```
[ogre.uri.edu]
Login name: iat (messages off)      In real life: Irena A. Trumba
Phone: 401-555-4444
Directory:  /usr/iat                Shell:  /bin/ksh
Last login:  Tue  May 17  03:21 on ttyp11
Unread mail since Sun May 15 19:19:33 1994
No plan
```

From this output you see that the user with user ID iat on *ogre.uri.edu* is named Irena A. Trumba. You see her phone number and the shell she uses (from the shell entry in */etc/passwd*). You see when she last logged in and that her mailbox has not been accessed since her last mail message arrived. You also see that she has no plan; this means that she has no *.plan* file (see Tip 584), not that she has no purpose in life.

You can give **finger** the -s option to get short output and the -l option to force long output.

For security reasons, you will find that many remote hosts provide only partial or no information to users trying to finger their users. You are more likely to encounter this problem when trying to finger users in commercial domains.

You can also sometimes get information on users by giving **finger** either the first or last name of the user. For example, you might find information on Irena Trumpa on *ogre.uri.edu*. You could try

```
$ finger irena@ogre.uri.edu
```

or

```
$ finger trumba@ogre.uri.edu
```

# Fingering a Remote Host

You can use the Finger service to find out who is logged in on a remote host. For example, to find out who is logged in on the system *trek.starfleet.mil*, use

```
$ finger @trek.starfleet.mil
```

You'll get a report listing the user ID, name, terminal, how long there has been no activity by that user, when he or she logged in, and other information, such as the office or other location he or she is logged in from. For example, the output might look like this:

| Login | Name | tty | idle | when | where |
|-------|------|-----|------|------|-------|
| picard | J.L.Picard | p4 | 4:11 | Fri 09:11 | |
| data | C.Data | *p1 | 0:02 | Tue 02:54 | data.shuttle.mil |
| bev | B.Crusher | *p5 | 27 | Sat 12:02 | |
| worf | L.Worf | p7 | | Wed 23:07 | |

If there is an asterisk before the terminal (tty) name, this user has turned off receiving messages. The idle time is specified in minutes and seconds, minutes (such as 27), or days (specified using a number followed by "d"). If there is no entry in the idle field, that user is currently active. Local users have no entry in the where field; remote users have an entry that shows how they were logged in.

You can finger your own computer using the command

```
$ finger
```

# T**IP** 584

# The .project and .plan Files

The **finger** command was first developed at the University of California at Berkeley and was designed to display information about students and faculty members. To help provide useful information, the **finger** command was set up to display two special files for a user, *.project* and *.plan*. For these files to work as intended, the search permission for others must be set on the user's home directory and the *.plan* and *.project* files must be readable by others.

If a user has a *.project* file, you will see the first line of this file when you finger this user; if this user has no *.project* file, nothing is displayed by **finger**. Also, **finger** will display the entire contents of the user's *.plan* file; if the user has no *.plan* file, finger will display

```
No Plan.
```

Here are some sample *.project* and *.plan* files.

```
$ cat .project
Working feverishly on a book of UNIX Tips!
$ cat .plan
I am working at home on this book between 5 AM and 8 AM and between
6 PM and 2 AM everyday.  You can reach me via e-mail or using my
unpublished telephone number during these hours.
```

When someone fingers the user with these *.project* and *.plan* files, the output will include the following lines:

```
Project:  Working feverishly on a book of UNIX Tips!
Plan:
I am working at home on this book between 5 AM and 8 AM and between
6 PM and 2 AM everyday.  You can reach me via e-mail or using my
unpublished telephone number during these hours.
```

There are plenty of good uses for *.project* and *.plan* files. For example, you can give people information on the location and time of a meeting by telling them to finger you. These files also let you act as an information resource on the Internet. (See Tip 708 for details.)

# Can You Change the Personal Information Someone Gets When Fingering You?

On some systems, a user can use the **chfn** (for *ch*ange *fin*ger) command to update some of the personal information displayed by **finger**. The information that can be changed can include the user's name, phone number, office location, and so on. If your system has the **chfn** command, you will be prompted for each of the fields you can change. You can blank out any of the fields by entering none. Because users on some systems have used this facility to change their personal information, be aware that you may not be getting accurate information when you finger someone.

# How Can You Tell If Someone Fingers You?

You'd like to know whenever someone fingers you on your local machine. Is there any way to find out?

Unfortunately, the answer is no. There is no way to know when someone fingers you! However, there are some techniques that provide some information when someone fingers you; see the FAQs in *comp.unix.questions* for details.

# Why finger Fails

For you to be able to finger someone on a remote machine, that machine has to have a Finger server, such as the **fingerd** program on UNIX systems, running on it. If it doesn't, your request will fail.

Sometimes when you finger a user on a remote system, you will get a message that tells you that this system refuses to connect remote users. Here is an example:

```
[arch9.att.com]
connect:  Connection refused
```

## TIP 588

# Fingering Coke Servers

Some clever people have hooked up vending machines so that you can use **finger** to determine the status of items in the machine. This was first done at Carnegie-Mellon University. Now the name Coke Server is used for a Finger server that displays information on some device other than a computer, such as a vending machine. For example, you can get information on the coke server at Carnegie-Mellon by using

```
$ finger @coke.elab.cs.cmu.edu
```

You will get output that tells you how many cans of each type of soft drink in the machine are cold, how many are warm, and whether each button will give you a warm or a cold soda. You can also get information on the vending machine that sells M&Ms by fingering the userid mnm as follows:

```
$ finger mnm@coke.elab.cs.cmu.edu
```

The output will tell you how full the machine is. Of course, the information on the coke and candy machines at CMU won't be very useful unless you plan to be in the vicinity of CMU in Pittsburgh! So you might find it useful to know that you can check the status of a soda vending machine at the Rochester Institute of Technology by using

```
$ finger drink@csh.rit.edu
```

You can also find out how to use the computerized Coke machine at the University of Wisconsin by using

```
$ finger coke@cs.wisc.edu
```

This won't be very useful unless you are in Madison, Wisconsin and have credit in your account.

# Logging In to Remote Systems via telnet

## Logging In to Remote Systems Using telnet

The **telnet** command provides an easy way to log in to remote systems. All you need to do to log in to a remote system is to issue this command followed by the name of the remote host. The following example shows how to log in to *math.unj.edu:*

```
$ telnet math.unj.edu
Trying ...
Connected to math.unj.edu
Escape character is '^]'
```

Sometimes you will not only need to log in to a remote system, but also to specify the port. This can be necessary when you are logging on to remote machines that offer some publicly accessible resource. To specify the port, you need only include the port number after the system name. For example, here is how you log in to port 3000 of the system *martini.eecs.umich.edu* to obtain geographical information about U.S. cities:

```
$ telnet martini.eecs.umich.edu 3000
Trying ...
Connected to martini.eecs.umich.edu
Escape character is '^]'.
```

Once you have made your telnet connection to a remote host, you will get a login: prompt. Log in as you ordinarily do. Note that some remote hosts are set up so that you do not need to give a password to log in.

# Using telnet Commands

Instead of giving **telnet** the name of a remote host, you can run a telnet session using the command

```
$ telnet
```

This starts a telnet session. You will get a prompt

```
telnet>
```

At this point you can enter a telnet command. For example, to connect to the remote host *astro.asu.edu,* use the telnet **open** command as follows:

```
telnet>open astro.asu.edu
```

Here is a list of the telnet commands that you can use at the "telnet>" prompt.

| Command | Function |
|---------|----------|
| **close** | Closes the current connection. |
| **display** | Shows operating parameters. |
| **mode** | Tries to enter line-by-line or character-at-a-time mode. |
| **open** | Connects to a site. |
| **quit** | Exits telnet session. |
| **send** | Transmits special characters ('send ?' for more). |
| **set** | Sets operating parameters ('set ?' for more). |
| **status** | Prints status information. |
| **toggle** | Toggles operating parameters ('toggle ?' for more). |
| **z** | Suspends telnet session. |
| **?** | Prints help information. |

# Suspending a telnet Connection

**TIP 591**

You can temporarily suspend a telnet session and run telnet commands directly.
To suspend a telnet connection, press CTRL-]. The resulting character is given when you make a telnet connection. When you press CTRL-], your remote connection is suspended, and you get the following prompt:

```
telnet>
```

You can return to your suspended connection by pressing the RETURN key.

If you are experiencing trouble with your remote connection, you can suspend your session and use the command

```
telnet> quit
```

You can end your session with the remote host with the telnet **close** command, as follows:

```
telnet> close
```

# Can You Suspend a telnet Session?

**TIP 592**

If your shell supports job control, you can use the **z** command at the telnet prompt to suspend a telnet session. This pauses **telnet** and returns you to your shell. You can run commands on the shell; **telnet** will remain in the background until you tell the shell to return to **telnet**. You do this using the **fg** command.

Because most hosts will automatically log a user off if there is no activity over a specified period of time, such as 30 minutes, you don't want to suspend a connection to a remote system you intend to resume for longer than this length of time.

# Why telnet Fails

Sometimes your attempt to log on to a remote host will fail. There are various reasons why this may occur. For example, if, when trying to telnet to *unj.edu*, you get a message

```
unj.edu: unknown host
```

the remote computer may currently be unavailable, the computer may not be part of the Internet, or you may have given an incorrect spelling for the host you meant.

If you attempt to reach a computer on the Internet, but your local network is unable to connect to this computer, you get a different message, for example:

```
Host is unreachable
```

There are some situations when you cannot give **telnet** the fully qualified domain name (FQDN), but instead you must supply the Internet Protocol (IP) number. For example, the command

```
$ telnet banana.un.edu
```

may not work, but the command

```
$ telnet 113.43.15.2
```

may work, where 113.43.15.2 is the IP number of *banana.un.edu*.

## Transferring Files with ftp

# Using ftp to Copy Files to and from Remote Machines

You can use the TCP/IP command **ftp** to copy files to or from a remote machine, as long as the remote machine is running software supporting **ftp** and is connected via a TCP/IP network to your machine.

TCP/IP software is available for a wide variety of operating systems other than UNIX, so that **ftp** can be used for copying files to and from a tremendous range of systems, including UNIX, DOS PC, Macintosh, VAX computers, and so on.

To use **ftp** to copy files, first enter the **ftp** command. You will then receive an ftp prompt. The following sample ftp session sets up a ftp connection with the host chicago and copies the file *articles* on chicago to your system:

```
$ ftp
ftp> open
(to) chicago
Connected to chicago
220   chicago FTP server ready
Name (chicago:khr): khr
331   password required for khr
Password:  xum22fip
230   user khr logged in
ftp> get articles
200   PORT command successful
150   ASCII data connection for articles (192.11.105.32,1440) (39 bytes).
256   ASCII Transfer complete.
local: articles  remote: articles
47 bytes received in 0.03 seconds (1.7 Kbytes/s)
```

You use the ftp **open** command to tell **ftp** that you want to make a connection to another machine. When you enter this command, you get the "(to)" prompt shown. After specifying the remote host chicago, the connection is made and the host chicago sends back message 220, as shown, and you are prompted for your name. When you supply this, chicago sends back the 331 message and you are prompted for your password. After supplying the correct password (which is not echoed back), you get message 230, which tells you that you are successfully logged in. You can now use the ftp **get** command to transfer the file *articles*. When you do this, chicago sends back a series of messages that tell you the transfer was completed.

# Using ftp Commands

**T**<sup>IP</sup>
**595**

Once you have established an ftp session with a remote host, you can run a variety of ftp commands. You can use the ftp **get** command to copy a file on the remote system to your own system. You can use the ftp **put** command to copy a file on your system to the remote system. You can copy more than one file from the remote system using the ftp **mget** command and the appropriate shell metacharacters. And you can copy more than one file on your system to the remote system using the ftp **mput** command. You can change directories on the remote machine using the ftp **cd** command and you can change directories on your local machine using the **lcd** command. You can print the name of the current directory with the ftp **pwd** command.

The following example shows the start of the ftp session used to copy all the files matching *chap* *(such as *chap1, chap2,* and so on) on the remote host to the local machine:

```
ftp>mget
(remote-files) chap*
mget chap1?  y
200  PORT command successful
150  ASCII data connection for chap1 (191.10.105.32,2211) (1280 bytes)
226  ASCII Transfer complete
local: chap1  remote: chap1
1290 bytes received in 0.11 seconds (11.8 Kbytes/s)
mget chap2? y
...
```

You could have eliminated the prompting used to ask you whether you want to transfer each file if you use the ftp **prompt** command. Note that you terminate an ftp session using the ftp **quit** command.

Here is a list of some of the most commonly used of the more than 50 different ftp commands. Look at the manual page for **ftp** (either using the **man** command or by reading it in the *Network User's and Administrator's Guide*) for details about all these ftp commands.

| ftp Command | Function |
| --- | --- |
| **append** | Appends a local file to a file on remote machine. |
| **ascii** | Sets the file transfer type to ASCII. |
| **bell** | Sounds a bell when file transfer is complete. |
| **binary** | Sets the file transfer type to binary. |
| **bye** | Terminates the ftp session. |
| **cd** | Changes current directory on the remote machine. |
| **close** | Terminates ftp connection to the current remote machine. |
| **delete** | Deletes file on remote machine. |
| **dir** | Prints listing of directory on remote machine. |
| **get** | Copies file on remote machine to local machine. |

| ftp Command | Function |
|---|---|
| **hash** | Prints toggle hash-sign (#) for each data block transferred. |
| **help** | Lists all ftp commands. |
| **lcd** | Changes current directory on local machine. |
| **ls** | Prints abbreviated listing of directory on remote machine. |
| **mget** | Copies specified remote files to local machine. |
| **mput** | Copies specified local files to remote host. |
| **open** | Sets up connection with remote host. |
| **prompt** | Toggles interactive prompting during multiple file transfer. |
| **put** | Copies local file to remote host. |
| **pwd** | Displays name of current directory on remote host. |
| **verbose** | Toggles verbose mode. |

# Copying a Binary File Using ftp

To use **ftp** to copy a binary file, such as an executable command, during your
ftp session, you must enter the **ftp** command

```
ftp> binary
```

Besides executable files, other files that may be binary include files generated by applications software,
such as word processors, database programs, and spreadsheets, compressed files, files of pictures or
sounds, and files produced by the **tar** program. (See Tip 606.)

# Finding Out Whether a Huge Download Is Still Running

It can take an extremely long time to download a huge file or group of files from a remote host using
the ftp **get** or **mget** command. In the middle of such a download, you may want to know if your
download is still running or if it has stopped for some reason! You can use the ftp **hash** command to
monitor the downloading of files. When you set the hash toggle to on, using

```
ftp> hash
```

each time a data block of 8192 bytes (or on some systems 4096 bytes) is sent, the toggle hash sign (#) will be printed. This lets you monitor the file transfer and see how many data blocks have already been transferred.

## Using ftp to Transfer Files from a DOS Machine

When you use **ftp** to copy a file on a DOS server, you first establish an ftp session with this machine, just as you would with any remote system. To change directories to find the file you are interested in, use the **cd** command. First, you will need to change to the DOS disk containing the file you want. For example,

```
ftp> cd C:
```

will put you on the C: drive. Once you have done this, you can change to the directory on the C: drive you are interested in. However, you need to use slashes instead of backslashes in the path on the DOS machine. For example, to change to the directory *public\math\results* on the C: drive, use the command

```
ftp> cd public/math/results
```

(If you forget to change the backslashes to slashes you will get an ftp error message). After you change to this directory, you can use

```
ftp> get primes
```

to transfer the file *c:\public\math\results\primes* to your system.

## Transferring Files to and from a Macintosh

You can use **ftp** to transfer files to and from a Macintosh. To do so, you need to know a little about Macintosh files and directories. First, when you connect to a Macintosh via **ftp**, the Macintosh will only ask you to supply a name and not a password. When you list files on the Macintosh using the ftp **dir** command, you may find both files and Macintosh folders, which are the equivalent to UNIX subdirectories; folders are shown with a trailing / (slash). For example, when connected to a Macintosh, you may find

```
ftp> dir
Addresses
Meeting Notes
Memos/
```

Here you see two files, *Addresses* and *Meeting Notes,* as well as the folder *Memos.* Note that the names of files on a Macintosh can contain spaces, as in *Meeting Notes.* When transferring such files using **ftp**, you need to place the name in quotes. For example, to transfer the file *Meeting Notes* to your system, giving it the name *notes,* use

```
ftp> get "Meeting Notes" notes
```

# Using Anonymous ftp to Copy Files

**TIP 600**

You can obtain a wide variety of public domain software on the Internet. Much of this software can be obtained via anonymous ftp. With anonymous ftp, users don't need to supply a specific password. Rather, systems offering files via anonymous ftp are configured to accept any string as a valid password. Sometimes a system will ask you to supply your e-mail address, your name, or some particular string as the password, but this is not required for logging in. The following session illustrates how anonymous ftp works for transferring ASCII files:

```
$ ftp zippo@abc.com
Connected to zippo.abc.com
220  zippo.ABC.COM  FTP server ready
Name (zippo.abc.com: qxj):  anonymous
331  Guest login ok, send e-mail address as password.
Password:  qxj@florida.edu
230  Guest login ok, access restrictions apply.
ftp> cd pub/crypto
250 CWD command successful.
ftp> get publickey
200 PORT command successful.
```

```
150 ASCII data connection for publickey (192.11.105.32,2229)  (17202
                                                                bytes)
256 Transfer complete
local: publickey remote: publickey
17202 bytes received in 19 seconds (0.90 Kbytes/s)
ftp> quit
221  Goodbye
```

# Using .netrc as a Shortcut for ftping to Remote Hosts

The *.netrc* file can be set up in a user's home directory as a way to provide a shortcut method to ftping to a machine (much like the *.rhosts* file for **rlogin**). The permissions on the *.netrc* file should be set to disallow read access by group and others (for example, mode 600 is good). A typical *.netrc* entry looks like this:

```
machine sunsite.unc.edu
login anonymous
password navarra@casbah.acns.nwu.edu
```

The entries can be separated by spaces, tabs, or newlines. Here we have an entry for the machine *sunsite.unc.edu* with the login name anonymous and password *navarra@casbah.acns.nwu.edu*. Note that some ftp clients require that you provide a password of the form *username@hostname*. In this way, we can anonymously ftp to sunsite without going through any login procedure. You can also do more than anonymous ftp by supplying a username and a password on the appropriate lines, but it's considered bad practice to have a real user account password in a file (even though the permissions are set so that no one else can read it).

The *.netrc* file can be used in conjunction with a shell HERE document to do batch anonymous ftping. As a simple example, you can run the following script to take a machine name as the first argument and a filename as the second argument. The script will ftp to the appropriate place and get the file

```
$ cat autoftp
#! /bin/sh
# Uncomment this if you don't have MODE set as an environmental
# variable.
#MODE=ascii
```

```
machine=$1
pathname="$2"
filename=basename $2
echo "This is auto ftp. You are connecting to $1"
echo "The file you requested is $pathname with mode $MODE"
ftp $machine << !EOF
$MODE
get $pathname $filename
bye
EOF
$ export MODE=bin
$ autoftp prep.ai.mit.edu /pub/tools/imake.tar
This is auto ftp. You are connecting to prep.ai.mit.edu
The file you requested is /pub/tools/imake.tar with mode bin
$ ls imake.tar
imake.tar
```

In this example, the variable MODE is set on the command line and the **autoftp** script is run. If you had previously set a default MODE (perhaps in a login script), then any time you run **autoftp**, it would use that mode by default.

However, there are drawbacks to using the *.netrc* file. For one thing, it takes up space for each machine for really no reason. If all we want to do is anonymous ftp, we can simply bypass any *.netrc* entry and just pass along any needed information directly in the script

```
#! /bin/sh
# Uncomment this if you don't have MODE set as an environmental
# variable.
#MODE=ascii
machine=$1
pathname="$2"
filename=`basename $2`
echo "This is auto ftp. You are connecting to $1"
echo "The file you requested is $pathname with mode $MODE"
# note use ftp -n to force login. Do not assume .netrc entry
ftp -n $machine << !EOF
user anonymous $USER@`hostname`
$MODE
get $pathname $filename
bye
EOF
```

This script is by no means robust. For one thing, it cannot get multiple files at once. For a more robust **autoftp** script, see the **aftp** script in the following tip.

# Automating Anonymous ftp

Here is a very useful perl script that you can use to automate anonymous ftp to a remote site.

```
#! /usr/bin/perl
# aftp -- A simple perl script to automate anonymous ftp to a site to
#         get file(s). Aftp comes with the con distribution but may also
#         be used separately. For more details using aftp, see the con
#         man page.
# Usage - aftp [b(in)|a(scii)] machine /full/path/name(s)
# Author: John Navarra (navarra@casbah.acns.nwu.edu)

# set up some variables. Edit these if not right on your machine.
$MODE=$ENV{'MODE'};
$FTP='/usr/ucb/ftp';
$ME=$ENV{'USER'};
$HOSTNAME=`hostname`;

# A "yes or no" subroutine.
sub y_or_n {
        local($prompt) = @_;
        print STDOUT $prompt;
        local($answer)=scalar(<STDIN>;            );
        if ( $answer =~ /^n/i )  {
           $MODE=( $MODE =~ ascii ) ? bin : ascii;
        }
}
# If aftp was not called with an ascii or bin option we will go thru
# some rigamorole to figure out the correct mode.
if ($ARGV[0] !~ /^-/) {
   &y_or_n("Transfer using $MODE mode? [yes] ");
}
while ($ARGV[0] =~ /^-/) {
```

```
   $_ = shift;
   if (/^-ascii|^-a/) {
      $MODE=ascii;
   }
   elsif (/^-bin|^-b/) {
      $MODE=bin;
   }
   else {
      print "aftp: not an option! Use -a[scii] or -b[in] \n";
      exit(0);
   }
}
$computer=shift;
print "Ftping to $computer using $MODE mode ... \n ";
# Let's do some ftp shall we?
open(FTP, "| $FTP -n $computer");
printf(FTP "user anonymous $ME@$HOSTNAME \n");
printf(FTP "$MODE \n" );
foreach $path (@ARGV) {
   ($basename = $path) =~ s!.*/!!;        # This mess gets basename
                                          #  from path

   if ($basename =~ /\*/ ) {              # See if we want multiple
                                          #  files
       ($dirpath = $path) =~ s!/[^/]*$!!; # This mess gets dirname
                                          # from path
       printf(FTP "cd $dirpath \n");
       printf(FTP "prompt \n");
       printf(FTP "mget $basename \n");
   }
   else {
       printf(FTP "get $path $basename \n");
       printf(FTP "\!echo got $basename \n");
   }
}
close (FTP);
print "Got'em! \n ";
```

**aftp** uses the enviromental variable MODE to determine which mode should be the default to transfer files. You can set MODE on the command line or in one of your startup scripts. However, if **aftp** is called with the **-a** (for *A*SCII) or **-b** (for *b*in) option, that mode will override MODE. The next argument for **aftp** is the machine name and the last argument is a list of filenames (which must be the full pathnames) to **ftp**. If the list contains a "*", it is assumed you want to **ftp** multiple files so the proper ftp commands are sent.

Here are a few runs. We want to contact the Mystery Science Theatre 3000 archive site to get the theme song, a Shadowrama Gif file, and any other pictures of Joel:

```
$ export MODE=bin # setting the value of MODE directly on the
# command-line.
$ aftp cs.odu.edu /pub/mst3k/sounds/theme.au \
  /pub/mst3k/images/shdrama.gif
Transfer using bin mode? [yes]   <HIT RETURN HERE>
Ftping to cs.odu.edu using bin mode ...
got theme.au
got shdrama.gif
Got'em!
$ ls
shdrama.gif      theme.au

$ aftp -bin cs.odu.edu /pub/mst3k/images/*joel* # We are not
                                       # prompted for mode
Ftping to cs.odu.edu using bin mode ...
Interactive mode off.   # This is a message from ftp not our program.
                   # Got'em!
$ ls
joelbot1.gif   joelbot2.gif   joeleats.gif   shdrama.gif   theme.au
```

# TIP 603

# Resolving Internet Addresses

Sometimes you may need to **ftp** anonymously to a remote host whose symbolic name (such as *ftp.nisc.sri.com*) is known to your computer, but whose Internet address (such as 192.33.33.22) is not known. When you attempt to **ftp** to such a site, you'll get an "unknown host" error message since the */etc/hosts* file does not contain an entry that provides address resolution of the symbolic name.

In such situations, you can use a name server on the Internet to resolve this. Create a file called */etc/resolv.conf* and put the following line in it:

```
nameserver 26.28.0.13
```

If you cannot write in */etc,* and your system adminstrator won't create this file, you still might be able to use the **nslookup** command. A typical usage would be

```
nslookup unknown-host 26.28.0.13
```

or

```
nslookup - 26.28.0.13    # to use interactively.
```

# Checking the Route to a Remote Host

**TIP 604**

Some systems have a command called **traceroute** that you can use to see the route from your system to a remote host. For example, to see the steps of the path from a system named *kosmos.wcc.govt.nz,* use

```
$ traceroute kosmos.wcc.govt.nz
```

If you run this command several times, you may see different routes as network connections vary over time.

# Handling Different File Types

# Converting Binary Files to ASCII Files

**TIP 605**

Sometimes you will need to convert a binary file to an ASCII file. For example, you may want to use e-mail to send a binary file over the Internet. The basic idea required to do this conversion is to group together blocks of eight bits to form bytes that correspond to ASCII characters. There is a UNIX utility called **uuencode** that performs this function.

For example, suppose you want to send the executable command **ptest**, a program that tests whether an integer is prime, to your friend Amanda. To produce an ASCII file that you can e-mail, you could first use the command line

```
$ uuencode primetest < ptest > tempmail
```

The name *primetest* is a tag you've attached to this file. This tag is required since it is used by the **uudecode** program to name the binary file it forms from the ASCII file *ptest*.

Next, you would use a program such as **mail** or **mailx** to send the file *tempmail* to Amanda. When you send her this message, you will need to tell how to recover the file, that is, to use the **uudecode** command. When Amanda reads her mail, saves the file *tempmail* into a file with this same name on her system, and runs the command

```
$ uudecode tempmail
```

she will recover the binary file you started with. And because you used the tag *primetest* when uuencoding this file, it will have the name *primetest* on her system.

Files that have been uuencoded and made available for transfer using **ftp** are usually given the filename extension *.uue*, for example, *primetest.uue*. If such a file is then compressed using **compress**, it will have the name *primetest.uue.Z*.

# TIP 606 — Working with tar Files

Many of the files that you download from remote hosts using **ftp** will be tar files. These are files that contain archives packed using the **tar** command. So when you unpack such a file, you will end up with a collection of files and directories. You will know that you have a tar file if its name ends with the filename extension *.tar*. Here are the steps you should follow to unpack a tar file, say *explorer.tar*.

First, make a new directory to hold the contents of this file, say *explorer*, and move the tar file *explorer.tar* to this new directory. Then change to this directory and run the command

```
$ tar -fvx explorer.tar
```

This will unpack the tar file and produce a collection of files and maybe directories. (The -f option tells **tar** that the name of the tar file *follows*, the -v option tells **tar** to display information on files as they are extracted, and the -x option tells **tar** to extract files.) At this point you might want to look at the files using the **ls** command and remove the original tar file.

You will also find that many files are tar files that have been compressed using the **compress** command. To unpack these, you have to use the **uncompress** command. For example, if you have retrieved the file *explorer.tar.Z,* you would first use

```
$ uncompress explorer.tar.Z
```

and then follow the same steps as before.

Similarly, if you encounter tar files compressed using a method other than **compress**, such as files compressed using **gzip** (such files will have the extension *.tar.gz*), you must first undo the compression using **zip -d** and then follow the steps outlined for extracting the files.

By the way, since filenames in DOS must have a single extension, the DOS extension *.taz* is used for tar files that have been compressed using **compress**, instead of the suffix *.tar.Z* used for this purpose on UNIX Systems.

# Transferring Compressed Files

When you explore the Internet, you will run into files compressed using one of a variety of different compression programs. Such files will have filename extensions, such as *.z* for files compressed using **pack** and *.Z* for files compressed using **compress**. A file could have been compressed on a UNIX system, a DOS PC, a Macintosh, or some other system. If you transfer a compressed file to your system, you will have to decompress it using the appropriate decompression program. If you don't have the decompression program, you can try to obtain it via anonymous **ftp**; use archie to look for a site. Here is a list of the most common compression programs, showing the corresponding decompression program and the filename extension used for files compressed with the program.

| Compression Program | Decompression Program | Filename Extension |
| --- | --- | --- |
| **compress** | **uncompress** | *.Z* |
| **gzip** | **zip -d** | *.gz* |
| **pack** | **unpack** | *.z* |

| Compression Program | Decompression Program | Filename Extension |
|---|---|---|
| Packit | unpit | *.pit* |
| pkzip | unzip41 | *.ZIP* |
| Stuffit | unsit | *.Sit* |
| zoo210 | zoo210 | *.zoo* |

# Recovering Corrupted tar Files

**608**

If you have a corrupted tar file, all may not be lost. You can try to recover it using the **tarx** utility that has been posted to *comp.sources.unix*. **tarx** uses a pattern-matching approach to identify tar header blocks, and will ignore lots of problems such as wrong checksums, read errors, and so on. You can obtain **tarx** via anonymous ftp from *keos.helsinki.fi* in */pub/archives/comp.sources.unix,* from *src.doc.ic.ac.uk* in */usenet/comp.archives/volume24/compression/tar,* and from *rs1.rrz.uni-koeln.de* in */.disk1/usenet/comp.archives/compression/tar.* You can use archie to find other sites if necessary.

# Creating tar Archives

**609**

You may want to create your own tar files, perhaps to archive some files or to prepare them for transfer to a remote system. You can create your own tar files using the **tar** command with the appropriate options. For example, suppose you want to pack the files *hamlet, macbeth, lear,* and *othello* into an archive with the name *tragedy.tar.* You can do this with the command

```
$ tar -cfv tragedy.tar hamlet macbeth lear othello
```

The options to **tar** used here are **-c** (for *c*reate), **-f** (for *f*ilename), and **-v** (for *v*erbose).

You may also want to compress the resulting tar file. To do this, use

```
$ compress tragedy.tar
```

The compressed file will be named *tragedy.tar.Z.*

There are other tools, such as **cpio**, for creating archives. See the Tips in Chapter 11 for details.

## Working with shar Files

**TIP 610**

Some of the files you'll find on the Internet and on USENET are **shar** (from *sh*ell *ar*chive) files. These are files containing an archive of files in the form of a shell script. Because of this form, it is very easy to unpack shar files to extract the individual files in them. When you get a mail message or copy a netnews article containing a shar file, the first thing to do is to save the message or article in a file. Then you need to edit this file to remove any headers that are present, leaving just the original shar file. To unpack the archive and extract the files stored there, you now need only run the **sh** command. This will run the file as a shell script that automatically unpacks the shar file. For example, suppose you want to unpack the shar file named *book.shar*. You would use

```
$ sh book.shar
```

Some systems include a command called **unshar** that does two things to a file. Let's say you have a file called *book* that contains a header followed by a shar file. First, the header is put into a separate file, in this case named *book.shar.hdr*. Second, the shar file is unpacked.

## Creating a shar File

**TIP 611**

It's easy to create a shell archive as long as your system has the **shar** command. Give this command the names of the files you want packed in the archive and redirect the output to the name of the file that you want to put this archive in. For instance, the command

```
$ shar preface chap1 chap2 chap3 appendix index > book.shar
```

packs the files *preface, chap1, chap2, chap3, appendix,* and *index* as a shar archive and puts this shar archive in the file *book.shar*.

Here is a version of the shar command that you can use if you don't have one on your system.

```
###################################################################
##
##   This is a shell command (shar) to combine
##   text files into a shar archive.  The original
```

```
##   files can be extracted by running the archive
##   file as a shell command (i.e., "sh archive-file").
##
#####################################################################

##
##   Initialize
##

diagnostic='eval echo >&2'
usage='USAGE: $0  files'
trap '$diagnostic "$0: Quitting Early"; /bin/rm -f $FILE; exit 1' \
1 2 3 15

if [ $# -eq 0 ]
then      $diagnostic $usage
     exit 1
fi

contents=$*
FILE=/tmp/SHAR$$
NAME="Ima G. Programmer"
ADDR="Well Labs"
MACH="...!xyzzy!IGP"
echo 'Output will be in shar.out'

##
##   Put out shar header.
##

>$FILE
echo "#################################################################"
 >>$FILE
echo "#" >>$FILE
echo "#  This is a shar archive.  Remove anything before" >>$FILE
echo "#  this banner  Extract with sh, not csh." >>$FILE
echo "#  Make this file executable, and run it as a shell.">>$FILE
echo "#  The rest of this file will extract:" >>$FILE
echo "#" >>$FILE
echo "#  " $contents >>$FILE
echo "#" >>$FILE
echo "#  Archive created:" `date` >>$FILE
```

```
echo "#" >>$FILE
echo "#  By:" $NAME >>$FILE
echo "#     " $ADDR >>$FILE
echo "#     " $MACH >>$FILE
echo
"#############################################################">>$FILE
echo "" >>$FILE


##
##  Process each file, and put it into $FILE with
##  the appropriate separator.
##

for file in $*

do   if [ ! -r $file ]
     then  $diagnostic "shar: $file cannot be archived"
           /bin/rm -f $FILE;
           exit 1;
     fi
separator="!E!O!F!$file"
    echo "echo" >>$FILE
    echo "echo +++++++++++++++++++++++++++++++++++++++++++++++++++"
 >>$FILE
    echo "echo extracting - $file 2>&1" >>$FILE
    echo "sed 's/^X//' > $file << '$separator'" >>$FILE
    sed 's/^/X/' <$file >>$FILE
    echo "$separator">>$FILE
    echo "echo ''" >>$FILE
    echo
"#############################################################">>$FILE
    echo "">>$FILE

##
## Use wc for primitive checksum
##

echo "echo Possible errors detected by  word count in $file:" >>$FILE
echo "echo ''" >>$FILE
echo "echo 'lines words characters'">>$FILE
echo "echo SENT:">>$FILE
echo "echo `wc $file`" >>$FILE
```

```
echo "echo RECEIVED:">>$FILE
echo "echo \`wc $file\`" >>$FILE
echo "echo ''">>$FILE
echo "echo Checksum and Block count for $file:" >>$FILE
echo "echo ''" >>$FILE
echo "echo 'Checksum block-count'">>$FILE
echo "echo SENT:">>$FILE
echo "echo `sum $file`" >>$FILE
echo "echo RECEIVED:">>$FILE
echo "echo \`sum $file\`" >>$FILE
echo "echo ''" >>$FILE
echo "chmod 700 $file" >>$FILE
echo "ls -l $file" >>$FILE
echo "echo ''" >>$FILE
done

##
## Finish up, move $FILE to shar.out and exit
##

echo "echo ">>$FILE
echo "echo Thats all Folks!" >>$FILE
echo "exit 0" >>$FILE
mv $FILE ./shar.out && chmod +rx shar.out || echo "shar:  could not \
 make shar.out: output is in $FILE" >&2
exit 0
```

# Using the Berkeley Remote Commands

## What Are the Berkeley Remote Commands?

The Berkeley remote commands, also known as the r* commands since their names all begin with "r", are used to carry out a variety of tasks on remote UNIX machines connected to your machine via a TCP/IP network. This family of commands includes **rlogin**, which logs in to remote hosts (see Tips

613-616); **rcp**, which transfers files (see Tip 617-620); **rsh**, which executes a command on a remote machine (see Tips 621-623); **rwho** and **rusers**, which are used to see who is logged in to remote machines (see Tip 624); and **rwall**, which is used to send a message to all users on your local network (see Tip 625). The Berkeley remote commands are used only on networks of UNIX computers, unlike the corresponding TCP/IP commands, which can be used on networks containing UNIX machines, DOS PCs, Macintoshes, and other types of computers.

# How to Log In to a Remote System with rlogin

**TIP 613**

You can use the **rlogin** (for *r*emote *login*) command to log in to a remote UNIX machine connected to your machine via a TCP/IP network. For example, to log in to the remote machine macademia, use the command

```
$ rlogin macademia
```

To log in to macademia, with the same user ID, it is necessary that macademia be in the host database of your local machine. If it is, and your machine can establish a connection to macademia, you will be automatically logged in without entering a password if you have an entry in the password database of macademia and your machine is in the file */etc/hosts.equiv* on macademia.

You can also be logged in without entering a password if there is a line in the *.rhosts* file in the home directory of the login on the remote machine, with either your local machine's name, if the login name is the same as yours, or your local machine's name and your user name.

Otherwise, as long as you have an entry in the password database of the remote machine, you can log in when you enter the correct password for your account on the remote machine. When you log in this way, you will not be able to run certain remote processes.

The **rlogin** command supplies the remote host with your user ID and tells this host what kind of terminal you are using by sending the value of TERM.

# Using rlogin to Log In to a Remote System Using a Different User ID

You can log in to a remote system using a different user ID by using the -l option of **rlogin**. For example, to log in to the remote system kalamazoo with user ID gix, use

```
$ rlogin -l gix
```

# Suspending an rlogin Connection

If you run a shell with job control, you can suspend an **rlogin** connection and return to it later. To do this, type

```
~CTRL-Z
```

When you suspend an **rlogin** connection, this connection becomes a stopped process on your local machine and you return to the machine from which you issued the **rlogin** command. You can reactivate the connection by typing **fg**, followed by RETURN. When you are logged in to a succession of machines using **rlogin**, you can return to your local machine by pressing ~ CTRL-Z. You can suspend only your last **rlogin** connection by pressing ~~ CTRL-Z.

# How Can You Abort an rlogin Connection?

You can abort an **rlogin** connection by pressing CTRL-D or typing **exit**, or ~. (tilde dot). This will return you to your original machine. If you have logged in to a succession of machines using **rlogin**, you can return to your local machine by typing ~. (tilde dot). If you type ~~. (tilde tilde dot), you will abort only your last connection.

# Copying Files on Remote Systems Using rcp

**T**IP **617**

You can copy a file on a remote host connected to your machine with a TCP/IP network using **rcp** (for *remote copy*), as long as you are allowed to do so. (See Tip 620.) For example, you can copy a file on a remote host, say the file */home/addresses* on the host verde, into a directory on your local machine, say */home/data*, giving it the same name, by using

```
$ rcp verde:/home/addresses    /home/data
```

If you want to change the name of this file, you must also give the new filename. So to change the name of this file to *list*, you would use

```
$ rcp verde:/home/addresses    /home/data/list
```

# Copying Directories on Remote Machines with rcp

**T**IP **618**

You can also copy entire directories using **rcp** with the **-r** (*recursive*) option. (See Tip 620 for when you are allowed to do so.) For example, to copy the directory */home/programs* on the remote host hook into the directory */home/misc* on your local machine, you could use

```
$ rcp -r hook:/home/programs   /home/misc
```

# Copying a File from Your Machine to a Remote Machine

**T**IP **619**

You can use **rcp** to copy a file from your local machine to a remote host connected to your machine on a TCP/IP network (as long as you are allowed to so; see Tip 620). For example, to copy the file */home/list* to the remote host halibut, to the directory */home/people*, you can use

```
$ rcp /home/list  halibut:/home/people
```

You could rename this file as */home/people/addresses* using

```
$ rcp /home/list  halibut:/home/data/addresses
```

# When Are You Allowed to Transfer Files Using rcp?

To be able to use **rcp** to transfer files to or from a remote host connected to your machine via a TCP/IP network, you must have an entry in the password database on that machine and furthermore, the machine you are using must be in the remote machine's list of trusted hosts. That is, your local machine must be listed in the remote host's */etc/host.equiv* file or in your *.rhosts* file on the remote host.

# Executing Commands on Remote Machines Using rsh

You can run a command on a remote system connected to your local host via a TCP/IP network using the **rsh** (for *r*emote *sh*ell) command. To be allowed to do so, you must have an entry in the password database on the remote machine and the machine you are using must be a trusted machine on this remote host, either by being listed in its */etc/hosts.equiv* file or by having an appropriate entry in your *.rhosts* file in your host directory on the remote machine. To run a command on a remote machine, you just need to give **rsh** the name of this machine and the command to run. For example, you can list the contents of the directory */home/info* on the remote host toad, by using

```
$ rsh toad ls /home/info
```

# Using rsh with Redirection Symbols and/or Metacharacters

When using **rsh** to run commands on remote hosts, you need to put quotes around shell metacharacters and redirection symbols in the commands you want run on remote hosts. For example, to append the file *frogs* to the file *newts* on the remote host noah, use

```
$ rsh noah cat frogs ">>" newts
```

If you used

```
$ rsh noah cat frogs >> newts
```

the file *frogs* on the host noah would be appended to your local file *newts,* not the file *newts* on noah.

# Do You Need to Run Commands on a Particular Remote Host Often?

If you find that you need to run commands on a particular remote host on your TCP/IP network often, you may want to set up a symbolic link so that you need only enter the name of the host to run a command on it. For example, suppose you run

```
$ ln -s /usr/sbin/rsh   /usr/hosts/cheese
```

and put */usr/hosts* in your search path. Then to list the files in the directory */usr/lib* on cheese, you need only type

```
$ cheese ls /usr/lib
```

When you do this, to remotely log in to cheese, you need only type

```
$ cheese
```

instead of the longer

```
$ rlogin cheese
```

# Using rusers and rwho to Find Out Who Is Logged In to Remote Machines

You can use the **rwho** command to find out who is logged in to the machines on your local network. The machines on the local network have to be running the **rwho** service daemon, **rwhod**, for you to get information on their current users. When your machine has not received a report from a machine for over five minutes, **rwho** assumes the machine is down, and doesn't report on users who were logged in to that machine. **rwho** also doesn't include users who have not had any activity for more than an hour. If you want to include such users, use the -**a** option of **rwho**.

You can find out who the current users are on a machine in your local network using the **rusers** command. A remote host will respond only if it is running the rusers service daemon, **rusersd**. You can get additional information on users, including when each user logged in, idle time, their terminal connection, and so on, using the -**l** option.

# Sending a Message to Everyone on Your Network

You can use the **rwall** (for *remote write all*) command to send a message to all users on a remote host. This will work as long as the remote host is running **rwalld**). For example, you can send a message to all users on the remote host pelee using the command:

```
$ rwall pelee
You are all invited to a party at John's Friday night.
Please RSVP via e-mail.  See you then!
^D
```

Users on pelee refusing to accept messages will not get this message. In general, **rwall** is reserved for use only by network administrators to warn users of networks and systems coming down. You should avoid casual use of **rwall**.

# Sending Faxes

## Sending Faxes from UNIX Systems

To be able to send and receive faxes from your UNIX system you need to have a fax-modem and the appropriate software supporting fax communications. This software should support sending text files and files in other formats as faxes. It should also support receiving and displaying faxes. You can find several different commercial software packages supporting fax communications on UNIX systems in the *Open Systems Product Directory,* published by UniForum. There are also commercial packages that support faxing large-format drawings from UNIX workstations. You can also find public domain software supporting fax for UNIX systems on the Internet. For example, look in the directory *pub/systems/fax-3.2.1.tar.Z* on the host *transit.ai.mit.edu.* (Tip 606 explains how to retrieve such a file.)

Another way to send faxes from UNIX machines is to use AT&T Mail and the accompanying PMX software. Using this service, you can send text files as faxes from your UNIX machine.

Finally, you can send faxes using the Internet Fax Server. See the following tip for details.

## Sending Faxes Using the Internet Fax Server

July 1993 saw the introduction of the Internet Fax service. Carl Malamud and Marshall Rose founded this service so that (eventually) documents could be sent via Internet e-mail to anyone with access to a fax machine. The service is based on a number of sites that have volunteered to provide coverage to a certain area—either a single fax machine, all the fax machines in a single location, or all the fax machines in a certain geographic area.

To use this service, you can use e-mail to send the document you want to fax to a special address, formed by inverting the telephone number of the target fax machine, inserting periods between the digits, tagging on the domain-name of the fax service, and prepending the target person's name. For example, to send a fax to Bodwyn Wook, whose organization is Bureau B and whose fax number is +1 908 555 4321, you would address the piece of mail to

```
Bodwyn_Wook/Bureau_B@1.2.3.4.5.5.5.8.0.9.1.tpc.int
```

When the piece of mail arrives at a *tpc.int* mail server, the rest of the address is processed and the message is forwarded to the appropriate server for that number (or it is bounced if no one services that area). The characters _ and / are special in the name field (to the left of the @); _ is mapped to a space and / to end-of-line (although the / will cause trouble for mail going over UUCP links). In the example described, the fax cover sheet might end up looking like this:

> Please deliver to:
> Bodwyn Wook
> Bureau B

How do you find out whether an area has coverage? First, mail sent to *tpc-coverage@town.hall.org* will return a list of covered areas.

Alternatively, some helpful programs are available to help with real-time coverage queries. You can get these by getting the file *rp.tar.Z* by anonymous ftp from *ftp.ice.uci.edu,* in the subdirectory *mrose/tpc.* The script *rpvalidate* (in the directory *client*) will, when fed a phone number, print either "accessible" or "not accessible". This tool uses **dig**, and a fairly recent version of **awk**—it's written to use **gawk** but **nawk** seems to work as well.

As of late December, 1993, coverage was available in parts of these countries or calling areas:

> North American Numbering Plan (United States/Canada/Mexico/Caribbean)
> New Zealand
> Australia
> Denmark
> Germany
> Netherlands
> United Kingdom

The package mentioned above also contains instructions on how to become a server, for yourself, your organization, or a geographic area.

# Chapter 10
## The Internet

# Using the Internet

## TIP 628

## What's the Internet?

The *Internet* is a network of computers that use common conventions for naming and addressing systems. No one owns the Internet. Instead, it is a collection of interconnected independent networks. People in over one hundred countries have access to the Internet. There are close to one million hosts known to the service that administers names for systems on the Internet, with an estimated total of over four million users.

The Internet is an extremely useful computer network. It is growing at a fantastic rate both in number of users and amount of traffic, so by the time you read this, there will probably be millions of additional Internet users.

There are many reasons why the Internet is growing so quickly. One reason is that the Internet provides a network for connections for e-mail messages throughout the world. Another reason is that you can find a tremendous variety of information on the Internet and can access this information using a wide variety of services. (See the following tips for how to use the Internet.)

## TIP 629

## Accessing the Internet

If you are a user on a multiuser system, your system administrator may already have connected your site to the Internet. If you are a user on such a system, you can access Internet services with the appropriate commands as described in later tips in this chapter. However, if you want to access the Internet from your own personal computer, you have two choices: connecting your system to the Internet directly or using one of the public-access providers. Unless you plan to become heavily involved with the Internet, we recommend that you use a public-access provider. To use one of these providers, you need a modem and the appropriate data communications software.

Most public-access providers charge a fee for using their system to access the Internet. These providers usually offer a wide range of Internet services, including e-mail, netnews, file transfer via **ftp**, and remote logon via **telnet**. You will want to find a nearby Internet access provider to keep your phone bills from getting out of hand (or one that has an 800 number). You probably will do better by choosing an access provider who charges a flat monthly rate rather than usage fees, since it's easy to find yourself connected to the Internet for long hours when you expect to be connected for only a few minutes. You should also try out an Internet access provider, when possible. Many providers allow you to log on as a guest to try out their services.

You can find a useful list of full-service public-access providers in the book *The Internet Complete Reference* by Harley Hahn and Rick Stout (Berkeley, CA: Osborne/McGraw-Hill, 1994). They include a list of public-access Internet service providers in the United States and Canada by area code, and a list of public-access service providers in Europe and the South Pacific by country. They provide the voice telephone number, e-mail address, and telephone number and login required for guest access, for each provider, when this information is available.

There are some Internet public-access providers who do not charge a fee. These are the *Freenets*. (See the following tip for details.) Although not paying money for services is nice, there are some disadvantages to using Freenets: limited services, erratic availability, and heavy use that causes performance problems.

# Free Internet Access

**TIP 630**

You may be able to obtain free access to some Internet services by joining a Freenet, which is an open-access computer system that charges no fees. You can find quite a few Freenets listed in the books *The Internet Complete Reference* by Hahn and Stout, and *Navigating the Internet* by Mark Gibbs and Richard Smith, (Carmel, IN: Howard W. Sams, 1993). The Cleveland Freenet, set up by Case Western Reserve University, is one such network. It is part of the National Telecomputing Public Network. You can register as a member of the Cleveland Freenet by logging on to one of the systems *freenet-in-a.cwru.edu, freenet-in-b.cwru.edu,* or *freenet-in-c.cwru.edu* as a guest user and use the menu interface to apply for an account. You will receive a logname and password after mailing the administrator a form. Once you have your account, you can use the Cleveland Freenet to send and receive e-mail, read netnews, participate in chat sessions, and use a variety of other Internet services.

# Methods for Accessing Internet Resources

Once you have located an Internet resource, you'll need to access it. There are three basic methods for doing so. The simplest and least interactive way to access information is via the **finger** command. (See Tip 632 for how to access information via **finger** and Tip 708 for how you can offer information via **finger**). Another way to obtain resources is by copying files on remote computers. To do this, use the **ftp** command. (See Tip 594 for information on this.) The third major way is to actually log in to a remote machine using the **telnet** command. Once you are logged in, you can access resources by running some specific commands. (See Tip 589 for how to use **telnet**.)

You will find the directions for which method to use to access particular information in lists of Internet Resources. (See Tip 701.) These lists tell you whether to use **finger**, **ftp**, or **telnet** to access particular resources.

# Using finger to Get Information

There are many information providers on the Internet that give their information via the **finger** command. All you need to do to gain access to this is to use **finger** with the appropriate host. For example, you can get information about the tropical storm forecast by running

```
$ finger forecase@typhoon.atmos.colostate.edu.
```

The following list includes some of the information you can get using **finger**.

| Information | Source |
| --- | --- |
| Aurora activity | *aurora@xi.uleth.ca* |
| Baseball scores | *jtchern@ocf.berkeley.edu* |
| *Billboard* charts | *buckmr@aix.rpi.edu* |
| Earthquake information | *quake@geophys.washington.edu* |
| NASA newsletter | *nasanews@space.mit.edu* |
| Tropical storm activity | *forecast@typhoon.atmos.colostate.edu* |

For a current list of such information services, consult the Updated Internet Service posted monthly to *alt.internet.services, comp.misc,* and *news.answers.*

# Using Anonymous ftp to Retrieve Files

One of the most common ways to obtain public domain software is to use anonymous ftp over the Internet. When you use anonymous ftp, you don't have to supply a particular password. When you make an anonymous ftp connection, enter "anonymous" as your name and supply either "guest" or your e-mail address as the password, depending on what the remote system asks for. Then follow the usual ftp commands. Remember that many large files are made available for anonymous ftp in compressed tar format. To copy these files using **ftp**, you must use the ftp **binary** command. When you get these files, you'll need to uncompress them and then use **tar** to recover the original files. Here is an example of an anonymous ftp session:

```
$ ftp math.unj.edu
Connected to math.unj.edu
220 math.unj.edu  FTP server ready
Name (math.unj.edu: gauss):  anonymous
331  Guest login ok, send ident as password
Password: gauss@cs.njsu.edu
230  Guest login ok, access restrictions apply
ftp> binary
200  Type set to I
ftp> cd pub/math
250  CWD command successful
ftp> get primelist.tar.Z
200  PORT command successful
150  Opening BINARY mode data connection for primelist.tar.Z (188828
     bytes).
226  Transfer complete 188828 bytes received in 1.7 seconds
ftp> quit
221  Goodbye.
```

# Learning More About the Internet

Until recently, there were no good books devoted entirely to the Internet and its services. Within the last year or two, many such books have appeared. For example, you can consult *The Internet Complete Reference* by Hahn and Stout (Osborne/McGraw-Hill, 1994), *The Whole Internet, User's Guide and Catalog* by Ed Krol (Sebastopol, CA: O'Reilly and Associates, 1992), *Navigating the Internet* by Gibbs and Smith (Howard W. Sams, 1993) and *Zen and the Art of the Internet, A Beginner's Guide* by Brendan Kehoe (Englewood Cliffs, NJ: Prentice-Hall, 1993).

Since the Internet is changing quickly, with many new services being developed, using published books probably won't keep you current. You should read netnews articles on these services, such as the FAQs in the newsgroup *news.answers*.

# About Internet Addresses

Each computer on the Internet can be addressed in one of two ways, by either name or number. First, each computer on the Internet has a name. For example, the full Internet name of the system discrete, owned by the mathematics department at the University of New Jersey, might be *discrete.math.unj.edu*. Here, *discrete* is the system name, *math* represents the group of all systems in the mathematics department, *unj* contains all systems at the University of New Jersey, and *edu* contains all systems at educational institutions in the United States. Second, the Internet number for this system might be 247.109.14.7. This number is assigned by the NSI Network Information Center. (See Tip 636.)

# How Do You Connect Your Computer to the Internet?

If you have your own machine or are a system administrator, you may want to connect your site to the Internet. There is a series of steps you need to follow to connect your site to the network. First, you have to obtain an IP network number for your site. You can do this by registering your site with the NSI Network Information Center (NIC). You can contact them at the following address: NSI, InterNIC Registration Services, 505 Huntmar Park Drive, Herndon, Virginia 22070, telephone: (703) 742-4777, (800) 444-4345, e-mail: *postmaster@internic.net*. They will provide you with the network number registration template.

Although every computer on the Internet has an address consisting of 32 bits, people find it much easier to use names for computers. And since most networking software uses an Internet address, there must be a way to translate the name of a system to an Internet address. This mapping is provided by the Domain Name System (DNS). You will need to establish a domain. You can do this by adding an entry to the distributed database used by the Internet for name-to-address resolution. If your domain

is in the United States, you will be part of one of six high-level domains shown in the following table:

| Domain | Members |
| --- | --- |
| *com* | Commercial organization |
| *edu* | Educational institutions |
| *gov* | Government organizations other than military |
| *int* | International organizations |
| *mil* | U.S. military organizations |
| *net* | Internet resources |
| *org* | Organizations not fitting into other domains |

If you are outside the United States, your highest level domain will have a two-letter country code, such as *au* for Australia, *ca* for Canada, or *uz* for Uzbekistan. In any case, once you have a domain, you can set up subdomains. For example, the domain *unj.edu* can set up domains *math.unj.edu, cs.unj.edu,* and *physics.unj.edu*. Each of these domains can set up subdomains if it wishes, and so on. The full name of a system is called its Fully Qualified Domain Name (FQDN). Beside an FQDN, each system on the Internet is uniquely identified by its Internet number. This consists of four positive integers, each less than 256. For example, *discrete.math.unj.edu* might have Internet number 247.109.14.7.

After registering your site and establishing your domain, you can install the necessary hardware and networking software and set up a connection to an Internet access point. You will need to access the Internet via an Internet Service Provider. For details, consult one of the references listed in Tip 634.

# The USENET and Netnews

**TIP 637**

## What's the USENET?

The USENET is not a network of computers. Instead, it is a global network providing an electronic bulletin board service called *netnews*. Netnews is organized into newsgroups that fall into a set of high-level categories. (See Tip 638 for more on this.) Like the Internet, there is no central control point for the USENET. News is transmitted throughout the USENET in a cooperative way using feeds from one site to another. System administrators make agreements with administrators on other systems to set up these news feeds. To get all the newsgroups of interest to users on a system, the administrator of this system may have to set up feeds for several different server systems. Most of the time these news feeds are provided free of charge. However, there are commercial services such as UUNet that charge for USENET news feeds. There are also companies that distribute information via netnews. The Clarinet, which provides information from newspaper news services, is one such example. (See Tip 666.)

**TIP 638**

## How Newsgroups Are Organized

Newsgroups on the USENET are organized by topic or geographical area. The first prefix of a newsgroup is used to denote a general topic area or a geographical area. Some of the prefixes used to denote topic areas are:

| Prefix | Topic Area |
|--------|-----------|
| *comp* | Computing |
| *news* | Netnews and the USENET |
| *rec* | Recreations, hobbies, and leisure time activities |
| *sci* | The sciences |
| *soc* | Social issues |
| *talk* | Discussions |
| *alt* | Alternative topics (almost anything can show up here!) |
| *misc* | Miscellaneous |

Many different prefixes are used to denote geographical areas. Here are some examples:

| Prefix | Area |
|--------|------|
| *chi* | Metropolitan Chicago |
| *na* | North America |
| *ne* | New England |
| *nj* | New Jersey |
| *ny* | New York |
| *ca* | California |
| *ba* | San Francisco Bay Area |

There are also prefixes used to denote organizations. These are used for newsgroups available only within a particular company. For example, newsgroups internal to AT&T have the prefix *att*.

A newsgroup is identified by a prefix, followed by a period, and a particular topic, or alternately, a topic followed by a period, followed by a subtopic. For example, the newsgroup *sci.crypt* contains articles about cryptography, while the newsgroup *comp.unix.questions* contains articles with questions about the UNIX System and answers to these questions.

# Where Can You Find a List of Current Newsgroups?

By now there are more than 5000 different newsgroups available on the USENET. The list of newsgroups is constantly changing as new ones are created and dormant ones removed. To see a current list of newsgroups (not including local and organizational newsgroups), look in the newsgroup *news.lists*, where such a list is posted periodically. You can also consult the useful list of newsgroups in *The Internet Complete Reference* by Hahn and Stout. This list is accurate as of May, 1993. Although the list will have changed some by the time you read it, you'll find their descriptions of the topics covered by newsgroups much better than those in the official *news.lists* list.

# TIP 640

## What's a Moderated Newsgroup?

Anyone can post anything to most newsgroups. This has its advantages and disadvantages. An advantage is that there is no censorship. A disadvantage is that there is no filtering of inane, offensive, bizarre, or worthless articles. To solve this problem, some newsgroups are *moderated*. All articles posted to a moderated newsgroup are routed to a moderator who selects articles that will be posted to the newsgroup.

The most popular of all moderated newsgroups is *rec.humor.funny*, which contains jokes deemed funny by its moderator, generally with no more than three jokes posted per day. Most people agree that the few jokes in *rec.humor.funny* are better than almost all the ones in *rec.humor*, which probably contains at least 20 times as much material!

# TIP 641

## A Little Help with USENET Lingo

There are some common abbreviations and slang used in netnews articles. You'll find it helpful to know the most common of these since they occur so often. One of the most important abbreviations is FAQ, which stands for Frequently Asked Question(s). There are special articles in many different newsgroups that pose and answer these FAQs. (See Tip 664 for more details.) Some of the other abbreviations you'll see include BTW (by the way), FOAF (friend of a friend), FYI (for your information), IMHO (in my humble opinion), PD (public domain), and the extremely important RTFM (read the . . . fine, fine manual). ;-)

There are some important slang words used on the USENET. Some of the most important of these words are "foo", "foobar", and "bar". These words are used to represent generic objects without referring to particular names. The first such object is often called "foo" and the second object (which needs to be distinguished from the first) is often called "bar". Sometimes the name "foobar" is also used for an object.

# Understanding "Smileys"

You won't really understand USENET communications unless you understand *smileys*. These are the small drawings made using ASCII characters that resemble faces. Different smileys are used to represent different feelings, attitudes, and intentions. You need to look at a smiley sideways to see it properly. Literally hundreds of different smileys have been invented and a large number are used frequently. Here are a few of the most commonly used smileys, together with some particularly clever ones:

| | |
|---|---|
| :-) | Smiling |
| :-D | Laughing |
| ;-) | Winking |
| :-( | Frowning |
| :-X | Sealed lips |
| l-l | Sleeping |
| 8-l | Surprised |
| :-{ | Mustached |
| (:)-) | Scuba diver |
| [:l] | Robot |
| @:l | Turban |

Because of the fundamental importance of smileys, you should make sure you understand what they mean. A misinterpreted smiley could lead to serious consequences! Fortunately, there are several sources to consult to figure out what an obscure smiley means, including *The Smiley Book* by David Sanderson (O'Reilly and Associates, 1993) and *The Unofficial Smiley Dictionary* available on the Internet either through periodic postings to various newsgroups or via Gopher from the system *pfsparc02.phil15.unisb.de* (Universitaet des Saarlandes). In the latter case, you will need to choose *INFO-SYSTEM BENUTZEN | Fun | Cartoons | Smilies :-)* from the Gopher menu. (See Tip 676 to learn about using Gopher.)

# TIP 643

# Reading Netnews

There are many different programs available for reading netnews. Among these programs are old standbys like **readnews**, **vnews**, and **rn**. Each of these programs has its proponents and is used extensively. Recently, many people have switched to one of the newer programs such as **nn**, **tin**, and **trn**. These new readers help users cope with the large number of articles posted. They provide features that let you screen out articles that are not of interest and let you read news articles in order on a specific topic. There are also several variants of newsreaders that have been designed to work with X Windows, including **xrn** and **xvnews** (based on **vnews**) and newsreaders based on GNU emacs, **gnews** and **gnus**.

Before deciding on a newsreader, first check whether it is available on your system. If it is, you should find documentation on this newsreader on your system. Otherwise, you can consult one or more of the books that cover netnews readers, such as *The Internet Complete Reference* by Hahn and Stout, or *UNIX Communications, Second Edition* by Bart Anderson, Bryan Costales, and Harry Henderson (Carmel, IN: Howard W. Sams, 1991).

If your system does not support a newsreader that you want to use, ask the administrator of your system to obtain a public domain copy from an archive and install it on your system. If you are your own system administrator, ask yourself to do this. (See Tip 670 for information about obtaining public domain software from source archives.)

# TIP 644

# Your .newsrc

Your *.newsrc* file in your home directory keeps track of the news articles that you have read (or at least, that your newsreader thinks you have "read"). If you look at this file, you will find a line for each newsgroup with the name of that newsgroup, a colon (:) or an exclamation mark (!), and a list of the numbers of the articles you have read from that newsgroup. These numbers are listed individually, separated by commas, or by runs. For example, the line

```
comp.unix.questions: 1-4574,4577,4601
```

indicates that you have read all articles in this newsgroup with numbers between 1 and 4574, inclusive, and the two articles in this newsgroup with numbers 4577 and 4601.

A colon following the name of a newsgroup means that you are subscribed to this newsgroup, while an exclamation mark means that you are unsubscribed to that newsgroup.

For example, the line

```
alt.whine! 1-8,11
```

means that you are unsubscribed to the newsgroup *alt.whine*, and you have read articles 1-8 and 11. (Who would subscribe to this newsgroup about whining and complaining?)

If you want to reread articles that you have previously read, or that your newsreader thought you read, you can edit your *.newsrc*. For example, to reread articles with numbers greater than 4570 in the newsgroup *comp.unix.questions*, just change the line in your *.newsrc* to

```
comp.unix.questions: 1-4570
```

Once you have done this, any newsreader you use will think you have only read articles with numbers 1-4570 in this newsgroup.

# Listing All Newsgroups Available to You

By now there are more than 5000 different newsgroups! (See Tip 639 to learn how to list them all.) Most systems don't carry all these newsgroups for various reasons, such as limited disk space, the limited interest of some topics, the off-color, obscene, profane, or politically incorrect nature of their articles, and so on. Nevertheless, there are probably hundreds of newsgroups carried on your system. There are times when you may want to list all of them. For example, when you **postnews**, you may want a list of newsgroups to which you can post the article. Or, you may just want to browse the list of newsgroups to find groups that may contain articles you would find of interest. To list all newsgroups, just print the contents of the file */usr/lib/news/newsgroups*, if such a file is available on your system (some systems configured in groups do not have this file). You'll find a list of newsgroups, together with a short description of the contents of each group, when such a description is available. By the way, some systems have a **newsgroups** command which you can use to get a list of newsgroups available on that system.

You should also note that many systems are set up so that just one machine in a group actually receives a full feed of netnews and stores the articles on disk. All other systems in the group go to that machine to retrieve articles only when someone starts reading news. If this is the case on your system, you will need to run the **getactive** command, which grabs a copy of the active file from the servers. This puts this list in the file *./active*.

# How to Start a New Newsgroup

**TIP 646**

If you think there is a need for a new newsgroup because no current newsgroup contains articles on a theme you think is important, you might want to try to set up a new newsgroup. The USENET has a well-established procedure for doing this. To propose a new newsgroup, you must submit a *Request for Discussion* (RFD) which you post to the newsgroup *news.announce.newsgroups* and to any other pertinent newsgroups; when you post the article, you list these other newsgroups after *news.announce.newgroups*. This ensures that your request goes to the moderator of that newsgroup. Any discussion of the merits of your proposal will take place in *news.groups*. If there is general agreement about the new newsgroup, a Call For Votes is posted to *news.announce.newgroups*. If the results are sufficiently positive (at least 2/3 yes votes and at least 100 yes votes more than no votes), your new group will be added to the USENET. Otherwise, your proposal will fail and cannot be reconsidered for at least six months.

# Using rn to Read Netnews

**TIP 647**

The news-reading program **rn**, a widely used newsreader, offers a tremendous range of features. For example, it lets you subscribe and unsubscribe to newsgroups, search for a newsgroup based on patterns, search for articles based on patterns or subjects, and search for text in an article. You begin reading news with **rn** by typing **rn**. If you don't already have a *.newsrc* file, **rn** will create one with a file of newsgroups kept by your system. If you already have one, **rn** will revise and update the file and then enter the level you use for selecting newsgroups to read. It will start at the beginning of your *.newsrc*, looking for newsgroups that contain articles that have not already been marked as "read." It supplies a list of the first newsgroups with unread news in your *.newsrc* and asks you whether you want to read articles in the first newsgroup with unread news. For example, upon starting **rn**, you might see

```
Unread articles in comp.unix.admin      258 articles
Unread articles in comp.unix.large       13 articles
```

```
Unread articles in comp.unix.misc        520 articles
Unread articles in comp.unix.questions   335 articles
Unread articles in comp.unix.shell       211 articles
etc.
********  258 unread articles in comp.unix.admin --- read now?
   [ynq]
```

If you want to read articles in this newsgroup, type **y** and you will see the first article not marked as "read" in this newsgroup. At this point you will have a range of options, such as reading the whole article, going to a different article, or searching for an article in this newsgroup based on pattern matching in the subject line, header, or anywhere in the article. (See Tip 653 for information on searching through articles by pattern matching.)

# Subscribing and Unsubscribing to Newsgroups with rn

You are subscribed to all newsgroups in your *.newsrc* when you start using **rn**. When **rn** encounters available newsgroups on your system not in your *.newsrc,* you are asked whether you want to add them to this file, which subscribes you to them. You can mark the current newsgroup by typing **u** when you are prompted at the current newsgroup level. For instance, to unsubscribe to *comp.unix.large*, you would do the following:

```
********  13 unread articles in comp.unix.large -- read new? [ynq] u
Unsubscribed to newsgroup comp.unix.large
```

You can check the current subscription status of newsgroups by typing L at the newsgroup prompt.

# Listing Newsgroups with rn

You can use the rn **l** command at the newsgroup level to list all newgroups, including both those you subscribe to and those to which you are unsubscribed, starting with certain prefixes. For example,

```
l comp.unix
```

will list all the newsgroups under *comp.unix*. Currently, there are more than 25 such newsgroups.

# Controlling rn with Switches

**TIP 650**

There are a number of command-line options, commonly known as switches, that you can use to control how **rn** starts. One particularly useful option is **-q**, which starts up **rn** so that you are not asked about any new newsgroups when you start. To start **rn** using this option, type

```
$ rn -q
```

In this way, you can bypass the annoying questions about whether you want to subscribe to a variety of newsgroups when you start reading news. Another useful switch is **-v**, which tells **rn** to echo all commands that you enter in **rn**.

You can also set options to **rn** using the RNINIT environmental variable. For example, to invoke the **-q** option when you run **rn**, use the command

```
$ RNINIT="-v"; export RNINIT
```

In the C shell, the command is

```
setenv RNINIT "-v"
```

# Searching for Newsgroups with rn

**TIP 651**

When using **rn** to read netnews, you can use pattern matching to search for newsgroups. At the newsgroup level, you enter a / (slash) or a ? (question mark), followed by the pattern you want to match in the name of a newsgroup. When you use the slash, **rn** will search through newsgroups in the order they are found in your *.newsrc*; when you use a backlash, **rn** will search backwards in your *.newsrc,* until the first newsgroup containing the pattern you specified is reached. For example, to find a newsgroup about multimedia, you would type **/multimedia**, as follows:

```
******** 87 unread articles in comp.unix.questions--read now? [ynq]
 /multimedia
Searching...
******** 12 unread articles in comp.multimedia--read now? [ynq]
```

# Listing Unread Articles with rn

When you use **rn** to read netnews, you can list all unread articles in a newsgroup by typing the = command after the "read now?" prompt. You will get a list of all unread articles and their subject lines in that newsgroup. For example, to list the unread articles in *comp.unix* questions, type = as follows:

```
******** 87 unread articles in comp.unix.questions -- read now?
 [ynq] =
```

# Searching for Articles with rn

With **rn**, you can use pattern matching to search for articles in a particular newsgroup that have subject lines containing a specified pattern.

When you are at the article level, enter a / (slash) or a ? (question mark), followed by the pattern you want to match in the subject line of an article. When you use the slash, you can search through articles beginning with your current location in the newsgroup in order of increasing article number.

Using a ? (question mark) will move you back from your current position through articles with smaller article numbers to the beginning of the newsgroup. You can also search through all articles in a newsgroup with a particular subject by using the ^N command.

# Screening Out Articles with rn

There are several different ways to kill articles when you use the **rn** newsreader. (By killing an article we mean marking it as "read" so that **rn** will not show it to you.) The simplest way is to use the **k** command at the prompt that comes up while reading an article. This marks as "read" all articles in the current newsgroup with the same subject as the current article. The second way is to use the **K** command. Not only does this mark all articles in the current newsgroup as "read", it also puts a line in the local kill file for this newsgroup that marks all articles with this subject as "read" whenever you enter that newsgroup.

The third, and most powerful, way to kill articles is to use the CTRL-K (^K) command. You can use this command at either the newsgroup or the article level. If you enter this command at the newsgroup level, you are able to edit your global kill file, which will mark articles with a given subject as "read" whenever a newsgroup is entered. If you enter this command at the article level, articles with the given subject will be marked as "read" whenever you enter this newsgroup.

Finally, use the **c** command to catch up on all unread articles. This kills everything!

# Reading Netnews with nn

To start reading netnews with **nn**, type **nn**, as follows:

```
$ nn
```

This will put you in the first newsgroup to which you are subscribed. If you wish to read articles only in a particular newsgroup, give the **nn** command the name of this newsgroup as an argument. For instance,

```
$ nn sci.math
```

puts you in the newsgroup *sci.math*. The **nn** newsreader will show you the authors and subjects of the unread articles in the newsgroup. Follow-up articles are indicated with > as their subject, follow-ups to follow-ups are indicated with >>, and so on. There are five different formats for presenting this information; you can toggle through them by typing the double quote (").

The next thing to do is to select which articles to read. To do so, you need only type the article ID, which is a letter from a to z as shown in the article list. You can select a range of articles to read by specifying the first and the last with a dash between them, so that a-e selects articles a, b, c, d, and e. One of the special features of **nn** is that you can select all articles on an entire thread with a common subject. For example, you can select all articles that have the same subject as article j by typing **j\***.

After selecting the articles you want to read, you can type **Z** to start reading them; you'll return to the same newsgroup when you are done reading them. If you type **X** instead, you won't return to the same newsgroup, but to the next one.

There are a number of commands to use when reading articles. Press SPACEBAR to move from one page to the next, **n** to go to the next article, and **p** to go to the previous article. You can save the article with a header by typing **s** and without a header by typing **o**. You can mail the article to someone by typing **m**. You can send an e-mail message to the author of an article by typing **r**.

# Using nn to Search Through All Articles on a Subject

Sometimes you may want to look at all the articles on a particular subject regardless of which newsgroup they appear in. You can do this with the **nn** newsreader. To do this, give **nn** the -m option, which tells it to merge all articles into one giant group; the -X option, which tells it to look at all newsgroups, including those to which you don't subscribe; and the -s option followed by the particular pattern you are searching for. For example, to search for all articles about lemurs, you might try

```
$ nn -mX  -slemurs
```

# Screening Out News Articles Using the nn Reader

When you read netnews, you will often find newsgroups cluttered with articles of absolutely no interest to you. When you read netnews using the **nn** reader, you can use a kill file to weed out some of the articles you don't want to read. You can use your kill file to weed out articles on a particular subject or from a particular person. For example, suppose you are reading *comp.unix.questions* and come across an article asking how to perform some editing tasks using **emacs**. If you are a **vi** user, you may want to kill the article posing the emacs question and all follow-up articles posted to this newsgroup. To do this, suppose you are in reading mode and you are reading a particular article. To kill this article, and all articles with the same subject, type **K** and you will receive the following prompt:

```
AUTO (K)ill or (S)elect (CR => Kill subject 1 month)
If you press the RETURN key, this article and all articles on the
same subject will be killed for 30 days.
```

# Screening Out News from a Particular Person with nn

Sometimes when you read netnews, you'll find a seemingly endless supply of articles written by the same person. Although some prolific posters of news have great wisdom, some people post articles that are utterly worthless to you. One nice feature of the **nn** newsreader is the ability to screen out articles by a particular person. Here is how you do this. Suppose you are using **nn** to read articles in the newsgroup *comp.unix.questions*. First type **K**, then work through the following sequence of prompts:

```
AUTO (k)ill or (s)elect (CR => Kill subject 30 days)k
AUTO KILL on (s)ubject of (n)ame n
KILL Name: Boris Badenoff
KILL in (g)roup 'comp.unix.questions' or in (a)ll groups?  a
Lifetime of entry in days (P)ermanent (30)  p
CONFIRM KILL Name perm:  Boris Badenoff y
```

You entered **k** at the first prompt so you could screen out (kill) articles. At the next prompt you entered **n** so you could screen out articles written by a particular person. At the next prompt you entered the name of the offending person, Boris Badenoff. Then you decided to kill all his articles in all groups, not just in the current newsgroup. You next decided to kill his articles permanently. Note that at this prompt you could have decided to kill his articles for a specified number of days. Finally, you confirmed the kill by entering **y** at the last prompt of this session.

# Posting a News Article

It's easy to post news articles. You just use the **postnews** or **Pnews** command. Before using **postnews** or **Pnews**, you should know which newsgroup you want to post the article to. Be especially careful when you decide how widely you distribute your article. It's annoying to netnews readers to have to filter through news articles that have been sent to inappropriate places. For example, if you post worldwide an article advertising a car for sale, someone in Sweden may ask you to drive it over for a test drive. You can limit the distribution of your article by using the distribution prompt you are presented by **postnews**. You should choose the narrowest distribution from the options available that will meet your needs. For example, an article with interest only to AT&T employees should be given the distribution att, and one advertising a car for sale in New Jersey should be given the distribution nj for New Jersey distribution. An article of general interest, such as a discussion of a new discovery in mathematics, should be given the distribution net that distributes it worldwide.

# Posting News Using rn

**TIP 660**

You can post an article in several ways using **rn**, by posting either a follow-up to an existing article or a new article. To post a follow-up article, you can use either the **f** or **F** command at the article prompt. If you use the **F** command, the original article will be placed in the follow-up article for you to use in your reply and **rn** will assume your follow-up is on the same topic. If you use the **f** command, the original article is not placed in the follow-up article and **rn** will ask you if you want to specify an unrelated topic. If you respond that you do, you will be able to specify a new topic.

# Posting News Using nn

**TIP 661**

You can post an article in several different ways using the **nn** newsreader. First, you can post an article as a follow-up to an article you are currently reading. You need only type **F** while reading the article selection list, or either **f** or **F** when reading an article. You can also post articles while using **nn** by using the **:post** command. You will be prompted for all the relevant information. When you are not reading netnews using **nn**, you can use the **nnpost** command. If you type

```
$ nnpost
```

you will be prompted for all relevant information in the same way as you are with the **:post** command from inside **nn**.

# How to Sign the News Articles You Post

When reading netnews, you may notice that many articles conclude with a "signature" consisting of one or more lines of information about the person posting the articles and possibly a line or two of text the poster feels conveys his or her philosophy of life. You can have a signature automatically added to every mail message you post through **postnews**, by using a *.signature* file. For instance, the contents of such a file may be

```
Life is a dream!
Jose Orez (chief scientist)   Intergalactic Computing Associates
Phone:  (909) 555-1234        e-mail:  joo@ica.com
```

You don't have to do anything special to have this signature appended to the articles you post. This will happen automatically each time you post an article.

You should restrict your *.signature* file to four or fewer lines. This limitation is enforced on some systems by the system administrator.

# Encoding and Decoding Articles

Sometimes you may want to post an article that could be considered offensive by some segment of the world, or maybe it really is offensive. For instance, suppose at lunch you heard a funny joke involving sex. You want to post it, but don't want to offend anyone. You can encrypt the article using rot13, which shifts each letter 13 positions down in the alphabet, wrapping around to the beginning of the alphabet, and then post it. For example, if you put your joke in a file named *offensive*, you can encrypt this file using rot13 and put the result into a new file named *oaf* with the following command line:

```
$ cat offensive | tr "[a-m][n-z][A-M][N-Z]" "[n-z][a-m][N-Z][A-M]" > oaf
```

By the way, you can decrypt a file that was encrypted with rot13 by using the identical command line. This means you can recover the original offensive joke from a file named *oaf* by using

```
$ cat oaf | tr "[a-m][n-z][A-M][N-Z]" "[n-z][a-m][N-Z][A-M]" >offensive
```

*You can automatically decrypt messages encrypted with rot13 when you are reading news with* **rn**, *via the* CTRL-X *command, or with* **nn**, *via the* D *command.*

# What Are FAQs?

**TIP 664**

Many newsgroups contain articles that pose and answer the most *frequently asked questions* (FAQs) that arise in that newsgroup. For example, you can find answers to common questions about the UNIX system posted in *comp.unix.questions*. The FAQs for a newsgroup are updated and posted periodically. FAQs are posted so readers avoid posting the same questions that other readers have posted and to help them quickly find answers to common questions. You'll find that newsgroups with FAQs are generally easier to read than those that don't have them. Before posting articles to a newsgroup, you should see whether that group has a FAQs posting. If it does, you should make sure your question isn't already on that list. If it is, and you ask the question anyway, you will find yourself under heavy attack by impatient readers of that newsgroup.

One extremely useful and interesting source of information on the Internet is the compilation of FAQs from different newsgroups posted to the group *news.answers*. You may find answers to questions you didn't even know you had by browsing through the FAQs from different newsgroups in *news.answers*.

You can obtain a complete list of netnews FAQs via anonymous ftp from *pit-manager.mit.edu* in the directory */pub/usenet/newsgroup*.

# Find Answers to UNIX Questions on Netnews

**TIP 665**

If you cannot find the answer to a question on the UNIX system in a book or by asking your friends, colleagues, or local gurus, you might want to post this question on netnews. There are several newsgroups available that you can use to solicit answers to questions you have about the UNIX system. When you have a general question, you can post it to the newsgroup *comp.unix.questions*. However, before you do so, you must consult the list of frequently asked questions (FAQs) on this newsgroup.

If you post a question already found in the FAQs, you will receive many nasty replies. But if your question in not among the FAQs and is not extremely esoteric, most likely many people will post an answer or send you a response via e-mail.

If you are a more advanced user, consider posting to the newsgroup *comp.unix.wizards*. Postings to this group tend to be extremely technical and the posters tend to have a lot of expertise, so make sure your question is carefully thought out and doesn't have an obvious answer.

# TIP 666 Reading an Electronic Newspaper

The *Clarinet* provides, for a fee, an electronic newspaper via netnews. The Clarinet distributes articles based on the United Press International wire service, using approximately 100 newsgroups, each with articles on a particular subject. More than 500 articles on news events, sports, science, technology, and business are posted daily. Also available are syndicated columns and a daily computer industry news magazine called *Newsbytes*. You can obtain details on Clarinet services by anonymous ftp to the directory */Clarinet* at *ftp.uu.net*. For information about subscribing to Clarinet, you can call them at (800) USE-NETS, send e-mail to *info@clarinet.com*, or write to Clarinet Communications, 124 King Street North, Waterloo, Ontario, Canada N2J 2X8.

# TIP 667 A Joke a Day?

Suppose you've had a bad day and need some humor to cheer you up, you want to put a good joke in a speech, or you want to impress your friends with your sense of humor. With a little work you can find funny jokes on the net. Your best bet is to read the moderated newsgroup *rec.humor.funny.* The jokes in this newsgroup have been screened by a moderator who generally has a decent sense of humor. Also, only a small number of jokes are posted each day.

On the other hand, you can also find some funny jokes in the newsgroup *rec.humor.* Unfortunately, there are hundreds of jokes posted to this group every day. Mixed in with a few funny jokes are hundreds of bad jokes and other unsuccessful attempts at humor. You'll have to read a lot of trash to find some pearls in this newsgroup, but you'll find a few. By the way, there are archive sites for jokes of particular types, such as light bulb jokes. You can find the location of these archives in a FAQ posted periodically to *rec.humor.*

# Finding Information on the Internet

## Methods for Finding Information on the Internet

The Internet offers a cornucopia of information. One serious problem is that it is often difficult to find out where to look for information that you may find useful or interesting. Fortunately, and unfortunately, there are many different places you can look to find sources of information on the Internet.

One of the first things you can do is to look at the list of Internet information sources posted to the newsgroup *news.answers.* Look for this in the Updated Internet Services List posted monthly.

A comprehensive listing of Internet Resources can be found in the chapter "Catalog of Internet Resources" in *The Internet Complete Reference* by Hahn and Stout. You can also refer to the chapter "Resources on the Internet" in the book *The Whole Internet* by Krol. This chapter includes a lengthy list of where to find information on the Internet organized by subject area. Among the services you can use to find local information on the Internet are the archie service (see Tip 671), the Internet Gopher (see Tip 676), the WAIS (see Tip 694), or the World Wide Web (see Tip 684). There may also be Internet mailing lists that provide information on topics of interest. (See Tips 698 and 699).

You can also use the InterNIC Directory and Database Service, which provides an easy-to-use front end for a variety of access methods, including WAIS, archie, the Internet Gopher, and the networking tools for obtaining these resources. (See Tip 669.)

## Using InterNIC Directory and Database Services

Some of the newest services for accessing Internet information are the InterNIC Directory and Database Services. There are three basic services: the Directory of Directories, Directory Services, and Database Services. The InterNIC Directory of Directories includes lists of ftp archives, Internet servers, and white and yellow page directories; library catalogs; and archives of data. It provides an easy-to-use menu-driven interface and a wide range of access tools, including WAIS, archie, and the Gopher. This service operates using keyword searches. There is no fee for accessing and using the basic capabilities of this service.

The InterNIC Directory Service provides you with a way to find e-mail addresses of other people on the Internet. It uses Netfind and X.500 to find users and organizations on the Internet and will also use its own database of users and organizations. This service is free.

InterNIC Database Services make it possible for educational organizations and other groups to share information with the community of Internet users. There is no fee for accessing these database services, but there is a fee for design, management, and maintenance of databases and storage of data for special groups.

To try out InterNIC services, you can use **telnet** to log in to *ds.internic.net*. You should use the login guest. To learn more about InterNIC services, you can go through a tutorial shell which can be started from the menu you are presented with upon logging on to this account. Also, for more information you can call the InterNIC Directory and Database Services at (908) 668-6587 or send e-mail to *admin@ds.internic.net*.

# TIP 670 Finding Public Domain Source Code on the Internet

First, as you have probably noticed, you'll find many tips in this book that tell you where to find useful public domain programs that you can run on your UNIX system.

You can often find the source code for useful programs in the USENET newsgroups devoted to the posting of source code. These newsgroups include *alt.sources, comp.sources.misc, comp.sources.unix*, and *comp.sources.x*.

You can also find out where to obtain useful public domain source code by consulting the archie database of anonymous ftp sites. (See Tip 671.)

Another good way of looking for public domain software is to check the monthly posting of a list of anonymous ftp sites and what they offer. This list is posted to the newsgroups *comp.misc, comp.sources.wanted*, and *alt.sources.wanted*.

Finally, if you have no luck finding public domain software that does what you need using the methods described, you can post a message to the newsgroups *comp.sources.wanted* and *alt.sources.wanted.* Be sure to describe your problem accurately and in sufficient detail. You will also need to specify the version of the UNIX system you are using.

# The archie System

The *archie system*, developed at McGill University in Montreal, is a particularly useful facility for locating resources on the Internet. This system lets you search through a database containing the names and locations of files available for public use on the Internet. Currently, more than 2 million files on more than 1000 servers are included in this database. The name archie was coined because "archie" is close to "archive", not because it is the name of the comic strip hero Archie Andrews. (But see Tips 681, 682, and 683 on Archie's friends Veronica and Jughead.)

You can search for files in two ways using **archie.** First, you can locate filenames that contain a specified string. Second, you can find the filenames of files that have descriptions containing a specified word.

To use **archie,** you need to have an archie client on your system, to log in to an archie server via **telnet,** or to send one of these servers an e-mail message. Currently, the recommended archie servers for the U.S. include *archie.rutgers.edu* (New Jersey), *archie.sura.net* (Maryland), *archie.internic.net* (New Jersey), and *archie.unl.edu* (Nebraska). Outside the United States, try *archie.edvz.uni-linz.ac.at* ( Austria ), *archie.univie.ac.at* ( Austria ), *archie.uqam.ca* ( Canada ), *archie.mcgill.ca* ( Canada ), *archie.doc.ic.ac.uk* ( United Kingdom ), *archie.cs.huji.ac.il* ( Israel ), *archie.funet.fi* ( Finland ), *archie.sogang.ac.kr* (South Korea), *archie.au* (Australia), *archie.ncu.edu.tw* (Taiwan), *archie.wide.ad.jp* (Japan), *archie.rediris.es* (Spain), or *archie.th-darmstadt.de* (Germany).

# Using the archie System via telnet

When you log in to an archie server via **telnet** (see Tip 589 for how this done), you should use the logname archie. Once you get the prompt

```
archie>
```

you can enter archie commands. For example,

```
archie> list
```

gives you the list of servers indexed by **archie** and the time they were last updated.

```
archie> servers
```

gives you a list of publicly available servers known to the site.

```
archie> help
help> ?
```

gives you a list of archie commands and what they do.

To do a search, you should first tell **archie** how to do a search using the archie **set search** command. There are four different options: **exact**, which requires the string to match a filename exactly; **regex**, which treats the search string as a regular expression in UNIX for matching purposes; **sub**, which requires the search string to match a substring of the filename; and **subcase**, which requires the search string to match a substring of the filename with no difference in case of characters. For example, to set a search to treat search strings as regular expressions, use

```
archie> set search regex
```

Once you have specified the type of search, use the archie **prog** command. For example, to find resources with the string "multimedia" in their filenames, use the command

```
archie> prog multimedia.
```

When the search is finished, your output will be the list of servers and filenames matching your search.

Sometimes, people who place files in archives on servers include a set of keywords or phrases to describe their files. You can search for files that have the string of interest to you in their keyword description using the archie **whatis** command. For example, to find the names of files that contain the string "earthquake" in their description, use the command

```
archie> whatis earthquake
```

Often you will find that the results of an archie search are quite long. To keep these results from scrolling across your screen, you can use a pager. To do so, use the archie command

```
archie> set pager
```

You can also limit the number of matches made by **archie** for your searches, since the first few matches may be sufficient. For example, you can limit matches to 10 using the archie command

```
archie> set maxhits 10
```

Here is a summary of many of the useful commands you can run on an archie server:

| Command | Function |
|---|---|
| **find** | Searches anonymous ftp database (same as **prog**) |
| **help ?** | Displays list of commands |
| **help** *command* | Displays help for specified command |
| **help set** *variable* | Displays help for specified variable |
| **mail** | Mails output of last search |
| **manpage** | Displays the manual page for archie |
| **prog** | Searches anonymous ftp database |
| **servers** | Displays list of archie servers |
| **set mailto** *address* | Specifies mail address for messages from archie |
| **set maxhits** *number* | Sets the maximum number of items to find |
| **set pager** | Displays output using pager |
| **set search exact** | Searches for an exact pattern |
| **set search sub** | Searches for pattern as substring |
| **set search regex** | Searches for a regular expression |
| **set sortby filename** | Sorts by alphabetizing filenames |
| **set sortby hostname** | Sorts by alphabetizing host names |
| **set sortby rsize** | Sorts in order of increasing size |
| **set sortby rtime** | Sorts by time and date, oldest first |
| **set sortby size** | Sorts in order of decreasing size |
| **set sortby time** | Sorts by time and date, newest first |
| **show** | Displays value of all variables |
| **whatis** | Searches the software description database |

# Having the archie Server Send You Results by E-Mail

When you log in to an archie server via **telnet**, you can have the server send you the results of a search via e-mail. To do this, you must first carry out your search. For example, suppose you use the following archie commands:

```
archie> set search exact
archie> prog tarx
```

After getting the results of the search on your terminal, you can use the following archie command to have the result of the search sent to you via e-mail:

```
archie> mail
```

If you want the results sent to a different e-mail address, you can use the archie **set mailto** command. For example, if you use

```
archie> set mailto ffred@walnut.una.edu
```

any e-mail sent to you by the archie server will go to *ffred@walnut.una.edu*.

# Accessing the archie System via E-Mail

You can access the archie system via e-mail when you want to do a search but don't want to spend the time interacting, logging on to a server, and issuing archie commands, or when you cannot log in to an archie server for whatever reason. To use **archie** in this way, your message should consist of a series of commands, one on a line, each beginning in column one of that line. For example, to find all files with filenames containing the string "phrenology", your message might look like this:

```
$ mail archie@archie.rutgers.edu
Subject:
prog phrenology
```

```
compress
```

You would get back a list of all files containing the string "phrenology" in their filenames and the location of these files. Since you used the **compress** command, the output will be compressed and encoded using **uuencode** before it is sent to you. You will have to undo this compression (see Tip 605) before reading the output. You can get more information about the archie commands you can use via e-mail by including a line with the command **help** in your message.

# Using an archie Client

If the archie client is installed on your system, you can use the archie command to do searches. For example, to use **archie** to search for the **tarx** program, you would run

```
$ archie -e tarx
```

Here the **-e** (*e*xact) option tells **archie** that you want an exact match. Because exact matches are the default, supplying the **-e** option here was optional.

The archie client connects to an archie server, which carries out the search and returns the results to you. You can redirect the output of this command to put the results of the search in a file. For example,

```
$ archie -e tarx > temp
```

will put the results of the search in the file *temp*.

You can limit the number of hits by using the **-m** option. For example,

```
$ archie -e -m10 tarx
```

will give you a maximum of 10 matches.

You can use the **-l** option to make the output of a search suitable for use by another UNIX command. For example, to find only the sites in Finland, with addresses ending in *.fi*, you can use

```
$ archie -e -l tarx | grep '.fi'
```

Here is a summary of the options you can give the archie command:

| Option | Function |
|--------|----------|
| **-c** | Searches for substrings, case-sensitive |
| **-e** | Searches for exact matches |
| **-r** | Searches for regular expression |
| **-s** | Searches for substrings |
| **-o** | Sends output to specified file |
| **-l** | Lists one item per line |
| **-t** | Sorts output by time and date |
| **-m** | Sets maximum number of items to find |
| **-h** | Sends requests to specified archie server |
| **-L** | Shows list of archie servers known |
| **-V** | Sets verbose mode for comments during search |

There is also an X Windows-based archie client, called **xarchie**. You will find using this client extremely easy.

# The Internet Gopher

**676**

The *Internet Gopher*, developed at the University of Minnesota, provides an information distribution system. The Gopher lets you browse through or search for information on servers that contain a wide range of information including telephone directories, bibliographic databases, weather, news, and so on.

To use the Gopher, you can either run client software on your system or use a public Gopher client. You can find client software for the Internet Gopher for different types of terminals via anonymous ftp to the directory */pub/gopher* on *boombox.micro.umn.edu.* By the way, client software for the Internet Gopher is also available from this source for the Macintosh and DOS PC.

# Public Gopher Clients

**677**

You can try out the Internet Gopher by using **telnet** to log on to a public Gopher client, most often with the logname gopher. You can find a list of public Gopher clients in the book *The*

*Internet Complete Reference* by Hahn and Stout. This list gives the locations, Internet addresses, and lognames to use for each public Gopher client. There are public Gopher clients in Australia, Chile, Denmark, Ecuador, Germany, Japan, Spain, and Sweden. There are more than a dozen public Gopher clients in the United States, including *gopher.msu.edu* (Michigan), *consultant.micro.umn.edu* (Minnesota), *scilibx.ucsc.edu* (California), and *gopher.uiuc.edu* (Illinois). To use these public Gopher clients, you simply need to **telnet** to any one of them and log in as gopher.

When you use a public Gopher client, you cannot save or print files, so you cannot do the same things you can if you were using a Gopher client on your own machine. You will only be able to request information using the e-mail option provided in many menus. You will also find that using a public Gopher client prevents you from doing some of the other things you can do when using a Gopher client on your own machine, such as starting telnet sessions on other remote systems.

# Learning More about the Internet Gopher

You can learn more about the Internet Gopher by reading the newsgroups *comp.infosystems.gopher* and *alt.gopher*. You should also read the gopher FAQs posted to these newsgroups and to *news.answers*, or obtainable via anonymous ftp from *rtfm.mit.edu* in the file *gopher-faq* in the directory */pub/usenet/news.answers*.

You'll find useful coverage of Gopher in the books *The Internet Complete Reference* by Hahn and Stout, *The Whole Internet, User's Guide and Catalog* by Krol, and *Navigating the Internet* by Gibbs and Smith.

# Starting and Using the Internet Gopher

Once you have a Gopher client installed on your system, you can start this service using the command

```
$ gopher
```

This sets up a session with the default Gopher server. If, instead of using the default server, you would like to be connected with a different Gopher server, give the name of this server after the command. For example,

```
$ gopher gopher.msu.edu
```

will connect you to the Gopher server at Michigan State University.

Once you are connected to the Gopher server, you are presented with a menu. This menu shows the different options that are available to you. Some of these options lead you to further menus and so on. Sometimes when using Gopher, you may work your way through a sequence of menus. If you want to return to some point in this sequence later, you can use a Gopher bookmark. Your Gopher client keeps track of all these bookmarks in your bookmark list. When you start Gopher, you can tell your Gopher client to use this bookmark list as the initial menu by using

```
$ gopher -b
```

By the way, if you use the X Windows system, you probably would prefer to use the **xgopher** program, rather than **gopher**, since **xgopher** takes advantage of the features of X Windows.

# T<sup>I</sup>P 680

# Using Gopher: An Illustrative Example

The following example of how Gopher is actually used should help illustrate its usefulness. Suppose you were visiting Northwestern University (NU) in Evanston, Illinois as a prospective student. After a full day of wandering around campus, you decide you are hungry and you ask someone where to find a good, affordable place to eat. Any good student at NU would tell you to check out Buffalo Joe's for their famous buffalo wings. Now imagine a few months later you were accepted to NU (because, after all, you are a good student) and you remember that you really enjoyed the buffalo wings at Buffalo Joe's—but you forgot where it was located! Never fear, try **gopher**:

```
# Here we know that the gopher server at Northwestern University is
  called
# gopher.nwu.edu. In fact, this is a common naming scheme -- but not
  always.
```

```
$ gopher gopher.nwu.edu
```

and the returned screen looks like this:

```
              Internet Gopher Information Client v1.12S


                Root gopher server: gopher.nwu.edu


   -->  1.  About Gopher at Northwestern.
        2.  Northwestern University Information/
        3.  News and Weather Reports/
        4.  FTP Sites/
        5.  Internet Libraries (via Michigan State)/
        6.  Internet Resources (via Michigan State)/
        7.  Local Restaurant Menus/
        8.  Other Gopher servers/
        9.  Recreation (via Minnesota)/
Press ? for Help, q to Quit, u to go up a menu         Page: 1/1
```

And voila! Choice number 7 is Local Restaurant Menus. So, you can use your arrow keys or just type "7" to go to that entry and the next menu that comes up looks like this:

```
                     Local Restaurant Menus

   -->  1.  Buffalo Joe's.
        2.  Carmen's.
        3.  Cross-Rhodes.
        4.  Da Vinci's.
        5.  Dave's Italian Kitchen.
        6.  Domino's.
        7.  Giordano's.
        8.  Gulliver's.
        9.  Jimmy John's.
       10.  Leona's.
       11.  Phoenix Inn.
       12.  Tsing Tao.
       13.  Unicorn Cafe.
       14.  Ying Yang's.
```

Wow! Someone already knew that Buffalo Joe's should be placed at the top (and not just because it was the first in alphabetical order! ;-). Anyway, a simple RETURN gets you this information:

```
                        Buffalo Joe's
                        -------------


Location: 812 Clark Street, Evanston
Phone: 328-5525


Buffalo Joe's Wings
-------------------
Tossed to order in Joe's own sauce,
they're served hot and buttery with
chilled celery sticks and ranch dressing.


Single order Chicken Wings ... 3.49
Mild, Spicy or Suicide.


Double order ... 6.25
```

[and more follows but you just want the address and wings anyway]

Pretty easy, isn't it? It is, assuming that you know that what you wanted was at Northwestern University and you know how to reach our Gopher server. Instead, if you didn't know how to reach our Gopher server (but you did know you wanted to reach NU), try typing "gopher" at your prompt. If you have a Gopher client installed, you will get some main menu, which, in addition to your local organizations info, will most likely have an entry like this:

```
      8.  Other Gopher servers/
```

Here we choose 8 and get:

```
      1.  Gophers at Northwestern/
      2.  Off Campus Gophers (via Minnesota)/
```

Choosing 2 gets:

```
  -->  1.  All the Gopher servers in the World/
       2.  Search titles in Gopherspace using veronica/
       3.  Africa/
       4.  Asia/
```

```
 5.  Europe/
 6.  International Organizations/
 7.  Middle East/
 8.  North America/
 9.  Pacific/
10.  South America/
11.  Terminal Based Information/
12.  WAIS Based Information/
```

This is a pretty common screen since it comes from the developers at UMN. Anyway, we want choice 8:

```
 1.  Canada/
 2.  Costa Rica/
 3.  Mexico/
 4.  USA/
```

Then choice 4 (yes, it can get tedious sometimes):

```
 9.  florida/
10.  georgia/
11.  hawaii/
12.  idaho/
13.  illinois/
14.  indiana/
15.  iowa/
16.  kansas/
17.  kentucky/
18.  louisiana/
...
```

Then choice 13 (we are getting closer):

```
 9.  Illinois State University/
10.  Institute for the Learning Sciences (Northwestern University)/
11.  Lake Forest College Math/CS/
12.  Lake Forest College, Lake Forest, IL/
13.  Loyola University, Chicago/
14.  Northeastern Illinois University, IL USA/
15.  Northern Illinois University/
16.  Northern Illinois University Chemistry Gopher/
```

```
17. Northwestern University/
18. Northwestern University, CTDNET/
19. Northwestern University, Department of Geological Sciences/
20. Northwestern University, EECS Department/
21. Northwestern University, Integrated Science Program/
22. Northwestern University, Mathematics Department/
```

Then choice 17 for the main NU Gopher server. Now, before we go on, note that we are connecting to the NU Gopher here. So, at this point, we can note exactly what that server is called by hitting the "=" sign at choice 17. Here we get the following info:

```
Name=Northwestern University
Type=1
Port=70
Path=
Host=gopher.nwu.edu
```

So the next time we want to reach NU, we can bypass all this nonsense and just type "gopher gopher.nwu.edu" as we did originally. To proceed, we get:

```
1.  About Gopher at Northwestern.
2.  Northwestern University Information/
3.  News and Weather Reports/
4.  FTP Sites/
5.  Internet Libraries (via Michigan State)/
6.  Internet Resources (via Michigan State)/
7.  Local Restaurant Menus/
8.  Other Gopher servers/
9.  Recreation (via Minnesota)/
```

And voila! We are back to that familiar screen and we know those wings are near!

# TIP 681

# Using Veronica to Search Gopherspace

There are over 1500 Gopher servers providing a wide range of information. How can you find something you need in Gopherspace, the space containing all the menus and information on all Gopher servers? One way is to use Veronica (named after the comic book character Veronica who is

Archie Andrew's friend and not from *Very Easy Rodent-Oriented Net-wide Index to Computerized Archives* as some people think!), a service developed at the University of Nevada. You can use Veronica to do a keyword search of most of the menus on most of the Gopher servers in Gopherspace. To use Veronica you select it as menu item in a Gopher menu which sets up a session for you with one of several Veronica servers in the world. Once you have established your session with a Veronica server, you will be asked for the words to search Gopherspace for.

# Using Veronica: An Illustrative Example

## TIP 682

The following real world use of Veronica illustrates its utility. We continue along the lines of Tip 680. We know those awesome buffalo wings mentioned in Tip 680 are at Northwestern. Any good prospective student will probably visit many universities and it is understandable that you might forget where you saw Buffalo Joe's (well, almost understandable!). Here is where Veronica comes in.

Like Archie (Veronica's friend), it allows you to specify certain keywords and it will search all over Gopherspace trying to find your entry in some gopher menu. Now it should be noted that there are many Veronica servers and many Gopher servers all over the world. And this vast system, due to the ever-changing nature of the Internet, is not always in sync. Thus, a query that works on one Veronica server may not always work on another.

It is useful to pick the server closest to your location so that you get results faster. Still, you may find that your query returns no response. In that case, it could be that the server is not responding or not updated (and not that you composed your query wrong). In this case, try a different server.

Now, back to our example. We know we want Buffalo Joe's but we forgot where it was. The first thing we need to do is find a Veronica server. Again, the easiest thing to do is type

```
$ gopher
```

If you look back at one of the Gopher screens previously, you will see that choice number 2 was

```
      1.  All the Gopher Servers in the World/
 --> 2.  Search titles in Gopherspace using veronica/
      3.  Africa/
      4.  Asia/
      5.  Europe/
      6.  International Organizations/
```

```
   7.  Middle East/
   8.  North America/
   9.  Pacific/
  10.  South America/
  11.  Terminal Based Information/
  12.  WAIS Based Information/
```

And this screen is common. So, we pick this choice to access Veronica and we get:

```
   1.
   2.  FAQ:  Frequently-Asked Questions about veronica   (1993/08/23).
   3.  How to compose  veronica queries (NEW June 24) READ ME!!.
   4.  Search Gopher Directory Titles at PSINet <?>
   5.  Search Gopher Directory Titles at SUNET <?>
   6.  Search Gopher Directory Titles at U. of Manitoba <?>
   7.  Search Gopher Directory Titles at University of Cologne <?>
   8.  Search gopherspace at PSINet <?>
   9.  Search gopherspace at SUNET <?>
  10.  Search gopherspace at U. of Manitoba <?>
  11.  Search gopherspace at University of Cologne <?>
```

Your screen may look at bit different here but the intention is the same. We want to search Gopherspace for Buffalo Joe's. Notice that we can search for Directory Titles or all of Gopherspace. In our case, the Buffalo Joe's menu was a file and not a directory title (like Local Restaurant Menus), so we choose 9:

```
       Search gopherspace at SUNET: Buffalo Joes


   1.  *** Too many connections - Try again soon. ***.
```

Whoops! Oh well, nothing is perfect. We will go back and choose 8:

```
+--------------------Search gopherspace at PSINet--------------------+
|  Words to search for Buffalo Joe                                   |
|                                      [Cancel ^G] [Accept - Enter]  |
+--------------------------------------------------------------------+
```

Here we input the words "Buffalo Joe". In this way, we are looking for entries that contain the words "Buffalo" AND "Joe". In fact, we could have used the word "AND" in our query and Veronica would know what we mean. If, instead, we had just used one of the words, we would probably get too many entries! Composing a useful Veronica query is not very hard. It is mostly common sense.

There are some special features that allow you to do more exact matching. And if you have a problem, try choice 3 on the menu above and you will get detailed instructions on how to compose Veronica queries. At last our search proves profitable! After a couple of seconds of "hunting," we get the following screen:

```
          Search gopherspace at PSINet: Buffalo Joe

-->  1.  Buffalo Joe's: meals are $3-$6.
     2.  Buffalo Joe's.
```

And there it is! Our old friend! Happy dining.

# Using Jughead to Search Your Regional Gopherspace

Sometimes you may want to search just a particular part of Gopherspace, say all the Gopher servers in the state of New Jersey, or all those in Scandanavia, and so on. If you use Veronica, there is no way to restrict your Gopherspace search to just servers in a particular region. *Jughead* (named after the comic book character Jughead, friend of Archie Andrews (and not from *Jonzy's Universal Gopher Hierarchy Excavation and Display*, as some people think) was developed at the University of Utah to solve this problem. To use Jughead for a particular part of Gopherspace, someone has to have set up a Jughead server that maintains a database of menu items within the particular part of Gopherspace you are interested in. To access Jughead, you need only choose the appropriate menu item from a Gopher server.

# The World Wide Web (WWW)

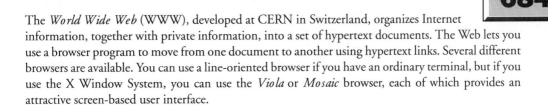

The *World Wide Web* (WWW), developed at CERN in Switzerland, organizes Internet information, together with private information, into a set of hypertext documents. The Web lets you use a browser program to move from one document to another using hypertext links. Several different browsers are available. You can use a line-oriented browser if you have an ordinary terminal, but if you use the X Window System, you can use the *Viola* or *Mosaic* browser, each of which provides an attractive screen-based user interface.

You can try out the WWW by using **telnet** to log in to the system *info.cern.ch*. Once you successfully log in to this system, you will be able to use a browser. You can obtain browsers for the WWW by using anonymous ftp to log in to a public WWW browser. Current public WWW browsers include three in the United States: *ukanaix.cc.ukans.edu* (Kansas), *www.njit.edu* (New Jersey), and *fatty.law.cornell.edu* (New York). There are also international browsers: *info.funet.fi* (Finland), *fserv.kfki.hu* (Hungary), *vms.huji.ac.il* (Israel), *sun.uakom.cs* (Slovakia), and *info.cern.ch* (Switzerland). Most of these do not require a login; some require that you log in as www.

You can obtain a browser using anonymous ftp to the system *info.cern.ch*. In the directory *pub/WWW/bin*, you will find directories for specific machines, each containing several browsers, including **www**, a line-oriented browser, and **viola**, an X-Windows browser. Mosaic, another useful X-Windows browser that supports multimedia applications, can be obtained using anonymous ftp from *ftp.ncs.uiuc.edu* in the directory */Web/xmosaic-binaries*. You need to select the appropriate version for your system from this directory.

You can find out more about the World Wide Web by reading the newsgroup *comp.infosystems.www*.

# TIP 685

# Using Mosaic

Mosaic is an increasingly popular tool you can use to discover, retrieve, and display information from the Internet. Mosaic provides a consistent, user-friendly interface to many Internet tools with dissimilar interfaces. You can access ftp, telnet, WAIS, Gopher, and Archie from Mosaic using a simple, point-and-click interface.

The following example illustrats how Mosaic is used. Suppose you have already installed Mosaic software on your system. You can start up Mosaic by using

```
Mosaic http://www-ns.rutgers.edu/htbin/archie_gateway
```

(This is an example of a Uniform Resource Locator (URL); see Tip 690 for details.) A Mosaic window will appear on your screen, including the following line and a text entry box:

```
This is a searchable index. Enter search keywords:
```

At this point you can enter the keywords of interest to you. For example, suppose you enter the keyword "xload" and then press RETURN. After a moderate delay (say of 2 or 3 minutes), you will get back a screen of citations of sources for the **xload** program, including the following:

```
gatekeeper.dec.com
    xload 749K (10-10-92) in /contrib/.mips-ultrix/bin/X11/
    Directory /contrib/src/cr1/X11R5/mips-ultirx/clients/xload
            (28-10-92)
    xload 1M  (07-10-92) in
            /contrib/scr/cr1/X11R5/mips-ultrix/clients/xload/
    Directory /contrib/src/cr1/X11R5/mit/clients/xload (28-10-92)
```

A portion of the text in each line will be highlighted (say in blue), while the rest of the text will be in normal text (say black). The highlighted text indicates a hypertext link to a document elsewhere on the Internet. If you click on the highlighted text,

```
/contrib/src/cr1/X11R5/mit/clients/xload
```

after a short delay, another screen will be displayed that contains a list of files, including *xload.c,* all highlighted as hypertext links. If you click on *xload.c* after a short wait, the source of this program will appear on your screen. If you click on the "Save As ..." button in the Mosaic window, you will be prompted with a file dialog box. You can enter the name for the save document, say *xload.c,* and click on the OK button.

# Where to Get Mosaic

**TIP 686**

You can obtain binaries via anonymous ftp for versions of Mosaic that run a wide variety of platforms, including many different UNIX platforms (such as Sun, SGI, IBM RS/6000, DEC Ultrix, and HP-UX), as well as Macintoshes and PCs running Microsoft Windows.

You can obtain binaries for Mosaic for each of the supported UNIX platforms via anonymous ftp from *ftp.ncsa.uiuc.edu* in the directory */Mosaic*. If you are using a machine for which such a binary version is available, you can retrieve this file and run Mosaic on your machine. If not, you may be able to port the source code for Mosaic to your particular machine by unpacking the source tree, editing the Makefile to specify your hardware platform and other options, make some modifications, and run **make**.

You can obtain binaries for Mosaic for the Macintosh from *ftp.ncsa.uiuc.edu* in the directory */Mac* and for the Windows environment in the directory */PC*. Look for *README, .doc,* or *.txt* files describing the current structure and software releases.

# Using Web Viewers

The Web contains a huge amount of text that can be browsed using Mosaic or some other browser. However, to take advantage of the hypermedia aspects of Mosaic, you will also need additional tools, called *viewers*. A viewer is a program that displays files containing information in a specific medium, such as audio, video, or graphics, in a platform-specific fashion. The viewers you need will depend on your platform; some may be included in the software supplied by your platform vendor. You may have to fetch others from the Internet. For example, on an SGI workstation, you may use the following viewers:

| Viewer | Medium |
|---|---|
| **mpeg_play** | Video |
| **showaudio** | Audio |
| **xv** | Graphics |
| **xpsview** | PostScript text |
| **xplaygizmo** | Control panel for other viewers |

To find out which viewers are available for your platform, first ask a local guru or system administrator. Next, you can use Mosaic to locate viewers. You can also consult the FAQ document on Mosaic to find such viewers.

# Configuring Mosaic for Specific Viewers

Mosaic obtains viewer bindings from the file *.mailcap* in your home directory. You can use the following extract of the *.mailcap* file on an SGI as a starting point to build your own *.mailcap* file:

```
audio/*;                  xplaygizmo -p showaudio %s
video/mpeg;               xplaygizmo -p mpeg_play %s
application/postscript;   xpsview %s
```

The *.mailcap* file defines a binding between a specific capability described in the left-hand column and a viewer described in the right-hand column that has that capability. The name of the target file is substituted for the %s token in the viewer description. A full description of the *.mailcap* file can be found in the Web.

# Configuring Mosaic to Spawn a Custom Viewer for Certain Files

You can configure Mosaic to use a viewer you provide whenever a file with a particular extension is encountered. For example, suppose you have the custom viewer called **ripples** that you want to use with certain audio files that have names ending with the extension *.ssw*. You should include the following line in your *.mailcap* file:

```
application/ssw;        ripples -s -Z %s
```

Then add a file to your home directory called *.mime.types*, containing the following:

```
application/ssw         ssw
```

This file creates a binding between file types, as indicated by their extension, and capabilities. The viewer is then identified by looking up the capability in the *.mailcap* file. This example indicates that files ending in *.ssw* require a capability of *application/ssw*. The *.mailcap* file indicates a viewer with this capability is **ripples**, that it should be invoked with the **-s** and **-Z** options, and that the filename should be substituted for the %s token. A full description of mime types may be found in the Web.

# Understanding Uniform Resource Locators

As you move your mouse around the screen and pass over the highlighted text segments or graphics, a line of information will appear just above the buttons at the bottom of the Mosaic window. This line, known as the *Uniform Resource Locator* (URL), is a description of the document that will be retrieved if you click on the text or graphics. A URL is like a filename but it contains two additional pieces of information: where the file lives in the network and how it should be retrieved. For example, here is a URL for a document describing Mosaic:

```
http://www.ncsa.uiuc.edu/SDG/Software/Mosaic/Docs/help-about.html
```

The first part of the URL, *http*, indicates that this document can be retrieved using the *HyperText Transfer Protocol*, an Internet protocol developed for the World Wide Web. There are other document retrieval methods including ftp, gopher, file, telnet, and news. The next part of the URL, *www.ncsa.uiuc.edu* is the network name of the machine containing the file. The last part of the URL, *SDG/Software/Mosaic/Docs/help-about.html*, is the pathname of the target file relative to a root that is local to the server.

Here are a few other examples of URLs:

```
gopher://tamuts.tamu.edu/11/.dir/subject.dir
ftp://csd4.csd.uwm.edu/pub/inet.services.html
telnet://idea.ag.uiuc.edu/
```

# TIP 691
# Saving Work with a Mosaic Hotlist

Mosaic allows you to create a list of favorite servers known as a *Hotlist*. Using simple menu commands, you can add the current page to the Hotlist or select a new page from the Hotlist. To find new pages to add to your Hotlist, you can use the Web to access the document.

```
http://www.ncsa.uiuc.edu/SDG/Software/Mosaic/Docs/whats-new.html
```

This document is updated frequently with announcements of new Web servers coming online. For example, the announcement for October 18, 1993 included the following line:

```
Rutgers University is now running a Web server
```

with Rutgers University highlighted. By clicking on the highlighted text, you can start down a path that leads to the archie server. You can save that page to your Hotlist, so you do not have to reconstruct the path the next time you want to use **archie**.

# What Is a Mosaic Home Page?

A *home page* is a starting point for exploring the Web. All organizations running Web servers provide a home page. This is the page you first access if you connect a server specifying only the server name and no file path. For example, if you type

```
Mosaic http: //www.ncsa.uiuc.edu
```

or select the "Open..." icon in the bottom of the Mosaic screen and type

```
http://www.ncsa.uiuc.edu
```

in the dialog box, you will retrieve the home page at NCSA. Home pages contain links to other documents supported by the local server and, often, references to other servers as well.

Mosaic may include a compiled-in reference to a home page that is specified in the source code. For the X version of Mosaic, you can specify your favorite home page with the X resource specification:

```
Mosaic*homeDocument:          http://my.favorite.com/my/favorite/file
```

This page is then used by default unless you specify another when you invoke Mosaic.

# Finding Out More about Mosaic

You can learn about Mosaic by using Mosaic itself. All the documentation is available online from various Web servers. Mosaic contains a small number of built-in links to documentation. Click on the Help icon in the upper-right corner of the Mosaic screen and select "About ...", "Manual ...", or "Demo ..." to get started. Just remember that each highlighted text segment or graphic is a hypertext link to another document, perhaps at the same site, perhaps halfway around the world. Click on the segment to follow the link.

You can also find out more about Mosaic from the FAQs that are posted periodically to *comp.infosystems.www*. You may also find the articles posted to this newsgroup useful.

# T**IP** 694 — Using WAIS to Search Databases

WAIS (for Wide Area Information Service) is a new service on the Internet that lets you search through databases by matching groups of words. This lets you find articles that you might be interested in based on some particular keywords they contain. The WAIS service can access more than 200 libraries. Each of these libraries has been created and maintained by volunteers and is available for free use.

To use WAIS, you will need to log in to a computer running WAIS client software. You can use your own system if it is running WAIS client software or you can use a computer on the Internet that provides WAIS to the public. For example, you can log in, via **telnet**, to a public WAIS client, such as *quake.think.com*, using wais as your login. The other current public WAIS clients you can access via **telnet** include *info.funet.fi* (Finland)—log in as wais; *swais.cwis.uci.edu* (California)—log in as swais; *nnsc.nsf.net* (Massachusetts)—log in as wais; *kudzu.cnidr.org* (North Carolina)—log in as wais; and *sunsite.unc.edu* (North Carolina)—log in as swais. Once you successfully log in to a public WAIS client, you can use **swais**, a character-oriented interface to WAIS. You can also access WAIS by using the Internet Gopher. (See Tips 676-680.)

You can install such a program on your own system. You should be able to find it via anonymous ftp to the directory *wais* on the system *think.com*.

# T**IP** 695 — Starting Off with WAIS

You can log in to a public WAIS client, using wais (or swais) as your logname. You will not need to supply a password, although some systems ask you to give your e-mail address as an identifier. The remote system will ask you your terminal type. After providing this, you will get a list of sources. You can select a current source from this menu. However, you generally should start your search by locating the libraries that might contain articles in which you have an interest. You can do this by querying the WAIS library named directory-of-servers. To do this, enter

```
/directory-of-servers
```

and press SPACE. You can then press RETURN to have the cursor move to the keyword line. For example, suppose you want articles about 3D movies. To get libraries that might contain articles on this topic, you provide it with some key words, with more words making it easier for WAIS to find a match. Here, we might try the following keywords:

```
cinema movies effects 3D stereoscopic
```

WAIS will give you a list of sources, number of lines, along with a score telling you how good a match is, with 1000 the maximum score used for the item with the most keyword matches. A score of 1000 does not guarantee a good match, however. You can move your cursor to a particular menu item and WAIS will give you information on this source.

Once you have done a search on the directory-of-servers, you can select particular servers using the list of sources menu. You can do this by first pressing **q** to end the paging program and **s** to return to this sources list. You then can select one or more sources using SPACE to select a source and = to unselect all sources. Once you have selected your sources, press RETURN to go to the keyword prompt and list your keywords. You can erase keywords with CTRL-U. Once you have listed your keywords, press RETURN again. You'll get a list of items showing their scores, sources, titles, and line numbers. To display an item, move to it in the menu and press RETURN. WAIS will give you information on this item.

# Choosing Good WAIS Sources

**TIP 696**

As described in Tip 695 you can use the directory-of-servers source to find sources that may contain information of interest to you. However, this is a rather general search and may not give you the best sources. Consequently, you may want to look at a summary of all WAIS sources. Such a summary containing brief descriptions of all WAIS sources, organized by categories, can be obtained via anonymous ftp from either *archive.orst.edu* in the file *src-list.txt* in the directory */pub/doc/wais* or *kirk.Bond.edu.au* in the file *src-list.txt* in */pub/Bond_Uni/doc/wais*.

# Finding More about WAIS

**TIP 697**

You can find out more about WAIS by reading the newsgroups *comp.infosystems.wais* and *alt.wais*. You should also read the FAQs posted periodically to these newsgroups and to *news.answers*. You can obtain these FAQs using anonymous ftp in the file *getting-started* in the directory

*/pub/usenet/news.answers/wais-faq* on *rtfm.mit.edu.* You may also find useful coverage of WAIS in the book *The Internet Complete Reference.*

# Mailing Lists

## TIP 698

## Internet Mailing Lists

There are close to 1000 different special-interest mailing lists available on the Internet. When you join one of these mailing lists, which function like electronic bulletin boards, you will automatically be sent all articles posted to that mailing list. The following sampling gives some idea of the wide range of mailing lists available on the Internet.

| Mailing List | Subject |
|---|---|
| AFRICA-L | The African people and the African continent |
| AIRCRAFT | Aircraft, helicopters, and air shows |
| AMNESTY | Amnesty International's urgent action appeals |
| AUDIO-L | Audio equipment and applications |
| BICYCLES | Bicycle equipment and racing |
| BIRDEAST | Birding Hotline for the Eastern U.S. |
| FILM-L | The cinema |
| FUSION | Nuclear fusion |
| HOCKEY-L | Collegiate hockey |
| HOMEBREW | Brewing and tasting of beer, ale, and mead |
| INFO-UNIX | Basic UNIX System Administration |
| MMEDIA-L | Multimedia in education and training |
| QUAKE-L | Use of computer networks after earthquakes |
| RAILROAD | Railroad and other transportation issues |
| SECURITY | Electronic, physical, and computer security |
| SHAKER | The history, artifacts, and beliefs of the Shakers |
| UNIX-SW | Announcement of new UNIX C public domain software |

See Tip 699 to learn how to obtain a list of Internet Mailing Lists and how to join these lists.

---

# The List of Lists

**T**<sup>IP</sup> **699**

You can find a description of over 800 mailing lists on the Internet in the book *Internet: Mailing Lists* edited by Edward T. L. Hardie and Vivian Neou (SRI Internet Information Series, Prentice-Hall, 1993). You can also download this list via anonymous ftp from *ftp.nisc.sri.com* in the file *interest-groups.Z* in the directory */netinfo*. Be sure to uncompress this file once you download it. You can also get a list of lists by sending a message to *mail-server@nisc.sri.com* containing the line

```
send netinfo/interest-groups
```

---

# Subscribing to a Mailing List

**T**<sup>IP</sup> **700**

To subscribe to a mailing list, you must send a message to the person maintaining this list. For instance, to join the mailing list "Fusion", you would send your request to *fusion-request@ZORCH.SF-BAY.ORG*. The person maintaining this list will then add you to its distribution.

Many mailing lists use the **listserv** program, which maintains mailing lists automatically. To subscribe to a mailing list that uses **listserv**, send a mail message to this server telling it that you want to subscribe to the mailing list. For example, you can subscribe to the mailing list PARAPSYCH on parapyschology by sending a message to *LISTSERV%RPICICGE@VM1.NODAK.EDU* that contains the line

```
SUB PSI
```

To remove yourself from this mailing list, you would send a message including the line

```
SIGNOFF PSI
```

# Internet Resources

**T**<sup>IP</sup> **701**

## Lists of Internet Resources

There are several sources of information on Internet resources. You can check the "Internet Services List," which is periodically posted to various newsgroups, including *news.answers*. This list can be obtained via anonymous ftp from *csd4.csd.uwm.edu* in the file *inet.services.txt* in the directory */pub*. You can also check Smith's BigFun List, which can be retrieved via anonymous ftp from *cerebus.cor.epa.gov* in the file *bigfun* in the directory */pub*.

You can also find useful lists of Internet resources in the books on the Internet mentioned in Tip 634. For example, there is a long list of Internet resources entitled "The Internet Navigator's Gazetteer" in the book *Navigating the Internet* by Gibbs and Smith. The book *The Internet Complete Reference* by Hahn and Stout, has an extensive list of Internet resources which the authors plan to maintain and update. If you want to add something to this list, mail your message to the authors of this book at *catalog@rain.org*. Another useful reference is the book *netguide* by Michael Wolff (New York: Random House, 1994) which provides an impressive list of services, information, and entertainment on the Internet as well as other parts of the "electronic superhighway." Another excellent reference is *The Internet Yellow Pages,* also by Hahn and Stout (Osborne/McGraw-Hill, 1994). In this book you'll find Internet resources organized in catalog form, much like the information in your phone company's *Yellow Pages*.

**T**<sup>IP</sup> **702**

## Accessing Libraries over the Internet

You can find out how to access the computerized libraries of many institutions throughout the world by reading a document which you can obtain via anonymous ftp from *ariel.unm.edu* with path */library/internet.library* or from *ftp.unt.edu* with path */library/libraries.txt*. You can also obtain a file describing strategies for using Internet library resources using anonymous ftp from *dla.ucop.edu* with path */pub/internet/libcat_guide*.

By the way, you can access the computerized resources of the Library of Congress using **telnet** to log in to *locis.loc.gov*.

# Finding Source Code for Mathematical Algorithms

You can obtain the source code for a wide variety of mathematical and scientific algorithms from the netlib archive at AT&T Bell Laboratories. You can obtain software from this archive via anonymous ftp to the system *research.att.com,* or via the mail server *netlib@research.att.com.* To find out how to use this mail server, send it a message consisting of the word "help".

# Books Available from the Internet Sites

You can get the full text of a variety of books using the Internet. The best source of these books is Project Gutenberg. Their specialties are classics with expired copyrights and various religious books. For example, you can get the text of *Aesop's Fables, Aladdin and the Wonderful Lamp, Moby Dick, O Pioneers!, Paradise Lost, Peter Pan, The Scarlet Letter, The Time Machine,* and *Tom Sawyer* from Project Gutenberg. To obtain the contents of books from Project Gutenberg, you can use anonymous ftp to *oes.orst.edu* with path */pub/etext,* to *mrcnext.cso.uiuc.edu* with path */pub/etext,* or to *info.umd.edu* with path */info/ReadingRoom/Fiction.* You can also use **telnet** to log in to *info.umd.ude* with login info.

You can obtain the text of other books from other Internet resources. For example, you can use anonymous ftp to *nic.funet.fi* to obtain the text of *A Christmas Carol, The Aeneid, Anne of Green Gables, The Call of the Wild, The Communist Manifesto, Discourse on Reason, The Invisible Man, Jabberwocky, The Legend of Sleepy Hollow, The Scarlet Pimpernel, Tom Sawyer, The Wonderful World of Oz,* and other books. You'll find the text for these books in the directory */pub/doc/etext.*

For a list of books available from the Internet archive sites, see the "Catalog of Internet Resources" chapter in *The Internet Complete Reference* by Hahn and Stout, or the other lists of resources mentioned in Tip 634.

# Webster's Dictionary Servers and Public Domain Thesaurus

You can check the spelling of words and get dictionary definitions using the online Webster's Dictionary. To access this online dictionary, use **telnet** to log in to *cs.indiana.edu* at port 2627 or *chem.ucsd.edu* with login webster to either system. When you log on, you are prompted for a word. If the word is not correctly spelled, the system will prompt you to choose among a number of similar words.

There are several places where you can get a copy of a public domain thesaurus of the English language. For example, you can get the 1911 version of *Roget's Thesaurus* via anonymous ftp from *clr.nmsu.edu* in */pub/lexica/thesauri/roget-1911*. You can also get a copy of a public domain thesaurus from Project Gutenberg at Illinois Benedictine College via anonymous ftp in the directory */pub/etext* on *mrcnext.cso.uiuc.edu*. A thesaurus is also available with Webster's; use the **-t** option to access it.

# Playing Games on the Internet

The Internet offers a plethora of information for you to use, but it also offers entertainment and recreational opportunities. There are a variety of games you can play on the Internet, including games you can download via anonymous ftp and play on your local machine. (See the books on Internet resources mentioned in Tip 701 to find such games.) There are also many interactive games you can play by remotely logging in to game servers. For example, you can play backgammon, chess, Diplomacy, Go and Scrabble with others on the Internet. See the "Catalog of Internet Resources" in the *Internet Complete Reference* by Hahn and Stout for the servers you can log in to to play each of these games.

You may enjoy participating in *Multiple User Dimensions (MUDs)* on the Internet. A MUD provides a virtual reality where players each take on a role, interacting with the game as they explore different dimensions of reality. MUDs can be either text based or graphics based. As you travel through a MUD you may solve puzzles, chat with other characters, create your own new part of the MUD's virtual reality, or battle monsters (just like real life). You can use **telnet** to log in to a MUD server. A MUD you might want to try is AlexMUD, based in Sweden. You can access AlexMUD by using **telnet** to log in to *mud.stacken.kth.se* at *port 4000*. (See Tip 589 to learn how to do this.) Also, try exploring Nightfall, a text-based social, virtual reality MUD (access through **telnet** to log in to *nova.tat.physik.uni-tuebingen.de* at port 4242) and the TinyTIM MUD, which contains more than

10,000 rooms, explored at one time or another by more than 2,000 players. You can access the TinyTIM MUD by using **telnet** to log in to yay.mdc.com at port 5440.

You can find a current listing of MUDs in "The Totally Unofficial List of Internet MUDs" posted to the newsgroups *rec.games.mud.misc* and *rec.games.mud.announce*. This list is also available using anonymous ftp from *rtfm.mit.edu* in the directory *pub/usenet/rec.games.mud.announce*. There is another useful list of MUDs in the "Catalog of Internet Resources" in The Internet Complete Reference by Hahn and Stout. To find out more about MUDs, you should read the article "MUDs, MUDs, Glorious MUDs" by Kevin M. Savetz in the March/April 1994 issue of *Internet World*. You may also want to read the USENET newsgroups on MUDs. These start with the prefix *rec.games.mud*. You may want to read the FAQs posted periodically to these newsgroups. They are also available via anonymous ftp from *ftp.math.okstate.edu* in the file *pub/muds/misc/mud-faq*. You can even attend a MUD conference. See the Savetz article mentioned earlier for details.

# Viewing Pictures from the Internet

**TIP 707**

There are a series of newsgroups on USENET where people post binary files of pictures in various formats. These are the newsgroups with names beginning with *alt.binaries.pictures*. For example, there are newsgroups that post pictures of fractals, fine art, tasteless material, and erotica; these are *alt.binaries.fractals, alt.binaries.fine-art.digitized, alt.binaries.pictures.tasteless,* and *alt.binaries.pictures.erotica,* respectively. To view these pictures, you'll need a picture viewer for pictures stored using several different formats, including GIF and JPEG. Animated pictures are also posted and stored in GL format. Here are the steps you need to follow to download and view such images.

First, save the netnews articles containing the file, or the series of articles containing the parts of the file, holding the data for the picture. These files have probably been stored in uuencoded format. (See Tip 605.) Combine the files holding these articles, remembering to strip out the article headers. Use the **uudecode** command to decode the uuencoded file. This will give you a file that contains the data for a formatted picture, which will be a *.gif* file, a *.jpg* file, or a *.gl* file (for GIF, JPEG, or GL formats, respectively). Finally, use the appropriate viewer to look at the picture or animation. You can get viewers from the sources listed in the FAQ on viewing pictures or from postings to the newsgroup *alt.binaries.pictures.utilities*.

To get more information about viewing pictures, read the FAQs on viewing pictures that is posted periodically to *news.answers* and is available via anonymous ftp from *rtmf.mit.edu* in the directory */pub/usenet/news.answers/pictures-faq* where the FAQs are divided into the files *part1, part2,* and *part3*.

# How to Become an Internet Resource

## How to Be an Internet Resource via finger

Perhaps the simplest way to act as an Internet resource is by using the capabilities of the **finger** command. To do this, use the *.project* and *.plan* files, since the contents of these files are printed when someone fingers your account. For example, to provide the latest beach conditions at the New Jersey shore, you could put the line

```
current New Jersey Shore conditions
```

in your *.project* file. You could also put in daily updates of weather conditions in your *.plan* file. For example, you may put the following in this file on a particularly nice day:

```
New Jersey Shore forecast for July 30, 1994.
Air temperature:  81-87 degrees Fahrenheit
Water temperature:  73 degrees Fahrenheit
Wind:  3-5 mph     Waves:  1-2 feet
Jellyfish:  None   Pollution:  None
```

## Offering Resources via Anonymous ftp

You can set up your own system so that you can offer files to remote users via anonymous ftp. When you do this, you give these users access to files you choose without giving them logins on your system. To set up anonymous ftp on your system, you can use the following procedure as a guide. See the instructions for your own system for more details.

Add the user ftp to your */etc/passwd* and */etc/shadow* files. Use an invalid password and a user shell that cannot be used, such as **/bin/true**.

Create the directory */var/home/ftp* so that you own it and not the user ftp, with the same group as user ftp. Create the subdirectories *bin, etc,* and *pub* in */var/home/ftp*.

Copy */usr/bin/ls* to the subdirectory */var/home/ftp/bin*.

Edit the copies of */etc/passwd* and */etc/shadow* so they only contain the following users: root, daemon, uucp, and ftp. Edit the copy of */etc/group* to contain the group other, which is the group assigned to the user ftp. Change permissions on the directories and files in the directories under */var/home/ftp* to the following:

| File or Directory | Owner | Group | Mode |
|---|---|---|---|
| ftp | ftp | other | 555 |
| ftp/bin | root | other | 555 |
| ftp/bin/ls | root | other | 111 |
| ftp/etc | root | other | 555 |
| ftp/etc/passwd | root | other | 444 |
| ftp/etc/shadow | root | other | 444 |
| ftp/etc/group | root | other | 444 |
| ftp/pub | ftp | other | 777 |

A complete procedure for setting up anonymous ftp under the SunOS is posted frequently to the newsgroup *comp.sys.sun.admin*. You can also obtain this by using anonymous ftp to retrieve the file */pub/sun-faq/anon-ftp.how-to* from *thor.ece.uc.edu*.

# Chapter 11

# System Administration
# for
# UNIX Systems

# Getting Started with System Administration

## System Administration via FACE Menus

**TIP 710**

One of the features under FACE (*F*ramed *A*ccess *C*ommand *E*nvironment) in SVR4 is System Administration from the menu level. This makes it easy to do a wide variety of system administration tasks using menus.

To use the system administration menu, you must have the root or sysadm permission. To access the sysadm menu interface, type

```
# sysadm
```

The first menu you will see presents a list of administrative categories. These categories include the following choices:

- ❏ Backup services
- ❏ Diagnostics
- ❏ File systems
- ❏ Machine
- ❏ Network services
- ❏ Ports
- ❏ Printers
- ❏ Restore service
- ❏ Software
- ❏ Storage devices
- ❏ System setup
- ❏ Users

You can navigate through this menu using the UP ARROW and DOWN ARROW keys; press ENTER to select one of the categories. When you do this, you will get another window that will offer a list of tasks in that category of administration. Continue selecting items in successive menus until you reach the particular task you wish to do.

# Where Can You Find Administrative Commands?

You can find commands for UNIX System V system administration in several different directories. These include */sbin, /usr/sbin, /usr/bin, /usr/etc,* and */etc.*

The */sbin* directory contains executables used in booting the system and in manual recovery from a system failure.

The */usr/sbin* directory contains executables for some administrative commands.

The */usr/bin* directory contains executable commands not critical to running in single-user mode.

The */etc* directory contains some basic administrative commands and many administrative directories. Some of the subdirectories of this directory that you might need to know about include:

| Subdirectory | Contents |
| --- | --- |
| /etc/bkup | Files for backups and restores |
| /etc/cron.d | Files controlling cron activities |
| /etc/default | Files assigning default system parameters |
| /etc/init.d | Storage location for files used when changing system states |
| /etc/lp | Local printer configuration files |
| /etc/mail | Local electronic mail administration files |
| /etc/rc?.d | Actual location for files used when changing states |
| /etc/saf | Files for local SAF administration |
| /etc/save.d | Location used by sysadm to back up data onto floppies |

The */usr/etc* directory contains the rest of the administrative commands.

# Becoming the Superuser

**712**

As a system administrator you will often need to become the *superuser*. The superuser is the user with username root and the uid 0. The root login is used by the system to carry out its basic functions; consequently, root can do almost anything. As a system administrator, you will want to change from your own login to root to carry out a variety of system administration tasks. For example, you will need to become a superuser to kill runaway processes owned by users on your system.

To become the superuser, use the **su** command. When you run this command, you will be prompted for the superuser password, as follows:

```
$ /bin/su -
password:  v12dgf8
#
```

Here, to run the **su** command, you use its full pathname, **/bin/su**, to make sure that you don't execute another command named **su** in your PATH. The - (dash) on the command line tells the **su** command that you want to change the shell environment to the environment of the superuser. For example, the home directory is set to the root directory / and PATH is set to include the directories where administrative commands are found. The password you supply (here v12dgf8) is not echoed, as usual. Then you get back the # prompt. To exit the superuser subshell, you type either CTRL-D or EXIT.

# System Startup and Shutdown

# Changing System States

**713**

UNIX System V has several different modes of operation. These modes are called *system states*. You will need to change these system states to do certain administrative tasks. The most important of these states are listed here:

| State | Name |
| --- | --- |
| 0 | Shutdown state |
| 1 | Administrative state |

| State | Name |
| --- | --- |
| s (or S) | Single-user state |
| 2 | Multiuser state |
| 3 | Remote file-sharing (RFS) state |
| 5 | Firmware state |
| 6 | Stop and reboot state |

Enter state 0, the *shutdown state*, to completely power down the machine. You need to do this if you want to move the machine or to change the hardware on your system, such as adding a new memory or communications board.

State 1, the *administrative state*, is used to start the operating system so that the full file system is available to the system administrator from the console, but not to other users.

State 2, the *multiuser state*, is the state in which file systems are mounted and multiuser services are available. This is the normal state of operation of UNIX systems unless they are sharing files using RFS.

State 3, the *RFS state,* is used to start the Remote File System, to connect the machine to an RFS network, and to mount and share resources over the network. This is the default run level.

State 5, the *firmware state*, is used to run special firmware commands and programs, such as booting the system from different boot files than usual.

State 6, the *stop and reboot state*, is used to stop the operating system, and then reboot to the state in the initdefault entry in the *inittab* file.

When your system is started up, it goes into either multiuser state (2) or RFS state (3). To change the default system state, you need to edit the */etc/inittab* file and change the initdefault line. For example, to bring up your system in RFS state (3) if it is now set up to go into multiuser state, change this line to

```
is:3:initdefault:
```

You may also want to change your system state once your machine is up and running. For example, to change your system from multiuser mode to RFS mode, use the command

```
# init 3
```

# System Shutdown

**TIP 714**

To shut down your system, you should use the **shutdown** command. This command sends a warning message and a final message, separated by 60 seconds, before its starts shutdown activities. By default, the command asks for confirmation before it starts killing processes and shutting down daemons. By using the -**y** option, you can have the system not ask for confirmation before going down, as in the following example.

```
# shutdown -y -g100
```

This tells your system not to ask for confirmation before going down, to go down 100 seconds after the warning message, and to go to the single-user (s) state.

You can also use shutdown to take your system to a lower state. For example, if your system is currently in state 3 (RFS), running

```
# shutdown -y g0 -i2
```

tells the system not to ask for confirmation and to go down immediately without a grace period to system state 2.

## System Customization

# Setting Up the System Profile Files

**TIP 715**

The system administrator of a UNIX computer needs to set up two profile files. The first of these is the system profile */etc/profile,* which is run for every user on login. The second is the skeleton *.profile* file used to get new users started before they create their own customized *.profile.* You can put this skeleton *.profile* in */etc/skel/.profile.* It will be copied to the home directory of a user when that user is added to the system by first entering the **sysadm** command and then selecting add and then users from successive menus.

Here is a sample */etc/profile* that you can edit to suit the particular needs of your system.

```
PATH=/bin:/usr/bin
LOGNAME=`logname`          #set LOGNAME to user's name
if [ "$LOGNAME" = root ]    # set a special PATH for root
then
      PATH=/sbin:/usr/sbin:/usr/bin:/etc
      PATH=$PATH:/letc;/usr/lbin
else
      PATH=$PATH:/usr/lbin:/usr/add-on/local/bin::
      trap : 2
      news -s     # report number of unread news items
      trap " 2
fi
trap "" 2 3
export LOGNAME       #make login name available to shell
. /etc/TIMEZONE      #make local time zone available to shell
export PATH
trap "trap " 2 " 2    # allow user to break out of
# message-of-the-day only
if mail -e             # check if mail is in user's mailbox
then
      echo "You have mail"
fi
umask 022
```

Here is a sample *.profile* that you can put in */etc/skel/.profile:*

```
stty echoe echo icanon ixon
stty erase
HOME=/home/$LOGNAME
PATH=:$HOME/bin:/bin:/usr/bin:/usr/local/bin
MAIL=/usr/mail/$LOGNAME
MAILPATH=/usr/mail/$LOGNAME
echo "Terminal?"
read term
TERM=$term
export HOME PATH TERMINFO TERM
umask 022
```

# Setting the System Date and Time

**TIP 716**

When you first set up your system, you will need to set the current date and time. For example, to set the date and time to October 6, 1994, 2:13 A.M., use

```
# date 1006021394
Oct 6 02:13  EDT  1994
```

You can also set the time zone used by your system by changing the */etc/TIMEZONE* file where the TZ environmental variable is set. For example, to set your time zone to Pacific Standard Time (PST), which is eight hours earlier than Greenwich Mean Time (GMT), specifying that you want to change to Pacific Daylight Time (PDT) when time is switched from standard time to daylight time, put the following lines in */etc/TIMEZONE:*

```
TZ=PST8PDT
export TZ
```

# Administering Users and Groups

# Adding and Deleting Users and Groups

**TIP 717**

You can add a new user to your system with the **useradd** command. For example, to add a user with the logname jose, use

```
#  useradd -m jose
```

The **-m** option is used to create a home directory for the login jose in */home/jose*. You may need to use the **chown** command to change the ownership of this directory from root to jose.

You can add a new login so that it expires on a particular day. You may want to do this if you are adding a user who may be a consultant working on a project of a specific duration. To do this, use the -e option of **useradd** followed by the expiration date. For example, the command

```
# useradd -e 11/30/95 jose
```

can be used to set up the login jose so that it expires on November 30, 1995. After this time, this login is not valid unless the system administrator enables it again.

You can use the **-f** option to set the number of days a login can be inactive before it is declared invalid. For instance, if you want to set up the login jose so that if it has not been used for more than 30 days, it becomes invalid, use

```
# useradd -f 30 -m jose
```

Any new login that you set up will be locked until a password has been added for it. To do this for the login jose, use

```
# passwd jose
```

You will be asked to type an initial password. This user will use the initial password the first time he logs in, after which he should change it to one only he knows.

# Locking an Unused Login

If you want to temporarily lock the account of a user, you can lock this login with the **-l** (*l*ock) option to the **passwd** command. For example, to lock the login jose, use

```
# passwd -l jose
```

To unlock an account locked in this way, the system administrator must run the **passwd** command again for this login.

You can also effectively lock out a user by setting the login shell of this user to **/bin/true**. An attempt to log in by this user will cause an immediate logoff.

# Deleting a User

**TIP 719**

You may want to delete a user to prevent this user from accessing your system, such as when someone quits your company or when a student leaves a university. For example, to delete the login jose, type

```
# userdel jose
```

If you also want to delete the home directory of jose, use

```
# userdel -r jose
```

Any files owned by jose that are not deleted when the home directory of jose is removed (if it is), will still be on the system and will still be owned by the user ID of the login jose.

# Eliminating a User's Account

**TIP 720**

Tip 719 shows you what actions to take to delete a user from your system by eliminating the owner's password and deleting his or her files. If you just do that, however, you may find out that other users have been using the files in this login. To avoid the problem of removing files used by other users, follow this procedure:

1.  Alter the user's passwd in */etc/passwd*. This will block any further logins.

2.  Look in */etc/group* to determine which other users belong to groups that include this user. You can do this using **grep**. Send mail to each of the others in these groups stating that the user's account is being closed, and will be unavailable after 30 days.

3.  Make the user's *$HOME* permissions 000, so that the directory is inaccessible to anyone.

4.  After a month (and after the files have been backed up so that they are available in an emergency), use the **find** command on **perms 000** and delete the *$HOME* directory.

Going through all these steps is easy to do manually if you have few users entering and leaving your system. If this happens often (at the end of a semester at a university, for example), it's easy to automate the whole process with a shell script. The drawback of doing so is that you'll need to remember to change permissions from 000 when someone complains about being denied access to the files.

# Setting Up a Restricted Shell Environment for Certain Users

Sometimes you may want to restrict the commands that certain users can run. Unfortunately, there is no easy method of restricting users in this way. There is a standard restricted shell, **/usr/lib/rsh** or **sh -r** on most machines, but this "restricted" environment is easy to break out of.

If you just want to provide a service to a certain group of users, a client-server approach is probably the most convenient. In this way, a server just listens on a certain port and the client accesses that port and the information is exchanged without much threat of break in.

If, however, you want to allow a user access to your machine with a shell, it is much harder to restrict what this user can do. It is possible to set up a mini-environment with the **chroot(8)** command. You will need to set up a whole new group of commands (and directories to put them in) for that restricted user. Thus, only those things you are willing to allow the user access to are explicitly available in this environment. Be warned, however, that setting up a "real" restricted environment is not very easy.

# Adding and Deleting Groups

Since permissions to read, write, and execute files (and directories) are assigned to owners, groups, and others, you will need to administer groups on your system. In particular, you will need to add and delete groups.

You can create new groups using the **groupadd** command. For example, you can use

```
# groupadd projectX
```

to add the name "project X" to */etc/group;* the system will assign a group ID number to this new group. After you create this group, you can use the **useradd** command with the **-g** option to add users to this group.

When a project is completed, you may want to delete a group from your system. You can do so using the **groupdel** command. For example, use the following command to delete the group projectX:

```
# groupdel projectX
```

## System Security

# Guidelines for Keeping Your System Secure

It is difficult to keep a system totally secure, but there is a wide variety of things you should do to reduce the risk that your system is compromised to a very low level. Here are some of them:

❑   Make sure that all login passwords are changed regularly. You can make sure this is done by enforcing password aging. (See Tip 728) Never give out passwords to users over the telephone, don't write passwords down, and don't give passwords to logins to people who do not absolutely need them.

❑   Use commands such as **useradd** and **passwd**, or the menu interface for system administration, to add users and to change passwords. This ensures that */etc/passwd* and */etc/shadow* are kept in synch.

❑   Protect the root password with extreme care. Close off permissions to superuser login directories so that no one can write to the bin or change the *.profile* of these logins.

❑   Set up passwords for administrative logins. (See Tip 725.)

❑   Remove logins that are no longer needed or lock out these accounts. (See Tips 718 and 719.)

❑   Limit the number of setuid programs (see Tip 729) to programs that must use this capability; remove all others.

❑   Check the log of superuser activity, */var/adm/sulog*, to monitor the activities of users who have used the **su** command to become root. Make sure they have not accessed system files or files of other users without their permission.

❑ Make sure login directories, profile files, and administrative files are not writable by others; if they are, you may have experienced a security breach.

❑ Make sure that sensitive information is stored in encrypted files, but note that such files are vulnerable to attack by tools such as the Crypt Breakers Workbench.

❑ Make sure that default permissions are set using the appropriate umask in */etc/profile*. Set up access permissions to systemwide files to restrict access to users.

❑ Make sure that authorized versions of commands allowing system access are used on your system, including **su**, **cu**, **ttymon**, **telnet**, and **login**. You can have serious security compromises if a user replaces one of these commands with the user's own version, changes the ownership permissions, or moves his or her own version ahead of the real ones in a user's PATH.

❑ Turn off the daemon for the trivial file transfer protocol, **tftpd** in */usr/etc/inetd.conf*.

❑ Never leave your system console unattended when you are logged in. It is best to log off, or at least to lock your terminal when taking a break.

❑ Keep your computer physically secure so that no one can steal it!

# Logging Unsuccessful Login Attempts

**T**<sub>I</sub>**P**
**724**

One way to see whether someone is trying to break into your system is to keep a log of unsuccessful login attempts. To do this, you turn on the built-in mechanism for logging unsuccessful login attempts on your system. Login attempts are logged after a user has made five consecutive unsuccessful attempts to log in. To turn on this mechanism, the system administrator needs to create a file */var/adm/loginlog*. The permissions for this file should be set with read and write permission for root only. Here are the steps you need to follow:

First, reset the default file creation privileges in a separate shell, using

```
# /bin/sh
# umask 066
```

Second, create the *loginlog* file with

```
# > /var/adm/loginlog
```

Next, change the group of this file to sys as follows:

```
# chgrp sys /var/adm/loginlog
```

Then, change the owner of the file to root:

```
# chown root /var/adm/loginlog
```

Finally, return from the level of the newly created shell using

```
# exit
```

# Assigning Passwords to Administrative Logins

There are a number of special logins assigned before a system is delivered. These are the administrative logins; these logins have special capabilities, but do not have the full capabilities of the root login. The administrative logins that you should know about are

| Login | Purpose |
| --- | --- |
| root | Controls the operating system |
| adm | Owns many system logging and accounting files |
| bin | Owns most user-accessible commands |
| sys | Owns some system files |
| uucp | Administers the Basic Networking Utilites |
| nuucp | Lets remote machines log in and transfer files |
| daemon | Owns some background processes and waits for events |
| lp | Administers the lp system |
| sysadm | Accesses the sysadm command |
| ovmsys | Owns the FACE executable program |

For example, to assign a password to adm, use

```
# passwd adm
```

You will receive the prompt "New Password:". After entering this new password, you will receive a second prompt "Re-enter new password:". If you enter the same string at both prompts, this string will be the password for this administrative login.

We recommend that you lock out all these logins except nuucp so you can only reach them from root.

# The /etc/passwd File

T**IP**
726

In earlier releases of the UNIX system, the */etc/passwd* file contained an encrypted version of a user's password. This led to possible security problems. This is no longer the case in UNIX System V Release 4.

The security problem in the earlier version of the UNIX system occurred because, since ordinary users could read */etc/passwd,* any user could run a program to encrypt words for a dictionary and other possibilities for passwords and compare them to the passwords stored in this file. If they found a match, they would have guessed the password for an account.

The basic purpose of */etc/passwd* is to identify each user to the system. There is a line in this file for each user. The contents of the lines in this file vary somewhat. For example, on some versions of UNIX System V Release 4, each line contains the following seven fields, separated by colons:

- ❑ User login ID
- ❑ Placeholder *x* (used to hold the password)
- ❑ User ID number
- ❑ Group ID number
- ❑ User's home directory
- ❑ Comment on the user (often the user's name)
- ❑ Default program executed when user logs in

# TIP 727

## What Is the /etc/shadow File?

The */etc/shadow* file is readable only by root. It is where encrypted passwords are stored in UNIX System V Release 4. This keeps other people from accessing the encrypted passwords to try and guess them. The */etc/shadow* file also includes information about password aging. The fields of this file include

❑  login

❑  For users with passwords, the encrypted password; NP (for no password); x (for the logins uucp, nuucp, and slan); *LK* for the listen login (logins with x and *LK* here are locked out accounts)

❑  Number of days between January 1, 1970 and the day when the password was last changed

❑  Minimum number of days required between password changes

❑  Maximum number of days a password is valid

❑  Number of days before expiration of a password that user is warned

❑  Number of days of inactivity allowed

❑  Absolute date when login may no longer be used

As an administrator, you can set up some variables that control what is allowed for passwords on your system:

| | |
|---|---|
| PASSLENGTH | Minimum length of a password (default is 6) |
| MINWEEKS | Number of weeks after changing a password during which it cannot be changed again |
| MAXWEEK | Number of weeks after changing password that user will be requested to change it on next log in |
| WARNWEEKS | Number of weeks before password will expire that user gets a warning |

# Setting Up Password Aging for a Login

You can make users change their passwords at particular intervals using the -x option of the **passwd** command. For example, if you use the command

```
# passwd -x 90 -n 10 inga
```

you will make the user inga change her password at least once every 90 days and you will prohibit her from changing her password again for 10 days after she has changed it. (This will keep her from changing back to her old password. However, this makes it impossible for her to change her password during these 10 days even if she thinks it has been compromised. If this is the case, she will have to ask her system administrator to change her password.)

You can warn users automatically that their passwords will expire with the -w (*w*arning) option to **passwd**. For example, the command

```
# passwd -w 5 inga
```

will warn the user inga each day that her password will expire starting five days before this is scheduled to occur. For example, three days before her password is scheduled to expire, she will see

```
Your password will expire in 3 days
```

# What Are Set User ID and Set Group ID Programs?

When you execute a program with its *set user ID* (suid) permission set, your effective user ID is set to the user ID of the owner of this file. For example, if you execute a program owned by root, you become superuser while you are running this program (such as when you run the **passwd** command). Also, when executing a program with its set group ID (sgid) permission set, your effective group ID is the group of the owner of the file. The suid and sgid permissions allow users access to resources generally not available to them.

# Setting User ID Permissions

To set the suid permission of a file you own, say on the file *salcomp,* type

```
$ chmod u+s salcomp
```

To remove this permission, type

```
$ chmod u-s salcomp
```

You can set the group ID permission of your own executable file, say *salcomp,* with

```
$ chmod g+s salcomp
```

To remove this permission, type

```
$ chmod g-s salcomp
```

To set the suid and sgid permissions, you can supply the **chmod** command with a string of four octal digits. The leftmost digit is used to change the suid or sgid permissions. The other changes the read, write, and execute permissions as described in Tip 130. If the first digit is 6, both the suid and the sgid permissions are set; if it is 4, the suid permission is set, but the sgid is not; if it is 2, the suid permission is not set but the sgid is; if it is 0 (or not given), neither the suid nor the sgid is set.

For example, the following command sets the suid permission on the program **salcomp**, but does not set the sgid permission:

```
$ chmod 4755 salcomp
```

# Security Problems with suid Programs

**TIP**
**731**

When you are the owner of a suid program, other users have all your privileges when
they run this program. This can lead to serious problems. For example, if you have included a command
allowing a shell escape such as an editor in a suid program, any user running this program could escape
to a shell with your privileges assigned to it. This user could copy, change, or delete your files or run
your programs. Because of these problems, many system administrators will not add new programs
that include suid or sgid permissions being set.

# Finding suid and sgid Programs

**TIP**
**732**

Since suid and sgid programs present potential security problems, you may want to
periodically list all the files with suid or sgid permissions set. If you find some files of this type that are
not among the ones that should be present on your system, you may have a security problem that
could allow a user to gain superuser privileges. To list all the suid and sgid files on your system, use
the command

```
# find / -perm -002000 -o -004000  -type f -print
```

You should compare your output with a list of these types of files that come with your version of the
UNIX system. You can find a list of all suid and sgid programs that come with various versions of the
UNIX system in Appendix B of the book *Practical UNIX Security* by Simson Garfinkel and Gene
Spafford (Sebastopol, CA: O'Reilly and Associates, 1991).

# Finding Files with No Owners

**TIP**
**733**

If files with no owners are present on your system, you may have a security problem.
For example, someone other than a valid user may have figured out a way to log in to your system and
set up a login, created some files, and then deleted the login. So, you will want to check for such files
if you suspect that your system has been compromised. On many systems, you can do this using the
**find** command with the **-nouser** option. Here is the command that you run:

```
# find / -nouser -print
```

*The output may contain files that were owned by valid users that you have deleted from your system.*

Similarly, you should check for files not owned by a valid group. You can do this using the command

```
# find / -nogroup -print
```

Of course, you can simultaneously look for files not owned by a valid login or not owned by a valid group with

```
# find / -nouser -o -nogroup -print
```

# TIP 734 — UNIX System Viruses

A *computer virus* is a software program that infects a system, causing it carry out certain undesired tasks and to replicate and spread the virus. A virus usually spreads itself by copying its code into executable programs. When a user runs an infected program, the virus copies itself into other executable programs that the user can modify. The virus, at some specified time or once infection has occurred, will carry out some specified task. This task can be destructive, such as removing important files, or can be benign and amusing, such as displaying messages on the screen.

Your UNIX system can become infected by a virus either when you install new software programs or download software from the Internet or some other bulletin board service. To avoid viruses you need to be extremely careful about where you get software programs. You should also make sure to put your system directories first in your PATH (see Tips 45 and 46) and do not allow directories containing executables or programs writable by anyone other than root.

You can sometimes detect infection of a file by a virus by noticing a change in the size of the file, the inode change time, the modify time, and the checksum of the file. You might want to periodically run shell scripts that check these things to try to detect viral attacks. One good reference where you can find some useful shell scripts to do this is the book *UNIX System Security* by Rik Farrow (Reading, MA: Addison Wesley, 1991).

# How to Find Out More about UNIX System Security

There are several useful books dealing with security on the UNIX system. These include *Practical UNIX Security* by Garfinkel and Spafford, *UNIX System Security* by Farrow, and *UNIX System Security* by Patrick Wood and Stephen Kochan (Indianapolis, IN: Hayden Books, 1985). You may also want to read the *Proceedings of the UNIX Security Workshop,* published annually by the USENIX Association; you can find out how to obtain these from USENIX at (510) 528-8649 or by e-mail at *office@usenix.org.*

You may also want to consult the newsgroups in the area *comp.security.*

## Communicating with Users

# Communicating with All Users

There are several different ways you can communicate with all the users on your system. For example, you can communicate a short message to users on a daily basis using the message-of-the-day file, */etc/motd.* The text you put in this file, using your favorite editor, will be displayed automatically when a user logs in.

You can put longer messages that your users might want to read when they log in or at a later time, in the */usr/news* directory. Users can read the news messages they have not yet read when they use the **news** command; to see all news messages, including those they have already read, they can use **news -a.**

To send a message to all users currently logged in to your system, you can use the **wall** command. You will want to do this when you must bring the system down in an emergency or to alert users that some scheduled maintenance is about to take place. For example, you might use **wall** as follows:

```
# wall
The system will be down in 1 minute.
Log off now!
CTRL-D
```

There is also an **rwall** command that you can use in a similar way to send messages to everyone logged in to a machine on your local network.

# Managing Your Disk Space

## Displaying Disk Space and Usage

You may be running out of disk space for users on your system. To see why this may be happening, you can display the disk space available on each file systems. To do this, use the following command:

```
# df -t
```

For each file system, you will see the mount point, related device, total number of blocks of memory, the number of files in the file system, the total number of blocks of memory and the total number of files available in that file system.

You can see how much space is being used by each directory using the **du** command. Its output shows the amount of space used in it and each directory below it.

## Using the du Command on Different Systems

The **du** command provides you with a detailed look or a brief summary of your disk usage. Some people get confused because the output of **du** indicates that they have used much more space than they expected. Worse is to have **du** make you think you're using less disk than you really are. Because of an unfortunate incompatibility among **du** commands on different versions of UNIX, you need to know which **du** program you are running to know how to interpret its output. Here are the major points:

❏ **/usr/5bin/du** is the System V version that reports disk usage in 512 byte blocks.

❏ **/bin/du** is the BSD version that reports disk usage in 1 Kbyte blocks.

❏ On SVR4 machines, the BSD version is in **/usr/ucb/du**, and the SVR4 version is in **/usr/bin/du**.

# What to Do If You Are Running Out of Disk Space

If you are running out of blocks of memory or the number of files you can create in a file system, you will need to take some actions. For example:

❏ You can archive files that are not needed onto floppy disks or cartridge tapes. These can be restored later if needed.

❏ You can delete files you no longer need. For example, you can delete or truncate administrative log files and spool files.

❏ You can ask users to clean up their file systems, deleting or archiving unneeded files.

❏ You can distribute files to different file systems with more room. For example, you can move users to file systems with lots of available space.

❏ You can compress files, if they have not already been compressed, to save disk space.

❏ Finally, you can buy more disks!

# Monitoring Files That Grow

There are a variety of files and directories that grow over time that you will need to monitor. In particular, you should regularly check the sizes of the log files on your system. These files keep track of different types of activities on your system. You will want to periodically delete or truncate such files, which include the following:

❑   */var/adm/sulog*, which contains a history of commands run by the superuser.

❑   */var/cron/log*, which contains a history of jobs kicked off by cron facilities.

❑   */var/adm/loginlog*, which monitors unsuccessful login attempts.

Since you will want to periodically delete or truncate these files, you will want to run cron jobs to do this. (See Tip 743) Other files and directories you need to monitor so they do not grow out of hand include

❑   /var/spool/uucp, which contains files waiting to be sent using the UUCP system; you'll want to delete files that cannot be sent that have been sitting in this directory for more than some period, say one week.

❑   */var/spool/uucppublic*, which contains files received by the UUCP system; you may want to delete files not retrieved by users after some period, say one month.

# Managing Processes

## Managing User Processes

**TIP 741**

When you use the **ps** command to list the commands that are running on your system, you may notice some processes that are causing problems. For example, a few processes may be using most of the CPU resources. Other processes may be using most of the system memory. There may be some steps you can take to improve the performance of your system by either killing or changing the priorities of such processes.

For example, you may have noticed that a process has used a large amount of time. This may mean that the process is in an infinite loop, some other error has occurred, or it may simply mean that a job is running correctly, but requires a large amount of time. You may want to kill a process using a large amount of time, but before you do consult with the user to see whether it is appropriate to do so.

Similarly, a process may be using a large percentage of the memory on your system. You may also want to kill such a process. You get information on the percentage of memory being used by a process from the %MEM field in the output of **ps -au** on BSD-related systems. You can also get information on memory use from the SZ field which gives the amount of nonshared virtual memory, in the output of **ps -el** on System V and **ps -au** on BSD.

You may also notice that some processes are using a large percentage of the CPU on the system. You will see this in the contents of the C or %CPU (for CPU utilization) column of the output of **ps -el** (or on BSD-related systems, **ps -au**). Again, you may want to kill such jobs after consulting with users. If you are using a version of the UNIX system that has the **renice** command (you can find it in the BSD compatibility package on SVR4), you can use this command to lower the priority of such jobs. For example, to lower the priority of the job with pid 7339, you use

```
# renice 4 -p 7339
```

You may also notice that one of your users is clogging the system with many similar jobs. This can be caused by poor shell programming, or some other problem; consult with the user before killing such processes and check how this user is writing shell programs. You may also ask users to run large, CPU-intensive jobs with low priorities using the **nice** command or to schedule such commands at off-peak hours using the **at** command.

# Managing Real-Time Processes

**TIP 742**

One of the features that System V Release 4 adds is support for real-time processes. Real-time processes are used in applications such as robotics, telephone switching, medical monitoring, and virtual reality programs.

UNIX System V Release 4 supports two configurable classes of processes with respect to scheduling. These are the *real-time class* and the *time-sharing class*. Each class has its own scheduling policy, but every real-time process has priority over every time-sharing process.

You can use the **priocntl** command to change the scheduling parameters of a process. You must be the superuser, or be running a shell with real-time priority, to change a process to real-time priority. Further, to change the scheduling parameters of a process to either real-time or time-sharing priority, you must be the superuser or your real or effective ID must match the real or effective ID of that process. Assuming you meet these requirements, here is how you use **priocntl** to set the scheduling class and priority of a process:

```
# priocntl -s -c RT -p 3 -i pid 1247
```

This sets the class of the process with process ID 1247 as real-time (RT) and assigns it a real-time priority value of 3.

# Scheduling Commands

You can use the *cron facility* to schedule commands. To schedule jobs, use the root *crontab* file. To edit this file, use the command

```
# crontab -e
```

This opens the root file in */var/spool/cron/crontabs* with the editor defined in your EDITOR variable. Entries in this file include six fields separated by spaces or tabs. The first five fields are integers identifying when the command is to be run and the sixth field is the command itself.

Of the five fields specifying the time a command is to be run, the first specifies the minute of each hour the command will be run (00 through 59); the second specifies the hours of each day the command will be run (0 through 23); the third field specifies the day of the month the command will be run (1 through 12); and the fifth field specifies the day of each week the command will be run (0 for Sunday through 6 for Saturday). The following line illustrates how jobs are specified in the *crontab* file:

```
00 16  *  *  1,2,3,4,5  /bin/su  root -c "/sbin/cleanup > /dev/null"
```

This line is used to schedule the command **/sbin/cleanup**, run as root, with its output discarded, at 4 A.M. every weekday (Monday through Friday).

# Scheduling Regular System Administration Activities

As a system administrator, you will want to schedule some regular administrative activities using the cron facility. Some of these activities include:

❑ Running backups on a regular schedule during times that your system is not used, which is most likely late at night or during early morning hours.

❑ Producing system activity reports for specific time periods.

❑ Checking the size of system logs and deleting or truncating them if they grow too large or contain out-of-date information.

❑ Printing reports at particular times when the printer is not being used for other purposes.

# Backing Up Your System

## Backup Basics

**TIP 745**

It's essential that you back up your system regularly. Since there is no way to recover deleted files in UNIX, retrieving them from a backup is the only way to avoid losing valuable information. Similarly, backup and recover are the only hope of recovering information if you have a disk crash, or suffer a corrupted disk segment. So you should perform system backups regularly and often. (See the strategies for backing up your system in Tip 752.)

There are several ways to generate backup copies of your files; these include the programs, **tar**, **dd**, **cpio**, and **dump**. With SVR4, new commands including **backup**, **restore**, **ufsdump**, and **ufsrestore** are available.

Backing up a system is important, and archiving files should make the files available for a long time. It's unfortunate that inconsistency and instability exist in the archiving programs. For example, **tar** is easy to use and has been available since the earliest UNIX systems, but it is being phased out, and no longer exists on some systems. **cpio**, its replacement, offers many more features, but is sometimes tricky to use. (For example, compatibility mode in SVR4 is not necessarily compatible with SVR3.2 and below.)

## Using tar for Backup

**TIP 746**

The **tar** (for *tape archiver*) will copy files to tape, floppy, or hard disk. To back up a file system, you need to be logged in as root or superuser. **tar** is normally set up with a default medium. In early UNIX systems, the default was the largest removable storage device on the system; on smaller systems the default will be the floppy drive. If you issue the command **tar** will start at the beginning

```
# tar c /
```

of the tape (c), and copy the entire file structure starting at the root (/). To copy only the user files in the */home* directory, use the command

```
# tar c /home
```

We recommend that you always use the **e** flag with **tar**; this prevents the archived files from being split across disks or tapes. The following script will back up your whole system to device rmt0:

```
# cd /
# tar ce  /dev/rmt0
```

# Making Selective Backups with tar

To make selective backups with **tar**, you need to create a list of the files to be included. The easiest way to do this is with the **find** command. The command

```
# find . -type f -print
```

will start in the current directory (.) and print all of the filenames. The command

```
# find . -type f -print > files.mine
```

will put the filenames into the file called *files.mine*. You can then edit the names in *files.mine* to include only those files you want to back up, and use the following command to archive those files:

```
# tar ce `cat files.mine`
```

# Restoring Files Archived with tar

Let's assume that someone accidently wiped out all of his or her files by doing an **rm \*** in your home directory. How could you restore the files? With **tar**, you can easily restore the entire missing directory tree. Use the command

```
# tar x /home/fred
```

to extract (**x**) and restore all of fred's files. **tar** also has a flag that lets you check what's on the tape before you restore anything. The **t** flag sends all the names of the files on the tape to the standard output, so the command

```
# tar t | prt
```

will send all the filenames on the tape to the printer. You can check the printout to make sure the files are on that tape. It's important to do this, not only to check for the existence of the file, but also to see the full pathname it has been stored under. **tar** will restore files with their original full pathname. This means that it may make up several levels of new directories in a restore.

# Backing Up with cpio

**TIP
749**

Although **tar** is easy to use, **cpio** offers many advantages for backups. It's supported on all UNIX systems, is flexible with many options, and will handle longer lists of files than **tar**. To make a full backup of your system using **cpio**, use the following commands:

```
# cd /
# find . -depth -print | cpio -ovc > /dev/ctape1
```

Running these commands will change the current directory to the root (/), **find** all the files, including those in lower directories (**-depth**), print a list of those (**-print**), pipe that list to **cpio** which will copy *o*ut (**o**), print a *v*erbose (**v**) listing of those files, and package them all into a single archive with a *c*ompatible (**c**) header, and send it to the cartridge tape drive.

At one time, you could do this in a more efficient way, saving memory and extra processes by using only the **find** command.

```
# find . -depth -print -cpio /dev/ctape1
```

However, the **-cpio** option to **find** is now considered obsolete, and will not be supported in future releases. Don't use it in system administration scripts.

# Making Incremental Backups with cpio

It's unnecessary to make a full backup of your system every time you work. In fact, you should adopt a strategy (see Tip 752) of occasionally backing up the whole system, and frequently backing up files that are actively used. The following command will back up only those files in the */home* file system that have been modified in the last day:

```
# cd /home
# find . -type f -depth -mtime 1 -print | cpio -ocv  > /dev/ctape1
```

The option **-type f** addresses only files, not devices, fifos, and so on, that have been modified one day ago. (**-mtime 1**)

If you are on a single-user system that has access to a larger UNIX system managed by professional staff, you can back up your system onto the larger one, and gain the benefits of having your backup files managed by the larger systems staff. The following script creates a cpio archive, and sends it to your login on the larger system:

```
# cd /home
# find . -type f -depth -mtime 1 -print | cpio -0cv > Jan0595.arc
# uuto -mp Jan0595.arc sysname!you
```

You can then log in to sysname, change directory to your archives, and use the **uupick** command to collect the cpio file. For example,

```
$ cd archives
$ uupick
from system small: file Jan0595 ? m
```

you respond with the **m** to the query in order to move the *Jan0595* file from the spool area into your directory.

# Restoring Files Archived with cpio

With **cpio** you can restore a single file, or an entire file system. The commands

```
# cd /
```

```
# cpio -ivdcmu  < /dev/ctape1
```

will change the current directory to root, and copy *in* (-**i**) the file on */dev/ctape1,* print a list of the files (-**v**), creating directories as needed (-**d**). The compatibility flag (-**c**) should always be used if copying across different systems. The (-**m**) flag retains the original modification times for the files, which are copied unconditionally (-**u**)—that is, replacing existing newer files with the same name. To copy in a specific filename, simply include it in the command line, as shown here.

```
# cpio -ivdcmu  /home/you/work/proposal/draft1  < /dev/ctape1
```

In this example, only the one file specified will be restored.

# Backup Strategies

**TIP 752**

How often should you back up your system? The answer depends on how often significant changes, those you would not want to lose in the event of a crash, are made in files on your system.

For a lightly used, single-user system, the following backup strategy may be sufficient: On the first day of the week, make a full system backup (starting at /). At the beginning of each day, make a backup of only those files that have been modified on the previous day. If your system crashes on Thursday, you could recover by restoring the complete system from the Monday backup, and the modified files from the Tuesday and Wednesday backups. For most users, the complete backup would involve several diskettes or a tape cartridge, but the incremental backups could be done to a single floppy each day. On the first day of the second week, do a full backup to a new tape, plus the daily modified backups. On the third week, recycle the first tape for a new full backup and recycle the first set of modified backup disks or tapes as well.

A more permanent strategy, that allows weekly and monthly archiving, can be created with a few extra tapes. On the first day of each week, make two full backups, removing one to off-site storage. If you have a flood or fire, you'll have one safe copy. Each day of the week, make backups of the modified files. After two weeks, reuse the modified backup tapes. After two months, retain the first full backup of the month off-site, and reuse the tapes from the second, third, and fourth weeks of that month. Over time, your off-site archive should contain a full monthly backup for every month, and one full weekly backup for the last month's worth of files. On-site you'll have a full weekly backup and daily modified file backups for this week only.

# TIP 753

# Compressing Files and Directories

If you are not using a file, you can reduce the amount of space it takes in your system by compressing it, using either the **compress** or the **pack** command. The command

```
# compress filename
```

will compress a normal text file by as much as 40%. The compressed file will have the name *filename.Z*. Using a wildcard with the command, as in

```
# compress *
```

will compress all files in the current directory.

To compress all files and subdirectories in your current directory, you can use the following script:

```
####################################################
##
##  Packall
##  This program packs an entire directory structure
##  or sub-structure.  If no args are given the
##  current directory is assumed to be the starting
##  point.  If a directory path name is given,
##  packall starts in that directory.  An arg
##  of "-" is passed to compress.
##
####################################################

PaTH="."
FLaGS=""
if test $2x = x
then
    if test $1x != x
    then
        if test -r $1
        then
            PaTH=$1
        else
```

```
            FLaGS=$1
        fi
    fi
else
    PaTH=$2
    FLaGS=$1
fi
find $PaTH -exec echo " " \; -a -print -a -exec compress $FLaGS {} \;
```

# Unpacking Files and Directories

**T**IP
**754**

The complement to the **compress** command is **uncompress** (and the complement
of the **pack** command is **unpack**). It reverses the compression and restores files to their original form.
This is a shell script that does the same for **packall**:

```
###########################################################
##
##  unpackall
##  This program unpacks an entire directory structure
##  or sub-structure.  If no args are given the
##  current directory is assumed to be the starting
##  point.  If a directory path name is given,
##  unpackall starts in that directory.  An arg
##  of "-" is passed to uncompress.
##
###########################################################

PaTH="."
FLaGS=""
if test $2x = x
then
    if test $1x != x
    then
        if test -r $1
        then
            PaTH=$1
        else
            FLaGS=$1
```

```
        fi
    fi
else
    PaTH=$2
    FLaGS=$1
fi
find $PaTH -exec echo " " \; -a -print -a -exec uncompress $FLaGS {} \;
```

# Archiving Files and Directories

**TIP 755**

You can use a similar set of commands to those in Tip 749 to archive your files. The **archive** command sends the file to be put on tape and stored offline by your system administrator.

Here is a procedure to pack all the files in a directory to one file before using the **archive** command.

```
cd dir
find . -print | cpio -ocvdm > filename.cpio
archive -m filename
```

The **archive** command may take a substantial amount of time to perform the archiving of your data. Therefore, do not remove the filename right away! Instead, run the **trail** command. **trail** returns a list of the files that you have archived. Only after the **trail** command returns the name of the file indicating a successful archive, should you use the **rm** command to remove the original files.

If you find that you need these files later, they are easy to retrieve. Use the following sequence of commands:

```
archive -r filename
cpio -icvdm < filename.cpio
```

This will unpack the files just as they were. The **-r** option on **archive** will retrieve the file, but leave a copy of it in the archive.

# Managing Your File Archives

**TIP 756**

Archives are normally used for long-term storage of files that are too good to throw away, but not needed enough to keep in active storage. They are exactly analogous to taking a collection of paper files to the attic or basement in case you ever need them again. The same thing happens to archive files as to files in your attic: soon you forget what's up there. A friend has boxes in her attic labeled, "DO NOT UNPACK, MOVE TO NEXT HOUSE."

In archiving as described above, you can bundle together 20 or 100 files under a descriptive name like *sources.cpio* and store it. Later, you can bundle another 20 or 100 files, call them *sources1.cpio* (or worse, call the second set *sources.cpio* so that you have two archived sets of different files with the same name). The **trail** command is of little help because it only returns information by the name archived. For example:

```
# trail

05/27/86   21:13:27      src/util1/util1.cpio
05/27/86   21:15:04      src/util2/util2.cpio
05/27/86   21:15:58      src/util3/util3.cpio
05/27/86   21:17:2       src/util4/util4.cpio
05/27/86   21:18:22      src/util5/util5.cpio
```

None of the archive commands give information about what it was that you stored.

You can save some information by adopting this procedure: Create a file called *.archived* in your home directory. Before you archive files using the procedures spelled out in Tip 755, enter the commands

```
# cd dir
# pwd >> $HOME/.archived
# date >> $HOME/.archived
# ls -al >> $HOME/.archived
```

This will append to your *.archived* file the directory, date, and listing information for each of the bundles of information you archive. Comparing this with the response of **trail** will give you an indication of what you have stored.

# Making Your Own Archive Files

You may be responsible for making your own archives. If your site doesn't offer formal archive service, or if you are your own system administrator, you need to take care of the physical details of archiving yourself.

Create a shell in your home directory named **writearc** with the following instruction:

```
#  find . -print | cpio -ocvdmB >/dev/rmt/0h
```

Next, make it executable. Ask your system administrator to mount a tape, and execute the **writearc** command from your home directory. If you are your own administrator, you'll have to mount the tape yourself.

# Erasing files from the Archives

To get rid of files that you have archived, use the command

```
#  archive -e filename
```

The -e option stands for *erase*.

If you have many archived files, you can automate their deletion by following this procedure. First, use the **trail** command to generate a file with the names of files currently in your archive. Make sure you're in your HOME directory when you do this.

```
# cd
# trail > mytrail
```

Next, edit the file you created (*mytrail* in the example) so that it contains only lines with the files you wish to remove from archive. Verify that your file (*mytrail*) contains only filenames that you really want to delete. Use the following sequence of commands to remove all the files included in the file (*mytrail*) from the archives:

```
for i in `cat mytrail | cut -f2`
do
echo "y" | archive -e $i
done
```

Note that any file deleted from the archive cannot be retrieved.

# Moving a User to a Different Login

Here is a procedure to pack all the files in a directory to one file before using the **cp** command to move them to a different login. You need to be root or superuser to do this, since many UNIX systems block regular users from using the **chown** (*ch*ange *own*er) command.

```
# find . -print | cpio -ocvdm > newfilename
# cp newfilename /filesystem/newlogin/rje/newfilename
# cd /filesystem/newlogin/rje
# chgrp newlogin newfilename
# chown newlogin newfilename
```

Then log in as the new login and use the command

```
$ cpio -icvdm < /filesystem/login/rje/newfilename
```

# Other Administrative Tips

# Checking System Activity

If you are having some problems with the performance of your system, you can use the **sar** (for *s*ystem *a*ctivity *r*eporting) command to obtain system activity information.

For example, your central processor unit (CPU) at any particular time is either busy or idle. When busy, the CPU is in either system mode or user mode; when idle, the processor is waiting either for something to do or for input/output completion. You can use the

```
# sar -u
```

command to see, for a series of time periods (which are of different lengths, such as 20 seconds or 1 minute, depending on your system) the percentage of time the CPU is in user mode, system mode, waiting for input/output completion, or is idle and waiting for something to do. Also, if your computer has a coprocessor, you will see the number of system calls per second that are executed on the coprocessor. You can detect a variety of problems from the information you get. For example, if the percentage of time the system is idle waiting for something to do is high, your system may have memory constraints. If you have a high waiting for input/output completion percentage, a disk slowdown may have occurred.

You can get information on disk activity using

```
# sar -d
```

For example, if your system has a hard disk and a floppy disk drive, the output of this command will show the percentage of time each disk was busy, the average number of requests outstanding, the number of read and write transfers to the device per second, the number of blocks transferred per second, and the average time in milliseconds that transfer requests waited in the queue and took to be completed.

# Formatting Disks and Tapes

**TIP 761**

You need to format disks and tapes before storing data on them. The commands you use will vary depending on the system you have. You will need to consult the manuals that come with your system to see how this is done on your system. However, the following examples for AT&T 3B2 computers should help you get started.

To store data on a floppy disk, you first have to format it. The command you can use to format a floppy disk installed into diskette drive 1 on your machine would be

```
# fmtflop -v /dev/rSA/diskette1
```

You do not have to format hard disks before using them, since the manufacturer of the disk will have done this. However, before you can use a new hard disk, you will have to add a volume table of contents (VTOC) to it. For example, suppose you have installed a second hard disk on your system. Before using it, run

```
# ftmhard /dev/rSA/disk2
```

You may also need to format cartridge tapes. To format a cartridge tape loaded into cartridge tape drive 1 on your machine, use

```
# ctcfmt -v /dev/rSA/ctape1
```

The system will verify that the formatting was done without error, since you used the -v (*verify*) option.

# Port Monitors

On the UNIX system, port monitors accept requests from peripheral devices, such as terminals or networks, and make sure that these requests are handled by the system. There are two types of port monitors in UNIX System V Release 4. These are **ttymon**, which listens to requests from terminals to log in, and **listen**, which listens to ports connected to the network.

To add, modify, remove, and track port monitors and services, you can use the Service Access Controller (SAC). When your machine enters multiuser state, the **sac** process starts; it is started from the line

```
sc:234:respawn:/usr/lib/saf/sac -t 300
```

in the */etc/inittab* file. **sac** reads the Service Access Facility (SAF) administrative file to determine which listener processes to start, which it then starts.

Creating port monitors and device drivers is complicated. But here are some basic things to know about:

❏ *Configuration scripts.* There are three types: one per system, used for all port monitors, named */etc/saf/_sysconfig;* one per port monitor, defining the environment of this monitor, named */etc/saf/pmtag/_config*, where pmtag is the name of the port monitor; and one per service, called *doconfig*, to override the defaults used by other configuration scripts.

❏ *Administration files.* Each port monitor has its own administration file.

❏ *Services.* You can add, enable, disable, or remove services for a port monitor using the **-a**, **-e**, **-d**, or **-r** options of the **pmadm** command, respectively.

❏ *Manipulating port monitors.* You can add, enable, disable, start, stop, or remove a port monitor using the **-a**, **-e**, **-d**, **-s**, **-k**, or **-r** options of the **sacadm** command, respectively.

# TIP 763

# Setting Up System Accounting

If you want to track usage of your system by user and charge customers for that usage, you will need to perform system accounting. Accounting is carried out using add-on utilities available on many different computers.

You can collect a wide range of data including how long a user is logged in, how much terminal lines were used, how many files each user has on disk. For each process, you can see who ran it, how long it took to run, how much CPU time it used, how much memory was used, which commands were run, and what the controlling terminal was.

You can set charges and bill for services based on this data. You can also charge for special services you perform such as setting up a new password for a user when this user loses his or her password, restoring lost files, archiving files for users, and so on.

To collect process accounting data, you need to set up a */var/spool/cron/crontabs/adm* file to periodically run the **ckpacct** (*check process accounting*) command, the **runacct** (*run accounting*) command, and the **monacct** (*monthly accounting*) command. The following entries are recommended for the *adm* file.

```
0    *  *  *    *    /usr/lib/acct/ckpacct
30   4  *  *    *    /usr/lib/acct/runacct 2> /var/adm/acct/nite/fd2log
30   9  *  5    *    /usr/lib/acct/monacct
```

This *adm* file sets up your system so that **ckpacct** is run every hour, checking that process accounting files do not exceed 1000 blocks; **runacct** is run every morning at 4:30 A.M. to collect daily process accounting information; and **monacct** is run at 9:30 A.M. on the fifth day of every month to collect monthly accounting information.

You will also need to put the following entry in */var/spool/cron/crontabs/root:*

```
30  22  *    *    4    /usr/lib/acct/dodisk
```

This runs the disk accounting functions at 10:30 P.M. on the fourth day of every month.

You can see terminal activity from the Daily Report. You will see the duration of the reporting period, how long the system was in multiuser mode, and the time each terminal was active, as well as other information, such as system usage on a per-user basis.

For more information on system accounting, see the chapter on this subject in the *Unix System V System Administrator's Guide* that is part of the *UNIX System V Release 4 Documentation Set.*

# Killing Processes on Your Machine

**TIP 764**

When you want to kill a process on UNIX, the normal sequence is to use the **ps** command to find out the process number and then use that number with the **kill** command. There has to be an easier way to do this without running two commands. How can you kill a process by specifying its name, rather than its number? Better yet, how can you kill a process by specifying a string that is in its name?

Here are several ways to do this. In each case, create a file named *skill* that contains one of these scripts:

```
pid=`/bin/ps -e | grep $1 | sed -e 's/^   *//' -e 's/ .*//'`
if [ "${pid}" != "" ]
then
    /bin/kill -9 ${pid}
fi
```

or

```
ps -el | grep $1 | grep -v grep | awk '{print $2}' | xargs kill
```

or

```
kill -9 `ps | grep $1 | grep -v grep | cut -c1-6`
```

# Shutting the Machine Down Safely

Unless otherwise impossible, always make sure the machine is properly shut down using the **shutdown** command (see Tip 714) or the **init** command (or the **halt** command on some systems) before turning off the power. These programs make sure information currently pending to disks is written there and all open files are closed. In addition, all other system processes are stopped. Without a proper system shutdown, you risk losing information or severely corrupting your file system.

If possible, try to attach your machine to a noninterruptible power supply, or at least a line which has very little power fluctuation.

# Some Useful Commands for Finding Out System Information

The following commands and their various options allow the administrator to find out crucial system administration information. You should check to see whether each of these commands is available on your system; many are standard UNIX commands, while others are found only on certain variants of UNIX.

| Command | Function |
| --- | --- |
| uname | Displays the name of the current system |
| arch | Displays the architecture of the current host |
| showrev | Shows machine and software revision information |
| iostat | Reports I/O statistics |
| vmstat | Reports virtual memory statistics |
| pstat | Prints system facts |
| lpstat | Displays the printer status information |
| mach | Displays the processor type of the current host |
| df | Reports free disk space on file systems |
| du | Summarizes disk usage |
| devinfo | Prints system device information |

| Command | Function |
|---|---|
| **mount**, **umount** | Mounts and unmounts file systems |
| **showmount** | Shows all remote mounts |
| **hostname** | Sets or prints current host system name |
| **ps** | Displays the status of current processes |
| **mps** | Displays status of current processes on an MP system |
| **uptime** | Shows how long system has been up |
| **model** | Prints detailed hardware model information |
| **nodename** | Assigns network node name or determines current name |
| **top** | Displays/updates information about top CPU processes |

# Use top If You Administer a Heavily Loaded Machine

**TIP 767**

**top** is a valuable system administration tool which is quite useful in diagnosing which processes are eating processor time on a heavily loaded machine. In normal use, **top** displays the top 15 processes on the system and periodically updates this information. Raw CPU percentage is used to rank the processes. If a number is given, then that top number of processes will be displayed instead of the default. In addition, there are various options available that limit your display to a restricted type of process.

**top** is not normally available in the standard distribution, but you can obtain **top** via anonymous ftp from *eecs.nwu.edu* in */pub/top* and from *ftp.germany.eu.net* in */pub/sysadmin/top*.

# How to Determine Swap Space Size

**TIP 768**

There is no clear-cut answer to the question about determining how much swap space you will need. As a general rule, you should set aside about 1.5 to 2 times the amount of real memory. However, you may find that you have set aside way too much or way too little disk space, depending on how much real memory you have and how busy your system is. For a small machine where not too many intensive things are going on, chances are you may not need much swap space at all. For really busy machines, you may want to increase the swap space beyond 2 times the amount of real memory. If you have the **pstat** command on your machine, you can use the -s option to find out how much swap space you have.

# TIP 769

# Disabling Printing of Banner Pages

The banner pages that always appear with print jobs are generally annoying and waste a lot of paper. Often, you do not want to see banner pages at all. You can turn off the printing of banners. Under the SunOS, for example, you can do this with the following method.

Put :sh: in the */etc/printcap* entry for the printer of interest. For SPARCprinters you will need to edit the *.param* for that printer. This file is located in the spool directory for that particular printer in SunOS4.X. Under SunOS5.x it is located under */etc/lp/printers/PRINTERNAME*. Change the line

```
BANNERPS=${DEFBANNER}; export BANNERPS
```

to

```
BANNERPS=; export BANNERPS
```

Also, you may want to turn off Job Log printing. You can do this by changing the line

```
PRINTJOBLOG=yes; export PRINTJOBLOG
```

to

```
PRINTJOBLOG=no; export PRINTJOBLOG
```

Under Xenix/SCO and most System V machines, you can set up the printer using the sysadm shell to not print banner pages.

You could also set up a systemwide alias in */etc/aliases* or */etc/profile* to use the **nobanner** option to **lp**:

```
alias lp = "lp -o nobanner $*"
```

# Finding Out More About System Administration

## Books on UNIX System Administration

**TIP 770**

There are many good books on System Administration. Here are some of them:

*UNIX System Administration Handbook* by Evi Nemeth, Garth Snyder and Scott Seebass (Englewood Cliffs, NJ: Prentice-Hall, 1989); *UNIX System V Release 4 Administration, Second Edition*, by David Fiedler, Bruce Hunter and Ben Smith (Carmel, IN: Howard W. Sams, 1991); *Essential System Administration* by Aeleen Frisch (O'Reilly and Associates, 1991); *System Performance Tuning* by Mike Loukides (O'Reilly and Associates, 1990); *UNIX Administration Guide for System V* by Rebecca Thomas and Rik Farrow (Prentice-Hall, 1988); the *UNIX System V System Administrator's Guide* and the *UNIX System V System Adminstration Reference Manual*, both part of the *UNIX System V Release 4 Documentation Set*.

## Newsgroups to Consult for Information on System Administration

**TIP 771**

You should read the USENET newsgroup *comp.unix.admin* to follow the discussion of topics of general interest to administrators of UNIX systems. You will probably also want to read the newsgroup(s) devoted to the type of machine you are using to run the UNIX system. The following newgroups address questions dealing with administration and general use for particular operating sytems. Usually, if you lack relevant or useful documentation, you will get useful information back when you post questions to the appropriate newsgroups.

| | | |
|---|---|---|
| *comp.os.linux.admin* | *comp.unix.aux* | *comp.unix.sys5.r3* |
| *comp.sys.next.sysadmin* | *comp.unix.bsd* | *comp.unix.sys5.r4* |
| *comp.sys.sgi.admin* | *comp.unix.cray* | *comp.unix.sysv286* |
| *comp.sys.sun.admin* | *comp.unix.large* | *comp.unix.sysv386* |
| *comp.unix.aix* | *comp.unix.solaris* | *comp.unix.ultrix* |
| *comp.unix.amiga* | *comp.unix.sys3* | *comp.unix.xenix.sco* |

# Chapter 12

## Network Administration

# Administering the UUCP System

## TIP 772 — Setting Up UUCP

Setting up and administering the UUCP system requires setting up and editing the files in the */etc/uucp* directory. Here is a list of the most important of these files and what they are used for:

❑ Set up the *Permissions* file to describe the access rights for other systems when they call your machine. (See Tip 784.)

❑ Set up the *Devices* file to list the devices present on your system and specify how to manipulate them to get through to the hardware connected to the devices. (See Tip 773.)

❑ Set up the *Dialers* file to describe how to dial a phone number on various types of modems attached to the system.

❑ Edit the *Systems* file to describe the systems known to your UUCP system and how to connect to each system. (See Tip 774.)

❑ Set up the *Dialcodes* file to describe symbolic names for phone number prefixes, so that numbers can be shortened.

❑ Set up the *Config* file to override some parameters used by the different UUCP protocols.

❑ Set up the *Grades* file to permit jobs to be partitioned into multiple queues with different priorities. (See Tip 775.)

❑ Set up the *Limits* file to limit the maximum number of UUCP system processes permitted to run simultaneously. This is used to make sure your system performance does not suffer from heavy UUCP system usage.

## TIP 773 — Editing Your Devices Files

To add new UUCP tty lines, you will need to edit your */etc/uucp/Devices* file. For each tty line to be used by UUCP, you need to add two lines to this file, one starting with "ACU" and the other with "Direct". The ACU line is used to specify the type of modem being used over this line; the Direct line is used by the **cu** command. Both types of line also specify the tty lines and the speeds permitted on these lines. For example, if you want to add tty line 21 with an AT&T 2296 modem, you would add the following lines for operation of this modem at 9600 bps:

```
ACU      term/21   -   9600   att2296
Direct   term/21   -   9600   direct
```

You also need to edit the *Devices* file to run UUCP across a LAN or TCP/IP network. For example, to set up UUCP to run across a TCP/IP network, use the line of the type

```
barinc   Any   TCP   -   \x000909099009999
```

This line indicates that the connection to the system barinc is to be made over TCP/IP to the Ethernet address of barinc provided in the last field.

# Editing Your Systems File

**TIP 774**

When you want to add a system to be contacted using the UUCP system, edit your */etc/uucp/Systems* file. For each system, you need to indicate the type of device to be used, the speed to use on that device, and the phone number to call, and you need to provide the chat script that describes how to connect to the remote system. The fields of */etc/uucp/Systems* are:

❏   Name of system

❏   Times to call it (such as "Evening" or "Any")

❏   Device type (such as "ACU")

❏   Speed to use

❏   Telephone number

For example, suppose you want to connect to the system fooinc. The entry in the *Systems* file might be

```
fooinc  Any  ACU  9600  5556666  in:--in:  nuucp  word: qox8z3
```

The chat script in this example tells UUCP to look for the characters "in:" (the last characters of "login:"). If they are not found in a few seconds, press RETURN and look again for them. Then send "nuucp", look for the string "word:" (the last characters of the string "password:") and, finally, send the string "qox8z3", which is the password for the nuucp login on fooinc.

# Defining UUCP Job Grades

**TIP 775**

You can set up different job grades to queue jobs to a remote computer by editing the */etc/uucp/Grades* file. Each entry in the *Grades* file has the following fields:

❑ User job grade

❑ System job grade

❑ Job size

❑ Permit type

❑ ID list

The user job grade is a name of up to 64 characters defined by the system administrator. The system job grade contains a one-character job grade assigned to the user job grade. The valid characters are uppercase and lowercase letters. There are 52 different priorities available, the highest priority specified by A and the lowest by z. The job size specifies the maximum job size in bytes that can be entered into the queue. The permit type is used to describe how the ID list should be interpreted. For example, if it contains "User", the ID list contains the logins of users permitted to use this job grade; if it contains "Group", the ID list contains the group names whose members are permitted to use the job grade.

The default *Grades* file specifies the three default grades: *high*, *medium*, and *low*. The default *Grades* file has the following entries:

```
high      F    Any      User      Any
medium    S    Any      User      Any
low       n    Any      User      Any
```

For example, the high priority queue is given priority "F", there is no file size limit ("Any") of jobs with this priority, and all users can send jobs with this priority.

Suppose you want to set up two other priority classes, *crucial* and *bottom*. Jobs queued with crucial priority need to get preferential treatment but they cannot be too large; jobs queued with bottom priority are of very low importance. You can edit the *Grades* file, adding the lines

```
crucial  B    5K    User      Any
bottom   x    Any   User      Any
```

This sets up the crucial priority so that it has priority "B" (only a queue with priority "A" would have higher priority), but only files of 5 kilobytes (5000 bytes) can be put into this queue and any user can use this priority. The bottom priority is set up with priority "x" (only queues with priorities "y" and "z" would have lower priority); any size file can be put into this queue and all users can use this priority.

# Checking on UUCP Administration

Since it is easy to make a mistake when editing the different files in */etc/uucp*, there is a special command that lets you check for any problems with the changes you made. In particular, you should check what you have allowed remote systems to do on your machine over UUCP connections.

When you have completed editing files in */etc/uucp*, you should run

```
# uucheck -v
```

In the output of this command you would see the results when **uucheck** checked the files and directories used by UUCP. You will also see what happens and what is allowed when a system logs in to your system as nuucp and your system calls another system via a UUCP connection. You will also see the commands machines can run on your system using the UUCP system.

# UUCP System Cleanup

You will want to run the cleanup script for the UUCP system periodically. We recommend you do this once a day, late at night. To do this, add the following line to the *crontab* file owned by root:

```
45 23  *   *   *   ulimit 5000; /usr/bin/su   uucp  -c \
"/etc/uucp/uudemon.cleanup" >/dev/null  2>&1
```

The command issued first increases the maximum file size to 5000 blocks and then runs the cleanup command under the uucp login.

# Machine Aliases

There are a number of occasions when it is useful for one machine to answer to a number of names—for example, when one machine is standing in for another which is broken; when you've merged two machines but the users' old e-mail addresses are widely known; or even when you want to call yourself to check that your own access method really works.

You can claim to be different names on both call-in and call-out by using the **MYNAME** command. For call-in:

```
LOGNAME=nuucp MYNAME=snowwhite
LOGNAME=huucp MYNAME=thorin
LOGNAME=ruucp MYNAME=gandalf
```

and so on. A machine calling in will think it is talking with the appropriately named machine. For call-out:

```
MACHINE=dopey:sneezy:grumpy MYNAME=snowwhite
MACHINE=balin:dwalin:ori:dori:nori MYNAME=thorin
MACHINE=gimli:boromir:legolas MYNAME=gandalf
```

will cause the central machine to adopt the correct name when it's placing calls to the others.

# Remote Execution of Commands with Arguments Containing Slashes

The **uuxqt** command will check all arguments to all commands against a list of shell special characters and, if there are any occurrences of the / character in any of them, against the paths given in the READ and WRITE clauses. The shell characters are ' ; & | ^ < > ( ) \t and \n, and if any of these are found, the command is automatically rejected. As for the READ and WRITE checks, the assumption is that any argument containing a / is a filename, and thus should be checked for legality. There are counter examples to this (for example, X.400 addresses), but there is no way around the problem at the moment.

# Protocols Used by UUCP

**T**IP
**780**

In UUCP terms, the "protocol" is how the data for each file is sent back and forth over the connection. Normally, this is negotiated at run time from a list hard-coded into each **uucico**, as modified by the configuration, just after the login has succeeded and the remote system name has been checked. It does not change throughout the conversation. There are only three protocols in common use: 'g', 'G', and 'e'. Many others have been written ('d', 'x', and 'f' are not uncommon), but these three are the only ones that seem to be widely available.

Protocol 'e' is the simplest. It is designed to be used only over an error-free communications channel, such as TCP/IP. It should not be used over anything that goes across an RS232 line, which generally excludes running it over any variety of modems (unless of course you have something like SLIP or PPP providing error correction). The protocol sends an initial packet containing the size of the file to be transferred, then the data is written in 4096-byte chunks until everything has been sent. (The underlying protocol suite may break up and reassemble these chunks if it so desires.)

Protocol 'g' is the original UUCP protocol, designed to be robust in the face of error, and yet provide good performance over the modems available at the time (1200 bps). It is a simple sliding window using 64-byte packets, permitting up to three packets to be outstanding at once. While it was designed to negotiate both parameters at run time, and it is possible to increase both (only if you have access to source code or enjoy patching binaries, alas), the stock release has these parameters hard-coded into it. Each packet has its own checksum. This protocol demands a clear 8-bit channel between the two ends of a connection.

Protocol 'G' is 'g' brought up to date. The maximum packet-size is 256 bytes and up to 7 packets can be outstanding. These limits are negotiated at run time if this protocol is selected. Again, a clear 8-bit channel is needed. Of the other protocols, 'd' is designed for use over multiplexed Datakit™ connections. It's similar to 'e' in that no extra error checking is done (that is, it depends on the underlying transport layer to do any error-detection and correction), but no initial packet containing the file size is sent. Instead, the protocol depends on a quirk of the underlying URP protocol—that a zero-length write is transported through the network and results in a zero-length read on the other end—to denote end-of-file.

Protocol 'x' was designed for use over X.25 connections. It's similar to 'g' except that there is no per-packet checksum, and the packet size is larger (512 versus 64).

Protocol 'f' originated in UCB and is available in some versions of UNIX. It is similar to 'g' except that it does *not* demand a clear 8-bit channel; in fact, it will happily run over a 7-bit channel with XON/XOFF flow control. It manages this by encoding all potentially troublesome data—for example, those bytes with ASCII value less than 32 or greater than 121 (decimal). It does not checksum every packet, but only has one checksum for the entire file (it was originally designed for X.25 links). However, the characters NULL and DLE (0 and 16) are used before this protocol starts up, and this may cause trouble for certain types of data switch (X.25 PADs are frequently confused by these). Other protocols do exist but will not be discussed here.

# 8-bit Clear Channels

**TIP 781**

Some protocols, notably 'g' and 'G', demand an 8-bit clear channel in order to work properly. Such a channel is sometimes harder to track down than you might think. If your computer is calling out through some variety of data switch to a modem, then to another modem and another data switch before it gets to the remote computer, there can be four connections which must all be set up correctly before these protocols will work properly.

Problems arise on the RS232 links. Each one must be configured for 8-bit characters and without XON/XOFF or any other type of in-band flow control. Start, stop, and parity bits are not included in the 8 bits, because these aren't transmitted through the dataswitch, nor between the modems. Similarly, out-of-band low control (normally hardware or RTS/CTS flow control) is fine; only those types of flow control that inject characters into (and remove character from) the datastream are harmful.

```
frodo Any TCP Any \x00020ace87031904
```

# Setting Up UUCP over a TLI Connection

**TIP 782**

Here is a "cheat sheet" which may help when setting up UUCP over a TLI connection. We show how to set up a connection running TCP/IP; it should be easy to adapt for other protocols—just replace "tcp" with the new protocol name. You will need to be root to execute these commands. You should also note that this allows direct access to **uucico**, no login or password is needed, and if you are using nondefault names for the various control files, you'll need to change the filenames as appropriate.

```
# first initialize network listener service over tcp
nlsadmin -i tcp

# add uucico service entry
nlsadmin -a101 -c"/usr/lib/uucp/uucico -r -iTLI -unuucp" \
-y"direct uucico" tcp

# set up tcp listener
un=`uname -n`
nlsadmin -l `/usr/etc/rfsaddr -h $un -p 2766` tcp

# set up Dialers entry. This may already exist, do not add if it does
echo 'tcp "" "" NLPS:000:001:101\N\C' >> /etc/uucp/Dialers

# set up Devices entry. This may already exist, do not add if it does
echo 'TCP,eGg - - TLI \D tcp' >> /etc/uucp/Devices

# add Systems file entry for each system
# remember to do this on the remote systems as well!
echo "remote_sys Any TCP - `/usr/etc/rfsaddr -h remote_sys -p 2766`" \
>> /etc/uucp/Systems

# start the listener
nlsadmin -s tcp
```

Since **uucico** tries systems file entries in the order they are encountered, you may wish to re-order the *Systems* file so that these (presumably fast) entries are tried first.

Some systems may require this one extra step. If, when running a trace, you find that you get connected but then **uucico** doesn't seem to start up, try adding this:

```
# add streams modules to be pushed
echo "service=uucico device=TCP push=tirdwr" >> /etc/uucp/Devconfig
```

## UUCP System Names

If you are planning to hook up to the big wide world over a UUCP link, you'll have to choose a unique name. This doesn't have to be the same as the hostname, but it will cut down on confusion if it is. Alas, there are currently something like 20,000 main sites in the UUCP maps, so, as you might imagine, it's very hard to find a system name that's both catchy and unique. This is known as *Harris' Lament*: "All the good ones are taken." Also, although your system name can be up to 256 characters long, UUCP only supports system names up to 14 characters (strictly speaking, it treats two systems whose names are not unique in the first 14 bytes as being the same system). This is a vast improvement over the situation of a few years ago, when system names were restricted to 6 characters. Of course, there were far fewer systems then.

For more information on this topic, look out for the README article posted periodically to the USENET newsgroup *comp.mail.maps*.

## UUCP System Security

## Using the Permissions File to Secure the UUCP System

You can use the *Permissions* file to control the access permitted to remote systems using the UUCP system to send files to your system, request files from your system, or execute commands on your system. You can customize the access permitted based on the remote system and the particular user ID associated with the request.

Each line in the */usr/lib/uucp/Permissions* file contains a LOGNAME entry and/or a MACHINE entry. The LOGNAME entry is used to associate a set of permissions with the name of a particular remote machine. Whenever a remote system uses the login ID given by LOGNAME entry, it is granted the permissions defined in the entry. The MACHINE entry is used to associate a set of permissions with a particular remote machine; these permissions are used when your local host calls the remote system with this MACHINE name or when your local host executes a **uux** request from this remote machine. Here is an example of an entry in */usr/lib/uucp/Permissions*:

```
LOGNAME=nuucp  MACHINE=alaska:hawaii:guam:samoa \
REQUEST=no  SENDFILES=call  READ=/usr/spool/uucppublic
COMMANDS=/bin/rmail
```

# Permissions for Multihop uuto

**TIP**
**785**

You can forward a file through multiple systems by using the command **uuto** *file machinea!machineb!person*. However, the *Permissions* files on *machinea* must be set up properly for this to work, because by default, forwarding a file in this way is disallowed.

Specifically, *machinea* must allow the originating machine to remotely execute the **uucp** command. This is done by adding something like this to the *Permissions* file:

```
MACHINE=machinea COMMANDS=rmail:uucp
```

Why do you have to do this? Well, what is really happening is that machinea is issuing the equivalent of this command:

```
uux machinea!uucp <file> machineb!person
```

and so the **uucp** command must be enabled in order for remote execution to take place. In general, for a uucp chain to work, each machine in the chain must allow the previous one to execute **uucp**.

Of course, if you want the chain to be two-way, then each machine must allow the subsequent one the same privilege, because that machine will be the preceding machine when a file comes back. The machine at the end of the chain doesn't need to allow **uucp** to be remotely executable, because **uucp** isn't executed on the final system in the chain. Instead, the file is placed in the requested location by **uuxqt**.

*If you don't explicitly put the* **rmail** *command into COMMANDS, that machine won't be able to send mail to your system, because the COMMANDS line you insert overrides the default one, rather than just adding to it. By default, the only command that can be remotely executed is* **rmail**.

Since it's convenient to be able to do this, you might wonder why it isn't set up this way by default. The answer is that in the mid-1980s, many releases of UUCP ago, there was a security hole when remote **uucp** was allowed. The idea that allowing remote UUCP is dangerous to the health of your system has entered UNIX folklore.

# TIP 786  UUCP System Command Restrictions

If you want to allow only some machines access to certain commands, there are various ways you can restrict things. Let's say you have a central machine with an outgoing FAX server, and you want only your internal machines to be able to access the service, to keep your phone bill down. The first level of security is just to add the names of the "friendly" systems to those systems that can access the command:

```
MACHINE=dopey:sneezy:grumpy COMMANDS=rmail:uucp:faxit
MACHINE=OTHER COMMANDS=rmail:uucp
```

This allows only those three systems to access the **faxit** command—everyone else can only execute **rmail** and **uucp**. If you want to tighten things up even more, to stop an outside machine from spoofing, or pretending to be, one of your internal machines, then you might want to make your internal systems use a different login (and password). To do this, you'll need to set up another account that looks mostly like the original nuucp one:

```
nuucp:x:10:10:External
UUCP:/var/spool/uucppublic:/usr/lib/uucp/uucico
luucp:x:11:10:Local UUCP:/var/spool/uucppublic:/usr/lib/uucp/uucico
```

Apart from the GCOS (name) field, there are two important changes; the account name is different and the UID is different.

Once you've changed the three local machines to log in using the luucp login, you can take the final step of editing the *Permissions* file:

```
LOGNAME=luucp VALIDATE=dopey:sneezy:grumpy \
COMMANDS=rmail:faxit:uucp
```

VALIDATE tells **uucico** that no systems other than those three may use the luucp login and password, and, further, that those three systems must use that login name. So system dwalin cannot use the luucp login, and system sneezy cannot use the nuucp login.

If you want even more security, you can explore the CALLBACK option, which specifies that when a system logs in, the call is dropped immediately and the central machine calls the remote system back. Take care with this option since two machines that both have CALLBACK set are never going to transfer any files!

# The UUCP System Security Log

You can get a report of the UUCP job transactions that attempted to violate system and user security measures by consulting the */var/spool/uucp/.Admin/security* file. Looking at this file will help you detect attacks on your system using the UUCP system. Attempted security violations include incidents where the requester fails security checks specified in the *Permissions* file or when the requester tries to access a protected destination file.

For an attempted violation of file transfer security, you will see the requester node name and user login, the destination node and user login, the destination filename, the source node name, the source file owner login, the source filename, the source file size in bytes, the modification date and time of the source file, and the data and time that transfer started and completed. For remote execution security incidents, you will see the requesting node name and user login, the destination user login, the date and time the command was executed by the server, and the command name and its options.

# Using the UUCP System to Keep Track of What You Allow Remote Systems to Do

How do you keep track of which systems can do what? There is a useful command called **uucheck** that generally lives in */usr/lib/uucp*. Run with no arguments, it checks your *Permissions* file for sanity (and since it uses the same routines as **uucico** and **uuxqt**, it thinks the same way as they do). However, if you run it with a -v flag, it will analyze the *Permissions* file and print an exhaustive list of who is allowed to do what. If you are trying to do complicated things with your UUCP permissions, you should be running this program after every change to make sure you've done things right.

# TIP 789

## Advanced UUCP Permissions

There are lots of things that can be done with UUCP Permissions, many more than can be covered here. An excellent reference is *Managing UUCP and USENET*, Tenth Edition, by Tim O'Reilly and Grace Todino (Sebastopol, CA: O'Reilly and Associates, 1992), which covers all aspects of UUCP administration.

# Diagnosing and Debugging UUCP Problems

# TIP 790

## Checking on Queued UUCP Jobs

You can get a list of all the systems to which your machine currently has a UUCP connection and those machines that could not be contacted by the UUCP system. To do this, use

```
# uustat -q
```

For each system in the output, you will see whether you currently have a UUCP connection to that system (TALKING) or you will get the reason why no UUCP connection could be made. For example, you might see a message like "WRONG TIME TO CALL".

# TIP 791

## Monitoring Live UUCP Connections

One way to figure out what is going wrong during a UUCP job is to watch a live connection attempt. You can do this using the **Uutry** command, in the following form,

```
# /usr/lib/uucp/Uutry -r system
```

where *system* is the name of the remote machine you are trying to connect to. You will get a detailed accounting of all the steps of the connection attempt. Some of the things that could be going wrong that you will be able to see from the output include use of a bad telephone number, a login problem after connecting to the remote machine, a problem with passwords, or a problem with permissions on the remote machine.

# Finding Out More About UUCP System Administration

You can find out more about UUCP system administration by consulting the *System Administrator's Reference Manual* that is part of the UNIX System V Release 4 *Document Set, UNIX Communications*, Second Edition, by Bert Costales and Harry Henderson (Carmel IN: Howard W. Sams, 1991), and *Managing UUCP and Usenet,* revised version by Tim O'Reilly and Dale Dougherty (O'Reilly and Associates, 1988).

# Running and Administrating TCP/IP

## Setting up TCP/IP

Before connecting to a TCP/IP network, you will need to obtain an Internet address.
Then you will need to install the Internet utilities on your system, if they are not already installed.

To connect your machine to a TCP/IP network, you will need to set up a network provider. This can be a LAN or a Wide Area Network (WAN). The steps you need to follow depend on which network you are using. When you have configured the network provider, you must configure TCP/IP to specify which provider to use to communicate with. This information is kept in */etc/inet/strcf.*

You will need to define the machines you would like to talk to in the file */etc/inet/hosts.* This file contains an entry for each machine you would like to communicate with. You should add new machines at the bottom of the file; there are entries in it for loopback testing even before you add entries for remote system. For each system, put the Internet address, host name, and host alias in the entry. For example, to communicate over TCP/IP with the remote host pluto, with alias planet, and Internet address *192.11.105.101*, put the following line in this file:

```
192.11.105.101    pluto    planet
```

To use TCP/IP as a transport provider for network services, such as RFS, UUCP, and so on, you will need to set up your TLI listener. Consult the *System Administrator's Reference Manual* to see how this is done.

To start up TCP/IP, first use the **shutdown** command to reboot your system, with

```
# /etc/shutdown -y -g0 -i6
```

Next, see whether the network daemon **inetd** is running. Use

```
# ps -ef | grep inetd
```

to do this. If you don't see it, stop the network with

```
# /etc/init/inetinit stop
```

and then restart the network with

```
# /etc/init/inetinit start
```

# Diagnosing Problems on a TCP/IP Network

There are several different things you can do to diagnose a problem on a TCP/IP network.

❑ You can use the **ping** command to determine if a particular host on your network is up or down. (See Tip 795.)

❑ You can use the **netstat** command to display the status of network traffic. (See Tip 796.)

❑ You should make sure the network daemon **inetd** is running. (See Tip 798.) On some systems, you should also make sure that the TLI daemon **tlid** is running.

❏ You can check your */etc/hosts* file to ensure that the entries of remote hosts are accurate. (See Tip 800.)

❏ You should check the accuracy of the lines in the file */etc/confnet.d/inet/interface*.

❏ If you run the Reverse ARP (RARP) protocol, you should check to see whether RARP is running.

❏ You should use **rlogin** command to connect to the first network device installed in the machine and to the local host to see if there are hardware or cable problems or if the configuration files are out-of-date.

# Using the ping Command

**TIP 795**

You can use the **ping** command to find out whether a host on your network is up or down. You need only give **ping** the name of the remote host. For example, to see whether the remote host hope is up, use

```
$ ping hope
```

If hope is up and receives the request sent to it over the network, you will receive the message

```
hope is alive
```

But if hope is down, or cannot receive the packet sent, you will receive the message

```
no answer from hope
```

You can also specify a timeout with the **ping** command. For example, the following command line sets the timeout for the request to 100 seconds, from the default of 20 seconds:

```
$ ping hope 100
```

Finally, if you think the remote host is up but is losing packets, you can use the -s option of **ping** (which is available on some, but not all, systems). This sends packets to the remote host continually until you press the BREAK key or a timeout is reached. The output will tell you whether any packets were lost.

# Displaying the Network Status with netstat

You can get a display of the current network status using the **netstat** command. The output of this command shows the status of network traffic in a tabular format. The information shown includes data on available routes and their status and on interfaces. The **netstat** command has many different options. Here are some you may find useful.

You can determine the state of communications controllers configured with a machine by running **netstat -i**. From the output you will be able to see how many packets a host thinks it has transmitted and how many it has received on each network. Also, to check the status of IP routers, run **netstat -r**.

# Diagnosing TCP/IP Troubles Using rlogin

You can use **rlogin** to diagnose some problems with your TCP/IP network. First, enter the command

```
# rlogin `uname -n`
```

If this command succeeds, you can send TCP packets and process them on the first network device associated with the machine, which is the machine you get by using **uname -n**. If this command is successful, but remote machines cannot log in to your machine using **rlogin**, you should check the hardware and cables of the first network device.

Next, enter the command

```
# rlogin localhost
```

If this is successful and the previous **rlogin** command was not, you should check the localhost entry in the file */etc/confnet.d/inet/interface*. Since some configuration files are dependent on **date**, you should update the inet-specific files using

```
# touch /etc/confnet.d/inet/interface
```

and then reboot your computer.

# Checking Your Network daemon inetd

One reason you may be having trouble with your TCP/IP network is that your network daemon **inetd** may not be running. To check whether it is, type

```
# ps -ef | grep inetd
```

If **inetd** is running on your system you will see a line for */usr/sbin/inetd* in the output. If you don't see a line for **inetd** in the output, you will need to restart **inetd** in one of two ways. You can use

```
# sacadm -p -s inetd
```

or you can reboot your computer.

# Sometimes inetd Isn't Called That

Some providers of SVR4 networking packages decided to rewrite many of the applications to run over TLI rather than over sockets. If you have one of these systems, you may find that **inetd** either doesn't exist, or has very limited functionality. You will need to find the name of the program that replaces it, and then use that name rather than **inetd** when you are following the instructions in some of the tips in this section. The name of the replacement server program should be found in the **man** pages or elsewhere in the provider's documentation.

Sometimes the replacement server program is called **tlid**. Additionally, if you are setting up your own services that run over TLI, you may find that you need to edit a different file, and that this file may have a slightly different format. For example, it may allow you to specify a list of modules that should be pushed onto the stream before the service is invoked.

# TIP 800

# TCP/IP Network Security

You can implement the security of your machine with respect to a TCP/IP network at either the host or user level, or both. The goal is to allow certain users the ability to do a remote login to your machine without a password, permitting these users to run remote commands on your machine and to limit other valid remote users so that they cannot run remote commands on your machine.

Use your */etc/hosts.equiv* file to list the remote hosts from which a user can log in to your machine without giving a password. Only the system administrator can change this file. Put the name of remote machines one on a line in *hosts.equiv*. For example, if your *hosts.equiv* contains

```
banana
lemon
orange
```

and you have added entries for all the users on these systems to your */etc/passwd* file, then all users on these three systems can log in to your system remotely using **rlogin** without supplying a password and they can use remote commands on your machine to connect to other remote machines.

You should note that by default, the *hosts.equiv* file on many machines has a + (plus sign) that allows all machines to be equivalent hosts. Since this is almost certainly not what you want, you should edit this file immediately and remove the +.

You can also enforce security at the user level. A user with a home directory on a remote machine can set up a file called *.rhosts* in this directory. An entry in *.rhosts* is either a host name, indicating that this user is trusted when accessing the system from the specified host, or a host name followed by a login name, indicating that the login name listed is trusted when accessing the system from the specified host. For instance, if mindy has the following *.rhosts* file in */home/mindy* on a system:

```
barbados
jamaica
cuba    ralph
cuba    portia
tobago
tobago  ralph
```

then the only trusted users are mindy, when logged on from barbados, jamaica, or tobago; ralph, when logged on from cuba or tobago, and portia, when logged on from cuba.

To ensure tight security, root should own all the *.rhosts* files and should deny write permission to remote users.

# Disabling Insecure TCP/IP Services

**TIP 801**

There are a number of different TCP/IP services that have security problems. To make your system more secure from compromise over your TCP/IP network, you should disable these services. For example, **tftp**, the trivial file transfer program, performs no authentication of users. Some versions of **tftp**, including those in versions of the SunOS prior to SunOS Release 4.0, allow files from the root directory to be stolen. To disable **tftp**, you need to comment out the tftp service in */etc/inetd.conf* by inserting a # (pound sign) as follows:

```
#tftp  dgram  udp    wait    root   /usr/etc/in.tftpd  in.tftpd
```

The finger service is also considered a security problem since it can be used to guess passwords by helping remote users guess valid user names and obtain other information that can be used to guess passwords. This service does not authenticate requesters of its service, nor does it provide an audit trail of service requests. To disable the finger service on your machine, comment out the finger service in */etc/inetd.conf* as follows:

```
#finger stream  tcp  nowait  root   /usr/etc/in.fingerd  in.fingerd
```

Since the **rwho** command can be used to transmit information to someone trying to guess passwords of accounts on your machine, you might want to disable it. Another reason to disable **rwho** is that running **rwhod**, the rwho daemon, eats up CPU resources on your machine. To disable rwho service on your machine, comment out this service in the system startup script which may be either */etc/inet/rc* or */etc/rc*. You can comment out three lines, as follows:

```
#if [ -f /usr/etc/in.rwho.d ]; then
#/usr/etc/in/who.d
#fi
```

# File Sharing

## TIP 802 — What Is File Sharing?

A *remote file system* allows computers on a network to act as servers to other computers on this network, called clients, so that clients can use resources on servers as if they were local resources. A single machine on a network can act as both a client and server, providing some resources for sharing and using the resources on other machines. Servers offer directory trees for access by clients of a network. Once a client has mounted one of these shared remote file systems on a local directory, remote files appear to the client, the users, and applications on the client as if they were on the local machine.

There are several advantages to sharing files using a remote file system. First, existing programs can run on different machines without changing these programs, since they can have the same files available to them anywhere in their directory trees. Many different users can run a program on a server as if it was on their local machines. This saves disk space on the client machines and allows clients access to a large variety of programs available on servers. System administration is also simplified tremendously by having programs on servers instead of on many different machines. Also, consistency of programs is much easier to maintain with file sharing. Finally, since different machines can act both as clients and servers, each machine can provide its own set of special programs to the other machines on a network, making a network of peer computers very powerful.

There are two remote file systems available on UNIX: NFS and RFS. Both are present in UNIX System V Release 4 and Release 4.2, and can be administered using a common package, DFS.

## TIP 803 — NFS Versus RFS—It's Not a War

The two file systems, NFS and RFS, are both remote file systems that can be used in networks of UNIX computers. However, they were developed with different goals in mind and both can be used on the same network.

The main goal of NFS is to provide file sharing across a network of machines that may be running many different operating systems, including DOS and VMS. It is also designed for easy recovery when servers fail and not to crash when clients fail. It does this at the price of not maintaining state information about clients accessing servers.

The main goal of RFS is to provide file sharing across a network of UNIX System V computers where this file sharing is as transparent as possible. RFS attempts to support UNIX file system semantics as closely as possible so that programs can run using remote files just as if they were using local files.

RFS supports the full semantics of UNIX system files operations, such as file locking, open with append mode, and so on. On the other hand, NFS uses its own network-locking facility, the Lock Manager, which support the style but not the semantics of UNIX system file operations.

Servers on RFS networks maintain the state of local resources and knows which clients have mounted each of its files. When an RFS client crashes, the server removes any file locks held by this client and carries out other cleanup activities. If an RFS server crashes, the client acts as if the files mounted from this server have been removed. On the other hand, servers on an NFS network do not maintain the state of local resources and do not know which clients have mounted their files. When an NFS client crashes, the server does not take any action. If a server crashes when trying to access a file shared on this server, he or she can either return an error after a specified timeout or block until the server comes up again.

# Sharing Resources

**TIP 804**

To make one of your local resources available for mounting by client machines, you will need to share this resource. To share either NFS or RFS resources, use the **share** command, which is part of the *Distributed File System* (DFS) administration package. For example, to share your directory */home/nancy/book* via NFS so that it is read-only (and not writable) by client machines, use the command

```
# share -F nfs -o ro /home/nancy/book
```

To share your directory */home/jan/memos reports* by the name REPORTS via RFS so that it is read-only by all clients except the client named hdqrs, who has both read and write permission on it, use

```
# share -F rfs -o ro,rw=hdqrs /home/jan/memos   REPORTS
```

# Unsharing Resources

**805**

If you have previously shared a resource, but you now want to make this unavailable for mounting, use the **unshare** command. For example, if you want to make the NFS resource */home/jeff/views* unavailable for mounting by remote clients, use

```
# unshare -F nfs /home/jeff/views
```

If you want to make the RFS resource named REPORTS unavailable for sharing, use

```
# unshare REPORTS
```

You don't have to use **-F rfs** in this command, since rfs is the default file type.

To make all the files you currently share—including both NFS and RFS resources—unavailable, use

```
# unshareall
```

To make just your NFS resource unavailable, use

```
# unshareall -F nfs
```

# Mounting Remote Resources

**806**

You can mount a resource shared by a server via NFS or RFS either explicitly, using the **mount** command, or automatically, using the */etc/vfstab* file, as long as your machine can reach the server of a network. (Note that on some systems, such as Suns, this file is */etc/mtab*.)

For example, on the server phoenix, you can mount the directory */usr/bin/viewers*, which phoenix has made available for sharing via NFS at the mount point */usr/lbin/viewers*. This makes read and write permissions available via the following:

```
# mount -F nfs -o rw phoenix:/usr/bin/viewers /usr/lbin/viewers
```

To see how to mount a file automatically when you boot your system, see the next tip.

# Automatically Mounting Remote Resources on Boot Up

To automatically mount a remote resource when you boot your system, use the */etc/vfstab* file. You will need to have created mount points for each remote resource you plan to mount. For example, suppose you want to automatically mount the resource */usr/viewers* from the server alaska via NFS with read and write permissions available. You have created the mount point */usr/lbin/viewers* for this resource. You have also set the permissions on this mount point to match those of */usr/viewers*. Put the following line in */etc/vfstab*:

```
alaska:/usr/viewers - /usr/lbin/viewers nfs - yes rw
```

# Unmounting Remote Resources

To unmount a file system, use the *umount* command. For example, to unmount the remote NFS resource */usr/lbin* on the server texas, use

```
# umount texas:/usr/lbin
```

You can unmount all the remote files mounted on your system using the **umountall** command. For example, to unmount all the NFS resources mounted on your system, use

```
# umountall -F nfs
```

# How to Find Out Why NFS Service Fails

**TIP 809**

Remote file sharing via NFS can fail from a problem with a server, a client, or a network. Here are some things you can check:

❑ Check that the NFS daemons are running by using the **nfsping** command, if it is available on your system. For example, to check whether the nfs daemon **nfsd** is running, use

```
$ nfsping -o nfsd
```

❑ Check that **mountd** on each server is available for RPC calls. Make sure the file */etc/init.d/nfs* has a block of lines starting with a line like

```
if [ -x /usr/lib/nfs/moutd]
```

❑ Make sure the **nfsd** daemons are running on servers; these are needed for remote mounts. There are four of these by default. Check that the */etc/init.d/nfs* file on each server has a block of lines starting with a line like

```
if [ -x /usr/lib/nfs/nfsd ]
```

❑ You can start these daemons without rebooting your system. To do so, you need to log in as a privileged user and use the following command:

```
# /usr/lib/nfs/nfsd -a 4
```

❑ If you are having performance problems you should make sure that the **biod** daemons are running on clients. You should look for a block of lines in each client's */etc/init.d/nfs* file that starts with a line like

```
if [ -x /usr/lib/nfs/biod ]
```

❑ You can enable the **biod** daemons without rebooting by logging in as a privileged user and using the following command:

```
# /usr/lib/nfs/biod 4
```

# Secure NFS

**TIP 810**

Because NFS servers authenticate a request to mount a file at the machine level and not at the user level, there are potential security problems with NFS. To take care of this problem, you can use *Secure NFS*, which can authenticate users when they make requests for mounting remote files. Secure NFS is based on *Secure RPC*, which lets servers and clients exchange encrypted information. To find out more about Secure NFS and Secure RPC, see the *Network User's and Administrator's Guide* that is part of the *UNIX System V Release 4 Document Set*.

# What Is Kerberos?

**TIP 811**

*Kerberos*, developed as part of Project Athena at MIT, is an authentication system for use on networks of clients and servers. You can use Kerberos to send sensitive information around a network and to restrict the use of various services on your network to valid users.

Kerberos includes a Ticket Granting Service that issues tickets for use of services. For example, after being logged in to a workstation running Kerberos for eight hours, network services will no longer run since your ticket for using these services has expired. To get a new ticket for running network services, you must use the **kinit** program, giving your logname and password again.

You can obtain the files for Kerberos via anonymous ftp from *athena-dist.mit.edu*. You can also obtain the source code for Kerberos, as well as articles on Kerberos and other documentation from M.I.T. To do this, write to the M.I.T. Software Center, W32-300, 20 Carlton Street, Cambridge, MA 02139.

# What Is NIS?

**TIP 812**

The *Network Information Service* (NIS), formerly known as *Yellow Pages* (YP), is a distributed network lookup service. It provides a way of identifying and locating resources and objects available on an NFS network and sets up a uniform, network-wide protocol and media independent storage and retrieval mechanism. This allows system administrators to distribute administrative databases, called *maps*, among different machines. The administrator can update these databases from a centralized site, automatically and reliably.

For details on NIS, consult the *Network User's and Administrator's Guide* in the *UNIX System V Release 4 Document Set.*

# Chapter 13

# Using Both DOS and UNIX

# Comparing Commands in DOS and UNIX

## Command Name Similarities and Differences

You may need to use both the UNIX operating system and DOS. You may also need to switch back and forth between the UNIX and DOS environments to perform some functions, perhaps even on the same machine. For example, in an office environment you may find it easier to do your mail administration and text formatting under UNIX, and your other applications, such as databases and spreadsheets, under DOS. The command structures in the two environments can be confusing, since some commands that perform analogous functions have the same or similar names, while the names of other commands that perform analogous functions are totally different.

Here are some of the similarities and differences between these environments that you should know about if you use both DOS and UNIX.

Sometimes the name of the command that carries out a function is the same in DOS and UNIX. For example, the DOS **cd** and the UNIX **cd** commands, if given a pathname as an argument, will change directories. DOS and UNIX both use **fdisk** to perform hard disk management. The DOS and UNIX **mkdir** command both make a directory, and **rmdir** removes a directory in both systems. And the DOS and UNIX **sort** commands sort fields in a file.

Other times, the commands for the same function may have similar names. The DOS **copy** command and the UNIX **cp** command both copy files. Likewise, the DOS **edlin** and the UNIX **ed** commands both invoke line editors.

Examples of unrelated names for commands with the same function are the DOS **rename** and the UNIX **mv** commands, which can both be used to rename a file in the current directory; the DOS **comp** and the UNIX **diff** commands, which compare two files to identify differences between them; and the DOS **delete** or **erase** command and the UNIX **rm** command, which are used to delete files.

There are other sources of confusion. For example, the DOS **cd** command, when given an argument, performs a change directory function similar to the UNIX **cd** command. However, the DOS **cd** *without* any arguments displays the current directory. In this situation it performs the same function as the UNIX **pwd** command.

Here is a summary of some of the more common UNIX commands and their DOS equivalents:

| UNIX | DOS | Function |
|------|-----|----------|
| cat | type | Lists the contents of a file |
| cd | cd | Changes directory (see also **pwd** command) |
| cp | copy | Copies a file or files |
| diff | comp | Compares files for differences |
| ed | edlin | Edits files |
| ls | dir | Lists files in a directory |
| mkdir | mkdir | Makes a directory |
| mv | rename | Renames a file |
| pwd | cd | Displays current directory (see also **cd** command) |
| rm | del | Removes a file or files |
| rmdir | rmdir | Removes a directory |
| sort | sort | Sorts contents of a file |
| vi | edit | Performs screen editing |

# Command Line Differences between DOS and UNIX

TIP
814

There are a number of important differences between DOS and UNIX that affect the command line. Keeping these differences in mind makes it easier to use both environments. For example:

| | |
|---|---|
| Case sensitivity | DOS treats lowercase and uppercase the same; UNIX distinguishes between cases. |
| Backslash, slash | DOS uses \ as delimiter in paths; UNIX uses / as delimiter in paths. |
| Filenames | DOS name is limited to 8 chars, extension to 3; UNIX name to 14 chars (256 in some versions). |
| Filename extensions | DOS supports, requires for certain filetypes; UNIX treats as optional. (See Tip 63.) |
| Wildcard matching | DOS and UNIX both use, but differently, depending on command. |

You should understand these differences before attempting to use command lines, since unpredictable results may occur when you use DOS commands in UNIX or vice versa.

# Using Familiar Commands in DOS and UNIX

There are ways to avoid having to remember all of the nuances of both DOS and UNIX commands. One solution for UNIX users who must use DOS frequently is to create a DOS batch file with a UNIX command name as the filename part of the batch file. For example, you can create a DOS batch file to perform the DOS **erase** command on a single file and call it *rm.bat*. The contents, when displayed back via the DOS **type** command, would look like this:

```
C:\> type rm.bat
erase %1
```

When you want to erase the DOS file called *junk*, you can do so with the command

```
C:\> rm junk
```

as long as the *rm.bat* file is in your DOS PATH. While you can write batch files with UNIX names to perform your most commonly used DOS functions, there are commercial products such as MKS Toolkit that do this by performing UNIX functions on DOS machines. (See Tips 850 through 854 for more information on this.)

DOS users who frequently use UNIX can write a UNIX shell script with a DOS command name and store it in a directory of executables, such as your own */bin* directory. For example, you can create a shell script named **del** to perform the UNIX **rm** command on a single file, which would look like this when displayed with the UNIX **cat** command:

```
$ cat del
rm $1
```

Then to delete the file named *errors*, you would simply type

```
$ del errors
```

You can create UNIX shell scripts with the names of DOS commands to perform your most commonly used UNIX functions, but you need to be careful about PATH conflicts if there is already a UNIX command with the name you choose. As an example, the UNIX **type** command will tell you what kind of file you are looking at. If you want to create a UNIX shell script called **type** to perform the same function as the DOS **type** command, you must ensure that your path is set correctly so that your shell script executes instead of the normal UNIX **type** command. (See Tips 43 through 46 for more information on setting up your UNIX PATH.)

There are also packages such as Mtools that let you perform DOS commands on UNIX machines. (See Tip 855.)

If you do not want to purchase packages or write scripts to perform command conversion, you should probably invest in a DOS command summary card to sit on top of your keyboard for use when you are in a DOS environment, and a UNIX command summary card for use in the UNIX environment.

# Running Both DOS and UNIX on the Same Machine

## Ways That You Can Use UNIX and DOS Together

If you need to run both DOS and UNIX, you can do so on the same PC. Before you can run DOS and UNIX on the same machine, you need to set up your PC to handle both environments. There are four ways you can do this, and the method depends on how you use the two operating systems together.

If the processor in your PC is an 8086, 80286, 80386, or 80486, you will be able to run both DOS and the UNIX operating system on the machine without any alterations or special CPU instructions, by simply partitioning your hard disk. (See Tips 817 and 819.)

You may want to use a DOS PC as a terminal to access your UNIX system. (See Tip 830.) This is useful if you work on both DOS and UNIX, but your DOS and UNIX machines are in different locations.

You may want to use DOS *under* the UNIX operating system, that is, run DOS commands from your UNIX shell. This is useful if you frequently share files and programs between DOS and UNIX. (See Tip 823.)

Finally, you may want to use DOS on a UNIX machine that does not have an 80x86 processor, such as a 680x0. To do this, you will need to obtain a DOS coprocessor board or DOS software emulator so that you can run DOS on your machine. (See Tip 821.)

## TIP 817 — Partitioning the Hard Disk

To run both the UNIX operating system and DOS on the same machine, you must partition the hard disk so that each has its own partition. You do this via either the UNIX **fdisk** command or the DOS **fdisk** command, depending on how you want to set up your environment. (See Tips 818 and 819.) Review the chapter on setting up the hard disk in your particular User's or Installation Guide before you attempt to partition the hard disk. You should make sure you know exactly how many megabytes your hard disk has before you attempt to segment it into partitions.

Since you will necessarily destroy data on partitions when you create and change them, you should carefully map out your strategy as to how much disk space you want for each of these operating systems before you do anything. If you are have a PC on a LAN, and have a system administrator for UNIX, ask the administrator to help you. If you have a single-user UNIX system, make sure you understand how partitions work, and what the disk requirements are for the combination of UNIX and DOS versions that you intend to run on your machine.

If you plan to run both DOS and UNIX on the same machine, you need to understand the impact of your choice of operating system for the first partition, and of the default active one. Since you can have only one active partition at a time, you should designate the one you want to boot at system startup to be the active one. The instructions for disk partitioning and partition activation should be in the User's Guide for both your DOS and UNIX operating systems.

The UNIX Operating System and its core utility packages take up around 15 to 20 megabytes of disk space. Allowing a minimum of 20 megabytes for the UNIX partition may let you run a minimum configuration of UNIX, without some of the utility packages, and DOS, merged in a partition. A merged partition is one where the two operating systems are in the same partition, with DOS running as a task of the UNIX operating system. This merge feature is provided by packages such as Merge386 by Locus Computing and VP/ix by Sunsoft. A rule of thumb has been the 80-20 rule: in a shared DOS and UNIX environment, 80 percent of the total disk space on your machine used for operating systems should be for UNIX and DOS merged, and the remaining 20 percent for DOS only.

If you run DOS 4.*x*, 5.*x*, or 6.*x* you do not have to worry about the size of the DOS partition; you can use system utilities to customize your partition. However, if you run DOS 3.*x* (which may be the case, especially since some LAN administrators still issue the DOS 3.*x* operating system for casual DOS users to avoid the added expense of a new version), you must load DOS 3.*x* into what is called primary DOS, which is the first 32 megabytes of the hard disk. Also, you need to consider this when you decide where to place your operating systems. If your hard disk is larger than 32 megabytes, you should also know that DOS versions 3.3 and later can take advantage of extended DOS (logical drive designation) for the remaining hard disk space, which means that applications and data can be stored in these partitions. DOS 3.2 and prior versions can only store data in DOS data partitions. (See Tips 818 and 819.)

# Allocating UNIX as the First Partition on Your Hard Disk

**TIP 818**

You should allocate the first partition to UNIX if you want to run UNIX most of the time, or if you intend to run Merge386 or VP/ix, which require this so that DOS can be loaded behind UNIX in the same partition. (See Tip 820.) To allocate the UNIX partition, boot the UNIX operating system from the boot floppy provided with the operating system. Next, partition your hard disk using the UNIX **fdisk** command by typing

```
# fdisk
```

A menu of options will appear on the screen, similar to this:

```
SELECT ONE OF THE FOLLOWING:
1.  Create a partition
2.  Change Active (Boot from) partition
3.  Delete a partition
4.  Exit (Update disk configuration and exit)
5.  Cancel (Exit without updating disk configuration)
```

If you choose 1, you will be asked what type of partition you want to create. You should select the one designated as a UNIX partition, which should be the first one listed. You will be told how many total cylinders your disk has, and asked how much of the disk you want to partition for UNIX. You will need to give some thought here to what operating system configurations you intend to run on your machine. (See Tip 820.) You should allocate 80 percent of the total disk space to UNIX. Once you have allocated UNIX as the first partition, you may create other partitions, such as primary DOS, extended DOS, or DOS data, up to the capacity of your hard disk, by using the same create partition option. (See Tip 819.) Once you have created all of the partitions you want to, you then make the UNIX partition active by selecting the change active partition option and following the instructions given.

While most people have 80386 or 80486 PCs, some 8086 and 80286 processor machines are still in use. If you have one of these, here are some things you will have to consider. These machines have small hard disks—as little as 20MB—so, using the 80 percent rule, the operating systems and their associated files would have to be something like 16MB for UNIX and 4MB for DOS. Even SVR4 without its utilities would have trouble loading in this small partition space! Even when using bigger disks with older versions of DOS, the fact that primary DOS must reside within the first 32MB only gives you a ratio of 24MB for the UNIX operating system and 8MB for the DOS operating system. So maybe it is time for you to upgrade to an 80486, or at least an 80386.

# Allocating DOS as the First Partition on Your Hard Disk

If you intend to use your machine mostly as a DOS PC, and only run UNIX occasionally, you should allocate the first partition as a DOS partition. To allocate DOS as the first partition, you need to first boot DOS from a floppy disk and then partition the hard disk using the DOS **fdisk** command. To do this, simply type

```
A:\> fdisk
```

A menu of options will appear on the screen, similar to this:

```
SELECT ONE OF THE FOLLOWING:
1.   Create DOS partition
2.   Change Active Partition
3.   Delete DOS Partition
4.   Display Partition Information
Press ESC to return to DOS
```

If you choose 1, you will be asked what type of partition you want to create. Select the one designated as a DOS partition, which should be the first one listed. You will be told how many total cylinders your disk has, and asked how much of the disk you want to partition for DOS. You will need to give some thought to what operating system configurations you intend to run on your machine. (See Tip

820.) You should allocate 20 percent of the total disk space to DOS. Once you have allocated DOS as the first partition, you may create other partitions, such as extended DOS, DOS data, and UNIX.

You do not have to worry about where the DOS operating system is loaded in the first partition if you are like most users running DOS 4.*x* or higher. (See the previous tip.) If you are running DOS 3.*x*, you need to consider the following information.

Since DOS treats the UNIX operating system as a non-DOS partition, if you make the DOS partition the first partition, you can use all of the 32MB of primary DOS for the operating system if you need to. You can then allocate the next partition as a non-DOS partition under which you can load the UNIX operating system, assuming that you have at least 15 to 20MB of disk space remaining. This gives you more room for each operating system. You can then add either DOS data or extended DOS partitions as required, up to the limit of the disk capacity. Once you have created all of the partitions you want to, you can then make the DOS partition active by selecting the change active partition option and following the instructions given.

# How to Decide Whether to Run Separate or Shared Environments

If you have allocated your partitions correctly, you now have one of two configurations that you can load operating systems onto: a UNIX partition followed by a DOS partition, or a DOS partition followed by a UNIX partition. You are now ready to load the operating systems into their partitions. Now you need to decide whether you want to run the DOS operating system *under* the UNIX operating system (see Tip 818) or as a separate environment. The reasons for doing one versus the other are discussed in the following paragraphs.

You can easily load each operating system in its own partition, but since only one partition can be active at a time, you will have to constantly activate and deactivate partitions to set up your environment. If you have a machine with an older 8086 processor, you must run DOS and UNIX as separate environments; with an 80286 or faster processor, there is another option, however. You can load both UNIX and DOS together in a single partition and then make them work together under the UNIX environment. (See Tip 818.) You can then load a separate stand-alone DOS environment under another partition to handle situations where your application will not run correctly in a merged operating system environment. There are advantages and disadvantages to a separate partition approach, as there also are for a shared partition approach.

For example, say you have loaded DOS and UNIX into separate partitions and do not have a UNIX partition that allows you to run DOS under UNIX, like Merge386 or VP/ix. You are using the UNIX operating system and you want to use DOS. You need to become a superuser, use the UNIX **fdisk** command to activate the DOS partition, log off of UNIX, then reboot the system to bring up DOS. When you want to go back to UNIX, you will have to use the DOS **fdisk** command to make active the UNIX partition and then reboot your computer to bring up the UNIX operating system.

If you seldom use one or the other environment, this may be an acceptable method. But if you frequently move between the two environments, this procedure is cumbersome. Also, the operating system you are running when you end your computer session is the one that will boot the next time you boot your computer, and it may not be the one under which you want to initially work. Thus, you may have to go through two boot procedures to bring up the operating system that you want.

As a second example, say you have DOS running under UNIX in the same partition using the Merge386 or VP/ix package. (See Tip 818.) You can run both UNIX and DOS operating system environments without having to change partitions, but when you issue UNIX commands in the DOS environment, they run slightly slower than they would in their native UNIX environment, and the same is true when you issue DOS commands in the UNIX environment. This is because an additional process must be started to run the commands in their nonnative environments. (See Tip 823.)

# Coprocessors for DOS and UNIX

**TIP 821**

If you are running UNIX on a processor other than an 80x86, you still may be able to run DOS on your UNIX machine by installing a coprocessor board that supports DOS. Machines that support such a board include 680x0 processors. Check with your computer vendor to find out whether there is such a board for your computer.

If your machine does not support DOS coprocessor boards, you need to use a software DOS emulator to run DOS on UNIX machines. The emulator typically provides emulation of either the CPU itself or of the IBM PC architecture, which includes the BIOS, the video adapter, the devices, and so on. Once you set up this emulation environment, you may load a version of MS-DOS on top of it. The DOS operating system may be a shrink-wrapped version, or it may be a customized DOS environment built into the PC architecture.

There are some publicly available software DOS emulators that are built for the old "workhorses" of the IBM PC environment, the 8086 and 8088 processors. The first one, built for emulation of an 8088 processor, works on a SUNOS 4.*x* environment. You can get the full source code for this through anonymous ftp from *cs.vu.nl* in the directory */pub/minix/simulator*. The code is written in C and, although written and tested on a SPARC, should port easily to other machines. Since it only emulates the CPU, you will have to acquire a BIOS and some additional device simulators. The software is licensed through Prentice-Hall; you may use it for educational or research purposes without obtaining written consent. For more information, contact the author, Andy Tanenbaum, at *ast@cs.vu.nl.*

The second publicly available DOS emulator is an alpha version of GDE, a package that emulates an 8088 with an 8087 coprocessor, and also emulates MS-DOS, with some BIOS support. The software was built for a number of target environments: SUN4/SUN3 SUNOS 4.x.x, MIPS, VAX Ultrix, RS6000 AIX 3.1, and SGI 4D. Most of the code is portable. This version is useful for someone who knows a fair amount about emulators and can work around some of their bugs. The source is licensed through GNU public license and it can be obtained through anonymous ftp from *scri.fsu.edu*, in the file */pub/hudgens/gde-0.3.tar.Z.* The author is J. H. Hudgens (*hudgens@scri.fsu.edu*).

The third emulator is a beta version of **pcm** (a *PC* emulator). This software emulates both an 8086 processor and an IBM PC environment with BIOS support. The target environments are SUN4, Apollo, and DEC machines. You must supply your own MS-DOS operating system to sit on top of the BIOS. The existing interface is X, but there is a crude tty interface for text programs. The source is licensed through GNU public license, obtained via anonymous ftp from *rtfm.mit.edu,* in the file */pub/pcm/pcm-0.65.tar.Z.* The author is Gary Beihl (*gary.beihl@columbiasc.ncr.com*).

For more information on building emulators, contact Robert Boucher at *boucher@sofkin.ca,* *boucher@asimov.ocunix.on.ca,* or *ah441k@Freenet.carleton.ca.*

# Running DOS under UNIX

## Using UNIX Commands to Access DOS Files

**TIP 822**

If you want to use DOS commands in the same environment as UNIX, you can run DOS under the UNIX operating system. If you don't need to run DOS applications, you can use basic DOS file manipulation commands that are included in some releases of UNIX without adding any additional software such as Merge (see the next tip) to your UNIX machine. For some versions of UNIX System V Release 4, you will find these commands in the Xenix Compatibility Package which may be one of the optional add-on packages included with your operating system.

These commands allow you to access DOS files by using the floppy disk drive on your UNIX machine. You can make and remove files and directories, display file and directory contents, copy files between DOS and UNIX, and format DOS disks.

For example, to make and remove DOS directories on your floppy, use the **dosmkdir** and **dosrmdir** commands. For example,

```
$ dosmkdir a:/newdir
```

makes the directory *newdir* on the DOS floppy, and

```
$ dosrmdir a:/newdir
```

removes it. Note that the path designation is the UNIX / (slash), not the DOS \ (backslash). You must use this format to specify files and directories when using these file manipulation commands.

To display the contents of a directory on your DOS floppy, use either the **dosls** command, which displays the contents in a format similar to the UNIX **ls** command, or the **dosdir** command, which displays the contents in DOS format similar to the DOS **dir** command. To display file contents, use

```
$ doscat a:/path/filename
```

where *filename* is in the directory *path* on your DOS floppy.

To copy a file from DOS to UNIX, use the format

```
$ doscp /path1/file1 /path2/file2
```

where *path1* is either the UNIX or DOS directory, depending on where the file is being copied from, and *file1* is the filename in *path1* to be copied; *path2* and *file2* are the receiving directory and file. For example, to copy the UNIX file */usr/data* to the file *dosdata* on the DOS floppy, use

```
$ doscp /usr/data a:/dosdata
```

To format a DOS floppy on your UNIX machine, type

```
$ dosformat a:
```

# Running DOS under UNIX

**TIP 823**

If you want to run DOS applications or use all of the DOS commands under UNIX, there are two commercial packages that do this: VP/ix from SunSoft and Merge from Locus Computing Corporation. These packages provide a virtual DOS environment—that is, they allow you to access programs and data files normally under the DOS partition and use them in the UNIX environment, as a task under UNIX. To the user, the sessions appear exactly as they would if you had changed partitions and booted DOS.

Merge and VP/ix are primarily intended for UNIX users who want to use DOS commands. There is also an implementation of Merge called Merge386 for 80386-based processors. Merge is available on UnixWare (the Univel network operating environment) for SVR4.2 UNIX machines. VP/ix is being planned for future integration onto SunSoft's Windows-based Wabi platform, which allows you to run Windows-based applications directly on Solaris 2, Sun Microsystems' implementation of UNIX SVR4.

These packages require that you load the UNIX operating system first before you install them into the UNIX environment. This new environment adds extensions to the UNIX kernel to handle the DOS commands and files. For example, under Merge386 you can enter the DOS environment from UNIX by simply typing

```
$ dos
```

The *autoexec.bat* and *config.sys* files that are created in your UNIX root directory by Merge are then executed to set up your DOS environment as it would be if you were running a stand-alone DOS session. You can run a normal DOS session and then return to the UNIX environment by typing

```
C:\> exit
```

at the DOS prompt.

You can also run DOS commands without having to enter into a DOS session. For example, if you want to list the contents of the current UNIX directory while running Merge under UNIX, you can type either

```
$ ls
```

or

```
$ dir
```

**dir** will execute a little slower than **ls** because a second process, a DOS one, needs to be started to run the DOS **dir** command.

You can do the converse from the DOS environment. If you are running DOS under the environment created by using Merge,

```
C:\> ls
```

will list the contents of the current DOS directory just as the DOS **dir** command does. Again, this will run a little slower than the native **dir** command, since a second process, a UNIX one, needs to be started to run the UNIX **ls** command.

# Setting Your PATH When Using Merge

The PATH environmental variable is used for both your UNIX and DOS commands run under UNIX. Hence, you need to make sure your PATH includes the directories where your UNIX commands are located and the Merge bin directories, which on most systems are */usr/dbin* and */usr/ldbin*. Usually, when you run the **dos** command, it will use the value of PATH; it changes it to DOS format and puts it in the DOS environment. You should also note that on some versions of Merge you use the DOSPATH environmental variable for your PATH in your DOS sessions; you will need to put your normal UNIX system bins and the Merge directories in DOSPATH for Merge to work properly.

*You can also set PATH for your DOS sessions in your rom, which is read when you start your DOS session.*

# Passing Environmental Variables to DOS

On some versions of Merge you can pass environmental variables to DOS sessions using the DOSENV environmental variable. The **dos** command will put any variables named in DOSENV into the DOS environment. For example,

```
$ PROMPT="your command?"; export PROMPT
$ TERM=AT386; export TERM
$ DOSENV=PROMPT,TERM; export DOSENV
```

When you run the **dos** command after typing these lines, the variables PROMPT and TERM will be included in your DOS environment with PROMPT="your command?" and TERM=AT386.

# Running DOS Applications under UNIX

If you have set up a virtual DOS environment under your UNIX environment using a package such as VP/ix or Merge (see Tip 823), you can invoke DOS applications directly from the UNIX shell. There are two ways to do this. The first way is to invoke the DOS application by typing the **dos** command followed by the DOS command line. For example, if you have the WordPerfect application loaded on your DOS machine, and you have defined your DOS PATH to include the directory where the *.exe* file for the application is stored, the UNIX command

```
$ dos wp
```

will suspend your UNIX session, start a DOS session, and then execute the DOS *wp.exe* file, which invokes the WordPerfect application. When you exit the application, you will leave the DOS session and return to your UNIX session.

An alternative way of doing this is to invoke the application directly from the UNIX shell. The UNIX command

```
$ wp
```

will also execute the WordPerfect application. The reason that you can directly invoke the application from the UNIX shell is that, when a package like Merge or VP/ix is running on your UNIX machine, the command interpreter for DOS recognizes that this command must be a DOS request, since it did not find a UNIX command or UNIX shell script with the same name. Therefore, you should avoid creating UNIX shell scripts with the same name as your DOS program. For example, having a UNIX shell script named **wp** would never allow the *wp.exe* file to execute. The DOS command interpreter will look for a DOS file with the filename *wp* and the extension *.exe* (or *.bat*) on the DOS machine and execute it. This direct method for invoking DOS commands is less efficient than invoking the DOS shell to run the application, since it only invokes the DOS environment during the execution of this one task, rather than exiting the UNIX system and starting an entire DOS session.

The VP/ix package supports LIM/EMS 3.2 and 4.2, which allow you to run DOS programs that require expanded memory under UNIX. You can also run DOS text-based applications from an asynchronous terminal attached to the UNIX machine, and reducing the need for intelligent PCs. In addition, DOS applications can use UNIX peripherals, such as a printer, without any additional drivers.

# Making DOS Applications Available on UNIX Machines

Suppose you have a DOS application such as *WordPerfect* running on your DOS PC. You want to free up your DOS disk file space and would like to be able to store the *wp.exe* file under the UNIX file system instead of the DOS file system, but still run it as a DOS application whenever you want to. For example, if you have *PC Interface*, you can copy the file to the UNIX file system, which is designated as DOS Drive D: (see Tip 833), by doing the following:

```
C:\> copy wp.exec d:
```

This will copy the file from the current directory on the C: drive to the current directory on the D: drive. Then copy all of WordPerfect's associated files into the same directory in which you put the *wp.exe* file. You can then execute the WordPerfect program, changing your current drive to Drive D: and issuing the command

```
D:\> wp
```

The program will run as it would normally.

As a second example, say you want to share a copy of the *wp.exe* file with another user (or users) running a shared DOS-UNIX environment such as Merge on another PC, and store it under the UNIX environment on this PC. If you have a terminal emulator capability (such as PC Interface) on your DOS PC and a shared DOS-UNIX environment such as Merge running on the other PC, you can use the file transfer function of your emulator to move the program file *wp.exe* to the UNIX machine running the Merge environment. You can then run the DOS application from the UNIX environment on this UNIX machine, whether you have a PC attached to it or just an ASCII terminal, by issuing the command

```
$ wp.exe
```

You can do this because the DOS command interpreter looks on both the DOS file system and the UNIX file system for *wp.exe*, since you are in a virtual environment where UNIX and DOS files are treated as though they were part of the same file system. (See Tip 826.)

If you had originally loaded the WordPerfect application on your PC using the tools supplied with the Merge package, you would be able to execute WordPerfect by using the command

```
$ wp
```

Here you do not need the *.exe* extension on the command line, since the DOS interpreter will look to see if the application was loaded using the Merge tools, and having found that it was, invoke the application.

# Running UNIX Commands When Using DOS under UNIX

TIP 828

You can run UNIX commands when you are running DOS under UNIX through the use of Merge. The way in which this is done varies with the particular version of Merge, so you will need to check the documentation that comes with your version of Merge for details.

On some versions you can use the **on unix** command. For example, you can run a command such as

```
C> ON UNIX GREP MICHIGAN ADDRESSES
```

Your output will come to your DOS session. You can also put such jobs into the background by including an & (ampersand) at the end of the command line. To exit from commands run with **on unix**, type CTRL-C. You should note that on some versions of Merge, you use **rununix** instead of **on unix**. Also, you should note that you need to use **ion unix** (for *interactive on unix*) to run interactive UNIX commands for some version of Merge.

You should also note that some versions of Merge let you use certain commands directly, that is, without using the **on unix** command. The usual set of commands supported in this way includes **cat**, **chmod**, **cp**, **grep**, **lp**, **ls**, **mv**, and **pr**.

## How to Find Out More about Running Both DOS and UNIX

You can find out more about running DOS under UNIX by reading the articles in the newsgroup *comp.unix.dos-under-unix*.

You can find out more about vendors and products that work on DOS and UNIX machines, make DOS and UNIX work together, and allow connections from DOS to UNIX machines by using the *Open Systems Products Directory* from UniForum.

You can find out more about how DOS and UNIX work together by consulting books such as *DOS Meets UNIX* by Dale Dougherty (Sebastopol, CA: Nutshell Press, 1988) and *The UNIX Guide for DOS Users* by Allen Taylor (Portland, OR: MIS Press, 1990).

## Terminal Emulators

## Setting Up Your DOS PC for Terminal Emulation

You may want to use your PC as though it were a terminal attached to a UNIX host to perform UNIX commands and transfer files from the DOS PC to the UNIX machine, or vice versa. This approach is useful if your UNIX machine is in a different location than your DOS machine. It also eliminates the need for a dedicated terminal to access UNIX.

To use your PC as a terminal, you will need to connect the two machines either directly or via dial-up modem. You will also need to obtain a terminal emulator package to make your PC act like a terminal, as well as enable it to transfer files to, and receive files from, the UNIX machine. (See Tips 831 and 832.)

To connect DOS machines to UNIX machines, you need both hardware and software designed for this purpose. While there are a few ways to connect networked machines, two of the most popular ones are RS232 serial and Ethernet. RS232 is the less expensive solution, requiring only a serial cable connecting the DOS and UNIX machine and the associated RS232 software. There are some drawbacks to this method, however, in the performance of the serial connection. Typical connections run at speeds from 1200 to 9600 bits per second.

An Ethernet connection gives you much faster data access speeds (up to 10 megabits per second) and allows you to run the TCP/IP protocol rather than the RS232 protocol, but requires more expensive hardware. An Ethernet board and the associated software are required on both the PC end and the UNIX host end, as is an Ethernet cable to connect them. Both of these connections are direct-connect, which requires that the machines be located in the same area, typically the same room.

If one machine is not close to the other, say in another building, you can still connect them, but you will need to use a modem at both the PC and UNIX host end, as well as the utility software for modem communications at both ends. While the data access speed available when using a modem is not as fast as direct-connect Ethernet, today's modems are capable of speeds up to 19,200 bits per second, which is faster than the maximum 9,600 bits per second available via direct-connect serial connections.

# Using a Terminal Emulator

You can access the UNIX environment from a DOS PC by installing *terminal emulator* software on your DOS PC. A terminal emulator does exactly what it sounds like it would do—it makes the PC act as though it were a terminal connected to the UNIX host. You can find commercially available terminal emulators for most of the industry-standard terminals, such as those from DEC, HP, Tektronix, and IBM. Two examples of robust emulators are PC-Interface by Locus Computing, and the ctrm package.

Whichever emulator you use, they all perform basically the same set of functions. First, they emulate (act like) a particular terminal, for example a VT100 or an HP2621. The keyboard sequences and screen displays on your DOS PC are all mapped to those of the terminal type you are emulating, so you can use familiar keystroke sequences and see the results the way you expect to. In fact, it should be transparent to you that you are working on a DOS PC instead of an attached UNIX console terminal.

Second, they allow you to escape from the UNIX-terminal mode to the DOS mode to run local DOS commands on your PC. This feature is helpful when you want to use a file created or transferred during a terminal emulator session in a DOS program.

Some of the emulators provide a screen interface that can be controlled through use of a hot key (which toggles you between the control screen and the terminal session).

To learn more about the capabilities of the commercially available terminal emulators, read the article on terminal emulators in the November, 1993 issue of *UNIXWorld*. This article compares 14 of the more popular emulators, including Windows-based products. This review discusses not only the basic emulator features, but some of the more advanced features available with some of these packages, such as running remote applications on the UNIX machine and performing remote printing or remote file access. (See also Tip 833.)

# TIP 832
# Using Emulators To Transfer Files

Almost all terminal emulators allow you to transfer files from DOS to UNIX, or vice versa. Almost all emulators let you transfer both ASCII text and binary files with error correction, using one of the common protocols such as kermit, xmodem, ymodem, or zmodem. In addition, these transferring scripts can be built into function keys. The transfers are typically centered around the UNIX host, so that transfers from DOS to UNIX are sometimes referred to as "transfers up" and from UNIX to DOS as "transfers down."

For example, using the kermit protocol which is available under the ctrm emulator, a file can be transfered from the UNIX machine to the PC with the **utopc** command, represented on PCs that emulate HP2621 terminals as the sequence <SHIFT-F3> (SHIFT key and function key F3 together). Keying this sequence displays back the command **utopc** and waits for you to type in the filename, in this case *asciifile.text*:

```
$ utopc asciifile.text
```

The screen changes to show that the transfer is taking place:

| Receiving File | Bytes | Corrected Errors | Time |
| --- | --- | --- | --- |
| asciifile.text | 1632 | 0 | 0:01 |

The transfer process puts the transferred file into the \\*ctrm* directory on the DOS PC and returns to the UNIX shell prompt. You can transfer a binary file (such as an executable program) by using the -i option, which is invoked by keying the <SHIFT-F5> keys. For example:

```
$ utopc -i binary.text
```

One important thing to note is that files transferred to the PC are restricted to the DOS naming convention of eight primary characters and a three-character extension. In the previous two examples, the resulting files created on the DOS PC would be called *asciifil.tex*, and *binary.tex*, respectively.

The kermit protocol under ctrm also allows you to transfer files from the DOS PC to the UNIX machine with the **pctou** command. By keying the sequence <SHIFT-F4>, you bring up the **pctou** command and type in the name of the file you wish to send up to the UNIX machine:

```
$ pctou dosfile.txt
```

The resulting screen would look something like

```
Sending File     Bytes    Corrected Errors    Time
------------     -----    ----------------    ----
dosfile.txt      94/94           0            0:01
```

You can also transfer binary files to the UNIX machine. For example, keying <SHIFT-F6> would invoke the **pctou -i** command, and

```
$ pctou -i command.com
```

would transfer the *command.com* file in its binary format. Since the DOS filenames are always a maximum of 12 characters (8 primary, 3 for the extension, and 1 for the dot), the files will always be created with the exact name supplied.

You can also run DOS commands from the UNIX environment when using the ctrm package. The command sequence

```
$ msdos doscommand
```

where *doscommand* is a DOS command such as **dir**, will invoke a DOS shell, execute the DOS command, and return you to your UNIX prompt.

# Advanced Terminal Emulator Features

**833**

Some emulators allow functions normally performed on one machine to be performed on the other in a familiar language format. A somewhat standard naming convention is to use the letter "u" in front of a DOS command to allow UNIX manipulation of DOS files. For example, PC Interface by Locus Computing uses a DOS command called **udir**, which performs a DOS directory function in UNIX format. The output of a directory listing of the D: drive (which is the UNIX drive that PC Interface attaches as a logical D: drive to the DOS machine) might look something like this:

```
D> udir
 Volume in drive D is UNXDRV
 Directory of D:\
 .                 .      dah drwxr-xr-x <DIR> 01-01-94 9:00a
 ..                       dah drwxr-xr-x <DIR> 01-01-94 9:00a
file.txt       FILE TXT   dah -rwxr-r- 22091 01-02-94  3:14p
unixreport     UNIXR{KEP} dah -rwxr-r- 21130 01-02-94  6:10p
```

where the UNIX filename is shown first, then its "mapped" name (the name that PC Interface internally generates based on how it can create a DOS filename and extension from the original UNIX filename), and then information about the file.

PC Interface also provides the DOS command **uren**, which allows you to rename either a source or target file that does not follow DOS naming conventions. For example, the sequences

```
D> uren unixfiletext unix.txt
D> uren unixr{kep} unix.rpt
```

allow you to rename the UNIX file *unixfiletext* to a DOS file called *unix.txt*, and then rename the internally generated DOS filename *unixr{kep}* to the UNIX filename *unix.rpt*.

Remote command execution is an advanced feature available with some emulators. With remote execution, you are not required to log in to the UNIX machine under a terminal emulation session. As long as you are attached to a UNIX host, you can run specific commands on your connected DOS PC that are executed as UNIX commands on the UNIX host. These commands must be background commands (that is, not interactive ones such as editors like **vi**). If you want to execute a UNIX command such as **grep**, however, you can do so by creating a DOS version of the file with the *.exe* extension. Under PC Interface, for example, you can use the ON utilities to allow you to create copies of the *on.exe* file with the UNIX name as the filename part. Working in the DOS directory *C:\utility*, the DOS sequence

```
C:\utility> copy on.exe grep.exe
C:\utility> grep "counter" dosfile
```

copies the file *on.exe* into a file called *grep.exe,* and then runs the **grep** command to find occurrences of the word "counter" in the file *dosfile* on the DOS disk.

Still another enhanced feature of terminal emulators is support for Windows. An example is the Microsoft Windows User Interface Program, with a built-in terminal emulator that runs under the Windows environment. This emulator can be configured for the terminal and communications settings that you desire, and can be invoked by selecting an icon with your mouse.

# Sending Compressed Files on UNIX and DOS

If you frequently send large files from DOS to UNIX, you'll appreciate how much time can be saved if you can send compressed files. You simply need to compress the file on DOS (or UNIX) with a program than can do the uncompression on UNIX (or DOS).

The most popular compression routine for UNIX is the **compress** program. A compatible version for DOS is provided in the MKS Toolkit by Mortice Kern Systems. You can compress a file on UNIX, transfer it to a DOS system, and then use MKS Tools **uncompress** to blow it back up on DOS.

Popular programs that do file compression and archiving on DOS are **pkzip** and **pkunzip**. These have become somewhat of an industry standard for software distribution. Much shareware, as well as CompuServe material, is distributed after being archived with **pkzip**. There is a UNIX-compatible version of these routines, called **zip** and **unzip**, which are compatible with **pkzip** and **pkunzip**. On the Internet, they are stored as **unz50p1** and **zip201**.

There are dozens of sites that have these sources. A few sites that have sources for both **unz50p1** (as well as **zip201**) are

| Host | File Name |
| --- | --- |
| *ifcss.org* | */software/unix/utils* |
| *nic.switch.ch* | */mirror/Info-Zip* |

| Host | File Name |
|------|-----------|
| *sunsite.unc.edu* | */pub/packages/TeX/archive-tools/info-zip* |
| *ftp.uu.net* | */pub/archiving/zip* |
| *sprite.cica.indiana.edu* | */pub/unix* |
| *ftp.inria.fr* | */system/arch-compr* |
| *wuarchive.wustl.edu* | */mirrors/misc/unix* |
| *svin02.info.win.tue.nl* | */pub/compression/zip* |

# TIP 835

# UNIX-to-DOS File Conversions

When you transfer files between UNIX and DOS machines, you receive them in the file format of the machine you transferred them *from*. In DOS, there are two programs that convert UNIX files to DOS and vice versa: **UNIX2DOS.EXE** and **DOS2UNIX.EXE**. **UNIX2DOS.EXE** converts the UNIX line terminator of CR (carriage return) to the DOS line terminator of CR-LF (carriage return and line feed). **DOS2UNIX.EXE** converts the DOS line terminator of CR-LF to UNIX's line terminator of CR. You probably have these two on your UNIX machine as well. Such programs are often included with UNIX, but if your machine doesn't have them, it's easy to create one. One way is to use the shell script provided in Tip 409. That script searches for CRs in lines of UNIX text that you would like to use on your DOS machine and strips them.

Another way is to use the **tr** command to get rid of the carriage returns. For example, to change the carriage returns at the end of text lines in the Macintosh file *macfile* to newlines in the file *unixfile,* use

```
$ tr '\015' '\012' < macfile > unixfile
```

To strip the carriage returns from the carriage-return/newline combination at the end of text lines in the DOS file *dosfile,* use

```
$ tr -s '\015' < dosfile
```

# Using tip to Connect to a DOS PC from a UNIX System

## Accessing DOS from a UNIX Machine Using tip

If you have an emulator that recognizes requests from a UNIX host on your PC (two examples are PC Remote and PC Anywhere), you can access the DOS machine from UNIX using the **tip** command, which allows you to connect to a remote machine and then access files. The remote machine may be a DOS PC.

You can use **tip** whether you are directly connected to a DOS PC or connected via a modem. To access the DOS PC, you need to know the connection port address or telephone number for the modem to which the DOS machine is connected. This information is in the */etc/remote* and */etc/phones* files on the UNIX host. (See Tips 575 through 581 for more details on **tip**.)

Once you have established the proper machine connections betwen your DOS and UNIX machines (see Tips 577 through 581), you can transfer files from the DOS PC to the UNIX machine, or from the UNIX machine to the DOS PC, with the **tip** commands. The **tip** commands use the concept of redirection in relation to the UNIX host in their format. (For example, ~< means the file is coming from DOS to UNIX, and ~> means the file is going to DOS from the UNIX machine.)

See Tips 576 through 578 for more details on using **tip** to transfer files between DOS and UNIX machines, as well as an example of file transfers to and from a UNIX machine.

# Networking DOS and UNIX Machines

## File Sharing Using NFS

You may want to make some of your files available to users on other systems. This is especially helpful if you have a master copy of a file on your machine that other users need to access and possibly update. You may also want to use files on other machines. You can do these things with file sharing.

NFS (Network File System) is a client-server-based file system that allows you to mount and access remote file systems across both heterogeneous and homogenous systems. NFS is widely used for file services on TCP/IP networks. It allows you to share files between computers. Using NFS, you can share files on your machines with other computers running UNIX, DOS, the Macintosh OS, or other operating systems. RFS (Remote File System) only allows file sharing among UNIX machines.

To mount remote disks or directories, you need to have NFS client software running on your machine. To make your disks accessible by other remote users, you need to have NFS server software running on your machine. In an NFS environment, machines can be both clients and servers.

You can run (PC)NFS systems on your DOS PC to share your DOS files with UNIX machines and vice versa. (PC)NFS is a class of system services that can run on Intel-based PCs, as well as some other PC architectures defined by the X/Open Group.

## Where to Get (PC)NFS Software for DOS PCs

There are a number of vendors offering commercial versions of (PC)NFS software. One example is PC-NFS from SunSelect. This package runs under MS-DOS and Windows, and provides terminal emulation and file transfer capabilities, along with the NFS capability to mount and share up to 14 network devices, including printers.

Other (PC)NFS software products are IBM TCP/IP from IBM; LAN Workplace and NetWare NFS from Novell (which lets you mount files from a NetWare Server); PathWay from The Wollongong Group; and PC/TCP from FTP Corp. These last two are also available for MS-Windows systems.

If you have diskless PCs on your network, you can mount them as a device from a remote server with the following products: PC-NFS from SunSelect, PC/TCP from FTP Corp., BW-NFS from Beame and Whiteside, and AIR for Windows from SPRY.

For more information on (PC)NFS and available products, read the newsgroup *comp.protocols.nfs*, which answers FAQs on the subject.

# Using TCP/IP to Connect DOS and UNIX Machines

You can connect your DOS PCs and UNIX machines using TCP/IP, which connects computers with different architectures. With TCP/IP you can use **telnet** to log in to remote machines that run other operating systems besides UNIX SVR4, in contrast to **rlogin**, which only allows you to log in to a remote UNIX system. (See Tips 589 through 593 for more information on **telnet**.)

You may use the **ftp** command to transfer files between the DOS PC and the UNIX machine. (See Tips 594 through 604 for information on how to transfer files using **ftp**.)

# Where to Get TCP/IP Software for DOS PCs

There are a number of commercially available packages for DOS that let you perform TCP/IP functions. One example is TCP/IP for DOS, by Locus Computing Corporation. This package allows DOS PCs to communicate with a variety of dissimilar host computers, and allows file transfer and remote command execution. A second package, PC/TCP for DOS, by FTP Software Inc., is an implementation of the TCP/IP protocol suite that includes file transfer (ftp client and ftp server), network printing and backup capabilities, and IBM 3270 emulation.

You can obtain X Window environment packages that run on DOS PCs. XoftWare for DOS, by AGE, integrates Novell TCP/IP drivers into the X server, allowing easy loading of network software and X software onto the DOS PC. (There is also a version of this package for DOS machines with Tiga accelerator boards, called XoftWare for Tiga/DOS, that gives you graphics equivalent to those displayed on a dedicated X terminal.)

# Using Macintosh PCs and UNIX Machines Together

## Using Terminal Emulators on Macintosh PCs to Access UNIX Hosts

If you want to use your Macintosh PC as a terminal connected to a UNIX machine, you can do this with one of a number of commercially available terminal emulation products. Since they all provide the same basic function of a VT-series terminal (such as a VT100), you should consider whether or not you need advanced terminal emulator features (see Tip 833) before you purchase one. In addition to Macintosh's own Serial Tool in the Communications Toolbox, there are products like Pathway Access, by The Wollongong Group; LAN Workplace, by Novell; VersaTerm, by Synergy Software; and TCP Connect II Basic, by InterCon Systems Corporation.

Examples of some of the additional features provided with these emulator packages are Mail and Usenet News (VersaTerm), **whois** and **finger** utilities (LAN Workplace), and client NFS (Pathway Access and TCP Connect II Basic).

## Using TCP/IP on Macintosh PCs

To connect Macintoshes to UNIX machines, use TCP/IP. Apple's MacTCP and other commercially available products provide TCP/IP networking functions form Macintoshes. One such product is VersaTerm with Versatilities, from Synergy Software. Besides providing the common functions of mail and file transfer while running on a LAN using TCP/IP, VersaTerm lets you remotely connect to a LAN running the TCP/IP protocol, using its built-in SLIP (for Serial Line IP) protocol as a Link Access Protocol (LAP) through MacTCP. If you already have a package that runs TCP/IP on your Macintosh, you can add SLIP functionality with products that provide the Link Access Protocol (LAP) for MacTCP such as SLIP LAP for MacTCP by TriSoft, or MacSLIP by Hyde Park.

In addition, all of the other Macintosh emulator products mentioned in Tip 841 support at least the basic TCP/IP protocol capabilities.

There are also free or nearly-free (shareware) TCP/IP packages available via anonymous ftp or on the CompuServe network. NCSA Telnet/tn3270 is one of the more frequently used freeware packages. If you want remote access, InterCon Systems has announced a version of SLIP LAP for MacTCP available on the Internet. Apple's ACES organization has put together a kit called the Macintosh Networking Kit that contains shareware and freeware for TCP/IP. You can contact them at (800)624-2237.

You can transfer files between Macintosh and UNIX machines if you are on a TCP/IP network by entering a **telnet** session and using the **ftp** command.

# File Sharing for Macintosh PCs

**TIP 843**

You may want your Macintosh to act as a client or server of a UNIX machine or vice versa. This is especially helpful if you have a master copy of a file on your machine that other users need to access and possibly update. You can do these things with file sharing via NFS.

There are a number of vendors providing (PC)NFS support for Macintosh PCs. PathWay NFS, from The Wollongong Group, and NFS/Share, from Intercon, both provide NFS client software. NFS/Share allows LocalTalk-connected Macintoshes to NFS-mount remote UNIX devices, using a LocalTalk to Ethernet gateway such as a Cayman GatorBox. GatorShare, from Cayman Systems, allows Macintosh PCs to mount NFS disks as Apple File Protocol volumes treated as remote drives on the Apple Chooser.

# Using UNIX Systems as Servers for Networked PCs

## Using the UNIX System as a File Server

You may be a user of a DOS PC with a disk drive that is small or is getting full quickly. If you are attached to a UNIX machine on a LAN, you can use the UNIX file system to store some of your data and retrieve it when you need it.

Certain emulator packages also let you access files on the UNIX system as though they were your own. You may choose to have these files on the UNIX machine for security reasons, or just to take advantage of a larger file storage capability than what is on your PC alone.

For example, the Host File Services mode under PC Interface allows you to treat the UNIX disk drive as a logical Drive D: extension of your PC disk drives. You can store files and retrieve them from the D: drive just as you would any other DOS drive. To retrieve the file *references* stored on the UNIX host and put it in the current directory on your C: drive, type

```
C:\> copy d:references c:
```

You can also use (PC)NFS software and associated server software to store files on and retrieve files from a UNIX host. See Tip 837 for more information on how to do this.

## Using the UNIX System as a Print Server

You may be a user of a DOS PC with a small printer (or no printer) attached to it. If you are attached to a UNIX machine on a LAN, you can use the printing capabilities available on the UNIX machine to supplement your own DOS printer. Here are some ways you can do this.

Certain emulator packages, such as PC Interface, from Locus Computing, allow you to use the UNIX system as a print server. A print server is a machine whose function is to accept printing requests from another machine such as a PC (or a number of PCs) and print them on the server's attached printer. If you don't have a printer attached to your PC, or you want to use a larger, faster printer attached to your UNIX host, PC Interface has a service called Host File Services that lets you log in to a UNIX machine and have access to its resources, including the printer.

To use the UNIX printer, you have to map it to one of the LPT channels (communications ports) on your PC, and have the **lp** spooler package installed on your UNIX machine. The DOS command sequence

```
C:\> printer LPT1 remote "lp -dvisijet"
```

sets up the environment so that any print requests to LPT1 on the DOS PC are sent to the remote UNIX host. The **lp** spooler command on your UNIX machine then prints these requests on the destination printer named *visijet.*

# Printing UNIX Files Locally on a DOS Printer

**TIP 846**

If your DOS machine is hooked up as a terminal to a UNIX host but you have a local DOS printer hooked up to the DOS machine, you can print ASCII files directly to the DOS printer using the following script:

```
#!/bin/sh
echo "\033[5i"
cat unixfile
echo "\033[4i"
```

This script takes a filename, here called *unixfile,* and sends the local XON/XOFF commands to the printer to print it. The #! sequence is used here so that the Bourne Shell can interpret the script correctly.

# Using LANs to Connect DOS PCs and UNIX Machines

## TIP 847

## File and Print Servers

LANs (Local Area Networks) are a configuration of machines on a network that let you talk to other machines like you (called peer-peer communications) or to a central machine to which you and others like you are connected (called client/server communications). The computers in a LAN do not have to be the same. However, to communicate with others on the LAN, they must use the same LAN protocols. If you use a DOS or a Macintosh in a LAN environment, you need to understand some of the different LAN architectures available for PCs to connect to UNIX machines and how to use them.

LANs have an NOS (network operating system) built specifically to perform the functions of peers, clients, and servers in a networked environment. Examples of NOSs are LAN Manager, by HP; NetWare and UnixWare, from Novell; LAN Manager, by Microsoft; and StarGROUP LAN Manager, from NCR. All of these allow machines on the LAN to act as both file and print servers.

One of the most popular network operating systems is NetWare, from Novell. It provides a full range of network services and software to users of DOS, Windows, Macintosh, and UNIX systems on a LAN. Netware networks consist of file/print servers, workstations, network adaptors and LAN drivers, and peripherals such as printers, modems, and fax machines.

A NetWare server can act as either a file server or a print server, thus providing Novell network access for UNIX and DOS systems. There are a number of products to let you do this, including NetWare NFS. (See Tip 838.) NetWare NFS has network interface software called NetWare Flex/IP, which provides a bidirectional print gateway and eliminates the need for TCP/IP software.

The DOS implementation of NetWare is called NetWare 386, which is a C-language product that runs on Macintosh and OS/2 80386 and 80486 processor environments as well, and allows file sharing through AFS, the Andrew File System scheme for the Macintosh, and NFS, the Network File System.

For more information, read *Inside Novell NetWare* by Debra Niedermiller-Chaffins (Carmel, IN: New Riders Publishing, 1992), *Intelligent LAN Management with Novell Netware* by Elenore Amon (Englewood Cliffs, NJ: Prentice Hall, 1991), *Novell's Guide to Integrating UNIX and NetWare*

*Networks* by James Gaskin (Alameda, CA: Sybex, 1993), or contact Novell directly at (800)772-UNIX).

# Using UnixWare for File and Print Servers

UnixWare is a version of UNIX System V Release 4.2 that contains network extensions designed to work with the NetWare environment. There are two versions of UnixWare. The Personal Edition version is for a single client and server user operating environment and comes with Locus Computing's Windows Merge (a DOS Merge package for Windows) and NetWare support. The Application Server version is for unlimited client and server users, and includes DOS Merge, TCP/IP and NFS, and the Fingertip Librarian for displaying manual pages. UnixWare supports UNIX SVR4.2, DOS and Windows applications, and supports both Motif and Open Look GUIs. You can perform file printing and file access by using either a Motif or an Open Look GUI.

For more information on UnixWare, see the May 1993 issue of UNIX Review, the *Rookie's Guide to UnixWare* by The Univel Group (Novell Press, 1993), or *Guide to the UNIX Desktop: UNIX SVR4.2* by UNIX System Laboratories (Summit, NJ: UNIX Press, 1992). Or contact Novell directly, at (809)-772-UNIX.

# Using LAN Managers as File and Print Servers

There are a few commercially available products that manage LAN environments. Microsoft offers a product called Microsoft LAN Manager that supports DOS and OS/2 clients and servers. HP also offers a product called LAN Manager that supports OS/2 as well as the HP3000 environment. NCR offers a product under its StarGROUP suite called StarGROUP LAN Manager, that is a UNIX implementation of Microsoft's LAN Manager. The product networks DOS and OS/2 clients and servers together. The UNIX version, called StarGROUP LAN Manager Server, integrates a UNIX server into the network. When configured together, these two products allow users to dial in to a UNIX server and run both DOS and UNIX applications, including multiple DOS client sessions under a UNIX session.

All of these packages allow the server to offer both print and file services to the client. Having a print server offloads the client to perform other tasks while a job is printing. Having a file server allows the PC to function with a smaller hard disk, since files are stored on the server and accessed only when needed.

An example of how file access from a server is accomplished under StarGROUP LAN Manager Server is the **net use** command. If you want to access files on the server, you can do so with a command in the format

```
C:\> net use X:   \\machine.serve\user
```

where *X:* is the drive on the server containing applications or files that you want to access, *machine.serve* is the network name given to *machine* acting as the file server, and *user* is the userid requesting access to the files.

You can access printers attached to the server with a command in the format

```
C:\> net use lptx:   \\machine.serve\printer
```

where *x* is the printer port designation (for example *lpt1*), *machine.serve* is the network name given to *machine* acting as the print server, and *printer* is the definition for the printer on the server.

# Using UNIX Tools on DOS and DOS Tools on UNIX

## TIP 850

## Using Toolkits to Perform UNIX Commands on a DOS PC

UNIX users working on DOS PCs often wish they could use familiar UNIX commands instead of unfamiliar DOS commands. To help solve this problem, a number of vendors have developed commercially available tools to provide UNIX commands on DOS.

One example of these tools is the MKS Toolkit from Mortice Kern Systems. The MKS Toolkit includes over 160 of the most commonly used UNIX commands. These commands let you perform tasks under DOS by using UNIX names and UNIX tasks for which there is no DOS equivalent. They let you operate as though you were under the Korn shell.

Some of the more common commands that overlap DOS functions are

| UNIX | DOS | Function |
|------|-----|----------|
| cat | type | Lists the contents of a file |
| cp | copy | Copies a file or files |
| ls | dir | Lists files in a directory |
| pwd | cd | Displays current directory |
| rm | del | Removes a file or files |
| vi | edit | Performs screen editing |

MKS Toolkit gives you tools to perform more complicated tasks that can be better done under the UNIX environment—for example, processes using **awk** or **sed**. These are some of the most common commands for which there is no DOS equivalent:

| Command | Function |
|---------|----------|
| awk | Performs data manipulation and file processing |
| diff | Displays differences between two files |
| head | Displays the first *n* lines of a file |
| grep | Searches a string in a file |
| od | Displays binary contents of a file |
| sed | Performs stream editing |

To emulate the Korn Shell (called KornShell in MKS Toolkit) in the UNIX environment under DOS, type

```
C:\> sh
```

This puts you into the UNIX system KornShell environment under the DOS *command.com* environment. To return to the DOS environment, simply type

```
C:\> exit
```

There is a **help** command to display the options for each of the commands in the MKS Toolkit. You invoke it by typing the **help** command and then the command you want to understand better. For example, to get options associated with the **grep** command, you would type

```
C:\> help grep
```

# Using Slashes and Backslashes under MKS Toolkit

One point of confusion between DOS and UNIX users is the use of the \ (backslash) for DOS file paths and the / (slash) for command options, and the use of the slash for UNIX file paths and the - (dash) for command options. If you have a version of DOS prior to 4.0, MKS Toolkit can help, through use of the **switch** command. The command

```
C:\> switch -
```

lets you change the option designation to a hyphen to match the UNIX structure; then you can use a slash as a file path designator and a hyphen as an option designator for both DOS and UNIX command sequences. This feature works for MKS Toolkit commands, but you should make sure any DOS applications you run support this naming convention, since a number of applications expect a backslash when creating or accessing files.

In DOS versions 4.0 and later, many DOS commands don't check to see what option designation you chose, so the **switch** command won't work. You will have to use a slash for DOS options and a dash for MKS Toolkit options if you are running one of these versions.

Another point to remember is that the backslash is a logical escape character in UNIX systems. For commands you execute under MKS Toolkit's Kornshell that require a filename to include a backslash, you must use another backslash before it to make sure that the shell recognizes it. For example,

```
C:\> sortit direc\\file
```

invokes a program called **sortit** and passes it the file *direc\file* to process.

# Using Pipes and Redirection under MKS Toolkit

The concept of pipes is a UNIX invention. A pipe is a method of allowing the results of a previous command to be passed on as input to another command. While DOS allows you some limited pipes using the **find**, **more**, and **sort** filters, UNIX allows you to build much longer pipes to pass results from processes to filters to programs, and so on.

You can send command output to other processes or files using MKS Toolkit just as you would normally do on a UNIX system. The pipe sequence is supported, so that

```
C:\> cat file | wc -l
```

will pipe the output of the **cat** command to **wc**, and display the number of lines counted in *file*, and

```
C:\> cat file | wc -l > newfile
```

will put the result into the file *newfile* instead of displaying it.

# Using uucp under DOS

The UUCP system is a set of programs that allows you to communicate with, copy files between, and execute commands on remote UNIX machines. There are also several commercial products that provide the UUCP system for DOS PCs. For example, UULINK, by Vortex Technology, lets you send and receive USENET articles as well as electronic mail. RamNet/UUCP, by Software Concepts Design, performs UUCP functions in the background, and can accept file transfer and remote execution requests. There is even a computer-based training application for DOS users called Using UUCP, by the Computer Technology Group, a division of Telemedia, Inc., that teaches you the basics of UUCP mail, file transfer, and remote command execution.

The MKS Toolkit includes a package for DOS machines called MKS UUCP. Once you have loaded the uucp utilities, you must configure the uucp environment with the **uuconfig** command. See the MKS Toolkit UUCP Guide for instructions on how to do this. Once you have configured your machine environment correctly, you will be able to run the complete set of UUCP commands as you would normally run them on your UNIX environment.

Suppose you want to send a file from your DOS PC to a UNIX machine. You first need to start up the two MKS Toolkit control programs: **mksos**, which interfaces with DOS to provide file access; and **mksuucp**, which provides background control for the UUCP suite. Next you can select a file, say *data*, and transfer it to a file called *newfile* in the public UUCP directory at a remote destination site called *other*, with the command

```
C:\> uucp -m data other!~/newfile
```

The **-m** option tells **uucp** to send mail back to you upon successful transfer.

You have the ability to execute commands remotely with the **uux** command, as in the following example:

```
C:\> uux cat distant!/work/info
```

This will list the contents of the file */work/info* on the remote site *distant*, assuming that you have read privileges for this file.

There is a help command for UUCP commands, available by typing

```
C:\> help uucp
```

at the DOS prompt.

For more detailed information on the MKS Toolkit UUCP commands, you should consult the MKS Toolkit UUCP and Mail manual. For more information on the UUCP system, see Chapters 9 and 12 of this book.

# Using MKS Toolkit with Other Network and Application Environments

MKS Toolkit works with a few of the most popular environments. If you are a Windows user, MKS Toolkit supports Windows 3.0 and higher. You can invoke Windows from both the DOS and UNIX (KornShell) environments and then use MKS utilities within the Windows environment. You can do the same thing if you are running DESQview on your PC, provided that QEMM has been installed.

If you are on a network that allows file sharing and you have the appropriate drivers installed, you need only have one copy of MKS Toolkit on a server that allows you to run MKS commands on any machine on the network.

Since setting up all of these environments depends heavily on your PC configuration, it's best to consult the reference manuals or user guides for the individual products before you attempt to do anything. The *MKS Toolkit Installation Manual* gives you some helpful instructions on using all of these environments with the package.

# Performing DOS Functions on UNIX Machines

Just as UNIX users want to use UNIX command structures while working in DOS, some DOS users might like to use familiar DOS commands while working in the UNIX environment.

Many UNIX systems have some ability to read MS-DOS-formatted disks. On XENIX/SCO machines, there are some combinations of **dosput, dosget, doscp, dosdir, dosformat,** and other related commands. If you do not have these commands on your UNIX machine, you might want to get a copy of Mtools, developed by Emmet Gray. Mtools is a commercially free package available for this purpose. It writes directly to the floppy device and does not require any special privileges. Mtools comes with its own command set including **Mdel, Mcd, Mdir, Mlabel, Mread, Mcopy, Mformat,** and **Mwrite.** Mtools works on a wide variety of architectures.

You can get Mtools via anonymous ftp from *thor.ece.uc.edu* in */pub/sun-faq/mtools-2.0.7.tar.Z* or *sifon.cc.mcgill.ca* in */pub/ftp_inc/unix/mtools*.

# Program Development under Both DOS and UNIX

## TIP 856

## C Programming in DOS for Portability

There are instances where you would like to be able to execute a program that was developed for use under DOS on a UNIX machine, or vice versa. A number of vendors have developed C and C++ language compilers for DOS machines. Examples are Borland International's Turbo C and Turbo C++, and Microsoft's QuickC. These products have taken C and C++ and added ANSI-conformant extensions to allow an increase in functionality on DOS-based machines. In addition, they have menu-driven interfaces that make C program development easier for novice programmers.

If you are familiar with C, but have not extensively used C++, Turbo C++ allows you to write both standard C programs and object-oriented C++ coding routines.

There are functions to convert UNIX-formatted values to DOS-formatted values, and vice versa. For example, Turbo C++ lets you convert the UNIX time/date value into DOS time and date fields using the **unixtodos** function, and vice versa with **dostounix**.

If you are writing programs that you are considering porting from a DOS environment to UNIX, or from UNIX to DOS, you should give your system call routines functional names. Then when you move the code to the other environment, you can easily locate and modify the system calls to fit your operating system.

You should also take advantage of the **#define** and **#ifdef** directives in routines to allow you to execute the correct code for your environment. As an example, you can define the names UNIX and DOS and then perform functions based on a condition check using the following construct:

```
#define UNIX
#define DOS
....
#ifdef UNIX
...UNIX-based routine code
#endif
#ifdef DOS
...DOS-based routine code
#endif
```

This format allows the correct environment to be included at compilation time.

You should also be aware of differences in the use of data types and character representations between UNIX and DOS and reflect this in your C code. Since UNIX uses 32-bit words and DOS uses 16-bit words, you can run into problems if you port a program from UNIX to DOS in which the use of declared integers (int types) assumes 32-bit words. You should also be aware that the DOS version of ASCII code contains more representations of characters than the UNIX version does, so there will be some characters that cannot be translated between the two.

# Using make for C Programs on DOS Machines

C programs typically contain one or more executables called object files, which in turn are made up of a number of source files. When you change a source or object file that is part of a program, you need to be sure that all of the interdependent files that make up the program are also updated so that they contain the latest version of code. UNIX has a **make** utility for recompiling and linking object modules. MKS make, part of the MKS Tookit from Mortice Kern Systems, provides this for DOS PCs. To use MKS make, you supply the rules describing interdependencies and the steps for rebuilding an object or program file in a file called the *makefile*. DOS C language compilers such as Borland's Turbo C and Microsoft C use slightly different terms in their makefile files, but the form is similar:

```
target target... : prerequisite prerequisite...
        commands
```

where *target* is a file made from other files, *prerequisite* is a list of files that the targets depend on directly or indirectly, and *commands* are the commands that remake the targets. Once you have built a makefile with the appropriate set of targets, prerequisites, and commands, you can rebuild a program or object module easily at any time by issuing the command

```
C:\> make
```

which looks for *makefile* in the current directory and rebuilds according to the instructions found in the file.

For more information on MKS make, read The MKS Toolkit Make manual, part of the Essential Development Tools for Programmers, by Mortice Kern Systems.

# Running the Same Applications Programs under DOS and UNIX

## Running Applications Software on Both DOS and UNIX Machines

Many popular database, spreadsheet, and word processing packages originally written for the DOS PC have been ported to the UNIX system. Examples are dBASE IV, by Ashton-Tate; Lotus 1-2-3, by Lotus Development; Word, by Microsoft; and WordPerfect, by the WordPerfect Corporation. Some of these applications were ported to earlier versions of UNIX because files could not be easily shared across networked DOS PCs and UNIX machines. You can now use these applications in their native DOS environment on a UNIX machine. If you have a PC running a merged DOS-UNIX environment such as DOS Merge, Merge386, or VP/ix (see Tip 823), you can run DOS applications under this merged environment and they will run as they would if they were run in a stand-alone DOS environment, with some minor differences.

One of the differences is in the use of / (slash) and \ (backslash) for referring to input and output files used by the application. If you are calling the application from the UNIX shell, you should remember that the DOS application requires the backslash naming convention. If your DOS program accepts an input file as an argument, invoking a program from the UNIX shell in the format

```
$ program  drive:\path\filename
```

will look for *filename* in *path* on *drive,* but

```
$ program drive:/path/filename
```

will not.

There are some issues in how the ports of applications originally developed for DOS behave on UNIX machines. One of the simplest is in file handling. UNIX systems use only a line feed (CTRL-J) at the end of a line, while DOS uses a combination of a carriage return (CTRL-M) followed by a line feed (CTRL-J). This can cause problems when you attempt to use a file created by a UNIX version of the application on the DOS application, and vice versa. If you have trouble reading in the file, you may need to convert it to the appropriate format using the **UNIX2DOS** or **DOS2UNIX** conversion utilities available with the DOS operating system. (See Tip 835.)

Despite the differences, most of the popular newer packages such as Lotus 1-2-3, MS Word, and WordPerfect allow you to transfer documents between a UNIX and a DOS machine using internal file conversion routines, as well as to transfer files to Windows, Macintosh, and OS/2 machines.

There are some differences that must be considered when you use a UNIX application that has been ported from its original DOS version. First, most DOS applications assume a single-user environment. Since the UNIX environment is multiuser, file access becomes an issue. The application must ensure permissions are set correctly by checking to make sure that a person attempting to update a file has permission to write to the file, and to read from it. The application also should check to see if more than one person is accessing the file simultaneously. Some applications restrict file access so that they run the same way they do in the DOS environment. As an example, in the UNIX version of dBASE IV, files such as the database file can be configured to be accessible by only person at a time. In particular, the dBASE IV command

```
$ .SET EXCLUSIVE ON
```

assures that database access is restricted to the current user.

Another issue that needs to be resolved in the UNIX version is file and directory security. Certain files and directories that are needed for application control should be restricted so that users cannot accidentally erase them, or at least, they should be encrypted. These files should be owned by root, and have read only permission by all others.

There are also printed output considerations. While there are LAN versions of some DOS applications that allow shared printing, most still depend on the existence of a printer attached to the DOS PC. The **set printer** command for these will most likely have to be changed on the UNIX version to access the UNIX spooler.

# Using X Windows on DOS PCs

## Using X Windows to Run Virtual Terminal Sessions

You can run DOS sessions along with X Windows sessions when you have the Merge software installed on your UNIX machine. (See Tip 823.) Even if you are not running **vtlmgr** (the control program to manage virtual terminal sessions) on your UNIX machine, you can run an X session under a virtual terminal on the console, and run full-screen DOS sessions in other virtual consoles. You can toggle between sessions by using a hot-key sequence (such as ALT-SYSREQ-functionkey), and return to the original home console with the sequence (ALT-SYSREQ-H). If you have executed **vtlmgr**, you can switch to other virtual terminals running DOS sessions or other activities.

You can also run DOS sessions inside **xterm** windows, but you will need to configure the **xterm** window properly to run the session. Finally, for Microsoft Windows users, you can also run Microsoft Windows under a DOS session within an X session.

*Simultaneous sessions of these types are a drain on the CPU, memory, and swap space. If you attempt to do too many things at once, you will notice a significant decrease in system performance.*

## Getting an X Server for Your DOS PC

You can run an X Window system server on your DOS PC. To find information on running X Window servers for PCs, consult the monthly posting by Daniel McCoy on *comp.windows.x*. The current copy of this article can be obtained via anonymous ftp from *ftp.x.org* in contrib as *XServers-NonUNIX.txt.Z*. You may also want to read the article on PC X Servers in the March 2, 1992 issue of *Open Systems Today*.

There are a number of commercial software packages that let you turn a PC running DOS and Windows into an X server. One of the most popular is DESQview/X from Quarterdeck Office Systems. This software runs on 386 or 486 PCs, and provides a complete range of interoperability between

DOS and UNIX environments, and has an optional TCP/IP Network Manager as well as OpenLook and Motif window managers. NCR's package, PC Xsight, allows multiple programs to be run on one or more computers concurrently from a single PC workstation.

Another product is eXceed, from Hummingbird Communications. This software supports DOS and Windows environments and uses Tektronix Serial Xpress, a high-speed serial protocol that can handle increased bandwidth needs for both the DOS/Windows environment and the UNIX host machine.

Two others are PC-Xware from NCD/GSS and eXodus 5.0 from White Pine Software. PC-Xware comes with its own internal TCP/IP stack from NetManage, and an X Remote protocol for remote access. eXodus supports Macintosh, DOS Windows, and NeXT machines with a consistent user interface across all three, and the Macintosh version supports Sun's OpenWindows.

Finally, there are XoftWare for DOS and Xoftware for Tiga/DOS, both by AGE. These packages turn 286, 386, and 486 DOS PCs into X servers, and have a hot-key function to go from X to DOS or Windows applications. They support high screen resolution and the Open Look, Motif, and DECwindows graphical user interfaces.

# Displaying PC Sessions on Your UNIX X Display

The X Window environment allows you to run multiple sessions on different parts of your screen. If you have software running on your X server that allows you to display output generated from a PC on your X Terminal, you can run an X Terminal session on one part of the screen and a PC session on another. An example of a product that allows you to do this is Net-I, by Programit. You can use this product to display PC sessions for a connected DOS or OS/2 PC on your UNIX machine's X Window System display.

# Running DOS under the X Window System with Merge

If you are running the X Window System and have Merge installed, the **dos** command will create a DOS display in a new X window. You can create multiple DOS windows in this way in your X

Windows session. To be able to use DOS under the X Window System, you need to set the value of the XMERGE environmental variable. For example, if you have a vga display, you would type

```
$ XMERGE=vga; export XMERGE
```

You should put this line in your X Window startup file which is usually *.xinitrc*.

You will need to bring up the pop-up menu in your DOS window by pressing ALT-D in the DOS window to be able to use your mouse in your DOS window or to do a variety of other functions.

To exit your DOS window, type **quit** in this window.

# Chapter 14

# Using and Customizing the X Window System

# Getting Started with the X Window System

## TIP 863 — What Is the X Window System?

The *X Window System* is a client-server windowing system that works independently of an operating system. It was originally developed by Project Athena at the Massachusetts Institute of Technology and is now owned and distributed by a nonprofit organization called the X Consortium Inc. It is the world's most widely used nonproprietary windowing system, and the de facto standard for windowing systems that run outside the proprietary Microsoft OS/Windows and Apple Macintosh environments. It is the windowing system typically used in conjunction with, among others, the UNIX Operating System.

Most commercial providers of the UNIX Operating System either include the X Window System in their UNIX package, or provide it as a supported add-on product. If you have such a package or product, start by installing and trying it out according to the manufacturer's instructions. The following tips will make the most sense if you have already played with the X Window System, at least a little bit.

## TIP 864 — Obtaining the X Window System

If your UNIX package does not include the X Window System, you can buy a supported X Window System package for it from one of several software houses that distribute such packages for standard versions of UNIX. These packages usually include a library of user interface objects, called an X Window System toolkit. Popular toolkits include Athena, a rudimentary toolkit included in the original MIT distribution, and two sophisticated commercial toolkits, MOTIF and OPEN LOOK. There are many different commercial sources for the X Window System. You can find a long list of these sources in the *Open Systems Product Directory* published by UniForum. For example, one widely distributed X Window System package for UNIX System V Release 4 is OSF/Motif for UNIX from INTERACTIVE. Be sure to follow exactly the software provider's instructions for installing your package.

# Obtaining a Public Domain Version of the X Window System

In the unlikely case that your software vendor can't find an X Window System package for your version of UNIX, and you are an experienced user of software manufacturing tools such as **make**, you can obtain the standard X Window System distribution by **ftp** from *ftp.x.org* (login as "anonymous"; provide your login in place of a password) and manufacture it for your system (after doing a complete system backup). You'll need a C compiler to use **make**. Don't try this without prior experience in software manufacturing; it may be easier to switch to a version of UNIX for which supported X Window System packages are available. You will also need a large amount of disk space for the X Window System; make sure this is available before beginning.

# Getting X Windows Software for Intel-Based UNIX Systems

There are several places to get X Windows software for Intel-based UNIX systems. These include several commercial options and several public domain versions. You can find a list of these sources in the FAQs in the newsgroup *comp.windows.x.i386unix.*

The best source for free X Windows software for Intel-based UNIX systems is XFree86. You can find sources for this software in these FAQs, as well as information about running XFree86.

# The Client-Server Model for X Windows

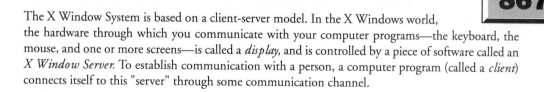

The X Window System is based on a client-server model. In the X Windows world, the hardware through which you communicate with your computer programs—the keyboard, the mouse, and one or more screens—is called a *display,* and is controlled by a piece of software called an *X Window Server.* To establish communication with a person, a computer program (called a *client*) connects itself to this "server" through some communication channel.

In the X Windows world, client software talks with the server through a predefined set of message formats called the *X Window System Protocol*. Messages sent by a client to the server are called *requests*, since they request actions by the server or information from it. Messages sent by the server to its clients are either "responses" that provide the requested information or feedback on the success or failure of the requested action, or "events" that tell the client that some event it might be interested in has taken place.

The X Window System is a *distributed* windowing platform, which means that, as long as two computers can communicate with each other at an acceptable speed, clients on one can use a server running on the other. For example, you can put the encyclopedia CD-ROM on a machine other than your own, but still run its software as a *remote client* to your desktop X server. When you do this, the encyclopedia program actually runs on the hardware of the second machine, but you communicate with it through the X server on your machine, so it looks and feels as though it were running on your computer instead of theirs.

The X Window System is a windowing platform independent of the operating systems on the machines on which it runs. This means that a client program running under UNIX, or on a Lisp Machine, can use an X server running on a stand-alone X Terminal, or under DOS on an old PC that's not up to running UNIX by itself any more. That old 386 might still be good for running an X Window Server, giving you access to your UNIX programs from a remote part of the house.

# TIP 868 — Window Managers

The window manager in X Windows is a special client that provides the set of features that produce the look and feel of the window system. These features include the window layout, the window borders, the way windows are created, how windows are moved, keyboard mappings, color mappings, onscreen menus, and so on. When a client needs to create a new window, the client and the server ask the window manager how this window should be displayed. Since the window manager is just a client, you can replace one window manager with another to change the look and feel of your window system.

There are more than 20 different window managers for the X Window System (see the FAQs for a list). The most commonly used window managers include **olwm** (the *Open Look Window Manager*); **mwm** (the *Motif Window Manager*); **gwm** (Bull's *Generic Windows Manager*), which can emulate other window managers using a built-in Lisp interpreter; **twm** (the *Tab Window Manager*, also called

Tom's *Window Manager*), which is a configurable tool for creating customized X Windows environments; and **tvtwm** (*Tom's Virtual Tab Window Manager*), based on **twm**, which provides a virtual desktop.

You can customize the menus and actions of your window manager. However, before doing so, you should spend some time using it and you should read the appropriate manual page. You will find directions for customizing the window manager on this manual page.

Some commercial applications have been built to work with a particular window manager, usually **olwm** or **mwm**. These were created with the appropriate toolkits available to programmers for developing applications running in the environment created by a particular window manager.

# Basic Hardware Requirements

**TIP 869**

Running the X Window System on a computer requires a high level of performance and a large amount of memory, since X Windows is complex and will not work well on machines with slow clock speeds. You will need a high-resolution graphics display, perhaps one that supports color, and a mouse or some other pointing device.

# X Terminals

**TIP 870**

*X terminals* are designed for use with the X Window System. These terminals have a large amount of memory and high-quality graphics screens. They do not have local disks or general-purpose CPUs. X terminals generally contain X server software in ROM. Clients connect to X terminals over a LAN. One of the major advantages of X terminals is that they can be less expensive than computers with general-purpose CPUs. However, when X terminals are used, the UNIX host they are connected to must be set up to support X terminals using **xdm** (the *X Display Manager*) or **xsm** (the *X Session Manager*).

You can find the latest information on X terminals, along with prices, posted quarterly by Jim Morton to the newsgroup *comp.windows.x.*

# TIP 871

## Display Sizes and Readability

For maximum productivity with the X Window System, get the largest monitor you can find. The amount of usable information you get from your screen depends on the physical size and number of the characters and symbols, more than on the number of pixels. For example, you can read more from a 19-inch screen with $1152 \times 900$ resolution than from a 14-inch screen with a $1280 \times 1024$ resolution.

The amount of material you can read from your display increases with the square of monitor size and resolution. A large $1600 \times 1280$ pixel display can show not twice, but four times as much text as an $800 \times 640$ pixel display.

The usable resolution of a color monitor depends more on its mesh size than on the electronics used to drive it. In calculating effective resolution, keep in mind that one inch equals 25.4 millimeters. For example, a 15-inch diagonal ($12 \times 9$ inches) screen with a .48 mm mesh has a maximum usable resolution of $12 \times 25.4 / .48$, that is, 635 pixels, even when driven by a $1024 \times 768$ framebuffer.

Color is glitzier, but your personal productivity will benefit more from larger size and higher resolution, even without color. Without a mesh to reduce resolution, you can sometimes buy a 1600-pixel monochrome monitor for less than you'd pay for an 800-pixel color monitor of the same physical size.

# Customizing and Running Your X Window System

# TIP 872

## Starting Up X Windows

The command that starts up the X Window System on your computer's console display, such as the **openwin** command on SUN workstations, is almost always a shell script. You can read this shell script to find out what happens to the arguments to your startup command. In **openwin**, they are passed through as arguments to the Xnews X server.

You can make your X server work faster with options that eliminate computationally expensive features you don't use. For example, if you don't use any of the old SunView applications, you can make Xnews on SUN workstations much faster with an initial command of

```
$ openwin -nosunview
```

instead of just **openwin**.

# Multiscreen Displays

You can have more than one screen as part of your display. Some of the hardware for additional screens may already be built into your workstation. For example, every SUN IPC with a color framebuffer also has a monochrome framebuffer for a second, monochrome screen. To use it, all you need is a second monitor—a monochrome one—to attach to this framebuffer.

When there are monitors attached to more than one framebuffer on your workstation, you can start up your server in multiscreen mode by specifying the framebuffer devices on the server startup command line. For example, on a SUN IPC with monitors attached to color and monochrome framebuffers, you can get two screens with the command

```
$ openwin -dev /dev/fb -dev /dev/bwtwo0
```

# Specifying on Which Screen to Display a Client

When starting up an X Window System client, you can use the **display** option to specify on which screen to display it. For example, on a workstation with a local server, you can specify the first screen (the one corresponding to the first -**dev** option on the multiscreen server's command line) with

```
"-display uunix:0.0"
```

and the second screen with

```
"-display unix:0.1"
```

This also works with the DISPLAY shell environment variable.

# Overriding the Value of DISPLAY

**875**

The DISPLAY shell environment variable, or the **-display** *<spec>* argument on the shell command line that starts up a client, can be used to tell the client to connect with a non-default X server and screen. If the value of DISPLAY and the *<spec>* on the command line differ, the command line will override the DISPLAY variable. In fact, client arguments given on the command line will override all other sources of client customization specs, including the resource files described in Tip 911. Command line arguments can be overridden only from within the client, by the application itself.

# Setting the DISPLAY Variable

**876**

The value of DISPLAY, or the *<spec>* part of a **-display** *<spec>* client command line argument, is composed of three parts. The first part of a DISPLAY value is separated from the rest by a : (colon). It tells the client which network endpoint, such as a specific network port on a specific system, it should connect itself to, to get to the server you want. It can be a system or port or terminal name, or the numerical address of a network port. The default value for this part, which is assumed if it is left blank, is the reserved name "unix", which points to the local UNIX system on which the client is running. It means "connect yourself to an X Window Server that's already running on the same computer as yourself."

The second part of a DISPLAY value is the number of a specific set of display hardware—keyboard, pointer, and screen(s)—and of the server that controls this hardware, and that the client is to connect itself to. It is there because on some computers, one can plug in a card to connect with a separate keyboard, pointer, and display monitor, for use by more than one user through more than one X Window System server process. On most computers there is only one display: the default, number zero. So the shortest and most common legal DISPLAY setting is

```
$ DISPLAY=:0; export DISPLAY
```

The last part of the $DISPLAY value or **-display** *<spec>* is the screen number, separated from the display (or server) number with a . (period). It is zero for the first screen, 1 for the second screen, and so on, in the order in which the **-dev** *</dev/frame-buffer>* arguments were given on the server (for example, **xnews**) startup command line or startup script (for example, **openwin**) command line. So, another way of specifying the default screen of the default local server would be

```
unix:0.0
```

# Two Common Problems You Can Have When Running an X Windows Program on a Remote Machine

**TIP 877**

There are two common problems that arise when you try to run a graphical program on a machine other than the console or the local machine. First, you may have forgotten to use the **xhost** command to allow a secondary host to access the graphical program. (See Tip 930.) Second, you may have forgotten to set your DISPLAY variable on the local machine. (See Tip 876.)

# Specifying Positions of Screens

**TIP 878**

With a multiscreen X server, your mouse cursor can be made to move smoothly between screens, sliding off the edge of one screen and onto the other. To do this, you must specify the positions of any additional screens relative to the first screen. For example, you can specify

```
$ openwin -dev /dev/fb -dev /dev/twtwo0 left
```

if your monochrome monitor is sitting to the left of the color one. Acceptable positions are left, right, top, and bottom.

# Using a Workspace to Save Setup Information

Under some window managers, such as Open Windows, you can set up the monitor however you want using various menus (such as the number of windows and their positions, sizes, whether they are iconified, colored, titled, and so on). This will create the appropriate entries in your startup files so every time you log in, your monitor will be as you like.

# The Session Script

Your actual work session under the X Window System is controlled by a session script. If you are using an "always running" server (or terminal, and so on) under **xdm**, the session script is taken from file *.xsession* in your home directory. If you start your session from a script that invokes **xinit** to run the server, your session script is *$HOME/.xinitrc*. Your session script is executed using your $SHELL, which defaults to **/bin/sh**.

Here is an example of a *.xinitrc* file:

```
# For 1152x900 color screen:
exec 1>$HOME/.openwin-out 2>$HOME/.openwin-err
xrdb $HOME/.Xdefaults                    # Load Users X11 resource database
$OPENWINHOME/lib/openwin-sys             # OpenWindows system initialization
xhost +`hostname`

xclock -update 1 -hl red -geometry 108x108--3+-8 &
xterm +ah -geometry 80x57--3--3 &
xterm +ah -C -name CONSOLE -geometry 80x8-115+-8 \
        -xrm 'CONSOLE*pointerColorBackground:yellow' \
        -xrm 'CONSOLE*pointerColor:blue' \
        -xrm 'CONSOLE*background:lightgoldenrodyellow' \
        -xrm 'CONSOLE*pointerShape:sailboat' &
xterm +ah -geometry 80x57+-4--3 &

olwm
```

See the following tips on how to customize your own *.xinitrc* file.

# Redirecting the Standard Error of Clients

If you start your X Window System from the console of your workstation, the diagnostic output (standard error) of your clients will be directed, by default, to that console, and may "break through" your X display screen. Since you will probably wish to save diagnostic output to a file anyway, just in case you might actually need it for debugging, the first line in your session script should be something like

```
exec 2>$HOME/client.err
```

Some X Window System clients have been (mis)designed to output diagnostic information to standard output instead of standard error. You can send this output to the same file as the standard error by putting the following at the head of your session script:

```
exec 2>$HOME/client.err >&2
```

If a client's diagnostics are verbose to the point of interfering with your use of the client error file, you can discard a specific client's standard output and standard error by redirecting them to */dev/null.* For example,

```
xhost + >/dev/null 2>&1
```

# Avoiding Hung Up Sessions

One of the most annoying situations that can arise in using the X Window System is to be left with a live session that cannot be gracefully terminated because, although the window manager client has quit, you continue to be connected to the now unmanaged server. Sometimes when this happens, the only way to recover control over your workstation is to reset and reboot it. To avoid this situation, the window manager's startup command should be the last command in your session script. Here is an example:

```
olwm 2>$HOME/olwm.err
```

It should be given without a terminal & (ampersand), so that when the window manager quits, the session script will exit, and **xinit** or **xdm** will safely terminate your session.

## TIP 883 — Setting Up and Starting Clients

X Windows clients inherit the keyboard map and the resource database values in effect when they first connect to the server. If you use **xmodmap** and **xrdb** to customize the behavior of other clients, be sure to run them synchronously (without a terminal &) before you start any other clients. It is a good idea to cluster all the customization clients (**xmodmap**, **xrdb**, **xset**, **xsetroot**, **xhost**) and run them all before starting any application clients.

Between output redirection and running customization clients at the beginning, and starting up the window manager at the end, your session script should list all the application clients you'd like to have available as you work.

All application client startup lines should be terminated with an & (ampersand) for asynchronous (background) execution. If you forget the terminal ampersand, your session script will never get to the lines that start subsequent application clients and the window manager.

## TIP 884 — Using the topLevelShell Widget

Most X Window System applications are built using the topLevelShell widget to communicate with the shell command line and with whatever window manager you are using. You can learn to use many of the facilities provided in this widget by reading the topLevelShell widget manual page.

Sometimes you may want to start up some applications from your session script even though you don't expect to use them immediately, just to have them available in the future, when you may need them, without waiting for them to start up. If an application was built using the topLevelShell widget, you can use the **-iconic** option on the command line in your session script to start it up in a pre-iconified state.

An application built with the topLevelShell widget can use any picture specified in a bitmap file as its icon picture. To specify the bitmap file, use the option

```
-xrm '*iconPixmap:<file>'
```

where *<file>* is the pathname, in your UNIX file system, of the bitmap file containing the picture you want.

# Creating a Bitmap File of a Picture

**TIP 885**

You can create a bitmap file of any picture you want using the **bitmap** utility. You can invoke **bitmap** from any shell window or shell script, including your session script if you wish. The resulting bitmap files can be used as sources for icons, cursors, background tiles, and other graphical objects.

# Labeling the Icon of an Application Client

**TIP 886**

You can control the text used to label any application client's icon with the following option:

```
-xrm '*iconLabel:<string>'
```

The *<string>* could be any string of visible characters, including blanks, and so on.

You can specify the font used to display any application client's icon label with the option

```
-xrm '*iconFont:<font>'
```

where *<font>* is any acceptable X Window System specification of a font listed in the output of **xlsfonts** for your display. Try

```
-xrm '*iconFont:*zapfchancery*'
```

# Specifying the Title in a Title Bar

You can specify any title you want to be displayed in the title bar of the window frame with which the window manager will decorate an application client. Use the option **-title**. For example:

```
-title 'This is my favorite hack'
```

Don't forget to put in quotes any title that contains spaces or other characters that are special to the shell.

# Saving Time Moving and Browsing Through Windows

You can minimize the time you spend moving and browsing through windows by carefully designing the layout of applications in your default screen and specifying the geometry of each application in your session script (*.xinitrc* or *.xsession*). The geometry option to X Window System applications has the form

```
-geometry <WIDTH>x<HEIGHT><+|-><X-OFFSET><+|-><Y-OFFSET>
```

It has three parts: the size (*<WIDTH>x<HEIGHT>*) of the application's main window; a pair of *<+|->* components specifying a reference corner; and an offset vector between corresponding corners of the application window and the whole screen.

The size (*<WIDTH>x<HEIGHT>*) part of the geometry argument is specified in pixels for graphics applications, and in character cells for text applications such as the **xterm** terminal emulator.

# Specifying the Reference Corner and Offset Values of Application Windows

The pair of signs preceding the x-offset and the y-offset for positioning the window specifies which of the four possible corners will serve as the reference corner for positioning a corner of the window relative to the corresponding corner of the screen. The pair (+,+) specifies the upper left-hand corner; (+,–) the lower left-hand corner; (–,+) the upper right; and (–,–) the lower right.

The pair of offset values specifies how far, toward the center of the screen, to displace the specified corner of the application window relative to the corresponding corner of the screen. So, for example,

```
+100-50
```

and

```
++100-+50
```

both mean "100 pixels horizontally toward the center (that is, to the right) and 50 pixels vertically toward the center (that is, up) from the lower left-hand corner of the screen, to the corresponding corner of the application window".

# Hiding Pixels of a Window

An *<x-offset>* or a *<y-offset>* value in a **-geometry** *<spec>* can be made negative in order to place a window partially offscreen. For example, to hide the leftmost ten pixels of a window by placing them offscreen, you should specify a y-sign and y-offset of + –10. On a small screen, it is sometimes useful to place the relatively useless edges and borders of application windows partially offscreen; for example, "+3+ –3" to hide a window's 3-pixel upper and right-hand borders.

# TIP 891

## Placing Windows Side by Side

If your screen is large enough, it is often helpful to be able to see two windows side by side, not obscuring each other, and to make each window as tall as your screen will accommodate. If you do this, you might set up more than one window on each side of your screen. Consider the following example taken from a session script with the font resource set to

```
*Font: -b&h-*-bold-r-*-*-14-*-*-*-m-*-*-*
```

for a 1600 x 1280 screen:

```
xclock -name "time" -geometry 113x113--5+-4 -update 1 &
xterm -geometry 80x83+-3+1 -name leftWxterm -C &
xterm -geometry 80x83+750+-4 -name rightNxterm &
xterm -geometry 80x83+13+-4 -name leftNExterm &
xterm -geometry 80x83+13--3 -name leftSExterm &
xterm -geometry 80x83+750--3 -name rightSxterm &
olwm 2>$HOME/olwm.err
```

In the above example, there are two sets of terminal emulator (*xterm*) windows side by side with each other: three on the left and two on the right.

In selecting among overlapping windows within each side-by-side set, it helps to have a readily accessible part of each window frame where it is never obscured by another window. The most readily accessible place to which one can move the mouse is an edge of the screen. Thus, in the left-hand set of **xterm**s above, the W(*est*) **xterm** can be selected by clicking on the left-hand edge of the screen, the NE by clicking on the left half of the top edge, and the SE by clicking on the left half of the bottom edge of the screen. Either of the right-hand **xterm**s can be selected by clicking on the right half of the top or the bottom edge.

# The xterm Client

## The xterm Client

**T**IP
**892**

The **xterm** (for *X term*inal) client provides a window for terminal emulation. In this window, you can execute UNIX commands, run shell scripts, or start other X clients. Usually when your system sets up your X environment, it creates an xterm window for you. You can create another xterm window using

```
$ xterm &
```

or selecting the appropriate menu option in the Workspace menu.

When you create a new window in either of these ways, the new window will appear, after the delay required for processing, in the default position with the default size for new windows. Your shell in this new window will be the shell specified by your SHELL environmental variable. Be sure to put the line

```
TERM=xterm
```

in your *.profile,* if appropriate, or to set TERM to xterm inside the window. This will allow you to run full-screen applications in the window in the way you want.

You can manage an xterm client by using the set of menus that come with it. Depending on the version of **xterm** you have, to bring up these menus, you either position the pointer and press the right mouse button or you press CTRL and one of the mouse buttons to get one of three different menus. By selecting menu items, you can perform a wide variety of functions, including redrawing the contents of the window, showing a talk window, killing processes running in the window, editing a block of text, selecting blocks of text for cutting and pasting to other screens, and so on.

# Killing an xterm Window

To kill an xterm window running your shell, you need only exit this shell. You can do so either with the **exit** command or by typing CTRL-D (or in the other ways specified in Chapter 3). You can also kill an **xterm** window by selecting the Exit choice in the **xterm** menu. When you kill an **xterm** window, all applications running in it are killed unless you ran them using **nohup**.

# Creating a Window for a Particular Command with xterm

Instead of running a shell in a new xterm window, you can specify a particular command to run inside the window. To do this, put -e followed by the command line you would like to run inside this window as the last argument to your **xterm** command line.

For example, you can run the **emacs** text editor on the file notes in an xterm window, using

```
$ xterm -e emacs notes &
```

To remote log in to the machine jersey and run a shell on jersey in an xterm window, use

```
$ xterm -e rlogin jersey &
```

When you finish the application, the window session will end and the window will disappear. This saves you the bother of removing the window yourself.

# Setting Color Options for xterm

You can set the foreground and background colors used for your screen when you use **xterm**. To set these colors to black and blue, respectively, use

```
$ xterm -fg black -bg blue &
```

You can see all the available colors on your system using the **xcolors** client, if this client is supported. When you have a monochrome display, you will have only two choices for these colors, generally black and white. You can switch the foreground and background colors by switching to reverse video, using

```
$ xterm -rv &
```

# Some X Clients to Know About

## Using the xclock Client

It is often useful to be able to see at a glance what time it is. You can make sure you have this information available by putting a line such as

```
xclock -analog -geometry 113x113--5+-4 &
```

in your *.xinitrc* or other session script file. It is best if you try never to obscure the clock, since you can forget the time very easily when having fun. But if it does get obscured anyway, positioning it in a corner, as in the example above, lets you select it with the mouse at any time to bring it up.

If you include the option **-update 1** on the **xclock** command line, your clock will be updated each second; if it is an analog clock, it will have a second hand that will move every second. It is best not to do this if your X Window Server is running on a remote terminal rather than directly on your UNIX machine. Redrawing the clock each second generates a lot of network traffic and can bring down a congested network quite easily.

## Mail Notification with xbiff

The **xbiff** client is used to display an icon of a mailbox in a small window on your screen. When a mail message arrives, your terminal beeps, the flag on the mailbox icon is raised, and in some implementations, the window switches to reverse video. You can reset the icon, bringing the flag back to its original position by reading the message or by clicking on the raised flag.

# Using xlock to Lock Your Workstation

**TIP 898**

Most X Window System distributions include **xlock**, a utility that keeps others from accessing your files from the X "desktop" while you are away from your desk. **xlock** will take over the screen and display a changing pattern designed to prevent phosphor burnout that might result from continuous display of an unchanging screen. This also hides what you had on the screen from any prying eyes. While **xlock** is running, it grabs the keyboard, so that no one can unlock your workstation without knowing your password.

The password **xlock** expects is the same one you use at login. If you mistype your password at **xlock**, just press RETURN twice and try again. **xlock** does not let you edit the password once you have started to type it.

Sometimes you may want to lock your workstation quickly when you suddenly need to leave or to hide your screen. See Tip 919 to see how to lock your shell by pressing just one key.

# How to Find Out Which X Windows Clients Are Available on Your System

**TIP 899**

To find out which other X Windows clients you can use, check out the *man1* subdirectory of the *man* directory in the X Window System package you are using. The files you see describe many interesting programs and useful tools. If any of the names intrigue you, just execute **man**. Or, if you've gotten this far and you prefer, execute **xman** with that filename (omit any suffixes or prefixes separated by periods, and shared by all manual pages in the directory, from the client name you use with **man** or **xman**). If your X Window System package is correctly installed, the appropriate manual page will be displayed on your screen. If what you read sounds useful or fun, try it out.

# Using the X Windows Calculator, xcalc

**TIP 900**

The **xcalc** client puts a display of a scientific calculator emulating either a Texas Instruments TI-30 or a Hewlett-Packard HP-10C in a window. To emulate a TI-30 (the default), use

```
$ xcalc &
```

To emulate a HP-10C that uses Reverse Polish Notation, use

```
$ xcalc -rpn &
```

Once you enter one of these commands, you will see a window with a calculator in it. You can give input to the calculator either by clicking on the first pointer button on buttons in the calculator window or by typing the numbers and symbols on the calculator using your keyboard.

You can kill your calculator by positioning the pointer on the calculator and typing **q** or **Q**, pressing CTRL-C, or clicking the third pointer button on the Ac key of the TI-30 or the On key of the HP-10C.

# X Windows-Based Editors

TIP 901

There are several X Windows-based text editors. Be careful when switching to one of these from your current text editor, since there can be a lot of overhead unlearning some of the editing commands you use on a daily basis.

For example, you can obtain a version of GNU **emacs** that includes X support from *prep.ai.mit.edu* in */pub/gnu*. You can also obtain Epoch, which is a modified version of GNU **emacs** with extra facilities useful in an X environment. Anonymous ftp sources include *cs.uiuc.edu* in *~ftp/pub/epoch-files/epoch*. Another version of GNU **emacs** that requires X Windows to run and includes support for multiple windows, input and display of extended characters, keymap support, and so on, is lucid **emacs**, available from *labrea.standford.edu* in */pub/gnu/lucid/directory*.

The **vi**-like microemacs editor **VILE** acts much like **vi** running in an **xterm** window. You can obtain it via anonymous ftp from *ftp.cayman.com* in *pub/vile*.

A large number of other X Windows-based text editors are described in the FAQs in *comp.windows.x*.

# X Windows-Based Mail Readers

TIP 902

An X Windows-based version of the mailer **mh**, called **xmh**, is included in the standard distribution of the X Window system. *MMH* (for *My Mail Handler*) is a Motif interface to the MH mail handler. It is available via anonymous ftp from *ftp.eos.ncsu.edu* in *pub/bill.tar.Z. MuMail* is an

X Windows-based Elm-like mailer. It is available from *sipb.mit.edu* in */pub/seyon/MUMAIL*. There are also a variety of commercial X Windows-based mailers, including *Z-Mail* with a Motif interface. See the FAQs in *comp.windows.x* for the latest information on X Windows-based mail readers.

## TIP 903 — X Windows-Based Paint Programs

The program *XPaint 2.1* is a color bitmap/pixmap editing tool that includes most of the standard features of paint programs. You can edit multiple images at the same time. You can obtain this program using anonymous ftp from *ftp.x.org* in the file *contrib/xpaint-2.1.0.tar.Z*. Other public domain and commercial software products of this type are listed in the FAQs in *comp.windows.x*.

## TIP 904 — X Windows-Based Drawing Programs

The **xfig** program is an object-oriented drawing program that supports compound objects. The format it uses can be converted to PostScript and several other formats. You can obtain this program from *ftp.x.org* in */contrib/R5fixes*. **xpic** is another object-oriented drawing program; it supports multiple font styles, point sizes, and line widths. However, **xpic** lacks some important features such as rotations and zooming. It is included in some versions of X Windows; look for the file *clients/xpic*). Other X Windows-based drawing programs, both public domain and commercial, are listed in the *comp.windows.x* FAQs.

## TIP 905 — Viewing Pictures with xv

You can view pictures in a wide variety of formats under the X Window System using the **xv** (for *X v*iew) program. You can also use this program to convert between formats, blow up and shrink pictures, change colors, and so on. You can obtain **xv** via anonymous ftp from *src.doc.ic.ac.uk* in */usenet/comp.sources.x/volume10* and from *relay.iunet.it* in */disk0/comp.sources/X/Volume10*.

# Grabbing Screen Images with xgrabsc

You can use the **xgrabsc** (for *X grab sc*reen) program to grab a rectangular screen image, such as a PostScript or X11 screen dump, and store it as a file. You can obtain the source for **xgrabsc** via anonymous ftp from *kappa.rice.edu* in */X11R4/bin/xgrabsc* or from *relay.iunet.it* in */disk0/comp.sources/X/Volume9.*

# X Windows-Based Clients for Internet Services

You can take advantage of X Windows-based clients for many different Internet services. Here is a list of some of these clients:

| Internet Service | X Windows Client |
| --- | --- |
| Gopher | **xgopher** |
| Archie | **xarchie** |
| Wais | **xwais** |
| Netnews | **xrn** |
| Netnews | **xvnews** |
| World Wide Web | **xmosaic** |

# Some Other Useful X Windows-Based Clients

There are a large number of different X Window System client programs available in the public domain. Some of these may already be installed on your system. Look in the X bin directory, which may be called */usr/X/bin* or */usr/bin/X11* on your system, to find out which clients you already have available.

Some of the clients you may find on your system include some amusing display programs, such as **aquarium**, which displays swimming fish in the screen background; **ico**, which displays a bouncing ball; **kaleid**, which displays a changing kaleidoscope; **xeyes**, which displays moving eyes that follow the pointer; **xgranite**, which displays a granite pattern in the background; and **xphoon**, which displays the phase of the moon in the background.

Be forewarned that any live animation clients, including some of those listed here, can bring down a network because of the large overhead in periodically redrawing a bitmap. This requires a large amount of data to be shipped over the network at frequent intervals, causing major network problems!

You can also obtain X Windows-based spreadsheets: for example, an X Windows-based version of **sc**, which supports Lotus files, from *vernam.cs.uwm.edu* in *xspread2.1.tar.Z*. There are quite a few different commercial X Windows-based project management software products. See the FAQs in *comp.windows.x* for details.

There are also X-based PostScript previewers, X-based troff previewers, X-based TeX previewers, X-based debuggers, X-based plotting programs, and so on. See the FAQs in *comp.windows.x* for more information.

# Resource Variables and Translations

## Using Resource Variables

In addition to shell command-line arguments, the behavior of X Window System clients and the appearance of their windows may be customized using *resource variables*. In the X Window System, a resource is not a commodity available in limited quantities, but rather a named variable that pertains to an object or a class of objects. An object may be an application or a component of an application, such as a widget (of the kind most applications are built from). When an application starts up, it reads in the current values of all applicable resource variables, stores them in a private copy of the resource database, and uses them to control its appearance and behavior.

Every application or other object in the X Window System has an individual name, which may be individually set for each instance of the object, and a class name, which is usually fixed and the same for all the objects in the class. For example, any instance of the **xterm** terminal emulator may be given a specified individual name with the **-name** *<newname>* command-line argument; but the class name of all the instances of **xterm** is XTerm (note that not only the X but also the following T are capitalized). The default instance name is usually a lowercase version of the class name—in this instance, "xterm".

The values of resource variables are usually specified in the form

> *objectName*resource*: value*

An example would be

```
xterm*scrollBar: on
```

Of they may be specified in the form

> *Class*resource*: value*

as in the following example:

```
XTerm*pointerShape: sailboat
```

*The latter assignment applies to all objects of class "XTerm", unless otherwise specified for an individual case, while the former does not apply unless "xterm" (the default) is still an instance's individual name.*

# Specifying Default Values of Resources

It is also possible to specify the default value that a resource is to have in any object having a resource of that name, unless otherwise specified. This is done by omitting the object name/class, and starting the assignment with just an asterisk. For example, to specify a font for all occasions, subject to exceptions as further specified, you would write

```
*Font:  *courier-bold-r-normal--12*
```

*"Font" is a class of resources whose individual names may be "font", "titleFont", "buttonFont", and so on.*

# The Resource Database

**Tip 911**

To be accessible to all clients, even those running on different host computers without access to your computer's disk, the authoritative copy of the resource database is stored on the server, as a property of its "root" or whole-screen window. Since every client makes a private copy of the resource database for its own use, it can override the common values with whatever exceptions were specified on its startup command line. Once a client starts, it usually ignores subsequent changes to the resource database. However, some clients (such as **olwm**—see Tip 868) request to be notified of changes to the resource database, and try to track those changes where possible.

When you first start to use an X Window Server, for example at the beginning of your *.xinitrc,* you need an **xrdb** command to populate the resource database with your preferred resource values. **xrdb** usually takes its input from a file, often called *$HOME/.Xdefaults* or *$HOME/.Xresources,* in which you have stored those values. Thus, the usual first line in a *$HOME/.xinitrc* is

```
xrdb -load $HOME/.Xresources
```

Like other customization clients at the beginning of your *.xinitrc,* **xrdb** should be run synchronously (without the & at the end), to make sure that it completes its task before any of your application clients (started with &) reads the resource database to configure itself.

Each resource specification in the file should be on a line of its own. If a single resource specification needs to be specified on more than one line, it may be continued to the next physical line with a \ (backslash). If the value of a resource includes more than one line of text (this is often the case with translations resources), the newlines embedded in its value must be written as *"\n."*

Resource values may include blank characters, such as spaces or tabs. Everything, beginning with the first nonblank character after the *":",* up to the next unescaped newline, becomes part of the stored value. Try to avoid the common yet difficult-to-find error of including invisible characters between the value you want and the end of the line. If, for example, you specify

```
xclock*hands: yellow
                    ^
                    |
             (invisible characters here)
```

the hands of the clock won't turn yellow, because **xclock** will look in the color database not for "yellow" but for "yellow<TAB>", and of course will not find any such color.

Some time after we first set up resource files, most of us tend to forget exactly why we decided to select certain values and not others. Fortunately, you can put comments about your choice in an X Window System resource file by prefixing each comment line with an ! (exclamation sign) in the first column.

Here is an example of a typical global resource file, *.Xdefaults*:

```
! .Xdefaults for 1152x900 color screen
*Font:   *courier-bold-r-normal--12*
*Scrollbar.JumpCursor:   True
*basicLocale:   C
*cursorColor:   red
*cursorMaskColor:       yellow
*displayLang:   C
*inputLang:   C
*numeric:   C
*saveLines:   1024
*scrollBar:   on
*timeFormat:   C
OpenWindows.AutoReReadMenuFile: true
OpenWindows.Beep:       always
OpenWindows.DragRightDistance:   100
OpenWindows.IconLocation:       top
OpenWindows.MultiClickTimeout:   4
OpenWindows.PopupJumpCursor:     True
OpenWindows.ScrollbarPlacement: right
OpenWindows.SelectDisplaysMenu: False
OpenWindows.SetInput:   followmouse
OpenWindows.WindowColor:        goldenrod
OpenWindows.WorkspaceColor:     turquoise
XTerm*cursorColor:      blue
XTerm*internalBorder:   2
XTerm*pointerColor:     yellow
XTerm*pointerColorBackground:   red
XTerm*scrollbar.background:     red
XTerm*scrollbar.foreground:     yellow
XTerm*scrollbar.thumb: \
   /usr/openwin/share/include/X11/bitmaps/black
XTerm*scrollbar.width:   7
XTerm*visualBell:       True
```

```
xclock*background:      blue
xclock*foreground:      white
xclock*hands:    yellow
```

# How to Find Out the Resources Available for Customizing an Application

To find out what resources are available to customize an application, read its manual page. For example, if you would like to specify the hand color of **xclock**, the **xclock(1)** manual page will tell you about the *hands* resource. If the value of a resource is of type *color,* you can specify any value in the output of the shell command **showrgb**.

# Choosing Fonts

The X Window System provides its users with hundreds of fonts for the display of text in various character sets, styles, weights, slants, heights, widths, spacings, and so on. You can use the **xlsfonts**, **xfd**, and **xfontsel** utilities (read their manual pages) to choose an appropriate font for assignment to just about any font-valued resource.

# Setting Boolean-Valued Resources

Boolean (true/false) valued resources can be set with a variety of equivalent constants. "Yes", "TRUE", and "on", and all of their lower- and uppercase variants, all mean the same thing. And similarly, "NO", "false", "Off" and their variants are all equivalent. Use whichever makes the most sense for a specific resource, and whichever makes your resource file easiest to read.

# Resources for Customizing Application-Specific Client Operation

Every X Window System client has special resources that customize application-specific aspects of its operation. For example, the VT100 emulator in **xterm** has resources that control the presence or absence of a scroll bar (and the associated capability to scroll back and forth through more lines than will fit in the one-screen window), and the number of lines to save for scrolling. With the lines

```
XTerm*scrollBar:        On
XTerm*saveLines:        1024
```

read into your resource database from a resource file, clients of the class XTerm will have scrolling enabled by default, and will save the last 1024 lines for access by scrolling.

# Using Pre-Existing Widgets

X Window System applications developers save time by using whatever preexisting widgets (packaged user interface objects) will work in their applications. In XTerm, for example, scrolling is controlled by a standard scroll bar widget from the Athena widget set. In time, you will learn to recognize widgets within applications on sight. This is useful because not only whole applications, but also individual widgets, can be customized with resource variables. The resources of each widget are described in its manual page. Note that the names of widget manual pages usually start with an uppercase letter (for example, Scrollbar).

Proprietary software distributions may include only the manual pages for special widget sets. For example, under the SUN Open windows distribution, the command

```
$ man Scrollbar
```

will document the Open Look scroll bar widget, and not the Athena scroll bar widget used in XTerm. The manual pages for the Athena widgets are available as part of the standard X Window System distributions from the X Window System Consortium. They are available by anonymous ftp from *ftp.x.org*.

# Customizing Widget Features with Resources

The special resources of each widget let you customize its special features. For example, the Athena scroll bar displays the location of the currently displayed text within the buffer of saved lines by tiling the corresponding part of the scroll bar window with a "thumb" bitmap. If you don't like the default stippling, you can choose a different bitmap, as shown in the following example:

```
XTerm*scrollbar.thumb:\
/usr/openwin/share/include/X11/bitmaps/black
```

This will give you a solid ("black") thumb. (The specific path of the *include* bitmap files will differ from system to system—the above works on the SUN OPENWIN distribution.)

Some resource variables are defined for all, or nearly all widgets. Such resources include *background-Pixmap* (a bitmap file path), or width and height. For example, the assignment

```
XTerm*scrollbar.width:    4
```

will change the width of XTerm's scroll bar to four pixels—and similar assignments will work for almost any widget.

# Using the Translations Table

One particularly useful resource variable, applicable to almost any client of widget, is the translations table. The value of this resource determines what the object (client or widget) will do in response to any event to which it is sensitive. The translations table contains a table of newline-separated lines, so each line but the last in a translation assignment must be terminated with "n". Each line starts with an event description, followed by a colon and one or more *actions*, possibly with parentheses-enclosed arguments, to be taken in response to the event. The available actions are listed in the manual page of each client or widget class.

By modifying the translations table, you can add an arbitrary number of additional *programmable functions keys* to XTerm. When doing this, it is necessary to prefix the list of new event translations with "#override". For example:

```
XTerm*VT100.Translations:        #override\
```

Without "#override", the list of new translations would replace the translation table for XTerm*VT100, instead of just overriding the respecified translations. If you forgot "#override", all the built-in event translations, predefined for every key on the keyboard, would be lost. (XTerm is sometimes used by other applications just to display text without accepting input. "Translations:" will yield an XTerm that will ignore all events.)

# Locking Your Console with a Single Key

One preprogrammed translation you will almost certainly want to have, if you use the X Window system in places where people who should not have access to your work may be present, is something like

```
<Key>L9:string("xlock -remote -mode random")string(0x0d)
```

This will let you lock your console with the press of a single key (in this case, the key L9 on the left-hand function keypad). If you need to take a break from your keyboard, just go to an **xterm** window with a shell prompt and press this key. The command to lock up your display will be sent with this one press, followed by RETURN. Since the ASCII RETURN character is not a printable character, it is represented as "0x0d".

# More on Using Translations Tables, Including Operating the Scroll Bar with a Mouse

With translations tables, you have complete control over what happens for any event: keyboard, mouse, even cursor entering and leaving a window ("Enter" and "Leave") or getting and losing keyboard focus

("Focus In" and "Focus Out"). For example, there is nothing to keep you from using the keyboard to do things normally done with the mouse, such as operating the scroll bar. The sequence

```
<Key>Up:scroll-back(1,halfpage)\n\
<Key>Down:scroll-forw(1,halfpage)\n\
```

will let you scroll back and forth in **xterm** with your UP ARROW and DOWN ARROW keys, a half-page per press.

If you use the above translation to operate scrolling from the keyboard, set the height of your **xterm** window to an odd number of lines. Because of truncation when the number of lines in a half-page is calculated, having an odd number of lines will always give you a line of continuity between pages, when you go from page to page by double-pressing the PGUP and PGDN keys.

# Using Translations to Send Strings from the Mouse

It is also possible to use translations to send strings, usually sent by keys on the keyboard, from the mouse instead. For example, you might want to be able to select a different window by moving the mouse, perform the default action in that window (such as reading the next item in a mail or news utility), and go back without taking your hand off the mouse. This can be done with the following translations:

```
~Shift ~Ctrl ~Meta <Btn3Down>:string(0x0d)\n\
~Shift ~Ctrl ~Meta <Btn3Motion>:ignore()\n\
```

The first of these translations sends a RETURN character when mouse button 3 is pressed. The second overrides the default translation of mouse motion with button 3 down, so that you don't need to stop the mouse in the target window while using the button to send a string.

# Conditioning New Translations

When changing the translation of an event for which a useful translation is already defined, as in the case of the button 3 events in Tip 921, it is a good idea to preserve your access to the standard actions by conditioning the new translation on a specific combination of modifier (SHIFT, CONTROL, meta, and so on) states. In the example above, the ~ (tilde) before each modifier conditions the translation on no modifier being pressed. So, if you still want to use the standard button 3 menu of XTerm, for example, it remains available when button 3 is used with the control modifier.

# Keyboard Maps and Utilities

## Changing Keyboard Maps

**T**IP
923

Every X Window System client that uses the keyboard obtains and uses a copy of the server's keyboard map as it was when the client first started up. The keyboard map maps each key on the keyboard to a key symbol, or *keysym*. By running the **xmodmap** utility before you start up your clients in *.xinitrc*, you can change the keyboard maps of all the clients to reconfigure the keyboard to suit your needs and preferences. **xmodmap** can also remap the numbering of mouse buttons—for example, if you use your left hand with the mouse.

Before you can use **xmodmap**, you need to know the keycode of the key to which you'd like to assign a different symbol, and the symbol or symbols you would like to assign to that key. The key code can be obtained with **xev**, a utility that opens two small windows, one inside the other, and then reports and describes all events that happen to those windows. You normally start **xev** from an XTerm window; event descriptions are sent as text and displayed in the text window from which **xev** was launched.

If you select one of the small **xev** windows with the mouse, and then press and release the key you are interested in, its key code and its current *keysym* will be reported in the descriptions of the KeyDown and KeyUp events you've generated. Each *keysym,* prefixed with "XK_", is listed in the file *include/X11/keysymdef.h* under the X directory (*/usr/openwin* on SUN Open Windows).

If you are used to a specific keyboard layout, or if you use two or more keyboards with different layouts, you can use **xmodmap** to change to compatible layouts. For example, since some keyboards reverse the relative location of the CAPS LOCK and CTRL-L *keysym,* the **xmodmap** manual page provides an example of using **xmodmap** to swap those keys. If you use **vi**, you will need the ESC key to be easy to reach, so if there's a grave/tilde key where you want ESC, you can swap them:

```
xmodmap -e 'keycode 106 = grave asciitilde' \
    -e 'keycode 93 = Escape'
```

Always use **xmodmap** to put the keys where your fingers expect them to be.

# Selecting Text from One Window and Sending it to Another Window

The X Window Server maintains a *selection buffer* with which you can select text from windows and send it to other windows as though it had come from the keyboard. In some applications, the text selection is done with mouse buttons (unless reassigned through a user's translations resource), while in others it is done with an onscreen button. The font selection utility **xfontsel**, for example, has an onscreen "select" button that puts the name of the currently displayed font in the selection buffer, from which it can be dropped into, for example, an editor window in which you are editing your font selections in a resource file.

# Putting Text in the Selection Buffer

XTerm's default translations let you put text in the selection buffer by depressing mouse button 1 (the conventional *select* mouse button) at the beginning of the text you wish to select, moving the mouse to the end of the selection, and then lifting it. If your selection goes beyond the end of the text on a line, the following newline is included in the selection and automatically sent with your text to the window in which you *drop* it by depressing the middle button.

You can select a word by quickly double-clicking button 1 over it, and a whole line with a triple click. You can select as many lines of text as you wish to drop into the receiving window at one time. This is particularly useful in transferring text between the windows of clients from different host machines.

On some versions of the X Window System, you can use the Edit function, which you can find on the **xterm** menu, to cut and paste from an **xterm** window. The Edit function lets you cut blocks of text from one area in the window and paste them to other areas of the window or to other windows, as long as the clients running in these windows support this function. You can also cut and paste blocks of text in an **xterm** window by using the scroll bars to locate the text you want to cut, selecting this text in the appropriate way, such as by pressing the left mouse button and sweeping the desired block and releasing the button, and then paste it into an editor screen or at the shell prompt to incorporate it into a command, using the Send, Copy, or Cut menu options to position this block where the cursor is.

# An Alternative to xclipboard

Although the X Window System comes with **xclipboard**, a special utility for dealing separately with several selected strings, it is often easier just to use an XTerm-shell window as a large "clipboard." Just give the command

```
$ cat > /dev/null
```

in the window you wish to use for this, drop the selected pieces of text into the window, and then select what you need from the text displayed in this window as you would from any other XTerm.

# Using the Content of the Selection Buffer from a Shell Script

The content of the selection buffer is stored as property "CUT_BUFFER0" of the server's root window. If you want to use it from a shell script, or from a **vi** macro that invokes a shell script, you can obtain it as the standard output of the shell command

```
eval echo `xprop -root CUT_BUFFER0|cut -c23-`
```

You can combine this capability with the translations resource of XTerm, which can specify actions that include the sending of strings that trigger arbitrary **vi** macros or shell scripts, to automate any action you would normally perform on a selected word or other text.

# Use a Backup Directory When Trying Something New

After all these specific hints, if you'd like to do something, and have a wild idea about how it could be done, try it. Of course, if you have a set of files that you need to modify for your experiment, save the unmodified versions in a backup directory before you try anything more. But, having done that, don't be afraid to experiment.

## Administering X Windows

### TIP 929 — Authorizing Users

On some versions of UNIX System V Release 4, you cannot use the X Window System if you have not been authorized by your system administrator. On some systems, the user agent for administration functions includes selections for administering the X system that can be used to allow users access to X Windows. However, other versions of UNIX System V Release 4 do not offer this capability. When this is the case, the system administrator needs to run programs to add users and to set environmental variables that support the X Window System. Such programs can usually be found in the directory */usr/X/adm*. The effect of running these programs is to set up users' *.profile* and other initialization files to support the X Window System. For example, in the OPEN LOOK environment, the command **oladduser** will add users and **olsetvar** will set OPEN LOOK environmental variables.

### TIP 930 — Using the xhost Client

When you are using the X Window System on a LAN, you can use the **xhost** client to control the machines on the network allowed to display windows on your display. You can allow all other machines on your network to display windows on your display with

```
$ xhost +
```

You can permit a machine on your network, say delaware, to display windows on your display with

```
$ xhost + delaware
```

You can prohibit all other machines on your network from displaying windows on your display with

```
$ xhost -
```

You can prohibit a particular machine, say jersey, from displaying windows on your display with

```
$ xhost - jersey
```

You can see which hosts are allowed to create windows on your machine by typing

```
$ xhost
```

You'll get a list of these hosts, one per line.

# Finding Out More about X Windows

## Where to Get More Information about X Windows

**TIP 931**

There are a variety of books on the X Window Systems. Users of the X Window System may want to consult *The X Window System: A User's Guide* by Niall Mansfield (Reading, MA: Addison-Wesley, 1991) and *The X Window System User's Guide* for XII, Release 5 by Valerie Quercia and Tim O'Reilly (Sebastopol, CA: O'Reilly and Associates, 1993). Programmers may want to consult *The X Windows System Toolkit, The Complete Programmer's Guide and Specification* by Paul Assente and Ralph Swick (Bedford, MA: Digital Press, 1990), the *Introduction to the X Window System* by Oliver Jones (Englewood Cliffs, NJ: Prentice-Hall, 1991) and *The X Window System: Programming and Applications* by Doug Young and John Pew (Prentice-Hall, 1992).

There are several periodicals devoted to the X Window System, including *The X Resource: A Practical Journal of the X Window System* and the *X Journal,* which is published bimonthly.

You should also read the newsgroups devoted to the X Window System, including *comp.windows.x* for a general discussion of the X Window System; *comp.x.announce* for announcements from the X Consortium; *comp.windows.x.apps* for a discussion on obtaining and using applications that run on X; *comp.windows.x.i386unix* for a discussion of X Window Systems for Intel-based UNIX PCs; *comp.windows.x* for a discussion on the X toolkit; and *comp.windows.x.motif* for a discussion on the

Motif graphical user interface. You will probably also want to read the FAQs posted periodically to *comp.windows.x* and to *news.answers.*

## TIP 932 — X Windows Conferences

There are several conferences on the X Window System that you might want to attend. The X Technical Conference is held in January in Boston. The XWorld Conference, which includes tutorials, presentations, and vendor exhibits, is held in March in New York City. Xhibition is a trade show and conference held in June in the San Francisco Bay Area; it includes tutorials, presentations, and vendor exhibits. There is also an annual conference of the European X User Group that includes presentations and vendor exhibits.

# Chapter 15

# Application Programming in C

# Program Development

## Documenting Your Programs

**TIP 933**

In order to design and write a program, you must know what you want it to do. Every serious programming effort should have a specification of the program's functions before any code is written. One way to write such a specification and to be sure that you understand what you want the program to do is to write the manual pages first. Explaining what the program does to a user is a good way to assure that you understand its operation.

UNIX provides a macro package for use in formatting manual pages with **troff**. You can see the definitions of the macros in the file *man.macs* in the directory */usr/ucblib/doctools/tmac*. The specific path may be different on your system, but the macros should be in *.../tmac/man.macs,* or */usr/lib/tmac/tmac.an.*

Here is a sample **troff** template that is a useful start for a manual page for your program:

```
.TH NAME 1  "Day Month Year"
.SH NAME
name - summary of function
.SH SYNOPSIS
.B name
[
.B -options
] [
.I arguments
]
.IX  "permuted index entries"
.SH DESCRIPTION
.B name
does this.
.SH OPTIONS
.LP
When relevant, describe here.
.SH ENVIRONMENT VARIABLES
.LP
List exported shell variables used by the tool here.
```

```
.SH EXAMPLE
.RS
.nf
put an example here
.fi
.ft R
.RE
```

Once you have written your manual page, format it with

```
nroff -man filename > progname
```

If you put formatted versions of your own manual pages in a specific directory, and add that directory name to MANPATH (see Tip 171), the UNIX **man** command can be used to display them.

# C Language Libraries

T IP
934

C is a very sparse language whose early versions did not have many of the capabilities usually incorporated into other programming languages. For example, such frequently used features as input/output operations and system calls were not part of C (and are still not in some implementations). Both were implemented for incorporation into a program as library functions. This is one of the reasons that C is used when porting between different operating systems is necessary.

By convention, the symbols, data types, and external names of functions are kept in header (*.h) files. Every C program needs to start with *#include* preprocessor directives, which read in the necessary files. By convention, the header filenames are placed in double quotes if they are private libraries, and in angle brackets if they refer to the standard system header directories. Thus, a program that used two system libraries and one private library would start with lines like

```
#include <stdio.h>
#include <ctype.h>
#include "/home/you/mylibe.h"
```

In this example, the header file *stdio.h* is the *st*andar*d i*nput and *o*utput library, and *ctype.h* is the *c*onvert *typ*es library which is used to convert alphanumeric strings into integers used for calculations within the program.

In System V Release 4, ANSI C was introduced. In ANSI C, the macros, header files, and libraries are part of the official language definition. ANSI C includes the following C header files:

| | | |
|---|---|---|
| <assert.h> | <ctype.h> | <errno.h> |
| <float.h> | <limits.h> | <locale.h> |
| <math.h> | <setjmp.h> | <signal.h> |
| <stdarg.h> | <stddef.h> | <stdio.h> |
| <stdlib> | <string.h> | <time.h> |

A conforming ANSI C program can only use this set of libraries.

## TIP 935

# What the cc Command Does

To convert the C language source code in a file, use the UNIX System C compiler, **cc**. The function of the **cc** command is to invoke, in the proper order, the following sequence of functions:

preprocessor
syntactic analyzer
compiler
assembler
optimizer (as part of assembler)
link-editing loader

**Preprocessor**    Prior to Release 4, **cc** invoked a separate preprocessor, **cpp**; in Release 4, the preprocessor is a logically separate function, but a separate **cpp** program is not invoked. Its functions include stripping out comments; reading in files (such as the *private.h* header file) specified in *#include* directives; keeping track of preprocessor macros defined with *#define* directives (and -**D** options to **cpp** or **cc**); and carrying out the substitutions specified by those macros. Since the macros usually reside in header files, changes in header files will change the behavior of executable products.

**Syntactic Analyzer**    The next step after the preprocessor is the C syntactic analyzer, a tool shared between **cc** and **lint**. The System V Release 4 version of **cc** actually uses one of three different behavioral variants of the syntactic analyzer, which implement the three syntactic modes available in Release 4: the "**t**" (transition mode), "**a**" (ANSI mode), and "**c**" (conformance mode).

Now that ANSI C is available, it is wisest to use the "c" version of the syntactic analyzer (the -**Xc** flag to the **cc** command), and write programs that will work on future compilers that will not accept pre-ANSI variants of C.

**Compiler**  cc's next step is to compile the syntactic analyzer's output into assembly language. Assembly language files have the suffix *.s*. **cc** does not normally leave the output of its compiler step in these files, but you can cause it to do so with the -**S** option. This option is useful if you need to manually check, and if necessary modify, the assembler code; such a step is not likely to be useful except when your program interacts very closely with the hardware it runs on.

**Assembler**  The next step for **cc** is to convert the assembly language output of the compilation step into machine language. This step is perfo. _ned by **as**, the assembler.

When given the -**O** option, **cc** also invokes an optional *Optimizer* that streamlines the assembly code. The result of this step is a file with a filename based on the original source file, but with an *.o* suffix. For example, the source file *prog.c* results in an object file *prog.o*. The -c argument can be used to make **cc** stop after this step.

**Link Editor**  The next and final step is carried out by the link editor, or loader, **ld**. **ld** can be invoked separately. However, by invoking it through **cc**, you make sure that the object is automatically linked with the standard C library, */lib/libc.so*. If **ld** is invoked independently, linking with the library */lib/libc.a* must be specified separately, with the -**l** option. **ld** loads a single executable with all the object (*\*.o*) files and all the library functions they call. In doing so, it "edits" the object code, replacing symbolic link references to external functions with their actual addresses in the executable program.

In Release 4, **ld** was changed to handle the Extensible Linking Format (ELF) for object binaries. In Release 3, static shared libraries were introduced to decrease both *a.out* size and memory consumption per process. The object modules from the libraries are no longer copied into the *a.out* file; rather, a special *a.out* section tells the kernel to link in the necessary libraries at fixed addresses.

In Release 4, dynamic linking, based on the SunOS 4.0 implementation, is supported. Dynamic linking allows object modules to be bound to the address space of a process at run time. Although programs under dynamic linking are marginally slower due to startup overhead, they are more efficient; since functions are linked on their first invocation, if they are never called, they are never linked.

# Naming Program Source Files

The C compiler requires that your source file be named with a *.c* extension, for example, *progname.c.* When you compile such a file, using

```
cc progname.c
```

the compiler creates a new file, a.out, which contains the executable module. *a.o ut* stands for *a*ssembler *ou*tput. Having all of the compiler's output given the same name is awkward at best. You can use the **-o** option to the compiler to specify the name you wish for the executable, as shown here.

```
cc -o progname progname.c
```

This example names the executable *progname.*

A common mistake that every programmer makes at least once is to pick the wrong name for a source file. For example, suppose you are writing a test program; it makes sense to call it *test.c,* and to call the executable module *test.* However, when you try to run the program, you'll actually be executing **/bin/test** or the **ksh** built-in **test**, rather than your executable *test.* If you follow our advice of not putting the current directory in your PATH, you'll always run the system command rather than the same-named one in the current directory (unless you call the command using its pathname, for example, **./progname**). If you give your program the same name as a shell built-in, the shell command will always be run instead of your program.

Avoid using UNIX command names as names for your program files.

# Never Write a Program from Scratch; Always Modify an Existing One

Program reuse is the key to high productivity. Start with something as simple as

```
main () {printf( "Hello, world.\n" ); }
```

Compile, link, debug, and run it. Now you have a development environment and working program. From this point on, all you have to do is modify a working program, not write a new one.

Better yet, find an existing program similar to your needs and modify it. Many people keep sources for all the products they have developed online (disks are cheap, good programmers aren't). Between your own sources and those of a network of colleagues, you should usually find something close to your needs as a starting point.

# Make One Modification at a Time

**TIP 938**

In the old days of programming, computer time was so scarce that programmers did "desk checks" of code. They tried to find multiple errors, correct them all, and then recompile. Doing this would introduce new errors while trying to fix old ones. For a program of any complexity, this creates a nightmare.

Compilation and link times on modern UNIX systems are so short that there is no reason to make and test more than one change at a time. If you make one change to a working program and it breaks, chances are pretty good that there is a bug in the change. This greatly simplifies debugging and fault isolation. Of course, there are times when several changes have to be made simultaneously—for example, when changing the composition of a data structure. Good design and an object-oriented attitude will keep these to a minimum. A side benefit of this tip is that you will always have a working program. It won't be complete, but you will always have something to show to demonstrate progress. Remember to keep a copy of the source to your last working version so you can back out of any change reliably.

# Write General Programs

**TIP 939**

During the development of a program, don't worry about efficiency. Express your application and algorithms in a clear and maintainable way. Only when the application is complete *and* you have demonstrated performance problems should you go back and begin optimization.

A typical software development project includes the need for many simple tools. Look beyond the immediate need and consider the general case. A small additional effort up front will be rewarded many times over later. For example, consider a program to perform a simple bit-order transformation on a stream of bytes. A little more thought might suggest that you may also want to transform the sense of the bits in the future. This thinking led to a program **bt.c** (bt for *bit twiddle*) that accepts two arguments, *-o* for order and *-s* for sense, that perform any combination of order and sense reversal on a byte stream.

```
/***************************************************************/
/*   bt.c - bit twiddle - filter to convert sense/order of input
 bits  */
/***************************************************************/

#include <stdio.h>

char *optstring = "os";
char *usage = "bt [-o] [-s]";

char table[256];

int sense = 0;
int order = 0;

/***************************************************************/

main(argc, argv)
int argc;
char *argv;
{
    int t;

    cmd_proc( argc, argv );          /* process cmd line args */

    gen_table();
    while( ( t = getchar() ) != EOF ) putchar( table[t] );

    exit(0);
}

/***************************************************************/

gen_table()
{
    int i;
```

```
    int j;
    int v;

    for( j = 0; j < 256; j++ ) {
        v = j;

        if( order ) {
            v = 0;
            for(i = 0; i < 8; i++ ) if( j & (1<<7-i) ) v |= (1<<i);
        }
        if( sense ) v ^= 0xff;

        table[j] = v;
    }
        return 0;
}

/******************************************************************/

cmd_proc(argc, argv )
int argc;                       /* number of args on command line
char **argv;                    /* pointer to the actual args
{

    extern  int getopt();
    extern  char *optarg;

    int  optchar;  /* option flag returned by getopt() call */

    while ((optchar = getopt(argc, argv, optstring )) != EOF) {

        switch( (char)optchar) {

        case 'o':
            order = 1;
            break;

        case 's':
            sense = 1;
```

```
            break;

    case '?':
            fprintf(stderr, "%s\n", usage );
            exit(1);
            break;
    } /* END: of switch */
}

            return 0;
}


/*****************************************************************/
```

# Don't Modify Bad Programs

**TIP 940**

Rewrite bad code. Eventually one of two things happens to all programmers. Either a small piece of good code grows monstrously beyond the framework originally conceived for it, or your initial approach to a problem is simply wrong. Regardless, don't hack it or patch it. Throw it away! For outgrown programs, analyze afresh the problem your monstrosity is supposed to solve. A likely outcome is a group of small routines, each of which solves a part of the problem. If your approach is wrong, go back to the literature and look for a better algorithm.

# Beauty Is Easier to Maintain

**TIP 941**

Keep your code beautiful. Small details of program layout such as vertical alignment of code and comments, white space around operators, consistent use of curly braces, and so on, are meaningless to the compiler. But they make a world of difference in the ease of reading a program and understanding its flow and function. During initial development and when making revisions, *always* keep your program layout clean. Any suggestions that you will "get back to it later" are self-deceiving. You won't get back to it, and you will be stuck with a mess to maintain.

# Parameterize Everything from the Start

This is a simple extra effort that will yield returns in ways you could not conceive of when you began. Our experience includes a voice editor program with window dimensions that had been parameterized using *#define* constants. This made it easy to change the window size by editing only one header file. Well after the initial development work was done it became necessary to change the window size dynamically during the execution of the program. It was a simple matter to introduce a size variable and change the value of *#define* from a constant to the name of that variable. Now, all references to *#define* symbol refer to a program variable instead of a constant. Like code layout, this must be made a part of your programming discipline. Even if you could go back and parameterize later, you lose the benefits of parameterization during program development. Every change is all the more painful.

## Using lint

# Use lint Before cc

The C compiler assumes that programmers know what they are doing, and it compiles any program of legal C code. Some lines of legal code, such as declaring several arguments to a function and then not using them, are more likely errors than clever programming. **lint** is a syntax checker that spots any anomalies and points them out, even if they would have compiled. It points out inconsistencies across several files. You should use **lint** with every program you write. It's as important a programming tool as an editor in preparing code. Use **lint** before you compile, and don't bother compiling until either the program lints without errors, or you are sure that you understand each of the warnings **lint** points out.

# lint Error Checking

An important reason to use **lint** before compiling is that **lint** not only finds syntax errors in ANSI C but also uncovers potential bugs, or problems with the code that would make it hard to port to another machine. In addition to simple syntax violations, **lint** also complains for the following reasons:

❑ Unreachable statements

❑ Loops not entered at the top

❑ Variables that are not used

❑ Function arguments that are never used

❑ Automatic variables that are used before they are assigned a value

❑ Functions that return values in some places, but not others

❑ Functions that are called with varying numbers of arguments

❑ Errors in the use of pointers to structures

❑ Ambiguous precedence operators

# Controlling lint Output

One difficulty in using **lint** is that it generates very long lists of warning messages that may not indicate a bug. Having to wade through many lines of warnings in order to look for potential bugs sometimes discourages programmers from making full use of **lint**.

There are "do not complain" options to **lint** that restrict its behavior. You should initially use **lint** without these options, determine whether warnings are not relevant, then turn options on in subsequent **lint** use. If you are developing a program as several separate modules, you may want to **lint** the module when you first develop it with none of the "do not complain" options turned on. As you alter and extend the module, you can disregard certain warnings that you know don't apply to your code. Three options that are useful for doing this are listed here:

**-h**        Do not apply heuristic tests to determine whether bugs are present, whether style can be improved, or to tighten code.

| | |
|---|---|
| **-v** | Do not complain about unused arguments in functions. |
| **-u** | Do not complain about variables and functions used and not defined, or defined and not used. |

# Inserting Directives in a Program to Affect lint

**TIP 946**

In addition to using the options discussed in Tip 945, you can put lint directives (which look like comments) into your source file to affect **lint**'s behavior:

| lint Directive | Meaning |
|---|---|
| /*NOTREACHED/* | Suppress comments about unreachable code. |
| /*VARARGSn/* | Suppress normal checking for variable number of arguments in a function. Data types of the first *n* arguments are checked. |
| /*NOSTRUCT*/ | Shut off strict type checking in the next expression. |
| /*ARGUSED*/ | Do not complain about unused arguments in the next function. |
| /*LINTLIBRARY*/ | Placed at the beginning of the file, this suppresses warnings about unused functions. |

## Using make

# Use make for All Programs

**TIP 947**

Use *makefiles* from the very start of program development. The benefits of the **make** program and *makefiles* are apparent for programs consisting of many source modules with complicated dependencies and program construction rules. However, use a *makefile* even for simple programs of one to a few source modules. Then you will have any special compiler options, as well as the libraries required for linking, all specified in one well-defined place. If your simple program starts to grow, you will already have the structure in place to support that growth.

# Components of a Makefile

**TIP 948**

The UNIX system programming environment provides a tool, **make**, that automatically keeps track of dependencies among files that make up a program, and makes it easy to create executable programs. In using **make**, you specify the way that parts of your program are dependent on other parts, or on other code. This specification of the dependencies underlying a program is placed in a *Makefile*.

When you run the command

```
$ make
```

the program looks for a file called *makefile* or *Makefile* in the current directory. The *makefile* is examined; source files that have been changed since they were last compiled are recompiled, and any file that depends on another that has been changed will also be recompiled. A *makefile* has several components to it, as follows.

❑ *Comments* In a *makefile*, comments can be inserted by using the # (pound) sign. Everything between the # (pound sign) and the next RETURN is ignored by **make**.

❑ *Variables* **make** allows you to define named variables similar to those used in the shell. For example, if you define *SOURCES=prog.c*, then the value of that variable, $(SOURCES), contains the names of source files for this program.

**make** has some built-in knowledge about program development and knows that files ending in a *.c* suffix are C source files, those ending in *.o* are object modules, those ending in *.a* are assembler files, and so on. You can also define the pathname of the product you are creating, and the flags (options) to be used by the C compiler.

❑ *Dependencies* Dependencies are specified by naming the target modules on the left, followed by a colon, followed by the modules on which the target depends.

❑ *Commands* The dependency line is followed by the commands that must be executed if one or more of the dependent modules has been changed. Command lines must be indented at least one tab stop from the left margin. Tabs are required; the equivalent number of spaces won't work.

# A Makefile Template

**TIP 949**

To demonstrate the use of **make**, here is a sample *makefile* capable of handling a program whose source directory contains two source files, *main.c* and *rest.c*; a header file *private.h* in a subdirectory (as is customarily done with header files) called *include*; and a *library, routine.a,* with sources in files *routine1.c, routine2.c,* and *routine3.c.*

A simple *makefile* for such an example might be

```
# A basic makefile to combine c sources
# private header files, and libraries.

HEADERS=include/private.h
SOURCES=main.c rest.c
PRODUCT=$(HOME)/bin/tool
LIB=routines.a
LIBSOURCES=routine1.c routine2.c routine3.c
CC=cc
CFLAGS=-g

all: $(PRODUCT)

$(PRODUCT): $(SOURCES)
        $(CC) $(CFLAGS) -o $(PRODUCT) $(SOURCES)

lint: $(PRODUCT)
        lint $(SOURCES) $(LIBSOURCES)
```

This example contains all the components of a makefile discussed in Tip 948 above. We gave the compiler itself a symbolic name (**CC=cc**) so that if, for example, we wanted to try a different compiler, the command **CC=newcc** is all that needs to be changed in the makefile.

# A More Complicated Makefile

**TIP 950**

The template in Tip 949 is usable, but it recompiles all the sources when **make** is invoked. It is more efficient to make the product depend only on the object (*.o*) files, thus reusing the objects if their sources have not been changed. To make sure that the objects are recompiled if either their source file or any of the headers has changed, you may include in the *makefile* an explicit inference rule (.c.o:) for converting C source files into object files. You can also specify flags for **lint**. These are called *$(LINTFLAGS),* since *$(LFLAGS)* is used by **make** to specify flags for **lex**.

This *makefile* supplies **ld** with the library of private routines it needs, and also makes sure that the private library is brought up-to-date if any of the header files of library routine source files are changed, and the product relinked if the library is changed.

Our template would now look like this:

```
# A more complicated makefile to combine c sources
# private header files, and libraries.

HEADERS=include/private.h
SOURCES=main.c rest.c
OBJECTS=main.o rest.o
PRODUCT=$(HOME)/bin/tool
LIB=routines.a
LIBSOURCES=routine1.c routine2.c routine3.c
LIBOBJECTS=$(LIB)(routine1.o) $(LIB)(routine2.o) $(LIB)(routine3.o)
INCLUDE=include
CC=cc
CFLAGS=-g -Xc
LINT=lint
LINTFLAGS=-Xc


all: $(PRODUCT)

$(PRODUCT): $(OBJECTS) $(LIB)
    $(CC) $(CFLAGS) -o $(PRODUCT) $(OBJECTS) $(LIB)

.c.o: $(HEADERS)
    $(CC) $(CFLAGS) -c -I$(INCLUDE) $<

$(LIB): $(HEADERS) $(LIBSOURCES)
    $(CC) $(CFLAGS) -c $(?:.o=.c)
    ar rv $(LIB) $?
    rm $?

.c.a:;

lint: $(PRODUCT)
    $(LINT) $(LINTFLAGS) $(SOURCES) $(LIBSOURCES)
```

The line ".c.a:;" disables the built-in **make** rule for building libraries out of their source files. Because of this line, **lint** will not use the built-in rule, which is slightly different, and which would have been invoked automatically (thus repeating, unnecessarily, some of the manufacturing steps) if it were not explicitly disabled or redefined.

# Using make Macros

**make** has five internally defined macros that are used in creating targets which have been used in the template in Tip 950. These are listed here:

- ❏ $* The filename of the dependent with the suffix deleted. It is evaluated only for inference rules.

- ❏ $@ The full name of the target. It is evaluated in explicitly named dependencies.

- ❏ $< Evaluated only in an inference rule and stands for the out-of-date module on which the target depends. In the *.c.o* rule above, it stands for the source (*.c*) files.

- ❏ $? Evaluated when explicit rules are used in the makefile. It is the list of all out of date modules, that is, all those that must be recompiled.

- ❏ $% Evaluated when the target is a library. For example, if you were attempting to make the library member component *lib(file.o)*, then $@ stands for *lib* and $% is the library component *file.o*.

# Avoiding Programming Mistakes

# Watch Out for Classic Programming Bugs!

Operator precedence can cause subtle programming bugs. For example,

```
if( a = getchar() != EOF )
```

is not the same as

```
if( ( a = getchar()) != EOF )
```

This is a classic bug made by all C programmers at least once on their path to proficiency. The expression in the **if** statement consists of three operands, **a**, **getchar**(), and **EOF** joined by two operators, = and !=. In the C language, the != operator is said to *bind* more tightly than =. This means that the expression formed by the != operator is evaluated first and the result of the evaluation becomes one of the operands of the = operation. The compiler treats the expression as though it were parenthesized:

```
if( a = ( getchar() != EOF )).
```

The value returned by **getchar**() is compared to EOF. If it is not equal to EOF, the value 1 is assigned to a; otherwise the value 0 is assigned to a. This occurs because the value of a relational expression is either 1 for **TRUE** or 0 for **FALSE**. By adding parentheses around the assignment

```
(a = getchar())
```

the value returned by **getchar**() is assigned to a, and then that value is compared with EOF.

# Avoid Assignment Bugs in C

Don't confuse assignment and comparison:

```
if( a = 3 ) {block of code}
```

is not the same as

```
if( a == 3 ) {block of code}
```

This is another classic bug that all programmers make at least once. The = operator forms an assignment expression that has the value of the right-hand operand and it assigns the value of the right-hand operand to the variable indicated by the left-hand operand. The expression

```
(a = 3)
```

assigns the value 3 to the variable *a*, but the expression also has the value 3. Thus, in the first case, **block of code** would always be executed, independent of the value of a at the time of evaluation, since the expression

```
(a = 3)
```

is always non-zero and thus, **TRUE**. The == operator forms a relational expression. It compares the value of the operands on its left and right and yields a value of 1 if they are equal, and 0 if they are not equal. In the second case, **block of code** is executed only if a is equal to 3, which is likely what you had intended. Programmers writing both C programs and shell scripts are particularly susceptible to this bug because the = operator is used both for assignment and as a relational in shell programming.

# Precedence of Logical Operators

The following bug is less common, but is included because it illustrates one of the few cases where the default binding of C is counterintuitive.

```
if( a & 0x1 && b & 0x2 ) {block of code}
```

is not the same as

```
if( (a & 0x1) && (b & 0x2) ) {block of code}
```

The precedence of the logical **AND** operator && is higher than that of the Boolean **AND** operator &. The first expression is evaluated as if it were written

```
if( a & ( 0x1 && b ) & 0x2 ).
```

That is, the expression

```
(0x1 && b )
```

is first evaluated. If *b* is non-zero, the expression will have the value 1; otherwise it will have the value 0. Then one of the expressions

```
( a & 0 & 2 )
```

or

```
( a & 1 & 2 )
```

will be evaluated. Since both

```
(0 & 2)
```

and

```
(1 & 2)
```

are equal to 0, the value of either expression will be 0, and *block of code* will never be executed. It would be more sensible if the Boolean **AND** operator bound tighter (that is, had a higher precedence, and was evaluated first), but it does not. A minor point as long as you remember to always parenthesize Boolean expressions.

# Don't Get Bitten by Byte Ordering

**TIP 955**

Be aware of byte ordering issues. Byte ordering describes the way that bytes are ordered in shorts and longs. It varies with machine architecture. If you only program in one machine architecture (for example, Sparc, Intel, or a 680x0), you may not even be aware of byte ordering issues. It becomes significant mainly if you exchange data between two different architectures, but it can also be a source of bugs when porting code between architectures. The best way to appreciate byte ordering is to execute the following program on various machines.

```
main() {
    union {
        char c[4];
        long l;
    } u;
    int i;
    for( i = 0; i < 4; i++ ) u.c[i] = i;
    printf( "u.l = 0x%08lx\n", u.l );
}
```

You should get the following results:

```
Big-Endian                        Little-Endian
----------------------            ----------------------
68010: u.l = 0x00010203           386:   u.l = 0x03020100
SPARC: u.l = 0x00010203
SGI:   u.l = 0x00010203
3B2:   u.l = 0x00010203
```

If you write a long into a UNIX file or communications pipe on one architecture, for example:

```
long l;
write( 1, &l, 4 );
```

and read it on another architecture with a different byte ordering:

```
long l;
read( 0, &l, 4 );
```

the results will not be what you expected. To avoid the problem, decompose the long into coefficients of powers of 256 and send the coefficients in a predefined order such as MSB first. For example, the long value

```
0x01020304
```

can be represented as

```
1 * 256^3 + 2 * 256^2 + 3 * 256^1 + 4 * 256^0
```

Send the coefficients 1, 2, 3, and 4 as a stream of bytes:

```
01 02 03 04.
```

Alternatively, you can write all data in ASCII using **printf**() and read it with **scanf**(). This makes less efficient use of storage space or transmission bandwidth but may be the easiest to implement. The terms "big-endian" and "little-endian" are often used to describe this difference. On a big-endian machine, the most significant byte of a multibyte object (such as a long) is stored at the lowest address. A good way to remember this is "big end first." A little-endian machine is the opposite: the least significant byte is stored in the lowest address (or "little end first").

# TIP 956

## Avoid the int Data Type

Never use the *int* data type. Always specify *char, short,* or *long* explicitly. Almost all (if not all) UNIX C compilers represent a *char* with one byte, a *short* with two bytes, and a *long* with four bytes. Unfortunately, such consistency is lacking for ints, which vary between two bytes or four bytes depending on the compiler, with some influence from the machine architecture. This inconsistency can yield problems when porting programs between environments with differing *int* sizes, especially when porting from a machine with four-byte ints to one with two-byte *int*s. For example, the following code works fine with four-byte *int*s but breaks with two-byte *int*s.

```
int i;
long a[100000];
for( i = 0; i < 100000; i++ ) a[i] = i;
```

On a two-byte *int* UNIX machine, the maximum value that *i* can represent is 32767. Adding one to that value yields –32768, not a reasonable value for an index in the array *a*.

Keep this in mind when you encounter bugs that appear to be dependent on the extent of some parameter, perhaps the size of a data file or an array.

# TIP 957

## Sizes of Variable Types

In order to avoid the problems pointed out in Tip 956, you need to know the sizes of the variable types on your machine. The following program helps you do this.

```
/* sizeof.c -  display variable sizes     */

#include <stdio.h>

main()
{
    printf("        char: %d\n", sizeof(char));
    printf("       short: %d\n", sizeof(short));
    printf("         int: %d\n", sizeof(int));
    printf("        long: %d\n", sizeof(long));
```

```
    printf("      unsigned:  %d\n", sizeof(unsigned));
    printf("         float:  %d\n", sizeof(float));
    printf("        double:  %d\n", sizeof(double));
```

If you compile and run **sizeof**, you'll get output something like this for your own machine:

```
$ sizeof
        char:  1
       short:  2
         int:  4
        long:  4
    unsigned:  4
       float:  4
      double:  8
```

# Dealing with Obscure Compiler Errors

**TIP 958**

The C preprocessor **/lib/cpp** is run automatically by the C compiler. It handles preprocessor directives such as macro substitution and conditional compilation. When you cannot locate the source of a compiler error, it sometimes helps to run just the preprocessor and examine the resulting file. Your compiler may have a command line option to run the preprocessor; in post-SVR4 systems, use

```
$ cc -E file.c ... > file.i
```

Or you can run it directly in some earlier systems as:

```
$ /lib/cpp file.c ... > file.i
```

You may have to include a **-I include_dir** option if your header files are in nonstandard locations and you use that option on the **cc** line.

The file *file.i* consists of the source file exactly as seen by the compiler. It includes all referenced headers, the values of macros, and code that is included through *#ifdef* directives. The line numbers differ from the original file but you should be able to locate the offending line by context.

# Disable the Compiler Optimizer for Obscure Bugs

Most compilers include a code optimizer that is invoked as part of the compilation process when the **-O** option is given to **cc**. The optimizer improves the efficiency of the compiled code. Unfortunately, in unusual circumstances, the optimizer may also introduce bugs.

If you have code that looks correct in all respects yet fails, try compiling it with the optimizer disabled. This is a lot easier than examining the assembly language output of the compiler, which is sometimes your only other recourse.

If you do find a case where the optimizer is responsible for a bug, be sure to inform the supplier of your compiler. If possible, try to isolate the problem to a small code fragment. However, it would not be surprising if the bug only appears in the context of a large source file, even though the bug is localized to a small region of the program.

# Use the vi % Command to Locate Balanced Enclosures

There are times when the compiler reports errors far from the point of actual cause, often on the last line of a file or the beginning of a new function definition. When the cause is not obvious, it might result from unbalanced curly braces or parentheses. The **vi** editor has a feature that makes it easy to isolate this type of problem.

If you have followed Tip 938 about making only one change at a time, the cause of the problem should already be localized to a single function. Place the cursor on the first left curly brace in the function. Enter the vi % command. **vi** will move the cursor to the balancing right curly brace. After a few iterations of the command, advancing the cursor to the next left curly brace on each iteration, the cause of the problem should be apparent.

# Program Style

## Establish a Consistent Program Layout across All Project Code

The closest thing to religion in C programming is program layout, especially the use of curly braces. Every style has its disciples convinced that their layout is THE layout. This topic is well beyond what can be covered in a few tips. See *C-Style Standards & Guidelines* by David Straker (New York, NY: Prentice-Hall International, 1991) for a thorough discussion. No matter what style you choose, use it consistently, day by day, year by year. When you return to some code you wrote five years ago and realize that it is just as readable as the code you wrote yesterday, you will be glad that you did.

If your project includes more than one programmer, establish agreement among all team members on a consistent style. Code written by any team member should appear as though it could have been written by any other team member. It will simplify shared development and maintenance of the resulting product.

## Removing Unneeded Code Correctly

Use **#ifdef** OMIT, not comments, to remove code. There are many occasions when you may want to temporarily remove a segment of code in a source file—for example, to test an alternate approach to an algorithm or bug fix. For a line or two it is usually all right to "comment out" the code, that is, surround the code to be deleted with the comment operators /* and */. For anything more than a couple of lines, though, this approach should not be used because of the likelihood that the code being "commented out" includes comments.

A better approach is to use the conditional compilation directives:

```
#ifdef OMIT
   (omitted code)
```

```
    ...
#endif
```

Use the symbol "OMIT" as the object of the **#ifdef** test to indicate that the following code is omitted. Be sure that you never define OMIT.

# Separate Functions with Comment Bars

To make your code readable, visually separate each function with a comment block. This makes each function easy to see, and provides you with an opportunity to add a short descriptive line. There are several ways to do this, and you should conform to whatever style is followed by your work group. Here's an example of using comment bars which separate functions, and also show indenting levels for internal modules. Include a comment consisting of a row of asterisks the full width of the screen to indicate the beginning of each function in a file. Within a function, include a comment bar at the indent level of the current code block to separate significant elements of code—for example a **for** or **while** loop, **switch** statement, and so on. Use a row of dashes to separate lesser elements, for example, cases of a **switch** statement. It improves readability significantly.

```
/* ********************************************** */
function()
{
    /* ********************************** */
    while( ... ) {

    }
    /* ********************************** */
    switch(...) {
    /* -------------------------------- */
    case():

    /* -------------------------------- */
    case():

    }
    /* ********************************** */
}
/* ********************************************** */
```

# Don't Include Vertical *'s in Comments

A popular style of commenting includes an * (asterisk) at the left margin of each line in the comment, as shown here.

```
/*   This is the body of a comment
 *   using a column of asterisks at the
 *   left text margin.
 *
 *   Don't do it!
 */
```

While this may initially look pretty and help identify comments, it is not a good idea. It is important to maintain comments as you maintain code, keeping the comments in agreement with the code they describe and including running commentary about changes. The asterisks only get in the way of subsequent editing.

```
/*   This is the body of a comment
     with no extra markings.

     Use it!
*/
```

# Name Temporary Variables Concisely and Consistently

All programs require local temporary variables with a scope of interest of only a few lines or so. For example, you may save the value returned by a function so that it can be tested and possibly used in an error message. Or you may need a copy of a pointer passed as a calling argument so that it can be incremented while saving the value of the calling argument for later use.

Use short variable names, perhaps *t* and *p*, respectively, for the above examples, and use them consistently in all of your functions. Long, descriptive variable names are appropriate for external variables, and sometimes locals with a long scope. But long variable names for short-lived temporary variables, especially ones that vary from function to function, only reduce readability.

# Use the getopts Facilities in All Programs and Scripts

All commands that you write should support the standard command line syntax described in the **intro**(1) man page. For example, all of the following command lines should be recognized equivalently.

```
command -a -b -c arg1 -d arg2
command -abc arg1 -d arg2
command -ab -carg1 -darg2
```

A command line parser that recognizes all variants described in **intro**(1) is nontrivial to write. Fortunately, the UNIX system provides a subroutine, **getopt**(3), that does most of the work for you. Following is a code fragment that recognizes the above command examples:

```
char *usage = "command [-a] [-b] [-c arg1] [-d arg2]";
char *optstring = "abc:d:";
extern  int getopt();
extern  char *optarg;

int optchar;   /* option flag returned by getopt() call */

while ((optchar = getopt(argc, argv, optstring )) != EOF) {
    switch( (char)optchar) {
    case 'a':
        a_flag = 1;
        break;
    case 'b':
        b_flag = 1;
        break;
    case 'c':
        c_val = optarg;
        break;
    case 'd':
        d_val = optarg;
        break;
```

```
    case '?':
        fprintf(stderr, "%s\n", usage );
        exit(1);
        break;
    } /* END: of switch */
}
```

For shell scripts, the built-in command **getopts(1)** provides a similar function:

```
while getopts "abc:d:" X
do
    case $X in
    a )     A_FLAG=1 ;;
    b )     B_FLAG=1 ;;
    c )     C_VALUE=$OPTARG ;;
    d )     D_VALUE=$OPTARG ;;
    \?)
        print -u2 - "Illegal option: -$OPTARG"
        exit
    ;;

    :)
        print -u2 - "Argument missing for option: -$OPTARG"
        exit
    ;;

    esac
done
```

See Tips 418 to 422 for other shell programming examples of **getopts**.

# Use a Consistent Loop Control in for() Loops

There are many ways to construct a loop to visit each member of an array. For example, each of the following loops set all members of the array *a* to 1.

```
#define SIZE 100
long a[SIZE];
short i;

for( i = 0; i < SIZE; i++ ) a[i] = 1;          /* BEST */
for( i = 1; i <= SIZE; i++ ) a[i-1] = 1;
for( i = SIZE-1; i >= 0; i-- ) a[i] = 1;
for( i = SIZE; i > 0; i-- ) a[i-1] = 1;
```

To improve readability and reduce errors, use only one form consistently in all your code. For efficiency reasons, the first example is the best choice because it avoids the subtraction of 1 in the index computation and because the conditional test of < instead of <= may be faster in certain architectures.

# Follow a Linked List in a for Statement

A **for** loop includes three statements, as shown here:

for( *stmt_1*; *stmt_2*; *stmt_3* ) {*block*}

Each of stmt_1, stmt_2, and stmt_3 may be null, consist of simple initialization, test, and increment operations, or include more complicated actions consistent with legal statement syntax. For example, you can visit every member of a linked list with the following fragment. The last item in the list is indicated by the value **NULL** in the "next" element.

```
struct foo {
    ...
    struct foo *next;
    ...
};
struct foo *root;

struct foo *p;

for( p = root; p != NULL; p = p->next ) { block }
```

In stmt_1 of the **for** loop, the pointer p is set to point to the head of the linked list; we won't worry here how the list was created or how root was set. The loop termination test statement, stmt_2, will be true as long as p doesn't point to the last element in the list. The loop increment statement, stmt_3, doesn't increment anything. Instead, it updates p to point to the next element in the list.

# Never Use Fixed Arrays, Always malloc() Storage

A sure mark of unreliable code is a fixed array storing anything, whether it is an input buffer or a symbol table. No matter how big you make the array, sooner or later someone will need a bigger one. And if you do build in large arrays, you are probably wasting a lot of storage for most applications of your program. Instead, use the **malloc**(3), **realloc**(3), and **free**(3) group of functions, which manage storage in a part of user memory known as the heap, for all arrays. Initially, allocate only an amount of storage for typical or light use of your program. When your initial allocation is consumed, call **realloc**() to expand the region. And, if your program no longer needs an array of storage, return it to the heap with **free**(). You will have to keep track of the quantity of storage actually used in each allocated array. That is a small price to pay for the reliability and convenience attained by eliminating all fixed limits for any resource.

# How to Troubleshoot malloc() Bugs

The **malloc**(3) family of routines provides an opportunity to make a couple of classic bugs: using storage that you have already returned with **free**(3), and failing to return storage with **free**(3) when you are done with it. The first one can yield all kinds of unexpected and unpleasant surprises. The second one yields a process that continually grows. While diligent programming can go a long way toward preventing these bugs, they will nevertheless happen to all programmers sooner or later and are often difficult to locate.

When you do get in trouble, one technique to help isolate the problem is to log every call to **malloc(3)**, **realloc(3)**, and **free(3)**, including the address returned by **malloc(3)** and **realloc(3)**; the address passed to **realloc(3)** and **free(3)**; a unique description of the location in the program where each was called; and the time of day.

After a crash or test session, sort the log using the memory address as the first key and time of day as the second key. You should find a pairing of **malloc(3)** (or **realloc(3)**) and **free(3)** for all addresses. If you don't, the description of the location may help you track down the faulty code.

# Always Test with Unexpected Input, Random Data, and /unix

A good test for the reliability of any program is to feed it unexpected input data. No program should dump core or terminate without an error message, no matter what input data is read. A program should be system-tested with various perversions, random lines of ASCII data, expected pathologies of the input data, and random binary data. An easy-to-remember source for a good test file is the UNIX system object file. It is not quite random but will certainly stress many programs.

```
$ my_prog < /unix
```

# Use a Program Block When Modifying Code

When you have to introduce local variables to an existing body of unfamiliar source code, perhaps during exploratory hacking, create a program block using a pair of curly braces. Any local variables you define within the block are local only to the block and changes to those variables will not have side effects on the code outside of the block. This can save you a lot of time ensuring that the names for your local variables are not used elsewhere in the program.

# Use Macros for Long Structure References

The C language provides an opportunity to construct nearly incomprehensible references to variables such as the following:

```
t = *xtp->xd_wrq->xq_next->xq_qinfo->xqi_putp;
```

You can eliminate a lot of typing bugs during development (and conserve your sanity) by defining a macro for the reference or portion of the reference as in

```
#define XQI_PUTP   *xtp->xd_wrq->xq_next->xq_qinfo->xqi_putp
#define XQ_QINFO   *xtp->xd_wrq->xq_next->xq_qinfo

t = XQI_PUTP;
t = XQ_QINFO->xqi_putp;
```

If your reference includes an array, you can substitute an index as follows:

```
#define XQ_NEXT(i)   *xtp->xd_wrq->xq_next[i]->xq_qinfo->xqi_putp

t = XQ_NEXT(3);
```

# Using the Conditional Expression Operator in Print Statements

There are several good reasons why the conditional expression operator (**a** ? **b** : **c**) should be avoided. These include a lack of readability and of a clear expression of the intended function. However, there is one area where they can contribute to the simplicity of expression of a program, as arguments of print statements. Consider, for example, the following code fragment that prints a string if a pointer to it is not **NULL** and prints a dash otherwise:

```
printf( "%15s\n", np->min != NULL ? np->min : "-" );
```

The alternative would be either two separate print statements or the use of an additional variable to save the results of an **if/else** block that tests the string pointer.

# Always Insert Matching Braces When Editing

It is easier to keep your braces balanced if you always enter the closing brace at the same time you enter the opening brace. Then go back and fill in the body of the code between the braces. If you wait until you reach the end of the body of code, you may forget the closing brace or enter too many. This is especially helpful if the body includes additional blocks also enclosed in braces.

# Error Handling

# Account for Every Program Termination Mechanism

There are few things in software more annoying than a program that does not do what it is supposed to do and then terminates without indicating why. Every possible abnormal termination mechanism should be identified and announced with an appropriate error indication, either a message to the screen or log, or a distinct exit code. For the developer's sake, the error indication should make it possible to determine the exact location in the program where the terminating condition was recognized.

It might appear that searching for all return statements from **main()**, and all calls to **exit()** from anywhere in the program, would suffice to identify all termination points. Each of these statements will certainly cause termination and should be announced, but there is another mechanism, signals, that can also cause termination. A program may wish to deal with a few signals, perhaps **SIGINT** or **SIGUSR1**, in a manner meaningful to the application. But that still leaves many others, almost all of which could yield unpleasant surprises. In addition to the signals needed specifically for the application, all other signals should be caught.

Since the signal catching routine is called with the signal number as its argument, only one catcher is needed for all residual signals. The catcher should announce the signal it was called with, perform any pretermination housekeeping, and then **exit**().

# Always Report All Errors

Many subroutines, and just about all system calls, may return an indication that an error of some sort has occurred. The error could arise from a problem with the calling arguments, the unavailability of a system resource, or a multitude of other causes. It is easy to get sloppy about error checking, especially with errors that "could never occur." However, your code will be much easier to debug initially and to maintain, and it will be much easier to track down obscure problems after delivery, if you follow this simple tip: Examine the return codes from *all* system and subroutine calls for error and report the errors in a manner appropriate for your application.

You may want to establish classes of errors with a different response for each class. For example, an invalid user input in an interactive program usually requires a simple reprimand. At the other extreme, some errors could only be caused by a program bug or by a malfunction in an external system component, hardware, or software. In this case, it is probably best to terminate execution of the application after an appropriate announcement of the error.

# Use a Consistent Error Message Syntax

You have probably seen programs that use a different style of error reporting for each error recognized. For example, an error returned by the **open**() system call might be announced with one of the following:

```
Can't open the input file.
**** Open returned a failure.
Where is the file <foo>?
The input file you specified can't be found or can't be read.
```

The existence of multiple styles in the same program suggest that it was written by several people or by one person over a period of time without any consideration for presenting a consistent, coherent interface to the user.

All error messages should follow the same grammatical construction, describing the error in terms that the typical user can understand and recover from, but also including adequate information to support developer and maintenance needs. For example, use the following message syntax for the **open**() failure described above:

```
fprintf( err_sp, "open( '%s' ) failed, errno = %d", filename, errno );
```

Always delimit the filename with single quotes so there is no confusion between the fixed and variable content of the message and always include the value of *errno* in case it is one that was not anticipated during development. In the specific case of an **open**() failure, you should probably first check for errors that are likely to result from a user failure—for example, a missing file or incorrect file access permissions—and report these with a more friendly and helpful message and save the above nastygram for the rest.

# Debugging Tips

## TIP 979 — Try to Avoid Bugs in the First Place

The best, surest way to make debugging your program easy is to avoid putting bugs in your program in the first place. While this may sound frivolous, bugs are not an inevitable part of all programs but arise through the actions of programmers. Just as programmers write programs with bugs, they can also write programs without them. If you follow the tips given elsewhere in this book, you will be well on your way toward writing defensive, robust, bug-free programs. But just in case a bug does creep in, this section contains tips on how to deal with it.

Debugging is the process of identifying the source of unintended behavior of a program. Just as there are a myriad of unintended behaviors, there are also many different techniques for identifying them. The ones you use will depend on your level of experience, the tools available, and most significantly, your own personal style.

# Preparing for Bugs: the -g option

TIP
980

Debugging tools such as **adb(1)**, **sdb(1)**, and **dbx(1)** if information is included in the executable file that, in the default case, is not included by the compiler. You must instruct the compiler, usually with the **-g** command line option, to include this additional debugging information. You can use a debugger with an executable compiled without the **-g** option, but its facilities will be severely limited. It is a good idea to include the **-g** option in the compilation of all source files during program development. That way you will be prepared for an unexpected core dump and won't have to recompile and try to reconstruct the failure to take a look at it.

# Preparing for Bugs: Logging Tools

TIP
981

Logging tools are an essential component of many programs both during development and after product delivery. The tools should support logging to a file, selection of logging information by a bit mask, and activation from the command line. In the days when user interfaces consisted only of a command line invocation or a dialog on the terminal, you could sometimes get by just sending the debugging information to the terminal, but a log file was still valuable. However, with modern graphical user interfaces, it is all but useless to send debugging information to the terminal and a log file is essential. A bit mask as compared to a debugging level allows you to select the specific type of information to include in the log. It is a good idea to designate a bit value for each major subsystem and reserve one for very temporary messages used only during debugging.

Including logging tools in a delivered product will add to the size of the executable program (because of the space consumed by the messages) and add slightly to the processor load (because of the decisions needed to include or omit a message). However, they can be invaluable in isolating problems in the field—for example, by producing a list of operator input and other major program events that led to a failure.

# Preparing for Bugs: the Signal Catcher

TIP
982

Tip 976 recommends catching all signals so that all program terminations can be identified. That suggestion promotes clean, documented terminations even in the presence of unexpected events such as division-by-zero. It also prevents the creation of a core file. However, during debugging, the core will very likely contain a wealth of information to help you identify the cause of the signal and should not be suppressed.

You can accommodate an orderly termination and still obtain a core file if you arrange to catch all signals, take care of any housekeeping in the signal catcher routine, set the **SIGQUIT** signal to **SIG_DFL**, and then send yourself a **SIGQUIT** signal. The following program illustrates the approach:

```
#include <stdio.h>
#include <sys/signal.h>

main()
{
    int i;
    sigprep();
    i = 3;
    i /= 0;
}


sigprep()
{
    int i;
    int sigcatch();
    for( i = 0; i < NSIG; i++ ) sigset( i, sigcatch );
}


sigcatch( sig )
int sig;
{
    fprintf( stderr, "sig = %d\n", sig );
    sigset( SIGQUIT, SIG_DFL );
    kill( getpid(), SIGQUIT );
    exit(1);
}
```

# TIP 983

# Techniques For Debugging

People have strong preferences about debugging techniques, sometimes without a rational basis for the preference. We present one variety here. Your approach may need to be quite different, but only you know what works best for you. There are at least three different approaches to debugging listed in order of undesirability (first is least undesirable): **printf()**'s, interactive debuggers, and integrated development environments.

Modern computers and compilers are so fast that the objection to using **printf()**'s or log calls because of compiling delays no longer applies except in extremely large (hundreds of thousands of lines of code) projects. It is just as fast to stick a few judicious **printf()**'s (or logging calls) in the code and recompile as to set breakpoints with a debugger. Debuggers are complicated and it takes a significant investment of time to learn the full breadth and scope of their facilities. Some programmers have never been willing to make that investment.

However, if you have a core dump, a debugger is the only way of examining the core file that may identify the cause of the dump. You should therefore become familiar with some basic commands such as displaying a stack trace and the value of variables. The next tip gives the bare minimum for a number of popular debuggers.

# Basic Debugging

**TIP 984**

Here are the debugger commands needed to display a stack trace, and the value of external and automatic variables for the **adb**(1), **sdb**(1), and **dbx**(1) debuggers:

|  | adb(1) | sdb(1) | dbx(1) |
|---|---|---|---|
| Invocation: | adb prog | sdb prog | dbx prog |
| Stack trace: | $c | t | where |
| External: | var/ | var/ | print var |

# Fixing Memory-Trashing Bugs

**TIP 985**

One of the nastiest bugs to find is code that unintentionally corrupts memory by violating the limits of an array or with an errant pointer reference. The bug is especially hard to catch because the effects of the bug can show up almost anywhere in the program, usually far away from the code that caused it. There are three areas of memory used by C programs: *bss* for external variables, the *stack* for automatic variables, and the *heap* for **malloc()**'ed storage.

Corruption of each of these areas has unique symptoms. Let's consider the case of a program that has an "off-by-one" bug in the index in an array of longs such that it writes one additional long beyond the proper end of the array.

If the array is external, the bug will modify the variable immediately following the referenced one. If the modified variable is a pointer, the bug will show up the next time the pointer is dereferenced and will likely produce a core dump from a bogus pointer. However, if the variable stores a numeric quantity—an account balance, for example—then the program will run fine but yield wrong results. If you suspect this type of bug, try rearranging the order of the declarations of the external variables. If the problem changes, you have a good clue to the cause. If the problem disappears, *don't*, repeat *don't*, under any circumstances think that you have fixed the problem. You have only deferred it until you or the next programmer adds a variable following the corrupting array.

If the array is automatic, the results may be quite similar to those above with one additional possibility. Function linkage information (function return addresses) are stored on the heap in addition to automatic variables and function arguments. Thus, an out-of-bound modification on the stack may corrupt a return address. The bug will show up when the function tries to return to the calling program. The return address is bogus, the program tries to return to the bogus address, and a core dump results. To isolate this bug, try moving a suspect automatic variable to an external variable.

The corruption of memory allocated from the heap yields yet another type of failure. To understand this, you must first understand a little about how **malloc(3)** works. **malloc(3)** requires a small amount of memory for housekeeping information which it interleaves with the memory it allocates for the user. Thus, if you modify memory out of bounds on the heap, you may corrupt **malloc(3)**'s housekeeping data. If you are lucky, this will show up as a failure of one of the **malloc(3)** routines (that is, **malloc(3)**, **realloc(3)**, **calloc(3)**, and so on) that will be announced with an error indication in the return code. Since you are following Tip 977, always checking return codes of all **malloc(3)** routines, you will know that you have a problem, but will have little information to identify its source. If you are not so lucky, you will get a core dump. Of the three memory areas, a corruption of the heap can be the most difficult to isolate. If your program structure permits, try a temporary shift to external storage or try allocating more storage than you require.

For example, try adding 100 to the size of all **malloc(3)** calls. If the bug disappears, you can identify the specific allocation causing the problem using a binary search technique. Add 100 to the **malloc(3)**'s in the first half of the program, then the second half, or the first quarter, or second quarter, and so on. It is not as bad as it sounds and may be your only recourse.

There is one more technique that may be helpful in isolating memory corruption bugs in some instances. If the array that you suspect you are referencing incorrectly is not critical to the correct flow of the program, try deleting all code where the values are written into the array.

# How to Find Useful Documentation

One of the important strengths of the UNIX system is that the principal user documentation, the system reference manuals (the "man pages") are of manageable size, easy to access, and devoid of the idiotspeak so common to a lot of other software documentation. Yet it is surprising how many UNIX system users are unaware of the reference manuals or don't understand their layout and notation. This probably arises because many users approach the system for a specific task and never take the time to explore its resources. Or they may have learned the system from one of the many popular texts and had no exposure to the underlying reference documents.

The reference manuals for your system are (short of the system source code) the ultimate authority on the behavior of your system. There are many variations, some small, some quite significant, among the UNIX systems sold by the major hardware and software vendors. No text intended for a broad audience can possibly keep up-to-date or reasonably cover all of the variations. Even the tutorial documentation supplied with UNIX systems is not adequately maintained and is often out-of-date relative to the current release. The vendor-supplied reference manuals are the closest you will come to a totally accurate description of the behavior of your system. Read them!

Most UNIX systems come with online manual pages. Execute the **man** command with an argument of "man" as follows:

```
man man
```

This will allow you to read the online documentation for the **man** command. Printed documentation may also have been shipped with your system, or it may be available as an option.

# The Meaning of the Funny Numbers in Parentheses after Commands and Routines

Throughout UNIX system documentation, including reference manuals, tutorials, text books, and periodicals, you often see command, system call, or subroutine names followed by a number in parentheses. The number identifies the chapter in the system reference manual where the command, system call, and so on, are described. By convention, the following assignments are used by all man pages:

1—commands
2—system calls
3—subroutines
4—file formats
5—miscellaneous
6—games
7—special files
8—maintenance

There is occasional use of the same name for commands, system calls, and perhaps other system resources. For example, **mkdir** is the name of both a command and a system call. The chapter number is therefore necessary, together with the name, to uniquely identify the system resource. A reference to **mkdir(1)** thus unambiguously indicates a command, while **mkdir(2)** is a system call.

# Read the Manual

The notation "RTFM" often appears in netnews postings, often in response to questions that are readily answered by the man pages. It stands for "Read the _____ Manual," where the blank is replaced with a word that might offend a few readers. Some examples are:

❑ What does the **cut(1)** command do? - RTFM

❑ What is the option to **ls(1)** to get a listing by file age? - RTFM

❑ How do you find out what options are available for the **cpio(1)** command? - RTFM

In short—RTFM.

# Browse the Documentation Periodically

While the title of this tip may sound flippant or glib, it is offered quite seriously. One of the weaknesses of the standard UNIX system documentation is that it presumes you know the names of the resources you need to accomplish your task. If you have a problem and are looking for a resource, there is no easy answer. For example, the documentation does not give a direct answer to the question: How do you find a command that compares two binary files?

For this, the permuted index would give you pointers to **diff**(1), **infocmp**(1), and **cmp**(1), and a review of the man pages for each command would then reveal that **cmp**(1) is the desired command. Some help is provided in finding these things on some UNIX systems. For example, on some implementations, the **man** command has a -**k** option. If you invoke

```
$ man -k keywords
```

**man** prints out one-line summaries from the *whatis* database that contain many of the keywords. The command **apropos** is essentially an alias for **man -k** and works the same way.

However, consider the following question: What are the commands for performing simple database operations on ASCII files? There is nothing in the main index or permuted index of the reference manual that suggests that you should look at **sort**(1), **cut**(1), **paste**(1), **join**(1), **comm**(1), **grep**(1), and so on.

How do you learn this? How do you learn about the -**k** option on the **man** command? How do you learn what subroutines are available in the C library? How do you learn what's new when you migrate to a new hardware platform? Regrettably, the only way is to set aside time each day or week as "nerd hours" and read the reference manual (remember RTFM?) cover to cover. The goal is not to learn the detailed operation of every option of every command, but rather to become familiar with what's available so when a need arises you will know if a solution exists and roughly where to look for the details.

# Follow the Models of Existing UNIX System Tools

There is a philosophy, a "UNIX way," that is embodied in the UNIX system commands and the means of plumbing the commands together. The "UNIX way" is certainly not the only way and some would argue that it is not the best way, but it is a way that UNIX users have become familiar with and have come to expect in the commands that they use on the UNIX system.

The UNIX system provides you the freedom and opportunity to develop any type of user interface to the commands that you write. Whether or not you like or agree with the "UNIX way," don't reinvent the wheel. Follow the "UNIX way." Follow the conventions described by example in the standard UNIX system commands. Read your input from *stdin* and write your output to *stdout* by default. Accept the specification of alternate input and output files with command line arguments. Use single-letter command line options. Don't litter the output of your command with noisy chitchat unless requested with a "verbose" option. In short, follow the existing model, don't invent a new one. The users of your programs will appreciate you for it.

## Write a Throwaway Program to Help You Understand a Feature

While the terseness of the UNIX system reference manual contributes to its strength, it also means that a lot has been left unsaid. Sometimes the only way to really understand how a feature works is to write a short program to test it. Don't be afraid to write a throwaway program. It may only take a few lines to eliminate your confusion, or it may take a hundred or many hundreds. No matter; it will be much easier to understand a feature in isolation in a simple test program than embedded in the context of your target application.

## Get into the Rhythm of Program Development

If you hop on a playground swing and give it a push, it will swing to and fro at a rate that it, not you, chooses. It has a natural period of oscillation that is determined by physics, not by the whims or desires of the rider. You could work very hard to make it go a little faster, but not much. Or, you could work very hard to make it go a little slower, but again, not much. Or, respecting the natural period of the swing, you could pump at just the right rate and swing back and forth almost effortlessly.

Program development is much like a swing. It has a natural pace, period, and rhythm. You can pour on the proverbial "Mongolian hordes," schedule every detail down to the last line of code, use every management trick in the book, and like the swing, the development may go a little faster, but not much. And like the swing, the effort is enormous.

You need to find the natural rhythm of program development, accept the pace of that development, and set schedules accordingly. You'll accomplish the same thing with much less effort and much more satisfaction.

# If You Don't Understand Something, Follow Its Threads Until You Master It

At one level, there is an elegant simplicity to the UNIX system. For example, it takes only one line to express a complete program:

```
main() { printf( "Hello, world.\n" ); }
```

Much can be accomplished at this simple level. If it serves the needs of your application, that's great, your development work will be a breeze. However, there inevitably comes a time when you will bump into the murkier corners of the UNIX system, and it often doesn't take long. For example, since the tty driver is buffering characters into lines, you can't read a character at a time from the tty without first plodding through nine pages of **termio**(7), adding a "*#include*" for at least one header file, declaring a couple of structures, and executing two **ioctl**(2) system calls. The UNIX system is full of snake pits like the above lurking just beneath the surface. A few others that come to mind: signals, the process level buffered I/O library, and kernel streams.

You may be able to deal with these at a superficial level with only partial understanding. However, without mastery, you will sooner or later get in trouble when things don't go as you hoped.

How do you master these features? The only practical way is to hack on each until you think you fully understand it, then hack on it some more. Write a small test program to play with the parameters of the feature; test the effects of each parameter independently and in combination; test for interactions with other system features; and so on. Follow the threads of each feature as far as they reach and through all the other features they touch. Only then will you be on your way from a junior programmer to a UNIX wizard.

# Preventing the Creation of Core Files

When a program malfunctions, it can create a core image, or simply a core that is useful in debugging the program. Use of the symbolic debugger, **sdb**, requires that you have a core file. If you're not planning to debug, however, the creation of a core file is a nuisance; a large core file can take up dozens of megabytes of your file system for no reason. To stop this from happening, you can try one of the following methods. If you are using **csh**, then put the following in your *.cshrc* file:

```
limit coredump 0
```

If you are using **ksh**, the **ulimit** command sets limits on the use of system resources, as shown here.

```
ulimit -c 1
```

This command limits the size of core files to 1 block (512 bytes).

Regardless of the shell you are using, if you create a directory named *core* in the directory you are executing the buggy program, the file system will not create a core file.

# Selecting a Shell to Use for the System Command

Imagine a C program that asks the user to type in a command string, and then uses the UNIX **system** command to execute the string the user typed. Such a program looks something like this:

```
main(int argc, char *argv[])
{
    char str[100];
    printf ("Please enter a command");
    gets (str);
system (str);
}
```

If you do this, the **system** command always executes a Bourne shell, since **/bin/sh** is written into the code. To have your program use a different shell, you need to use the system call to **exec** the new shell with the command as its argument. For example,

```
system ("exec /bin/ksh -c 'COMMAND'");
```

will have the system call invoke **/bin/sh**, which will exec **ksh**, which will then run the command.

# Generating International Characters

**TIP 996**

Sometimes you may need to generate the extended ASCII characters from the keyboard in order to use the appropriate foreign characters needed in different languages. Since the manual pages don't discuss how to generate or translate international character sets, here is a tip on how it can be done.

The **setlocale**() and **chrtbl**() functions are part of the XPG3 standard for internationalization of applications. The first question is what is meant by international characters. If you're on the console, you only have available the PC extended ASCII character set. This supports only a subset of the characters needed for full internationalization. It may be impossible to do what you want with this set, since it generally supplies only lowercase "international" characters. In addition, unless the file system supports storage in directory entries (and, in particular, the UNIX utilities support the idea) of 8-bit names, you will have to do input/output translation of the characters so that they may be stored as 7-bit values. This is generally done by making the scan codes generated by the keys report a 7-bit value, thus replacing American ASCII with a local version.

It's important that you have 8-bit clean programs. For example, if you're using **xterm**, you must set the eightBitInput and resources. You would then use the ALT key to set the eighth bit, which gives you international characters. When you have the keyboard working, make sure that your display can handle 8-bit characters. For X Windows, you can select an ISO font. For X Windows, the latin1 font is a 16-point font from the ISO 8859 standard called Latin 1. X (when using the same fonts) automatically has the advantage of being the same representation everywhere.

## Using lex

# What Is lex?

**TIP 997**

The **lex** command is a program generator for simple lexical processing. Strings and expressions are searched for and C routines are executed when they are found. The following tips should be used as a prototype for others to use as a starting point for their own **lex** script. Often an experienced programmer will know what needs to be done with **lex** but will forget the simple things like the syntax of the delimiters between the various sections of a **lex** script. These tips provide templates or prototypes and include all of the **lex** punctuation and examples of the syntax. They are meant to jog the memory of someone already familiar with the concepts.

# TIP 998 — An Example of a lex Script

The following is a complete **lex** script that recognizes several types of lexical tokens in the input stream. The script stores the value of the token in a structure called 'yylval' and then prints its type and value. Tokens consisting of numerics including a decimal point (Ex: 123.456, 123., or .456) are labeled FLOAT; numerics without a decimal point (Ex: 123) are NUM; anything in quotes is a STRING; and an initial alpha possibly followed by an alphanumeric is an IDENTIFIER.

```
%{

/********************************************************************/
/*      example.1  - example lexical analyzer */*/
/********************************************************************/

    #include <string.h>

    double atof();

    struct yylval {
        float   flt;
        int     num;
        char    *str;
    } yylval;

%}


%%

([0-9]+\.[0-9]*)|([0-9]*\.[0-9]+) {
            yylval.flt = (float) atof( yytext );
            printf( "FLOAT: %f\n", yylval.flt );
            }
```

```
[0-9]+              {
            yylval.num = atoi( yytext );
            printf( "NUM: %d\n", yylval.num );
            }


[a-zA-Z_][a-zA-Z_0-9]* {
            yylval.str = strdup( yytext );
            printf( "IDENTIFIER: '%s'\n", yylval.str );
            }


\"[^"\n]*           {
            if( yytext[yyleng-1] == '\\' ) {
               yytext[yyleng-1] = '\0';    /* trash \ */
               yyleng--;                    /* and adjust for it */
               yymore();                    /* get some more text */
            }
            else {
               yylval.str = strdup( yytext+1 ); /* strip leading " */
               input();                          /* eat trailing " */
               printf( "STRING: '%s'\n", yylval.str );
            }
            }


.                   ;
\n                  ;

    %%
```

# How to Use This Template

Type the entire script in Tip 998 starting with the '%{' and ending with the final '%%' into a file named *example.l.* Use the **lex(1)** command to translate the script into a C program.

```
$ lex example.l
```

**lex** outputs the program into the file *lex.yy.c*. This name is built into **lex** and cannot be given by the user. Compile the C program, link with the **lex** library, and save the executable in the file *example:*

```
$ cc -o example lex.yy.c -ll
```

Run the executable:

```
$ example
```

And type some input, ending it with an EOF (usually ^D). Or just hit your INTR key (usually DEL or ^C). Here is an example of some input and the resulting output:

```
123
NUM: 123
12.86
FLOAT: 12.860000
"Hello, World"
STRING: 'Hello, World'
a_label_123
IDENTIFIER: 'a_label_123'
```

# How to Extend the Template to Other Uses

The example in Tip 999 is a classic UNIX filter: it reads from *stdin* and writes to *stdout*. There are probably some useful things you could do with a **lex** program like the above. However, it is far more common to use **lex** to generate a lexical analyzer that is used in conjunction with another program, very often with a **yacc(1)** parser. The following example is a modification of the program in the previous tip. It now includes a **main()** that calls the lexical analyzer and deals with the tokens it returns. Ordinarily the **main()** would be in a separate file but it's in the **lex** script for brevity. The **lex** part of the code no longer prints the token type and value but simply returns the token type for **main()** to process.

```
%{
/*******************************************************************/
/*      example.l  - example lexical analyzer                      */
/*******************************************************************/

#include <string.h>
double atof();
struct yylval {
    float flt;
    int   num;
    char  *str;
} yylval;

#define FLOAT          1
#define NUM            2
#define IDENTIFIER     3
#define STRING         4

main()
{
    int token;

    while( (token = yylex()) > 0 ) {

        switch( token ) {
        case FLOAT:
            printf( "FLOAT: %f\n", yylval.flt );
            break;

        case NUM:
            printf( "NUM: %d\n", yylval.num );
            break;

        case IDENTIFIER:
            printf( "IDENTIFIER: '%s'\n", yylval.str );
            break;
```

```
        case STRING:
                printf( "STRING: '%s'\n", yylval.str );
                break;
        default:
                printf( "Unexpected value returned by yylex()
                '%d'\n", token );
                break;
                }
        }
}

/****************************************************************/

%}

%%

([0-9]+\.[0-9]*)|([0-9]*\.[0-9]+) {
        yylval.flt = (float) atof( yytext );
        return FLOAT;
        }


[0-9]+           {
        yylval.num = atoi( yytext );
        return NUM;
        }


[a-zA-Z_][a-zA-Z_0-9]* {
        yylval.str = strdup( yytext );
        return IDENTIFIER;
        }

\"[^"\n]*        {
        if( yytext[yyleng-1] == '\\' ) {
            yytext[yyleng-1] = '\0';      /* trash \ */
            yyleng--;                     /* and adjust for it */
            yymore();                     /* get some more text */
        }
        else {
            yylval.str = strdup( yytext+1 );   /* strip leading " */
```

```
              input();                          /* eat trailing " */
              return STRING;
          }
          }


      .                   ;
   \n                      ;

   %%
```

## Porting Software

## Porting to SVR4

**TIP 1001**

There are lots of differences, some subtle, some blatant, between the sets of system and library calls of UCB- and System V-derived systems. (By *UCB-derived* we mean the various BSD releases and other software environments derived from the University of California at Berkeley version, the best-known being SunOS. We exclude other v7-derived environments such as Xenix.) Each offers calls which are not available in the other, and there are important differences between even the same routines. Just because a system or library call has the same name in both places doesn't mean it works the same way!

By design, SVR4 is essentially a union of both environments, with few things being left out (and some of those because they have been superceded by technology, or because they were not found to be in widespread use). Software written in a UCB environment is generally easily ported to SVR4, as long as it doesn't depend on things like *libkvm* or the idiosyncrasies of the operating system or hardware.

In this section we will cover some of the main points to bear in mind when porting software from UCB to SVR4. These tips range from the trivial to the convoluted. You may want to skim these tips the first time through, and then if you think you are having problems with a specific routine, look for a tip with that in the title.

To find more information on this topic, two books that are of great help: the *UNIX SVR4 Migration and Compatibility Guide*, part of the *UNIX System V Release 4 Document Set*, and *POSIX Programming* by Donald Levine (Sebastopol, CA: O'Reilly and Associates, 1991).

# TIP 1002

# How to Use ranlib

The *makefile* for almost any BSD or Sun source code is likely to call **ranlib**. This program rebuilds the header of an archive library, thus making searching the library much faster. This has long been done by **ar** and **ld** in System V. Since the header includes the absolute pathname of the library, **ranlib** has to be called after a library has been installed, but before it can be used, and is generally done as the last part of installation.

Thwarting a *makefile* that calls this program can be done in at least two ways. The first is to edit the *makefile* and look for invocations of **ranlib**, such as

```
RANLIB=ranlib
```

and replace them with

```
RANLIB=:
```

(The command : is a shell built-in which does nothing and returns TRUE.) If **ranlib** is called explicitly, then you have a little more editing to do. The crude-but-effective alternative is to link */usr/bin/true* to */usr/bin/ranlib* (it can be anywhere in the standard PATH).

# TIP 1003

# BSD Compatibility Mode

To ease the pain of transition, a way of building programs is available that tries to emulate the way that some UCB calls work; it also provides some calls that aren't in SVR4 (or that are there but under different names). The emulation mostly consists of wrappers around base SVR4 routines, and it does not try to be a complete replacement.

Nevertheless, if you want a quick and dirty method of seeing if a piece of Sun or BSD software will compile and run in your environment, it's worth trying BSD Compatibility Mode. This consists of a set of include files and a small number of libraries, plus a pair of scripts, replacements for **cc** and **ld** which make use of them. You can use this mode merely by using */usr/ucb/cc* rather than **cc**. Most makefiles will contain a line like this:

```
CC=cc
```

which should be changed to

```
CC=/usr/ucb/cc
```

This will pull in BSD-like include files (in */usr/ucbinclude*) and libraries (*/usr/ucblib*). If the makefile calls **cc** explicitly, then it's easier to go through it and replace lines like this:

```
cc -c $(CFLAGS) foo.c
```

with

```
$(CC) -c $(CFLAGS) foo.c
```

and then insert the definition of **CC** at the top of the *makefile*. That way, when you've stopped using BSD compatibility mode, you only have to edit one line in the *makefile*.

If the *makefile* calls the loader explicitly, you will also need

```
LD=/usr/ucb/ld
```

or the equivalent (but see the discussion that follows).

These two programs (*/usr/ucb/cc* and */usr/ucb/ld*) are normally shell scripts that simply use the **-I** flag to **cc** and the **-YP** flag to **ld** to pull in the appropriate set of *include* files and libraries.

It is possible to use the *ucbinclude* files and libraries stand-alone, by putting something like this onto the (regular) **cc** and **ld** lines:

```
cc:    -I/usr/ucbinclude
cc/ld:  -L/usr/ucblib -lucb
```

but you should be extremely careful in how you do this, because pitfalls abound. There are routines that have the same name but different effects in both the UCB and the regular C library. The signal routines are probably the best known (and one of the most vexatious), but there are others. Hence, if you have an **ld** command line, or you are mixing-and-matching between System V and UCB libraries, you should use something like this on the build lines in your makefiles:

```
cc: -lc -L/usr/ucb -lucb
ld: -lc -L/usr/ucb -lucb -lc
```

This way the standard C library is searched before the UCB emulation one, and any references to unresolved routines will be resolved from the System V rather than from the UCB library. This means, for example, that you get System V signals rather than UCB ones. Rescanning the C library after the UCB allows any routines referenced by the UCB library to be resolved as well. (Note that **cc** automatically scans the System V C library last.)

For further reading, see Tip 1002 on **ranlib**, or the *UNIX SVR4 Migration and Compatibility Guide*.

# TIP 1004 — More on BSD Compatibility Mode

Actually, there are more parts to BSD Compatibility Mode than just the replacements for **cc**, **ld**, and all the files they use and reference. The differences between UCB and SV systems extend further than just the system and library calls; some of the commands are different, too.

UCB versions of some of these can also be found in */usr/ucb*, including such favorites as **biff**, **chown**, **df**, **du**, **echo**, **hostname**, **install**, **ls** and **mt**. So, if you have a script that is looking for any of these, and that isn't working, or is working oddly because **ls** is returning one too many fields, try putting this at the top of the script:

```
PATH=/usr/ucb:$PATH
```

Or modify the existing line, setting PATH to something so that */usr/ucb* comes before */usr/bin*, as shown here.

```
PATH=/usr/bin:/etc:/usr/etc
```

becomes

```
PATH=/usr/ucb:/usr/bin:/etc:/usr/etc
```

If there isn't a "PATH=" line, then you need to concern yourself with shell script security! For further reading, try the *UNIX SVR4 Migration and Compatibility Guide*.

# Using index and rindex, strcasecmp and strncasecmp, bcopy, bcmp, and bzero

In BSD/Sun software, you will frequently find calls to string and memory handling routines which don't exist in SVR4. Conversion for most of these is simple, and **index** and **rindex** are trivial:

```
#define index strchr
#define rindex    strrchr
```

The next three have almost exact equivalents in SVR4 and can be converted by macros:

```
#define bcopy(source, target, count)  memmove (target, source, count)
#define bcmp(source, target, count)  memcmp (target, source, count)
#define bzero(source, count)  memset (source, 0, count)
```

Note that the target and source parameters for **bcopy** and **cmp** are backwards from those expected by **memmove** and **memcmp**, so if you try

```
#define bcmp memcmp
```

and you are testing for more than simple equality, then you will get a value which is the opposite to what you are expecting. Also, **bcopy** is defined to handle overlapping copies, but **memcpy** is not, which is why you should use **memmove** instead. The return values from the other routines are also different, but this rarely causes a problem.

Alas, there are no exact equivalents for **strcasecmp** and **strncasecmp** in SVR4. However, versions of them can often be found hidden in other system libraries, such as *libnet* or *libresolv.* Obviously this is manufacturer-dependent, and either or both of these libraries may not exist on a particular system. Good versions of these can be found from many places on the net, the best possibly being in the source for **nntp** (derived from BSD sources).

# Using getrusage

**TIP 1006**

**getrusage** is a routine that reports on resource utilization of a process and its children. Most of its functionality is not supported in SVR4, the exception being the user and system time used by the current process. This information can be found by using the **times(2)** system call, but note that the data is returned in a different format (it's measured in clock ticks, not in seconds/microseconds), so some conversion is in order. For example:

```
#include <sys/types.h>
#include <sys/times.h>
#include <sys/limits.h>

struct tms buffer;
struct timeval ru_utime;

time (&buffer);
ru_utime.tv_sec = tms.tms_utime / CLK_TCK;
ru_utime.tv_usec = ( tms.tms_utime % CLK_TCK ) * 1000000 / CLK_TCK;
```

# SVR4 Equivalent for getdtablesize

**TIP 1007**

**getdtablesize** is a routine provided in BSD/Sun systems to determine how many file descriptors can be opened by any process at one time. This is provided in SVR4 by **getrlimit**, so a quick and dirty substitute function might be

```
#include <sys/time.h>
#include <sys/resource.h>

long
getdtablesize ()
{
    struct rlimit rl;

    getrlimit ( RLIMIT_NOFILE, &rl );
    return rl.rlim.cur;
}
```

# stdio Buffering with setlinebuf and setbuffer

Have you ever wondered why that last **printf** before your program core-dumped didn't seem to actually write anything? That's because of *stdio* buffering—characters that get processed by the *stdio* routines (all the routines which take a FILE * argument) are held in an internal buffer until something happens to force them to really be written.

*stdio* buffering in SVR4 is a superset of that found in BSD/Sun systems. By default, an output stream is line-buffered if it points at a terminal, unbuffered if it is *stderr,* and normally buffered otherwise.

Normal buffering means that any bytes written to the stream are held in an internally allocated buffer of size BUFSIZ until either BUFSIZ bytes have been written, or **fflush** is called. A stream that is line-buffered will also write when a newline is written, or when input is requested from that stream. Bytes written to an unbuffered stream are written immediately. This behavior may be modified with the routines *setbuf* and *setvbuf.*

Conversion of software from BSD/Sun to SVR4 in this situation is simple enough. There are only two routines to consider, *setbuf* and *setvbuf* being identical.

```
setlinebuf (stream);
```

becomes

```
setvbuf (stream, (char *) NULL), _IOLBF, BUFSIZ);

setbuffer (stream, buffer);
```

becomes

```
setvbuf (stream, buffer, _IOFBF, sizeof(buffer));
```

However, *setlinebuf* can be used while the stream is active, and *setbuf* cannot. There is no direct replacement for this functionality—if you really need it, you'll have to use *freopen* to get a new stream, and then set up buffering on that.

# Differences in Regular Expressions

"^[^']*'[^']*$? Looks like tty line noise to me.

A number of regular expression (RE) compilation and execution routines are provided in SVR4, but none of them exactly match the functionality of *re_comp* and *re_exec* in BSD. Fortunately, the SVR4 and BSD routines have the same RE grammar and syntax, because converting an RE from one form to another is generally not an afternoon's pleasant diversion.

For a fast porting job, it's probably easiest to use *regcmp* and *regex,* although these are not exact replacements. They do handle the same RE grammar, but their return values are backwards from the BSD routines, and *regcmp* returns a pointer to the compiled expression, whereas *re_cmp* hides the compiled expression internally.

So, to convert the routines, you might use something like the following. For UCB:

```
if (( error_message = re_comp (pattern)) != NULL )
    error...

matched = ( re_exec ( buffer ) == 1 );
```

For SVR4:

```
char *compiled_pattern;

if (( compiled_pattern = regcmp (pattern)) == NULL)
    error...

matched = ( regex ( compiled_pattern, buffer ) != NULL);
```

Additionally, you may need to include *libgen.h* or some other include file, and to link with an extra library, generally *libgen,* if the regular expression routines are not kept in the standard C library.

# Handling Signals

The signal routines are probably the best-known example of routines that have the same name but are significantly different between System V and UCB systems. Because of their wide utility, they are generally the most worrisome.

The big difference between System V and UCB signals is that System V signal handlers are reset when caught, but UCB signals aren't. What does that mean? It means that in the UCB universe, once you have installed a signal handler (by using **signal(3)**), it stays installed, and all instances of that type of signal will be caught by the signal handler you have specified, until you define a different handler. In System V you have to redefine the handler after *every* signal of that type. In other words, in System V, signal handlers are one-shot, whereas in UCB they are persistent.

Making porting between SVR4 and BSD more difficult is the fact that there are two varieties of signals in both UCB and System V—each has basic and advanced signals. All of these variants are merged in POSIX signals, which are (generally) available in SVR4 systems, but this harmony can take a fair amount of work to achieve.

If the application you are trying to port is using UCB advanced signals, things aren't too bad, and you can get away with only using some macros and let the preprocessor do the hard work for you.

```
#define sigvec        sigaction
#define sv_handler    sa_handler
#define sv_mask       sa_mask
#define sv_flags      sa_flags
#define sv_onstack    sa_flags
```

**sigpause()** and **sigsetmask()** are almost directly replaced by **sigsuspend()** and **sigprocmask()**, and **sigblock(mask)** is almost **sigprocmask (SIG_BLOCK, mask)**. The difference lies in the return of the old signal mask—BSD signals return this as the return code of the function, and POSIX signals send it back as an extra parameter, so if the program wants the old signal mask, then a little coding is necessary. Other features of BSD extended signals are also available, such as **sigaltstack()** for **sigstack()**, **siginterrupt()** (look at the **SA_NODEFER** flag in **sigaction()**), and the saving of the context in use when the signal occurred (see **SA_SIGINFO**, same place).

Unfortunately, changing from simple UCB to POSIX signals is not as trivial. The first thing to do is to inspect the signal handlers and find out whether they simply catch the signal, clean up, and exit. If they do, you can probably leave them alone and let them be invoked via the System V **signal(2)** routine. The SVR4 and UCB routines have the same name and, in this case, do the same job. If, however, they are called more than once, or if they are being used to communicate between processes, then you need to change the calls.

```
signal ( SIGINT, SIG_IGN );
```

becomes

```
sigset_t blocked_sigs;
sigemptyset ( &blocked_sigs );
sigaddset ( &blocked_sigs, SIGINT );
sigprocmask ( SIG_BLOCK, &blocked_sigs, (sigset_t *) 0) );
```

This may look horrifying, but it isn't really. In this example, the four lines declare an uninitialized set of signals, initialize this set to empty, add the SIGINT signal to the set, and block those signals referenced in the set. If you want to block multiple signals, then you can call **sigaddset**() multiple times, once for each signal you want to block, before calling **Bsigprocmask**.

Here's an example of the code change needed when you actually want to catch a signal:

```
signal ( SIGINT, int_handler() );
```

becomes

```
struct sigaction act;
act.sa_flags = act.sa_mask = 0;
act.sa_handler = int_handler;
sigaction ( SIGINT, &act, (struct sigaction *) 0 );
```

In this example, a signal action structure is declared, the signal action is not reset to default when caught, the mask associated with this action is set to zero, the handler address is given, and then the structure is passed into the kernel for the desired action to take place.

# Using getwd to Find the Current Directory

The routine for finding out the current working directory is slightly different between System V and UCB. This is another one which is usually easy to change:

```
#include <sys/param.h>
#define getwd(path)      getcwd(path, MAXPATHLEN)
```

Most code only uses the pointer returned by **getwd**(), passing a **NULL** pointer to ensure that nothing is copied into the optional storage area. If the code is using the parameter, then you should check that the variable path is large enough to store any possible return value. (This value is defined by MAXPATHLEN in */usr/include/sys/param.h*). Check the declaration of the variable passed, or where storage is allocated for it, to be sure.

There are other differences. For example, in case of error, **getwd**() places an error message in the area pointed to by *path,* while **getcwd**() merely returns an error code.

# Using gethostname to Find the Machine Name

The routine for finding out the machine name is rather different on System V than it is on UCB, and they even have different names. What UCB calls a system name, System V calls a hostname. Just to confuse things even more, the *utsname* structure has a field called *sysname,* but this is used to describe the type of operating system being run (for example, "System V"), and the *hostname* field is what you want to look at. Sometimes these two are the same anyway. A wrapper function for **gethostname** might look like this:

```
#include <sys/utsname.h>
gethostname (name, length)
char *name;
int length;
{
    struct utsname un;

    uname(&un);
    strncpy(name, un.nodename, length);
}
```

Of course, appropriate error checking should really be added.

# Finding Out More about C under UNIX

## TIP 1013

## How to Find Out More

There are several places to look for more information about program development. One of the first is the UNIX system documentation. The UNIX System V Release 4 *Programmer's Guide* contains descriptions of the C compiler, and the **lint**, **lex**, and **make** programs. The *Programmer's Reference Manual* contains the manual pages for the programming tools, as well as for all of the library routines.

There are several netnews groups that are sources of useful information, including:

    comp.lang.c
    comp.unix.internals
    comp.unix.wizards
    comp.unix.programmer

Guides that are useful for UNIX program development include *The C Programming Language,* second edition, by Brian W. Kernighan and Dennis Ritchie (Prentice-Hall, 1988); *Advanced UNIX Programming* by Marc Rochkind (Prentice-Hall, 1985); *Advanced Programmer's Guide to UNIX System V* by Rebecca Thomas, Lawrence R. Rogers, and Jean L. Yates (Osborne/McGraw-Hill, 1986); *The UNIX Programming Environment* by Brian W. Kernighan and Rob Pike (Prentice-Hall, 1984); P *OSIX Programmer's Guide* by Donald Lewine (O'Reilly and Associates, 1991); *Advanced Programming in the UNIX Environment* by W. Richard Stevens (Reading, MA: Addison-Wesley, 1992) and *The Standard C Library* by P.J. Plauger (Englewood Cliffs, NJ: Prentice-Hall, 1992). The best book we've seen on software development independent of computer environment is *Code Complete: A Practical Handbook of Software Construction* by Steve McConnell (Redmond, WA: Microsoft Press, 1993).

## TIP 1014

## Getting a C Compiler for Your Machine

In the past few years, there has been some movement to restrict the distribution of UNIX software to only that which is essential. In some cases, this means that your distribution may not have come with a C compiler (or you were forced to pay extra for it). And even if you did, you might not have an ANSI C compiler. If either is the case, the FSF (Free Software Foundation) has a free ANSI C compiler called **gcc**. It is widely used throughout the world and is constantly being improved. The main site for GNU software is *prep.ai.mit.edu* in the directory */pub/gnu,* but there are many other sites that mirror the GNU software distribution:

ASIA:                    *utsun.s.u-tokyo.ac.jp:/ftpsync/prep*

AUSTRALIA:          *archie.oz.au:/gnu (archie.oz or archie.oz.au for ACSnet)*

AFRICA:               *ftp.sun.ac.za:/pub/gnu*

MIDDLE-EAST:      *ftp.technion.ac.il:/pub/unsupported/gnu*

EUROPE:              *irisa.irisa.fr:/pub/gnu*

CANADA:             *ftp.cs.ubc.ca:/mirror2/gnu*

USA:                    *wuarchive.wustl.edu:/mirrors/gnu*

# Index

*(Organized According to Tip Number)*

# Index